Inventing the Charles River

Inventing the Charles River

Karl Haglund

Published in Cooperation with the Charles River Conservancy

The MIT Press   Cambridge, Massachusetts   London, England

This book was set in Bembo by The MIT Press
Printed and bound in the United States of America.

Library of Congress Cataloging-in-Publication Data
Haglund, Karl.
     Inventing the Charles River / Karl Haglund.
          p. cm.
     Includes biblographical reference and index.
     ISBN 0-262-08307-8 (alk. paper)
          1. Charles River (Mass.)—History. 2. Charles River Valley (Mass.)—
History. 3. Boston Region (Mass.)—History. 4. City and town life—
Massachusetts—Charles River Valley—History. 5. Landscape—Social
aspects—Massachusetts—Charles River Valley—History. 6. River engineer-
ing—Massachusetts—Charles River—History. 7. City planning—
Massachusetts—Boston region—History. I. Title.

F72.C46 H33 2002
333.78'45'097444—dc21
                                                                2002022919

10 9 8 7 6 5 4 3 2

The publisher and the Charles River Conservancy are grateful to the many people whose contributions helped support the publication of this volume. Major sponsors include Claire and Jay Baldwin, Lyme Properties, Muriel and Norman Leventhal, the Narnia Fund, and Mary and Edgar Schein.

For Karen

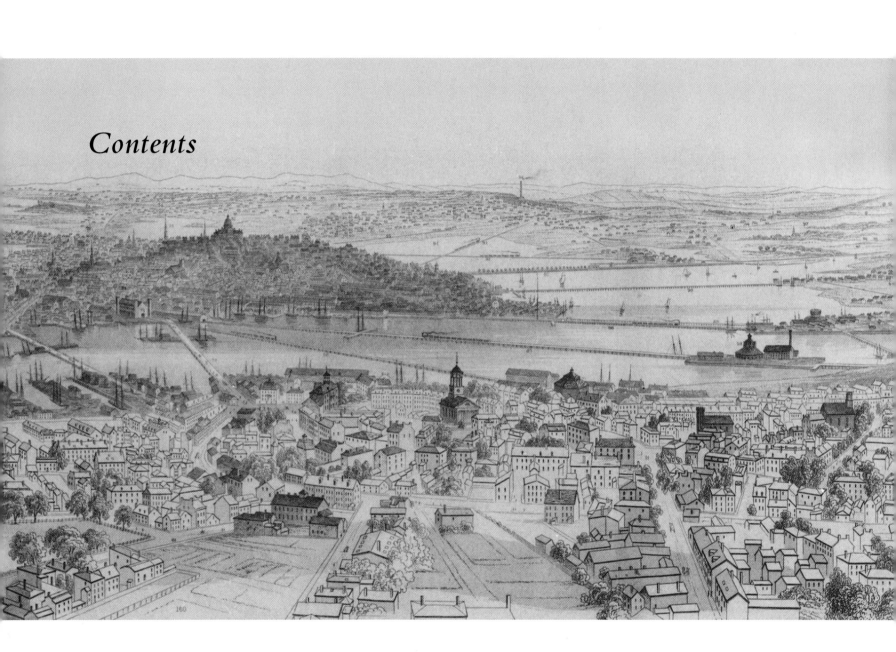

Contents

Foreword

Renata von Tscharner
President, the Charles River Conservancy

Frontispiece Few places combine so much beauty and civic pride as this stately allée. In the 1960s Cambridge activists chained themselves to its trees to prevent their being cut down as part of a "road improvement" scheme. In the spring of 2001 the Charles River Conservancy led a coalition of over twenty-five groups in opposing legislation that would have separated the River parklands from the parkways and transferred their management to two state departments.

Twenty years ago I left my native Switzerland and settled in Cambridge, Massachusetts, close to the Charles River. From the first time I saw the river I was captivated by its glittering expanse rimmed by sinuous parkways and inspiring vistas. But there was more to it than that: a stroll along the shoreline invited reverie; there was a sense of the infinite about this waterscape, even the heroic.

In childhood I had learned to swim in icy mountain streams. On confronting the Charles, my first impulse was to plunge right in. Of that I was quickly disabused, advised by neighbors and friends that a mother of small children did not have the right to put her health at such risk. Pollution levels were still too high, they said.

Soon I found other pleasures on and along the Charles. I roamed the river parklands by bike and roller blades. On the first of every May, my children and I would cross to the middle of the Weeks Footbridge at dawn, flowers in our hair, to welcome the rising sun with song and dance. By canoe and kayak I explored the upper reaches of the river. For my fiftieth birthday I received a wet suit, extending by a month into the fall the time when I could slip a windsurfer into the water and skim across the basin. If I could not swim, at least I could glide!

As an urban planner I have long been intrigued by the notion of place: how it is made; how people relate to it; how it shapes personal and collective identity. Over time I found the Charles, and particularly its parklands, drawing more and more of my professional interest. Eventually I decided to expand my knowledge of the river in a Cambridge sort of way, by offering a course at the Radcliffe Seminars. There my students challenged me to understand the circumstances that led to the "invention" of the river. For we quickly began to see that what appeared at first to be transparently "natural" was in its entirety a human creation. But as we searched for clues to the steps in this creation, we also became aware of a disturbing reality: this river invented with so much care was desperately in need of renewal.

The seminar led to an ongoing involvement with the Charles River Parklands. When I heard that an old friend had launched a park conservancy in New York, it struck me that the

Charles needed something similar. How might one initiate such an organization? Just where I had stopped, I decided—with another seminar. But this time, instead of landscape design students, I would invite friends and colleagues from my days as an urban planner, along with community activists and environmentalists.

Among those invited to speak before this diverse group was Karl Haglund, an MDC planner who was primarily engaged in planning for the river's "lost half mile" below the Boston Museum of Science but who was also helping to create a master plan for the renewal of all the river parklands. Karl volunteered to lead a boat tour as the culminating activity for our seminar. On a fine afternoon in the fall of 1999, we cast off from the dock at Herter Park and headed down river. Soon the combination of sun, water, and the passing shoreline had its way. All of us became intoxicated with the beauty of the place.

Karl shared with us his encyclopedic knowledge of the river and inspired us with his dedication to its use as parkland. As entranced as we all were that day, this was no simple exercise in landscape architecture or recreation planning. What we all began to see was the broad outline of a vision, a dream of a civil society centered around the democratic common ground of a magnificent parkland, the anchor of a great metropolitan park system.

I soon learned that Karl was not only a planner but a scholar of the river. As part of his graduate work at MIT he had written a dissertation on the epoch of brilliant invention and slow decline that had led to the present parklands. A reading of that dissertation was a revelation for me. Its chapters carefully chronicled the social, intellectual, and political forces that have shaped the basin. From the utopian musings of a nineteenth-century Scottish insomniac seeking a cure in Boston, to the monumental struggles over the river crossing schemes of the Big Dig, Karl told the river's story across the span of two centuries in an elegantly phrased, richly illustrated narrative. I saw immediately that this story demanded a larger audience.

In the three years since that idyllic tour, much has come to pass. The seminar led to the founding of the Charles River Conservancy. Understanding of the central role of the Charles River Parklands in the life of metropolitan Boston has increased among government leaders as well as the public, and the Commonwealth of Massachusetts is slowly moving toward funding the Charles River Basin master plan. With the plan now in general circulation and a wide-ranging discussion of how best to renew the parklands under way, the publication of *Inventing the Charles River* could not be more timely. The conservancy is pleased to have helped ensure its publication by providing staff support and finding sponsors willing to help offset some of the costs of production, and to have helped expand its scope by commissioning architectural photographer Peter Vanderwarker to create a series of pictures that complement the historic photos and drawings Karl has gathered.

While 150 years have passed since the notion of creating the parklands first was raised, the work remains unfinished. To read this book is to enter into the process of reimagining this landscape. In this way the parklands will continue to be a collective work of self-invention, an artifact of our own time and ethos. There is much to be done. Parkways must be protected, plantings renewed, bridges rebuilt, swimming made available once again, traffic calmed, and paths improved.

The challenge is formidable, but for those of us who have heard the river's song, it must be answered. *Inventing the Charles River* will help focus the work that we must do. The Charles River Parklands have the potential to become a world-class amenity that we can leave with pride to those who follow us. I invite you to join in this effort.

Acknowledgments

This project began in a conversation with Richard Rabinowitz and Sam Bass Warner, Jr., twenty years ago at the American History Workshop. It is my hope that what follows reflects their commitment to public history in the service of the community.

The research for this work has benefited from the generous help of many people and institutions. They include the Lina Coffey, Randall Mannella, and Catharina Slautterback, Boston Athenaeum; Lisa Tuite, The Boston Globe; John Dorsey, Aaron Schmidt, Eugene Zepp, and Roberta Zonghi, Boston Public Library; Richard Fitzgerald, Boston Society of Architects; Sean Noel, Boston University Special Collections; Nancy Richard, Bostonian Society; William Marchione, Brighton-Allston Historical Society; Kit Rawlins, Maeve Strucker, and Charles Sullivan, Cambridge Historical Commission; Dennis Carlone, Carlone & Associates; Kristen Swett, City of Boston Archive; Mary Daniels, Librarian, Special Collections, Frances Loeb Library, Harvard Graduate School of Design; Michele Clark, Frederick Law Olmsted National Historic Site; Kyle Carey, Brian Sullivan, and Melanie Halloran, Harvard University Archives; David Cobb, Harvard Map Collection; Roni Pick, Mapping Boston Foundation; Charles Beveridge, The Olmsted Papers, American University; Martha Clark and Maxine Trost, Massachusetts State Archive; the late Albert Swanson, Metropolitan District Commission; George Sanborn, Massachusetts State Transportation Library; Nicole Lapenta, MIT Museum; Janet Heywood, Mount Auburn Cemetery; Rob Roche, Shepley Bulfinch Richardson and Abbott; Lorna Condon, Society for the Preservation of New England Antiquities; and Beverly Schenk, Watertown Free Public Library.

The images that illuminate this story have been generously shared by Chan Krieger & Associates, Thomas Dahill, Bob von Elgg, Alex Gerard, Lajos Heder and Mags Harries, Jerry Howard, Landslides, Laurence Lowry, Bob O'Connor, John Powell, JoAnn Robinson, Peter Roudebush, Moshe Safdie and Associates, Arthur Shurcliff, Sylvia Stagg-Giuliano, James Storrow, Robert S. Sturgis, Steven Sylvester of Harvard College Library, Yanni Tsipis, Peter Vanderwarker, and Michael Zapf. Peter Vanderwarker expertly produced most of the contemporary images in chapter 12 to match the historic photographs.

For providing images I am also indebted to the staffs of the Barletta Company, Boston Herald, Boston Symphony Orchestra Archive, Brooklyn Museum of Art, Fundación Colección Thyssen-Bornemisza, Harvard Business School, Harvard College Library, Harvard University Art Museums, Hollis Taggart Galleries, Library of Congress, Middlesex Canal Association, Middlesex Registry of Deeds, Museum of Fine Arts, Museum of Hamburgische Geschichte, New York Public Library, Public Library of Brookline, Staatsarchiv Hamburg, State Library of Massachusetts, and Worcester Art Museum.

Their own knowledge and experience of the Charles has been shared with much enthusiasm and delight by Mark DeVoto, Isabella Halsted, John Moot, John Sears, and Patricia Sekler.

Most of all, this research has been made possible by the unfailing support of Sean Fisher of the Metropolitan District Commission Archives and Charles Sullivan of the Cambridge Historical Commission.

Permission from the Arnold Arboretum of Harvard University is gratefully acknowledged to include material in chapter 4 that was previously published in *Arnoldia*.

Source material, critical commentary, and research in progress were generously shared by Steve Carr, Tom Carter, Chris Greene, Gert Gröning, Julian Hillenkamp, Arleyn Levee, David Luberoff, Karen Madsen, Keith Morgan, Nancy Seasholes, Charles Sullivan, and Cynthia Zaitzevsky.

Julia O'Brien, the Director of Planning of the Metropolitan District Commission, has offered many thoughtful discussions about the Boston Metropolitan Park System and about this project. At the MDC the planning office provided a sense of perspective and a welcome *esprit*.

For friendship and support during the years of research and writing, I am grateful to Doug Anderson, Lloyd Baird, the late Jim Baum, Grant Bennett, Clayton Christensen, Carter Cornwall, Gary Crittenden, Paul Dredge, Don Eddington, Bob Fletcher, Chris Kimball, George McPhee, Richard Rabinowitz, and Bret Wunderli. Special thanks to Deborah Barlow, Gerald Horne, Tony Kimball, Tom Eagar, Katie and Tony Strike, and Sherry Kafka Wagner.

Harold Bauman, Carl Steinitz, and the late Kevin Lynch shared their understanding of history, cities, and landscapes. Leo Marx and Sam Bass Warner, Jr., gave thoughtful analysis and engaging criticism of the dissertation on which this book is based. As advisor and teacher, Stanford Anderson offered generous encouragement over many years.

Max Hall read a draft outline and shared his great editorial skill as well as his cheerful spirit and his appreciation of the river. For carefully reading all or substantial parts of the manuscript, I am indebted to Bob Fletcher, Grettle Haglund, Paul Haglund, Richard Haglund, Steve Kaiser, Bill Kuttner, John Sears, Nancy Seasholes, Charles Sullivan, and Jack Wofford. Karen Madsen gave insightful comments on the entire manuscript at a critical time. Our son David has cheerfully read almost every draft of every chapter, and his good judgment has improved the narrative from beginning to end.

The staff, volunteers, directors, and advisory board of the Charles River Conservancy have made this project possible: Kristin Mallek, Amelia Raven, and Fritz Nelson; Jay Baldwin, Catherine Donaher, and Mark Kraczkiewicz of the board of directors; John Moot, Barbara Norfleet, Patricia Platt, and Jane Zirpoli of the board of advisors; Lisa Schmid Alvord and Joel Alvord, Shary Page Berg, Liz Curtis, David and Katharine Davis, Laurie Gould, Betsy Harper, Candace Roosevelt, Elizabeth Sprague, Ellen Stevens, Mary and Roger Webb; Robert Cowden, Peter Golden, and Peter Munkenbeck. Susannah Hollister did exceptional work in collecting and organizing the images. Renata von Tscharner, the founder of the conservancy, has provided consistent encouragement and support for this book and the bold vision of its connection to the future of the parklands.

Larry Cohen, Michael Sims, and Yasuyo Iguchi of the MIT Press have generously given this project extraordinary patience and great professional skill.

My parents, Grettle and Richard, my wife's parents, Helen and Dee Call, Elizabeth Haglund, and my brothers and sisters have steadfastly supported this work. Most of all, I am grateful for the sustaining love and good cheer of my wife Karen and our children, Anna, Erik, David, Thomas, and Evan.

Introduction

Today the Charles at Boston . . . does not appear actually to flow at all. It is more like a great mirror held to the city's most favoring profile.
David McCord, 1948

The once-tidal reach of the Charles River, extending almost nine miles upstream from Boston Harbor to the low dam just above Watertown Square, has been called Boston's "Central Park." An open seam between Boston and Cambridge, this portion of the Charles looks to all appearances tranquil and almost unchanging, one of the most visible and carefully preserved natural features of Boston.

In fact, nothing could be further from the truth. Two hundred years ago Cambridge was separated from Boston by more than two miles of open water—three times the present distance—and by thousands of acres of salt marshes and open, unsettled lands extending in all directions from the river's meandering shores. In the nineteenth century the shallow basin, its nine-mile length edged with mud flats and broad salt marshes, was dammed for mills and filled for commercial and residential ventures. At low tide the bays of the lower Charles became vast expanses of noisome, sewage-laden mudflats.

Before the basin's fragmentary creation could begin, the river first had to be imagined as a public space. In a plan for the Boston metropolis published in 1844, the Charles was envisioned as a great public space and as the focal point of the region. The clarity of this metropolitan perspective, and the first phase of its startlingly rapid realization in the 1890s, brought immediate acclaim in Europe and America. Exhibits on metropolitan Boston's parks were included in the Paris Exposition of 1900, in several international fairs held in Buffalo, St. Louis, and Portland between 1901 and 1905, and at an international competition for the planning of Greater Berlin in 1910. The Boston regional park system was quickly recognized as the most notable scheme of comprehensive metropolitan park planning in the United States and the first such organization of land in the world.[1]

Once imagined, three signal interventions made possible the physical construction of this vision: the acquisition of the river banks by the Cambridge and Metropolitan Park Commissions in the 1890s; the construction of the Charles River Dam between 1903 and 1910; and the completion in 1936 of the Storrow Memorial Embankment, now universally known as the Esplanade. The transfer of the riverfront to the public domain was the essential first step. The dam stabilized the level of the river and forever covered the fetid mudflats. The creation of the Esplanade greatly enlarged the open margins of the river's shores and established the centerpiece of the "water park" that Bostonians had fantasized about since the middle of the nineteenth century.

The new public spaces along the Charles changed the way Bostonians perceived their city. The basin, with its expansive views of Boston and Cambridge, has become one of the two fundamental points of reference against which the visual character of the city is measured and remembered (Boston Common is the other).[2] The view from the river suggests an apparent clarity and visual order in a city otherwise well known for its bewildering and irregular geography. The basin has been called the city's most distinguishing physical feature.[3] Its form is straightforward: from below the Longfellow Bridge to Boston University, the basin is one extensive, almost regular space. Upstream, although the river narrows and bends and the views are much less expansive, we imagine this part of the Charles as a seamless extension of the paths and parkways along both shores.

River Stories

Perhaps because the image of the Charles is so distinct and its physical development so apparently obvious, its history has merited only passing mention in larger stories that might have paid it more attention.[4] And these stories have missed crucial differences, not only between the Charles River Basin and other public spaces created in metropolitan Boston, but also between the Charles and its most direct precedent, the designs by Frederick Law Olmsted for the Back Bay Fens (figures 4.22, 4.23). Discussions of public parks in nineteenth-century Boston usually focused on existing natural scenery that ought to be preserved. But the river was recognized as early as the 1820s as an enormously difficult sanitary

hazard, a reclamation project and not a "reservation" of unique or characteristic New England scenery.[5]

It would be hard to imagine a greater contrast in the treatment of urban rivers than between the Fens and the Charles Basin, in metaphorical as well as formal terms. Olmsted conceived and executed the Fens as a single, unified work. His design deliberately and successfully obscured almost all of the visual connections with the city around it. The Charles Basin, on the other hand, was imagined by many people as an expansive, open landscape. It has been built in fragments, here and there, and even now is under construction.

Both the Fens and the Charles are entirely designed spaces, "works of man rather than of nature,"[6] but even the barest outline of the history of the Charles is largely unknown. Few realize that the open space of the river between Cambridge and Boston is a complete transformation of a now-obliterated natural landscape, a transformation that proceeded over three or four generations.

After sketching the grand vision for the river of 1844 and the park debates in Boston after the Civil War, the narrative that follows will focus on the public discourse in two periods of the river's history: from 1890 to 1903, when the riverbanks were acquired and the Charles River Dam was approved; and the five years from 1989 to 1994, when the crossing of the river by the Central Artery/Tunnel project (the "Big Dig") was finally resolved. In the invention of the Charles River, who propounded the visions of the river's future? How were these visions shared? What of the early schemes was realized? How had Bostonians' views of the public realm changed by the last decade of the twentieth century?

Refinement and Professional Culture

At the core of these questions is the cultural matrix in which discussions of the city's design have taken place. The sustaining energy that recreated the Charles as an open, public landscape was rooted in European aristocratic traditions. Studies of public spaces in nineteenth-century America have focused on "moral order" and "civilizing the cities," but only recently have the historical origins

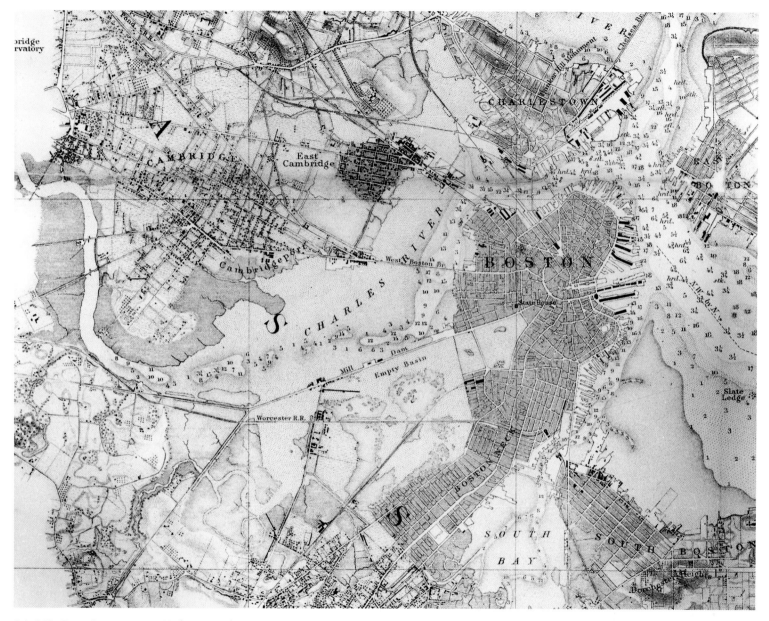

I.1 U.S. Coast Survey, *Boston Harbor, Massachusetts*, 1857.

I.2 The Charles River and Mount Auburn Street, Cambridge (left), 1878.

of this widely shared yearning for "the refinement of America" been carefully revealed.[7] The establishment of Boston's parks shows how this aspiration for refinement—as much as the fear of disorder and the impulse to civilize newcomers to the metropolis—enabled the city's urban visionaries to cultivate support for parks and public spaces among several generations of Boston and Cambridge elite. The aura of artistic and genteel elegance that suffused the sketches and drawings and the verbal representations of the Charles created a shared vision of the river that sustained continuing public investment in the basin's physical spaces.

These shared images not only illuminated the commitment to parks and public spaces; over time they helped alter the perception of the entire city. Eighteenth-century drawings of American cities, direct descendants of earlier European illustrations, conventionally presented urban centers behind a foreground of thriving waterfront commerce. By the end of the nineteenth century, the American invention of the skyscraper and its interpretation by photographers (especially in New York City) profoundly altered our sense of the modern city. Yet while capitalists in other American cities rushed to build the most thoroughly modern skyscrapers, conservative city fathers in Boston continued to enforce downtown height restrictions and imposed new height limits along the Charles.[8]

At some point early in the twentieth century, the popular views of the city from Boston Harbor were overtaken in popularity by photographs taken from across the Charles River looking

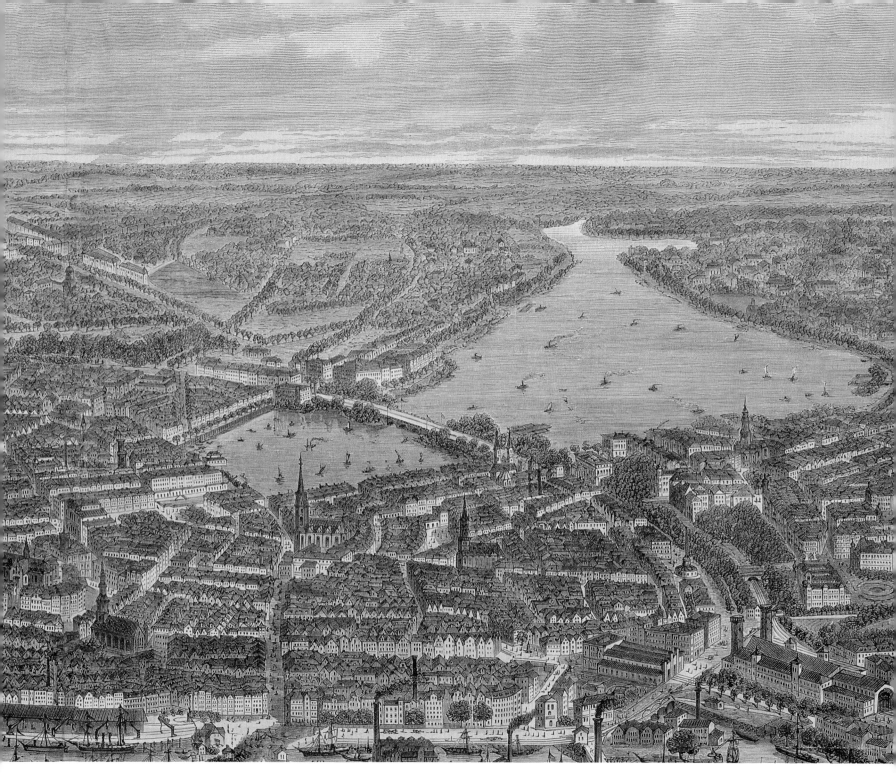

I.3 The Alster Basin, Hamburg, about 1870, frequently compared with
the Charles River Basin in the nineteenth century.

toward Beacon Hill, a horizontal urban image edged in tranquil blues and greens. Upstream of the Back Bay and on the Cambridge side, the city's universities erected the first tall buildings along the basin, in the 1960s; commercial developers soon followed their example. In the building boom of the 1980s, towers in downtown Boston went higher and higher, and dramatically transformed the long views from across the Charles. Although the skyscrapers now visible from the basin alter the sense of a linear, emerald-edged city, they are still sometimes half-wished away by the persistence of the older vision.

As the unifying effects of the older culture declined, and the new professional mode boldly extended its reach, public discussions of civic design in Boston were completely transformed. The post–Civil War park debates in Boston, and the park construction that followed, established a high-water mark for the culture of refinement. These public dialogues, as they were recorded in newspapers and other records, were high-toned exchanges among cultivated gentlemen, certain of their domain. Boston's city fathers also acknowledged the advance of professional culture, and they sought out Olmsted and other designers for competent technical advice, but they remained fully and finally in control.

This explicit commitment to subordinating professional competence in the service of an overarching public realm also marked the controversy over the first Charles River Dam when, after years of witnessing contentious and inconclusive arguments, James Storrow persuaded the legislature in 1902 to hire the best professional engineer it could find. The transformation wrought along the shores of the basin by the completion of the dam in 1910 did not, however, attain the appearance of refinement to which the city aspired, the Boston Society of Architects campaigned actively to enhance the river by creating new islands and bridges. In 1936 the Storrow Memorial Embankment—now known as the Esplanade—was dedicated, but only after the first genuinely acrimonious debate in Boston over highways.

Less than fifteen years after Bostonians created the Esplanade as the centerpiece of their "Emerald Metropolis," Storrow Drive, a limited-access highway, was pushed through the riverfront from

I.4 "Seawall on Charles River. Looking East toward Main Street." Cambridge, about 1897.

Soldiers Field Road in Brighton to Boston's West End, in spite of powerful public opposition.

The final landmark in the twentieth-century transformation of the basin was the controversy in the 1990s over the Central Artery/Tunnel project, in particular that part of the design known as Scheme Z, the river crossing over the mouth of the Charles. The artery project was driven by a tenacious commitment to demolish the elevated Central Artery through downtown Boston and rebuild it underground, with new buildings and public spaces where the old highway had been. Many observers of the artery sought a equally compelling vision for the project's proposed design for the Charles River bridges and the derelict spaces just beyond Boston, where more lanes of elevated highway were proposed than would be taken down in the center of the city.

Ultimately, an extraordinary public discussions about the Charles River Crossing of the Central Artery foundered over incommensurable issues. No one found ways of weighing betterments to traffic flow against the effects of massive, shadow-casting bridges and ramps on the urban life and visual character of the city. And just as in the 1850s it had been considered unseemly to discuss the benefits that would accrue to the owners of property adjacent to the proposed Central Park in New York, in the 1990s little public discussion compared the interests of downtown Boston property owners who would benefit from the new underground artery with the effects of all the new elevated roads and ramps to be built in neighborhoods north and south of downtown—in South Boston, the West End, Cambridge, and Somerville.[9]

The prospect of increasingly fragmented professional discourse troubled Charles W. Eliot as early as 1854—fifteen years before he became the president of Harvard: "The different professions are not different roads converging on the same end; they are different roads, which starting from the same vantage point diverge forever, for all we know."[10] In his subsequent efforts to make the university the ultimate guarantor of expert authority, President Eliot contributed to what finally became a great discontinuity in public life. As the historian Thomas Bender has outlined, a model was created of disciplinary rather than civic professionalism; of experts who abandoned their ties to places; of a "community without locality" based on professional relationships rather than face-to-face discourse among neighbors and citizens.[11]

When the unifying civic connections fray, once-fixed elements in the life of the community may lose their hold. Boston Common is arguably the city's most sacred public space, yet the weight of its three centuries in the history of the city was not enough to prevent the construction in the late 1950s of an underground parking garage on its western edge.[12] The Charles River Basin, by contrast, was shaped by promoters of landmaking and bridges and railroads before it was taken by acclamation into the public realm in the 1890s; given its much shorter past, it is not surprising to find along the river continuing conflicts between land development, ever-increasing auto traffic, and the claims of the community.

In the history of America's cities, the invention of the basin is an uncommon and remarkable landmark. The place of the Charles in the city of the twenty-first century will depend on a renewal of the civic vision that created this extraordinary legacy.

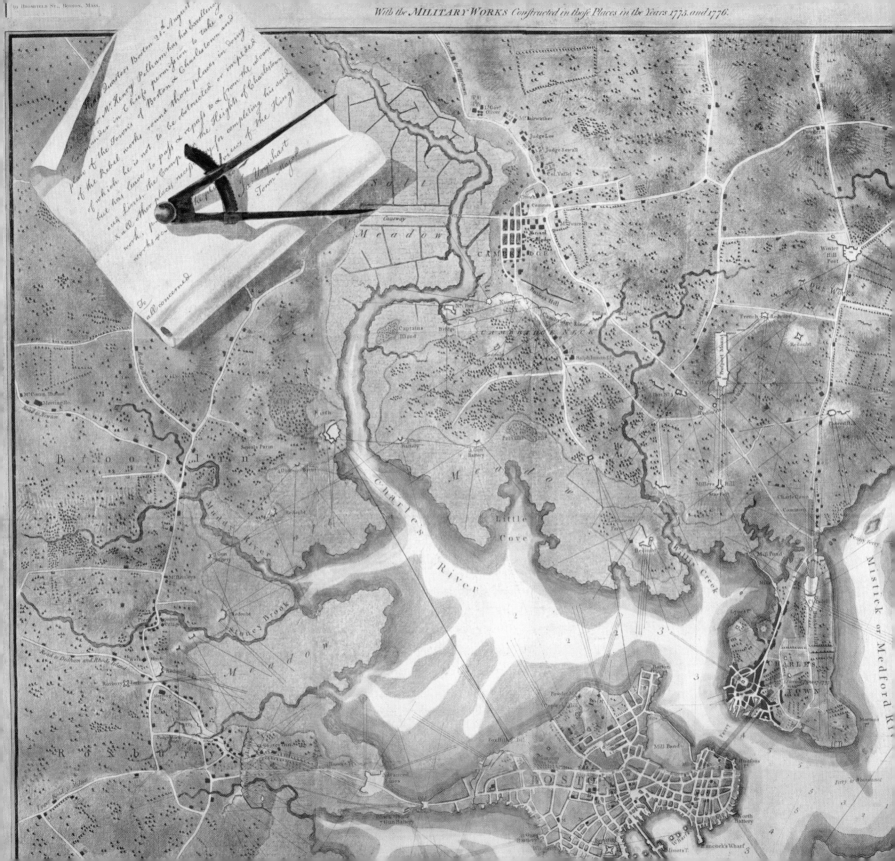

1

Earth Work

*It had often been said that a Boston man's ideas were limited by the
extent of the Common; that he could comprehend forty-one acres, but not
forty-two.*

Boston Post, June 17, 1874

Earth work is more durable than any other human work.

Charles W. Eliot, address to the American Society of Landscape
Architects, 1911

The earliest known maps showing the full extent of the tidal
Charles River basin from Boston to Watertown were drawn late in
the eighteenth century. Today these maps evoke startling and unfamiliar realms—scattered uplands separated by broad salt marshes,
mudflats that flooded at high tide. Prepared during the
Revolutionary War to document the colonists' fortifications in
Boston and Cambridge (frontispiece), these maps document a
physical reality that had changed very little since the first English
colonists settled in Boston a hundred and fifty years before. Since
the founding of Boston in 1630, the town's inhabitants contrived
only minor alterations to the region's topography.[1]

Beginning soon after the American Revolution, however,
the schemes of capitalists and builders began to make over their
surroundings. The leading citizens of the community shared an
almost limitless faith in the engineering of what were known
throughout the country as "internal improvements." Too late they
realized that these ingenious enterprises, in particular the mill
dams, bridges, and land fills, had turned the region's shallow, meandering rivers into open sewers, creating in the process sanitary hazards that could not be ignored. Yet it was the constrictions of the
region's environmental structure—the surficial remains of its geological past, which the improvers fought so tirelessly to overcome—that became the basis for every visionary scheme for the
Boston region.

The Topography of the River

The Charles River estuary, in its full tidal expanse, is almost beyond
imagining today. Nineteenth-century drawings, paintings, and

Frontispiece Henry Pelham, *A Plan of Boston in New England with its Environs,*
1777, detail

photographs of the river suggest the character of these broad salt marshes, although only hinting at their extent. Fragments of similar, once-extensive marshes can still be seen in Boston along the Mystic and Neponset Rivers; further north and south of the city, acres of salt-marsh meadows remain, dotted with rocky, tree-covered islands and flooded at high tide.

Although it is only about twenty-five miles over land from the source of the Charles in Hopkinton to the mouth of the river in Boston Harbor, the river's meandering course is almost eighty miles long. About ten miles from the harbor, the meager, unhurried stream flows across the center of a ring of hills that defines the perimeter of what geologists call the Boston Basin (figure 1.1). On the north, the hills follow a relatively straight line along a single escarpment from Waltham to Lynn. South of Waltham the basin's rim is obscured as the elevations increase more gradually; the Blue Hills form a more visible and dramatic edge just beyond the escarpment. Inside the fault lines of the basin the relatively soft sedimentary soils are manifest in a wide expanse of bays and marshes, not only of the Charles but also of the Mystic and the Neponset Rivers to the north and south.[2] The higher ground is dominated by southeast-facing drumlins, built up by the last glaciers ten thousand years before.[3]

The tidal estuary of the Charles extends eight miles upstream of the harbor to Watertown Square. Charles Eliot concluded in 1892 that the river's physical character "is and always was peculiar":

> In the first place, the so-called "River" is not a river. It is a tidal estuary, a shallow and muddy trough, broad in its seaward part, narrow and tortuous in its inward extension. . . . When the tide is out, the upper mile of the trough in Watertown is drained practically dry; the four succeeding miles of channel retain only from one to ten feet of water, and the bottom of the lower basin is exposed over at least half its area.[4]

Except for the river edges of the Boston and Charlestown peninsulas, almost the entire length of the estuary was rimmed with salt marsh.

At the boundary between fresh and salt water, the indigenous people had established a large settlement, perhaps as early as six thousand years ago, and had occupied the site continuously for over four thousand years (figures 1.2, 1.3).[5] The Algonkian name for this place was *Mushauwomuk*, "where there is a big river," and the name seems to have encompassed the entire river valley, not just the river itself.[6] A plague decimated almost the entire Native American population of the Bay Colony in 1617–1618, and the rich fishing grounds along the lower Charles were relinquished without resistance or compensation. The small community that remained joined John Eliot's "Praying Indians" in Natick in 1650. During King Philip's War, they were forcibly relocated and held on Deer Island in Boston Harbor, returning to settle in small communities along the Charles in Newton, Wellesley, and Medfield. By 1690 the Algonkian had deeded away all their claims in the Charles River Valley.[7]

Captain John Smith, after his second voyage to New England in 1615, published a description of the region and included a map in the second and subsequent editions. Smith himself proposed the name "New England" and described in his text the "Countrie of the Massachusetts" (the name of the local Algonkian tribe). Not surprisingly, the map itself ascribes the naming of "the most remarqueable parts" to "the high and mighty Prince Charles" (figure 1.4, to the left of the lion and the unicorn). The prince's own name was given to the river located between Cape Anna (after his mother) and Cape James (for his father).[8]

The English colonists later abbreviated the Algonkian name for the Charles River valley as "Shawmut" and applied it to the peninsula alone. From the beginning of settlement the colonists oriented the new town toward the harbor, as early engravings such as the well-known Bonner map of 1722 make clear (figure 1.5). The three hills of the peninsula's "Trimountain"—Cotton (later Beacon), and West (later Mt. Vernon)—separated much of the growing town from the river. The Charles lapped up against the western edge of the peninsula, where the Common sloped down from the Trimountain, and the mouth of the Charles was fixed on early maps just beyond the North Cove.[9]

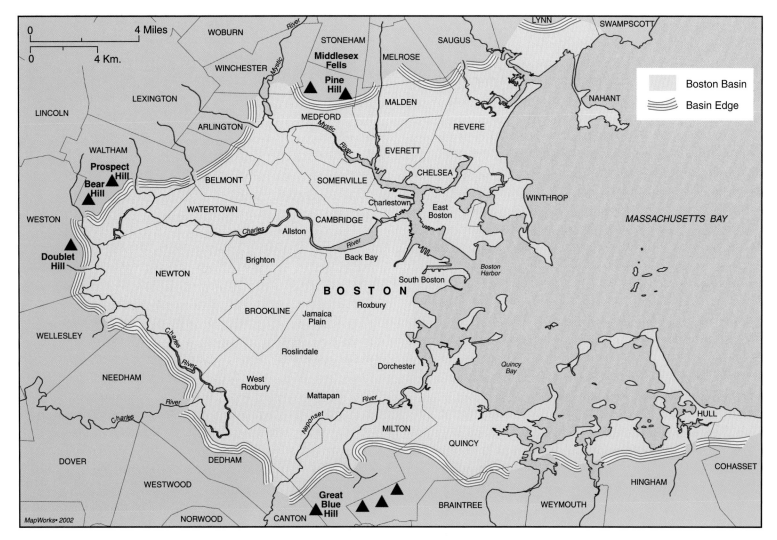

1.1 The Charles River Basin, extending from the harbor to Watertown Square, was subject to the ebb and flow of the tides until the completion of a temporary dam near the harbor in 1908. The Charles Basin is not to be confused with the Boston Basin, the relatively flat landscape inside the ring of hills and escarpments that surround Boston and the nearby cities. The hills extend from Lynn on the North Shore west to Waltham and south and east to Quincy on the South Shore, forming a ring around the Greater Boston area.

1.2 Perhaps as early as six thousand years ago, indigenous people established a large settlement along the Charles near Watertown Square and occupied the site continuously for more than four thousand years. This bronze relief by Claire Nivola was completed for Paul Revere Park in Charlestown in 1999.

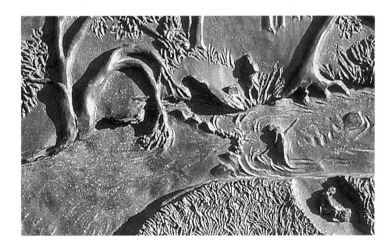

1.3 Thomas Morton, one of the early settlers of Mount Wollaston (now Quincy, Massachusetts), wrote in 1637 that "there is a fish called shads, by some allizes [alewives], that at the spring of the year pass up the rivers to spawn in the ponds, and are taken in such multitudes in every river that hath a pond at the end, that the Inhabitants dung their ground with them." In this detail of Claire Nivola's bronze relief, a native standing in the river is catching fish at the weir made of stones and brush.

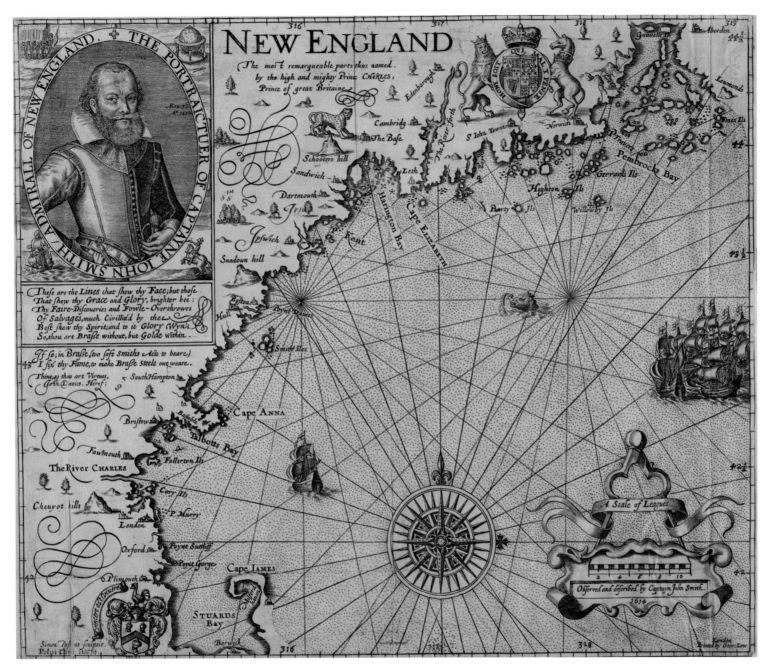

1.4 The first printed map to use the name "New England" was prepared by Captain John Smith in 1615. Many of the names on the map have changed or moved; a town named Boston appears on the map above the Smith Islands, and Cape James and Stuards Bay have long since been rechristened. But a few prominent names remain—including the River Charles, named for Prince Charles, then fifteen years old.

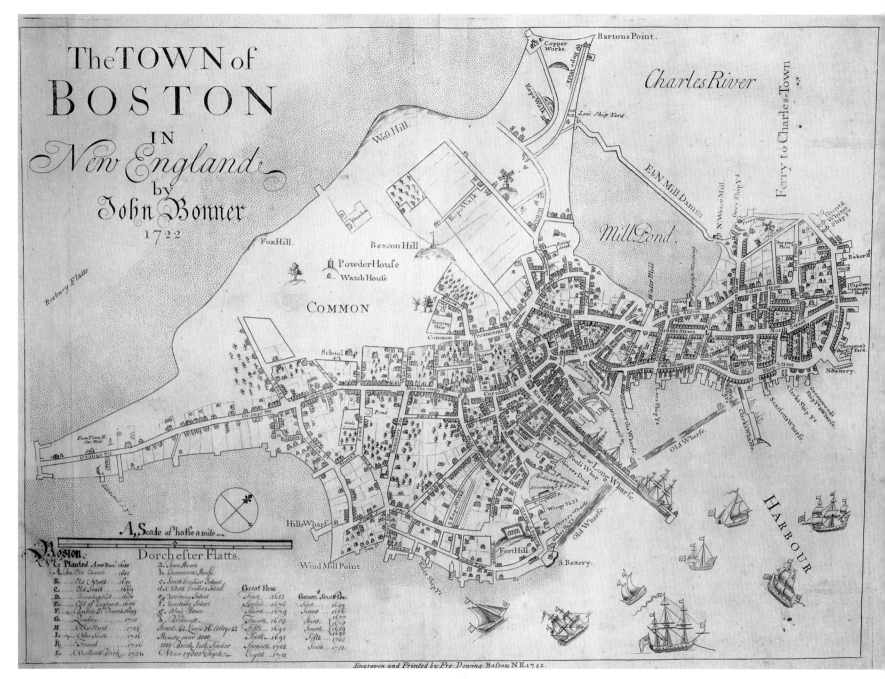

1.5 John Bonner's map of 1722, the oldest surviving map of Boston, shows the mill and dam built across the cove on the north end of the Shawmut peninsula (upper right). West of the Common are the Roxbury Flats (later called Back Bay). A 1777 map by Thomas Page noted that the flats were "dry at low water."

The broad extent of the lower Charles and its tributaries cut off Boston from the surrounding countryside and from the settlements at Charlestown and Newtowne (as Cambridge was known until 1638). The mouth of the river, between Charlestown and Boston, was less than a third of a mile across, but for a hundred and fifty years, ferries offered the only passage linking the two towns (figure 1.6, center). Like Boston, the Charlestown peninsula was mostly well-drained upland, without the extensive marshes or mudflats of Cambridge or Roxbury. Immediately upstream of the harbor were Boston's North Cove and the broader expanse of Gibbons' Creek (on some maps marked as Willis Creek, later Miller's Creek, and finally Miller's River). Grave's Neck, now the densely settled community of East Cambridge, was a small island at high tide, cut off from both Cambridge and Charlestown. The shallow flats of Oyster Bank Bay along the southern edge of Cambridge were separated from the uplands by the "Great Marsh." On the Boston side, Stony Brook and the Muddy River flowed into the wide and irregular expanse of Back Bay, known earlier as the Roxbury Flats (figure 1.6).[10]

The breadth of the Back Bay at its widest point, from Boston Neck (today the intersection of Washington and East Berkeley Streets) to the mouth of Little Cove in Cambridge (now the intersection of Brookline and Auburn Streets, just east of Central Square) was over a mile (more than three times its present width at the Harvard Bridge). At high tide the level of the basin rose nine feet above the low-water mark; extreme high tide was as much as fifteen feet above low water.

Upriver, at Captain's Island (now Magazine Beach), the Charles narrows and veers almost due north. Twice a day the expanse of marshes on the south side of the river (present-day Soldiers Field and the Harvard Business School campus) were flooded by the incoming tide (figure 1.6, upper left). The trip from Boston to Cambridge, across Boston Neck and then skirting the marshes on the south side of the bay, was eight miles. By ferry to Charlestown, the journey to Cambridge was about half as far.[11]

1.6   Henry Pelham, *A Plan of Boston in New England with its Environs,* 1777.

Mill Dams and Wharves

In this "watery landscape" the harvesting of salt hay in the marshes began, undramatically, the alteration of the estuary's natural landscape by the English settlers (figure 1.7). Far more conspicuous in "the inexorable encroachment of land upon water that has marked the history of Boston" was the construction of wharves on the harbor side of the peninsula, also begun in the first years of settlement. At the end of the eighteenth century, as the city expanded to the west, mill dams and bridges built along the rivers hastened the creation of new land. The mill dams created shallow ponds, and sooner or later the production of the mills was exceeded in value by the prospect of creating new lands by filling the ponds. Bridges, especially when their construction necessitated long causeways across shallow marsh land, attracted fill at their abutments the way ships attract barnacles.[12]

The grist mill in Watertown, erected by 1634, was the first dam on the Charles and is generally regarded as the first dam in the Bay Colony. The dam is not mentioned in the records of the General Court, perhaps because the right to construct a fish weir had already been given on the same site two years earlier. The mill creek may have been dug at the same time, creating an island in

1.7 "Summer Showers," Martin Heade's 1870 painting of a marsh near Newburyport, Massachusetts, delineates a coastal estuary bounded by rocky uplands. The marshes along the edge of Cambridge and Watertown looked much like this in the years before the settlements were extended to the river's edge.

Chapter 1

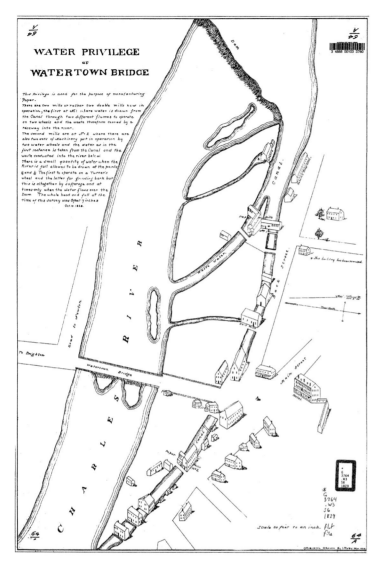

1.8   In 1632 the General Court authorized the construction of a weir on the Charles at the fall line in Watertown, which marked the upstream extent of the tidal river. Two years later a mill dam was built on the same site.

Watertown Square. Built just beyond the head of the tide, the dam established the upper limit of navigation on the river (figure 1.8).[13]

The difficulty of maneuvering through the shallow channels downstream of Watertown was one reason for the selection of the site for Newtowne. As the first capital of the Bay Colony, the town was to be accessible to the harbor, but also defensible against pirates or attacks from the mother country to revoke the colony's charter. A low hill above the river overlooked both the town and the landing below, and Town Creek, which followed a curving line just west of Creek Lane (now Eliot Street) and then turned sharply south below Water (now Dunster) Street and drained into the river. A ferry was established from the foot of Water Street to Little Cambridge across the river (a separate parish in 1679, chartered as the town of Brighton in 1807). The founding of Harvard College in 1636 compensated in part for the loss of the seat of government, which was moved to Boston two years later. A town wharf was built in 1651, and in 1660–1662 the Great Bridge (on the site of the present Anderson Bridge) was financed by a levy against the whole colony, the first bridge below the mill dam in Watertown. Extending from the foot of Wood Street (later Boylston, now John F. Kennedy Street), the bridge attracted sufficient traffic that Water Street was eclipsed as the center of commerce in Cambridge (figures 1.9, 1.10).[14]

After the Watertown dam and gristmill, the next mill privilege to be granted was in 1643 for a dam across the cove on the north end of the Shawmut Peninsula. There the proprietors were required to erect "one or more corne mills, and maynteyne the same for ever." A narrow island (running roughly along the line of what is now Causeway Street) created a path across the cove at low tide, and served as the foundation for a mill dam across the cove (figure 1.5). The mill owners also dug a channel from the mill pond to the Great Cove (also known as Town Cove), which separated the North End from the rest of Boston; bridges over the channel were built at North and Hanover Streets. The fouling of the river and the harbor was presaged by a determination in 1656 that the bridge at North Street was the only place in the town where "beasts entralls and garbidg" could be dumped without a fine.[15]

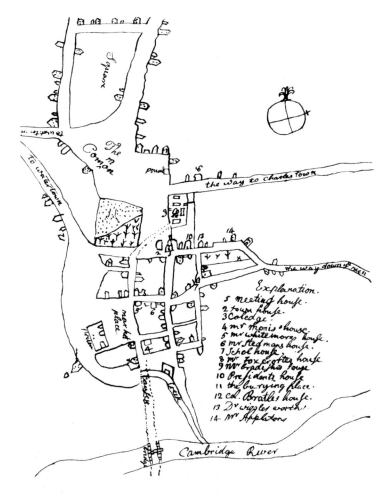

1.9 The oldest extant map of Cambridge dates from about 1748. Although crudely drawn, the map confirms the location of Town Creek (now Eliot Street) and its passage under the "causey" (causeway) to the bridge over the "Cambridge River." The map's legend lists the meetinghouses, the college, and the houses of some of the town's prominent citizens.

1.10 The town of Cambridge as it appeared in 1775 was reconstructed in this 1947 diorama at Harvard's Widener Library. At the lower left is Harvard Yard; the town dock is at the lower right corner. The Boston peninsula is separated from Cambridge by the wide expanse of the Back Bay.

With these few exceptions—the mill dams at Watertown Square and North Cove in Boston, the first Great Bridge in Cambridge—the river and its margins remained largely unaltered from the founding of the Bay Colony until the end of the Revolutionary War. The Charles was the principal route to Boston from Cambridge and points west, but through the eighteenth century the city remained oriented to the harbor and saw itself as a seaport, the principal gateway to England and the Continent. The construction of Long Wharf, begun in 1711, heightened that waterfront perspective (figure 1.11). Beginning at King (now State) Street and extending well beyond Town Cove into the harbor, Long Wharf created what "amounted to a dramatic road from Boston to the sea . . . the obvious avenue to Boston from the part of the world that really mattered."[16]

A South East View of the Great Town of BOSTON in New England in America.

Printed for Carington Bowles Map & Printseller at N.o 69 in St Pauls Church Yard. London.

1.11 For its first hundred and fifty years, Boston saw itself as a seaport, the principal gateway in the colonies to England and the Continent. Shipping on the Charles was important, but the distance between bridges made the river a topographical obstacle, hindering travel between Boston and the surrounding settlements. This painting by J. Carwitham is based on a drawing by John Bonner from about 1725.

The insular character of the city began to change at the end of the eighteenth century as bridges were built linking Boston with the mainland. The replacement of the ferry to Charlestown (from present-day Washington Street to City Square) was discussed in Boston town meeting as early as 1720, when, according to Governor Hutchinson, it was "looked upon as a Quixote enterprise." In 1738 a proposal to construct a bridge from Boston to Lechmere Point was denied by the General Court, although discussions of bridges recurred intermittently until after the Revolutionary War. In 1785, the legislature denied another petition for a bridge to Lechmere Point, this time from Andrew Cabot, who had purchased the confiscated Phipps farm at one end of the proposed bridge. Instead, the right to build a toll bridge from Boston to Charlestown (just downstream of today's Charlestown Bridge) was awarded to Thomas Russell, John Hancock, and eighty-two other incorporators. To compensate Harvard College for the loss of its ferry privilege (granted in 1640), the proprietors were obligated to pay the college £200 annually. Fifteen hundred feet long and forty-two feet wide, with a thirty-foot draw near the center, the bridge cost £1500 and was the only permanent bridge of any size in America (figures 1.12, 1.13). At the time there were, for example, no bridges at all over the Merrimack, the Connecticut, the Hudson, the Delaware, the Susquehanna, or the Potomac.[17]

The dedication ceremonies on the eleventh anniversary of the Battle of Bunker Hill in 1786 attracted "almost every respectable character in publick and private life" in Boston. The bridge was hailed as a triumph of technology, and shortened the route to Boston for merchants and farmers in Charlestown, Malden, and Medford (at the time, these three cities together were about twice as large as the population of Cambridge). A banquet for six hundred people was served on Breed's Hill; a poem composed for the occasion, titled "On the flourishing State of Charlestown," summarized the pastoral ideal to which the town aspired, "Where city life with rural sweets is join'd."[18]

1.12 The replacement of the Charlestown ferry with a bridge in 1786 established the only permanent bridge of any size in America. The bridge's proprietors were required to compensate Harvard College for the loss of income from the ferry privilege, which had been granted to the college in 1640.

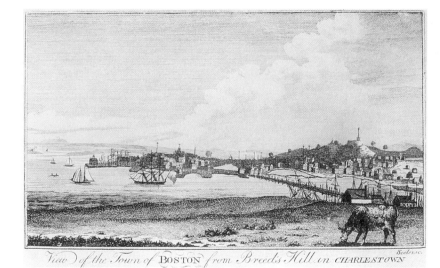

View of the Town of BOSTON *from Breed's Hill in* CHARLESTOWN

1.13 The view of Boston from Breed's Hill in Charlestown at the end of the eighteenth century reveals the prominence of the Trimountain and the lantern on the top of Beacon Hill. At fifteen hundred feet in length, forty-two feet wide, with a thirty-foot draw near the center, the Charles River Bridge was a visual emblem of Boston's zeal to expand trade.

The zeal to expand trade with the hinterlands that drove the construction of the Charles River Bridge also resulted in the first major canal project in Massachusetts. Secretary of War Henry Knox commissioned a survey for a canal from the Charles to the Connecticut River in 1791, and a company was incorporated the following year. Knox's venture was a false start; a more feasible canal venture was organized two years later to link Boston with the Merrimack River. Designed by Loammi Baldwin of Charlestown, the last section linking the canal with the mill pond south of Charlestown neck was opened on New Year's Eve in 1803 (figures 1.14, 1.15). It was described in the 1808 report on roads and canals of the U.S. Treasury secretary as "the greatest work of the kind" in America.[19]

Five years later, the canal company rented part of the Almshouse Wharf in Boston's West End (east of the future site of Massachusetts General Hospital) and built offices and storage sheds. The annual report for 1808 noted that "a line of direct communication has been fixed" between the wharf in Boston and the canal's termination in Charlestown "by means of buoys and ropes, so that our boats could pass over against the wind and across the tide."[20] Floating buoys marked the location of the cables, which were heavily weighted and rested on the river bottom until the canal boatmen pulled them up as they guided their cargoes across Charles River Bay (figure 1.16). From there barges continued on the canal through the former mill pond past Haymarket to the Town Dock.[21]

The Middlesex Canal struggled to make a profit for two decades; although the value of the stock increased considerably, shareholders paid a hundred assessments of varying amounts during those years. The canal business was marginal until the establishment of the Lowell mills in 1822; the company's best years were the mid-1830s—just as the Boston and Lowell Railroad opened. The payment of dividends ended in 1845, and seven years later the directors voted to remove the dilapidated bridges over the canal, to "cause the canal under said bridges to be filled up," and to sell the remaining property of the corporation.[22]

The Charles River Bridge, however, made money from the first. Its success opened people's eyes, not only to the prospects for new development in Boston, Charlestown, and the towns to the north, but also to the financial prospects for toll bridges linking Boston more directly to Cambridge and the towns to the west. The proprietors of the West Boston Bridge (replaced in 1907 by the Longfellow Bridge) did not wait for a charter, but proceeded in 1793 to sell 200 shares in three hours. This speculative fever alarmed a number of conservative Bostonians; it would be cured, John Adams predicted, "by a few bankruptcies which may daily be expected, I had almost said, desired." Two months later the New York markets crashed.[23] A newspaper editorial argued that the new bridge with its more direct access to Cambridge would raise the temptations and therefore the expenses of Harvard College students.[24] The high profits from the existing bridge suggested to some that it held an undeserved monopoly, and not surprisingly, the Charles River Bridge proprietors objected to the new bridge. They were placated by an extension of their right to collect tolls an additional thirty years, and the new bridge was approved.[25]

Built in 1793, the bridge extended from Cambridge Street in Boston over the river to a causeway that ended at Pelham's Island (figure 1.17). More than twice as long (3,483 feet) as the Charles River Bridge, it also required a causeway 3,344 feet across the Cambridge marshes. It also hastened the growth of Boston's West End, where prosperous merchants like Harrison Gray Otis built fine residences.

Across the river, the new bridge created aspirations for international trade among the proprietors of the new village of Cambridgeport.[26] Within a year after the West Boston Bridge was completed, half a dozen buildings had been constructed on Pelham's Island (near present-day Lafayette Square). Canals and dikes were built to drain the marshland around the island and define clear navigation channels, streets were laid out, and house lots plotted. In 1805 Cambridgeport was declared a U.S. port of delivery, and the Cambridge and Concord Turnpike (now Broadway) and the Middlesex Turnpike (now Hampshire Street) were authorized. A year later the population of the Port was estimated at a thousand people. Lumber, coal, and stone wharves along the causeway and the canals relied upon the river for transportation,

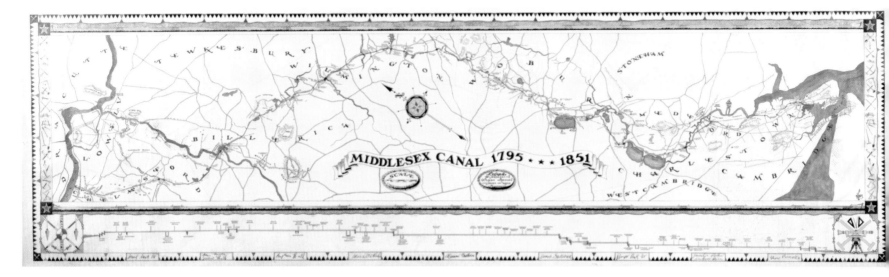

1.14 Opened in 1803, the Middlesex Canal was described by the U.S. Secretary of the Treasury as "the greatest work of the kind" in the entire country. The canal linked Boston to the Merrimack River valley and to the growing cities further north and west.

1.15   Like Boston, Charlestown was connected to the mainland by a narrow neck of land that separated the Mystic River (upper left) from the Charles. The Middlesex Canal emptied into the old mill pond at the meeting point of the Charles and Miller's Rivers.

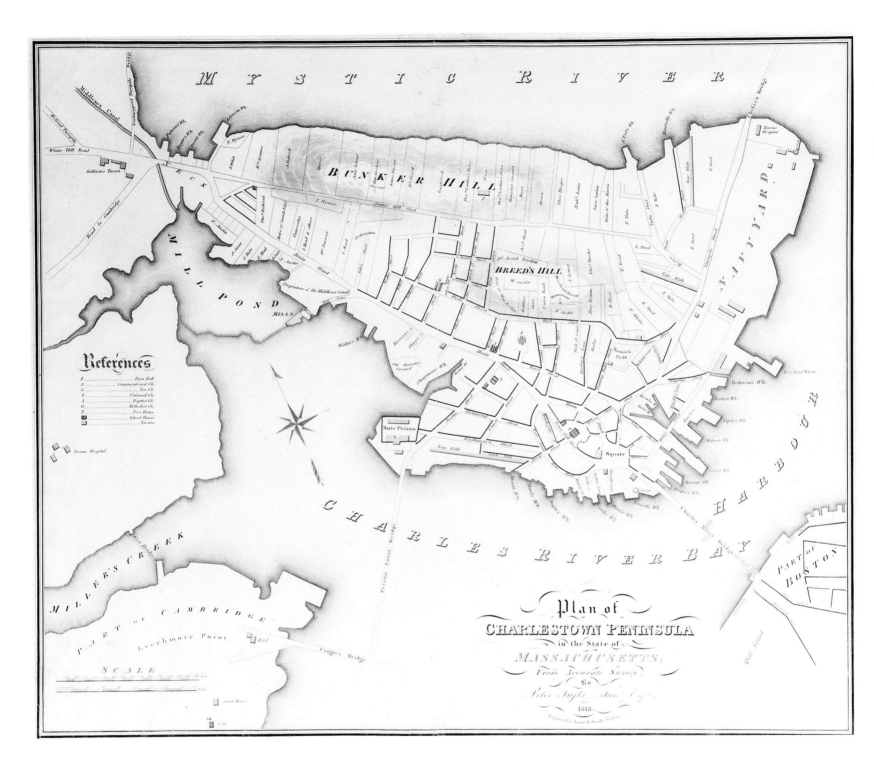

Plan of
CHARLESTOWN PENINSULA
in the State of
MASSACHUSETTS,
From Accurate Survey
By
Peter Tufts, Jun. Esq.
1818.

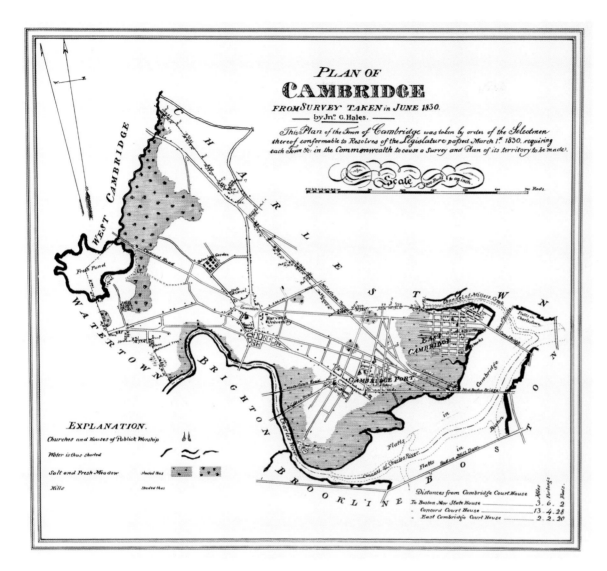

1.17 The West Boston Bridge (lower right, running from Cambridge Street in Boston to Main Street in Cambridge) was approved after the owners of the Charles River Bridge downstream were granted the right to collect tolls for thirty years beyond their original charter. Marshes were drained to transform Pelham's Island into the new village of Cambridgeport at the west end of the bridge, in the hope of creating an important destination for international trade.

1.16 A system of ropes and floating buoys allowed canal boats to cross the Charles from the mill pond near Charlestown Neck to the company offices at Almshouse Wharf in Boston's West End. From there boats continued to the mill pond at North Cove (lower right) and to the canal (now Canal Street) that emptied into Boston Harbor.

1.18 In 1816, the U.S. Arsenal at the Charlestown Navy Yard was moved seven miles up the Charles to Watertown from its exposed location on Boston Harbor. One consequence was that the war department demanded that all new bridges on the river from the harbor to the arsenal be built with draws. This would become a major issue eighty years later when the West Boston Bridge was replaced.

but the town never fulfilled the commercial aspirations of its proprietors. A half-mile stretch of woods isolated the village from Old Cambridge, and much of the Great Marsh still remained, a hindrance to development on the east. The West Boston Bridge proprietors built the River Street and Western Avenue Bridges to link their first bridge with Brighton, but the center of commerce had shifted to East Cambridge. In twenty-five years, the only outside capital the village attracted was the state powder magazine, built on Captain's Island near the river's edge in 1818.[27]

The following year the U.S. War Department determined that an upstream location was more secure against foreign attack and relocated the navy's arsenal from Charlestown to Watertown (figure 1.18). One consequence of this move was the war department's jurisdiction over bridges on the Charles, including a stipulation that draws were required between the arsenal and the harbor.[28]

The rise of East Cambridge also began with bridge construction, this time promoted by Andrew Craigie. Although he was not an incorporator, Craigie was a member of the first board of directors for the Middlesex Canal. He began buying land (secretly directing friends and relatives) in East Cambridge near the terminus of the canal soon after construction started. By 1805 he controlled all the upland of East Cambridge and petitioned the General Court for approval of a bridge from his properties to Boston. Over the next two years the Middlesex Canal owners and the Newburyport Turnpike proprietors also applied to the legislature for a bridge from Boston to East Cambridge, then finally agreed to join with Craigie in a single company.[29]

Disagreements over the location were resolved, and Loammi Baldwin designed a structure to connect Leverett Street in the West End with Lechmere's Point (figure 1.19). Among the leading opponents of Craigie's Canal Bridge were the proprietors of the West Boston Bridge. Their charter required an annual payment to Harvard College, the holder of the original ferry privilege from Boston to Charlestown. The Canal Bridge company agreed to pay half of the annual annuity owed by the West Boston Bridge to the college. The Charles River Bridge owners, however, did not oppose this third river crossing. They were collecting almost $20,000 a year in tolls, and the value of their stock had tripled.[30]

That was not, however, the end of the controversy. At one point some investors in Cambridgeport refused to allow the construction of Cambridge Street across their property because it would provide a straight thoroughfare from the Canal Bridge and East Cambridge to the center of Old Cambridge (figure 1.17); petitions and counterpetitions were filed with the legislature. The charter was, in the end, awarded to Craigie, and the bridge finally opened in August 1809.[31]

Craigie then turned to developing the 300 acres he held in East Cambridge, which he had purchased for less than $20,000. He

1.19 Charles Bulfinch was a Boston selectman when he drew the plan for what is now known as the Bulfinch Triangle. In his plan, the mill dam became a street along the edge of the Charles; Merrimack and Charlestown (now North Washington) Streets defined the other two sides of the triangle.

sold sixty shares at $6,000 each and later named some of the streets after the new shareholders. After lobbying Middlesex County officials and making a gift of $24,000 to the county, Craigie persuaded them to relocate the courthouse to East Cambridge. A grand gala was held to celebrate the opening of the courthouse, designed by Charles Bulfinch and completed in 1816. The following year the New England Glass Company opened northeast of Bridge Street, the most succesful of the early enterprises that made East Cambridge the center of industry along the lower basin.[32]

Damming the Back Bay

Here and there, especially near the new bridges, marshes were drained and filled to create new land. At the turn of the nineteenth century, the scale of these operations dramatically increased. In the Back Bay the "first instance of dumping the tops of hills into coves" began in 1799. The Mount Vernon Proprietors had acquired property on the southwest slope of the Trimountain from the agent of John Singleton Copley, who had left Boston twenty years before, never to return. When Copley learned of the sale, he thought the price was far too low and refused to sign the deed. (Lawsuits over the sale continued into the 1830s.) The proprietors then commissioned two surveys, one by Bulfinch and another by Mather Withington, the proprietors' surveyor. Bulfinch's grandiose design made a square (as the proprietors had renamed the westernmost peak) 460 feet long and 190 feet wide of the top of Mount Vernon; the surveyor's simpler plan, which was chosen, required cutting down the hill by fifty or sixty feet. A gravity railroad was constructed to dump the gravel from the hill into the river, making land that became Charles Street. The railroad has been described as the first in America, and the land transaction was the largest in Boston up to that time.[33]

Beacon Hill was the next peak of Boston's Trimountain to go. First proposed in a contentious town meeting in 1804, an agreement to fill the Mill Pond for house lots was finally approved three years later; the town would get the one-eighth of the land. An extension of the Mill Creek would be built parallel to the new Canal Street, allowing water to continue to flow from the Charles through the canal to the harbor. Charles Bulfinch was appointed to the committee to resolve the arrangement of the new streets and drew the plan that is now known as the Bulfinch Triangle (figure 1.19). The filling went on for twenty-one years (figure 1.20), and when the remains of Beacon Hill proved insufficient, the gravel from the hill was supplemented with mud from tidal flats.[34]

These early land-making efforts would soon be overwhelmed in scale by a scheme proposed for the Back Bay. Its original intention was to replace the mills that had been lost in the filling of the Mill Pond, but it was finally the failure of this grandiose milling enterprise that changed "the shape of Boston more completely than any other single undertaking in its history."[35]

In June 1813 Uriah Cotting and others petitioned the legislature to establish the Boston and Roxbury Mill Corporation and to allow the new company to dam both the Back Bay and the South Boston Bay, connecting them by raceways across Boston Neck to create tidal ponds for generating power (figure 1.21). The Back Bay mill dam would extend from the corner of the Common at the foot of Beacon Street to Gravelly Point in Roxbury (today the intersection of Commonwealth and Massachusetts Avenues). To help defray the cost, a toll road would be built on top of the dam that would connect with the Worcester Turnpike (now Route 9). The following year another scheme proposed to add to the original plan two additional dams, one across the Charles (near the present Harvard Bridge) and the other across the Miller's River in Cambridge.[36]

A town committee reported that there were few objections to the scheme; the mill dams would retain in Boston large amounts of capital "now forcing their way in distant and inconvenient situations," would create "new sources of employment," and would render valuable an extensive tract of land owned by the town. The committee recommended approval of the plan, provided that a portion of the shares in the corporation were made available to all who wished to purchase them.[37]

The legislature then held hearings and issued a report that endorsed the Cotting scheme with some changes. Bridges already

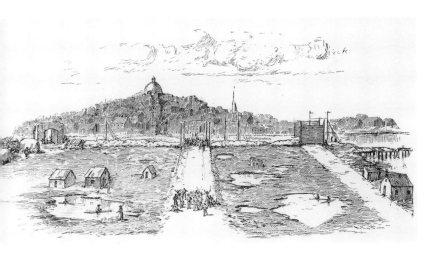

1.20   In this lithograph from the late 1820s, Causeway and Traverse Streets are barely cow paths, and the filling of the Bulfinch Triangle is still unfinished. The masts of sailing ships are visible above the edge of the canal, which linked the river and the mill pond with Town Cove and the harbor. On the horizon are the houses on Beacon Hill and the dome of the State House.

impeded navigation in both South Bay and the Back Bay, and the Back Bay was very rarely navigated, making both bodies of water "almost a *waste*" for commercial traffic. The new water-powered mills would give Boston an edge over New York and Philadelphia, whose factories were dependent on steam power. The mills would employ as many as 10,000 people and require $8,000,000 in capital.[38]

Passed in 1814, the act of incorporation altered the terms of the project. South Bay would be the full basin, rather than the empty basin, and the dam across Back Bay would extend from Beacon Street to Sewall's Point in Brookline (now Kenmore Square), rather than to Gravelly Point. A third dam, the "Short Dam," was also authorized, from Gravelly Point to the relocated Back Bay dam (figure 1.22). Although the deliberations of the legislature show no objections to the project because of its effects on public health, the act gave the Board of Health the authority to require that the flats in the empty basin be kept covered with water. At the close of its session that year the legislature approved the charter with only fifty of the five hundred legislators present and voting.[39]

The sanitary hazards of Boston's rivers have in recent times been described as a post–Civil War issue, created by the city's phenomenal growth in the last third of the nineteenth century.[40] In fact, the problem was prophesied in 1814, before the dam across the Back Bay was built: One Boston resident, in a letter to the editor of the *Daily Advertiser* the day after the charter was approved, wrote that the mill dams would create an "empty mud-basin, reeking with filth, abhorrent to the smell and disgusting to the eye."[41]

The project, as described by Cotting in his public stock offering in 1818, was seen entirely in economic terms. It had been delayed by the War of 1812, and now the need for mill sites in Boston was greater in New England than elsewhere. The population was increasing faster than the agriculture and manufacturing enterprises to support them, and the region's only advantage was the "superabundant productiveness in men." Boston had the opportunity, unmatched by any other city in the world, to create all of the water power necessary for its future manufactories, and tide mill power would be 10 percent less cost-

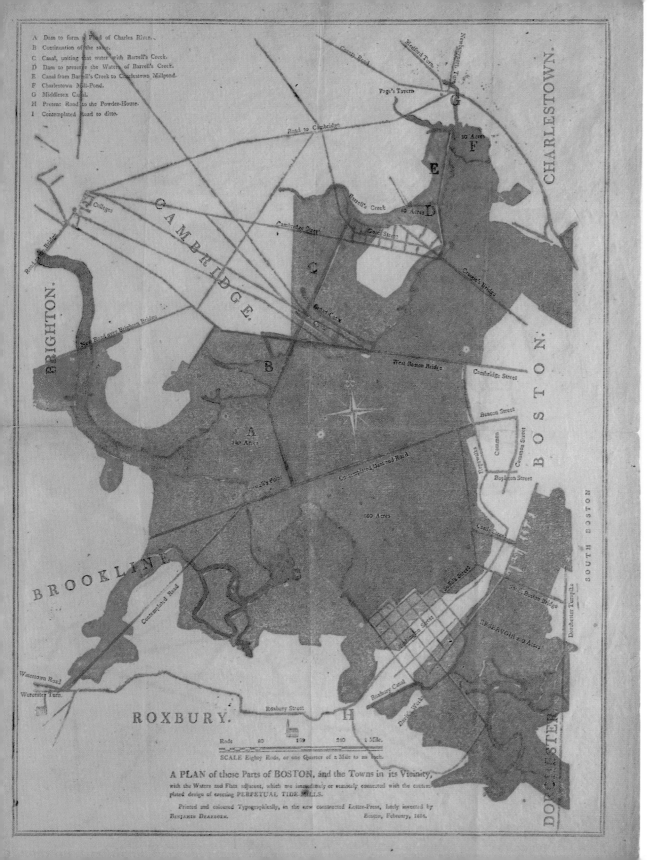

A Dam to form a Pond of Charles River.
B Continuation of the same.
C Canal, uniting that water with Barrell's Creek.
D Dam to preserve the Waters of Barrell's Creek.
E Canal from Barrell's Creek to Charlestown Millpond.
F Charlestown Mill-Pond.
G Middlesex Canal.
H Present Road to the Powder-House.
I Contemplated Road to ditto.

CHARLESTOWN.

BRIGHTON.

CAMBRIDGE.

BOSTON.

SOUTH BOSTON

BROOKLINE.

ROXBURY.

DORCHESTER.

Rods   50   100   210   ¼ Mile.
SCALE Eighty Rods, or one Quarter of a Mile to an Inch.

A PLAN of those Parts of BOSTON, and the Towns in its Vicinity,
with the Waters and Flats adjacent, which are immediately or remotely connected with the contemplated design of erecting PERPETUAL TIDE-MILLS.

Printed and coloured Typographically, in the new constructed Letter-Press, lately invented by
BENJAMIN DEARBORN.   Boston, February, 1814.

1.21 The first of several proposals to dam the Back Bay was submitted to the legislature in 1813. A year later, this scheme by Benjamin Dearborn suggested three dams on the Charles, one near the present Harvard Bridge and another across Barrell's Creek.

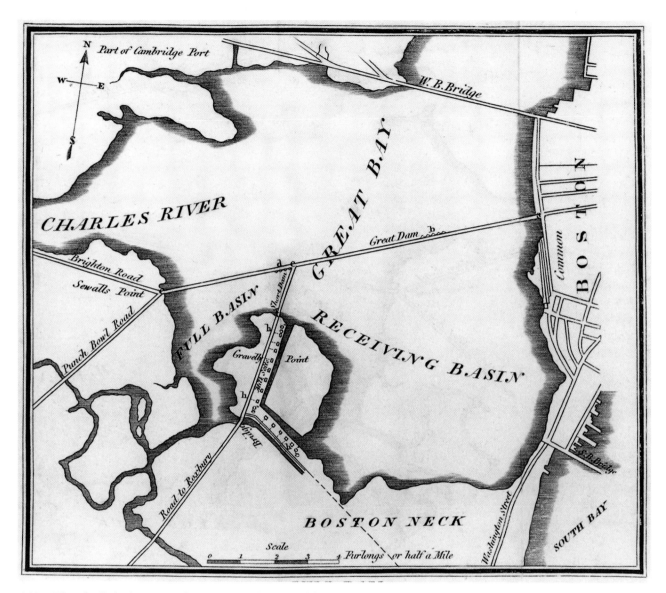

1.22 When finally built in 1821, the "Great Dam" extended from the corner of Beacon and Charles Street to Sewall's Point in Brookline (now Kenmore Square). As this map shows, a "Short Dam" separated the "Full Basin" from the "Receiving Basin." Eighty-one mills, according to the project's promoters, would employ ten thousand people. Only a few Bostonians entertained the possibility that the Back Bay might become an "empty mud-basin, reeking with filth."

ly than steam power, on which other cities relied. To assure prospective stockholders, Cotting noted the skepticism that greeted the proposal for the Charles River Bridge, whose stock was now worth six times its original price. The mill dams would not only generate power, but the primary dam would also function as a toll road connecting the foot of Beacon Street with the Worcester Turnpike. His pointed final lines observed that "If the public do not have all these improvements it will not be the fault of URIAH COTTING."[42]

The stock subscription sold out in a few hours, the dam was constructed, and Western Avenue, the new toll road (now Beacon Street), was opened in July 1821. In the opening day address, General William Sumner observed that three decades earlier, Boston Neck was the only land route from Boston to the Mainland.

> It was then, our town resembled a hand, but it was a closed one. It is now opened and well spread. Charlestown, Cambridge, South Boston, and Craigie's Bridge have added each a finger, and lately our enterprising citizens have joined the firm and substantial thumb over which we now ride.[43]

The Charles River Bridge Case

In 1823, only two years after the toll road on the Mill Dam had opened, a petition for yet another bridge on the Charles was filed by John Skinner and Isaac Warren, the first act in a controversy that would take more than twenty years to resolve. The proposed Warren Bridge was to be located less than three hundred feet upstream of the Charlestown abutments of the Charles River Bridge of 1786 (figure 1.23), and it was to be toll-free after six years. Wharf owners objected to the prospect of further obstructions to navigation, and Harvard College filed remonstrances to the General Court. The petition for the new bridge was resubmitted in each of the next three sessions, but the legislature took no action. In 1826 a legislative committee summarily rejected the petition.[44]

The following year, the petitioners alleged that the thirty-year extension of the forty-year charter for the Charles River Bridge (granted in 1793 when the West Boston Bridge was approved) had been obtained by fraud. Although the proprietors objected strenuously, the yearly profits and the greatly increased value of the stock left many unsympathetic to their claims of abridged property rights. In March the House and Senate ignored committee proposals for compromise and authorized the charter. Toll collection would cease after the initial capital plus expenses were recouped, but no later than six years after completion. In the first of several legal landmarks in the case, Governor Levi Lincoln vetoed the bill, the first use of the executive veto by a Massachusetts governor. A year later a nearly identical bill was approved and signed by the governor. The new bill did oblige the Warren Bridge to pay half the annuity owed to Harvard College by the Charles River Bridge proprietors.[45]

The corporation was organized in April 1828, and in June work began. That same month, a bill in equity was filed by the Charles River Bridge proprietors (whose legal counsel included Daniel Webster) with the state Supreme Judicial Court, asking for an injunction to halt the construction. A few days after the hearing in August, the injunction was denied. The bridge was opened on Christmas Day, but the court decision in favor of the Warren Bridge was not announced until January 1830. The plaintiffs appealed to the U.S. Supreme Court. Receipts on the Charles River Bridge for first half of 1829 were only $6,000, down from $15,000 for the first six months of the previous year.[46]

The first arguments before the Supreme Court were presented in March 1831, but less than a week later the Court, failing to reach a decision, ordered the case continued. A motion for reargument was accepted in 1833, but the arguments were not presented. One justice died and another resigned the following year; Andrew Jackson nominated two new justices in January 1835, and in the same month Webster recommended that the Charles River Bridge plaintiffs seek a settlement through the state legislature. In the spring of 1835 Chief Justice Marshall died, and a backlog of sixty cases piled up before Roger B. Taney was confirmed as the new chief justice.[47]

Meanwhile, the Warren Bridge had collected tolls equal to the cost of the bridge by early 1832. Rather than declaring the bridge free and open, the proprietors asked to have the toll privilege extended to cover their potential liability in the still-pending case. For the years 1832 to 1834 the Warren Bridge averaged about $22,000 per year in tolls, with profits increasing from about $12,000 to a little more than $16,000. During that time toll receipts for the Charles River Bridge declined by over half (to an average of about $12,000 per year); the bridge was still profitable, however, and net income had increased from $6,541 to $9,383.[48]

Impatient with the failure of the two corporations to reach a settlement, the legislature rejected a series of compromises. In the absence of new legislation, the Warren Bridge became the property of the state, and therefore free of tolls, on March 2, 1836, and the Warren Bridge Corporation was dissolved. There was a celebration in Charlestown, but in Cambridge Harvard's treasurer reported that the college's stock in the old bridge was now worthless.[49]

The Supreme Court finally heard arguments in the bridge case in January 1837. Simon Greenleaf was granted a leave of absence from Harvard Law School to argue the defendants' case, a milestone in the history of academic freedom, since Harvard's financial interests were with the plaintiff's side. Daniel Webster argued for the proprietors that the new charter indirectly destroyed the old. Justice Story wrote Charles Sumner a few days later that the arguments on both sides were "a glorious exhibition for old Massachusetts."[50]

Less than three weeks later, the Court decided in favor of the Warren Bridge. Story said in a letter to his wife that "a case of grosser injustice, or more oppressive legislation, never existed. I feel humiliated, as I think everyone here is, by the act which has now been confirmed."[51]

The Charles River Bridge proprietors were still obligated to maintain the bridge, to tend the draw, and to pay Harvard $666 each year. They petitioned the legislature for release from those obligations and for compensation for the loss of their property. The legislature not only refused to offer compensation, but declined even to study the value of their franchise. The bridge corporation responded by raising the draw and closing the bridge. Four years later, in 1841, the legislature approved a bill offering a $25,000 settlement to the proprietors. The act also reinstated the tolls for no more than two years, to repair the bridge and to compensate the stockholders. In 1847, the legislature granted Harvard $3,333.30 compensation for the loss of the college's annuity during years when the state had ownership of the bridge. The college's "ancient" ferry privilege, granted in 1640, was over.[52]

In writing for the majority, Chief Justice Taney observed that the Charles River Bridge had destroyed Harvard's ferry privilege, and the bridge charter did not require Harvard's consent. The legislature then had authorized the West Boston Bridge with no hint that the extension of the Charles River charter for an additional thirty years was compensation. If the case were decided in favor of the old bridge, Chief Justice Taney saw the turnpike corporations "awakening from their sleep and calling upon this court to put down the improvements which have taken their place."[53]

The Supreme Court's decision was seen by many as a victory for the promotion of growth and technology. The financial success of the Warren Bridge was repeated in 1846 by a group of Cambridge investors, who determined to buy the Canal and West Boston Bridges or to build a third bridge in between. Almost immediately the proprietors of the Canal Bridge voted to sell. The new owners collected tolls sufficient to recover their investment and to rebuild the bridge six years later; in 1858 both bridges were turned over to the city, now "free public avenues forever."[54]

The future, however, was not to be found in the construction of more bridges or turnpikes. New engines of prosperity had arrived in Boston in 1835 with the opening of railroads connecting Boston with Providence, Worcester, and Lowell. Steam-driven locomotion captivated the imagination of writers and reformers as well as capitalists, and hastened the transformation of the basin.

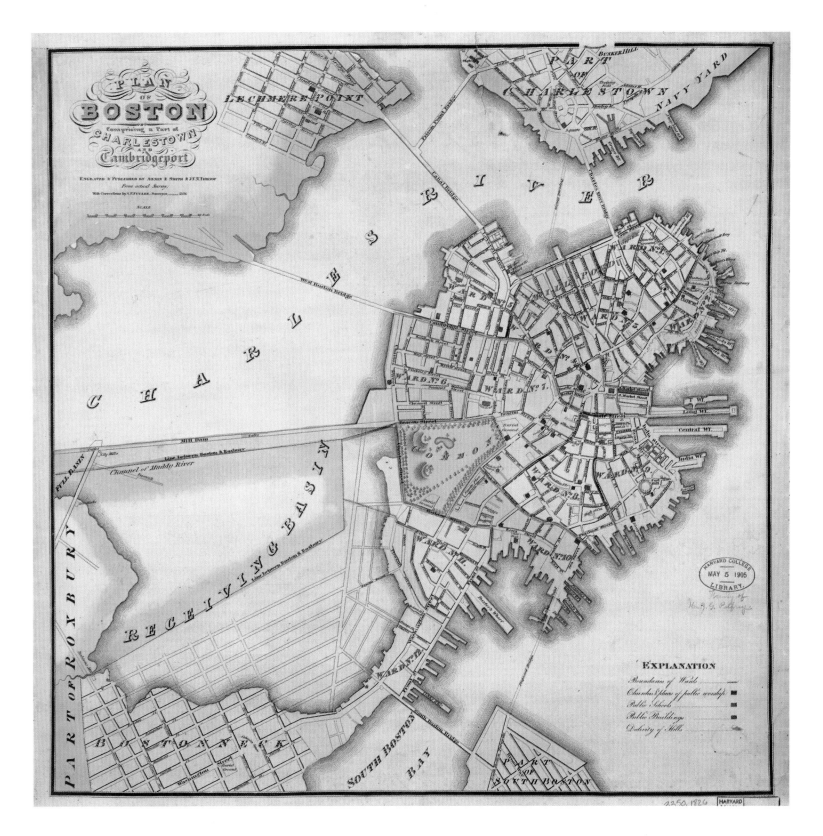

1.23 Construction on the Warren Bridge (shown in dashed lines) had not yet begun when this 1826 map was printed. The road to the new bridge in Charlestown's City Square was only a few yards from the Charles River Bridge, but the new bridge would cross the river on a line that provided a more direct route to Beacon Hill. The bridge was also to become toll-free after six years. Seeing a threat to their toll revenues, the proprietors of the older bridge sued. The Massachusetts Supreme Judicial Court denied their motion, the bridge was completed in 1828, and the case was immediately appealed to the U.S. Supreme Court. When the Court finally ruled in favor of the Warren Bridge owners seven years later, the Charles River Bridge proprietors raised the draw of their bridge, tacitly asserting that if they could not collect tolls, no one could use their bridge. Both bridges became property of the state—and toll free—in 1847.

shall be happy to explain. — The City Authorities can readily consult the People. — ... to be laid before the City Authorities, and at a next Session of the Legislature, your final sanction may be obtained. — Other Plans may be advertised for; and, the best adopted: so ... Permit me now, to respect acknowledgment of respect & esteem. — Your obed.t & very humble Servant — Rob.t F. Gourlay.

narlboro Hotel, Boston, May 9 1844

The New City

of

Boston

to be

laid out

as Taste, &

Convenience

may

dictate

Charles River

Charles River

Charles River

Distributing Railway

West Boston Bridge

Mill Dam Avenue

Rail-way

Distributing Rail-way

Canal Rail-way

Distributing The Boulevards, Rail-way, may

Causeway St.

Hanover Street

Ann St.

Commercial St.

Docks

Wharves & Warehouses

Long Wharf

State St.

Docks

Harbou

Harbou

The Botanic The ... Gardens

The Elysean Fields

Western Circus Island-way

Rail-way

Boulevard

The New City, &

Beacon St.

Cambridge St.

Tremont St.

Court St.

School St.

Winter St.

West St.

Bedford St.

Summer St.

Essex St.

Beach St.

Church St.

Eliot St.

Tremont St.

Broad St.

Wharves

2

The Science of City Building

Surveyors—men accustomed to look across valleys without thought of falling in, and through hills as though transparent—men of imagination too powerful to be distracted with little objects, and men of independence, who will neither be biased nor misdirected by petty interests, should be called upon to decide as to lines of communication.

Robert Gourlay, *Plans for the improvement of Edinburgh*, 1829

Readers of poetry see the factory-village and the railway, and fancy that the poetry of the landscape is broken up by these; for these works of art are not yet consecrated in their reading; but the poet sees them fall within the great Order not less than the beehive or the spider's geometric web. Nature adopts them very fast into her vital circles and the gliding train of cars she loves like her own.

Ralph Waldo Emerson, "The Poet," 1844

The streams, the islands, and the promontories,—all may be made to harmonize in one grand panorama, to display striking and enchanting scenes such as the imagination, once awakened, may conceive better than it is possible to describe.

Robert Gourlay, *Plans for . . . the City of Boston*, 1844

In 1843 an eccentric insomniac named Robert Gourlay arrived in Boston for medical treatment. Claiming to have been sleepless for almost six years, he passed the time developing what he called "the Science of City Building." A year after his arrival in the city, he drew up what has been called "the first great plan for Boston." Centered visually and symbolically on an island to be created in the center of the Charles called the "Elysian Fields," with a "New Town" on filled land in the Back Bay, the plan would make of Boston a metropolis that offered health, comfort, and economic prosperity to all in a gloriously preserved natural setting. The design of the city would become a science, and its work would be directed by Boston's citizens.[1]

Frontispiece Robert Gourlay, *General Plan for enlarging and improving the City of Boston* (Boston, 1844), detail.

At the time of Gourlay's arrival, Boston was entangled with the issue of private rights and public actions, as ventures that had once been seen as belonging entirely to the private sphere—including roads, bridges, and other public works—lobbied for more active public support or intervention. Between the 1780s and the middle of the nineteenth century the state legislature labored to define the range and limits of private rights and public actions, and Massachusetts, like other states, moved from "acquiescence as state policy" to more vigorous intervention in commercial and social issues. Tasks such as the construction of turnpikes, initially viewed as opportunities for chartered corporations and limited monopolies, were more strictly regulated or taken over as legitimate activities of state and local government. The profound social consequences of schemes for canals and railroads, even when their effects were manifest in the character and form of cities and towns, were seldom easy to see at the time these internal improvements were chartered by the state. As these effects became more severe, government acquiescence was replaced by the creation of what has been called the "reform state."[2]

Yet even before roads, bridges, canals, and railroads began to shape American cities, Renaissance ideas of city life had been transplanted from the courts of Europe to England and then to the American colonies. This impetus toward more urbane cities, as Richard Bushman has recently documented, was emblematic of a "culture of refinement." Its roots have been traced to about 1690, and it comprised manners, dress, conversation, the decorative arts—all the trappings of what came to be called polite society.

In the process of identifying what was proper and refined, the culture of refinement scrutinized houses, gardens, public buildings, even city plans. If the standards of its "beautification campaign" were not met, persons, houses, even whole neighborhoods would be judged improper, ugly, uncivilized.[3]

As a cultural system, refinement clashed with the values of capitalism and republicanism. Refinement "was worldly, not godly, it was hierarchical not egalitarian, and it favored leisure and con-

sumption over work and thrift." But capitalist markets, it turns out, required both "frantic getting and energetic spending"; together these two cultural systems of refinement and capitalism created our economy of consumption. In the larger community, they also allowed self-interest—the impulse to impress, to define social standing, to establish one's importance—to be joined with civic betterments that advanced all classes in the community. City fathers could sponsor the creation or improvement of public spaces that not only increased the value of their own real estate but would also provide "breathing spaces" near densely inhabited tenements and elevate the manners and morals of the lower classes.[4]

Thomas Jefferson's distrust of cities and his famous defense of "those who labour in the earth" as God's chosen people, like his opposition to the development of manufacturing in America, was rooted in an ideal of America as a "middle landscape," harmoniously situated between the culture of cities and the wilds of nature. Leo Marx has persuasively argued that Jefferson's view was not a simple agrarianism, but a rejection of economic standards as the ultimate measure of society. The loss to the economy of keeping factories in Europe would be made up, Jefferson was convinced, in the "happiness and permanence of government."[5] Both the upward-striving aspirants to refinement and the intellectuals who rejected the utilitarian mode in favor of a pastoral middle ground could join in seeking dignified public landscapes that expressed the hopes of the new republic.

By the end of the eighteenth century, the spirit of gentility had encouraged a decided preference for straight streets and some sense of urban grandeur in the colonies. One witness to this new civic sense was Josiah Quincy, whose son later served four terms as mayor of Boston. In 1773 he visited cities and towns on the eastern seaboard as far south as Charleston, South Carolina, and compared their appearance and orderliness. "The streets of Philadelphia," he wrote, "intersect each other at right angles; and it is probably the most regular, best laid out city in the world."[6]

The medieval street patterns of Boston were based on topography and on the predilections of the town's builders, not on European ideas, and left little room for the new taste in city design.

2.1   The Joseph Barrell Mansion on Pleasant Hill (later known as Cobble Hill) in Charlestown (on the far right in this 1810 view) overlooks the flats and open water of the Charles. Thomas Grave's house and barn at Lechmere Point are on the left and the Canal (Craigie's) Bridge in the right foreground.

Instead, the desire for gentility in the eighteenth-century town was manifest in more elegant residences, in church buildings such as Christ Church (Old North), Old South, and King's Chapel, and in new public buildings such as the old State House.[7] Beyond the city elegant country seats were constructed, including several famous estates along the Charles.

After the Revolutionary War, signs of refinement in Boston multiplied at a lively pace. No single person epitomizes the transformation more than Charles Bulfinch, architect of the new State House (1795–1798), several churches, a number of the most elegant Federal-era residences, whole blocks of townhouses, and street plans for several sections of the growing town.[8] To the north of Boston across the Charles, Bulfinch designed a country seat for Joseph Barrell, his first patron; its location confirms the open and

undeveloped character of much of the surrounding towns (figure 2.1). The wide expanse of water just upstream of the bridge at the junction of the Charles and Miller's Rivers still lent an air of remoteness to the undeveloped hills and flats west of Charlestown neck, in spite of the much increased traffic through Charlestown that followed the opening of the first Charles River Bridge. In 1791 the Boston merchant Joseph Barrell purchased two hundred acres overlooking the two rivers, including a fifty-foot rise known as "Cobble Hill," as the site for a new suburban estate. Bulfinch's design for the Barrell mansion included the first oval parlor built in Boston, expressed on the principal facade in a bow-front exterior wall with a curved portico above. This eastern outlook commanded "a superb view over the garden and Charles River, [with] Boston with its many spires in plain sight" (figure 2.2).[9]

Barrell hired an English landscape gardener to design the grounds, which included "lawns, trees, gardens, terraces, greenhouses, fish-ponds, dove-cotes, poultry-yard, stable, coach-house, a well-stocked barn, and an attractive boat-house." Trout and goldfish were "domesticated" in a fish pond on axis with the oval parlor; liveried boatmen were employed to pilot a barge across the

2.2　The Barrell Mansion was designed by Charles Bulfinch, a graduate of Harvard College and Barrell's protégé. The house marked the first appearance of an elliptical parlor in a Boston house design.

2.3　The grounds of the Barrell mansion were lavishly planted by an English landscape gardener. The deed, still on file in the Middlesex County Courthouse, shows the fish pond and the poplar grove on axis with the main house, with a "Bathing House" on the water's edge. In good weather liveried boatmen rowed Barrell across the river in a barge.

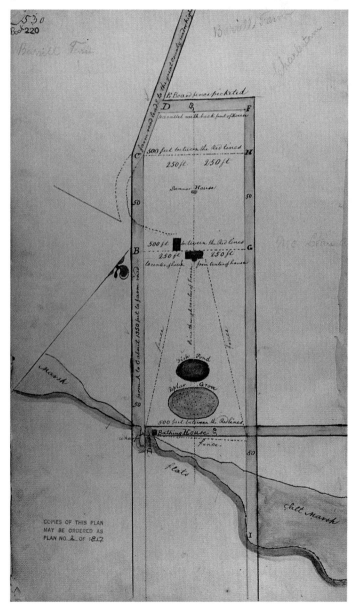

river, a pleasant alternative in good weather to the land route through Charlestown and then across the new bridge. Barrell's use of a landscape gardener was uncommon in the eighteenth century; both buildings and landscapes were more often the work of gentlemen amateurs (figure 2.3).[10]

Barrell was not alone in his preference for country living. Although the village of Brookline was perhaps the most popular place for rural estates beginning in the late 1750s, several notable villas were built in the lower Charles River valley (figure 2.4). In 1791, the same year that Barrell acquired his Charlestown property, Andrew Craigie bought the 1759 Vassall estate just west of Old Cambridge (now the Longfellow National Historic Site). Originally eighty-seven acres, Craigie added over fifty more acres to the estate. He also built a dam to create a small lake and turned the property into a working farm. Theodore Lyman bought thirty acres along the river in Waltham in 1793, and Christopher Gore built an estate a mile upriver from Lyman a decade later. By then, what began as an acceptable alternative for a few of Boston's merchant princes became the predominant fashion. In 1809 Harrison Gray Otis acquired twelve acres on the top of Strawberry Hill in Watertown with glorious views up and down the river valley. Otis named the estate "Oakley" and hired Bulfinch to enlarge the hun-

2.4 The north side of the Charles River valley between Waltham and Cambridge was the site of several notable country seats in 1830, including the estates of Harrison Gray Otis in Watertown, and Christopher Gore and Theodore Lyman in Waltham.

dred-year-old house. Bulfinch added an elliptical salon with an open portico above, making the front facade a near twin to the Barrell estate in Charlestown (figure 2.5). A contemporary described these areas of country estates as "the border land between the region of agriculture and the region of horticulture."[11]

In 1816, after Joseph Barrell's death, his estate in Charlestown attracted the interest of the new Massachusetts General Hospital, organized five years before. Asylums in Europe had pioneered an approach to the treatment of the insane that came to be known as "moral management." The connection between mind and body was seen as fundamental and was reinforced by open, naturalistic settings, representing in the landscape the absence of constraint that was a hallmark of the new regime. The founders of the McLean Asylum, organized in 1816, were persuaded that the Barrell estate would be an ideal site for the new institution. The state had constructed a prison not far away on the river's edge in Charlestown in 1805, also designed by Bulfinch, but its unadorned granite facades were probably not seen as a significant intrusion on the pastoral views from the grounds of the Barrell mansion. The Barrell estate offered not only a superbly planted site but also easy access from its own wharf across the Charles to the waterfront site that the new hospital had purchased in Boston's West End (figures 2.6–2.8).[12]

2.5 When Charles Bulfinch enlarged a hundred-year-old house in Watertown for Harrison Gray Otis, he added an elliptical parlor on the front facade of the estate that Otis named "Oakley" (shown in a sketch from 1816).

2.7 Pedestrians on the West Boston Bridge enjoyed a view downstream that included (from left to right) the Massachusetts General Hospital, the Harvard Medical School, and the Charles Street Jail.

2.6 The trustees of the new Massachusetts General Hospital acquired Pleasant Hill from the Barrell estate in 1816 as an asylum even before the first hospital building was constructed in the West End. Bulfinch was commissioned to add flanking wings on either side of his earlier country house design; a third story was later added to the main building.

2.8 At low tide in 1853, the grounds of both the hospital and the medical school were edged in mudflats.

According to Josiah Quincy, in his first inaugural address as mayor in 1823, fresh air was now a matter of the general welfare. "The sons of fortune can seek refuge in purer atmosphere. But necessity condemns the poor to remain and inhale the noxious effluvia," he said; the city, therefore, should provide for its poorest citizens "that surest pledge of health, a pure atmosphere."[13] Along with his active interests in a new market, the city water supply, the sewerage system, and the city's burial places, these concerns would guide Quincy's actions to improve Boston Common.

The forty-odd acres of the Common had been acquired by the proprietors of the Massachusetts Bay Company from the Reverend William Blaxton in 1634, four years after the settlers moved across the river from Charlestown and nine years after Blaxton had settled alone on the Shawmut peninsula. As early as 1674 this public space was described by the English visitor John Josselyn as "a small, but pleasant Common where the Gallants a little before Sun-set walk with their Marmalet-Madams, as we do in Morefields, &c till the nine a clock Bell rings them home to their respective habitations, when presently the Constables walk their rounds to see good orders kept, and to take up loose people."[14] Much of the Common was regularly used as a cattle pasture and a military parade ground.

In 1784 a new row of trees was planted along the Tremont Street mall (figures 2.9–2.10). Eleven years later, land opposite the mall was sold by the town to pay for a new almshouse, and Colonnade Row (another Bulfinch design) was constructed in 1810. These new rowhouses provided views across the Common to the Back Bay and the hills of Brookline and Brighton. As the harbor side of the Shawmut peninsula was more densely built up, Bostonians became increasingly attached to the wide vistas and the fresh southwest breezes across the Back Bay and the Charles.[15]

The benefits of fresh, moisture-bearing breezes would be an issue in the repurchase of land on the edge of the Common that the town had given away in 1794. The ropewalks on Fort Hill had burned that year, and a portion of the mud flats west of Charles Street was granted to the ropewalk proprietors, who filled them. There were fires in the new ropewalks in 1806 and 1819, which likely alarmed the residents of the newly settled areas nearby. The proprietors offered to sell the land back to the city, and the purchase was made in 1824 for $55,000.[16]

Immediately a dispute arose over the disposition of the land. At a town meeting that year the matter was referred to a committee. They objected to the purchase of land until a dispute with the Boston & Roxbury Mill Corporation was resolved, and they also opposed any residential construction on filled lands; the building foundations would be unstable, the city would lose money, and most important, the vitality of the city would decline. Boston was free of disease, according to the committee report, because

> there is over the open space, which it is now proposed to alienate, a constant current of fresh air, which revives and purifies the entire atmosphere of the City. . . . This incessant stream . . . comes . . . into the noxious atmosphere of a crowded population, diluting the force of disease.[17]

Five questions were submitted to the voters: Should upland and flats west of Charles Street be sold? Should the Common remain open? Should the dispute with the mill corporation be settled by renewing their grant but forbidding the construction of buildings? Should the upland and flats southwest of the Common be sold? Should the city construct a cemetery west of the Common? The voters rejected all but the second proposition, which directed that the Common would be "forever after kept open and free of buildings of any kind, for the use of the citizens."[18] The stewardship of both the Common and the flats (filled in 1830) was clearly established. Yet more than thirty years would pass before this new land was finally developed as the Public Garden.

The city's burial grounds had been the subject of controversy for some years by the time Josiah Quincy was elected mayor in 1823. As one of several actions he immediately took to promote public health, Quincy organized a Joint Committee on Urban Interments to report "on the expediency of prohibiting or limiting the erection of any New Cemeteries or tombs within the

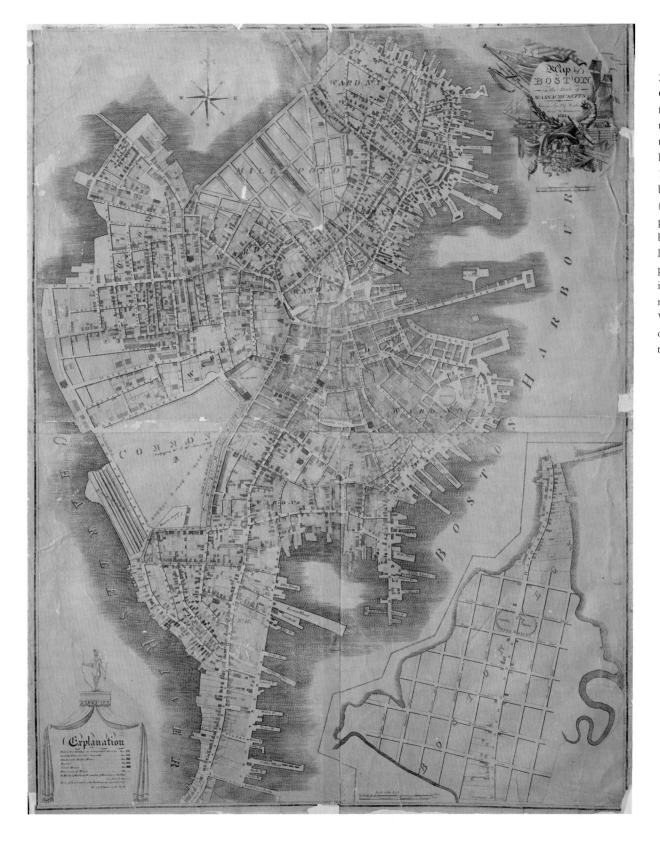

2.9 The western edge of Boston Common, which slopes dramatically from the top of Beacon Hill, ended at the river. A narrow strip of flats along the river edge of the Common beyond Charles Street was deeded in 1794 to the proprietors of the burned-out rope walks on Fort Hill (on the east side of the Shawmut peninsula), who then filled it; it was bought back by the city thirty years later. The Common was first used as a pasture and parade ground; the planting of rows of trees and more elaborate fencing after the Revolutionary War made the streets along the edges of the Common's forty acres among the city's most desirable locations.

2.10 Voters in 1824 determined that the Common would be "forever after kept open and free of buildings of any kind, for the use of the citizens."

precincts of the city." The committee recommended restricting, and ultimately ending, burial within the city's limits. A second committee was appointed to select a site for an "extramural cemetery," but no site was selected, and no report was ever written. A burial ordinance did pass in 1826, closing the King's Chapel, Old Granary, and Central (Common) burying grounds, as well as the old section of the Copp's Hill Burying Ground in the North End.

That left only the newer section of Copp's Hill and the South Burying Ground on the Neck Lands (now part of the South End). Quincy also tried unsuccessfully to close the Middle Burial Ground on the Common in order to extend the mall.[19]

Land takings by the state or by local governments were uncommon and could be highly controversial, as a similar effort in Cambridge about the same time plainly showed. In 1823, a group of landowners who lived near the Cambridge Common presented a petition to the town meeting for "setting out trees, fencing in certain parts, etc." While the Common was owned by the town, it was not fenced, and travelers on such new roads as the Concord Turnpike and the "Craigie" road from East Cambridge to

Watertown were unable to pass over it in all directions. Nothing was done immediately, but seven years later the petitioners supported an act of the legislature that authorized them to enclose the Common at their own expense, to level the surface, and to plant trees, for "public use only, as a public park, promenade, and place for military parade." Two commissioners were appointed to lay out new boundaries for the Common and the adjacent roads (figure 2.11).[20]

The act provoked strenuous opposition from the turnpike interests, who petitioned for a new highway across the Common. Among those opposed was eighty-year-old Jeduthun Wellington, who twenty-seven years before had laid out a turnpike running on a straight line from the West Boston Bridge to Concord, passing by the Wellington family farm (in what is now Belmont Center). The

2.11 Cambridge lagged behind Boston in its refinement of public spaces. This 1809 view across the common shows (from left to right) Harvard College, the First Parish Church, the Old Burying Ground, and Christ Church. Although trees lined the edges of the town common, the common itself was ragged and unfenced. A dispute over the Concord Turnpike's encroachment on the common resulted in what was described at the time as the largest town meeting in the history of Cambridge. In 1830 a group of landowners successfully petitioned the General Court for the right to enclose the common for "public use only, as a public park, promenade, and place for military parade."

conflict led to the largest town meeting in Cambridge history in the Old Cambridge meetinghouse, where enclosure of the Common was approved. The meetings were so contentious that the parish, which owned the meetinghouse, decided that it no longer wished to host such occasions. The building was then sold to Harvard, and a new town hall was built in Cambridgeport.[21]

Wellington filed a petition for redress with the state legislature, asserting that the enclosure would require travelers "to pass the said Common, in their travel to and from the city of Boston, by a circuitous route, considerably increasing the distance," simply "to gratify the taste for ornament of a few individuals." His petition was finally rejected by the Supreme Judicial Court two years later, and enclosure of the Common proceeded.[22]

Mount Auburn Cemetery

As vigorously as the citizenry of Cambridge and Boston defended and improved their commons, the undisputed landmark of refinement in antebellum Boston was the Mount Auburn Cemetery, chartered in 1831. Although organized by Boston's elite, the cemetery has been open to the public with few restrictions since its founding. Its organizers extolled the physically restorative and morally elevating force of the cemetery's "natural" scenery, advancing the general acceptance of the landscape aesthetic that would guide the creation of public parks in succeeding decades. General Henry Dearborn and Jacob Bigelow, the most active of the founders, also designed Mt. Auburn's landscapes and buildings.[23]

Jacob Bigelow grew up in rural Sudbury, studied at Harvard College and the University of Pennsylvania Medical School, and then settled in Boston to teach medical botany at Harvard. His Harvard classmate Alexander Everett, then a student in the law offices of John Quincy Adams, introduced him into Boston social and intellectual circles, and Bigelow was elected to membership in the Anthology Club, the Boston Athenaeum, the Massachusetts Historical Society, and the American Association for the Advancement of Science. In November 1825, Bigelow invited a number of friends to discuss the development of a rural cemetery.

Two members of the group investigated several sites. The owner of the Aspinwall estate in Brookline refused to sell, and properties along Western Avenue near the Charles were too costly and topographically uninteresting.[24]

That same year George Brimmer, a college friend of Bigelow's, purchased the remnant of the Simon Stone farm on the eastern edge of Watertown, just across the river from the Brighton marshes. Since the turn of the century the property had been a favorite resort of Harvard students, who called the area "Sweet Auburn" after Oliver Goldsmith's poem. In the middle of the old farm a glacial moraine rose 125 feet above the river, surrounded by an irregular landscape of ponds and dells.[25]

Although signs of change were appearing in the rural landscapes around Boston, Mt. Auburn offered pastoral views in all directions. Toward Cambridge were the generous grounds of Elmwood and Andrew Craigie's farm; just to the northwest was Oakley (Harrison Gray Otis, who knew nothing of horticulture, had sold the house in 1825). To the west of Brimmer's property was the new Watertown Arsenal, moved from the Charlestown Navy Yard in 1819. Its two-story red brick buildings were designed "in a plain, neat substantial manner" by Alexander Parris and arranged symmetrically around a small parade ground; they would hardly have disturbed the scenic prospects (figure 1.18).[26] Further upstream near the Charles were the country places of the Gores and the Lymans; west of their estates was the new mill of the Boston Manufacturing Company, built in Waltham in 1815, a more substantial enterprise than the arsenal but also more remote. In the distance was Prospect Hill. To the east the outlook from the cemetery offered distant views across the Back Bay to Boston and the heights of Dorchester. South of the low hills of Brighton and Brookline were the Blue Hills; looking north, the heights of Arlington obscured the hills in Medford and Lynn. Brimmer originally planned to erect a country estate on the old farm.

In 1829 the Massachusetts Horticultural Society was chartered by the General Court, in the words of General Dearborn, its first president, to be "a branch of our domestic industry" and an "association of men of taste, of influence, and industry." The following year some of the society's founders, including Dearborn and Bigelow, met with Brimmer. They determined to organize a rural cemetery under the auspices of the society, not as an independent institution, and Brimmer agreed to sell his property, which he had not developed, at a loss. In December Bigelow announced a plan for the cemetery and a separate experimental garden. A few months later the legislature amended the society's charter, allowing it to establish a rural cemetery and to "plant and embellish the same with shrubbery, flowers, trees, walks, and other rural ornaments" (figure 2.12).[27]

Justice Joseph Story, by now a member of the cemetery committee, was the unanimous choice to speak at the consecration of the new cemetery. His address included a picturesque description of the views from Mt. Auburn of the Charles and the surrounding hills:

All around us there breathes a solemn calm, as if we were in the bosom of a wilderness, broken only by the breeze as it murmurs through the tops of the forest. Ascend but a few steps, and what a change of scenery to surprise and delight us. We seem, as it were, in an instant, to pass from confines of death to the bright and balmy regions of life. Below us flows the winding Charles, with its rippling current, like the stream of time hastening to the ocean of eternity. In the distance, the city—at once the object of our admiration and our love—rears its proud eminences, its glittering spires, its lofty towers, its graceful mansions, its curling smoke, its crowded haunts of business and pleasure, which speak to the eye, and yet leave a noiseless loneliness on the ear. Again we turn, and the walls of our venerable University rise before us. . . . Again we turn, and the cultivated farm, the neat cottage, the village church, the sparkling lake, the rich valley, and the distant hills, are before us, through opening vistas, and we breathe amidst the fresh and varied labors of man.

These comforting views offered "every variety of natural and artificial scenery, which is fitted to awaken emotions of the highest and most affecting character. We stand," concluded Story, "upon the borders of two worlds" (figures 2.13–2.14).[28]

Many who were drawn to Mt. Auburn found a less sobering, downright cheerful aspect in its picturesque variety. The actress Fanny Kemble found it to be "a pleasure garden," not "a place of graves." Judging from the growing number of visitors—and their behavior—many others agreed with the actress. Soon after Dearborn resigned in 1834, Story took over and persuaded the cemetery committee to exclude all but proprietors on Sundays, and to prohibit all carriages except those holding nontransferable tickets, to be issued annually. Such regulations were criticized, and some suggested that the cemetery association was a private speculation. Story countered that Mt. Auburn was "in the truest and noblest sense a public institution," open to all "upon easy and equal terms"—the price of a lot. There were many, however, for whom that cost was beyond reach; over time, the regulations were reduced, and more and more residents resorted to the cemetery for outdoor excursions.[29]

A more serious disagreement among the founders was the division of expenditures between the cemetery and the gardens. Story and Bigelow wanted to build the chapel, tower, and gate that were in the original plans, which would necessarily reduce the funds for horticultural experiments. Late in 1834, Story chaired a committee to separate the two interests, and soon thereafter he became the first president of the Proprietors of Mt. Auburn Cemetery. Bigelow, the gentleman architect, designed the Gothic chapel, the Egyptian gate, and the crenellated observation tower.[30]

2.12 The buildings and grounds of Mount Auburn Cemetery were designed by Henry Dearborn and Jacob Bigelow, two members of the Massachusetts Horticultural Society who promoted the rural cemetery as a project of the society a year after its founding in 1829. The earliest "Plan of Mt. Auburn," by Alexander Wadsworth in 1831, hints at the contours in a faded blue-gray. Mount Auburn itself is ringed by a road and was later crowned by the observation tower. The lesser hills to the north and east are named Laurel, Pine, Cedar, Juniper, Harvard, and Temple. The three largest ponds are also named: Garden, Forest, and Meadow. Most of the carriageways are named for trees, and in typical Boston fashion the irregular drive surrounding the cemetery changes names half a dozen times—Garden, Maple, Magnolia, Mountain, Walnut, Cypress, Pine.

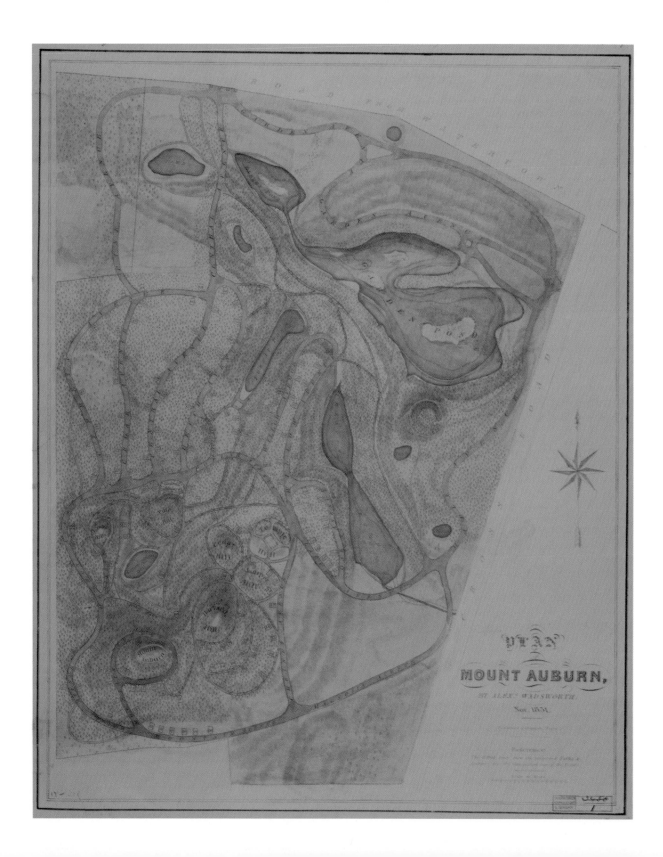

2.13 Like many other residents and visitors, the actress Fanny Kemble found the Mount Auburn Cemetery to be "a pleasure garden," not "a place of graves," as this view looking toward Fresh Pond from the top of Mount Auburn suggests.

2.14 At the consecration of the cemetery, Joseph Story described "the winding Charles, with its rippling current, like the stream of time hastening to the ocean of eternity." As late as 1900, it was still possible to find glimpses of such pastoral landscapes.

Boston Railroads

At the same time its citizens were aspiring to greater refinement in the visual character of the constructed city, the development of mills in the Back Bay and of various industrial enterprises in East Cambridge accelerated the transformation of Boston's landscape. These conflicts would be multiplied as the first Massachusetts railroads were chartered and began building tracks, bridges, and causeways into the city. While restrictions about financing, rates, and fees were included in the railroads' corporate charters, the charters also granted powers of eminent domain as well as great latitude in the choice of routes and in the location of terminals, bridges, and other structures. Although at odds with the growing sense of urban gentility, the fascination of Americans with railroads accelerated the national love for mobility.

The vigorous debate on the development of railroads in Massachusetts was circumscribed by the state's financial straits in the aftermath of the War of 1812. The prosperity of neighboring New York, especially after the opening of the Erie Canal, deepened the general sense of the Bay State's economic stagnation. New York City celebrated its access to vast new markets in the Midwest and beyond while Boston still lacked year-round transportation even to Worcester County and the Berkshires. The state was divided topographically into four regions, isolated from each other by hills and river valleys running north and south. The construction of the Blackstone Canal pushed Worcester into the domain of Providence, and the Connecticut River towns increasingly shuttled their freight to and from New Haven and New York. While the Middlesex Canal gave Boston merchants access to the Merrimack Valley and southern New Hampshire, the once-prosperous coastal towns like Salem and Newburyport found no replacement for the declining China trade.

Nathan Hale, the editor of the *Boston Advertiser*, painted a bleak picture of the state's economy:

> Between the close of 1825 and the beginning of 1831 gloom and despondency seemed to settle down upon Massachusetts. Her sons left her to build up rival states and cities, and her fairest and richest daughters were courted away to grace more prosperous lands. The grass began to invade the wharves and pavements of her commercial centers and the paint to desert the front of her villages.[31]

He was certain that the state should immediately underwrite railroad connections to western Massachusetts and New York. Many others shared his view. Harrison Gray Otis, in his inaugural address as mayor two years later, complained that

> All parts of the Union but New England are alive to the importance of establishing and perfecting the means of communication by land and water. The magic of raising states and cities in our country to sudden greatness seems mainly to consist in the instituting of canals and railroads. . . . The state and city must be up and doing, or the streams of our prosperity will seek new channels. . . . Our planet cannot stand still but may go backward without a miracle. . . . The apathy hitherto prevailing, in relation to this scheme, is unaccountable.[32]

Census figures and business profits supported a pessimistic reading of the state's economy.

About 1823 Loammi Baldwin II, son of the engineer of the Middlesex Canal, was hired by the directors of the Bunker Hill Monument to design their proposed obelisk. But when the project for a short canal to transport stone from the Quincy granite quarries to the harbor failed, it was Gridley Bryant and not Baldwin who found another way. Bryant was a contractor as well as a student of mechanics and natural philosophy; his solution was a horse-drawn railroad. With the backing of Thomas Handasyd Perkins (already one of Boston's merchant princes and soon to be the largest shareholder in the new venture), Bryant petitioned the legislature—and found them less than enthusiastic. Their response, he said, was a series of questions: "What do we know about railroads? Who ever heard of such a thing? Is it right to take people's land for a project that no one knows anything about? We have corporations enough already." In spite of such doubts from the General Court, a charter was finally passed in 1826.[33]

The Quincy Granite Railway was a modest success; but out of it came a series of ingenious mechanical developments by Bryant, all of which encouraged a group of investors to take up what they called "the railroad scheme," hatched in "the obscure chamber and studied privacy," to promote state support of railroad construction in the Commonwealth. Seeking to create a general enthusiasm sufficient to overcome the fears of opponents, the railroad supporters organized the Massachusetts Rail Road Association. Their most novel form of promotion was the construction of a model railroad in Faneuil Hall.[34]

Revealing aspects of the debate on state funding are found in Hale's persistent promotion of railroads in the *Advertiser*. In describing the urgent economic need for railroads, Hale wrote that Boston's market once extended into Rhode Island, Connecticut, New Hampshire, Vermont, and even western New York; now, in the wake of the Erie Canal, it had shrunk to a circle "descried from the cupola of the State House." To prevent the city's death, it would be necessary to actively support the development of steamships and railroads.[35] (Hale described the view from the State House to emphasize the limited vision of Boston's citizens; fifty years later this view would be invoked to promote an expanded, metropolitan view of the city's opportunities.)

The scale of state investment proposed by railroad promoters frightened many of the Commonwealth's citizens. Joseph Buckingham, editor of the *Boston Courier*, wrote that a railroad to Albany would cost "little less than the market value of the whole territory of Massachusetts" which, "if practicable, every person of common sense knows would be as useless as a railroad from Boston to the moon." Charles Francis Adams would later write that Boston had once held the lead over other American cities because of the "early progressive spirit" manifest in the development of the Middlesex Canal and the Granite Railway. As he saw it, pessimism like Buckingham's explained why Boston lost that lead and never regained it.[36]

Adams did acknowledge that the technological innovations of the railroads were paralleled by the need to invent new administrative and professional modes of operation: "Just as during the Revolution physicians, farmers and booksellers were turned into generals, so half a century later editors and merchants served as railroad presidents, while mechanics and school masters became engineers and surveyors." The Boston & Worcester (later the Boston & Albany) pioneered this new scale of management.[37]

The directors and managers of the new railroads were granted powers of eminent domain and given almost complete freedom to determine routes and locate terminals, decisions that seemed of no great moment in the 1830s. The state's Board of Internal Improvements said in 1829 that it was not appropriate for the board to determine the locations of railroad stations, since the companies needed to negotiate with towns along their routes.[38]

The directors of the Boston & Worcester went further; they avoided public discussion of routes and terminals until they had signed all the required real estate contracts. The railroad's charter was also amended so that bridges could be located across the Charles wherever the directors wanted, as long as they got the consent of bridge proprietors if they proposed to locate within one hundred feet of an existing toll bridge. The company considered four possibilities. A route to Lechmere Point would save money, since the railroad could connect with the Boston & Lowell, but would require many grade crossings in Cambridge. Constructing a railroad crossing upstream of the West Boston Bridge meant a terminal on Charles Street in Boston, on the wrong side of town and separated from the harbor. The directors tried negotiating with the owners of the Mill Dam for a right-of-way along Western Avenue (now Beacon Street), but concluded the price was too high. The railroad's weak financial position led to an agreement with the South Cove Corporation, chartered in 1833, with the promise of access to deepwater berths, which the South Cove proprietors never delivered.[39]

The result was a railroad causeway across the Back Bay (figure 2.15). The Boston Water Power Company was certain that the causeway violated their corporate charter; the Boston and Worcester was equally sure that taking a right-of-way from a corporation was no different from taking the property of individuals, which right was allowed in the railroad's charter. The courts

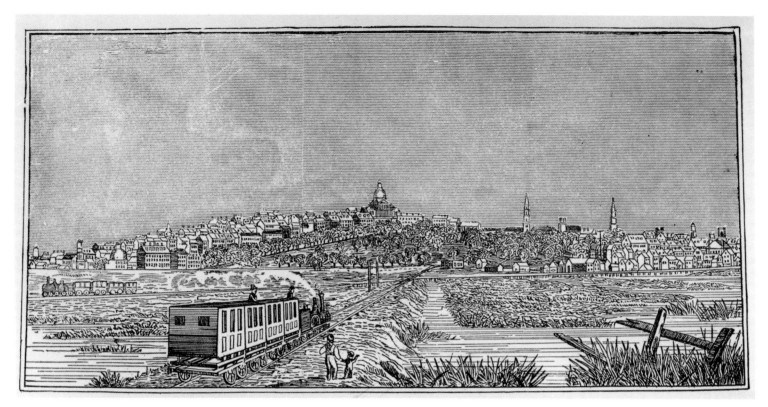

2.15 The first steam locomotive in New England was operated from the Tremont Street terminus of the Boston & Worcester Railroad in 1834, and lines to Worchester, Providence, and Lowell were opened the following year. In the foreground of this 1839 engraving is a train from Providence; a train bound for Worcester is show at the far left.

declined to grant an injunction against the railroad, the Water Power Company's stock declined by half, and the case was finally resolved in the railroad's favor seven years later.[40]

In March 1834 the Boston & Worcester was the first railroad to run a steam locomotive in New England. The *Evening Transcript* recorded the city's sudden fascination:

> Crowds of people were assembled yesterday at the Tremont street terminus of the Worcester Railroad, to witness the operation of the Locomotive Engine. It was the first time we ever saw one in motion, and we candidly confess that we cannot describe the singular sensation we experienced, except by comparing to that which one feels when anticipation is fulfilled and hope realized. We noted it as marking the accomplishment of one of the mighty projects of the age, and the mind, casting its eye back upon the past, as it was borne irresistibly onward, lost itself in contemplation of the probable future.

Regular service as far as Newton was established by mid-May, and the formal opening of the line all the way to Worcester was celebrated on July 4, 1835. A few weeks later, Christopher Columbus Baldwin, the respected librarian of the American Antiquarian Society, recorded in his diary the singular event of his thirty-fourth birthday: he saw a "Rail Way Car" for the first time. "What an object of wonder!" he wrote. "How marvelous it is in every particular! It appears like a thing of life. . . . I cannot describe the strange sensations produced on seeing the train of cars come up. And when I started in them for Boston, it seemed like a dream."[41]

The Boston & Providence line also constructed a causeway across the Back Bay, hastening the decline of the mills. Further downstream, at the confluence of the Miller's River with the Charles, the construction of the Boston & Lowell Railroad accelerated the industrial development that Andrew Craigie had earlier promoted in East Cambridge (figure 2.16).

Because the railroads came so early to Boston, and because the state allowed the construction of tracks and trestles across state-owned tidelands, Boston was spared a pattern that would later be

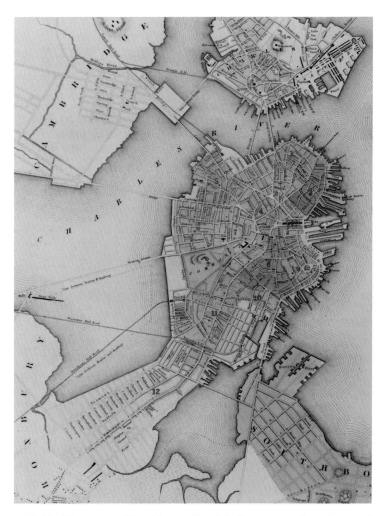

2.16 The Worcester and Providence railroads built causeways that crisscrossed in the receiving basin, south of the Back Bay Mill Dam (left center in this 1838 map). The Boston Water Power Company sued the Boston & Worcester for disrupting the operation of the Mill Dam, but the courts declined to halt the construction. The mills along the cross dam of the bay, never as prosperous as their proprietors had hoped, were finished. In East Cambridge, the Lowell and Charlestown Branch railroads had cut across the once-pastoral view from the McLean Asylum grounds.

repeated in so many other American cities, where the advancement of railroads often required the destruction of already established industrial tracts and residential neighborhoods.[42] But this appropriation of open marshes and mudflats, while avoiding the centers of existing cities and towns, helped inaugurate a scale of land making that completely transformed Boston and the surrounding towns.

The supreme deference to the railroads' charters is also revealed in the feeble responses to the protests of the McLean Asylum, which began only four years after the Boston & Lowell built tracks through Charlestown along the asylum's western boundary (figures 2.17, 2.18). The hospital board ordered its first legal action against an attempt by the Charlestown Branch Railroad to connect with the Boston & Worcester. More than two years later, the hospital, expecting five thousand dollars in damages, was awarded six hundred. The intended uses of quiet and secluded grounds of the hospital for exercise and refreshment "have been impaired and well-nigh prevented by the encroachments of traffic, with its noise and its risks," N. I. Bowditch wrote in a history of the hospital. "Those spacious and beautiful grounds, with their fertile soil and pleasant undulations of surface, are not only completely encircled by railroads, but their breadth is twice cut through by them."[43] Litigation by the hospital continued for fifty years, and ended only when the asylum moved to Belmont in 1895 and sold the estate to the Boston & Maine Railroad (which by then had consolidated the interests of the earlier railroads in Cambridge and Somerville).

The arrival of the Boston & Lowell north of the city also hastened the demise of the last of the Trimountain's three peaks. Between May and October 1835, the top sixty-five feet of Pemberton Hill was dumped north of Causeway Street, to make land for depots and rail yards. A similar pattern of filling and railroad construction took place in South Cove and at the east edge of Back Bay.[44]

By the 1840s, according to one account, the Mill Dam had become a walking place for fashionable young people; Thomas Handasyd Perkins's granddaughter recalled that the dam was "the resort of couples on the eve of an engagement." That could have

2.17 This etching from about 1851 shows the main building of Massachusetts General Hospital (now known as the Bulfinch Pavilion) in the foreground and the McLean Asylum across the river (upper left). In between are a railroad roundhouse and the long railroad trestle of the Fitchburg Railroad.

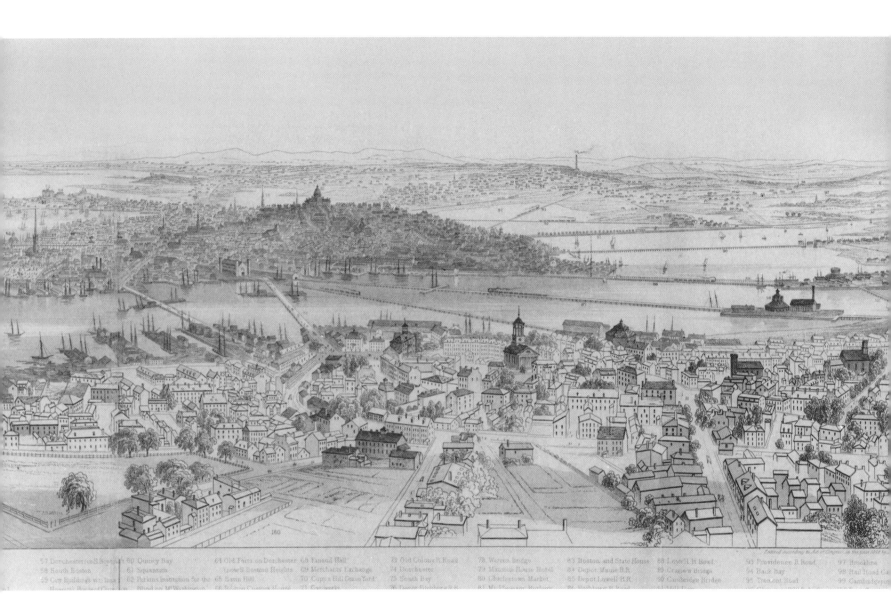

57 Dorchester or S.Boston   60 Quincy Bay   64 Old Point on Dorchester 68 Faneuil Hall   73 Old Colony R Road   78 Warren Bridge   83 Boston and State House   88 Lowell R Road   93 Providence R Road   97 Brookline
58 South Boston   61 Squantum   above S.Boston Heights 69 Merchants Exchange   74 Dorchester   79 Maison House Hotel   84 Depot Maine R.R.   89 Craigies Bridge   94 Back Bay   98 Rail Road Ca
59 City Buildings we have   62 Perkins Institution for the 65 Savin Hill   70 Copp's Hill Grave Yard 75 South Bay   80 Charlestown Market   85 Depot Lowell R.R.   90 Cambridge Bridge   95 Tremont Road   99 Cambridge
   Harvard Hospital Grou   Blind on Mt Washington 66 Boston Custom House   71 Eastpoint   76 Depot Brighton R R   81 Mt Vernon Harbour   86 Brighton R Road

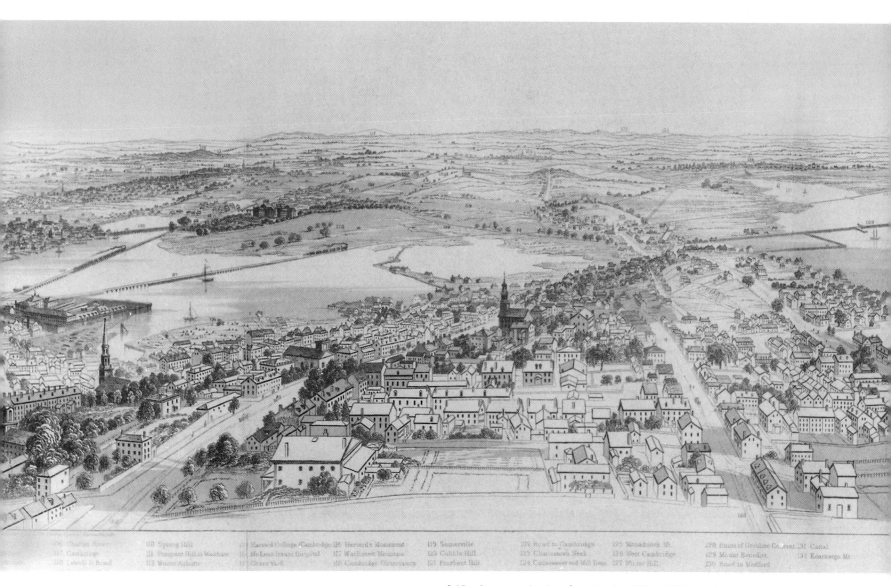

2.18 A panoramic view from Bunker Hill in 1848 greatly exaggerates the scale of the Charles, giving the appearance that there was ample room for the railroads to share the river with the surrounding neighborhoods. Railroad trestles cross over the Miller's River and the lower Charles to stations on Causeway Street. Upstream are the Craigie Bridge (now the dam), the West Boston (now Longfellow) Bridge, and the 1821 Mill Dam across the Back Bay. The landscaped grounds of the McLean Asylum are on the right of the smokestacks of East Cambridge (center).

been true only when the tides were high or the winds were favorable. As early as 1830 Mayor Harrison Gray Otis observed in his inaugural that "the condition of the flats west of the neck is regarded by eminent physicians as becoming pregnant with danger to the health of the city." The construction of the railroad causeways soon thereafter only aggravated the sanitary hazard. By 1849 a special committee of Boston's Board of Aldermen was directed to investigate. They described the "huge ventilator" that nature had designed to pour "fresh and health-giving breezes" across the Charles into the streets of the city; through ignorance or folly this beneficent creation had been destroyed. The basin had become a "nasty and stagnant" backwater:

> In fact, the Back Bay, at this hour, is nothing less than a great cesspool, into which is daily deposited all the filth of a large and increasing population. And it is a cesspool of the worst kind,—contrived, as it were for the purpose of contamination and not of relief; for it is an open one, and, therefore, exposed continually to the action of the sun and weather, and every west wind sends its pestilential exhalations across the entire City.[45]

The dire forecast made by the anonymous writer in the *Advertiser* in 1814 had come to pass.

"Elysian Fields": Boston's First City Plan

The terrible conditions along the lower Charles and its tributaries excited the imagination of an extraordinarily eccentric visitor to Boston in 1843–1844. In those years Robert Gourlay, a native of Scotland, wrote a series of letters to the mayor, the governor, and the legislature, and produced at least two remarkable drawings and lengthy accompanying texts—work that has recently been called visionary and prophetic, the "first great plan for Boston."[46] Yet the only public reaction to his Boston visions uncovered to date are the letters to Gourlay that he published in his own tracts.

Born in 1778, he left Scotland at the age of 29, pursued by the law because of his outspoken advocacy of electoral reform. In

England his work with agricultural laborers was marked by the publication of a series of tracts with titles like *Tyranny of Poor Laws Exemplified* (1815) and *The Village System, Being a Scheme for the Gradual Abolition of Pauperism, and Immediate Employment and Provisioning of the People* (1817). Harried by opponents, Gourlay emigrated to New York in 1817 to establish an emigration society to aid the poor, but he left almost immediately and settled in Upper Canada. There his inquiries into the effects of land speculation soon antagonized the province's ruling council. He was tried and acquitted twice for seditious libel, then arrested for failing to comply with an 1819 order banishing him from Upper Canada. When he demanded a trial on the issue of his banishment, he was jailed for six months until the case was heard, which he lost. After returning to England he was imprisoned on a charge of insanity.[47]

Gourlay came to Boston in 1843 seeking treatment for acute insomnia. He had gone sleepless for six weeks in 1833 and for five months in 1837; now, six years later, he claimed he had been without sleep for "five years and eight months, with the exception of two hours." Yet it was this "extraordinary calamity" of wakefulness, he claimed, together with a vivid imagination, that led to his extensive plans. He was able to bring objects to his mind's eye for study, which he then "arranged, and rearranged at pleasure, as readily as though material substances were present. . . . Thus are watches of the night often beguiled."[48]

This preoccupation with cities did not, however, begin in Boston. On his way to Canada in 1817, he traveled through Detroit and there was shown a plan for the extension of the city. It struck him then that city building might be reduced to "a science of incalculable value," especially in America "where thousands of cities are yet to be founded." His systematic study of this new science began a decade later, when he completed the first of a projected series on the subject in Edinburgh in 1829. He was detained in New York in 1834, where he says he spent many hours contemplating "improvements of the city," although he produced only a single plan.[49]

His initial schemes for Boston were almost bizarre in their cramped and peculiar scope. After four months in the city, Gourlay wrote three letters to Mayor Martin Brimmer in June and July 1843. The first letter proposed grazing sheep on the Common, twice a day for three hours. A month later he wrote to suggest a pagoda and flower garden on the Common (figure 2.19). Entry to the first floor of the pagoda would be free, but there would be a charge for the upper floors and for entry into the garden. His third letter described the "wretched appearance" of the Common and offered his services to the city to improve it. Two days later Gourlay wrote the president of the city's Common Council and sent the mayor copies of the letters he had earlier addressed to him. Mayor Brimmer replied that the council did not believe it was authorized "to place a building of any kind" on the Common; that right had been reserved by the citizens to themselves. Furthermore, the council did not believe it was expedient to graze sheep there. Although rebuffed, Gourlay published his letters and the mayor's response, together with illustrations, as a small pamphlet in September.[50]

Nothing in his barely developed ideas for New York or his quixotic sketches to improve Boston Common prepares us for the startling and prophetic imagination of his May 1844 "General Plan, for Enlarging and Improving the City of Boston" (figure 2.20). Addressed to Governor George Nixon Briggs and the governor's council, the drawing of the city included a utopian description of the future city across the top of the large sheet, together with a proposal for a society to promote "the Science of City Building." The very next day he wrote a letter, also to the governor's council, acknowledging that at first sight his plan might strike many as "fanciful and extravagant." In June and July he wrote three more letters responding to the "many remarks" he received about his plan.[51]

Equally striking was the extended written elaboration of this plan that Gourlay addressed to the legislature in September 1844 in a single lengthy letter (seventeen pages in the pamphlet he later published). These more expansive schemes he saw as in harmony with the "great purpose" of his life, which he described as bettering the conditions of the laboring classes. Whatever the opposition he stirred up, he remained a visionary optimist, believing that if society would

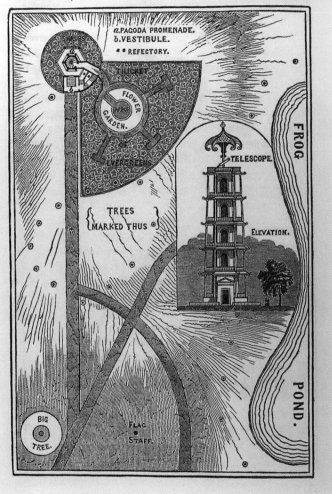

2.19 Robert Gourlay produced a series of eccentric plans and letters during a stay in Boston in 1843–1844 for the treatment of insomnia. His first scheme was for a pagoda and flower garden on the Common, whose appearance he thought was "wretched," and he magnanimously offered his services as an "agriculturist" to improve the Common's "green and yellow melancholy."

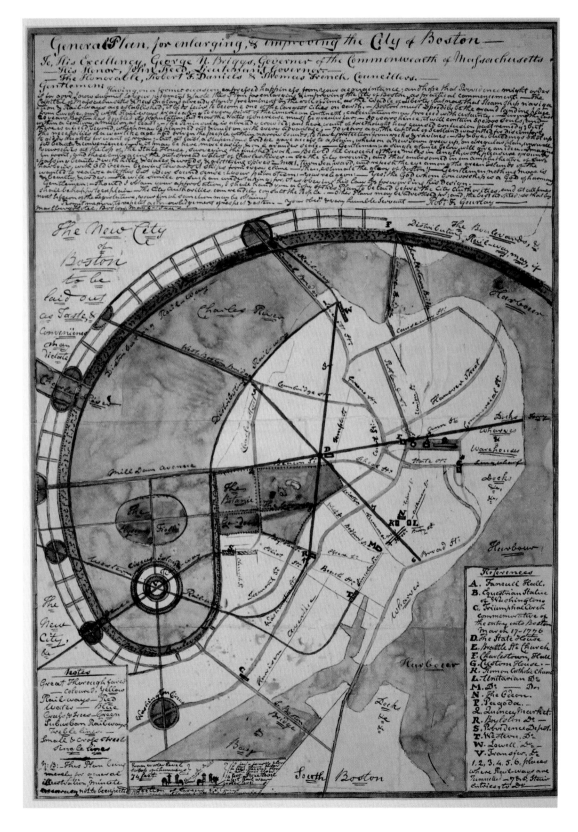

2.20   Gourlay's letters and his first quixotic scheme for the Common are even more startling when measured against the prophetic vision of his 1844 "General Plan, for enlarging and Improving the City of Boston." Gourlay believed in the power of transportation technology to better the conditions of the laboring classes, and his plans showed an expanded network of railroads converging on an island in the Back Bay.

give us Steam-ships and Railroads in abundance; let all be educated and have fair opportunity; let wild lands be rightly laid out, and honestly disposed of;—then, poor-laws and poor-rates may everywhere be dispensed with: pauperism will cease.[52]

Gourlay's confident view of the transforming power of transportation technology was widely shared in his time, but he was equally sanguine about the movement of masses of people from country to country:

> Emigration and immigration have been so neglected and misunderstood, that both are decried. Europeans deplore and retard the former; while Native Americans are banding together against the latter! Oh, miserable folly and infatuation!—Oh, that all were enlightened,—that all may see, how all may be benefitted, and contribute to each other's happiness.
>
> I have effected nothing, but Time, the greatest reformer, will solve the problem, and harmonize every jarring element. Steamship navigation will speedily bring nations together, and railroads will entwine the branches of the human family in indissoluble union. Prepare then for the grand interchange of civilities. Let the landing-place from Europe give kindly welcome to strangers; and, let their first impressions, in Boston, be those of delight and admiration.[53]

The May 9 plan and the series of letters that followed—widely circulated among the city's leadership—are important to this story for several reasons. In recognizing both the geographical limitations and the opportunities of the city, his ideas went well beyond the boundaries of the city of Boston as its citizens saw it. He predicted the city's population fifty and a hundred years hence with startling accuracy. Only nine years after the arrival of steam trains in Boston, Gourlay described a resolution to the topographic constrictions that have confounded railroad access to and through the city (a conflict that the city's planners have yet to resolve, a hundred and fifty years later). He anticipated both the growth and the character of the suburbs that railroads and streetcars would generate. Gourlay appealed to a wide range of disparate

interests in describing its future, and although his drawings were unskilled, the textual images he set down were dazzling. He conceived a plan for the Charles River as a single, defined, publicly created space, susceptible to reasoned analysis and purposeful design. And that plan made the region's natural landmarks the framework for the growth of the metropolis.

Gourlay's plans appealed to Boston's many-faceted vanities—the city's sense of history, the aspirations of its literary pantheon, the high-mindedness of its citizens' moral sensibilities—and its increasing prosperity. If Boston followed his lead, Gourlay told his readers, the Cradle of Liberty would become "the cradle of the arts and sciences," guided by a society for advancing "The Science of City Building" that would both gather and distribute plans for "buildings of every description, villages and cities; and a central point, either to draw intelligence from, or to send intelligence to,—hints, essays, plans, etc." There was nothing, he said, more commendable than "efforts to secure the almighty dollar, provided, that it is ever looked to as a means, not an end." In fact, the city's merchants would be stimulated to become rich so they might rightly apply their wealth to "the utmost enjoyment of this world." And since Boston's citizens were already exemplary in "orderly moral and religious habits," it would be easy for them to understand the relationship between physical order and "mental refinement, enjoyment, and perfection." The inhabitants' united mental and moral faculties would guide the destiny that history and geography now thrust upon it.[54]

Gourlay understood that until the advent of steam technology, the region's geography had been a substantial hindrance. This, too, was part of the city's destiny. The "watery waste" surrounding Boston had been purposefully designed so that its citizens should be "penned up, and thence feel discomfort"—so that they would be driven to take advantage of the region's "peculiar position and structure" and build a metropolis that would surpass all other cities, ancient and modern.[55]

No city, Gourlay claimed, had the advantages Boston now possessed. Boston had doubled in population in the previous twenty years, but that was much less than Philadelphia and New York had grown during those two decades. Gourlay was certain that the doubling of population would accelerate prodigiously; there would be 500,000 people in fifty years, and a million a hundred years hence. Boston would become the "grand landing-place from Europe . . . with rail-ways eradiating to every point of the continent." To accommodate this expansion, he proposed for the city a pattern of what he called "distributing" and "sub-urban" railways (the texts of his letters and maps suggest that these "sub-urban" railroads were underground). The crossing of the Providence and Worcester railroads in the Mill Dam's receiving basin would be the center for a new "Circus Island" in the middle of a reconfigured Back Bay (figure 2.21). Downstream of this crossing was another island, the "Elysian Fields." New rail lines along Mill Dam Avenue (Beacon Street), the West Boston Bridge, and a line from the Lowell station just north of Causeway Street intersected underground beneath the State House. The extended Lowell line would turn west and connect with the Worcester railroad, since many travelers were only passing through from Lowell or Portland to Providence or New York. (This idea of linking Boston's northern and southern rail lines was revived in the 1910s, included in the 1970s as part of the Central Artery project, then dropped and taken up again in the 1990s.)[56]

The heart of Gourlay's scheme was a proposal for a "New Town" (his phrase) on the mudflats of the Back Bay (figure 2.22). The lack of forethought in the spatial organization of the Shawmut peninsula had created "confusion past remedy," but the nearby flats and surrounding lands offered the opportunity to repair the defects in the fabric of the historic city. It was not necessary to accept these lands as they were, or to wait for private initiatives to produce, piecemeal, whatever the city might become. The scale of action required far exceeded earlier efforts like the Charles Street flats or the Mill Pond. The city should immediately consider developing the 2,000 acres of worthless mudflats in the Back Bay, which would be transformed according to this plan into an urban district of immense value. The Boston Water Power Company had property rights that would be overridden, but since it was clear that they could never carry out this vast plan without

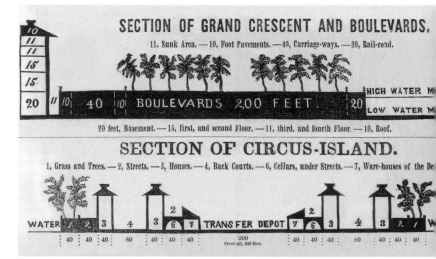

2.21 At the center of the "Circus Island" in the Charles would be a "transfer depot" where the trains from North Station, South Station, and Park Square would meet—today called the "North-South Rail Link." Gourlay's plans were dismissed. His idea of a central rail link was revived at least three times in the twentieth century, although it still remains unbuilt.

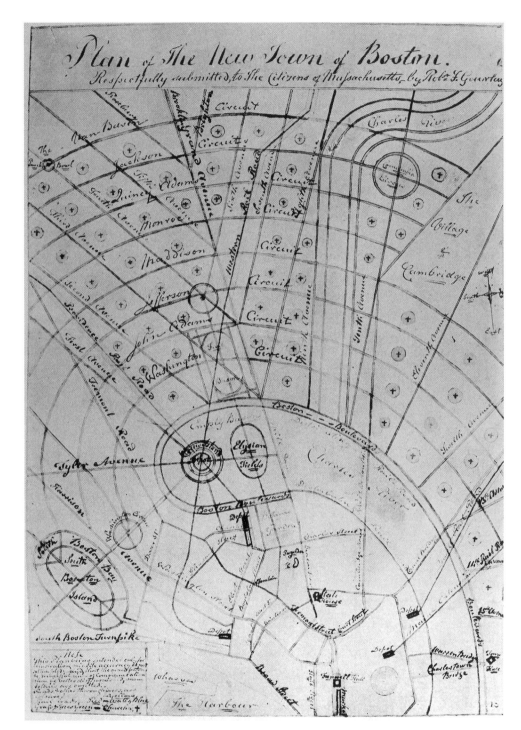

2.22 The landscape architect Fletcher Steele, who published in 1915 this less-known version of Gourlay's plan for a "New Town" in the Back Bay, called him one of the first modern city planners. Gourlay believed that only the state was capable of filling the 2,000 acres of worthless mudflats in the Back Bay, which would be transformed into an urban district of immense value.

legislative action, the corporation would "cheerfully and liberally" cooperate in this scheme. The important issue, said Gourlay, was to adopt the best possible plan—his or a better one—before streets and buildings laid out and the expense of such forethought was increased.[57]

Gourlay's last letter elaborated on the deficiencies of the city's street network in great detail, especially the lack of light and air on the narrow streets that created sinks of disease and infection. In the New Town there should be yard space for every house, where children would play and their elders would garden to "soften their hearts and better their affections." Legislation should protect such spaces against the threat of rapacity. Since "railroads diminish distance," it would no longer be necessary to crowd the buildings of the city together when the luxury of space could now be afforded without the slightest inconvenience.[58]

Perhaps because Gourlay's drawing focused on the Boston peninsula and on a dramatically reshaped Charles River, subsequent evaluations by historians have neglected the regional context, which he carefully elaborated in the accompanying text. This larger area was encompassed within two concentric circles extending from the State House, the first at a distance of two and a half miles, the second six miles out. The General Court, wrote Gourlay, should pass a special act to create the new town in the Back Bay, then a second act to govern the planning of the remaining lands within the first circle, and finally a third act extending out to the six-mile circle. Boston should also see to the natural abundance that graced the margins of the city:

> Within the space enclosed by the outer circle round Boston, (call it BOSTON BOUNDS), fine improvements may be made at little cost, merely by connecting and exhibiting to the greatest advantage those rare and beautiful features which Nature has here thrown together for the hand of man to work upon.
>
> The high grounds near Roxbury, Chelsea, etc., Mt. Auburn, Fresh Pond, Spy Pond, etc., the streams, the islands, and the promontories,—all may be made to harmonize in one grand panorama, to display striking and enchanting

scenes such as the imagination, once awakened, may conceive better than it is possible to describe.

> How easily could PATHS and RIDES and DRIVES be conducted round about, and among all these fascinating objects! How agreeable it would be to have public carriages, hourly, to carry up to each place in turn, allowing sufficient time for strangers to be satisfied; to have a steamboat in connection running from Squantum Point touching at certain promontories, islands, etc., and landing at Winthrop Head!—All this needs but legislation, for, if set about, it would pay, and yield unspeakable gratification.[59]

In the center of these natural features would be the completely reshaped landscape of the Charles River. Gourlay's beneficent view of railways allowed for a single "distributing" railroad lining the edge of the basin alongside a broad tree-lined boulevard; this, too, he described in visual and visionary phrases:

> Imagine yourselves at the top of the State House surveying the finished work. Behold the crescent of three miles in length, with pleasure-grounds in front, and these embracing the outspread waters of Charles River. See the city around, and that embosomed in an amphitheatre of surpassing beauty,—with hills, and dales, and woods, and glittering spires? Next, turn sea-ward, and refresh the eye among the green islands of the harbor, with the old ocean bearing towards it ships from every clime. Then, estimate the glory of Boston!!
>
> Gentlemen:—Nothing more is wanted to realize all this, but your sound sense, your patriotism, your religion:—yes, the God whom you worship is a god of harmony, and beauty, and order. He will smile on such an undertaking; for, it is obeying his law and forwarding his design.[60]

In this expansive metropolis, new modes of transportation would provide mobility to all classes; the honest disposition of newly filled lands would offer abundant opportunities; and the glorious natural landmarks of the region would induce refinement and gentility—if Bostonians would only avail themselves of their spectacular providence.

The Pastoral Design

As it happens, Gourlay was neither the earliest nor the most extravagant enthusiast to describe a harmonious middle landscape in which railroads steamed cheerily through a rich and variegated natural setting. In 1831, only two years after the first successful run of George Stephenson's steam locomotive, Charles Caldwell delivered an address at the Louisville Branch of the National Lyceum (subsequently published in the *North American Review*) titled "Thoughts on the Moral and Other Indirect Influences of Railroads." A student of Benjamin Rush at the University of Pennsylvania and later founder of the Louisville Medical Institute (now the University of Louisville), Caldwell argued that railroads would bring together whole nations into unified, refined, and highly educated societies, with all of the advantages and few of the vices of crowded populations. Their effects would make the inhabitants of different nations "morally one"—or at least remove prejudices and instill mutual regard, "and thus prepare the way to peace."[61]

How would this wonder come to pass? Caldwell appealed to the law of nature that required every thing to produce after its kind:

> Objects of exalted power and grandeur elevate the mind that seriously dwells on them, and impart to it greater compass and strength. Alpine scenery and an embattled ocean deepen contemplation, and give their own sublimity to the conceptions of beholders. The same will be true of our system of Rail-roads.

Such improvement would not come and go like shadows, but would permanently improve the American genius.[62]

Only slightly less effusive than Caldwell, Gourlay with his Boston plan appealed directly to both the utilitarian and the pastoral modes of the American myth. Leo Marx has carefully described how in the 1840s the most formidable challenge to the myth was articulated. In that decade, barely ten years after the first successful railroads were constructed in America, native writers introduced the figure that Marx has called "the machine in the garden." In its earliest expressions, in the works of Hawthorne and Thoreau, for example, this figure was expressed as a simple reverie in an ordinary landscape—suddenly and harshly interrupted by the frightful noise of a steam locomotive. In less literal and more anguished forms, the machine's disruption of the American pastoral is an image that has haunted our literature ever since.[63]

The antidote for this distress was offered in the same decade, in Ralph Waldo Emerson's essay "The Poet":

> For as it is dislocation and detachment from the life of God that makes things ugly, the poet who re-attaches things to nature and the Whole—reattaching even artificial things and violation of nature, to nature, by a deeper insight—disposes very easily of the most disagreeable facts. Readers of poetry see the factory-village and the railway, and fancy that the poetry of the landscape is broken up by these; for these works of art are not yet consecrated in their reading; but the poet sees them fall within the great Order not less than the beehive or the spider's geometric web. Nature adopts them very fast into her vital circles and the gliding train of cars she loves like her own.[64]

Not only poets and writers but also intellectuals working in visual modes could take this way out. In 1836, the painter Thomas Cole had written that "a meager utilitarianism seems ready to absorb every feeling and sentiment, and what is sometimes called improvement in its march makes us fear that the bright and tender flowers of the imagination will be crushed beneath its iron tramp." Yet a few years later, in a number of Cole's Catskill landscapes, as in the work of many other American painters, "a minuscule but conspicuous, often centrally located railroad is made to blend seamlessly into a pastoral prospect."[65]

This melding of pastoral New World landscapes with steam locomotives—the most potent symbol of nineteenth-century technology—soon became a commonplace in popular culture. The Eastern Railroad was begun in 1836 between East Boston and Salem, and was extended by 1842 to Portland, Maine. The line was rerouted across the Charles in 1854. The Eastern's route not only provided competition for the Boston & Maine along the New England coast; it also helped transform Boston's North Shore into an area of upper-class summer estates. In 1847 the *Boston Times* described the route of the railroad as "a glorious ride of nine miles, with a sea view all the way on one side and groves and highly cultivated farms all about."[66]

Gourlay's vision of "the streams, the islands, and the promontories," however, offered more than newly accessible scenery. His plan for Boston, crudely mapped but richly imagined in its accompanying text, was more than a simple urban version of the American pastoral, more than an intellectual application of Emerson's injunction to reattach manmade technology to the natural world. He aimed to overcome a fundamental limitation of the pastoral vision, which is essentially static and lacking the means to reach the promised paradise.[67] His vision of the middle landscape—promontories, rivers, and reflecting basins lined with railroad tracks in the very center of the future metropolis—linked free and fair access to land with a hitherto unimagined freedom of movement. Transportation and the public realm would be inseparably joined.

2.23 Alhough Hawthorne wrote that the shriek of a locomotive whistle in the countryside was "harsh above all other harshness," his neighbor Emerson countered that Nature adopts the factory village and the railroad "into her vital circles and the gliding train of cars she loves like her own." In this 1846 view of Swampscott, the painter Thomas Doughty followed Emerson's view, and made the railroad an agreeable, almost invisible element in the pastoral landscape.

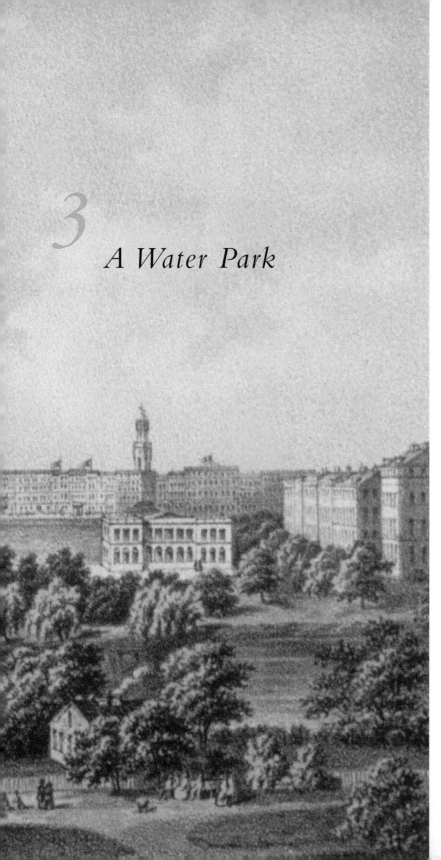

3

A Water Park

Although Gourlay harassed the mayor, the city council, the legislature, and the governor, several historians of Boston have concluded that his extravagant designs left no trace on the city. In their view, his scheme was "wholly unrealistic" and had "little to do with the actual problems confronting the builders of the Back Bay"; consequently, "nothing came of all this imaginative planning." It is true that the only written evidence of any reaction by the city fathers to his plans is in the pamphlets Gourlay himself published. Yet Gourlay not only addressed the sanitary, transportation, and development issues of the Back Bay, he also described the regional context in which they should be resolved, and concluded that action by the state would be required.[1]

Professional designers have found more wisdom in Gourlay's plans than historians. Warren Manning worked in the Olmsted office from 1888 to 1896 and then opened his own office. He shared a copy of Gourlay's plan with Fletcher Steele, another Boston landscape architect, who published a laudatory article in *Landscape Architecture* in 1915. Steele called Gourlay one of the first modern city planners, because his proposal addressed "the replanning of old cities, provision for future expansion, the coordination of traffic systems, housing and garden cities, small open spaces and

Frontispiece "View of Hamburg," from George Snelling, *Remarks,* 1860.

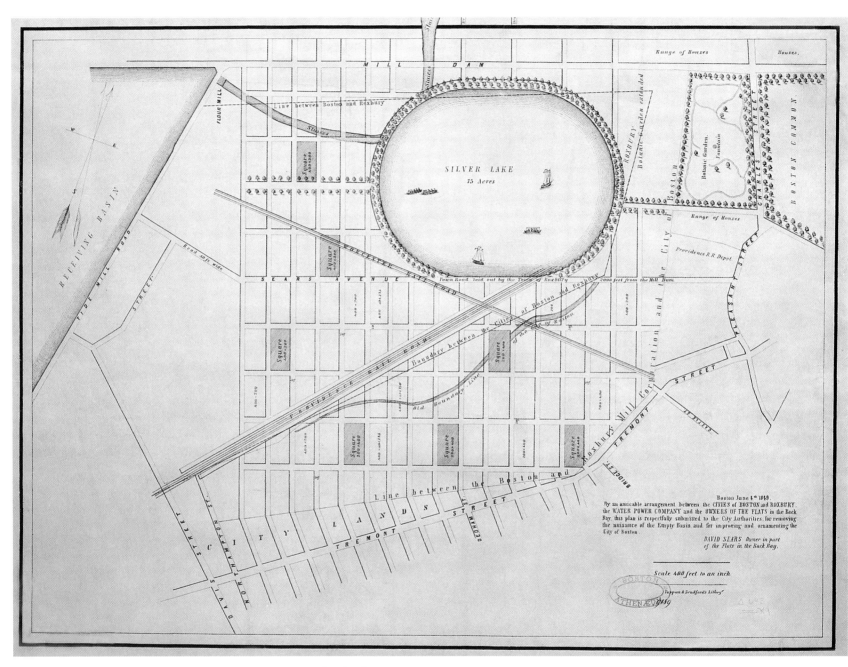

3.1   Several prominent Bostonians took exception to the plan for turning
most of the Back Bay into house lots. In 1849 David Sears published a plan
for the Back Bay that included a seventy-five-acre "Silver Lake" in the center
of a grid of streets, bringing salt water into the center of the new quarter of
the city. There were as many as a half dozen other plans for leaving part of the
Back Bay as open water.

park systems." In their recent study of Boston's "Past Futures," Alex Krieger and Lisa Green echoed Steele's judgment, calling Gourlay's map and text the first great plan for the city.[2]

When Bostonians addressed the city's future, however, their plans were incremental and far less imaginative. The prosperous David Sears published a much more modest proposal five years later. After purchasing several parcels of mud flats in the Back Bay beginning as early as 1822, Sears petitioned the city regarding a plan he called "Silver Lake" (figure 3.1). A grid of streets would abut the dam, and in the center a tree-lined boulevard would open onto a seventy-five acre lake, bringing salt water into the center of the new quarter of the city. One channel would carry water into the lake under a row of house lots, but the channel from the lake into the Charles would apparently be open to view. The adjacent Botanic Garden would be extended one block west, with the corner of the lake opening onto the Garden. Health-giving salt air breezes would then carry across the lake to the Common.[3]

Sears's sketch for "Silver Lake" hints at some of the complex issues that would have to be resolved in any development of the Back Bay. Ownership of the mud flats was divided between the state, the Boston Water Power Company and the Boston & Roxbury Mill Corporation. The railroad interests seem to be ignored in the plan; streets and lots were platted without regard to the existing tracks. Perhaps Sears was thinking of Gourlay's "suburban" railways. There were as many as half-dozen other plans for leaving part of the Back Bay as open water.[4]

The Design of the Back Bay

By the early 1850s, the Commonwealth had determined to resolve the conflicting claims of the mill owners, the state, and private owners of flats in Back Bay (figure 3.2). The result was a striking contrast with the circumstances in the bay fed by the Miller's River on the border between Charlestown, Somerville, and East Cambridge. There, the state had undisputed title in Commonwealth tidelands, yet the railroads were granted great latitude by the state in building over and in the river. Lawsuits, in par-

ticular the series of actions filed by the McLean Asylum, were also decided in favor of the railroads. In resolving the claims in the Back Bay, however, the legislature intervened because the state was one of the parties involved in the dispute.[5]

The first legislative commission to take up the question of the Back Bay was appointed in 1848 and filed a report two years later. They concluded that the Back Bay flats "are lost for every valuable purpose, and may be filled and made into dry land without public injury." The land was more valuable than the water right, and a compromise was required between the state and any other parties with rights in the bay. The primary claimants were the Boston and Roxbury Mill Corporation, established by the original charter to construct the Mill Dam and the mills, and the Boston Water Power Company, incorporated in 1824 to purchase water power from the Mill Corporation. In 1832 the Water Power Company acquired the mills and all the land south of the mill dam; in the same agreement the Mill Corporation retained the roads and the land north of the mill dam.[6]

The resolution of the various claims to the flats and the choice of alternatives for "improvement" of the Back Bay were assigned to a second commission. This board agreed with the first report that made land would be worth more than the franchise in water power; they made nine recommendations about the process of filling the bay, but sidestepped the arguments among the various claimants. Instead, another commission was proposed.[7]

The third commission, originally called the Commissioners on Boston Harbor and the Back Bay, would not hear testimony opposing the proposed filling of Back Bay, claiming that the General Court had clearly expressed its intention to fill the basin. David Sears offered to give up his interest in the flats if the commissioners would build a lake of at least twenty-five acres; the lake would be the setting for music, skating, boating, and fireworks. The following year Sears wrote the governor to say that if lake were not built, "what might now easily be made beautiful and attractive will give place to narrow and filthy streets, with bad sewerage and imperfect ventilation, and filled with a sickly population, and with receptacles of misery, vice and crime." His appeal was ignored.[8] The commission

3.2   From the dome of the State House in 1858 the mud flats in the Back Bay were plainly visible, as were the few mills along the "Cross Dam" (upper right). A legislative commission had concluded that the Back Bay flats were "lost for every valuable purpose, and may be filled and made into dry land without public injury."

reached agreement with the Mill Corporation and the Water Power Company and signed indentures with them in June 1854. In the agreement with the Mill Corporation, the state released to the corporation the flats between the mill dam and a parallel line running two hundred feet to the north. The corporation had to build a seawall on the new property line and fill the flats according to the plans of the state. They also released their right in the flats south of the dam and the right to collect tolls on the mill dam road after 1863.[9]

The indenture with the Water Power Company extinguished the company's right to flow water over the flats; in return the company received half of the state's flats below the high tide line, an additional 102 acres. The Commonwealth retained the area closest to the Common, bounded on the north by Beacon Street, on the west by a line between Fairfield and Exeter Streets, and on the south by Providence Street (from Exeter to Berkeley) and Boylston Street (from Berkeley to Arlington). In the original plan, the streets were named according to an incomprehensible system of roman numerals and letters based on the width of the streets and the order in which they were laid out. A second indenture between the Commonwealth and the Water Power Company in September 1854 opened the way for the company to begin filling its section of Back Bay, which began in May 1855.[10]

With no money to fill its land, the state sold the block on the south side of the Mill Dam (now Beacon Street) between Arlington and Berkeley Streets to two private parties, and used the proceeds to hire two railroad contractors to haul fill. Since most of the hills of the Shawmut Peninsula had been cut down and built upon, gravel to fill the Back Bay was found in Needham. For several years, three trains, each with 35 cars, made 25 trips a day and filled an average of two house lots each day (figure 3.3).[11]

3.3 To begin filling the Back Bay, the Commonwealth contracted with Norman Munson and George Goss, partners in several contracts with the railroads who had never undertaken anything remotely as large. Gravel was brought by train from Needham, nine miles from Boston, where trains were loaded with a steam shovel—a recent invention—built by John Souther at the Globe Locomotive Works in South Boston. In 1859 three trains running day and night, each with thirty-five cars, made a total of twenty-five trips in twenty-four hours, carrying a total of twenty-five hundred cubic yads, enough to fill nearly two house lots each day. Although the pace slowed considerably in subsequent years, landmaking in the Back Bay was essentially complete by the early 1880s.

The city of Boston had no claims to flats in Back Bay, but had reached an agreement in 1827 with the Mill Corporation that allowed the city to lay drains into the receiving basin and to dig mud from the flats. The state was skeptical about releasing any flats in Back Bay to the city; the 1855 Back Bay Commission did not believe that "any grant of land [in the Back Bay to Boston] is . . . expedient or that the city can prudently be clothed with the power of establishing a generous system of streets or an efficient system of drainage for that vast area." The city, according to the commission, "has used, and now uses, the Back Bay as a cesspool."[12]

The state made a series of proposals to the city, each of them committing the city to add some made land to the Public Garden and to keep it "forever open." For two years the proposals were rejected or countered with "uncooperative and rapacious" demands. Contemporary observers criticized the city for "ignorance and want of tact and wisdom" in their conduct of the negotiations.[13] A settlement was finally reached, not with the commission but with a joint committee of the legislature, although the reasons for the city's change of mind remain obscure. In December 1856 a Tripartite Agreement was executed between the Commonwealth, the city, and the Water Power Company. The state would donate to the city a wedge of flats so that the western boundary of the Public Garden would be perpendicular to the mill dam (now Beacon Street). A new street (now Arlington Street) would be built on this line, and the city and the state would each build half of the road. The city gave up the right to dig mud from the flats.[14]

The disposition of the Public Garden was finally settled by the city's approval of an act of the legislature in 1859, which decreed that the land would remain a park. The act did allow for a single exception, the construction of a building for horticultural purposes or for use as a new city hall, should the city wish to propose it. A competition for the design of the Public Garden was held in 1859, and construction was completed by the early 1860s (figure 3.4).[15]

The plan for the Back Bay had been modified in December 1856, changing the design for Commonwealth Avenue. Originally, it was to be one hundred twenty feet wide; the new plan widened it to two hundred feet. The committee's justification for the change acknowledged the benefits of connected public space: The modification "would give to the plan a feature of great magnificence, not existing elsewhere in this country. . . . This feature would make the territory attractive and desirable as a place of residence to an extent which, in the first place, would enhance the prices of the land and facilitate sales; and in the second place, would confer a lasting and permanent benefit upon the public by providing a broad and ornamental avenue connecting the Common and public garden in Boston with the picturesque and pleasing suburban territory."[16]

3.4   The state made a series of proposals to the city, each of them committing the city to add some of the made land to the Public Garden and to keep it "forever open." For two years the proposals were rejected or countered with "uncooperative and rapacious" demands. The disposition of the Public Garden was finally settled by the city's approval of an act of the legislature in 1859, which decreed that the land would remain a park.

VIEW OF THE PUBLIC GARDEN & BOSTON COMMON.
FROM ARLINGTON ST.
Published by F. B. STEWART & Co.

The Public Garden and the Commonwealth Avenue Mall were a local manifestation of what the landscape gardener Andrew Jackson Downing had a few years earlier called "Parkomania," an enthusiasm that only increased following the completion of New York City's Central Park, designed by Frederick Law Olmsted and Calvert Vaux. *Scientific American* in 1856 described the New York park as "an enterprise which we advise every city in the country to imitate." By the end of the decade, according to an article Olmsted wrote on parks for the *New American Cyclopedia*, new public grounds were underway in Philadelphia, Baltimore, Brooklyn, Hartford, and Detroit.[17]

The enthusiasm for the Commonwealth Avenue Mall was not universal, however, as the proposal for "Silver Lake" had already suggested. In 1859, George Snelling wrote an impassioned memorial to the legislature that argued against a boulevard in the center of the Back Bay. The record he created is important for two reasons. It is one of the earliest collections in Boston of arguments in favor of urban open space. And it is apparently the first publication to illustrate Hamburg's Alster Basin as the appropriate model for Boston's civic aspirations. Although Boston's setting on the Charles would sometimes be likened to London, Paris, Venice, and other waterfront cities, pictures and descriptions of Hamburg were by far the most frequent comparison in discussions of the city's future over the next seventy years.

It would be a mistake to fill the entire empty basin under the terms of the Tripartite Agreement, Snelling asserted, first in a letter to the *Boston Transcript* in April 1858 and then a year later in his memorial to the legislature. Instead, Marlborough and Newbury Streets should face a seven-hundred-foot-wide basin (figure 3.5). Filling the center of the empty basin would rob the city of an invaluable source of life-giving fresh air. The southwest wind, Snelling argued, "blows directly over the Common; and, taking its bracing qualities from the wide area of water over which it now passes—water renewed from the ocean twice in twenty-four hours—it bears health and refreshment to every part of this crowded and closely built city."[18]

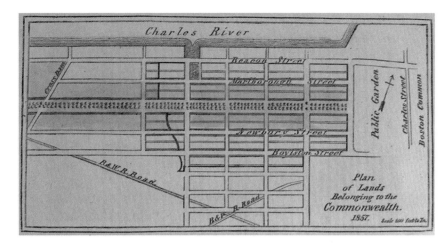

3.5 In 1859, after the city of Boston and the Commonwealth had finally reached a compromise about the filling of the Back Bay, the prominent Bostonian George Snelling apparently persuaded the governor and others that it would be a calamity if fresh breezes off the Charles from the west no longer freshened the air of the new Public Garden and Boston Common. In a letter to the legislature that year, Snelling included a plan of the Back Bay, with all the space set aside for Commonwealth Avenue—both the mall itself and the parallel roads along the mall—tinted in blue to indicate how this area could be preserved as open water.

The memorial was deferred to the next session of the General Court. One December day Snelling was walking across the Common when he met Governor Nathaniel P. Banks, who reported that he was making "a personal survey of the territory in question." Pointing to the area of the empty basin that would be made into dry land, Snelling warned that the sun would beat on it all day, accumulating heat that would last all night. He contrasted Hingham, with its prevailing summer winds over land, and Nahant, a resort because of its ocean breezes. Then he described for the governor the *Alster-damm* in Hamburg (figure 3.6). The freshwater basin was about as large an area as Boston Common, with "magnificent edifices" on three sides; on the fourth side, a public promenade separated the Inner Alster from the outer basin. Boston, Snelling told the governor, had in the

Back Bay the same elements that Hamburg had incorporated in creating the Alster. The two men arranged an appointment for the next day. In that meeting the governor requested a copy of a view of Hamburg, although he feared Snelling's proposal was too late.[19]

After unsatisfactory responses from legislators, Snelling determined to reprint his memorial, together with testimonials he had solicited in support of his proposed revision to the Back Bay plan. The respondents argued on three principal grounds—civic refinement (and with it increased property values), public health, and justice for the poor. Some argued for all three. E. Y. Robbins found the Common "a great opening into the country," where citizens could not only "inspire the fresh breeze" but also "commune with rural nature." Either through foresight or a happy accident, the Common opens to the southwest, the direction of the prevailing winds in summer, when fresh air is most beneficial. Daily laborers, he wrote, cannot escape to the country as the rich do; "Necessity holds them prisoners in the city." It would be a cruel injustice if considerations of gain robbed them of "free breath." In signing the memorial to the legislature, former mayor Josiah Quincy "deviated from a rule of conduct" he had prescribed for himself, to avoid questions of local improvement. He found Snelling's plan vital to the future health and comfort of the city's inhabitants. Edward Jarvis copied tables showing mortality and causes of death in English cities, and came to an unambiguous conclusion: "*decrease of life* goes in a positive ratio, hand in hand, with the increase of *density of population*."[20]

Senator Charles Sumner, writing from Washington, D.C., thanked Snelling for intervening to save the Common "by keeping it open to the western breezes and to the setting sun." He knew well the "value of water in scenery," and he cited a friend's view that a landscape without water was "like a face without eyes"; he also understood the value of open spaces as "*out-of door ventilators*." Orville Dewey thought the Common "the loveliest view of land and water and distant horizon that ever was opened into the heart of any great city . . . except Naples." Neither London nor New York offered anything like it. The unmodified Back Bay plan,

according to an unnamed gentleman just returned from Europe, was closing off air and water from the Common and "*spoiling the finest promenade in the world.*"[21]

After the Civil War, the argument for the city's beautification would more and more often be tied to higher land values. But in the letters collected by Snelling in 1859, only John Dix joined the two issues. He pointed out that in every city in the world where a waterfront existed, unappropriated by commercial interests, it was occupied by the wealthiest inhabitants. As examples he cited St. Petersburg, Hamburg, Dresden, Frankfurt, Florence, Naples, Charleston, and Chicago. The most pragmatic approach was argued by William Parrott. If Snelling's view ultimately were proved wrong, "the remedy is easy. The section may be filled in." The city should simply act on what Dix called the "dollar principle." It would be a mistake *not* to leave the center of the Back Bay unfilled; not a dollar would be lost if Snelling's proposal were adopted. It would mean simply that the cost of filling would not be spent now.[22]

As Snelling saw it, the villains in this story were "a company of Boston land speculators, encouraged by politicians" who eagerly accepted their lavish estimates of the state's financial gain. The well-being of the community was being sacrificed to the narrow financial interests of a few brokers in property.[23]

Two years later, in his 1861 inaugural, Governor John Andrew endorsed Snelling's proposal, suggesting that a basin in the center of the Back Bay might "secure to the public health" the benefits contemplated by the 1814 legislation that had authorized the creation of the full basin.[24] But none of these arguments would be persuasive, and talk of new parks for Boston was set aside by the outbreak of the Civil War.

The lasting legacy of Snelling's campaign was the introduction of images of Alster Basin into Boston's discussions of its future. In his 1860 reprinting of the previous year's memorial to the legislature, Snelling included an engraving of the Inner Alster as well as two newspaper articles describing the "crystal lake" at the center of the most beautiful part of Hamburg.[25] As the focus of Boston's aspirations, Hamburg was a striking choice. According to

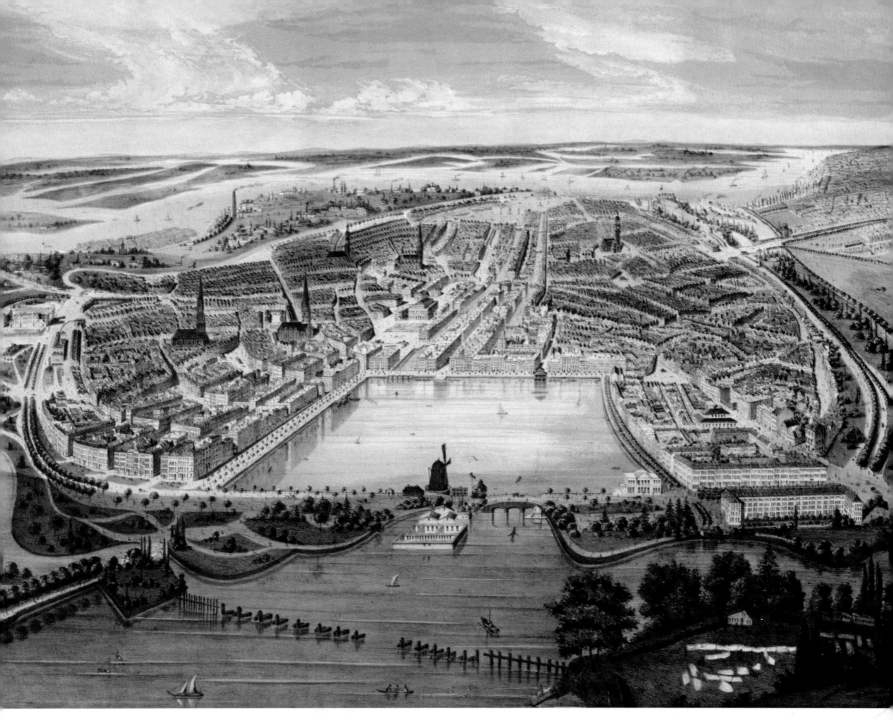

3.6 This bird's-eye view of Hamburg's Alster Basin dates from the middle of the nineteenth century, about the time Snelling included a drawing of the Alster in his petition to the legislature, the first time the Alster was proposed as a model for the development of the Charles River Basin.

one of the newspaper articles Snelling cited, the city was widely known as a commercial center but never celebrated for its beauty.[26] Founded in the ninth century at the meeting point of the Bille, Alster, and Elbe rivers, the city began almost immediately filling marshes and constructing canals. By 1235 A.D. a mill dam had been built across the Alster. A new fortification was built around the city in 1615–1626 during the Thirty Years War, and what is now the Inner Alster was left as open water inside the wall (figure 3.7). At the same time a new quarter of the city was laid out west of the Alster, reinforcing the perimeter of structures overlooking the basin. By the nineteenth century the urbane character of the basin was clearly established. Photographs and drawings of the city from the 1860s reveal why Bostonians found the reshaping of Hamburg's rivers a worthy pattern (figures 3.8–3.10).[27]

3.7   Over five centuries before Boston began reshaping the Charles, the city of Hamburg had transformed the Alster River in the center of the city. By 1235 a mill dam had been built on the lower Alster. This view from the late sixteenth century shows the Alster mill pond (top center) outside the city walls. New fortifications were built between 1615 and 1626 during the Thirty Years War that extended around the mill pond, incorporating what came to be called the inner Alster Basin inside the walls.

3.8 By the middle of the nineteenth century, a fashionable neighborhood had grown up around the lower Alster.

3.9 An elaborate swimming pavilion was constructed along one edge of the Alster in 1869. Open at first only to men and boys, the swimming facilities were expanded in 1901 and a separate entrance was provided to allow public bathing for women.

3.10 For a visit by the Kaiser to the city of Hamburg in 1887, a steam launch was outfitted with a swan on the prow.

In the end, Snelling's petition was ignored by the General Court, and the filling of the Back Bay proceeded according to the 1850s agreements. More than half of the state's land was filled by 1864, when the rate of filling was cut back; the remaining Commonwealth land was finished in 1876. The Boston Water Power Company finished its larger share of the flats in the 1880s (figures 3.11–3.12).[28]

3.11, 3.12 Although the plan for Back Bay has received extravagant praise, it is really quite simple. Its most distinguishing characteristics were the narrow, deep lots; height restrictions, and the expanse of Commonwealth Avenue extending west from the Public Garden, widened from one hundred twenty feet in the original scheme to two hundred feet in the final plan.

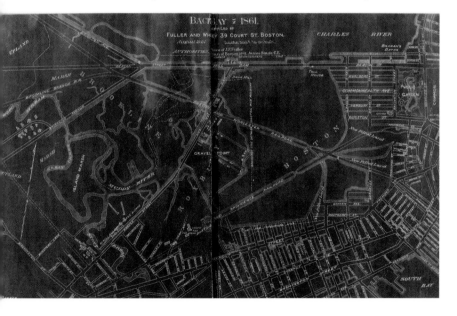
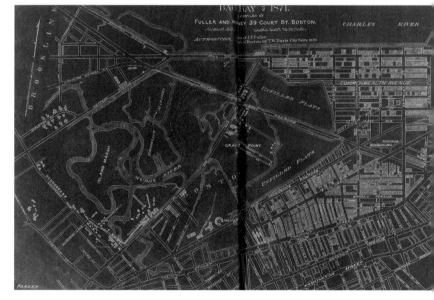

On the Water

While Gourlay, Sears, and Snelling promoted the basin as a scenic opportunity and a source of the public health, a few people were venturing out on the water, or jumping in. As early as 1800, Thomas Brattle built a bathhouse on his estate near the Brick Wharf at the foot of Ash Street in Cambridge. Several drownings must have occurred in the Charles judging from a formal vote by Harvard College to thank Brattle for "his kind and generous attention to the interest of humanity especially as they respect the preservation of the lives of the students of the College."[29] Judging from subsequent designs, the bathhouse was probably a wooden cage, open on the top, which allowed river water to flow through the structure (figure 3.13). Harvard built its own bathhouses about 1810 and 1841, and the Cambridge Humane Society built another bathhouse near the Great Bridge in 1830.[30]

In Boston, a growing concern for public health in the city's tenement neighborhoods led to a city council resolution to support public bathhouses in 1860, and to the construction of six floating bathhouses six years later. Four were located along the harbor, at the foot of Broad Street, near L Street in South Boston, in the South End, and in East Boston; and two were attached to bridges in the Charles, near the West End at the West Boston Bridge, and at the Warren Bridge, between the North End and Charlestown (figures 3.14–3.16).[31]

Boating on the Charles also dates from before the Civil War. A group of Harvard College students bought a thirty-seven-foot, six-oared boat in 1844, which they kept in Brighton; two years later they built a boathouse below the College Wharf on the Cambridge side (figures 3.17, 3.18). Racing was perhaps less important than rowing to favorite spots like the Spring Hotel in Watertown, or downstream to Braman's Baths, the Parker House,

3.13 Bath houses were constructed in the Charles River by Harvard College or by alumni in 1800, 1813, and 1841. They were probably built over the water, with a wooden cage below the surface that allowed the river to flow through the lower part of the structure, much like this bathhouse pictured in 1898. Privately owned bathhouses were also operating along the river in Boston in the mid-nineteenth century.

3.14 In 1866 the city of Boston organized a "beach bath" at L Street in South Boston and five floating bathhouses like this one, attached to the old West Boston Bridge in 1898. Women and girls were allowed in the bathhouse for two hours in the morning and two hours in the afternoon; the rest of the day was restricted for use by men and boys.

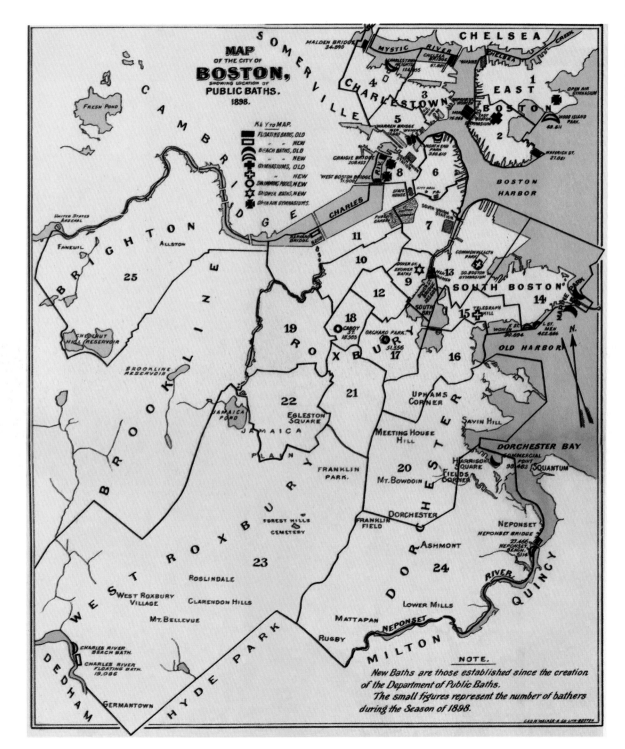

3.15 By 1898, the city of Boston managed thirteen floating baths, including five along the lower Charles. In that year the city organized a separate Bath Department.

3.16 Two bathhouses are visible in this postcard taken sometime after 1907 of the park at Charlesbank and the Cambridge (later Longfellow) Bridge. One bathhouse is partly hidden by the women's field house on the edge of the park; the other (lower right) represents a design devised by one of the bath commissioners and first introduced in 1898, with the tank of the bathhouse open to the sky for "perfect ventilation."

3.17 A group of Harvard College students bought a thirty-seven-foot, six-oared boat in 1844. By the time of this 1857 drawing in *Ballou's Pictorial Companion*, boat races had become a popular sport. Here the "Volant," sponsored by the Charles River Association, defeated the "Huron," owned by a club of Harvard College students that included J. J. Storrow. (Forty years later Storrow's son led the successful campaign for the Charles River dam.) On the left of the drawing, its roof crowded with spectators, are Braman's Baths on the north side of Back Street.

3.19 Workers at the Riverside Press organized a rowing club in 1869 and built a boathouse between River Street and Western Avenue.

3.18 Crimson as the Harvard color first appeared at a regatta in 1858, when a crew that included tutor Charles W. Eliot purchased six China silk scarves at Hovey's department store and tied them around their heads. The crew defeated six boats in a three-mile race that day and won a six-mile race two weeks later. By 1910 the color was formally adopted by the university.

3.20 Organized in 1851, the Union Boat Club built this elaborately decorated boat house on Brimmer Street in 1870. The oldest boat club in Boston and the second-oldest American club, the Union erected a grandstand on the upstream side of the boat house for viewing the boat races.

3.21 At the bend in the river just east of Mount Auburn, the Winchester estate in Cambridge included this pavilion on the Charles. An arch on the lower level of the facade allowed for boats to be rowed inside for storage.

or the theater, with "perhaps half the crew stretched on the floor boards all the long pull home." The Union Boat Club was organized in 1851, and by the middle of the decade *Ballou's Pictorial Companion* was recording organized races between clubs. Braman's Bathhouse often served as both the grandstand and the finish line. Workers at the Riverside Press organized a boat club in 1869, and Union replaced its old boathouse on Brimmer Street the following year (figures 3.19, 3.20). Several private boathouses were also built on the Charles (figure 3.21).[32]

Filling the Charles

In the fall of 1869, for reasons that remain obscure, a bill was presented to the General Court to approve substantial additional fill north of the new seawall on the water side of Beacon Street, in the main channel of the lower Charles. Hearings on the bill called forth vociferous protests from some of the city's most prominent citizens and established for the next thirty years the terms for public discourse on the river as a public space.

As it happened, the state's hearings on filling the Charles began about the same time that Boston's city fathers reopened the debate on public parks. On November 5, there were hearings on both issues, and E. H. Derby testified at both hearings. After speaking first to the legislative committee on the Charles River, Derby then testified at the Boston park hearings, where he began by observing that he had just come from a committee "assembled rather to diminish our recreation enjoyments, and breathing places." It was much more satisfying, he said, to speak at a gathering with the opposite purpose. Led by Oliver Wendell Holmes, the witnesses at the Charles River hearings outlined all the arguments for developing the river as a water park—though it would be more than thirty years before the first steps were taken to that end.[33]

The committee was officially chartered to look at improvements to the Mystic, the Miller's, and the Charles Rivers, as well as South Bay, Fort Point Channel, and Dorchester Bay. The hearings, however, addressed only the Charles River. The chairman announced at the first hearing that the committee would assume that the flats from the West Boston Bridge to the cross dam would be filled for a distance of fourteen hundred feet from the shore, reducing the channel of the river to between three and five hundred feet (figure 3.22). As it turned out, no one testified in favor of the proposal or described any benefits that would follow from it. Following introductory presentations by counsel for the opponents, various experts testified against the scheme. The engineering authorities described how shoaling in the harbor would increase. Medical doctors described the spread of diseases that would follow and presented statistics on mortality. Real estate bro-

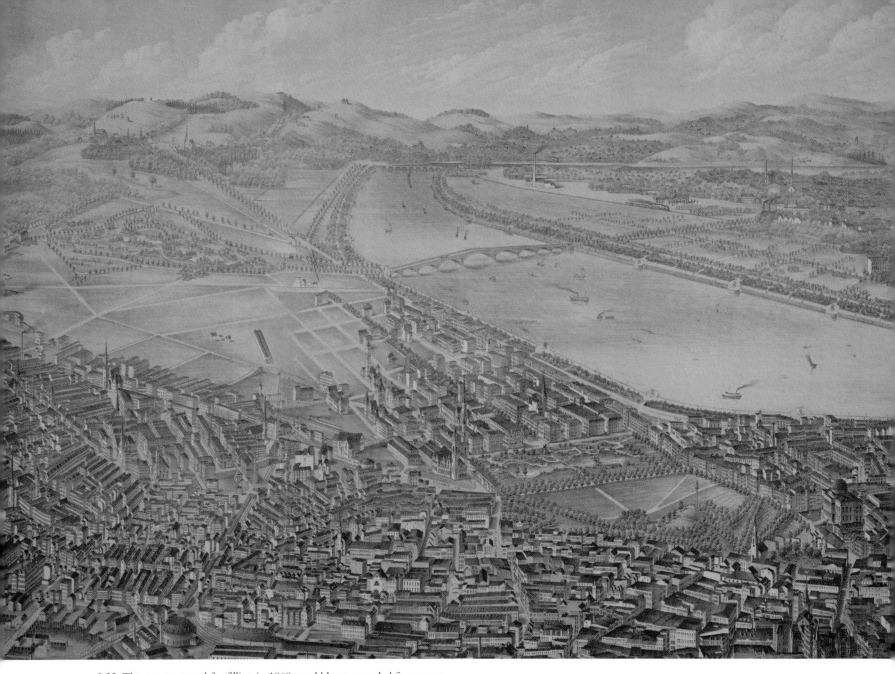

3.22 The area proposed for filling in 1869 would have extended from a proposed bridge at Massachusetts Avenue (center) to the West Boston Bridge (far right). Back Bay was turning into house lots (a project that took more than twenty-five years) but the land across the river in Cambridge remained largely undeveloped. This 1880 bird's-eye view of Boston and Cambridge shows the progress of new construction on the Boston side.

kers enumerated the precipitous decline in property values on the water side of Brimmer and Beacon Streets, because of the loss of fresh air and the view of the water and the country beyond. And the community's loss of trust in the state's prior commitments would be shattered.[34]

The most elaborate testimony was presented by Dr. Holmes, who described his strong attachment to the water side of the new streets in the Back Bay. He acknowledged a classic dilemma of expert witnesses: His expertise followed, in part, from his personal interest in the issue. Holmes emphasized, however, that this matter was not a concern just for the few wealthy residents who had built along the river. He was only one of many citizens of Boston who would be "distressed in mind, body, and estate" if the plan were realized. "In mind, as it threatens one of the principal comforts and enjoyments of our lives. In body, as it contemplates cutting us off from the great air reservoir to which, in the hotter months, we look as the safeguard of our health. In estate, because we have invested our property and our children's inheritance." He put the choice before the committee in the most dramatic terms:

> Nothing short of a convulsion of nature, an earthquake, an inundation, a great fire, or the invasion of a hostile army would produce greater dismay, or entail more insupportable losses than the realization of this revolutionary project.

The exposed mudflats were preferable to a much narrower channel, which would likely be developed as East Cambridge had been, where the smoke and noise of numerous factories made the area "as nearly uninhabitable" as any part of Boston's suburbs, with the exception of the neighborhood near the soapworks in Cambridgeport. Holmes concurred with the widely held view that vitiated air caused or severely aggravated fevers, childhood diseases, cholera, scrofula, and consumption.[35]

Although analogies between urban life and the human body were centuries old, Holmes extended this imagery almost to parody.[36] A great city, he said, has "a collective life, like individual organized beings." Its brain was the municipal government, its muscles the police and "other active servants." Above all, a city required breathing organs. A densely developed city with no internal breathing spaces was like a fish or reptile, breathing with gills; a city with large air spaces was like a higher animal, with lungs. Boston was "peculiarly favored in having both sets of organs. the common and public garden one lung, this [Charles River] basin the other." The proposal before the legislature would cut out the larger part of the right lung and "sell it as the lights and liver of four-footed beasts are sold in the market." He concluded his testimony by paraphrasing a poem:

> Down the river did glide, with wind and tide,
>   A pig with vast celerity;
> And the Devil he grinned, for he saw all the while
> How it *cut its own throat;* and he thought with a smile
> Of the Bay State's financial prosperity.

Several legislators' questioned Holmes's claim that the air in the Back Bay remained salubrious after passing over the reeking mudflats at low tide. Holmes did not back down; the air was far better, he said, than it would be if more of the river were filled. When asked if there was anything offensive in the appearance of the mud flats, Holmes responded that he would not "go out of the sight and smell of these flats. That is the best proof I can give of what they are. Three times I have had a chance to choose my residence, and each time I have got nearer and nearer to the flats."[37]

Dr. George Derby, secretary of the state Board of Health, was asked whether, if filling the river any further would be a disaster of such magnitude, then why wasn't the filling now underway in the Back Bay—the filling that created the house lots Holmes had bought and built upon—equally a mistake? Weren't the opponents of filling the Charles arguing that Boston be put into a straitjacket, where no more change would be allowed? Derby deflected the question by repeating that "any material abridgment of that water area" would be bad for the city.[38] Nathan Matthews, formerly president of the Boston Water Power Company, and Colonel Newell Thompson, who had served as auctioneer for the Commonwealth lands in the Back Bay, testified that that the money brought in from the sale of new lots would not come close to compensating for the damage claims that would be brought by the owners whose newly built row houses faced the river. Two weeks later four other doctors testified: the city physician, a member of the Harvard Medical School faculty, a doctor from the Old Ladies Asylum on Revere Street (which backed on the river), and a surgeon from the City Hospital.[39]

Holmes solicited letters on the issue, and a number of them were included in the committee's report. Louis Agassiz asked whether it was possible that there were men ignorant of the value of "such a large sheet of sea water, bathing, invigorating and refreshing its surroundings?" He hoped such "vandalism" would not be tolerated; if it came to that, there would be "in Cambridge a host of radical friends ready to be extreme conservatives in this matter." The letters George Snelling had collected ten years earlier were also published by the committee.[40]

In the face of unanimous testimony against the proposal, the committee took no action. These arguments against filling the basin—shoaling in the harbor, increased pollution in the river, and cutting off air and light from the houses on the water side of Beacon Street—would be employed against the proposals for a Charles River dam for the next thirty years.

Resuming the Park Debates

For all those who opposed it, the proposed filling of the Charles was a straightforward question. The park debates, on the other hand, were not so easily resolved. After a group of citizens petitioned the city council on the subject in the fall of 1869, a joint committee was established. Two hearings were held in November of that year, and they were preceded by numerous editorials and letters on the subject in Boston newspapers. In many of the articles and in the hearings, the creation of a park along the banks of the Charles was listed as one of the highest priorities.[41]

Boston's natural setting, so extravagantly celebrated in Gourlay's descriptions of the region, was used as an argument both for and against the expenditure of public funds for parks. One of the most influential essays was written by Horace W. S. Cleveland,

a native of Lancaster, Massachusetts, who had worked as a landscape designer in Boston from 1854 to 1868. Soon after moving to Chicago in the spring of 1869, Cleveland published an essay, *The Public Grounds of Chicago*, with an appended discussion titled "What Boston May Do." He asserted that every city should follow "its own style of adornment appropriate to its 'moral and physical character.'" Boston had neither "the necessity or the power" to construct a large central park, and with sea breezes on three sides together with the seventy-five acres of the Common and the Public Garden, the city was adequately supplied with ventilation. If Boston wanted a park comprising attractions of natural scenery, it would have to go beyond the city limits; the best site in the region was the territory around Spot Pond in Arlington.[42]

A visitor coming to Boston for the first time could not ride a mile in any direction without finding great beauty in the region's natural features and evidence everywhere of taste and culture, in the humblest cottages as well as the most extravagant villas. Such a visitor might fairly ask (and Cleveland emphasized that the question was not "an imaginary one"), "What do you Bostonians want of a park, with such wealth of natural beauty all around you, and almost every foot of it so tastefully improved by private hands?"[43]

All that Boston needed to do was finish and adorn the roads that connected these delightful scenes, and so make a park of the "whole surrounding country." Such a plan would exert a moral influence far beyond any that would follow from the creation of a single large park. Was this not, Cleveland asked, the "most simple and practicable scheme" that could be devised? He doubted the city's will to realize even this simple idea, however, and could not resist saying that Chicago was preparing to create a series of parks and reservations in her third decade that Boston was finding impossible to do "in the third century of her existence." Not surprisingly, the argument of Cleveland's imaginary visitor was cited in an editorial in the *Boston Evening Transcript* opposing public expenditure for parks the day after the second hearing.[44]

With one exception, the witnesses at the hearings were in favor of parks. There was much discussion of large and small parks,

parks close to the city and rural parks accessible by public conveyance. A few speakers asked whether the parks were for the rich, the poor, or for both. Settling these questions would require "very liberal views of space and time," according to Elizur Wright. He argued that a city park should be large (at least two thousand acres), well wooded and well watered, with the finest lake scenery, natural or artificial, and "should be capable of being made a museum for the study of every branch of natural history, as well as an attractive retreat into the domain of wild Nature herself. It should not only have luxuriant gardens, groves, and forests, but rocks that are both instructive and sublime." Such a park, he said, had been discovered by Governor John Winthrop in 1631 at what was now known as Spot Pond. For two more decades, Wright would campaign to acquire the area as a public reservation. He was also one of several who expressed the view that if "Boston makes a park that will only do for the present municipality of that name, a large Boston will soon have to make another."[45]

Three weeks after the hearings, on December 2, the landscape gardener Robert Morris Copeland (who had been Cleveland's partner in the 1850s) published a remarkable editorial in the *Boston Advertiser* that elaborated on Cleveland's suburban parkway and added to it a series of parks he thought should be realized in Boston's near future. All the towns surrounding the city, he wrote, "are now Boston and are populated with our citizens, who come here to earn money, and go home to enjoy it." Whether or not annexation proceeded, park sites should be acquired beyond the present city limits now. Parks would not only invigorate Boston's citizens, but also increase the wealth of the city. Public open spaces, wrote Copeland, were no more a debt than the store in which a merchant keeps goods for sale.[46]

Copeland's proposal matched Gourlay's 1844 plan in its expansive view of the future city, and described in captivating detail the reservations and grand boulevards that would surround Boston. He agreed with Cleveland's assessment of the picturesque scenery in the region, but he went beyond his former partner's ideas and advocated public acquisition of the most significant natural areas. Near the city there were two superb opportunities for large parks;

the first extended from the Back Bay basin (the full basin, not the receiving basin) to Parker Hill, the second included the Roxbury highlands and the valley of Stony Brook. The Charles River Basin would be filled with fresh water from Stony and Muddy Brooks, and provide a striking foreground to the hill beyond.[47]

A grand boulevard would extend from Squantum Point on the south and continue in a great arc around the city all the way to Chelsea (now Revere) Beach. In between it would pass by the Bussey Farm (now the Arnold Arboretum) and the Chestnut Hill Reservoir, then cross the Charles on its way to Wellington Hill in Belmont. The hill, the falls of Beaver Brook, and the East Lexington meadow would become a park of five to eight hundred acres. The boulevard might then divide, with the western branch enjoying the view inland to Mount Wachusett and Monadnock; joined again, the road would then pass between Spy Pond and Fresh Pond across Arlington to Spot Pond and continue to the beach at Chelsea. That was not the end, however; bridges and ferries would connect the harbor islands and complete the circle back to Squantum Point. This scheme would open up lands for development in every suburban community, and make Boston "truly the most beautiful city in America."[48]

Like Gourlay, Copeland believed that since all the surrounding communities would benefit, it would be reasonable for the legislature "to appoint a metropolitan commission with power to under take this plan." Even the future upkeep of the parks was addressed. The commission would condemn the necessary properties to construct the boulevard, then offer the improved lands for sale, providing enough to maintain all the public grounds in good order. Copeland's metropolitan plan would "unite and harmonize every interest," including all those who have advocated other park schemes as well as every property owner within twelve miles of the State House.[49]

The opposite approach was taken by Uriel H. Crocker, a Boston lawyer, in a letter to the *Advertiser* published two days after Copeland's plan had appeared in the paper. Crocker focused on creating a single road, less than four miles in length, from the Mill Dam (now Beacon Street) at Hereford Street to Corey's Hill and

then continuing to Chestnut Hill Reservoir (figure 3.23). This approach was "superior to all hitherto offered" for at least five reasons. First, it would be centrally situated (as contrasted with the proposed parks in Dorchester or Spot Pond). It incorporated natural features that already existed. Corey's Hill offered one of the most expansive views in the metropolitan area, but it was private and inaccessible; the reservoir was already a favorite resort for walking and driving; and the Back Bay (described in language later echoed by Eliot) offered an expansive open space "furnished by nature without cost," large enough to cool the breezes that passed over it, with room for all who wanted to row or sail, an attractive site for a drive and promenade along its shores. At Craigie's Bridge, a two- or three-foot dam could be constructed to keep the mud flats continually covered. The plan would meet the wants of both rich and poor, "those who ride and those who walk." It could be done for little expense: The promenade on the river would have to be built, but the route beyond the river to Corey's Hill and the reservoir was already beautiful enough that they could be left for a time as they are. Finally, this four-mile park would be accessible to far more people than a compact park of the same size.[50]

Although modest in comparison with Copeland's grand scheme, Crocker's plan echoed Copeland's ideas about the importance of connected open space. It would give the city "a continuous line of ornamental grounds" from the State House to Chestnut Hill. This was far superior to the plans that took a "compact" area like Central Park in which "a drive of considerable length might be made to wind so ingeniously that those who passed over it should not be made unpleasantly aware of the fact that they were riding round and round within narrow and confined limits." Crocker couched his ideas in rich visual language:

> The manner in which the proposed park unites and combines the varied charms of the Chestnut Hill reservoir, of Corey's Hill, and of the large tidal basin of Charles River, seems to us peculiarly happy. Either one of these, the two rural lakes among the hills, the lofty elevation with its wide-reaching view of country on the one side and of city and ocean on the other, in the west the green hills and valleys, in the east the red bricks of the city and the blue of the ocean, and on the north and south the white houses of the suburbs swarming over the green fields for miles away—or the broad body of salt water, large enough for thousands to sail or row upon without crowding—either one of these elements, we say, would alone suffice to make a park famous; to make it a place of which a city might well be proud; but to unite all these in one pleasure ground is to do something worthy of Boston.

In addition to writing the committee on parks, Crocker wrote two newspaper articles. The second article concluded (with a visual metaphor that never caught on) that the park scheme "would give a golden spoke to the Hub of the Universe."[51]

Crocker shared with Copeland a regional view of the responsibility as well as the opportunity for public parks. The bill he drafted for the legislature proposed a metropolitan (not a Boston) commission, empowered to take land outside the city limits, with nine members—the mayor of Boston, four members appointed by the Boston City Council, and four appointed by the governor.[52]

While the bill was under consideration in the General Court, a number of Bostonians wrote to Frederick Law Olmsted and asked for his help (figure 3.24). Several urged him to testify before the legislature. He declined to do so, but he did agree to speak at a meeting of the American Social Science Association on February 25, 1870.[53] His talk, "Public Parks and the Enlargement of Towns," did not discuss any of the Boston park schemes. He did echo Gourlay and Copeland in asserting that "the Boston of today

3.23 In the Boston debates on public parks after the Civil War, engineers, landscape gardeners, and interested citizens came forward with plans to connect open space through the city, ranging from modest to grand. U. H. Crocker, a Boston lawyer, took a circumspect approach, suggesting a four-mile road from the mill dam at Hereford Street to Corey's Hill and the Chestnut Hill Reservoir that incorporated landscape elements "furnished by nature without cost." This "continuous line of ornamental grounds," wrote Crocker, "would give a golden spoke to the Hub of the Universe."

3.24 By 1870, when Frederick Law Olmsted first spoke at a public meeting in Boston, he had completed with his partner Calvert Vaux the design and construction of Central Park.

3.25 The landscape gardener Robert Morris Copeland proposed two large parks for the city. One extended from the Back Bay to Parker (now Mission) Hill, the other included the Roxbury highlands and the valley of Stony Brook. He also described a grand boulevard that would extend in a great arc around the city from Squantum Point in the south to Chelsea (now Revere) Beach. Another element of the grand design of parks he deemed "worthy of Boston" was Copeland's concern for social equality. Integral to the park plan was accessibility to "all classes of population," a sentiment echoed by the new mayor, Samuel Cobb.

is the mere nucleus of the Boston that is to be. It is practically certain that it is to extend over many miles of country now thoroughly rural in character."[54]

The bill, which required approval by two-thirds of the eligible voters in Boston, passed the state legislature on May 27. Just before the city election, a handbill was circulated that claimed the parks outside the city limits would be paid for by city residents, a line of reasoning that would plague all future proposals for metropolitan government. In fact, a special commission was to be appointed to assess the surrounding cities and towns. Out of fifteen thousand voters, the bill fell short of the required margin by about nine hundred votes.[55]

A new petition was presented to the City Council in December, but the council took no action for three years. Essays and exhortations continued to appear in the local press, and in 1872 Copeland revised his earlier editorial and published it as a pamphlet titled *The Most Beautiful City in America: Essay and Plan for the Improvement of the City of Boston*. Some of the major features of his first plan remained, including the park joining the Back Bay with Parker Hill, Fort Hill in Roxbury, Williams Park in West Roxbury, and the Stony Brook valley (figure 3.25). The Back Bay would be dammed to create a "sheet or lake of fresh water, diversified by islands, and crossed by the great avenues on suitable bridges."[56]

Copeland changed his mind about some elements of his 1869 plan. The suggested parks were all located within the city limits, an acknowledgment, perhaps, of the failed referendum. And although he agreed that the Back Bay was now the city's finest residential district and that the residents would be delighted with a park along the Charles Basin, he now said that all of the city's streams, even those of "small volume," would be needed to support manufacturing. The Neponset River already demonstrated this general rule, and in time, "every foot of the Charles River bank will be wanted for yards and wharves." The harbor islands would likely be used for residences or commercial ventures (for example, private resorts), but should not be improved by the public unless they could be connected to the mainland with bridges and made accessible to "all classes of population."[57]

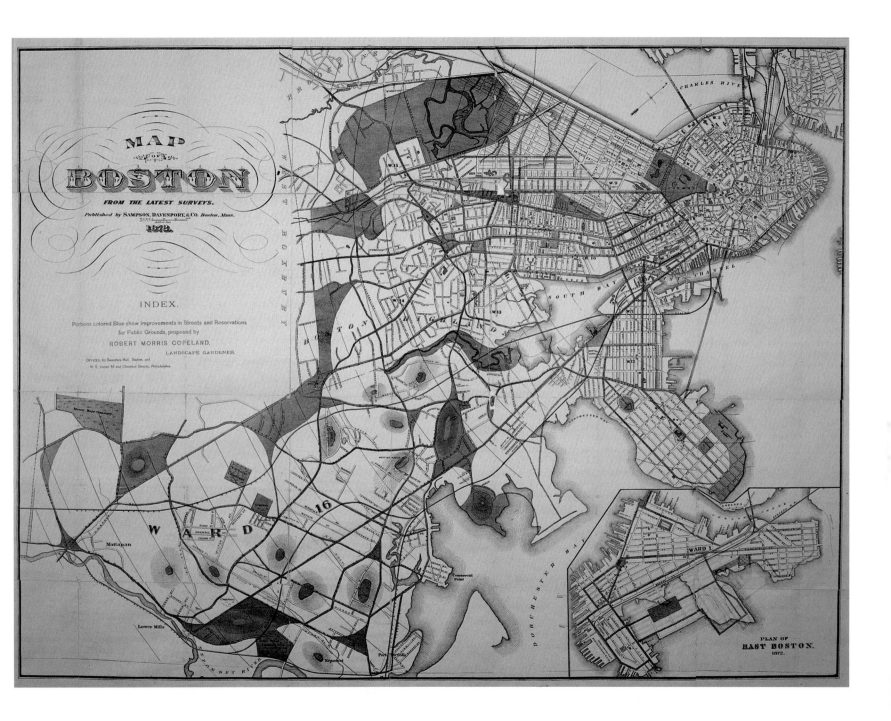

In his inaugural in 1874, the city's new mayor, Samuel Cobb, renewed the call for the establishment of public parks, and a month later a special commission was appointed by the city council. In June two more hearings were held. Most of people who spoke supported a "water park" on either the Back Bay or the Charles, and a petition was presented with fifteen hundred signatures in favor of a Back Bay water park. Among the most articulate speakers at the hearings was Richard Henry Dana. He claimed that the Charles River was an opportunity not available to any other city, because "a park in the heart of the city with sea water was worth ten thousand parks out of the reach of the people, especially of the poorer portion of the population." The city should never have built houses on the north side of Beacon Street, Dana said; where there should be "a great public driveway," there was instead "a contemptible scavenger's street, thirty feet wide, backing up against the unmentionable parts of private houses" (see figure 3.54). Boston should not only construct the water park; the city should consider building another row of house lots to create a suitably dignified frontage on the park.[58] Public health remained a great concern. "Pure atmosphere" was the surest guarantor of well-being, said one speaker (quoting an address fifty years before by Mayor Josiah Quincy), "not merely in the wide street and splendid avenue, *but in every lane, in every court and every alley.*"[59]

The engineer Ernest W. Bowditch, who had been associated with Copeland for three years until Copeland's death in 1874, described a plan that drew heavily on Copeland's earlier ideas. By including several public reservoirs and rural cemeteries, the acquisition of land would be reduced, and the region's water supplies would be protected. With the exception of land in Cambridge around Fresh Pond, most of the proposed parks were inside Boston city limits. The following year he revised his scheme; to the southern and western parks of his previous plan he added parks north of the city, including Spy, Mystic, and Spot Ponds, Prospect Hill in Malden, and Chelsea Beach, making a full circle from Chelsea to Squantum. Anticipating Olmsted's later designs, he included the valley of Muddy River to connect Back Bay with Jamaica Pond. As others had suggested earlier, he argued that the cost of these parks should be divided between Boston and the surrounding towns (figure 3.26).[60]

The special commission filed its brief report in December 1874. It began by comparing park acreage in Boston with New York, Brooklyn, Philadelphia, Baltimore, and Chicago. Boston suffered in the analysis, with only 115 acres; Brooklyn (the next lowest) had already acquired 550 acres, and Philadelphia headed the list with 3,074 acres. The report then summarized the financial benefits of park construction, drawing on data from the same six cities. Since the start of park construction in New York, the city's real estate valuation had increased 91 percent, but the three wards around Central Park had increased more than $200 million (over 700 percent), and the park had cost only $14 million. In the other four cities, total valuation increased from 21 to 143 percent, but the property surrounding new parks increased from 100 to more than 400 percent. Following the financial analysis was a brief consideration of the sanitary problems of the city, and the public health benefits that would follow from building parks.[61]

Although far less expansive than Copeland's or Bowditch's plan, the commissioners emphatically endorsed immediate action, since "every day's delay will add so greatly to the cost." They repeated Cleveland's view that the city did not need a large "Central Park," but should instead build a series of parks of various sizes "connected by broad driveways." Looking out from the center of the city, they suggested laying out a series of parks of moderate size "between the third and fourth mile circles." Land for a second band of larger parks beyond the first series should be purchased but need not be improved. Since any park acquisitions would require legislation, however, it would be imprudent to recommend specific sites until the City Council was granted the power to act.[62]

3.26 Many of the reservations later incorporated into the Boston and metropolitan parks were included in a plan prepared by the engineer Ernest Bowditch in 1875. He too thought that Boston did not need a "Central Park," but rather a series of open spaces linked in a coherent system. In this plan, the valley of the Muddy River connected the Back Bay with Jamaica Pond, an idea later incorporated by Olmsted in his "continuous chain of pleasure grounds," now known as the Emerald Necklace.

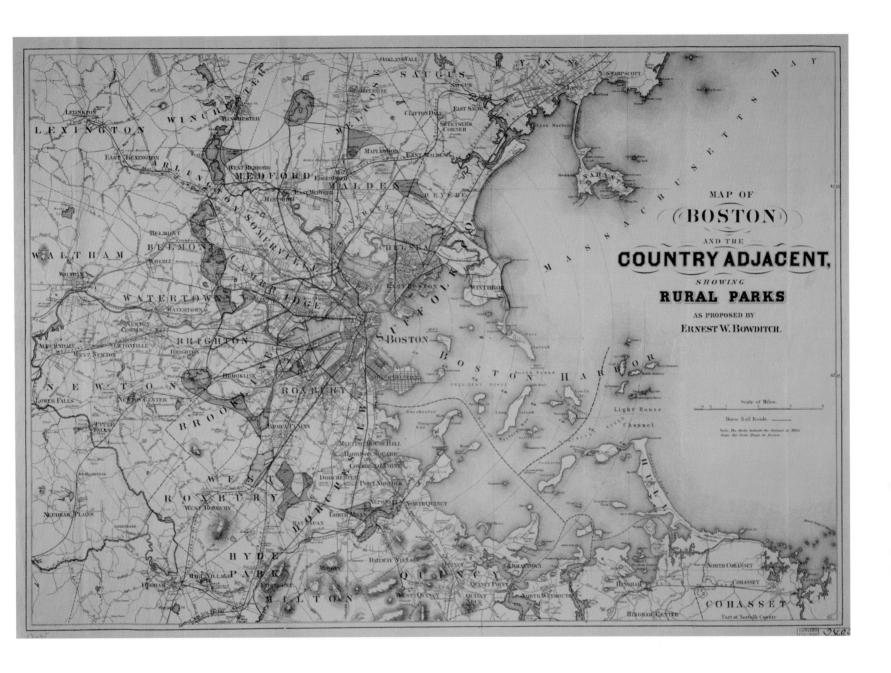

Despite considerable opposition in the council, an order was finally passed petitioning the General Court for a new parks bill. The act approved by the legislature followed the city's order closely, including a provision that allowed not only Boston but also adjoining cities and towns to take land for parks. Three park commissioners would be appointed by the mayor, and all appropriations had to be approved by a two-thirds majority in both branches of the City Council. The bill was passed by Boston voters in June 1875.[63]

The Charles River Embankment Company

In Cambridge, the first proposals for public spaces along the river came from a private venture, on land first acquired as part of a railroad scheme. Charles Davenport was an apprentice carriage builder when he took over his master's business in 1832. Davenport built the first omnibuses in New England in 1833–1834 and the first modern railroad passenger cars in America in 1836–1837, and soon outgrew his cramped shop in Central Square. In 1842 he established a new plant on Main Street, on a property that ran out into the flats of the Charles River. Six years later Davenport was one of three incorporators of the Union Railroad, chartered to build a line from the Fitchburg Railroad in Somerville across the Cambridgeport flats to Brookline. It would cross the Charles at Cottage Farm and connect with the Boston & Worcester Railroad, filling in one crucial link from the west to the deep-water piers in Charlestown and East Boston (figure 3.27).[64]

In 1846, two years before the founding of the Union Railroad, the Chelsea Branch Railroad was incorporated to connect East Boston with Chelsea, another move to link the expanding rail network north of the city with Boston Harbor. The Chelsea Branch was renamed the Grand Junction in 1848, when it was authorized to cross the Mystic River into Somerville and tie into the Boston & Maine and other northern railroads. Five years later the Union line was authorized to lease its property in Cambridgeport to the Grand Junction, and the Boston & Worcester agreed to help construct the tracks from Brookline

through Cambridge and Somerville in exchange for lease rights to harborfront property in East Boston.[65]

More than 80 percent of the rail line across Cambridge was built on a high embankment across marshes and mudflats. With few culverts, the embankment reduced the flow of water over the marshes, drying out the land and making it more attractive for development. But the marshes on the river side—and the rail line itself—attracted industries and discouraged residential development on the river side of Cambridgeport. Service began in 1855, but soon thereafter a bridge was washed out by a storm. The Boston & Worcester refused to invest in rebuilding the line and sued the Grand Junction; a decade later, the Worcester line was authorized by the legislature to take over the Grand Junction. In 1868 the Boston & Worcester merged with the Western Railroad (which was operating the route from Worcester to Albany) to create the Boston & Albany Railroad. The new company reconstructed the Grand Junction tracks, and the line through Cambridge began operating again in 1869; it was (and still is) the only practical connection between northern and southern railroads in Boston.[66]

Davenport, meanwhile, closed his business in 1856 and pursued other interests for the rest of his long life. Chief among these was the Charles River Embankment Company. During a visit to Havana in the 1850s, Davenport "saw the small embankment on the bay there, where the people sat under the palms, enjoying the breezes." Returning to Cambridge, he eventually purchased three-quarters of the flats between the West Boston and Cottage Farm Bridges, and in 1868 began circulating a series of proposals for water parks on both sides of the river (figure 3.28).[67]

In 1882 Boston and Cambridge agreed to construct a new bridge across the widest part of the basin at Massachusetts Avenue, and in turn Cambridge and the Embankment Company negotiated the transfer of land for an approach to the bridge and the creation of a two-hundred-foot esplanade behind a new seawall along the river in exchange for a postponement by the city of any tax increases during construction. Frederick Viaux drafted a street plan for the company in 1889, which was published in the 1894 Cambridge atlas (figure 3.29). The building restrictions established by the Embankment Company reinforced the substantial images of Davenport's drawings. They included a twenty-foot building setback from the esplanade, a prohibition against commercial and industrial buildings, minimum and maximum heights of three to eight stories, and a restriction of building materials to brick, stone, or iron.[68]

Construction on the seawall began in 1883, but the company went bankrupt in the depression ten years later. Davenport had clearly underestimated, among other things, the difficulty of selling house lots on the water side of the railroad line whose franchise he once shared. Only the Riverbank Court apartments, the city armory, the Metropolitan Storage Warehouse, and a few other smaller buildings were completed.[69] The land for the Cambridge Esplanade was set aside, but the unoccupied, water-filled lots remained unsold for two decades (figures 3.30, 3.31).

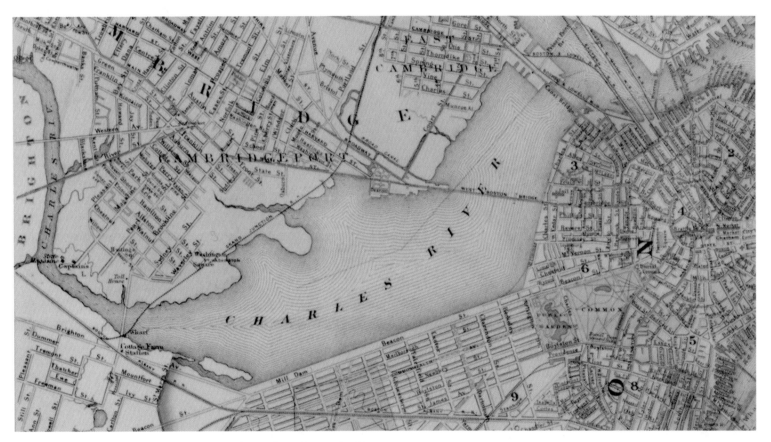

3.27 Charles Davenport began acquiring marshland along the Cambridge side of the Charles in the 1840s, and in 1853 he was one of three partners who incorporated as the Union Railroad Company and were granted the right to build a line across the marshes south of Cambridgeport. The ragged edges of mudflats and marsh, already split by the development along the West Boston Bridge, were now divided by an embankment that extended from the Brookline Bridge to Main Street. The marsh land north of the railroad, now dammed off from the river, offered large tracts for industrial development

A VIEW AS THE BASIN WILL LOOK WHEN COMPLETED.

NEW BOSTON AND CHARLES RIVER BASIN.

3.28 Although his Union Railroad had been taken over by the Grand Junction, Davenport still hoped to develop the land on the water side of the rail line. In the 1870s he began, as "the first projector of the Embankment," to promote a residential development patterned after the Back Bay (where MIT now stands).

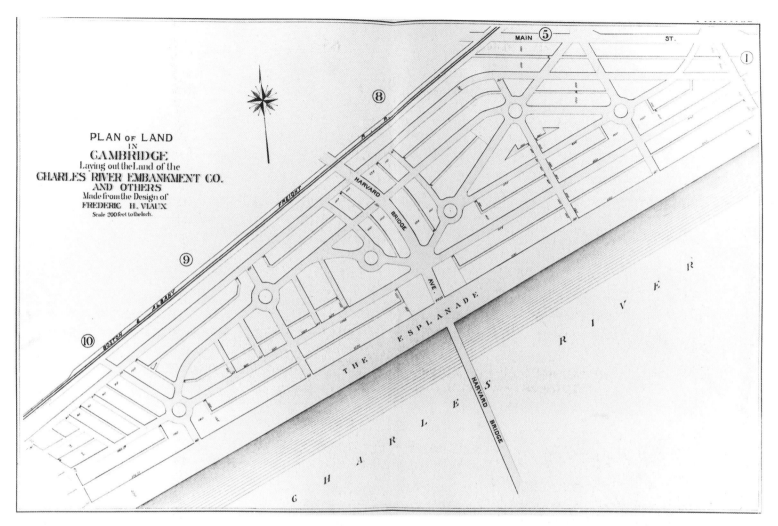

3.29 Boston and Cambridge agreed in 1882 to construct a new bridge across the widest part of the basin, and Davenport hired Frederick Viaux to draft this street plan to incorporate the bridge into his plans for a grand residential neighborhood on the Cambridge side. A parcel two hundred feet wide was deeded to the city to create "The Esplanade." Across the back of the development were the railroad tracks in the right-of-way once owned by the Union Railroad.

3.30 Even after the seawall was constructed, clamdiggers still ventured out onto the mudflats along the Cambridge Esplanade at low tide. The trees along the Esplanade have recently been planted. On the horizon at the Cambridge end of the Harvard Bridge in this photograph from about 1900 are the Riverbank Court Apartments (now MIT's Ashdown House).

3.31 The Charles River Embankment Company deeded the land for the Cambridge Esplanade to the city, but the unoccupied, water-filled lots remained unsold for two decades. Davenport had likely underestimated the difficulty of selling land on the water side of a rail line. This view of the Harvard Bridge looking toward Boston was taken soon after the bridge's completion in 1891.

The Boston Park Commission was finally appointed in July 1875, and two months later another public hearing was held. The notice of the hearing in the city newspapers invited "civil and landscape engineers" and other citizens to comment on lands for public parks. Then the commissioners began keeping daily office hours, and at least eighty people came to the office during the winter of 1875–1876. Many of them presented papers or plans, and by the spring almost every possible site in the city had been endorsed by someone. In October the commissioners asked Olmsted to join them in a visit to proposed park sites. The following spring, as they were making final decisions, they again invited Olmsted to inspect the parks. Only a draft of Olmsted's observations survives; it focuses on four of the proposed sites. He strongly endorsed the Charles River Embankment and Jamaica Pond, and suggested some changes in the boundaries of the parks proposed for West Roxbury (now Franklin Park) and Back Bay, (including Parker Hill). He also reviewed the plans for the roads leading to the parks and suggested "greater liberality in the new parkways and bolder and more sweeping improvements of existing streets leading toward the parks."[70]

The commission's 1876 report was a landmark not only for Boston but in the history of American park development. More than that, the report mirrors the vision and commitment of the park commissioners. Given the lengthy deliberations of the city fathers on the subject, reflected in the skepticism of observers like H. W. S. Cleveland, this commitment was crucial in later allowing the Olmsted office the freedom to develop the park designs.

Four criteria were established for selecting parks and parkways. The first was "*Accessibility*, for all classes of citizens by walking, driving, riding, or by means of horse or steam cars." "*Economy*" required the choice of lands that as much as possible were not producing income and would not disturb the business or domestic growth of the city. "*Adaptability*" called for identifying lands with appropriate natural features, that would require the least cost for development. Finally, properties with "*Sanitary advantages*" for park development would become "unhealthy if neglected or built upon."[71]

Waterfront parks were recommended at City Point, Savin Hill, on the harbor, and on the Charles River. Two urban parks were suggested, on Parker Hill overlooking Back Bay, and at South Bay. Four miles from the center of the city land should be acquired adjacent to the Chestnut Hill reservoir in Brighton and for the West Roxbury Park. Jamaica Pond would be linked by parkways be Parker Hill and Franklin Park (figure 3.32).[72]

The report described each proposed park in some detail. The Charles River Embankment would extend from Leverett Street to Cottage Farm Bridge and would provide space for "walks, drives, saddle-pads, and boat-landings," and a parkway two hundred feet wide. The perspective drawing in the report did not show new row houses facing on the basin, as Dana had suggested the year before (figure 3.33). The commissioners hoped to connect the embankment with Brighton Park, but the best route would be through Brookline, and the park act did not grant the authority to create a parkway in another jurisdiction.[73]

A meeting in Faneuil Hall in June 1876 enthusiastically endorsed the commissioners' recommendations. Richard Henry Dana claimed that Boston lagged behind every city in America in providing parks. Edwin Clarke identified the issue at the root of every debate on the cost of parks: it was difficult to compute the educational or sanitary value of parks "on any scale that the market acknowledges." That value was nonetheless "real, substantial, and potent." The city council, however, did not support the suggested appropriation of five million dollars, and the report was ignored for a year. Opposition to the parks came from several directions. The city was still recovering from the Great Fire of November 1872 and from the crash of 1873. A sewer bond was pending and the parks were seen as competing for those funds.[74]

The council finally approved $450,000 for the Back Bay park in 1877, perhaps hoping that inadequate funding would kill the entire project. The commissioners proceeded with land acquisition, which was largely completed by March 1878. As the city had done with the design of the Public Garden two decades earlier, the commissioners decided to hold an open competition. The first prize was awarded to Hermann Grundel (a florist, according

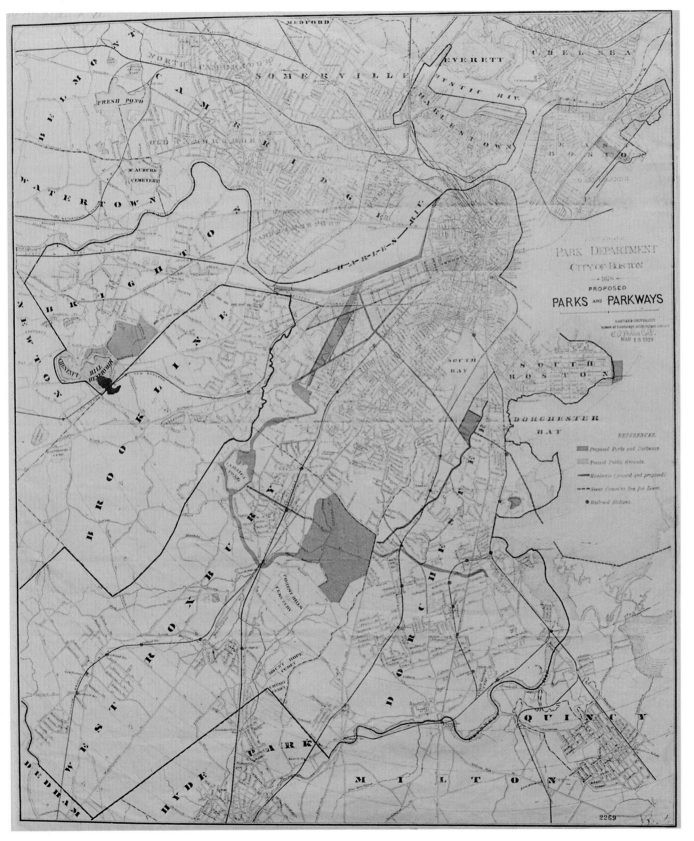

3.32 The commissioners of the Boston Park Department, organized in 1875, published this plan the following year. It proposed parks in numerous locations, many chosen for their natural features that could become pleasant public open spaces at modest expense to the city. Though gentle curves connected Jamaica Pond with Roxbury (later Franklin) Park, straight lines and sharp angles characterized the plan north of the pond.

3.33 The filling of house lots in the Back Bay was a little more than half finished when the Boston Park Department proposed the construction of a park
along the river—and a new parkway with a row of houses facing the river to
create a proper river facade. Many of the property owners on the water side
of Beacon Street, quite attached to their views of the river, vocally opposed
the idea.

to the city directory), but the commissioners were not satisfied
with the plan. A few months later they hired Olmsted to complete
a design for the park.[75]

The Back Bay Fens and the Muddy River

The primary purpose of the Back Bay park was sanitary improvement, by providing storage for flood water from Stony Brook.
Olmsted hoped to join that objective with the construction of a
salt marsh. This would not be a re-creation, since much of the Fens
had always been open water or mud flats. In fact, his new marsh
would require the diversion of the Muddy River and Stony Brook
into conduits running into the Charles, followed by extraordinarily careful engineering of the substructure beneath the proposed
plantings of wetland shrubs and grasses.[76]

The clarity and appeal of Olmsted's naturalistic landscapes
are apparent even in the site plans, particularly in comparison with
the park commission's original plan of 1876 (figures 3.34, 3.35). In

a letter to the chairman of the Brookline park commission in
1890, Olmsted described how at the center of the city would be

the broad dignified, urban residence street—Commonwealth
Avenue—with its formal tree-shaded central mall. This
extends to the cross street called Westchester Park [now
Massachusetts Avenue], where the avenue turns a slight angle
and the formal arrangement yields to a gracefully curving
drive and walk embellished by long irregularly planted,
undulating grass plots, which prepare the mind for the strong
contrast to everything urban presented by the next link in
the chain, called the Back Bay Fens. This is a ground of considerable breadth and extent, which in its general aspect, will
appear a fortunately preserved reservation of a typical small
passage of New England sea shore landscape, including a salt
creek bordered in part by salt meadows and in part by gravelly shores, both hemmed in by steep, irregular sylvan banks.
There will be in it no shaven lawns or pastured meadows: the
planted ground above the salt marsh being occupied by

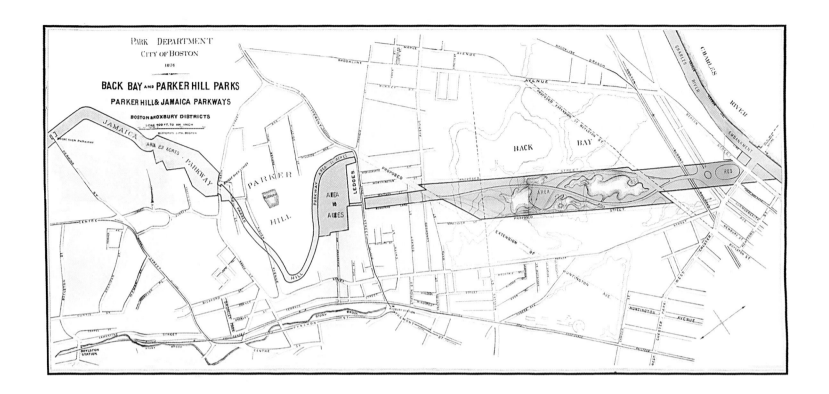

3.34 In an 1876 plan prepared by the Boston Park Department, a pair of long, narrow trapezoids connected the Charles River with Parker (now Mission) Hill. The boundaries of the proposed Back Bay Park and the alignment of the new streets were driven by the skewed geometry of the existing streets.

bushes or low, creeping flowering plants, in a condition suggestive of natural wilderness.[77]

Construction on the park, which Olmsted persuaded the Boston commissioners to rename the Back Bay Fens, was largely complete by 1890.

Olmsted's description of the Fens was written to persuade the Brookline park board to join with Boston so that the landscape of the Fens could be extended up the valley of the Muddy River to Jamaica Pond. Although the area was included in Bowditch's 1875 plan, the Boston park commissioners had not included it in their report the following year. The residential areas along the Muddy River were declining in both Boston and Brookline. Near Brookline Village were forty condemned houses, an uncharacteristic departure from the town's tradition of careful stewardship guarded by an elite group of educated and prosperous residents.

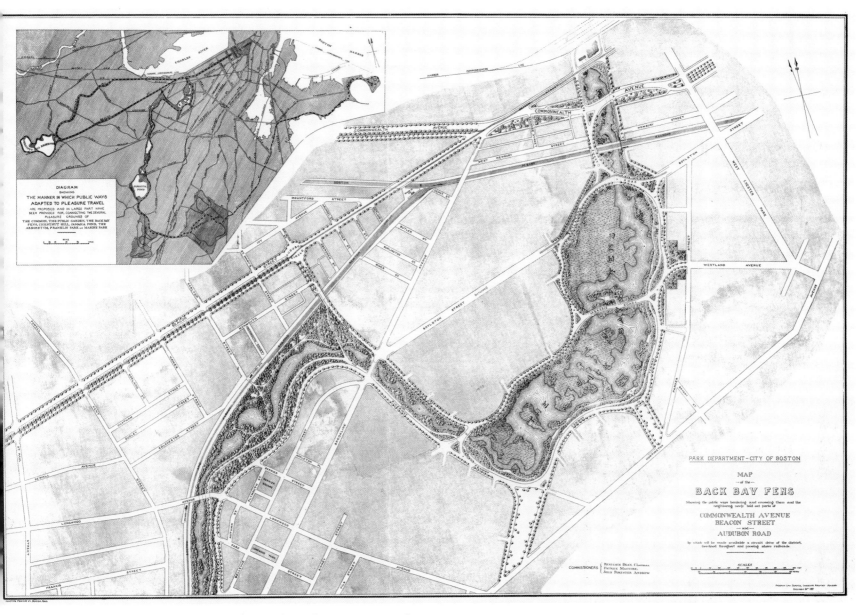

3.35 The Back Bay Fens, wrote Olmsted to the park commissioners of
Brookline, "will appear [as] a fortunately preserved reservation of a typical
small passage of New England sea shore landscape." The inset map from this
1887 plan of the Back Bay Fens shows the "continuous chain of pleasure-
grounds," including a series of parkways all the way to Castle Island on the
Harbor.

3.36 Olmsted's naturalistic landscape for the lower Muddy River Valley required extensive regrading of the existing site to achieve the picturesque effect he envisioned. On the right in this 1892 photograph is Christ's Church, Longwood.

3.37 The greatly altered landforms of Olmsted's design for the Muddy River are essential to fulfilling the park's flood control function. This image from about 1900 shows how the rich palette of plant materials obscures—almost makes invisible—the substantial subsurface engineering work, imparting the illusion of a natural landscape.

Chapter 3

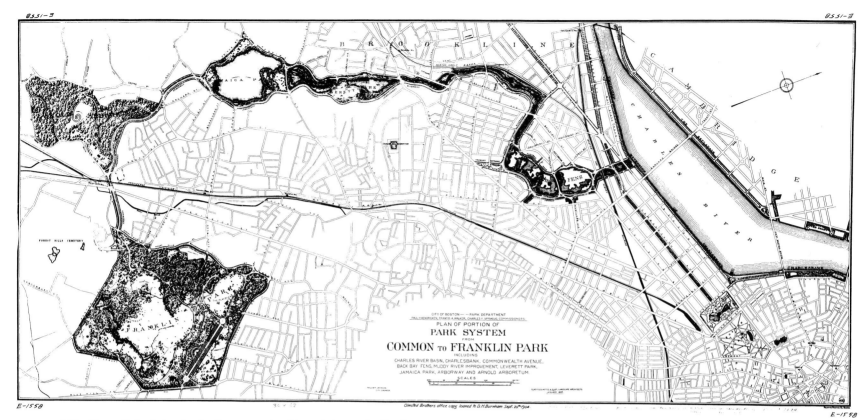

3.38 Olmsted's final plan for the Fens not only addressed the regular flooding of the Muddy River but also threaded an undulating landscape along the boundary of Boston and Brookline. The gently curving parkways, at least in the time of horse-drawn carriages, created scenic vistas of the water course and the parks. The Back Bay Fens met the Charles River just beyond Commonwealth Avenue, upstream of the Harvard Bridge.

The river was overloaded with sewage, and much of it was a breeding ground for mosquitoes.[78]

In 1880, about a year after Olmsted prepared the first drawings for the Back Bay, he sketched his first "Suggestion" of a plan for the valley. It was published in the park reports of both Boston and Brookline, and his revised scheme the following year was approved by the two park boards. Both communities, however, made unrealistically small appropriations for the work. Construction was delayed for years by difficulties in land acquisi-

tion, and in 1890 Olmsted revised the design and recommended that the boundary between the two towns be changed, which required an act of the General Court. The construction of the Muddy River, largely completed by 1893 (figures 3.36, 3.37), filled in the last link of Boston's "continuous chain of pleasure-grounds" (figure 3.38).[79] Although Olmsted had been skeptical at first, he found in the Boston park commission a willing and energetic client. In less than twenty years, over two thousand acres had been acquired and developed as part of the public domain.

Charlesbank

The Boston park report of 1876 had imagined a Back Bay reservation linked to an embankment along the Charles River. Four years later, however, the board determined to begin with a smaller park along the Charles, extending from Leverett Street (at the Craigie Bridge) only as far as the West Boston Bridge. Constructing a new seawall and filling the river (figure 3.39) required approval of the harbor commissioners, a lengthy process, and a preliminary design was not prepared by Olmsted until 1887. The plan was straightforward: an outdoor gymnasium for men and boys at one end, a similar area for women and girls at the other end, and a large greensward edged with benches and lights extending for most of the park's length along the river (figures 3.40, 3.41).[80]

An open fence surrounded the men's running track and gymnastic apparatus, opened in 1889 (figure 3.42), although it is unclear whether the absence of planting around the men's gymnasium was the landscape architects' preference or the consequence of limited space. For the women's gymnasium, completed two years later, the running track was arranged around a "turf playground for little girls" and heavily screened by a dense planting of shrubs (figures 3.43–3.45). On the side of each gymnasium was a two-story "lavatory building" with offices on the first floor; the second floor provided lavatories and a turnstile entrance to the outdoor gymnasium. The equipment at Charlesbank was designed by Dudley Sargent, who had been appointed director of the new Hemenway Gymnasium at Harvard by President Eliot in 1879.[81]

Between April and December 1890, there were 95,602 visits to the men's gymnasium, an average of almost 450 each day. The following year lights were added and the number of visits was 169,591, with 46,548 visits after seven in the evening. In 1891, the women's gymnasium opened and averaged almost 1100 weekday visits betwen June and the end of October. The children's play

3.39 A seawall along Boston's West End was constructed in the late 1860s just beyond Charles Street. The cupola of the Charles Street Jail is visible in this 1886 photograph (right center), looking upstream from Craigie Bridge.

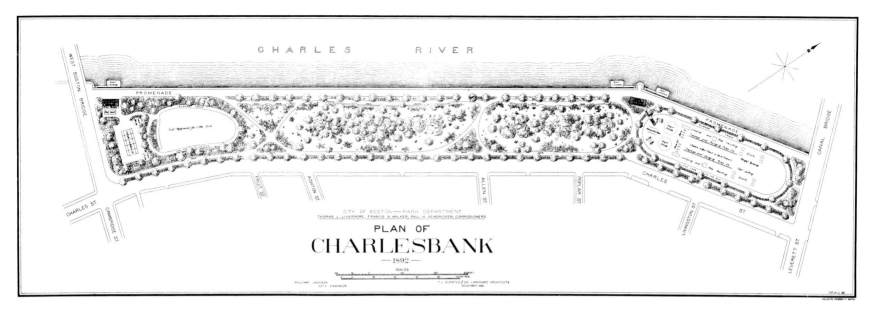

3.40 A preliminary plan for Charlesbank was approved by the park commissioners in 1887. This revised plan from 1892 shows the park as it was built.

areas also included three "sand courts" (sometimes called "sand gardens"), which had been introduced in the North End by a group of Boston women in 1886.[82] The first open-air gymnasium in a public park, Charlesbank was also the first public park on the Boston side of the basin.

Olmsted later explained to the metropolitan park commissioners that the Charlesbank had been "designed solely with reference to itself" and "as an isolated feature for the enjoyment and health of the crowded working class population near by." It was therefore very different, he said, from the treatment that would be suitable for the continuous esplanades planned for other sections of the river banks. Yet the greensward, the largest portion of the park, was described as "planted in the character of a natural grove," to screen the view and "smother the roar of the streets"; and it was not until 1898, by order of the park board, that the "turf and tree-covered mounds were thrown open to women and to children under fourteen years of age," reflecting a continuing concern with creating and preserving scenery. [83]

3.41 A new seawall was constructed to provide space for Charlesbank, which included a waterfront promenade along the edge of the river, with gas lights and benches along most of its length. The contours of the greensward provided informal spaces for children and adults.

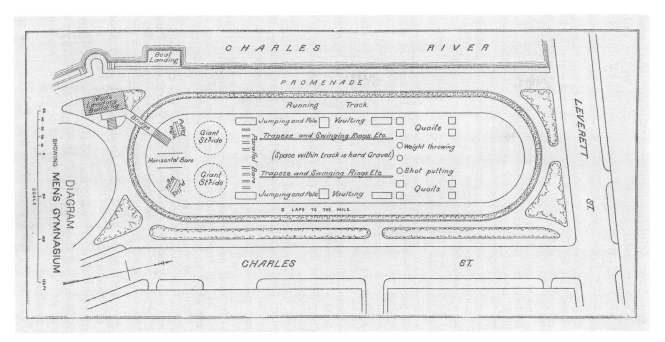

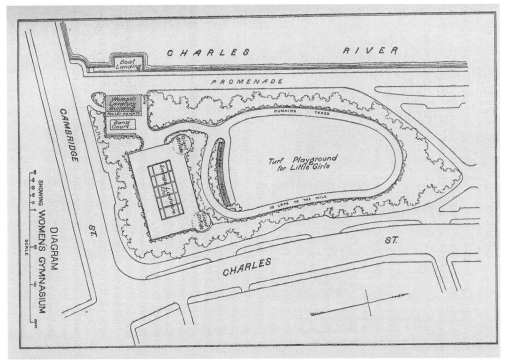

3.42 The men's outdoor gymnasium was opened first, in 1889. On the upstream end was the "Men's Lavatory Building" with the entrance to the outdoor exercise area on a bridge from the second floor over the public walkway and the fenced-in running track. "Wheelmen" were allowed to use the track in the forenoon, or when the track was not wanted in the afternoon by runners.

3.43 Included in the women's gymnasium, which opened in 1891, was a children's play area with "sand courts." Sometimes called "sand gardens," the idea had been introduced by a group of women in the North End in 1886. In this plan, the sand courts are located in the upper left; around the "Turf Playground for Little Girls" is a running track. Both the men's and women's gymnasiums included two areas for the "Giant Stride," an apparatus that used ropes and a tall pole for exercises.

3.44 Rope climbers and on-lookers are photographed here in the play area labeled "Swings, Ladders, etc." in the plan. The equipment in this area include twelve swinging ropes and five "serpentine ladders united, with guard-rails."

3.45 The preliminary plan for Charlesbank Park was completed in 1887; the park was finished five years later. Olmsted later said the park had been "designed solely with reference to itself . . . as an isolated feature for the enjoyment and health of the crowded working class population near by."

Longfellow Meadows and Longfellow Park

Upstream, in Brighton and Cambridge, the clash between residential growth and industrial development provoked the beginning of riverfront landscape improvement. In 1870, Henry Longfellow, his family, and several of his friends gave seventy acres of marshland on the Brighton side of the river to Harvard College, motivated in part by the legislature's approval that year of a large abattoir just upstream in Brighton, but also to protect the view of the Brighton Hills from the upstairs study of his house on Brattle Street (figure 3.46). Twenty years later, with a gift from Henry Lee Higginson of thirty-one acres adjoining what was then called the Longfellow Marshes, the university established Soldiers Field as the new athletic fields of the college.

Higginson's words at the dedication suggest how different the marshes were before the athletic structures and high-speed roads were constructed there. Soldiers Field was a "great lovely plain, bordered by the sunset and other irreclaimable gifts of the sky and landscape, and set forever there in memory of valor and of love."[84]

In 1887, Longfellow's children donated two acres of land in front of his house to the Longfellow Memorial Association, which had been founded five years earlier. The open land would connect the Longfellow House and Brattle Street with the river at the point where Mt. Auburn Street touched the water's edge at high tide. Charles Eliot, who had just returned from a lengthy European tour after a two-year apprenticeship with Olmsted, agreed to do the design; it would be his first park.[85]

3.46 Salt-marsh hay was still harvested in the Brighton marshes at the time the poet Henry Wadsworth Longfellow, some members of his family, and several friends donated seventy acres of the marsh to Harvard College. In the distance, just beyond the bend in the river, is the tower of Harvard's Memorial Hall (begun in 1870 and still under construction at the time of this 1872 engraving, it was finally finished six years later).

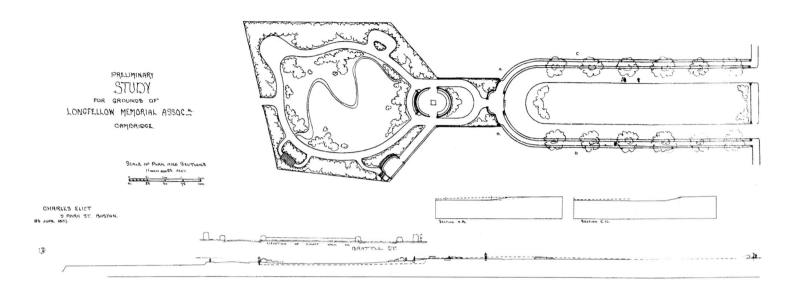

3.47 Longfellow Park was donated by the poet's family to connect the Longfellow House on Brattle Street with the Charles River and the Brighton marshes beyond. The natural terrace divided the site into what Charles Eliot, in this preliminary sketch of 1887 for his first park design, called "the green" and "the garden." The minimal design of the green was to evoke a sense of "the village green of old times."

The long, narrow site was divided by a "steep terrace-like bank," which offered pleasing views over the river marshes to the hills of Brookline. Eliot determined that the monument or memorial should be located on the edge of this terrace in the center of a stone exedra. The natural terrace divided the site into what Eliot called "the green" and "the garden." A road was required along the edges of the green to provide access to the properties along either side, which would make the area "a wholly public place." A minimal design for this portion of the site would reinforce the memory of "the village green of old times." A low wall would separate the green from Brattle Street, with a line of maple or elm trees along the edges of a loop road extending to the memorial (figure 3.47).[86]

The design of the garden, the lower portion of the site, should be adapted "to the use and enjoyment of all orderly citizens, and of women and children in particular." It was to be quiet and restful and "would be spoilt by flower beds"; the only plantings in the design were lawn, shrubs, and trees. Water from a spring on the site would be led across the oval of the garden. The northeast corner of the garden was higher than the other corners, and the view was even better than from the exedra, because it included the woods and tower of Mt. Auburn Cemetery (figure 3.48).[87] Even this first park design by Eliot, and his careful explanation of it to the Longfellow Memorial Association, revealed his inclination to magnify the site's scenic characteristics through landscape design as well as his interest in preserving and enhancing what have come to be called cultural landscapes.

Chapter 3

3.48 The terrace that defined the edge of the garden appears in the left center of this photograph. Wide walkways and abundant greenery create a sense of refined open space. Linking the house with the river, Longfellow Park is an early example of Eliot's interest in preserving and enhancing what have come to be called cultural landscapes. This view shows how Eliot's design was modified by the addition of monumental granite steps, the work of Boston architects S. Howard Walker and Herbert R. Best. The steps were removed in 1914 for the present monument, which was designed by Daniel Chester French and Henry Bacon.

Public Health and the River

Longfellow Park, Charlesbank, and the Back Bay Fens were constructed about the same time, and suggest an increasing refinement of the public spaces in Boston and Cambridge. In fact, it was argued at the time that these park developments represented a series of hopelessly inadequate gestures against a rapidly rising tide of industrial expansion throughout the metropolis. During the park debates of the 1870s, the refinement of the Commonwealth Avenue Mall in the Back Bay was contrasted with the sewage that every elegant new house in the neighborhood was dumping directly into the Charles.

Across the river, the residents of East Cambridge found themselves in the middle of one of Boston's booming industrial centers. By 1854, half a dozen railroad lines had been built across what had once known as "Charles River Bay," including the Boston & Lowell in 1835; the Boston & Maine (from Portland via Haverhill) in 1844; and the Eastern Railroad (originally constructed in 1838 between East Boston and Salem) in 1854. All the lines opened depots in Boston, three on Causeway Street and one at Haymarket (figure 3.49).[88] In this area of the lower basin there were no contested property rights, as there had been with the mill corporation in the Back Bay; the Commonwealth held title to all the "flowed tidelands" (the land that was under water at low tide) of the Charles. The railroads were nonetheless given complete freedom in their choice of routes into the city from the north.

One consequence was the creation of a maze of moveable bridges in the lower half mile of the Charles, hastening the decline of shipping on the river. A more serious result was the expansion of industries like meatpacking, attracted by the availability of rail transportation on the open sewer that the Miller's River had become (figure 3.50). By the 1870s, the tenants of the riverbanks included two meatpacking companies in Cambridge and seven in Somerville. The largest was John P. Squires & Co., founded in 1842 in Boston. The company expanded from its quarters in Faneuil Hall to East Cambridge in 1855. By 1868, Squires employed 330 people, owned three acres of buildings with a processing capacity of 7,000 swine, and booked a third of the Cunard Line's total cargo capacity to Liverpool. At its peak in the 1890s, the company's operation covered twenty-two acres and employed a thousand people, making it one of the largest businesses in Boston. All of its waste was dumped into the stagnant Miller's River.[89]

Complaints from Boston, Cambridge, and Somerville about the area around the Miller's River led to the creation of the state Board of Health in 1869, and three years later a Joint Board of the Harbor Commissioners and the Board of Health was established to abate the nuisance. In its 1873 report, the Board of Health wrote that there was "no territory of equal extent within the borders of Massachusetts in so foul and so dangerous a condition, and none

3.49 Railroads from the north and west expanded their rail yards in the Miller's River and built new terminals along Causeway Street in Boston. The bridges in this 1877 view include three former toll bridges, the Charles River and Warren Bridges (left) and the Craigie Bridge (right); in between are the railroad trestles of the Fitchburg, Boston & Maine, Eastern, and Boston & Lowell Railroads, each with its own terminal building (the Boston & Maine terminal was in Haymarket Square).

3.50 By 1879, the tenants of the riverbanks included two meatpacking companies in Cambridge and seven in Somerville. The largest was John P. Squires & Co. (in the center of this bird's-eye view, west of Bridge Street), founded in 1842 in Boston. By 1868, Squires had pens with a capacity of 7,000 swine. The McLean Asylum (lower right) is surrounded by railroad tracks, but would remain here another twenty-five years before moving to Belmont.

in which so virulent forms of epidemic disease, if ever introduced would be likely to commit such ravages as in the Miller's River District and its immediate surroundings." Squires's lawyer responded that the problem was "in the neighborhood, in the people who inhabit the tenement houses about there and who are allowed to throw their filth upon the ground or into the basins of Miller's River." The board recommended chartering an abattoir, as had been done in Brighton, but failed to make a finding against any individual companies.[90]

In 1874 Cambridge and Somerville built sewers and filled in the remaining open water around the packing plants. The two cities, acting under the state health legislation, were immediately sued by the Commonwealth under another new state ordinance regulating waterways. Chapter 149 of the Acts of 1866 (now Chapter 91) gave the state harbor commissioners jurisdiction over construction in Commonwealth tidelands. In 1873, the Boston & Lowell Railroad wanted to expand its rail yards and decided to fill north of the Prison Point Bridge. The Board of Harbor Commissioners sued the railroad as well as Cambridge and Somerville for their unlicensed filling operations. The Supreme Judicial Court decided in favor of the commissioners against the railroad, although the company had to pay only for damages since the suit begun. The most extensive filling occurred in 1878, covering the flats on either side of the Prison Point Bridge. Another round of filling in 1896 turned the last remnants of the old Charles Bay and the Miller's River into a virtual canal, extending under the Prison Point Bridge to what was left of the main channel of the Charles.[91]

Although conditions in the neighborhood of the Miller's River were somewhat improved, the pollution of the marshes and mud flats along the Charles remained a great concern, as increasing numbers of residential and commercial structures were erected along the river banks. In 1878 the Boston Board of Health published a map with the mud flats in Boston and Cambridge crosshatched in bright red and the prevailing winds across the flats marked by arrows (figure 3.51). The board observed that "large areas have been at once, and frequently, enveloped in an atmos-phere of stench so strong as to arouse the sleeping, terrify the weak, and nauseate and exasperate nearly everybody. . . . It visits the rich and the poor alike. It fills the sick-chamber and the office. . . . It travels in a belt half way across the city, and at that distance seems to have lost none of its potency, and, although its source is miles away, you feel it is directly at your feet." The largest polluted areas shown on the map were the remnants of the Back Bay and the Miller's River.[92]

The town of Brighton also attracted industries that viewed the Charles as a free and open sewer. A cattle market was established there in 1775 to supply the Continental army during the siege of Boston, and by 1790 the business had become the largest meatpacker in Massachusetts. A disagreement in 1807 over the construction of a new road to provide better access to the market led to the creation of Brighton as an independent town. By 1869, more than forty slaughterhouses were scattered through the town, dumping offal into ponds and small streams. That year, of the 120 deaths recorded, 41 (including a number of children) were blamed on the unsanitary practices of the meatpacking business. The legislature established the "Butchers Slaughtering and Melting Association," granted the association the exclusive right for the processing of beef within a six-mile radius of Boston, and a new abattoir was constructed along the river across from the Watertown Arsenal (figures 3.52, 3.53). Instead of several dozen small, unhealthy operations, one large processing plant now dumped its offal directly into the river. On the east side of Brighton, along the Charles near Brookline, smaller businesses—the Bowker Fertilizer Works, the Boston Fresh Tripe Works, the Boston Glue Works— also drained into the river.[93]

3.51 The Massachusetts Board of Health was created in 1869 to address the pollution of the Miller's River, who wrote three years later that no territory in the state was in "so foul and dangerous a condition." The board published a map in 1878 "Showing the Sources of SOME OF THE OFFENSIVE ODORS perceived in Boston." The most polluted areas of the river were shaded, and arrows indicated the direction of the prevailing winds, as a guide to avoiding the miasmas emanating from the river.

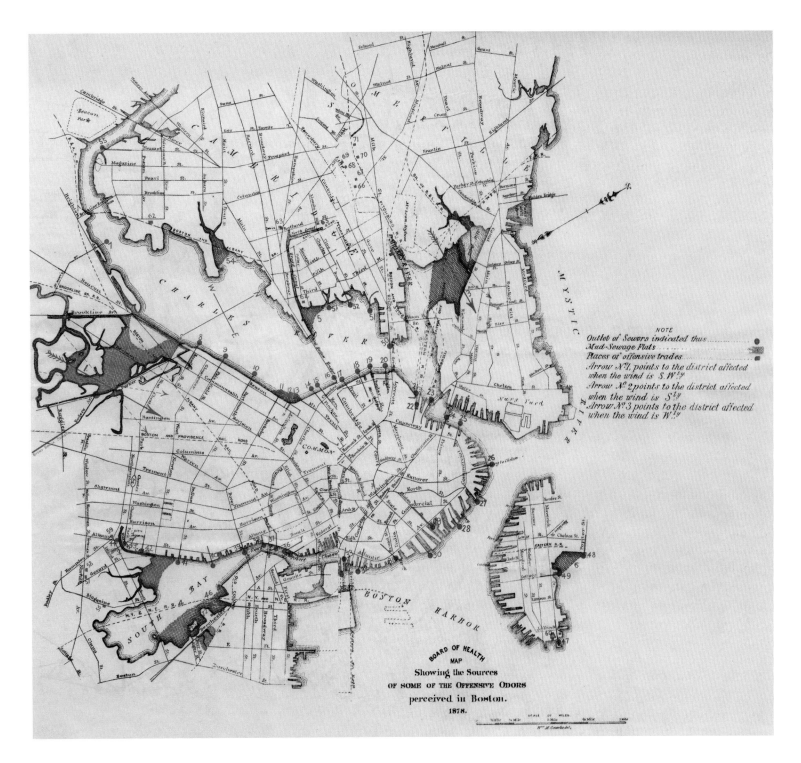

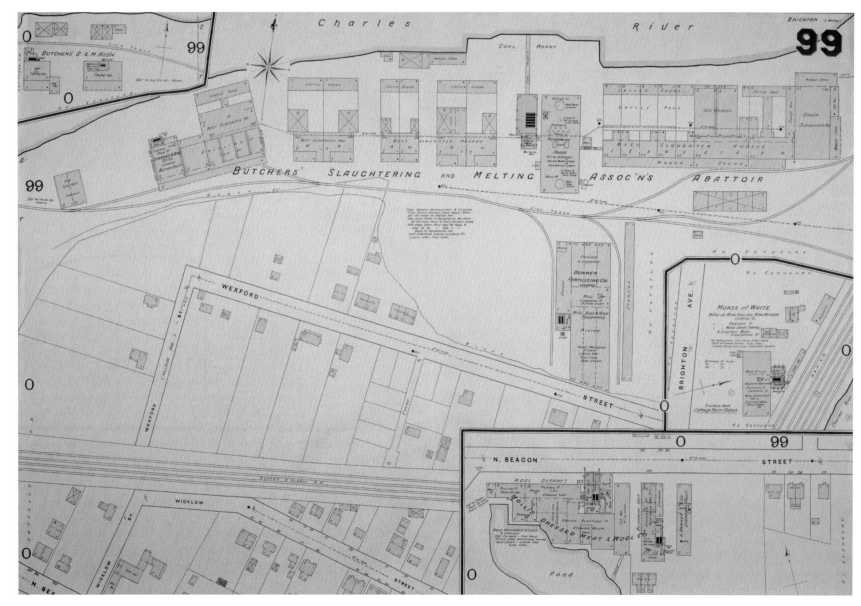

3.52 The Brighton Abattoir was established in 1870 by the "Butcher's Slaughtering and Melting Association" to consolidate the smaller slaughterhouses that were scattered throughout the town, and it was granted a monopoly on the processing of cattle within a six-mile radius of Boston.

3.53 Although its appearance from a distance was no worse than other industries, the Brighton Abbatoir was one of the major polluters of both air and
water along the river. This 1909 view was taken from just beyond the boat
landing at the Watertown Arsenal, marked by a cannon at the left corner of
the projecting seawall.

In the summer of 1892 Old Cambridge was subjected to such "disagreeable and probably injurious emanations" from the river that people had to close their windows at low tide. Several hundred residents, including many of the town's physicians, petitioned the state Board of Health for relief.[94]

Sanborn fire insurance maps from the 1880s show prisons in Boston and Charlestown, slaughterhouses in East Cambridge and Brighton, and Charles Davenport's partially filled, bankrupt development in Cambridge. The roundhouses and yards of the Boston & Albany Railroad filled most of the area that had once been "Cottage Farm"; shabby commercial ventures and tenements extended from the harbor to Watertown. Even along the Back Bay, the view from the river was unchanged from Richard Henry Dana's 1874 description: "a contemptible scavenger's street, thirty feet wide, backing up against the unmentionable parts of private houses" (figure 3.54).[95]

Such was the state of the Charles River Basin at the time the new Metropolitan Park Commission proposed to reclaim it for the public domain.

3.54 Although residents of the water side of Beacon Street may have enjoyed great views of the river, Back Street—the alley that ran along the river behind their elegant row houses—was still a "contemptible scavenger's street" in 1892, when Childe Hassam painted this view looking toward Beacon Hill and the golden dome of the State House.

MAP
OF THE
METROPOLITAN DISTRICT
OF
BOSTON
MASSACHUSETTS

Showing the existing public reservations
and such new
OPEN SPACES
as are proposed by Charles Eliot, Landscape Architect
in his report to the
Metropolitan Park Commission
Dated January 2d 1893

4

The Emerald Metropolis

The provision of ample open spaces for public recreation and the promotion of public health is now universally regarded as an essential feature in the proper equipment of urban communities. . . . There are already . . . well settled expanses of suburban population [in Boston], with acres and acres of streets and houses where a few years ago were pastures and woodland, possessing no open space whatever.

Sylvester Baxter, 1893

Thus has nature placed and preserved at the very gates of Boston riches of scenery such as Chicago or Denver or many another American city would give millions to create, if it were possible. Stupid indeed will be the people of greater Boston if they fail to perceive and attend to their interests in this matter before the opportunity is lost.

Charles Eliot, 1893

At the height of the Panic of 1893, Charles Francis Adams and his brother Henry "packed up our troubles and made for Chicago" to see the World's Columbian Exposition. Like thousands of others, they were captivated and astonished by the fantastic ensemble of images they saw there—neoclassical buildings all perfectly white, arrayed according to Frederick Law Olmsted's general plan to display "the successful grouping in harmonious relationships of vast and magnificent structures." Employing the talents of America's best architects, the fair's "White City" generated enormous enthusiasm for what soon came to be called the City Beautiful movement.[1] The buildings of the Exposition comprised a grandiose and overwhelming representation of a society remade by professional expertise (figure 4.1).

In his autobiography, Henry Adams puzzled over the exhibits and the architecture of the exposition. These extraordinary white structures had been "artistically induced to pass the summer on the shore of Lake Michigan"; the question was, did they seem at home there? More than that, Adams wondered whether Americans were at home in the fair's idealized New World city.[2] But neither Henry nor his brother, in their published works or private writings, connected the urban visions they saw in Chicago with Charles's labors as chairman of the Metropolitan Park Commission in Boston.

Frontispiece *Map of the Metropolitan District of Boston, Massachusetts, Showing the Existing Public Reservations and Such New Open Space as are Proposed by Charles Eliot, Landscape Architect,* January 2, 1893.

In January 1893 the six-month-old park commission had completed its first report, written by Sylvester Baxter, the commission's secretary, and Charles Eliot, its landscape architect; Adams wrote the introduction. Their report addressed the urban environment, but not by focusing on the city center, as Chicago's White City had done. Nor did they advocate complete control of suburban development—street plans and public transportation as well as parks—an approach that Olmsted and others had unsuccessfully urged in New York City in the 1870s.[3] Looking instead to the margins and the interstitial spaces of the region, they envisioned an "Emerald Metropolis." More than a city in a park, more, even, than a *system* of parks, it was a visual definition of the region's structure that could be sustained, they were convinced, even in the face of unimagined growth. The Emerald Metropolis would help Bostonians feel at home by preserving what Eliot called "the rock-hills, the stream banks, and the bay and the sea shores" of greater Boston—the natural edges, paths, and landmarks of the region.

Eliot and Baxter moved to shape the region by reserving as open space large tracts hitherto unbuildable but now on the verge of development, the shores of rivers and beaches still marshy or shabbily built up, and the most picturesque remaining fragments of the aboriginal New England landscape. In their metropolitan vision, the *natural* features of the area—the hills, the rivers, and the shores—should establish the armature for urban development, not the haphazard assemblage of streets, lots, railroads, and streetcar lines. Once set aside, these reservations would add forever to the fitness of the city for human habitation, joining unique and characteristic landscapes to the place-making power of the city's historic and cultural landmarks. The park commission's plan offered the citizenry of Boston an opportunity to see the metropolis in an entirely new way. In painterly terms, the figure and ground of the region would be reversed: The natural features, not the built environment, would constitute the visual structure of greater Boston (figure 4.2).

4.2 The park plan extended to the rock hills—the forest reservations along the ring of hills that surround Boston about ten miles from the State House. The radial spokes of the park system were the three rivers—the Mystic, the Charles, and the Neponset. The beaches of the bay and seashores comprised the third element of the plan. A system of parkways connected the reservations. In this metropolitan vision, the natural landmarks of the region—the hills, the rivers, and the shores—would be "reserved" as the framework for urban development, before the construction of streets, railroads, and streetcar lines.

DIAGRAM OF THE PARKS & PARKWAYS OF THE BOSTON METROPOLITAN DISTRICT.
TO ACCOMPANY REPORT OF OLMSTED, OLMSTED & ELIOT, DATED DEC.1.1896.

OPEN SPACES SECURED BY LOCAL AUTHORITIES.

SCALE OF MILES

OPEN SPACES SECURED BY METROPOLITAN COMMISSION

The proposed reservations represented the first metropolitan application of the idea of "reserving" natural landmarks that began with Yosemite, Yellowstone, the Adirondacks, and Niagara Falls.[4] It is impossible to attribute the authorship of the metropolitan park system to a single creator. Yet it is clear that the strenuous efforts of a small number of citizens were crucial to the transformation of metropolitan Boston's image of itself.

Sylvester Baxter, after concluding that he could not afford MIT's recently opened architecture school (the first in America, founded in 1869), went to work for the *Boston Daily Advertiser* in 1871. He probably read Bowditch's proposal in the *Advertiser* in 1874 advocating a metropolitan park system. From 1875 to 1877, Baxter studied at the universities of Leipzig and Berlin and was particularly interested in German municipal administration.[5] On his return to Boston, he joined Elizur Wright and others in the campaign to preserve "Stone's Woods" in Malden, Medford, and Winchester. He advocated a new name for the area—the "Middlesex Fells"—and wrote Olmsted (who had not yet moved to Boston) about the Fells in 1880.[6]

Baxter's interests extended over an extraordinary range. In 1881 he joined an archeological expedition to investigate Zuni ruins in the southwest, and the following year he wrote an article about the visit of several Zuni chiefs to Washington and Boston (on the beach at Deer Island in Boston Harbor the Zuni conducted a sunrise ceremony). In 1888 Baxter wrote to Edward Bellamy about collaborating to realize the ideals in Bellamy's *Looking Backward*; when the Nationalist Club of Boston was organized in that year, Baxter became the secretary (and he later wrote an introduction that was included in several editions of *Looking Backward*). He also wrote several books of poetry and a history of Spanish Colonial architecture in Mexico after wintering there with the landscape painter Frederick Church.[7] His abiding interest, however, was his vision for what he named "Greater Boston." Although he never studied architecture, Baxter made his own way to what Gourlay had called "the science of city building" (figure 4.3).

4.3 After four years at the *Boston Daily Advertiser,* Sylvester Baxter studied municipal administration in Germany in 1887–1888. When he returned to Boston he became involved in the campaign to preserve the Middlesex Fells in Malden, Medford, and Winchester.

For Charles Eliot, periods of contentment and tranquility (especially when he was walking in rural Boston or camping on the Maine coast) alternated in his adolescence with recurring episodes of self-doubt and depression. His mother died when he was nine, and by the time he began his studies at Harvard, his father had been president of the college for ten years and was already an Olympian figure in American higher education. The burden of family privilege and accomplishment heightened Charles's anxieties when as an upperclassman he realized that he "could find no practical bent or ambition anywhere about me." At one point in his senior year he came near to giving up his studies entirely.[8]

Not long after graduation, conversations with his uncle Robert Peabody (an architect who lived near Frederick Law Olmsted in Brookline) persuaded Eliot that he should become a landscape architect. Since there was then no recognized training for the field, he determined to enter Harvard's Bussey Institution, where the Department of Agriculture and Horticulture was located. The following spring, Eliot was introduced to Olmsted by Peabody, and was immediately offered an apprenticeship. Within a week he had dropped out of his classes and taken his first inspection tour with Olmsted as a full-time employee and the first apprentice in the Olmsted office. He soon discovered how well his endeavors outside of school had prepared him for his profession— the childhood drawing lessons, the adolescent mapping of imaginary towns and real neighborhoods (like Norton's Woods in Cambridge), the long hikes around Boston, the summers during college organizing a group of friends to study the natural sciences on Mt. Desert Island.[9]

After an apprenticeship of two years, he left for Europe. Following Olmsted's advice, Eliot ignored the monuments of the "Grand Tour" in favor of lengthy studies, carefully documented, of public parks, botanical gardens, and city streets. Most of one winter he spent reading landscape books in the British Museum. He returned with an extraordinary breadth of professional knowledge—from landscape construction to styles and philosophies of design.[10] After five years of managing his own office, he was well equipped for his part in the creation of the metropolitan park system (figure 4.4).

In contrast to Eliot's years of preparation, Charles Francis Adams claimed to have "blundered into" his role as the first chairman of both the temporary and the permanent park commissions. Rejecting the family traditions in politics, history, and literature, after college he consciously "endeavored to strike out a new path and fastened [himself], not, as Mr. Emerson recommends, to a star but to the locomotive-engine." He was the first commissioner of railroads in Massachusetts, and later became the president of the Union Pacific Railroad. Yet his friendship with Olmsted, his work with Eliot on a proposed town site in Garfield, Utah, for the Union Pacific, and his unhappiness with the transformation of the city of Quincy by what he called the "development fiends" drew him to the work of organizing the park system.[11]

4.4   After a two-year apprenticeship in the Olmsted office in Brookline, Charles Eliot left for a year in Europe. Following Olmsted's advice, he ignored the "Grand Tour" and instead studied public parks and gardens. In 1887 he opened his own office; after actively promoting a metropolitan park system, he was hired as the new park commission's consulting landscape architect.

Defining the Region

The framework of ideas behind the parks and reservations went back at least half a century, but the immediate precedents were a series of articles written by Baxter and Charles Eliot. In a February 1890 editorial in the new periodical *Garden and Forest*, Charles Sprague Sargent (the director of the new Arnold Arboretum) urged the preservation of the ancient Waverly Oaks in suburban Waltham and Belmont (figures 4.5–4.7). Eliot's published reply a few weeks later began by acknowledging the pressing need for public squares and playgrounds, as well as the failure of the cities and towns around Boston to act. Addressing that need would probably require a metropolitan commission, just as a similar authority for sanitary sewerage had finally been created in 1889 after decades of bickering among the cities and towns of the region. The pri-

4.6 Charles Sprague Sargent, the director of the new Arnold Arboretum, promoted the protection of the ancient Waverly Oaks near Beaver Brook in 1890. The picturesque brook, with its ponds and shallow water falls, marked the boundary between Belmont and Waltham. Eliot hoped to reserve the area for public enjoyment through a private trust that would hold "small and well-distributed parcels of land . . . just as the Public Library holds books and the Art Museum pictures—for the use and enjoyment of the public."

4.5 By the 1860s, the Waverley Oaks had become a favorite destination of Boston painters, including Winslow Homer, who painted this scene of two women walking in the woods.

4.7 This 1895 image suggests the majestic presence of the oaks. Complications in the title prevented their acquisition by the Trustees of Reservations, which Eliot had helped organize. Instead, Beaver Brook was the first acquisition of the Metropolitan Park Commission in 1893.

mary concern of Eliot's letter, however, was not the future prospect of government action; that would require months or years to organize. Instead, Eliot described a scheme that could immediately preserve not only the Waverly Oaks, but also many of "the finest bits of natural scenery" in the region. He looked out from the State House and saw, within a ten-mile radius, many still-surviving remnants of the New England wilderness. There were half a dozen scenes of uncommon beauty, "well known to all lovers of nature near Boston . . . in daily danger of utter destruction." Eliot urged the immediate creation of a trust to hold "small and well-distributed parcels of land . . . just as the Public Library holds books and the Art Museum pictures—for the use and enjoyment of the public." Generous men and women would bequeath these irreplaceable properties to such an association, just as others give works of art to the city's museums.[12]

Although Eliot did not note the distinction in his 1890 letter to *Garden and Forest*, the analogy with the art museum and the public library suggested *two* approaches to preserving open space, one private and the other public. Even before the campaign to organize the trustees was completed, Eliot and Baxter moved—first separately and then jointly—to promote a public regional parks authority. Eliot wrote a letter to his boyhood friend Governor William Russell in December 1890, recommending that the State Board of Health develop a plan for metropolitan reservations.[13]

Three months later, Baxter wrote a series of articles in the *Boston Herald* about what he called "Greater Boston." His articles set the opportunity for regional parks in the context of metropolitan government, and addressed a much wider audience than *Garden and Forest*. He, too, scanned the ten-mile view from the State House, but he described an image that was the very inverse of Eliot's fast-disappearing landscapes. From that height he observed "a billowy sea of buildings stretching away in nearly every direction, apparently without interruption, as far as the feet of the chain of hills that encircles the borders of the bay from Lynn around to Milton." The constructed pattern of buildings paid little heed to the configuration of town boundaries, and the limits of Boston covered only a fraction of the true city. The proper man-

agement of this Greater Boston called for a metropolitan commission with the authority for all the major public services—water supply, sewerage, fire, police, schools, highways, transit, parks.[14]

Baxter's appeal for regional action built on prior discussions of water and sanitary issues. As early as the 1870s, the threat to the public water supply in the region prompted proposals for metropolitan solutions, including annexation and the creation of regional authorities. Boston did expand substantially between 1867 and 1874, annexing Roxbury, Dorchester, Charlestown, Brighton, and West Roxbury. In 1874 annexation was rejected by the voters in Brookline, marking, in political terms, the end of the movement in the region. The problems of water supply and sewerage, however, continued to worsen. An editorial in the Boston *Daily Advertiser* in 1872 asked "whether the interest of the metropolitan community . . . would not be better served . . . for the purposes of water supply and drainage if it were treated as one district, and were placed under the care of a single board, aided by the best engineering skill available." Finally in 1886 a state commission on the "General System of Drainage for the Valleys of the Mystic, Blackstone and Charles Rivers" recommended a regional sewerage system to be managed by "a central agency and authority, which can for this special purpose override town boundaries and disregard local susceptibilities." Three years later the Metropolitan Sewerage Commission was established.[15]

The creation of commissions with limited, functional jurisdictions was less politically threatening, but also, in Baxter's view, ultimately far less effective than genuinely regional government. He saw the disparity between the richer and poorer cities and towns of the region as an unnecessary evil, open to correction if the appropriate administrative structure were created and then supported by a tradition of honest, competent civil service. His arguments in the *Herald* for a new governmental structure were clear and direct:

The true Boston—geographical Boston, as distinguished from political Boston—comprises all that territory lying around the city which is covered by a compact mass of population, with social and business interests substantially identical. Nothing but a legal fiction stands in the way of its being known as such. The interests of this great metropolitan district now require that that fiction should disappear.

Of all the public functions to be managed in the metropolitan district, Baxter reserved his lengthiest description for a chain of pleasure grounds under regional administration, extending in a sweeping arc around the city from Lynn Beach and the Lynn Woods to the "mountain-like" Blue Hills range. Taken together with the recently completed parks in the city of Boston, these large woodland reservations would constitute one of the grandest park-systems in the world.[16]

Olmsted urged Baxter to publish the *Herald* articles, and soon after *Greater Boston* appeared, Eliot read it and proposed to Baxter that they work together to realize the metropolitan park system.[17] The two men immediately set out to construct a constituency for their ideas. Starting with the governing board of the Appalachian Mountain Club, Eliot helped organize a standing committee of twenty-nine to consider a new organization, which set to work in the spring of 1890. As an energetic member of the committee, Baxter drew on his ties to newspaper editors and writers across the state and to other veterans of the twenty-year-old campaign to preserve the Middlesex Fells. The organizing process was not always smooth, as Eliot complained to his wife Mary. He described one committee meeting held to plan for the public hearings as "a farce" that ended in the usual result—Eliot was delegated to solicit other speakers, to speak himself, and to send postcards "to make sure of an attendance."[18] The legislation to create a privately endowed Trustees of Public Reservations was signed in May of 1891.[19]

At the urging of Eliot and Baxter, the Trustees of Public Reservations agreed to organize a meeting of park commissions from across Greater Boston in December. After public hearings the following spring, the temporary Metropolitan Park Commission was authorized by the legislature in June 1892.

Among Baxter's primary concerns were the administrative inefficiencies and parochial jealousies of the myriad cities and towns in the Boston Basin. Eliot also knew first-hand how the wariness of town officials affected the development of public open space. From his extensive explorations of the region's fringes, he knew that town boundaries often bisected the most scenic areas, especially along ponds and river valleys; it would be senseless, he said, for one town to act without the other, but too often one town had refused to spend money for fear the adjoining town would enjoy what it had paid for.[20]

It was clear that these local interests would have to be drawn together. To that end the new metropolitan park commissioners planned a series of twelve day-trips in the fall of 1892, and invited city officials and prominent residents of the towns to join them. The secretary's minutes recount the itinerary of these "tours of inspection" (ten of them in the five weeks from mid-September to mid-October), which took the commissioners and their guests throughout the metropolitan district.[21]

Two trips were given to exploring the shores of the harbor and the bay by steam launch, one from East Boston to Nahant, Lynn, Swampscott, and the Saugus River, and one to Castle Island, Quincy Bay, Peddock's Island, then south to Hingham and the Fore River. The tours of the Fells and the Blue Hills each took a day. On the trip to Revere (figure 4.8) they traveled by train to Winthrop, where they were met by carriages on loan from the livery service at Franklin Park. After driving past the beautiful grounds of the Chelsea Naval Hospital, they took a launch up the Mystic River, passing the two small parks then under construction in Charlestown below Bunker Hill Street and at Tuft's Mill Pond.[22]

Again and again the minutes of these journeys underline a fascination with grand and scenic views. On Milton Hill the commissioners found one of the "noblest prospects" in the neighborhood of Boston. The outlook down the valley of the Saugus River toward the meadowland, the serpentine stream, and the uplands "formed a picture of exceptional charm." The view from the twin summits of Prospect Hill in Waltham was "wide and glorious." Thompson's Island presented "a remarkable appearance with its well grown plantations of trees," an example of what ought to be done on the other harbor islands.[23]

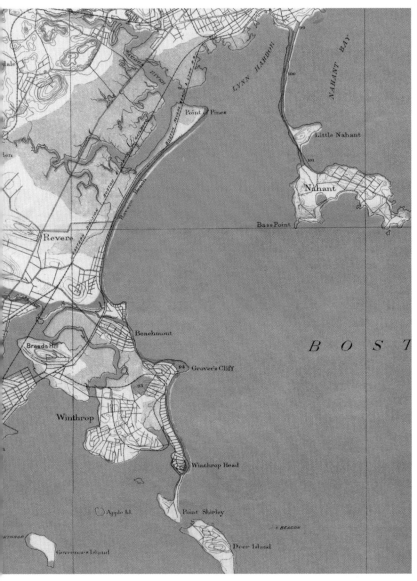

4.8 The most visionary acts of the park commission were not the preservation of undeveloped landscapes but the schemes to reclaim the riverbanks and beaches, which were occupied by tenements and industries. Revere Beach provided the longest natural beach in the metropolitan area, its sweeping curve offering magnificent views of Nahant and the ocean beyond. Its transformation required the relocation of streets and railroads and the demolition of numerous shanties and saloons.

The travelers also noted the unique and distinctive landscapes on their inspection tours; they were deeply impressed with the remarkable beauty of the landscape of the ancient Waverly Oaks in Belmont and with the need to preserve them for the public. The only disturbing sight noted by Baxter during the first ten trips was a collection of "ugly fish houses and an equally ugly Hotel" on Nahant Beach, but he thought it was nonetheless one of the most beautiful sites on the Massachusetts coast. The places they visited were unfamiliar to most of the members; Baxter wrote that the outings "were like voyages of discovery about home."[24]

The last inspection, on the first day of November, was of the Charles River between Boston and Watertown. Baxter's account of this tour is twice as long as his other entries in the minute book, and is filled with harsh judgments about the condition of the river. The entourage included the secretary and engineer of the Boston Park Commission, the chairman of the State Board of Health, two members of the Harbor and Land Commission, all but one of the members of the Cambridge Park Committee, two members of the Charles River Improvement Commission, and Frederick Law Olmsted (who had not come on the previous outings).[25]

The Charles River tour began with a walk along the edge of Charlesbank Park, with Olmsted as guide. The group then crossed over the Harvard Bridge to inspect the work of the Charles River Embankment Company and continued on to Captain's Island and Soldiers Field. The Charles River shore "was marred by industries merely in search of cheap land," with no need of water transportation, and made ugly by "squalid hovels, dump heaps and other nuisances." Its banks were "inky black" with foul sewage deposits, though they should be a popular pleasure ground. The commission had visited several scenic estates on other tours, but on this trip they visited the grounds of the old Stickney place in Watertown, once a beautiful country house "but now fast going to decay" because of the undesirable developments along the river.[26]

Two weeks later the commissioners met to review their findings. Adams and Baxter submitted written comments, so the minutes record only the observations of Philip Chase and William de las Casas (the other two commissioners), and Charles Eliot. The two commissioners agreed that the Charles River was the most important site to be addressed, and that the Fells (figure 4.9) should be the second priority. Eliot thought the most significant subject had not yet been addressed, which was providing "numerous small spaces" throughout the region. The ocean beaches and the reforestation of the harbor islands should be considered next. Then should follow the provision of "pleasant routes" to the bay and sea shores "and incidentally to the heart of the City"; the river valleys would be the most natural locations.[27]

During the following two months, the board considered the terms of the legislation to establish a permanent commission. In January Adams's draft of a report was approved, and the board voted to publish Baxter's report over his own signature; Eliot's report was published as the third part of the document. The legislature's joint committee on public reservations reported favorably on the temporary commissioners' bill.[28]

Picturing the Park System

The rationale for the Metropolitan Park System as outlined in the 1893 report drew on a reservoir of ideas that had now gained widespread acceptance as a critical aspect of the culture of refinement. Eliot summarized the need for the visible presence of nature in the genteel city:

> The life history of humanity has proved nothing more clearly than that crowded populations, if they would live in health and happiness, must have space for air, for light, for exercise, for rest, and for the enjoyment of that peaceful beauty of nature which, because it is the opposite of the noisy ugliness of towns, is so wonderfully refreshing to the tired souls of townspeople.[29]

These general principles gave strong support for the *concept* of the park system. Like Gourlay, Crocker, Copeland, and others before and since who have projected Greater Boston into the future, Baxter and Eliot linked urban images with profound moral obligations. The real genius of Baxter and Eliot's plan, though, was not in its rationale, but

in its integration and extension, in visual and practical terms, of a series of earlier, fragmentary proposals for the Boston region.

Here, as throughout the two men's writings, images were crucial to their visionary narratives. During the report's preparation Eliot had written to the commissioners that his special work for the park commission was "the picturing by printed words, photographs, and maps of those open spaces which are still obtainable near Boston." The details of the "legal machinery" could all be resolved once this picturing aroused the necessary public support.[30]

As secretary and landscape architect to the commission, Baxter and Eliot submitted separate and strikingly different reports, but both documents were generously illustrated with diverse maps and views: fifteen photographs, a dozen line drawings, and a dozen black and white maps and site plans, including foldout maps of the Middlesex Fells and the Blue Hills, and a twenty-four by twenty-four-inch color map of existing and proposed open space.[31]

The Report of the Secretary

The first part of Baxter's eighty-page report addressed three questions: the need for metropolitan open space; the "Logical Method of solving this Problem"; and the value to the region, as well as the advantages to the cities and towns, of contributing to reservations outside their boundaries. Elaborating on the image he first presented in his 1891 article on "Greater Boston," Baxter suggested that an observer looking out from the State House at the area within ten or twelve miles of Boston would see what appeared to be one city, set in a region of striking landscape diversity. The residents of the southern half of the region were well provided with parks, parkways, and playgrounds, but the rest of the area had "almost nothing of the kind." Part of the region had made itself into one municipality (a circumlocution for Boston's annexation of the surrounding towns), while the rest of the area was cut up along "political and not natural lines." If these circumstances continued, much of the region was "in danger of becoming a vast

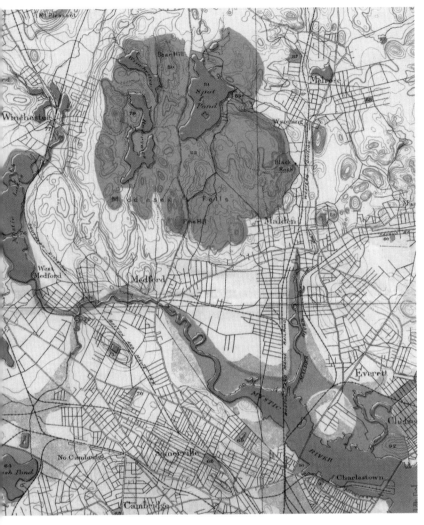

4.9 Measured against the demand for "the more absolutely utilitarian improvements," public open space seemed a luxury. Yet Eliot maintained that without the reservation of natural scenery, like Spot Pond, the Middlesex Fells (center), and the Mystic River marshes (lower right), these communities would someday discover that their suburban charm had vanished.

desert of homes, factories and stores, spreading over and overwhelming the natural features of the landscape."[32]

Other large American cities—Chicago, Minneapolis, Washington, D.C.—had taken steps at or near their founding to anticipate the future. Boston had instead followed a process of "gradual community dis-integration." Many of the "ancient villages" of the region had split into several new towns, as Charlestown, for example, had been divided to create Somerville, Woburn, and Winchester. More recently, these suburbs had seemed to be the answer to the evils of crowded city tenement-houses, but now many of them were becoming acres of houses and streets unrelieved by any public open space.[33]

In greater Boston, the creation of a single municipal authority appeared to be out of the question. And local jealousies persisted, in spite of the growing number of cities and towns enacting parks legislation. The current owner of Norton's Woods in Cambridge (bordering the city of Somerville) for some time had allowed its use as a neighborhood pleasure ground, and making the area a public park had been much discussed. But the city of Cambridge was not interested in acquiring the property because it was on the edge of the city, and Somerville didn't have the authority or the money to take it.[34]

A final obstacle noted by Baxter was the rapid growth of many of the suburbs around Boston. The new residents of these communities were demanding schools, streets, and water and sewer service, yet the increases in land values and local tax revenues were lagging behind, even as complaints about higher taxes were increasing. Measured against the demand for "the more absolutely utilitarian improvements," public open space seemed a luxury. Yet without the reservation of natural scenery, these communities would someday discover that their suburban charm had vanished.[35]

The way out of these dilemmas was for the Commonwealth to lend its credit to the communities of the district, a method already tested in the Metropolitan Sewerage Act passed four years previously. Cities and towns could then take advantage of the state's lower cost of credit and avoid excessive short-term taxation. And for one million dollars (far less, Baxter pointed out, than the two and a half million dollars the national government was then spending for harbor fortifications in just one small town on Boston Bay) a metropolitan commission could purchase at least one of the harbor islands, Revere Beach, the lands along the Snake Creek Valley in Chelsea and Revere, the Middlesex Fells (figure 4.10), a reservation along the Mystic River, the Muddy Pond woods, and the Blue Hills—and still leave a large amount to secure land and rights along the Charles, the Neponset, and the Mystic to protect against their pollution.[36]

In addition, the temporary park commission had already received offers of cooperation from private individuals "of public spirit and of large means" that would protect other picturesque and historic landscapes. Such areas included the Waverley Oaks in Waltham and Belmont, the region of Pranker's Pond in Saugus, and a stretch of the Charles in Weston. And the protection of the region's water supplies (for example in the Lynn Woods, the Fells, and the Blue Hills, and along the Charles) would lead to cooperation between water boards and the park commission and create opportunities to preserve additional tracts of open land. Olmsted's "recreative treatment" of the Back Bay Fens showed that the most pleasing remedy to a sanitary hazard could also be the cheapest.[37]

In reviewing the sites that should constitute a "general system of open spaces for public recreation and the promotion of health," Baxter based his discussion on the commission's series of inspection tours and on the conversations during those inspections with park commissioners and other local officials. In Baxter's view, this provided first-hand knowledge of both the natural features of the region and the needs and wants of the communities. The discussion of particular open spaces that followed was organized geographically, starting with Boston Bay. Then the report reviewed the sites north and west of the city, discussed the problems and prospects for the Charles River, continued with potential open spaces south of Boston, and concluded with a review of the lakes and ponds of the region.[38]

The pollution of the rivers presented a threat to public health, but the alternative use of the Charles was already realized between Riverside in Newton and center of Waltham. Canoeing

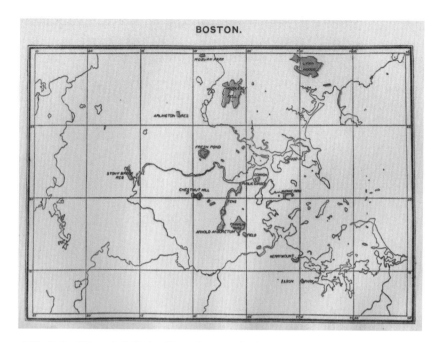

4.10 In justifying their "scientific park system," Eliot and Baxter compared the open spaces in Boston with Paris and London. By this standard, Boston was sorely deficient in providing for parks and reservations.

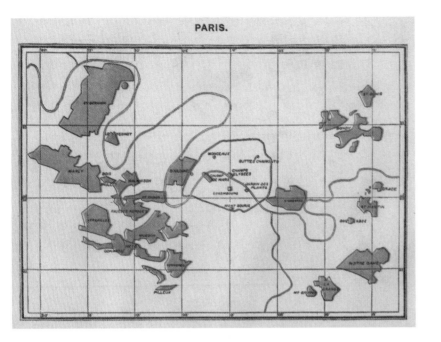

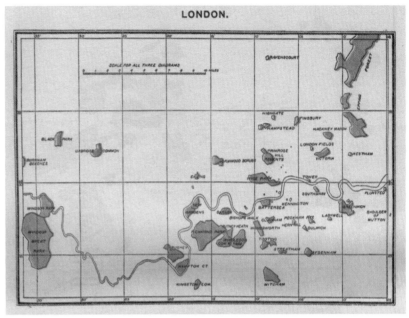

and boating there had made Riverside among the most popular resorts in the region. Another example was the Muddy River. Its sanitary hazards could have been remediated with sewers or canals, but "the cheapest way turned out to be the most beautiful way." Already much of the river banks were public: Charlesbank and the proposed embankment in Boston, the Embankment Company's Esplanade and the Longfellow Memorial Garden in Cambridge, the Watertown Arsenal, and Soldiers Field in Brighton.[39]

In the third part of his report, Baxter addressed two particular concerns, "Special Pleasure-ways, or Roads for Light Traffic," and local pleasure grounds and playgrounds. Eliot had listed these two issues as among his highest priorities in the board's discussion on November 12, and he described the opportunity to incorporate parkways into the metropolitan park system twice (though almost figuratively) in his own report. Baxter once again focused on establishing a clear precedent for action. In endorsing a series of special roadways to link the metropolitan parks and reservations, Baxter cited the Illinois boulevard act, which allowed the Chicago park commissioners to gain the consent of municipal authorities and abutting land owners to connect parks with such pleasure roads. Good and bad examples of roadway planning in Boston were also noted. Commonwealth Avenue, the parkways of the Emerald Necklace, the planned improvements to Blue Hill Avenue, and the proposed parkway from the Arnold Arboretum to Stony Brook were made possible because the annexation of several adjoining towns had given the city of Boston the necessary geographical range. By contrast, the region north of the Charles River, cut up into many small cities and towns, lacked not only extensive parks but also clearly delineated routes to the center of Boston.[40]

As Olmsted had transformed the disjointed schemes of the Boston Park Department in his designs for what became the Emerald Necklace, Eliot unified the proposals of Gourlay, Crocker, Copeland, and others for metropolitan reservations of open space. His summation is a startling but almost certainly unconscious echo of Gourlay's "grand panorama" of "the streams, the islands, and the promontories." In Eliot's words, the "rock hills, the stream banks, and the bay and sea shores," were both "the available and the valuable sites for public open space." These three images—the hills, the rivers, and the shores—also provided a simple and legible visual framework for the metropolitan district.[41]

Eliot began by noting that the great population centers of the world "have now accepted the teachings of bitter experience, and have provided themselves with the necessary and desirable open areas, albeit at immense expense and with great difficulty" (figure 4.10). The people of the metropolitan district of Boston, on the other hand, had the opportunity of doing so while the cost was still modest. Then the concern should be the basis of selecting such public open space.[42]

A study of the natural features of the region, Eliot believed, would "bring forth the facts in the case" and result in the "scientific selection" of lands for public open space. His report, therefore, was divided logically into three parts. First was a physical and historical geography of the parks district, with each section of text carefully cross-referenced to several drawings and photographs. Next was a study of the way in which the "peculiar geography" of the metropolitan district ought to govern the selection of public open spaces. Finally, the report documented the opportunities for acquiring open space according to these governing principles.[43]

The analysis of the region's physical geography began with the "Rock Foundation" of the metropolitan district, exposed in two bands north and south of the city. The Wellington Hills, from Waltham to Cape Ann, presented a "steep, wall-like front," about one hundred feet high (figure 4.11), punctuated with a few higher summits like Bear Hill in Stoneham (325 feet) and Burrill's Hill

4.11 During the preparation of the 1893 report, Eliot wrote to the park commissioners that his "special work" for the commission was "the picturing by printed words, photographs, and maps those open spaces which are still attainable near Boston." The report included a dozen sketches of "the hills, the rivers, and the shores," like this view of the Malden cliffs.

4.12 Eliot claimed that the scenery in the Blue Hills was superior to the public woods of Paris and Epping Forest in London. This sketch shows a view of the Blue Hills from Muddy Pond Woods.

in Lynn (285 feet). On the south, the Blue Hills were divided into a dozen rounded hills, much higher than the northern ridges, from three to six hundred feet above sea level (figure 4.12). In between the two ranges of hills, the sea had flowed over the ancient rocks and created Boston Bay. The underlying rock was exposed in only a few places: against the sea at Swampscott and Cohasset, Nahant and Squantum, and the outer islands; on land, in the ledges of Roxbury Puddingstone and a few other places; and at some of the falls in the rivers.[44]

On this stony foundation, between the exposed hills and the ocean, was a variegated pattern of "Glacial Rubbish." The retreating ice flows left rounded hills in Chelsea and in the harbor, with ridges and hollows scattered here and there. But most of the debris had been scoured into level plains, with few sharply defined valleys, leaving the streams to wander in an "unusually aimless" way (figure 4.13). Rainwater was caught in the hollows, or dammed behind glacial drift, making for numerous ponds and swamps, a

4.13 The landscape in and around Chelsea was marked by what Eliot called "Glacial Rubbish," which left meandering streams such as Snake Creek, depicted here, as well as numerous ponds and swamps. Eliot delighted in these natural landforms.

striking addition to the "already wonderfully varied and picturesque" landscape. Into this landscape the sea moved in and out, on the north extending the salt creeks to the rock highlands, on the south "flowing about the half-sunken drumlins."[45]

Eliot then delineated the "Effects of Human Occupancy" on this landscape, that is to say, the visible marks of the first two hundred years of European settlement. What he saw was as pleasing as the natural landforms:

> Generation after generation labored with the trees and stones, and at last the rounded hills stood forth as mounds of green, marked and divided by walls of field stones, and sometimes crowned . . . with the white churches of the victors. . . . After two hundred years of these arduous labors, the neighborhood of Boston was a lovely land. The broad or narrow marshes still lay open to the sun and air, through them the salt creeks wound inland twice a day, about them lay fields and pastures backed by woods upon the steeper slopes, and across their sunny levels looked the windows of many scattered houses and many separate villages.

But that idyllic landscape was disappearing under waves of urban and suburban immigration in the nineteenth century. Eliot described how factories had taken over the riverbanks, building tenements for the workers, "always with their backs to the stream," so that the rivers and brooks were "at one blow made both foul and ugly."[46]

Eliot then shifted to a cryptic discussion of governing principles. Land for building upon was scarce, and so all the lesser mudflats and marshes in the heart of the city should be filled, to increase the taxable real estate and to reduce sanitary nuisances. On the other hand, filling the water courses presented great dangers, and should not go too far; the larger streams, both salt and fresh, could not "safely be meddled with." Public ownership of the stream banks would preserve the most important of the many scenic elements of the city, preventing harmful uses and encouraging beneficial ones like recreation. Since the principal rivers flow toward the center of the city, public lands along the rivers would also offer sorely needed routes from the suburbs to the city and to

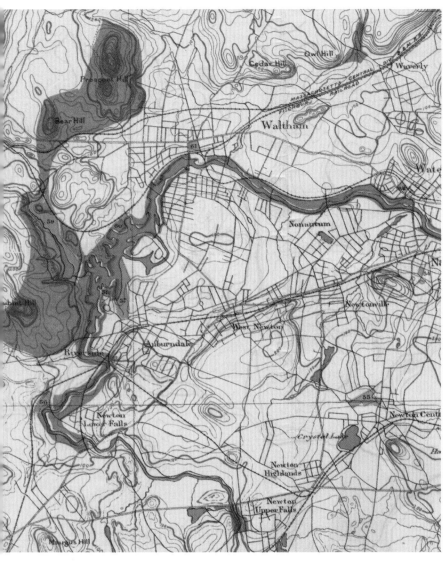

4.14 By linking Prospect Hill, the highest area in Waltham, with Bear Hill and Doublet Hill, Eliot connected the proposed western forest reservation with the Charles. He sought to preserve not only distinct landscape types, but also to preserve or create connections between them. Prospect Hill was to be the western forest reservation, providing geographical balance to the park system, but it was never acquired from the city of Waltham.

the bay beyond. These roads along ponds and streams would also mean that "good houses" would have "their fronts, and not their back yards, turned towards water-side roads."[47]

For the lands in the proposed reservations, private ownership would be not only harmful to the general welfare, but bad "public financial policy." If the larger spaces were not purchased in time, they could never be had. Therefore, "All scientific planning of open spaces proceeds thus from the greater to the less." The larger reservations would offer not only the "fresh air and play-room" of smaller spaces but also the "free pleasures of the open world of which small spaces can give no hint." Although the smaller parks in every neighborhood were crucial, they should be a local responsibility.[48]

In considering the sites available for acquisition consistent with these principles, Eliot recapitulated the image of "the hills, the rivers, and the shores." And while Baxter's observations regarding the proposed sites had been more general, Eliot pointed out particular issues of design and management. An example was Prospect Hill in Waltham. Baxter described the site's place in the park system; Eliot mapped the connection between Prospect Hill, the Charles River, and Doublet Hill to the south (figure 4.14). To emphasize the wild state of the Blue Hills, he noted that they constituted "such a barrier that the railroads, 'the creators of suburbs,' have completely avoided them." Their scenery was finer than the public woods of Paris, and far surpassed Epping Forest in London. Once acquired, the hills should cost little for maintenance and nothing for improvement for many years. All the large reservations—the Fells, Muddy Pond, the Blue Hills—could be acquired now for a million dollars, "only as many dollars as there are inhabitants of the metropolitan district."[49]

The ponds and streams of the region presented an opposite set of challenges. While the burgeoning population of greater Boston had avoided the hills, it had, "like the waters, settled in the valleys." A first look might suggest that public ownership would be almost impossible, but it should not be abandoned without careful study. Even small streams would benefit from public ownership; at Cheese-Cake Brook in Newton, for example, the stream bed was preserved by building roadways on either side (figure 4.15). The

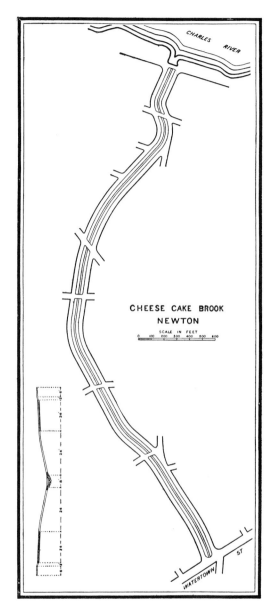

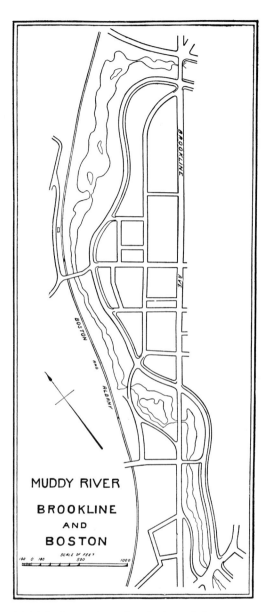

4.15 The advantages of public ownership of even small streams in suburban developments was noted in the park plan. Cheese-Cake Brook in Newton could be preserved by building roadways on either side. The roadways would allow houses to have, in Eliot's words, "their fronts, and not their back yards, turned towards water-side roads," increasing the value of the land on either side of the stream.

4.16 The larger rivers, the Charles and the Muddy, also showed the advantages of riverside transportation. This plan for the Muddy River suggests how railroads and parkways could be integrated with the design for the rivers and streams.

pollution of the stream was prevented, a handsome roadway created, and the value of the adjacent property would increase more than the cost of the small amount of land taken by the public. The larger rivers, the Charles and the Muddy, showed the same advantages at work. A map of the Muddy River diagrammed the relationship of the railroad (now the trolley line) on one side and the parkway on the other (figure 4.16).[50]

The bay and sea shores appeared as Boston's one great "open space," comprising one fourth of all the surface within a fifteen-mile circle of the State House. Yet while the waters were free to all, the shores were not. Only Nahant Beach, a highway, belonged to the public. The first task of a metropolitan commission should be the acquisition of the beaches from Great Head in Winthrop to Point of Pines in Revere. Here, too, parkways were essential to the

4.17 Maurice Prendergast was one of several Boston painters whose work included scenes in the metropolitan parks, like this watercolor of Revere Beach.

image of the emerald metropolis. In the future, Revere Beach should be "a place of residence, equipped with a broad esplanade and drive, and lined with houses and hotels facing the south-east and the sea" (figure 4.17).[51]

Eliot's proposal to reserve the rivers and their margins, in spite of their then-degraded state, was unique in a system of park development.[52] Near the end of his report, Eliot sketched the symmetry the proposed river reservations added to the metropolitan plan:

> As the ocean at Revere Beach was reached by a ten-mile drive from Winchester down the valley of the Mystic River, so now the bay shore at Squaw Rock is reached by a ten-mile drive from Dedham down the lovelier valley of the Neponset. Half-way between these northern and southern riverways we find Charles River, leading, by another course of ten miles, from Waltham through the very centre of the metropolitan district to the basin just west of the State House. Nature appears to have placed these streams just where they can best serve the needs of the crowded populations gathering fast about them.

There was also a natural symmetry in the proposed forest reservations—Lynn Woods and the Fells north of the city, Muddy Pond and the Blue Hills on the south, the Waverly Oaks and Hemlock Gorge to the west. Taking no credit for perceiving this order in the region's topography, Eliot said it was simply "due to nature"; he brought his professional judgment of the public needs for open space and "the district's financial powers" to that inherent symmetry.[53]

The Report of the Commissioners

The recommendations of the board, drafted by Adams, were considerably more cautious than Baxter and Eliot's expansive schemes. The commissioners were satisfied with the need to organize a metropolitan district, and argued that it should include all the communities served by suburban railroads around Boston. Together these twelve cities and twenty-four towns, with 888,000 residents, comprised forty percent of the state's population.[54]

The scheme of park development outlined in the 1893 report could not, in the commissioners' view, "be carried out in its entirety at once." Nor would it be wise or economical to do so. Many common needs of the city and its suburbs were already recognized: police, drainage, water supply, transportation. To these acknowledged needs should be added open-space reservations. A single example was sufficient to document this requirement—the movement in summer toward the ocean by rich and poor. The islands and beaches of greater Boston should be public, but that could not be done except through "combined actions."[55]

The report included a bill to create the administrative machinery for a permanent metropolitan park board, and under "ordinary circumstances" they would have gone no further. But the commissioners determined that two of the proposed open spaces required immediate action, the Fells and the Blue Hills; delay would involve irreparable injury and much greater future expense. While the schemes suggested in the report were attractive, the board declined to make further recommendations.[56]

Assembling the Reservations and Parkways

The effort of picturing the metropolitan parks in the 1893 report, aimed at Boston's "both high-handed and liberal" Yankee aristocracy, was a complete success. The report became a best seller, according to Adams's biographer, and the General Court distributed 9,000 copies. The parks bill was passed by the legislature and signed by Governor Russell, permanently establishing the Metropolitan Park Commission (MPC) on June 3, 1893. Charles Dalton, chairman of the Boston Park Commission, thought the report would be one of the most important contributions to the literature of public parks ever made. Adams observed to the board that "Our work is chiefly educational. We cannot expect to accomplish practical results immediately, but to prepare the public to do something in these directions some years hence."[57]

Eliot, however, had other intentions. He moved with what now seems almost incomprehensible speed to map the reservation boundaries, and the park commission acquired almost seven thou-

sand acres of mostly open land in its first eighteen months. Its first taking was Beaver Brook, including the Waverly Oaks, which (in the face of title difficulties) the Trustees of Reservations had tried unsuccessfully to acquire. More than 5,500 acres were acquired for the Blue Hills and the Middlesex Fells, two of the three large reservations in the 1893 plan (Prospect Hill, the reservation proposed for the western portion of the district, was never acquired from the city of Waltham). Another 475 acres was taken along Stony Brook.[58]

In 1896 Eliot successfully argued for the acquisition of over a hundred privately owned structures along Revere Beach, including eighty-one buildings on the beach itself.[59] An elaborate bathhouse was constructed with changing rooms for a thousand bathers and a laundry that could wash, wring, and press 500 suits an hour. In the back was parking for a thousand bicycles. Across the boulevard a series of simple but elegantly detailed pavilions and a bandstand were constructed (figures 4.18–4.21).

The acquisition of the reservations proceeded with little apparent opposition. The land takings followed a lengthy process that typically included topographical surveys by the engineering department; review of the surveys by the landscape architects and the plotting of taking lines; cost estimates and a review of both the design and the financial aspects of the plans; usually some modification of the original plans; the preparation of taking plans based on surveys; and finally, the preparation of the necessary papers by the law department. Although this was a lengthy and tedious process, Eliot's familiarity with the natural areas around Boston, and the involvement of local officials and the Metropolitan Park commissioners in touring the proposed reservations, greatly accelerated the extensive acquisitions in the early years.[60]

Eliot pressed vigorously to acquire as much of the identified reservation land as possible, but he struggled in vain to persuade the park board to develop what he called "general plans" for each reservation before roads and structures were built. When the pace of acquisition slowed in 1896, he organized a project to document the current state of vegetation throughout the park system. Published in 1898 (after Eliot's death at the age of thirty-seven the

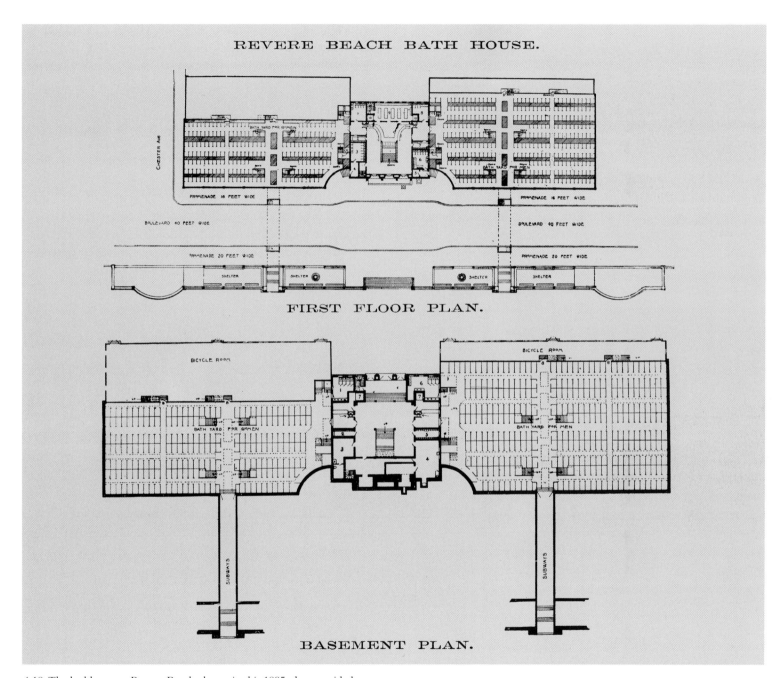

4.18 The bathhouse at Revere Beach, shown in this 1895 plan, provided passageways under the boulevard to the open shelters and the beach.

4.19 A bathhouse (left) was built on the landward side of the boulevard. On each side of the bathhouse were five hundred open-air "rooms" arranged in two tiers, with space behind to store a thousand bicycles. The laundry could wash, wring, and press five hundred swimsuits per hour.

4.20 Over a hundred private structures, including eighty-one on Revere Beach itself, were demolished to open the sweeping views of the ocean along the longest natural beach in greater Boston.

4.21 The popularity of Revere Beach is apparent in this photograph from the 1930s.

previous year), *Vegetation and Scenery* is a detailed complement to Eliot's planning principles outlined in the 1893 report. Although it does not address riverine landscapes, the *Vegetation* report reveals fundamental attitudes toward the management of landscapes.[61]

The MPC report had advocated a "scientific" selection of lands, but Eliot averred that the vegetation study would merely record the existing conditions in the reservations, and was not "an historical or even a scientific inquiry." But what did Eliot mean by "historical" and "scientific"? Certainly the *Vegetation* report documented his earlier statements that both the beauty and ugliness of the existing vegetation were primarily the work of men, "chopped over, or completely cleared, or pastured, or burnt over, time and time again." While the reservations were sharply distinguishable in their topography, recent human actions had made the vegetation of the woodlands very much alike and "remarkably uninteresting."[62]

Then why—apart from a few scattered natural and geologic oddities—had these parks been acquired? Natural reservations, Eliot had said, "were the cathedrals of the modern world," and the Boston metropolitan reservations had been acquired as a "treasure

of scenery." The stewards of the park system should "control, guide, and modify the vegetation generally that the reservations may be slowly but surely induced to present the greatest possible variety, interest, and beauty of the landscape." In the preparation of *Vegetation and Scenery*, Eliot encouraged Arthur Shurcliff, then an apprentice at Olmsted, Olmsted & Eliot, to sketch "before" and "after" scenes in the reservations, after the manner of the English landscape gardener Humphrey Repton. They were included in the printed report to suggest the enhancement of the landscape through the judicious use of the ax (figures 4.22, 4.23).[63]

Standing in the way of such landscape improvements, Eliot wrote, was a "small but influential body of refined persons" who opposed such efforts to adapt landscapes to new requirements. These people "talk of 'letting Nature alone' or 'keeping nature natural,' as if such a thing were possible in a world which was made for man." The idea that it might be sacrilegious to control or modify the existing verdure was nonsense. Even the six thousand acres of the Blue Hills, situated as it was on the rim of the metropolis, did not constitute a wilderness; in fact, the vegetation was "really artificial in a high degree."[64]

Eliot's priorities for both the large and small reservations were clear: first, to safeguard, through public acquisition, the scenery of these natural areas before it was too late; second, to make that scenery accessible to the public; finally, to enrich and enhance the beauty of the reservations.[65]

Even if there should be sufficient public support to accomplish the first and second of these tasks, could the enhancement of scenery ever be justified at public expense, when "ordinary people will never appreciate the difference"? In the *Vegetation* report, Eliot answered emphatically in the affirmative. Following Olmsted, he argued that in the presence of "unaccustomed beauty or grandeur," even the average person experienced "sensations and emotions, the causes of which are unrecognized and even unknown." In Eliot's mind this principle was the basis for the public commitment to schools, libraries, and art museums. It was well exemplified in many already completed public parks, and for him it was the foundation for the metropolitan reservations.[66]

4.22 Eliot acknowledged that in many areas the second-growth vegetation of the metropolitan reservations was decidedly uninteresting. To illustrate the benefits of vegetation management, he asked Arthur Shurcliff (who was an apprentice in the Olmsted office) to sketch several views in the reservations. This drawing illustrates a "tree-clogged notch in the Middlesex Fells."

4.23 Providing for "reservations of scenery" would require regular clearing of vegetation. Eliot argued that little of the local area was truly wilderness, and hence notions of "keeping nature natural" were misguided.

It was the new Cambridge Park Commission and not the MPC, however, that acquired the first parklands along the Charles. As in much else before and since, the city of Cambridge determined to go its own way in the development of the riverfront. In spite of Eliot's active leadership in the founding of the Trustees of Public Reservations, only four of the 180 donors to the organization in 1892 were from Cambridge, and no one from Cambridge signed the petition to the legislature that year in support of creating a temporary Metropolitan Park Commission. Four of the five members of the newly appointed Cambridge Park Committee did come along on November 1 for the last of the twelve metropolitan open space tours organized by Eliot and Baxter.[67]

At the end of November the Cambridge committee urged the city not to wait for the Commonwealth to "come to the relief of the imperilled communities, and prosecute this work as a great sanitary necessity."[68] Cambridge should act on its own immediately and establish a permanent park commission.

The 1892 committee report described opportunities in several wards of the city, but its most extensive comments were directed to the urgency as well as the opportunity for public space along the Charles. The river was graphically described: "Along the bottom and banks of the Charles River is deposited a bed of apparently putrescible sludge, consisting of decomposed animal and vegetable matter from the shores, and noxious filth from the sewers. . . . It is therefore evident that the river can be thoroughly purified only by controlling its banks, putting them in proper condition to be kept clean, and dredging the filth from its bottom." The solution was also within the city's reach: "Cambridge holds the key to the situation; for that part of the river bank that is most unsightly, the most offensive, and the most menacing and is susceptible of the greatest improvement by being made attractive, valuable and healthful, lies within its borders." The cost to the city would be more than justified as a "sanitary necessity [and] as a conservator of public morality and popular contentment." But it was also a financial imperative: it would reduce the tax rate by increasing property values.[69]

When the permanent park commission first met in July 1893, one of its first official acts was to hire Charles Eliot as the commission's consulting landscape architect. Eliot's first report in December emphatically reaffirmed the value of the river frontage. It should be developed as five contiguous sections, each with its own character: "The Front," between Craigie's Bridge and the Broad Canal; "The Esplanade," on either side of the Harvard Bridge; "Captain's Island," the widest tract along the river; "The River Road," from Captain's Island to Cambridge (now Mount Auburn) Hospital; and "Elmwood Way," the connection between the river and the already developed reservation around Fresh Pond (figures 4.24, 4.25). The benefits were obvious:

> Here is a total of eight hundred acres of permanently open space provided by nature without cost to Cambridge. All of this area was, until lately, unavailable for purposes of public recreation, and, except by boats, most it remains so. . . . These priceless spaces still lie unused, like money hoarded in a stocking, yielding no return to their owners. If Cambridge is to invest money in public recreation grounds, a just economy demands that such money shall first be placed where it will bring into use for public enjoyment, these now unused and inaccessible spaces with their ample air, light, and outlook.[70]

In January 1894 the city took by eminent domain almost all the riverfront within its borders, the first public parkland to be acquired along the basin.[71]

Following the lead of George Snelling, Charles Davenport, and the Metropolitan Park Commission, Cambridge officials also promoted the example of the Alster Basin in Hamburg. Henry Yerxa, a member of the temporary park committee and now the chair of the park commission, published a lengthy report of his 1894 travels in the *Cambridge Chronicle* titled "European Out-Door Life." Included were photographs, one from Berlin and three of the Alster. Yerxa noted that the people in those cities spent much more time in the open air "than is the custom in our New England cities or even country towns." While this might be due in part to climatic conditions, he believed the governments did much more to

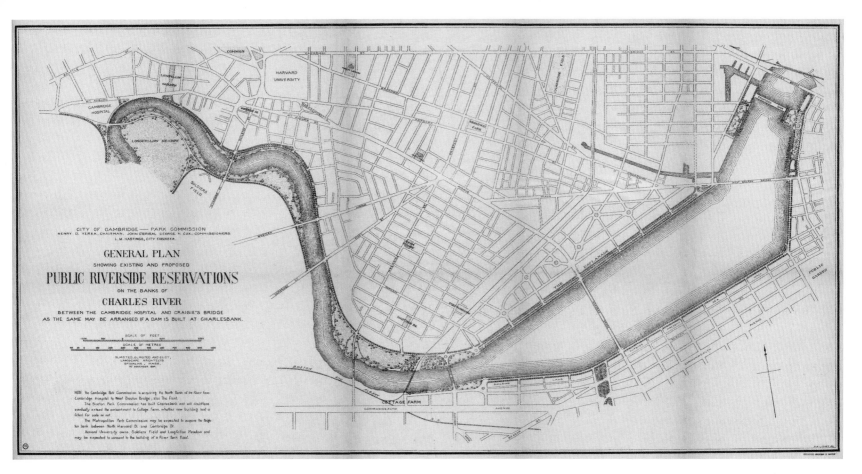

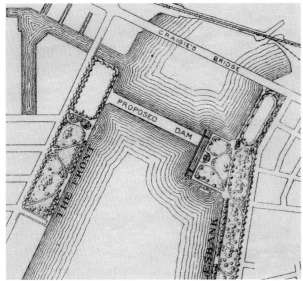

4.24 Charles Eliot produced conceptual plans for the Charles River Basin in 1894. His plan for the city of Cambridge recommended developing the riverfront as five contiguous sections: The Front, the Esplanade, Captain's Island, the River Road, and Elmwood Way.

4.25 The Front proved the most difficult to develop. Eliot's 1894 plan showed a planted park with a small boat landing at the north end. A more detailed plan completed a year later divided the space between a swimming beach and a playground. In 1899 another revision was done, but it, too, was indefinitely postponed.

4.26 The Cambridge Park Commission constructed the first small segment of Charles River Road (now Memorial Drive) just upstream of Boylston (now John F. Kennedy) Street, as an "object lesson" to demonstrate the future appearance of the parkway. The first London plane trees (popularly known as sycamores) were planted in 1897.

foster such outdoor life. In his lengthy description of Hamburg, he noted the bronze statue of Schiller along the banks of the Alster, and rhetorically asked, "How long shall it be before a bronze statue of our own Longfellow shall rise upon the banks of the Charles he loved so well and which he has done so much honor?"[72]

The Charles, Yerxa asserted, was actually superior to the Alster, because of the "beautiful winding of the river back into the hills . . . and the cool southwesterly winds [which] sweep down from an open country during the heated season." There could be no better ambition for Cambridge residents than to change "not only the face of nature along the banks of our Charles," but also the faces of the "weary and heavy laden . . . and the faces of the children of our city."[73]

As an "object lesson" in the improvement of the river, the commission determined to begin in the neighborhood at the foot of Boylston Street (figure 4.26). There the marsh lands were "filthy and obnoxious," and the buildings were "totally unfit for human habitation." It also appeared that along that stretch, "park-like effects might be most quickly and easily obtained." After some difficulty filling the marshy banks of the river, the area was graded, the first section of Charles River Road from Boylston to Bath (now Hawthorne) Street was paved, and the first London plane tree was planted on April 22, 1897 (figures 4.27, 4.28).[74]

Extending the parkway east from Boylston Street to the Cambridge Esplanade proved more difficult. The Casino boathouse was moved from Bath Street to DeWolfe Street in 1895, the

4.27 In 1870 the poet Henry Wadsworth Longfellow, several members of his family, and a few friends donated seventy acres of Brighton marshes to Harvard; Henry Lee Higginson donated an additional thirty-one acres twenty years later, and the site was dedicated as Soldiers Field. Grandstands and several structures had been erected at the time of this 1897 view, but much of the marsh still remained along the river.

4.28 In 1907 Harvard's second Weld Boathouse was completed (lower left), and the plane trees along Charles River Road were flourishing. Across the river the speedway, built by the Metropolitan Park Commission in 1899, is visible beyond Newell Boathouse (right center).

4.29 In 1898 the riverfront below the Boylston Street (now Anderson) Bridge was occupied by wharves and a long coal storage shed rented by Harvard College to Richardson and Bacon (note the name on the shed roof). Downstream are two Harvard boathouses and a boat-builder's shop. The neighborhood along the river was then known as Riverside.

4.30 Richardson and Bacon's coal wharf (above) was demolished for the construction of the parkway east of Boylston (now John F. Kennedy) Street. By 1902 the "Richardson and Bacon" sign on the roof had been reduced to "Ric."

Weld Boathouse was moved and remodeled two years later, and in 1901 the Harvard varsity boathouse at Winthrop's Wharf and the adjoining boat builders' shop (at the foot of DeWolfe Street) were demolished. It took five more years before the College coal wharf was removed and the adjoining building partially demolished (figures 4.29, 4.30). The beach at Captain's Island (now Magazine Beach) drew large crowds after it was opened in 1899 (figures 4.31, 4.32), but the extension of the parkway from Boylston Street to the beach was blocked by the buildings of the Riverside Press, on the river's edge between Western Avenue and River Street. By the fall of 1914, the structures in the way of the parkway had been demolished, a seawall had been constructed, and the river road from the Cambridge (now Longfellow) Bridge to Mt. Auburn Street was finally opened (figures 4.33–4.36).[75]

In spite of the association of low-lying wetlands with disease, there were some who were deeply distressed by the filling of the marshes. James Russell Lowell had written eloquently about the marshes in "Indian Summer Reverie."[76] Though he acknowledged that there were those who saw nothing in the marshes "but levels brown and bare," he carefully described the range of colors across the seasons:

> In Spring they lie one broad expanse of green,
> O'er which the light winds run with glimmering feet:
> Here, yellower stripes track out the creek unseen,
> There, darker growths o'er hidden ditches meet.

4.31 In 1899 the powder magazine at Captain's Island (now Magazine Beach) was remodeled and the slope was sanded to accommodate swimming, but demand "exceeded all expectations" and two temporary bathhouses were constructed the following year.

4.32 The beaches along the Charles were immensely popular at the turn of the century, although the views were hardly pastoral. Opposite Captain's Island were the tanks of the Brookline Gas Company and the yards of the Boston & Albany Railroad.

4.33 James Russell Lowell was born near the river at "Elmwood" and, except for eight years in London, he lived his entire life there. This stand of trees close by came to be known as the "Lowell Willows," an acknowledgment of the river references in the poet's work.

4.34 The first section of seawall was built on either side of the future site of the Harvard Bridge in 1883 by the Cambridge Embankment Company. This 1898 photograph shows a hydraulic dredge at work downstream from the now-completed bridge.

4.35 Hydraulic dredges were used for most of the filling, but the construction of the seawalls and parkways along the river still required horsepower and much handwork, as shown in this 1903 photograph taken upstream of the Harvard Bridge.

4.36 The East Cambridge Embankment was extended in 1898 by the park commission after the city assumed control of Davenport's failed development. The photograph shows the placing of stone ballast on the wooden, pile-supported platform on which the seawall was built. Earthen fill or dredged material was then dumped on top of the stone ballast.

Although only remnants of the marshes remained in Brighton and Cambridge, they were still seen as important wildlife habitat and an important aspect of the surrounding communities' natural patrimony. William Brewster, the Harvard ornithologist, had grown up in Cambridge and gone birding in his school days with the sculptor Daniel Chester French. In his view,

> The work of reclaiming—or as some of us prefer to characterize it, of destroying—the Charles River Marshes has progressed rapidly and relentlessly of late. Although not as yet nearing completion, it has already resulted in the total obliteration or very serious disfigurement of most of these once primitive and beautiful salt meadows.

"More practical men," said Brewster, did not appreciate the marshes the way Longfellow, Lowell, and a few others did; to such men the marshes "were but waste lands, unsightly to the eye and more or less prejudicial to the health of humankind."[77]

It was not, however, only practical men who felt this way. Charles Eliot reported to the Metropolitan Park Commissioners in 1897, for example, that the ten miles of salt-marsh river bank "must sooner or later be made usable" (figures 4.37, 4.38).[78]

4.37 An 1899 photograph shows the ragged edge of the river at Mount Auburn Hospital, before the landscape improvements were begun.

4.38 One year later, the marshes were drained, regraded, and planted in grass. William Brewster, professor of ornithology at Harvard, thought that what was called reclamation by some was actually the relentless destruction of "once primitive and beautiful salt meadows."

In November 1893, Frederick Law Olmsted wrote to Eliot and Olmsted's son John (after they had become his partners and the firm renamed "Olmsted, Olmsted & Eliot"):

> nothing else compares in importance to us with the Boston work, meaning the Metropolitan quite equally with the city work. The two together will be the most important work of our profession now in hand anywhere in the world. . . . In your probable life-time, Muddy River, Blue Hills, the Fells, Waverly Oaks, Charles River, the Beaches will be points to date from in the history of American Landscape Architecture, as much as Central Park. They will be the opening of new chapters in the art.[79]

Yet Charles Francis Adams, in spite of the commission's initial success in acquiring land, found the press of administrative details increasingly frustrating. In the fall of 1894 he wrote in his diary that the board had spent the day at Middlesex Fells and "gravely pondered divers problems involving the purchase with public money of land at 10c a foot for which private money would not give 2." The following June, after a visit with the commission to the Fells, Adams noted that he was "bored to death and fast getting cross." His private impatience notwithstanding, when his resignation from the board was made public two days later, he noted that it was "the successful ending of a successful piece of work."[80]

When he looked back two decades later on his time with the park board, Adams was still startled by the speed of the commission's progress: "Wholly opposed to the policy of rapid growth and what I could not but regard as premature development, I found myself powerless to check it. I was, in fact, frightened at our success in the work we had to do." By then, however, he had come to believe that he had never in his life done "work more useful or so permanent in character . . . as saving to the people of Massachusetts the Blue Hills and the Middlesex Fells."[81]

By the time of Eliot's death in the spring of 1897, Revere Beach was complete. Extensive land takings had been made along the Charles River, including all of the lower Charles to Watertown and Hemlock Gorge on the upper Charles. The park system included almost seven thousand acres. Takings had also been made for the first five parkways, at the Blue Hills, the Fells, Revere Beach, and along the Neponset River and the Mystic Valley. Including interest to be paid, the cost of these acquisitions was $6,800,000.[82]

At the end of 1900 a total of nine thousand acres had been acquired in thirteen reservations, and the nine constructed parkways included an additional six hundred acres. A note of caution appeared in the commission's report for that year, suggesting that "the cost of any further additions must be weighed with the utmost caution against their advantages."[83]

Baxter and others were convinced that the endeavor of "picturing" the parks should not end with the 1893 report, and should be extended well beyond Boston. Baxter found the turn of the century an appropriate moment to celebrate the park system in Boston, and wrote a lengthy, profusely illustrated essay in May for the *Boston Herald* (figures 4.39). That same year the Metropolitan Park Commissioners commissioned a one-ton plaster model of the metropolitan area for the Paris Exposition (figures 4.40–4.42). The model was later exhibited at the Pan-American Exhibition in Buffalo (1901), at the Louisiana Purchase Exposition in St. Louis (1904), and at the Lewis and Clark Centennial Exposition in Portland, Oregon (1905). A 1905 article by the secretary of the national City Parks Association on "The Development of Park Systems in American Cities" included a lengthy description of the Boston metropolitan parks and suggested that "readers have doubtless so identified the park movement with Boston as to be almost totally ignorant that anything of a similar nature has been undertaken elsewhere."[84]

In 1910 the international competition for the planning of Greater Berlin resulted in an influential exhibition and a widely circulated two-volume catalog. A lavishly illustrated chapter on American park systems described their significance as the basis for city plans and their importance in relieving urban congestion. Several pages were devoted to the Boston city and metropolitan

WONDERFUL PROGRESS DURING THE PAST SEVEN YEARS

4.39   Baxter was committed to continuing the Metropolitan Park Commissions's efforts to "picture" the metropolitan park system, and in 1900 he published in the *Boston Herald* a richly illustrated report on the progress of the parks. The framed scenes depict various sites of improved open spaces. By now almost nine thousand acres had been acquired, and the reclamation of derelict lands like Revere Beach was attracting Boston's citizens beyond all expectations.

OF WORK ON THE GREAT METROPOLITAN PARK SYSTEM.

parks, with a full-page map of the metropolitan park system and photographs of the Blue Hills and Revere Beach. The section of the exhibit on American parks was later mounted separately in several German cities.[85]

By the beginning of the twentieth century, the successful prosecution of Baxter and Eliot's plan for metropolitan parks had brought almost the entire length of the lower Charles River in Boston and Watertown into the public realm. The Cambridge Park Commission had acquired most of the north bank of the river and had constructed large sections of the riverfront parkway. To a number of the citizens of greater Boston, it was time to reopen the debate on damming the Charles so that the great water park could at last be realized.

4.40 Working double shifts for eight months, twenty-one people built this model of metropolitan Boston for the Paris Exposition of 1900. The model, eleven feet in diameter and weighing one ton, was later exhibited at international fairs in Buffalo, St. Louis, and Portland, Oregon. The metropolitan park system was widely acclaimed by city planners in England and Germany, who recognized its importance as a successful example of structuring a regional plan around reservations and natural landmarks.

4.41 It took six months to make a wax model; then plaster casts were made in ten sections. The handpainted surface depicted 250 miles of railroads, 300 miles of streams, 2,750 miles of streets, and 157,000 dwellings, and was "planted" with 200,000 trees. Even the Frog Pond on Boston Common was shown in scale.

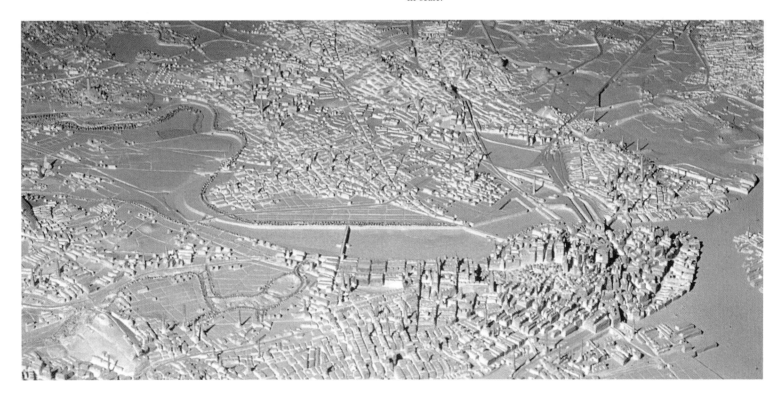

4.42 The model's three-dimensional relief reveals the dense development of the Boston peninsula, and the undeveloped and open lands in Cambridge and Brighton.

Damming the Basin

The broad Basin, surrounded as it will be by handsome promenades, is destined to become the central "court of honor" of the metropolitan district.

Charles Eliot, 1896

Under your nose . . . rose now and then the stench from mudflats and sewage that the sluggish current of the Charles and the sluggish tides that penetrated to the basin did not avail to drain properly. However, this was chiefly noticeable in summer, when Beacon Street people were expected to be out of town.

George Santayana, recalling his boyhood home on the water side of Beacon Street

A dam across the main channel of the lower Charles was part of the 1814 scheme for tide mills in the Back Bay, but only the Great Dam (underneath present-day Beacon Street) and the Cross Dam were built in 1821. By the 1870s, however, damming the river appeared to many to be the only solution to the increasingly foul state of the lower basin; twenty years later, a state-funded board published a plan for the river showing a dam just above Craigie's Bridge (figure 5.1).[1]

The Water Side of Beacon Street

The tensions engendered in the small world of elite Boston society by the proposal to dam the Charles are nowhere better described than in John Marquand's novel *The Late George Apley,* which the author once observed was based on the Boston he knew all too well. The first hint of the controversy came in a letter to George from his father Thomas. The father had recently heard some disturbing rumors that "a small group of hare-brained meddlers [was] agitating to have the Charles River dammed," covering forever the flats behind the Apley house on the water side of Beacon Street, which Thomas enjoyed watching at low tide. When a group of mostly "younger men" started up a campaign for the dam, the senior Apley was among the first to organize the opposition, with the aim of stopping what was clearly an encroachment on the rights of property owners. Thomas took the drastic step of

Frontispiece "Closing Off the Basin, October 20, 1908"

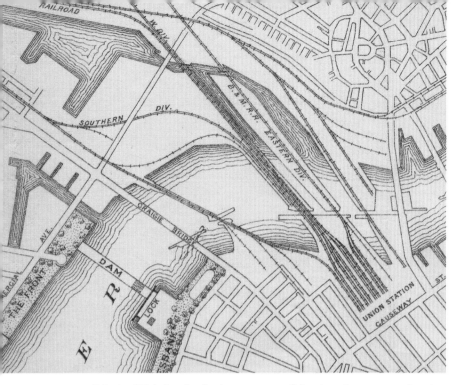

5.1 An 1894 plan for the improvement of the river shows a new dam just above the Lechmere Canal, a concession to the commercial boat traffic to East Cambridge. The dam itself is a narrow structure, extending from Olmsted's Charlesbank to "The Front," a park proposed in East Cambridge.

writing an angry letter to the *Boston Evening Transcript* to say that it was beyond his "ability to see . . . why Boston should want another pool of stagnant water at her gates":

> There are enough stagnant pools in the Fens already. . . . It will be done to gratify the unbalanced whim of a small group who believe there are not sufficient places for the citizens of Boston to walk and play. It is not the purpose of those who built upon the Charles River to have playgrounds in their back yards. The Boston Common was intended for recreation, and also the Public Gardens; and these generous contributions to the city's welfare are enough.

His son George took the opposite side in the controversy, the only time in his life that he "crossed his father."[2]

Some years later the son delivered a memorial sketch of his father to the Centennial Club. In the sketch he recalled a scene in his father's private office that followed the publication of the father's letter to the editor. In vain the senior Apley advocated his own position: "I do not care as much for the water, as I do for the principle of the thing. It is a bitter blow, at my time of life, to know that my son has turned traitor to his class. . . . This talk about the common good is arrant Socialism and nonsense. You and I do not stand for the common good. We stand for a small class. . . . " George responded by citing the opinions of men respected by his father who favored the dam, but Thomas was unmoved. To him this was clearly the end of the city he once knew; the great men of Boston from his youth were gone, and the stuff of which they were made was not to be found in his son's generation.[3]

George nonetheless stood steadfast in support of the dam. He lent his name to the cause, and "was actually present at several State House hearings, though he did not speak." George's wife sided with her father-in-law, and the strain between father and son caused George's mother "to take to her bed." Tension in the family did not dissipate until George's sister announced her engagement some months later.[4]

As he retold the story of their intense disagreement to the members of his club, George wondered if "in certain respects" his father was right after all. Perhaps the city *had* fallen to the static state of ancestor worship, in which "the achievements of the past are beyond our present capacities"[5]

The Charles River Improvement Commissions

Although a dam on the lower Charles was discussed at the time the Boston Park Department was organized in 1876, the campaign in favor of a dam became a lively issue in 1891, when the legislature appointed a commission on the improvement of the Charles. The board included the mayors of Boston, Cambridge, and Newton, and the chairman of the Watertown board of selectmen. The governor appointed three additional board members, one of whom was Charles Eliot.[6] Although all the members of the commission were "familiar enough" with the state of the river, they began by taking a tow boat up and down the length of the basin, and then held a series of public hearings. After weighing the "solid and pertinent facts" and the "diverse and conflicting" opinions, the commission presented their conclusions in an 1892 report written by Eliot.[7]

The report began by observing that the natural or physical character of the river "is and always was peculiar." Below Watertown the Charles is not a river but a tidal estuary, "broad in its seaward part, narrow and tortuous in its inward extension, and filled and almost emptied by the tide twice every day." Although the shoreline was greatly altered near the harbor, further upstream "the natural rim of this tidal trough is the ragged edge of a salt marsh. These marshes are plains of mud . . . covered with salt grasses and penetrated by numerous crooked and narrow creeks." The river's historical development was "equally distinctive and peculiar," characterized above all by large and small landfill ventures and ever-increasing pollution.[8]

The commission's conclusions established the framework for the next decade of debate on the river. Although no engineering studies were completed, the report stated unequivocally that the Charles was no longer the source of harbor scour it once was, a consequence of the filling upstream and the piles of the railroad bridges at its mouth. The river had become "relatively unimportant as a highway," and to most people in the metropolitan district it now served primarily as a barrier to travel. For far too many people, it had also become a "dangerous nuisance." Where the Charles was wide, there seemed to be no hesitation by enterprises like Davenport's Charles River Embankment Company in Cambridge and the Boston Water Poer Company to fill and improve the marshes. Above Cottage Farm, where the river narrows, the owners on one side seemed fearful of "unsightly occupation" of the opposite side, and so did nothing. All the property owners might develop a binding plan, but if they did not, they "must expect to see their shore lands taken from them by right of eminent domain." If the owners could not cooperate, there should be legislation allowing cities and towns to work together.[9]

By this time, seven of the sixteen miles of riverbank between Boston and Watertown were already owned by public or "semi-public institutions"—Harvard, the Cambridge hospital and the Cambridge cemetery, and the Watertown Arsenal. (The city of Cambridge did not acquire its river front until 1894.) The two-and-a-half miles of the Back Bay were "dedicated in the public mind, if not in fact, to the custody of the Boston Park Commission"; an embankment along the Boston side of the river had been authorized by the legislature in 1893 (though it was not completed until 1910). Only two miles were occupied by "practically irremovable" industrial concerns (the three largest were the Boston & Albany Railroad, the Brookline Gas Company, and the Brighton Abattoir) and five miles were in private hands. In this optimistic view, the remaining three or four miles of riverfront could be acquired without great difficulty for public use.[10]

Although the commercial use of the river had declined, the report recommended that the opportunity for boat traffic be maintained. The hindrance to boat traffic presented by the twelve drawbridges and five railroad bridges could be removed if the existing bridges were replaced by drawless spans elevated above the river. At North Station, the railroad "bridges" were so wide that they "fairly roof the river," serving "as rent-free switching yards, where engines engaged in making up trains cross and recross continually." A single broad high-level bridge would eliminate the conflict with barge and tow-boat traffic on the river, as such elevated railroad approaches at terminals in Philadelphia and London had shown.[11]

The commission's second report, published in 1893, was much briefer than the first. It included a draft bill creating a commission with the authority to make improvements. It also recommended granting the authority to Boston and Cambridge to construct embankments along the entire frontage of the river.[12]

The general court chose not to create a new commission. Instead, only a week after the permanent Metropolitan Park Commission (MPC) was established in June 1893, the state legislature authorized the Joint Board on the Improvement of the Charles River, consisting of the park commission and the State

Board of Health. The joint board was to investigate the sanitary conditions of the river between the Charles River Bridge at the mouth of the harbor and the Waltham town line, and also to prepare plans for improvement of "the beds, shores and waters" of the river and the "removal of nuisances therefrom." A sum of five thousand dollars was authorized to employ "engineers and experts." The board appointed Frederick Stearns (the engineer for the board of health) as engineer, Olmsted, Olmsted & Eliot as landscape architects, and Dr. Robert Greenleaf as sanitary consultant. In a departure from common practice, the joint board did not hold any public hearings.[13]

The 1894 report of the joint board pointed out that at the Charlesbank Park the commercial use of the river "has already been abandoned in favor of the more profitable use thereof for purposes of residence and recreation."[14] River traffic would decline further after the federal government approved the construction of the new Cambridge (now Longfellow) Bridge without a draw; the legislature later compensated wharf owners above the bridge on the Cambridge side for their losses.

The board also endorsed the twenty-year-old idea of new house lots north of Beacon Street. The idea seemed sound: the houses facing the river should be "worthy adjuncts to the superb location," and there would be "better policing and care which all public grounds receive when the neighboring householders walk through them habitually, or constantly have them under view." The report cited an excerpt from Mayor Nathan Matthews's inaugural address in 1891:

> We have in this [Charles River] basin the opportunity for making the finest water park in any city in the country; an opportunity which should be grasped before it is too late. The eventual solution of this whole problem should . . . be an imitation of the plan adopted by the city of Hamburg, under similar circumstances.

The first five plates in the report were of the Alster Basin in Hamburg, and the text noted that "some of the finest of the private houses, the principal hotels, and such shops as are usually found in the better quarters of a city" faced directly onto the Alster. A photograph of boating on the Thames near London was also included, to suggest that the outdoor life along the Alster in Hamburg was "not peculiar to the German nation" (figures 5.2–5.4).[15]

5.2 The reports of the park commissions and the state boards also included photographs of the sewer outfalls along the riverfront, like this one near the corner of Brimmer and Beacon Streets.

5.3 Views of the Hamburg's Alster Basin were included in the reports of the state boards that investigated the river, and were also promoted in the first reports of the Metropolitan and Cambridge Park Commissions. This photograph from the 1890s shows the highly developed landscape along the Alster, which included landscaped paths and numerous formal and informal boat landings.

5.4 The elegant Lombard Bridge separated the inner and outer basins of the Alster. The 1894 joint board report quoted the 1891 inaugural address of Mayor Nathan Matthews, who urged Boston to imitate the development of the Alster Basin. In 1884, during a year's travel and study in Europe, the Boston landscape architect Charles Eliot had visited Hamburg and had written that the city's "water parks [were] such as Boston should have made of the Back Bay."

The report also included a remarkable map, not quite four feet long, of the existing conditions along the river (figures 5.5, 5.6). For the first time, the existing state of the entire basin was documented on a single sheet of paper, a persuasive argument for the essential unity of both the problems and the prospects for the Charles. The map showed two prisons, three coal-burning power plants, numerous shabby commercial ventures (including the extensive slaughterhouses in East Cambridge and Brighton), a large, bankrupt, half-filled residential development (today the site of MIT), and "temporary" railroad trestles filling half the space between Craigie's Bridge and the harbor. The only park in the river was the Charlesbank, along Boston's West End.

In 1894 the Board of Harbor and land Commissioners held hearings on the joint board's recommendation to dam the river. To represent them at the hearings the opponents of the dam hired several engineering experts and as counsel two former governors, John Long and William Russell (who had signed the legislation establishing both the Metropolitan Park Commission and the joint board). At the second hearing, Long delivered an impassioned opening statement on behalf of his Beacon Street clients:

> There was sprung upon this community suddenly one of the most radical changes in the natural situation of the city of Boston that has ever been suggested, a plan to put up a permanent dam obstructing navigation, changing a body of salt water to fresh, affecting millions of property, affecting commercial interests, raising great questions of sanitation, unprecedented, for this is no parallel to it—

The indignation of the remonstrants was only heightened by accusations that the opponents of a dam were selfishly guarding their property interests against the welfare of the community.[17]

Among the speakers in favor of the dam was Harvard president Charles W. Eliot, who introduced himself "with considerable reluctance" as a citizen of Cambridge, having "no representative quality whatever." Eliot pointedly observed that among all the witnesses, "there is not one of the citizens who have testified here, including myself, whose opinion upon these expert questions is of any value whatever." In fact, every question that had been raised had already been addressed in the report of the joint board.[18]

This was not an issue of individual property owners and their rights, Eliot argued, but "a question for the happiness and health of the five or six hundred thousand people that belong to this metropolitan district." Perhaps after expert testimony had been presented, everyone in favor would change their minds, but "at present the principal opposition, we all know, proceeds from property owners on the water side of Beacon Street." In an appeal to logic that fell on deaf ears, Eliot concluded by observing that the proposal to build a dam was entirely separate from the plan to build a row of houses facing the basin. In fact, since the cost of not building a dam would be much greater than the cost of building one, there would be more pressure on the state to create and sell new house lots if a dam were *not* built.[19]

The remonstrants countered with several well-known local experts on their side, including Dwight Porter, a professor of hydraulic and sanitary engineering at MIT, and Colonel George E. Waring, who early in his career had been the drainage engineer for Central Park in New York. The proponents of the dam responded by asking Frederick Stearns and William Sedgewick of the State Board of Health to testify. Since the Harbor Commission had no money for new studies, the testimony consisted largely of citations from previous studies of the river and the harbor, and of conflicting judgments about the conclusions of those studies from the experts hired by the two sides.

Turning the tables on Eliot, Gamaliel Bradford attacked the supposedly disinterested testimony of the joint board's experts— Eliot's son, the landscape architect, and the health board's engineer—as well as the experience of the joint board's members. Comparing the boards with the authority and experience of the state and federal supreme courts, he pointed out that the Metropolitan Park Commission was only two years old: "They are not trained men in their line. They are only reputable citizens who take this position. And I think their opinion is entitled to just so much weight as their individual character carries with it, and no

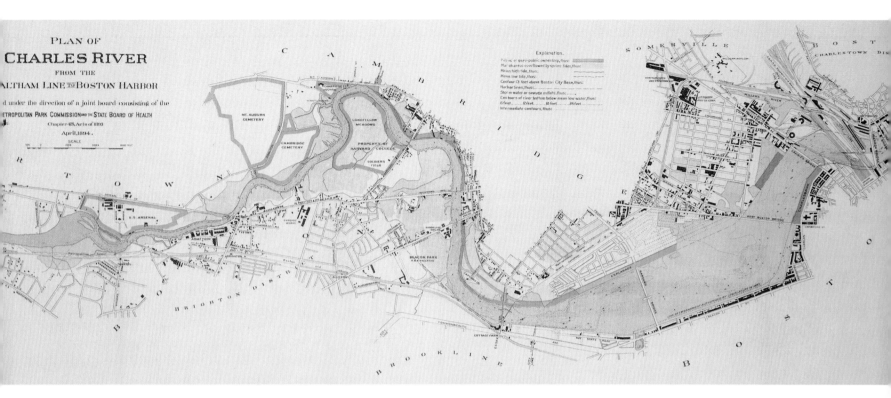

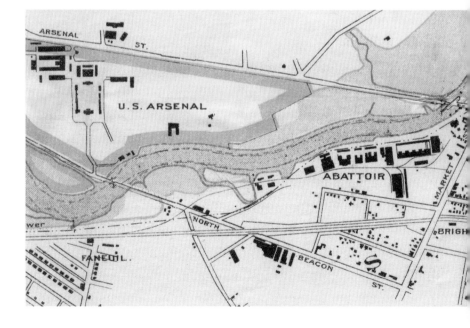

5.5 A joint board comprising the Metropolitan Park Commission and the State Board of Health published this remarkable map of existing conditions along the basin in 1894. Between Watertown and Boston Harbor were two prisons, three coal-burning power plants, numerous shabby commercial ventures, a bankrupt residential development in Cambridgeport (today the MIT campus) and acres of "temporary" railroad trestles below Craigie's Bridge. Charlesbank, along Boston's West End, was the only public space along the river.

5.6 The 1894 map included detailed outlines of the major structures along the river, including the Brighton Abattoir and the Watertown Arsenal downstream of the North Beacon Street Bridge.

more." He suggested that if a dam were built, Stearns would be the engineer to direct it. And as for "young Mr. Eliot,"

> he sees in these marshes a splendid opportunity to develop a landscape gardening park. He sees he may find employment probably for years in a most congenial occupation, and that he can make himself a reputation that will spread all over the country, and perhaps last for centuries.

By accepting fees from the joint board, Stearns and Eliot's judgments were rendered suspect.[20]

At the conclusion of the hearings, the Harbor and Land Commission determined that no one could say what the effect of a dam would be. In the absence of overwhelming evidence in favor of the proposal, the commissioners were unwilling to risk the "incalculable injury" that might result to the harbor and the city.[21]

The board's failure to act was recalled in George Santayana's autobiography. He grew up at 302 Beacon Street, the water side, in those favored houses where every room was "initially attractive," with either the sun on the street side or the view over the water. The summer sunsets were "more gorgeous, good Bostonians believed, than sunsets anywhere else in the world," and Santayana's limited experience did "not belie them." As for the view of Cambridge, "darkness added to distance [and] made the shabby bank opposite inoffensive." But there were two "counter-effects discovered eventually by enthusiastic purchasers":

> Under your nose was a mean backyard, unpaved, with clothes or at least clotheslines stretched across it; and mean plank fences divided it from other back yards of the same description, with an occasional shed or stable to vary the prospect. Under your nose too—and this was the second counter-effect—rose now and then the stench from mudflats and sewage that the sluggish current of the Charles and the sluggish tides that penetrated to the Basin did not avail to drain properly.

So why did the residents remain on the water side of Beacon? Because the smell "was chiefly noticeable in summer, when Beacon Street people were expected to be out of town; they made no loud complaints; and the democracy in general was not yet aroused to the importance of town planning for its own sake. The age was still enamoured of *laissez-faire;* and its advantages were indeed undeniable. For the government it meant a minimum of work, and for the public it meant a minimum of government."[22]

Although the construction of the dam and the creation of the basin would later be reckoned among the city's signal accomplishments, Bostonians who shared the views of the fictional Thomas Apley successfully blocked those projects for another decade.

Parkways and Bridge Schemes

Beyond addressing the importance of the dam and its relationship to the proposed park along the river, Eliot's work for the Charles River Improvement Commission and the joint board made plain his view of the relationship of parkways and public open space. The 1894 report of the joint board indicated that the advantage of "a continuous parkway from Waltham to Boston" was so obvious that it need only be mentioned. Roads built on the borders of the public reservations along the Charles would benefit both private owners and the public treasury—and to reinforce the point, Eliot drew the proposed parkways at the same scale as the map of the existing conditions (figure 5.7).[23]

In 1894 a $300,000 appropriation for land acquisition along the river was passed, and the following April the Metropolitan Park Commission made the first takings on the Boston side of the Charles, extending from the Western Avenue Bridge all the way to the Abattoir above the Arsenal Street Bridge.[24]

Ironically, the first parkway construction by the MPC—and the first permanent improvement on the riverfront—was a project that seems quite out of character with Olmsted and Eliot's resolute statements on the restorative effects of natural scenery. In 1896 Olmsted had said unequivocally that "if motion is accelerated, park ground will be put to a use quite inconsistent with its main purpose. In other words, a park is a preserve of scenery, and as such it is no place for the driver's speedway." Yet according to the joint

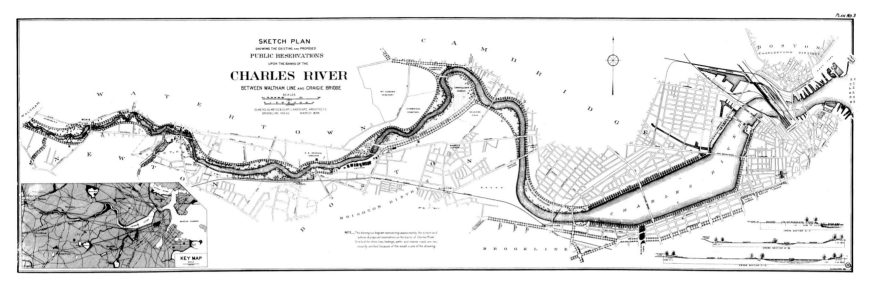

5.7 The 1894 "Sketch Plan" prepared by Charles Eliot for the joint board showed parkways on both sides of the Charles. The plan also includes a dam just above Craigie's Bridge. The strongest objections to the plan were aroused by the proposal for a row of house lots on new fill north of the existing houses on the water side of Beacon Street.

board's 1894 report, the remaining marshland adjoining Harvard's Soldiers Field was the only location along the river where a mile-long speedway could be constructed, uninterrupted by cross streets (figures 5.8, 5.9). Perhaps the speedway on the Charles was seen as politically unavoidable; the discussion of it is surprisingly brief. Completed in 1899, the project included not only a two-mile track for carriages and the roadway from North Harvard Street to the Arsenal Street bridge, but also space for a bicycle track and structures to accommodate a stables, a house for the superintendent, and a police station.[25] The speedway was immensely popular, and continued in active use into the 1950s.

Eliot's work for the Metropolitan Park Commission and the Charles River Improvement Commission also led to sketches for two proposed bridges whose design and location he believed would enhance the public realm. To replace the old structure at Cottage Farm, he proposed the "Charlesmouth Bridge" further downstream, where it would connect the Charles with the new parkways laid out by Olmsted along the Muddy River. The new bridge would also mark the passage from the "Marsh Section" to the "Basin Section" of the lower Charles, and would create a fine view extending all the way to the State House (figures 5.10, 5.11).[26]

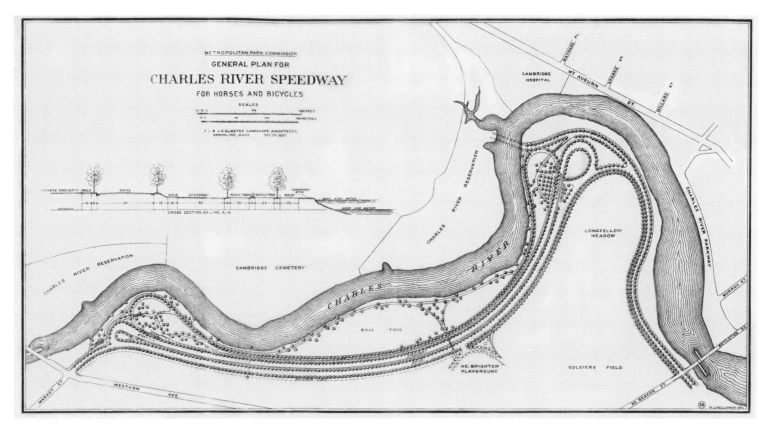

5.8 In the 1894 plan for the Charles Basin, Charles Eliot included a speedway for horses and bicycles along the edge of the Longfellow Meadows. Four years later the final design was completed, and the speedway opened in 1899.

5.9 On weekends the mile-long uninterrupted course (between the Harvard athletic fields and what is now Herter Park in Allston) was a popular attraction for carriage races. The speedway was actively used until the late 1950s, when the first phase of the Metropolitan Boston Arts Center (now the Christian A. Herter Center) was built on the site.

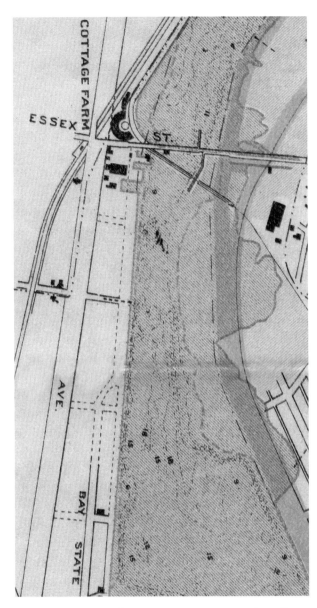

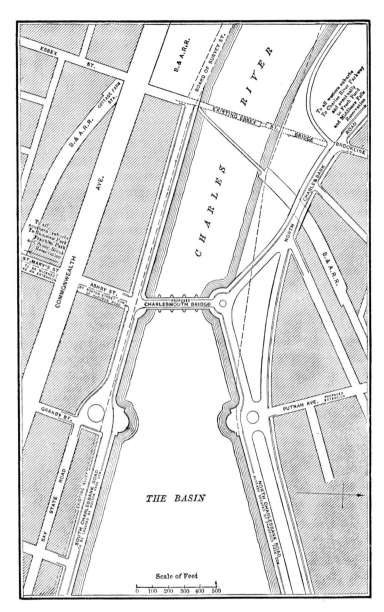

5.10 The location of the existing Essex Street (now Boston University) Bridge was upstream just far enough to miss the long view down the basin; the diagonal of the railroad bridge was also unattractive. In the ongoing reconstruction of bridges across the Charles, Eliot saw the potential for improvement along this stretch of the river and the opportunity for more striking vistas.

5.11 Eliot proposed a new "Charlesmouth Bridge" just downstream of the old Essex Street Bridge, to capture the long view looking toward Beacon Hill and East Cambridge. Overlooks on both sides of the river were located at new traffic circles east of the proposed bridge.

In 1892 the improvement commission had suggested a single high-level bridge behind North Station to make the river more accessible for boating. At that time the objection of the railroads was sufficient to block any new legislation, and the work of the improvement commission was later seen, in the case of the railroads at least, to be "wholly fruitless." Two years after the improvement commission's report, in an unpublished letter, Eliot proposed a more radical solution. To avoid the full cost of "a suitable union station on the mainland of Boston," Eliot wrote, the railroads have covered the Charles with a series of timber platforms, which they use as "a rent-free switching yard and terminal" (figures 5.12, 5.13). In his opinion, state and national legislation allowed this only on a temporary basis, and he hoped that sooner or later the renewal of these permits would be refused and the railroads would then build a terminal on the north side of the river. That would allow bridges and park lands "susceptible of fine architectural treatment."[27]

In a drawing to accompany the letter, Eliot diagrammed a pair of new bridges. One would connect from City Square in Charlestown diagonally across the river, replacing the Warren Bridge. A landscaped boulevard would extend from the river along the line of Canal Street to Haymarket. The second bridge would connect the new Union Station to Leverett and Charles Streets at Craigie's Bridge, just downstream of Olmsted's Charlesbank Park. On the Cambridge side, Union Station would be connected by a landscaped boulevard along the river to Craigie's Bridge and "The Front," a park proposed for the water's edge (figure 5.14).[28]

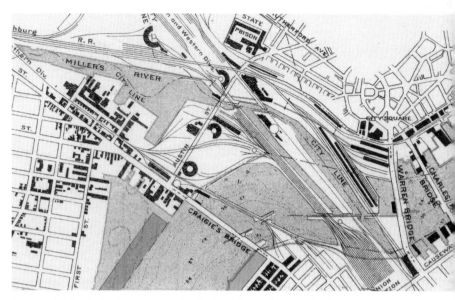

5.13 In 1892 Charles Eliot proposed a single high-level railroad bridge over the Charles to replace the numerous trestles that had nearly covered the Miller's and Charles Rivers below Craigie's Bridge.

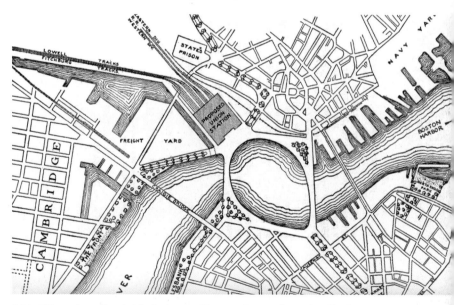

5.14 When the railroads blocked any efforts at change along the Charles, Eliot proposed a more radical solution in an unpublished letter: removal of the station to the north side of the river, with a grand view of a new pair of bridges to Boston.

5.12 More than half the water surface of the Charles below Craigie's Bridge was covered by rail yards and sidings, built under "temporary" permits.

The Cambridge Bridge

Nothing came of Eliot's visionary bridge schemes, but soon after the acquisition of almost the entire riverfront as public space, the legislature approved a new Cambridge Bridge. The realization of its design, which attracted widespread public interest, was a singular milestone in the campaign for the basin. Renamed for Henry Wadsworth Longfellow in 1927, the bridge is one of the great landmarks of Boston, its present rusting and dilapidated condition notwithstanding, and arguably the finest bridge in the city. Building it, however, was no simple matter, requiring what was described at the time as a campaign of "Drawless Bridge Agitation" in Congress after the proposed design was rejected by the U.S. War Department.

A drawless structure had been considered by the Boston Transit Commission in the mid–1890s as a replacement for the old Charles River Bridge connecting Boston and Charlestown, since frequent openings of a draw would enormously disrupt the schedule of the elevated transit line to be built in the middle of the new bridge. The commission determined that it might take as long as two or three years for legislation to override the War Department's objections and designed the new swing bridge at a higher elevation than the old one. If drawbridges on the Charles were later declared unnecessary, the new Charlestown bridge could be permanently closed, and in the meantime its height would require far less frequent openings than the old bridge.[29]

The replacement of the existing West Boston Bridge was authorized in the spring of 1898, and by June William Jackson had been appointed chief engineer for the bridge commission. Jackson had been the city engineer for Boston since 1885; he was also the chief engineer for the Harvard Bridge (1887–1891) and the Charlestown Bridge (1896–1900). Almost immediately Jackson hired as consulting architect Edmund Wheelwright, who had been the city architect for Boston from 1891 to 1895. Wheelwright had studied architecture at MIT after graduating from Harvard College in 1876; Jackson left MIT a month before graduating in 1868 to take a position working on the Chestnut Hill Reservoir in the city engineer's office.[30]

The early studies for the Cambridge Bridge showed that highway traffic was increasing, while commercial traffic on the river continued to decline. The new bridge was expected to be the primary rapid transit link between Boston and Cambridge, and avoiding delays caused by bridge openings was at least as important here as it was for the Charlestown Bridge. In deference to the War Department, however, a bridge design with a draw located on one side of a central island was drawn up. After further studies, the commission approved a drawless bridge and determined to hold hearings at the beginning of 1899. The mayors of Boston and Cambridge and the presidents of the Boston Elevated Railway and the Citizens' Trade Association testified, as did the secretary of the Metropolitan Park Commission and President Eliot of Harvard. The Board of Engineers of the War Department held their own hearing, and rejected the proposal for a drawless bridge as an obstacle to navigation; the board also rejected the drawbridge and island scheme because it would reduce the tidal flow from the river into the harbor and create an unsafe draw passage.[31]

Undaunted, the bridge commission decided in June 1899 to appeal to Congress, which was in recess until December. To prepare the state's congressional delegation, the commissioners took them on a boat tour during the summer. They pointed out the declining boat traffic on the river and the completed and proposed park improvements along the shore. They noted that the Charles "is practically unique among American rivers," because seventeen miles of its banks, from Craigie's Bridge to Dedham, were already public reservations, or soon would be.[32]

At the same time, Wheelwright and Jackson undertook detailed design studies. A stone arched design was rejected because of its estimated cost of five million dollars. Its width and low elevation above the water (twenty-five feet at the center span) would have been "low and dark." They considered a central trussed arch above the road surface. Reluctant to abandon a masonry structure, Wheelwright sketched a steel structure with masonry piers, marked by stone towers in the center and at both ends of the bridge.[33]

As a contingency, the designers developed a drawbridge with three sets of masonry towers (figure 5.15). The central towers (one

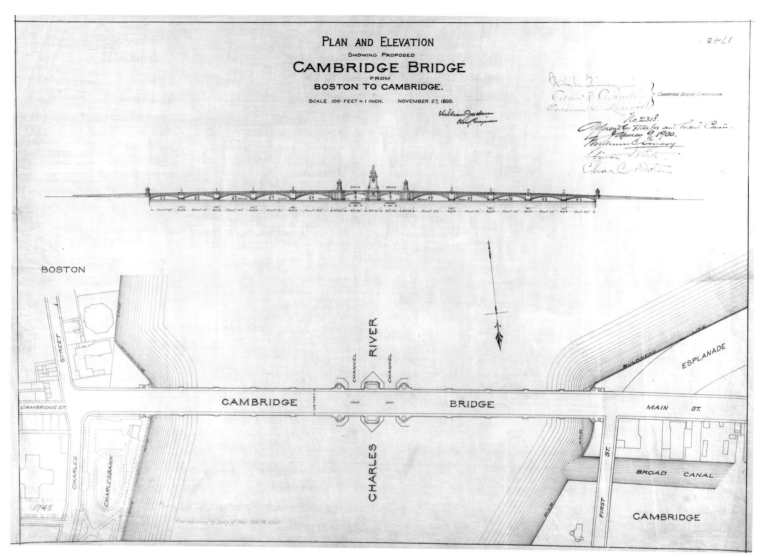

PLAN AND ELEVATION
SHOWING PROPOSED
CAMBRIDGE BRIDGE
FROM
BOSTON TO CAMBRIDGE.

SCALE 100 FEET = 1 INCH.   NOVEMBER 27, 1899.

5.15 Since the U. S. War Department had declined to approve bridges on the Charles without draws, Edmund Wheelwright prepared a design for the new Cambridge Bridge with six towers in the center. The two towers in the middle, twice as high as the towers on either side, concealed the two pairs of drawbridges in their raised position. A notation along the lower edge of the plan confirms the approval of this design by the War Department in February 1900.

hundred feet above the roadway) and the two pairs of side towers would conceal the leaves of the open draw bridges. This design was submitted to the War Department, with the expectation that the design could be built immediately if Congress rejected a drawless design.[34]

The following February the War Department approved the six-tower drawbridge design, just as Congress began hearings on the bill to approve a fixed-span bridge. The bridge commission's report quoted at length the testimony of the mayor of Cambridge, who referred to the plans to make the river "a great water park." Sadly, the mayor observed, little attention has been paid to the four bridges across the broad section of the basin—Craigie's, West Boston, Harvard, and Brookline—"none of which has beauty, dignity, or architectural pretension." Three of the structures were unsightly pile bridges, "grotesquely inconsistent with the present plans for the future of the river." And while the aesthetic character of the proposed fixed bridge was important, as were the lower maintenance and construction costs, the most important factor was the problem a draw bridge would create for rapid transit across the bridge.[35]

Amendments to the bill required the state to compensate upstream wharf owners and gave the War Department approval of the pier locations, and the bill was finally passed at the end of March (figures 5.16–5.19).[36]

5.16 Oversize blocks of granite were mortared into the towers of the new Cambridge Bridge, and scaffolding was erected in the river so that stones on the piers of the four center towers could be carved in place. The prow of a Viking ship was carved on each of the four piers, the consequence of a misguided Harvard professor's well-publicized efforts to prove that Leif Eriksson had sailed up the Charles around the year 1000 A.D. The city seals of Cambridge and Boston were also carved into the stonework.

5.17 The old West Boston Bridge connected Cambridge Street in Boston with Main Street in Cambridge. To maintain the existing street alignment, a temporary bridge was erected while the new Cambridge Bridge was built (it was renamed in 1927 after Henry Wadsworth Longfellow). Tied to the upstream side of the temporary bridge were one of Boston's floating bathhouses and a shack offering boats for rent.

5.18 To meet the U.S. War Department's requirement for a twenty-seven-foot clearance above the water, the architect Edmund Wheelwright designed a series of graceful arched spans and four imposing, exquisitely detailed center towers for the new bridge.

5.19 The Longfellow Bridge set a new standard for bridge design in Boston, a standard that some argue has been met only once since, in the John W. Weeks Bridge, the only footbridge across the Charles, built by Harvard to connect the new Business School in Allston with the Harvard houses in Cambridge.

Five years after the 1894 hearings on the dam, Frederick Law Olmsted, Jr., wrote a letter to the *Boston Herald*, endorsing an upstream location for the dam. It was better, he said, to stabilize the river for part of its length than not at all. The dam at Craigie's Bridge could be built later, and if it were, the only objection to a second dam near Cottage Farm would be its effect on boating. Olmsted suggested that in all the comparisons of the Charles with the Thames, everyone in Boston was forgetting how people managed to row at Oxford in spite of the number of locks there.[37]

James Storrow, an investment banker and past captain of the Harvard crew, thought the idea of a dam at Cottage Farm was "an absurd proposition," and in 1901 he organized a new campaign for a dam at the mouth of the basin. He had recently given up his law practice and gone to work with the investment banker Henry Higginson. Together with his wife Helen Osborne Storrow he had actively supported children's philanthropies in the city, including settlement houses, Girl Scouts, and Newsboys; he was also elected to the school committee that year.[38]

By now several significant factors had turned in favor of building the dam on the site originally proposed at Craigie's Bridge. The metropolitan sewer had been completed. All of the wharf rights in Cambridge and all but three in Boston had been relinquished, largely as a result of the negotiations with property owners for the bill passed by Congress to permit a drawless bridge as a replacement for the West Boston Bridge.[39]

All of these factors added weight to the earlier findings of the joint board. A dam was a less expensive solution to the problem of the flats than filling or dredging. It would provide a recreation area "the cost of which sinks into insignificance compared with the prices that have been paid for parks and open spaces within the city limits and surrounding suburbs." And the recently constructed parks in other parts of the city were not enough. As Storrow would later testify, the children of the North End will not find their way to Franklin Park more than once or twice in their lives; as their ordinary playground, "it might as well be on another planet."[40]

And time had worked against the opponents of a dam. George Waring, the sanitary engineer who had testified on their side in 1894, had died of yellow fever in Havana. Of their former counsel, ex-governor William Russell had died, and John Long was in Washington in Roosevelt's cabinet. There was now almost universal support for the measure: all of Boston's newspapers, the city governments of Boston, Cambridge, Newton, and Watertown, the State Board of Health, and the Metropolitan Park Commission.[41]

Higginson was the first signatory in a widely circulated pamphlet (probably put together by Storrow) asking that the matter be "duly investigated by the proper authorities." Once again Back Bay was compared with the Alster Basin in Hamburg and the Thames, but the old proposal for a new row of house lots facing the river was dropped. Ten thousand letters were mailed out, and five thousand postcards and two thousand letters in favor came back. Storrow introduced legislation in 1901, but failed to meet the notice requirements. He then presented a bill authorizing a commission to study the problem. At the commission hearings the following year, Storrow observed that this would be the third or fourth commission to take up the problem; there would continue to be more commissions, until the whole question "is made sufficiently plain that the ordinary citizen can understand it and be satisfied with the justice of the result"—a high and optimistic standard for public discourse.[42]

This time the commission was given an appropriation to study the issue, and the commission's members represented both civic and professional authority: Henry Pritchett, the president of MIT, had been superintendent of the U.S. Coast Survey; Colonel Samuel M. Mansfield had supervised improvements in the Boston Harbor shipping channel as an officer in the corps of engineers; Richard Henry Dana was well known in the community and would have the confidence of people in Boston and Cambridge.[43]

The supporters of the project engaged as counsel Nathan Matthews, the former mayor who had endorsed the dam as early as his inaugural in 1891 and who lived on the water side of Beacon Street. Storrow also got the endorsement of John J. Fitzgerald, the three-term congressman representing the North End and the West

End. The Roman Catholic vicar general and the Episcopal bishop of Eastern Massachusetts supported the project on behalf of the tenement neighborhoods near the river. Storrow's committee negotiated with many of the riverfront property owners in Cambridge and their objections were withdrawn. The Associated Board of Trade and the Citizens Association of Boston had opposed the project in 1894, and they, too, changed their position.[44]

The opponents of the dam presented a petition signed by seventy-six residents of Beacon Street. They claimed there was no evidence to show that a dam would not increase shoaling in the harbor. Professor Dwight Porter once again attacked every argument in support of the proposal. The Alster Basin, he said, was not analogous; it was sixty miles from the sea, it was eight hundred miles further north, and no sewer drainage was ever permitted into the Alster Basin. The Charles would never be used for boating or skating, the air and water temperature of a fresh-water basin would be higher in the summer, and the incidence of malaria in the basin, already recognized by the Metropolitan Park Commission in 1893, would increase. The basin would become offensive "both to sight and to smell."[45]

Gamaliel Bradford, who eight years before had challenged the judgment of the joint board's experts, claimed at the 1901–1902 hearings that the whole idea was a conspiracy on the part of Cambridge and Harvard College, since "the President of the United States, the outgoing and incoming Secretaries of the Navy, both of the Senators from Massachusetts, and, I suppose, some of the members of Congress, are all loyal sons of Harvard."[46] Although he was also a Harvard graduate, he nonetheless opposed the dam: "It is not that I love Harvard less," he said, "but that I love Boston more." It was true that Storrow and Higginson had rowed for Harvard, and Storrow had coached the college crew. Bradford may also have known that a committee on athletics of Harvard's Board of Overseers had discussed the proposed dam and that all the members "pledged to do everything in their power to carry out our plans for it."[47]

By now Storrow was convinced that all the experts except Porter supported the dam. In his opening testimony for the peti-

tioners in favor, James Storrow showed several photographs of the basin at low tide that depicted slimy exposed seawalls, sewer outfalls, and polluted mudflats. He quoted a resident of Beacon Street who lived near one of the private sewers, who opposed the dam because "he considered the right to drain into that basin 'a priceless privilege.'" Storrow outlined the history of the proposal and the reasons it had not been passed, which he attributed primarily to the lack of funding for the various commissions that had considered it and the ample financial support provided by those who opposed the dam, who solicited expert testimony against it in previous hearings. His conclusion reflected complete confidence in the ability of experts to find a solution, once the community agreed on what it wanted: "nothing in this matter in any way really presents a difficult *engineering* problem. It is merely a question of doing certain things if they are worth doing at a certain cost."[48]

As in 1894, President Eliot also testified in favor. His son Charles had been in the middle of the riverfront design work for the metropolitan commissioners as well as for the Cambridge park commission at the time of his death in 1897 at the age of thirty-seven. President Eliot had finished a lengthy biography of his son just before the hearings began.[49] He forcefully advanced his interest in the river and in the planning of Boston:

It is my feeling that the proposed improvement of the Charles River Basin and the banks of the river is of the greatest interest to thousands of people. The principal ground for favoring the improvement of the basin has seldom been put forward. It is to increase the health and happiness of four hundred thousand people who live within an easy walk of this seven-mile park which nature has really provided.

I wonder if any member of this committee has walked of a June or an October evening along the Charlesbank and noted the thousands who use it. The sight of the people gathered on the Charlesbank park on any fair evening between the first of May and the first of November would go far to convince any person, who really believes that cities exist and that commonwealths exist to promote the well-being of the people, that this great improvement of the Charles River Basin and of the banks of the Charles River is a thing fit to be done by this intelligent Commonwealth. There are, of course, objections, but these objections, after all, seem to me to be of second rank, because great modern communities do not exist ultimately for commerce, but commerce exists for them. Nor do municipalities exist for profit in money, but for the people who live in them, and the supreme object of any city should be the happiness of the community.[50]

Almost three months later, after eleven hearings and almost six hundred pages of testimony, the committee concluded that the two outstanding questions were technical: shoaling in Boston Harbor and the pollution of the river. These issues were placed in the hands of the committee's chief engineer, John R. Freeman.

A graduate of MIT and a member of the MIT Corporation, John Freeman had recently completed a report on the water supply for New York City and was widely known and respected in his profession (figure 5.20). He knew most of the men on both sides of the controversy; several were friends or former classmates.[51] As an engineer, Freeman concluded that the proposal in 1894 had failed "from lack of investigation and presentation complete enough to satisfy the conservatives and the honest doubters . . . insufficient exact reliable data was at the bottom of all the difficulties."[52]

He recognized the political aspects of the proposal, but he also felt there were significant ethical issues involved for those whose expertise was sought by the community. He "almost began to envy those experts of the court room whose lawyer friends tell them what they are expected to prove." He was especially contemptuous of Dwight Porter's testimony for the opposition:

> For an expert to do what a certain engineer friend of ours . . . did in the Charles River Dam case, leaves a very unpleasant odor, and I believe that every time that you or anyone of us enters a lay case as a partisan for hire, he dulls his keenness of perception of the truth and impairs his moral strength and his highest usefulness.

5.20 John Freeman, acknowledged as the father of hydrologic engineering in America, was the chief engineer of the 1903 Committee on Charles River Dam. He identified twenty-three major issues that should be addressed to determine if the dam was justified. The final report of almost six hundred pages concluded that the dam was a "great public improvement" and "need not cost a dollar more" than the sanitary improvements that the cities of Boston and Cambridge and the Commonwealth would have to build even without the dam.

Freeman's own rule was not to allow himself "to be used by a lawyer for the manufacture of testimony," and not to participate in legal disputes unless he was "well convinced of the merits and justice" of the side that sought his services.[53]

He originally thought he was to be only an advisor to the committee, and was already over-committed, apparently the usual condition of his professional life. In addition the scope of the survey had been underestimated, the appropriation was inadequate, and the report deadline was unrealistic. He soon determined that there was no satisfactory existing survey of the basin, and that the authorized study on mosquitoes should be expanded into a real bacteriological survey. He was directed to meet with representatives of the railroads, and toward the end of his work he was also asked to consider other sites and to revise the report and the cost estimates.[54]

Because so much had been said on both sides of the argument with so little basis in actual investigation of the issues, Freeman exhaustively set forth in his report the outstanding questions as he saw them:

1. In general, the benefits and disadvantages resulting from proposed dam.
2. Best type of dam, complete or half tide.
3. Best location.
   (a)   Just above Broad canal.
   (b)   Just above Lechmere canal.
   (c)   At Craigie bridge.
4. Most advantageous elevation of water surface; grade 8, Boston base, or higher. Effect on ground-water levels of neighboring territory.
5. Fresh water basin *v.* salt water; comparative advantages.
6. Necessity for large tidal sluices.
7. Present condition of Fens basin; analogy to proposed basin.
8. Quantity of upland water flowing into the proposed basin.
9. Purity of this upland water.
10. Extent of the present pollution of Charles River basin; means of lessening this.

11. Amounts of pollution admissible without offence.
12. Remedies for the unavoidable pollution.
13. Means for circulating water in Fens basin and Cambridge canals.
14. Lessening pollution of basin by extending separate system of sewerage.
15. Effect of stagnation of water in proposed Charles River basin.
16. Effect of this stagnant fresh water basin on health; malaria.
17. Effect of lessening the tidal prism upon the shoaling of Boston harbor.
18. Effect of dam upon navigation and commerce in Charles River basin, in Cambridge canals and in upper harbor.
19. Storm flood levels in proposed basin; frequency or probability of ever flooding the marshes after dam is built.
20. Cost of dam and lock, with and without special tidal sluices.
21. Cost of marginal conduits for increasing cleanliness of waters of basin.
22. Cost of making good any injury to navigation resulting from dam.
23. Cost of dredging foul sludge banks.
24. Cost of shore line improvements.[55]

To answer these questions, twenty separate studies were undertaken. Since dredging and other operations had substantially altered the river bottom, a new survey of the basin was prepared. The effect of the tidal basin on air and water temperatures was analyzed. Chemical and bacterial analysis of the water was completed, and a separate study by a pathologist reviewed malarial conditions. Because of the frequent comparison in previous hearings and newspaper articles of the basin with the Fens, separate studies compared the circumstances of the two rivers. (Among other conclusions, this analysis suggested that the pollution in the Fens from Stony Brook first became serious in 1897, and it could be substantially reduced at low cost.) Studies were done of sewage overflow and dilution, and a separate investigation was made of the pollution in the Broad and Lechmere Canals. The amount of water entering the basin was measured for two months, and the flood discharge of the Charles and Stony Brook was investigated. The geology of Boston Harbor was reviewed, a map of harbor dredging was prepared, the velocity of harbor currents was measured, and borings of silt deposits were taken. At Freeman's request, the city engineers in Boston and Cambridge conducted or reviewed studies of the progress on separating sewage and storm water discharge, and of the benefits to the rivers and canals of constructing marginal conduits.

In addition to discussing these issues "briefly" (forty-four pages), in the final report Freeman insisted on including appendixes outlining the methods, the data, and their interpretation. He, like Storrow, believed that after all the years this question had been debated in Boston, anyone who was interested should have a "full and convenient opportunity to judge of the adequacy of the new data secured and of the reasonableness of our conclusions."[56]

The deadline for the report was January 14, 1903. The next day Freeman wrote a friend that "the Committee submitted its Report yesterday noon together with a statement that the Engineer's Report and the appendices were *in the hands of* the printer. Literally, this may be understood that the printer has hold of one end while I have hold of the other end." Freeman finally turned in the last proofs in April.[57]

Completed after almost a year of constant overtime for Freeman and his assistants, the final report was unequivocal in its conclusions:

> It appears that the advantages of the dam and the basin at nearly constant level largely overbalance the possible disadvantages; that sanitary conditions will be improved, and danger of malaria not increased; that interests of navigation and manufacturing will be bettered; that the harbor will not be shoaled by loss of tidal currents; that a magnificent opportunity for wholesome recreation and the enjoyment of a more beautiful landscape will be made possible by the construction of this dam.[58]

As a result of the survey's careful estimates, the "remarkable fact appears that this *great public improvement* . . . need not cost a dollar

more" than the cities of Boston and Cambridge and the metropolitan district were already committed to spending for the bridge, sewer, and sanitary construction that would be necessary with or without the basin.[59]

Satisfied with Freeman's flood of evidence, the legislature at last created the Charles River Basin Commission to design and construct the dam.

Constructing the Dam

Since the site for the dam extended from Charlesbank Park in Boston to the proposed park at "The Front" in Cambridge, the decision to build an earthen dam created an opportunity to connect these first two riverfront parks (figure 5.21). Soon after the basin commission began work, Guy Lowell was retained by the basin commission as the consulting architect and landscape architect.[60] He was probably responsible for the idea that the dam could be made much wider than the design of the roadway and the locks required. Initially, the planned width of the dam had been determined by the length of the two locks. The lock for commercial boats on the Boston side was more than twice as long as the space required for the small boat lock on the Cambridge side of the dam. By making the dam a uniform width, the height of the retaining walls on the basin side could be reduced, and the expense for additional fill would be nearly balanced by the savings in the size of the walls. The park would be increased to almost seven acres, and its cost would be one-eighth that of an equal amount of nearby land in Boston, and about one-fourth that of an equivalent parcel in Cambridge (figure 5.22).[61]

Hiram A. Miller, who had supervised the building of the Wachusett Reservoir, was appointed chief engineer. His staff determined almost immediately that the tidal flow in the river would make it impossible for deposited fill to remain in place, unless a temporary "shut-off dam" were constructed. And to maintain the commercial boat traffic on the river, the lock would have to be constructed before the shut-off dam blocked passage across the rest of the lower channel. The shipping companies also insisted on a

5.21 The first published perspective of the Charles River Dam from 1904 showed a large lock on the Boston side and a bay of sluice gates (which included a passageway for small boats) on the Cambridge side. The proposed park on the surface of the dam was almost five hundred feet wide next to the lock, and tapered on the north end to a little over two hundred feet wide.

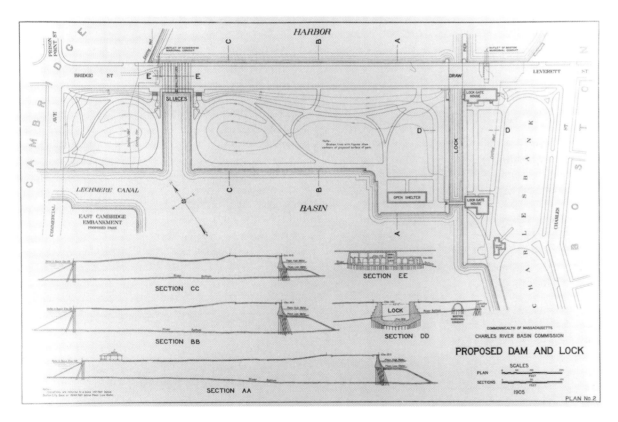

5.22 Guy Lowell, the consulting architect and landscape architect for the dam, is likely the source of the final outline of the dam. By widening the dam, the seawall on the upstream side would be lower and less expensive, covering the cost of additional fill to create a larger park on the surface of the dam.

lock eighteen feet deep at low water, which would require additional costs for separate sluices (rather than using one of the sluices as the commercial lock). Miller's staff set as the design benchmark the greatest flood in the past seventy-five years, which occurred in February 1886. The capacity of the sluice gates was established at ten percent higher than the 1886 flood.[62]

By January 1907 almost ten thousand piles had been driven to support the construction of the lock, the seawalls, and the Boston Marginal Conduit. The conduit had been authorized as a part of the dam legislation, to carry sewer overflow and discharge it below the dam (figures 5.23, 5.24).[63]

The shut-off dam required six rows of piles, with six-inch pine sheeting driven between the middle piles. The sheeting was cut off three feet below mean low water, and earth was filled on both sides and covered with rip-rap to prevent scouring. Above the six rows of piles, running from the Cambridge side to the lock cofferdam, eighty-six gates were built of six- by eight-inch timber, each ten feet wide and fifteen feet high, and held above the river by ropes. On October 20, 1908, all the ropes holding the gates were cut in seven seconds by a team of men with axes scurrying across the tops of the gates (figure 5.25). Because a drought had severely reduced the river's flow, it would have taken many days to fill the basin with fresh water. Instead the sluices were opened and salt water from the harbor filled the basin in a few hours. As soon as the gates were in place, dredges began immediately dumping fill up to the tops of the gates, making an earthen dam with a wooden core (figures 5.26, 5.27).[64]

Two of the engineers traveled to Europe to study locks at Bremerhaven, Kiel, and Bruges. The staff determined to use caisson lock gates installed on two four-wheel trucks, rather than the more common mitering gates (sometimes called scissor locks). The sliding locks could be heated in winter, they would require less room than miter locks, and they could take pressure in both directions, from flood waters flowing downstream and from storm tides pushing in from the harbor (figure 5.28).[65]

5.23 After the cofferdam was constructed around the area of the lock, a forest of piles was driven to support the weight of the lock, the new bridge, and the lock houses. By January 1907, 9,969 piles were in place.

5.24 The lock (lower right) was constructed first, so that ships could pass through it once the temporary dam was completed. The sixteen-foot diameter opening (lower left), is the Boston Marginal Conduit, designed to carry the dry-weather flow from Stony Brook and the storm overflow on the Boston side of the lower basin.

5.25 A temporary dam with eighty-two shut-off gates was built to close off the basin. Each gate was ten feet wide by fifteen feet high, built of six-by-eight-inch timber, and was held above the water by ropes. On October 20, 1908, all the ropes were cut in seven seconds and the gates dropped into place.

5.27 Concrete retaining walls were poured up- and downstream to encase the temporary wooden gates in the middle of the permanent dam. On the left in this April 1909 photo are the piers for the viaduct of the Boston Elevated Railroad Company. Just upstream of the viaduct piers is the retaining wall of the dam (in the center of the photo), a concrete structure faced with cut granite blocks.

5.26 Once the gates of the temporary dam were in place, dredges immediately piled earth on the shut-off gates.

5.28 Instead of the more common mitering gates, caisson gates were used, running on two four-wheel trucks perpendicular to the lock. The gates were heated to permit boat passage in the winter, and compartments in the gates allowed for access to the trucks at the bottom of the gates.

In addition to the park on the dam, Lowell designed five structures in the park. The two lock gate houses were located adjacent to Charlesbank. The upper lock house was a one-story structure to protect the sliding lock mechanism. The two-story lower lock house included a residence for the lock superintendent, with an attached tower for the draw bridge tender (figure 5.29). Soon after the dam was completed, the superintendent's residence was converted to a police station. On the north side of the lock was an elegant open pavilion. At the Cambridge end of the dam a stable and boathouse were built for the park police (figures 5.30-5.33).

5.30 The stables and boathouse were constructed for the park police. The sluiceway (upper right) allowed for the passage of small boats through the dam; larger boats went through the lock at the other end of the dam. Although still passable, all but a few feet of the sluiceway is now covered by the Museum of Science parking garage. To frame the vista of this newly enhanced cityscape (and to screen the railroad yards downstream), Robert Peabody created the arched viaduct for the Boston Elevated Railway (now the MBTA Green Line). The Metropolitan Coal Company (left) was one of many industries that still lined the Lechmere Canal at the time the dam and the park were completed.

5.29 Guy Lowell, the consulting architect and landscape architect to the Basin Commission, designed a stables, boat house, two lock houses (lower left and center), and an open pavilion on the dam; he also did the planting plan for the seven acres of newly filled parkland.

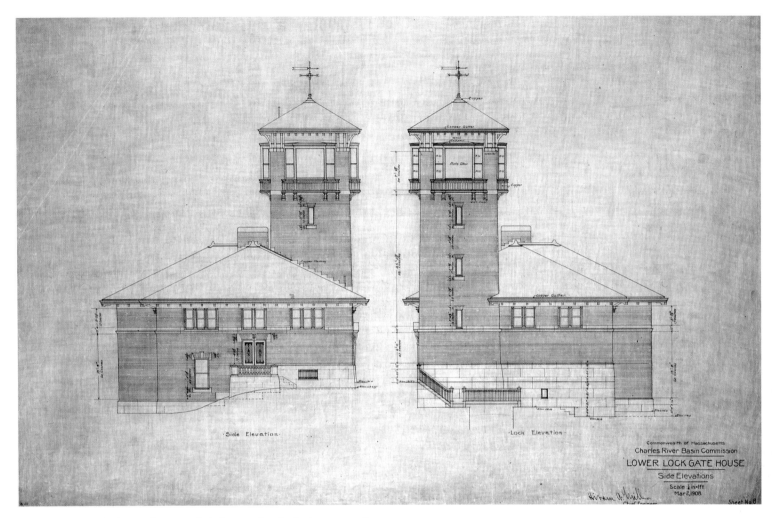

·Side Elevation·

·Lock Elevation·

Commonwealth of Massachusetts
Charles River Basin Commission
LOWER LOCK GATE HOUSE
Side Elevations
Scale ½ in=1ft
Mar 2,1908.
Sheet No.8.

5.31 The lower lock gate house included space for the lock gate on the ground floor and the residence of the superintendent on the main floor. Soon after the building was completed the superintendent's quarters were converted for use as a police station.

Charles River Basin, Boston, Mass.

5.32 The landscape on the dam provided large lawn areas between the walk along the water's edge and the roadway next to the viaduct. It served as a greensward connecting the proposed park at "The Front" in East Cambridge (left center) to the gymnasiums and open lawns at Charlesbank. The boathouse and stables for the metropolitan park police are just to the right of the drawbridge over Lechmere Canal (center).

Sketch of open Shelter for Park,
in connection with New Charles River Dam.
Guy Lowell, Architect.   Boston.

Elevations.
Scale 1/8" = 1'0".

5.33 The office of Guy Lowell drew this watercolor sketch of the open shelter on the dam opposite the upper lock gate house.

The Boston Embankment

The Charles River Basin Commission was authorized to construct not only the dam and locks but also the Boston Embankment. An extension of the open space at Charlesbank, the Embankment would be about three hundred feet wide between the new Cambridge (now Longfellow) Bridge and Berkeley Street; it would bend to parallel Back Street to Charlesgate West. Although the common practice was to make new land by building a granite seawall and then filling behind it, the fill for the Embankment was dredged while construction of a concrete seawall proceeded along the edge of the area to be filled. At the same time, the Boston Marginal Conduit, a major addition to the Boston sewer system, was constructed behind the seawall along the entire length of the new Embankment.

When the Embankment was essentially complete in 1910, it was turned over to the Metropolitan Park Commission. The new parkland was the realization of ideas dating from Gourlay's 1844 proposal and the public meetings after the Civil War that endorsed a water park on the Charles. The Metropolitan Park Commission had put off planting trees or installing benches the entire length of the new park, in part because of a proposed subway extension under the embankment. Another continuing obstacle to development was the opposition of the residents of Beacon Street, even though many of the houses on the Boston side of the basin were closed from late spring to early fall. Their resistance was officially acknowledged by the Metropolitan Park Commission, whose 1911 report defended their cautious lack of landscape development along the basin (figure 5.34). The commission's inaction "has arisen in most instances from a desire to avoid serious mistakes, and from consideration for the plainly expressed disinclination of property owners in the neighborhood of the basin to have its present clean-shaven formal look and the uninterrupted vista from their houses interfered with." Instead of a public driveway, recommended by the Basin Commission, the abutters insisted on maintaining Back Street as it was, a small, private street that ran along the edge of the embankment.[66] Uriel Crocker's son George, recalling his father's proposal for a park along the lower basin, thought the property owners on the water side of Beacon Street "had succeeded in saying to the public, 'You may come down and look at the basin if you wish, but you must walk, and you must walk in the sun. You must not have any public boathouses, bathhouses, trees, restaurants, or anything of the kind.'"[67]

A Picture of Still Life

The dam covered the mudflats along the river and stabilized the water level from Boston to Watertown. As a public open space, however, many people declared the basin a failure: "It is, indeed, a wondrous picture—of still life. The breathing space is there, plenty of it, the broad sheet of almost currentless water is there, but the people—where are they? They are not there."[68] The new concrete seawall on the Boston side of the basin continued to reflect the waves blown up on the wide expanse of water by the prevailing winds. If anything, the water was more choppy than before the dam was built. Although the lower Charles was a "scenic and sanitary triumph, it failed to live up to expectations as a water park." The Boston architect Robert Bellows said that the basin "resembles a huge bath tub, and the oarsman feels like a piece of soap in it. It is an extremely wide and uninteresting body of water." A report on metropolitan improvements, written only a year after the work on the basin was completed, called it "a windswept lake of magnificent distances."[69]

For a number of Bostonians, the water park was a great disappointment.

Harvard Bridge, looking toward Cambridge. Mass.

5.34 The Charles River Basin Commission was also authorized to construct the Boston Embankment on the Boston side of the river above the dam. About three hundred feet wide on the Beacon Hill flat and one hundred feet wide along Back Bay, it extended from Cambridge Street to Charlesgate West. This view of the embankment looks from the Harvard Bridge toward the Riverbank Court apartments (now MIT's Ashdown House) in Cambridge.

6

The Colleges and the Esplanades

As an engineer I am unable to advise my friends to put money into permanent buildings for an institution [MIT] which by the time it gets to be vigorously performing its use is faced by a continually increasing expense to protect it against the encroachments of the sea, with a distant future when submergence is inevitable.

Hiram Mills to the president of MIT, 1912

People come here from the West and turn up their noses at the Charles river basin. They state flatly what they would do with that basin if people out West had the handling of it. It would be "something else than a wash basin with some ducks in it."

Cambridge Tribune, 1928

In no city is unification of public sentiment more difficult to obtain. In none are more numerous or more various plans offered every time a public improvement is proposed. . . . Will the thing be done? Who can tell? This is Boston.

The New York Times, on the plan to build a four-lane highway as part of the new Esplanade, 1929

Today, there is only one esplanade on the Charles—the one with the Hatch Shell and the fireworks, on the Boston side. But from the first proposal of the new Boston Park Department in 1876 to the completion of the islands and lagoons in 1936, the area was officially called the Boston Embankment. The Esplanade was across the river in Cambridge. The name showed up first in the 1870s on the maps and drawings of Charles Davenport, then in the street plans and park proposals of the city of Cambridge a decade later. But at some point after the completion of the Boston Embankment in 1910, the name crossed the river to stay.[1]

In the last decade of the nineteenth century, few signs of active life or leisure could be seen along the river—mostly rowers on the water and a few athletes at Harvard's recently dedicated Soldiers Field. Then came the studied eclecticism of Carey Cage, a small structure for indoor sports, and Harvard Stadium, the largest reinforced concrete structure in the world at the time. In 1903, the Charles River Dam was approved, and new parks and parkways were built. Moving at a measured pace, Boston's universities discovered the riverbanks.

Frontispiece *New Boston Civic Advance Campaign,* December 1910, detail

Visions of the Basin

A year before the gates of the temporary dam were dropped to fill the basin in 1908, a radical approach to the basin's improvement was published by the landscape architect Arthur Shurcliff. He had been working in the office of Olmsted, Olmsted & Eliot (later Olmsted Brothers) in Brookline since 1896, and he had worked on several of the firm's projects on both sides of the river. In his autobiography, written forty years later, Shurcliff recalled first sketching a plan for a large island in the middle of the Charles in about 1905. The following year Shurcliff drew an even larger island, adding two new bridges at Dartmouth and Deerfield Streets (figure 6.1). In his 1906 proposal the island was lined with structures; a later version left most of the island open, with buildings and monuments at each end.[2]

About the same time, Ralph Adams Cram also drew up a perspective sketch for what he called "St. Botolph's Island," graced by an elegant new bridge and a large Gothic cathedral to St. Paul at one end and a large "Metropolitan Building" at the other (figure 6.2). A formal axis extended the full length of the island, whose dimensions, Cram noted, "more or less closely followed" those of the *Cité* in Paris.[3]

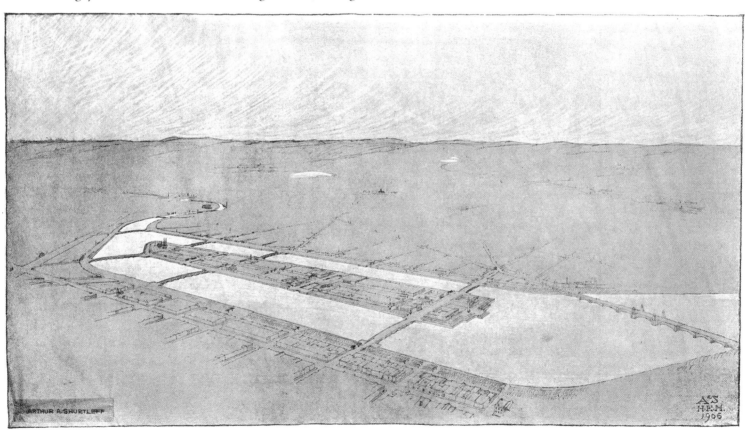

6.1 Since Gourlay's first drawing of an island in the Charles in 1844 (frontispiece, chapter 3), the idea has reappeared again and again. About 1905 Arthur Shurcliff began a series of island sketches. In this 1906 drawing, published the following year in a report cosponsored by the Boston Society of Architects, long rows of buildings and playgrounds extend the full length of the island. Two new bridges are shown at Dartmouth and Deerfield Streets, upstream and downstream from the Harvard Bridge (completed in 1891).

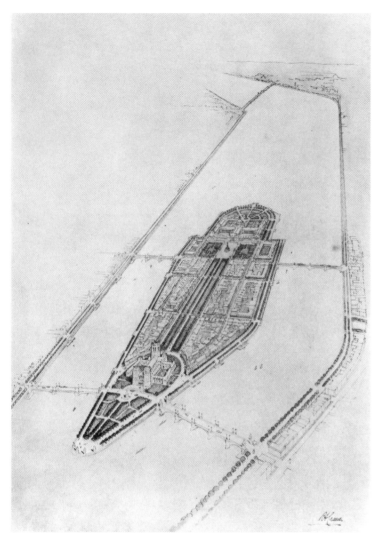

6.2 In the society's 1907 report, Ralph Adams Cram, the Boston architect whose works include the Cathedral of St. John the Divine in New York City, proposed an island with a new bridge and a cathedral at one end and a large civic plaza facing the "Metropolitan Building" at the other end.

Two of these island sketches by Shurcliff and Cram were included in a 1907 publication of the Boston Society of Architects sponsored by the Chamber of Commerce, the Boston Merchants Association, and a number of other groups. The basin was one of thirteen major areas that were studied in the report of the society's Committee on Municipal Improvement (the other sites included Copley Square, the Fenway, and several major street improvements). The report included an illustrated comparison of the Charles River with London, Paris, Rome, and Hamburg, all drawn to the same scale (figure 6.3). Niagara, Detroit, and Jackson Park in Chicago were also mentioned, as were the European examples of the Margaretheninsel in Budapest and the Moldau in Prague. Cram claimed in the report that "from an artistic standpoint" the basin was "empty, vague, and uninteresting." Looking from above the water's surface "the eye refuses to take in distances greater than 750 feet"; by leaving a channel of that width on the Boston side of the proposed island the rowing course would be improved (there was no mention of sailing) and the city would gain "an element of distinguished beauty that would have a distinct pecuniary value." Shurcliff's island also proposed a narrower channel on the Cambridge side, wider than the Seine at the Louvre in Paris, allowing a waterway on the Boston side of the same width as the Thames in London.[4]

The idea of artificial islands in the Charles was endorsed by the mayor of Boston and was also incorporated in the 1911 report of the Joint Board on Metropolitan Improvements, a commission established by the legislature to consider public works, highways, the harbor, and issues of civic beautification. The joint board went so far as to suggest the island as a site for MIT, which had outgrown its quarters in the Back Bay, and the architectural firm of Bellows & Gray drew up an island scheme that would expand over time (figures 6.4, 6.5).[5] Islands in the Charles would continue to fascinate Bostonians for the rest of the century.

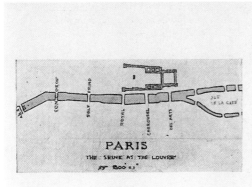

FIGURE 28.

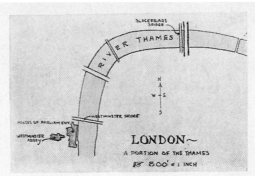

FIGURE 30.

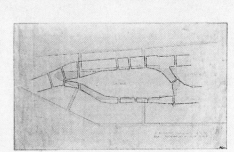

FIGURE 26. Island No. 1 Compared with Paris.

FIGURE 29.

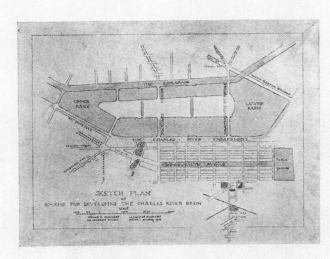

FIGURE 27. Island No. 2 and Surroundings.

FIGURE 31.

6.3 Rivers in Paris, London, Rome, and Hamburg were drawn at the same scale, to illustrate how an island in the basin would reduce the visual and physical separation of Boston and Cambridge and create "a feature of extraordinary beauty." Any city in Europe, said Cram, "would seize on such a chance with avidity."

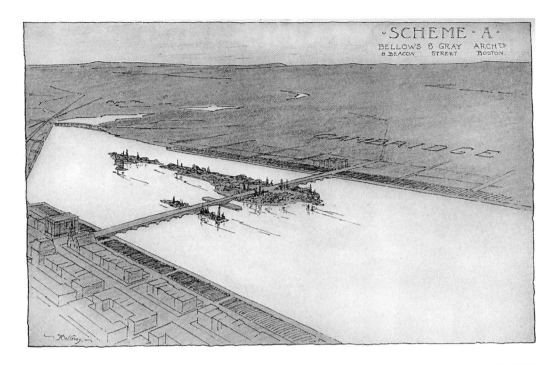

6.4 "A Small Island, For Recreation and Boating Purposes Only," Bellows & Gray Architects, 1911.

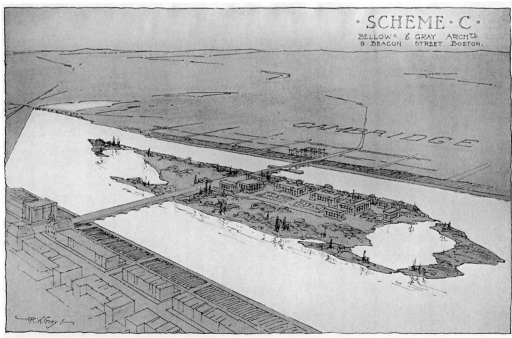

6.5 "Larger Island, For Recreation and Other Purposes," Bellows & Gray Architects, 1911. This scheme for an expandable island, the architects thought, might have particular appeal for MIT, long since overcrowded in a few buildings in Back Bay. The institute could make new land in the river as its departments grew.

In 1909, a group of seven Boston business and professional leaders held a dinner for about two hundred people to organize "Boston–1915." The seven included the lawyer Louis Brandeis and James Storrow, at the time president of the Boston Merchants Association; the active leadership of merchant Edward Filene earned for the group's objectives the nickname "the Filenium." Their intention was to develop an exposition for the city, "not an ordinary fair but a graphic display of a living, working city, a display of Boston as a going concern."[6]

A first exposition was held in November 1909 at the old Museum of Fine Arts building in Copley Square, with several hundred exhibits by public and private Boston organizations. The exhibits focused a disproportionate level of attention on the Charles River. The basin had a room of its own, with a dozen photographs of the Charles and the Alster Basin in Hamburg and a rendering of Cram's island proposal.[7]

Boston–1915 also began publishing a monthly journal called *New Boston* (figure 6.6), and in 1911 the magazine included a harshly critical article on the failure of the basin as a recreation area. In a subsequent issue, *New Boston* followed with essays by Shurcliff and Bellows on their island proposals and a detailed, illustrated description of the Alster Basin written by Arthur Comey, a landscape architect and planning consultant in Cambridge. Shorter articles endorsing the proposed basin development were written by Mayor John Fitzgerald and several other prominent Bostonians.[8]

One of the secretaries of Boston–1915 suggested putting aside the proposed capital improvements such as islands and parkways in favor of activities that might be organized and promoted immediately. His suggestions included band concerts, refreshments, fireworks, electrical displays, an annual "Charles River Basin Fete," official water sports contests, and moving pictures on floating screens. The subjects for moving pictures might include "tuberculosis, the safe and sane Fourth, pure milk and the fly, . . . historical pictures, views of other cities, city planning schemes and popular dramas and humorous pictures."[9]

6.6 In 1909, a group of Boston businessmen organized "Boston–1915," a campaign that was to culminate in an international exhibition. Their journal *New Boston* devoted considerable attention to improving the basin as a recreation space. The December 1910 issue included several essays about the basin and featured an island on the cover, with a biplane and a dirigible circling overhead. As the cover illustration revealed, island schemes focused on the center of the basin, rather than its edges. The narrow Boston Embankment (upper right) had just been filled.

After the end of the First World War, the idea of a memorial island in the Charles was revived again. The mayor of Boston appointed a committee for a veterans' memorial in 1921 chaired by the architect Charles Coolidge; its members included Cram, Shurcliff, and the sculptor Cyrus Dallin. The imposing memorial building proposed in their final report was to be constructed as part of a new Harvard Bridge (figure 6.7). Since the island would shorten the span of the bridge by eight hundred feet and reduce its estimated cost by $1,600,000, the memorial structure's projected cost of two million dollars would be nearly paid for. Five years later the MDC's annual report noted that proposals for islands and embankments either at the center of the basin or along the edges of the river had been widely discussed, to reduce the length and consequently the cost of bridge structures, since a bridge or tunnel at Dartmouth Street was thought to be needed sooner or later.[10] The *Cambridge Tribune* published another memorial proposal in 1928, with the observation that "people come here from the West and turn up their noses at the Charles river basin. They state flatly what they would do with that basin if people out West had the handling of it. It would be 'something else than a wash basin with some ducks in it.'"[11]

A more subtle design proposal was also never executed. With the basin no longer tidal following the completion of the dam, Olmsted's ingenious solution to the problem of salt water in the Muddy River was no longer necessary. In 1910 changes in the original design were recommended by John C. Olmsted, Frederick Law Olmsted, Jr., and Arthur Shurcliff. Their proposed revision was ignored, as was their 1921 proposal; instead the area was used as a dump for fill from subway construction.[12]

6.7 After the first World War, an island seemed to some an ideal place for a war memorial. This 1920 "Memorial to Boston Soldiers, Sailors and Marines" was recommended by a committee appointed by the mayor of Boston which included both Arthur Shurcliff and Ralph Adams Cram.

Even before the dam was approved, the plans for parks and parkways along the river had immediate consequences for the planning of Boston's universities. Under Charles W. Eliot, president from 1869 to 1909, Harvard had avoided buying land in Riverside, as the neighborhood south of Mt. Auburn Street was then called. However, the appeal of the area increased considerably as the Cambridge Park Department began work on the first section of Charles River Road (now Memorial Drive) and the Basin Commission was authorized to build the dam. Over a period of at least a decade Harvard asked several respected firms to prepare plans for connecting the Old Yard with the river; in addition, official and unofficial proposals were developed, not only for landscaped boulevards, but also for constructing new college buildings along the Charles.

Several of the university's consultants thought these efforts at campus planning were long overdue. After supervising the grounds of the college from 1887 to 1890, the landscape architect Charles Eliot (the president's son) concluded that "permitting donors of buildings and gates to choose their sites is fatal to general effect. Outside the quadrangle the Yard is already a jumble of badly placed buildings and roads."[13]

In the fall of 1894, the Board of Overseers approved two resolutions, one to develop a plan for Harvard's properties and the second recommending the appointment of an advisory committee to approve all plans for the future development of the university. The committee would be composed of members of Harvard's governing boards as well as appropriate professional advisors. The following spring the president and fellows rejected both ideas, but they did inform the overseers that they had solicited plans for open areas, roads, and future building sites from the Olmsted office, the architects Charles Follen McKim and H. H. Richardson, and others (figure 6.8).[14]

6.8 After some years of complaints, the Harvard Board of Overseers in 1894 determined to develop a plan for the university's growth. Two years later this plan was submitted by an unknown designer. It included an axis extending from Kirkland Street and Memorial Hall all the way to the river. A tree-lined boulevard opened onto semicircular plazas at Massachusetts Avenue and at the river parkway.

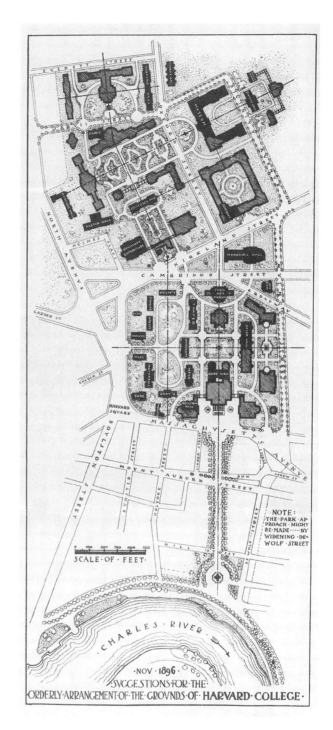

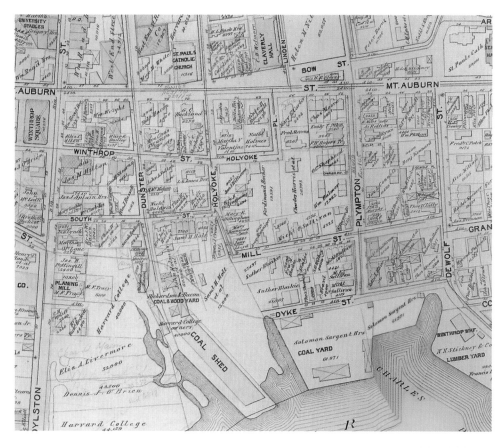

6.9 Although Harvard owned several parcels between the old yard and the river, the university actually sold land in that area as late as 1898. Most of the riverfront was in private hands.

6.10 By the 1890s several boathouses had been built between River Street and Boylston (now John F. Kennedy) Street, but commercial activities like coal and lumber yards dominated the riverfront. This photograph was taken from the smokestack of the West End Street Railway power plant, located across the road from the first Weld Boathouse (on the site of what is now Eliot House).

The following year Harvard's treasurer asked McKim (who had been a student at Harvard and was then living in New York) for a copy of a drawing that McKim had prepared sometime before. In his reply McKim described the plan's objectives, including "the possibility for a front door or connecting link" between the university and the river. A broad "alleyway," planted with elm trees four abreast like the Beacon Street Mall on Boston Common, would "afford numerous plots for the development of the University upon a definite system." When the plan was conceived, McKim had also asked about the likelihood of acquiring the whole area and demolishing what McKim disdainfully called the "inch-plank architecture" of the Riverside neighborhood (figure 6.9, 6.10). His recollection in 1896 was that the cost of acquiring the

entire district had been estimated at $450,000. McKim concluded his note with an observation about the university's haphazard building program: "What difficulties may stand in the way of this plan I do not know; but this I do know—that *some* plan is woefully needed at Harvard to restore, at least in a measure, the sense of order and repose which belong chiefly to her early buildings."[15]

The first Harvard buildings on the river were erected at Soldiers Field. Seventy acres of the Brighton marshlands had been donated by Henry Longfellow, his family, and a few friends in 1870; Henry Higginson had given another thirty-one acres in 1890 to honor six college classmates who had died in the Civil War. At the dedication of the field, Higginson gave what Samuel Eliot Morison later described as "one of the Major's simple, manly addresses." Higginson urged his listeners to remember that the fellows from Yale and Princeton were their brothers; Harvard should "beat them fairly if we can, and believe that they will play the game just as we do." He described the playing fields as a "great lovely plain, bordered by the sunset and other irreclaimable gifts of the sky and landscape, and set forever there in memory of valor and of love."[16]

The meadows would not remain an open "lovely plain" for long—Harvard began almost immediately to occupy the landscape with imposing, quite permanent structures for sports that demanded more than well-kept lawns. Carey Cage, completed in 1897, was the first university building designed by a member of the faculty of the School of Architecture. Newell Boathouse (1899) was the work of Robert Peabody, and replaced a long series of wooden boathouses on the river. Like the Carey Cage, it was built of concrete, a material that members of the engineering faculty were experimenting with; its facades and articulated roof were clad with slate shingles. Seven years later Peabody designed the Weld Boathouse, just downstream of the old wooden bridge at Boylston (now John F. Kennedy) Street and directly in front of the coal-burning power plant of the West End Street Railway (see figure 4.28).[17]

Nothing built since has matched the monumental change to the old Longfellow Meadow that came with the construction of the Harvard Stadium in 1902–1903 (figure 6.11). At the time the

6.11 The architects Charles McKim and Daniel Burnham were responsible for the Harvard stadium's system of classical proportions and its open orientation to the river, which created a striking setting not only for football but also for the occasional presentation of Greek theater at daybreak.

largest poured concrete structure in the world, the stadium has been described as "functionally almost perfect, structurally innovated and aesthetically advanced." And it was built in the middle of an extended, passionately argued debate on college sports in general and football in particular. Teddy Roosevelt convened a meeting on the subject at the White House and invited representatives from Harvard, Yale, and Princeton. The Harvard faculty voted more than once to drop football; President Eliot, in a section of his 1903–1904 annual report titled "The Evils of Football," wrote that "worse preparation for the real struggles and contests of life can hardly be imagined." Yet the stadium was built.[18]

A collaboration of professors in architecture, civil, and mechanical engineering, the stadium involved new techniques for pouring and erecting concrete that required modification during the course of construction. The system of classical proportions, and the decision to orient the open end of the stadium to the river, were contributed by McKim and Daniel Burnham.[19]

The athletic facilities at Soldiers Field accelerated the interest in connecting the Old Yard and Massachusetts Avenue with the river parkway and the stadium. The Olmsted office prepared one approach based on widening DeWolfe Street (figure 6.12); a later plan drew a straight axis tying the river with the buildings in the Old Yard (figure 6.13). In 1902 Harvard alumni raised $50,000 and proposed to enlarge and landscape DeWolfe Street, with the city, the state, and the Metropolitan Park Commission also contributing.[20]

The appeal of axial spatial arrangement taught at the Ecole des Beaux Arts in Paris was reinforced by the publicity surrounding the planning for Stanford University by Olmsted and Charles Coolidge (1886–1888) and for the University of Chicago by Henry Ives Cobb (1893). At Harvard it was manifest not only in most of the proposed street alterations, but also in the surviving proposals for buildings along the river from the time of McKim's letter until the final drawings for new freshman dormitories were completed in 1912. An unsigned drawing, perhaps by Charles Wetmore and probably completed before 1902, shows a massive open quadrangle facing the river, with buildings disposed symmetrically around the edges. A large new bridge crosses the river at Dunster Street, just downstream from the old span. A 1909 drawing by Wetmore's firm retains the grand quadrangle and the new bridge, with a new boulevard ending in an arc of ninety degrees to provide an imposing entrance to the new stadium (figure 6.14).[21] Even the early sketches done by Charles Coolidge after his firm was selected to design the new dormitories were organized on a grid plan, with only the roadway following the bend of the river.

None of these plans would be realized, however, unless the university acquired the land. This President Eliot was reluctant to do because of the increasing hostitlity in Cambridge to any plan that would increase the amount of tax-exempt property. A 1909 *Harper's* article, which accompanied the Wetmore drawing of the river properties, indicated that state legislation was pending to increase the taxation on educational institutions (the article also noted that as early as 1895, Wetmore commenced buying property in the area with a view to "making the development on a dividend-paying basis"). As late as 1898, Harvard sold land between

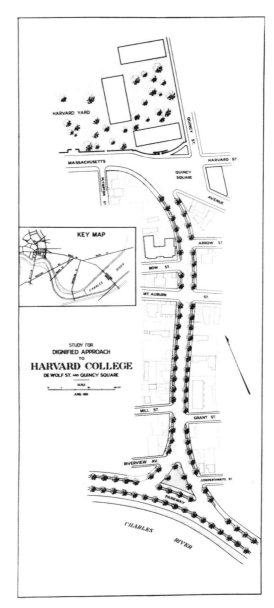

6.12 Frederick Law Olmsted, Jr., and John C. Olmsted completed a series of studies for "A Dignified Approach to Harvard College." Drawings in 1897 considered the widening of DeWolfe and Plympton Streets, maintaining a straight connection between Massachusetts Avenue and the Charles; a study four years later took a less formal approach to widening DeWolfe Street, with the road curved and planted at both ends, obscuring a direct view of the river.

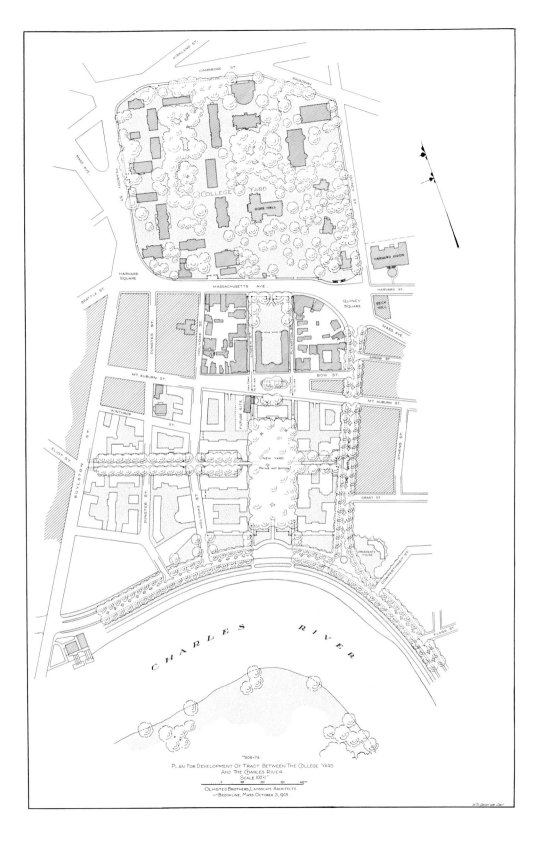

6.13 A 1903 plan by Olmsted Brothers for the development of the Riverside lands closely follows their earlier map and does not include the parcel owned by the West End Street Railway (now the site of Eliot House). Plympton Street, closed in the plan, was to become the center of the "New Yard," with irregularly shaped buildings (much more irregular than in the Old Yard) grouped on either side. A long, tree-lined pedestrian axis extended from DeWolfe to Boylston Street.

6.14 The New York architects Warren and Wetmore produced the most grandiose riverside plan in 1909, with "The Great Projected Quadrangle, the Memorial Bridge, and the Boulevard to the Stadium." The quadrangle was twice the width proposed by the Olmsteds, with nine almost identical buildings in straight rows along the three closed sides. A new bridge extends from the west side of the quadrangle, and the road across the river bends ninety degrees to an oval plaza on the broad side of the stadium (which is closed on the river side).

Massachusetts Avenue and the river. Eliot had determined that the opportunity could not be addressed immediately, or he knew that a group of alumni would act instead—which they soon did. Edward Forbes had been an undergraduate at Harvard from 1891 to 1895, when some of the university's early plans for building in Riverside were first discussed, and by the time he returned to Cambridge after two years at Oxford he was convinced that the university ought to "make use of the Charles River as did Oxford, of its river." The director of the Fogg Museum from 1909 to 1944, Forbes had a love of the visual arts that included a concern for landscape architecture and city planning. In the late 1890s he helped to secure Governor Hutchinson's Field in Milton for the Trustees of Reservations.[22]

When Forbes's brother Cameron heard about the proposed widening of DeWolfe Street in 1902, he wrote Edward from Florence and suggested that a group of ten men each contribute fifty thousand dollars "to buy the land to be improved, not only by this boulevard but by the river park." Soon thereafter Edward organized the Harvard Riverside Associates, and an acquisition plan was completed by January of the following year. The area bounded by the river and Boylston, Mt. Auburn, and DeWolfe Streets totaled almost 610,000 square feet, only 141,000 square feet of which were owned by Harvard or by university-related student clubs. Forbes solicited letters endorsing the plan from Charles Eliot Norton, Henry Higginson, and President Eliot, who made it clear that the university would not provide any funds. By mid-March of 1903, the associates had raised $100,000 and had acquired two-thirds of the planned 468,000 square feet of land (figure 6.15).[23] Although the project was private, its public benefits were immediately endorsed in the press. When the plan was made public in the *Boston Globe* in mid-March, the paper noted that "the value of the

6.15 An undated map shows the land owned, optioned, or purchased by the Harvard Riverside Associates, a group organized by Edward Forbes. Two-thirds of the property bounded by Boylston, Mount Auburn, and DeWolfe Streets was acquired and then donated, with restrictive covenants, to the university. The green line on the map indicates the outline of the "New Yard," where the Harvard houses were later built.

broad open space in front of the college buildings can hardly be estimated. It would make it possible to drive the entire length of Cambridge without leaving the park system."[24]

The associates turned over the land to the university when planning was begun for freshman dormitories along the river but retained the right to review the architectural proposals (figure 6.16). They required that part of the land be kept open and that vistas to the river and the parkway be developed; they also participated actively in the design process for the new buildings, which were completed in 1913 (figures 6.17, 6.18). A formal visual connection linking the river with Harvard Yard, however, was never built.[25]

Five years before, a graduate program in business administration was organized. Those opposed to it assumed, as Morison noted in the university's tercentenary history, "that it was to be a mere school of successful money-making," which Morison admitted "has not been absent from the students' minds." In fact, the program was so popular that it almost immediately outgrew its temporary home on the top floor of Widener Library. The university turned its attention to the eastern half of the Brighton marshes (figure 6.19) and held a design competition, won by the New York firm of McKim, Mead and White (figures 6.20–6.22). A single donor, the New York banker George F. Baker, gave the entire estimated cost of five million dollars, and the new campus was dedicated in 1927.[26] The fictional George Apley had earlier supported the Charles River Dam; he later wrote his son that the new school of business was "one of the most damnable examples of the materialism which we face." He had, "of course," not seen it, and when he motored by it he "looked the other way." George Baker took the opposite view, suggesting at the time of his gift that the school would "give a new start to better business standards."[27]

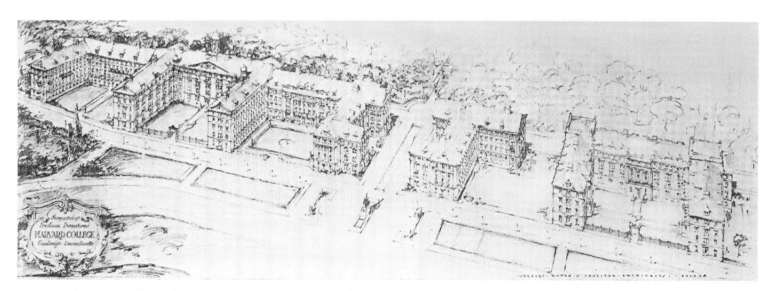

6.16 An early sketch by Charles Coolidge retained the axial planning of earlier riverfront schemes, with the new freshman dormitories lined up in a row along a straight street set back from Charles River Road, the city's new parkway (renamed Memorial Drive in 1923), which followed the curve of the river.

6.17 The final design for Smith, Standish, and Gore Halls eliminated the separate, straight roadway and reoriented Standish Hall to follow the curve of the parkway and the river. McKinlock Hall (right) was completed in 1925.

6.18 This aerial view from about 1920 shows the Weld Boathouse, the Boston Elevated power plant, and Smith Hall on Boylston Street, with the subway yards across the street. On the other side of the river temporary bleachers have closed in the north end of Harvard Stadium.

6.19 The Brighton marshes were almost entirely open in 1875, when this photograph was taken from Harvard's nearly completed Memorial Hall. Gore Hall (now the site of Widener Library) and Boylston Hall mark the edge of what would become the college's "New Yard" (right center).

6.20 In the competition for the design of the Harvard Business School, the plan by Charles Coolidge was drawn to show the relationship of the new campus to the stadium across the street and to the dormitories Coolidge had designed on the north side of the river.

6.21 Coolidge's design, which was not chosen, was organized around a large quadrangle on which the library faced. Smaller irregular quadrangles were created by the dormitories and classroom buildings. An allée of trees between the dormitories led to the river, which was almost invisible from the central open space.

6.22 The winning design for the Business School, by the New York firm of McKim, Mead & White, also located a quadrangle in front of the library, but turned the library to face the Charles; the dormitories were splayed slightly to follow the curve of the river. Large tracts of land nearby were occupied by industrial structures and rail yards in this 1955 photograph—and still are today.

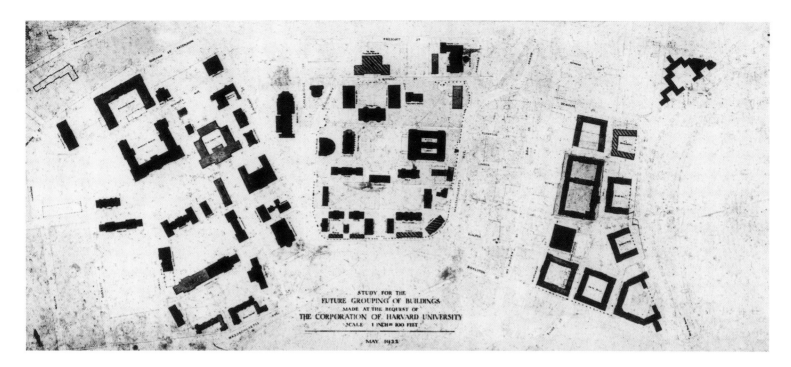

STUDY FOR THE
FUTURE GROUPING OF BUILDINGS
MADE AT THE REQUEST OF
THE CORPORATION OF HARVARD UNIVERSITY
SCALE 1 INCH = 100 FEET

MAY 1922

The freshmen dormitories and the new business school were far from the end of President Lowell's ambitions for the riverfront. In a speech in 1907, before he became president, Lowell asserted that the university needed to establish "a group of colleges, each of which will be national and democratic." Harvard should eliminate the exclusive private dormitories that Wetmore and other investors had been providing for the sons of wealthy families since the late 1880s and, by bringing students and faculty together in their daily lives, restore the spirit that had animated the college when its extent was limited to the Old Yard. Yet Lowell believed that such a drastic alteration in the college's structure could not be made all at once, and he carefully referred to the three new dormitories as "freshman halls."[28]

The idea of residential colleges was as old as Oxford and Cambridge. Woodrow Wilson, during his tenure as president of Princeton, had promoted a college plan at the turn of the century, and Yale was offered the funds to implement such a plan by Edward Harkness, a Yale graduate, in 1926. When Yale dallied,

6.23 President Lowell had planned the freshman dormitories along the river with the hope of making them into residential houses for upperclassmen modeled on the colleges of Oxford and Cambridge. By 1922, seven years before President Lowell presented the proposal to the faculty, Charles Coolidge had resolved the essential elements of the site plan for the river houses.

Harkness requested an appointment with Lowell in October 1928. Three months later, the *New York Times* announced that Harvard had accepted a pledge from Harkness of more than eleven million dollars to build seven colleges. Douglass Shand-Tucci, who has carefully documented the creation and design of the colleges, suggests that "the witticism that Lowell had realized Princeton's idea with Yale's money is very nearly the truth."[29]

In the end, Lowell's democratic aims were reflected in a considerable alteration to the grandiose, axial designs that had dominated the university's early plans along the Charles (figures 6.23–6.25). The new buildings were aligned to follow the curve of the parkway, bringing them in much closer relation to the public space along the water's edge.

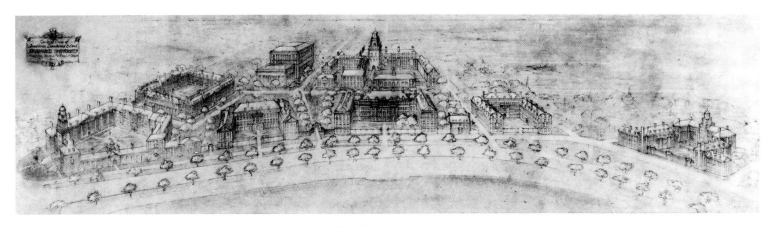

6.24 This 1928 rendering shows how the new buildings were added beside and behind the earlier dormitories. DeWolfe and Plympton Streets remained open, but the idea of a formal connection to the Old Yard was abandoned. Holyoke, Dunster, and Linden Streets were closed between Winthrop Street and the river, heightening (even after the gates of the quadrangles facing the river were kept locked) the sense of a grand pedestrian boulevard along Memorial Drive.

6.25 The triangular parcel on which Dunster House was built called for a much more complex massing to meet the house's spatial requirements. The architect Hugh Shepley succeeded not only in creating a central quadrangle and two smaller spaces facing the river, a variation on the open spaces of the earlier freshman dormitories; he also stepped the roof lines on either side of the tower to meet the residences on the adjoining blocks—a striking contrast to the simpler massing of the earlier structures.

MIT Moves to Cambridge

Unlike Harvard's acquisition of property along the river, which was conducted under the cover of anonymous real estate agents, the decision of MIT to move to Cambridge was the subject of very public discussion. Incorporated in 1861, the Massachusetts Institute of Technology offered its first classes four years later. By the turn of the century, the institute had clearly outgrown its limited space in the Back Bay. Although the school had by now trained some of the country's best-known engineers, MIT was not wealthy, certainly not by the standards of many of the much older New England colleges. Charles W. Eliot taught chemistry at MIT for four years before accepting the presidency at Harvard in 1869, and he recognized the success of the institute, in particular by comparison with Harvard's struggling Lawrence Scientific School. He proposed a merger to each of the four new presidents of the institute between 1870 and 1900, and his fourth proposal in 1900 became entangled with MIT's search for a new campus.[30]

Henry Pritchett, who became president in that year (and who was appointed to chair the commission on the proposed Charles River dam established the following year), endorsed the plan to move the institute from the Back Bay to a location still to be determined in his annual report of 1902. Apparently no action was taken during the next year, but in January 1904 the *Boston Daily Advertiser* announced that the institute and Harvard had agreed to merge. The school's faculty and staff vigorously protested, but upriver, anticipating that MIT would approve the merger, a group of men that included Henry Higginson and Andrew Carnegie purchased the riverfront property in Brighton east of Soldiers Field as the site for the institute's new campus (the site later built upon by the Harvard Business School, figure 6.19). After more than a year of debate, the MIT faculty voted against the merger by a margin of fifty-six to seven. About 3,200 alumni were invited to send in ballots; 2,900 voted, of which 2,035 were opposed. The Technology Corporation nonetheless approved the merger, twenty-three to fifteen, in June 1905.[31]

In September the state's Supreme Judicial Court denied the institute's title to the land it occupied on Boylston Street in Boston (which had been purchased with funds MIT received as a land-grant college) and enjoined the corporation from either selling the property or building new structures on the land. Without the anticipated proceeds from the sale of its old site, the school was unable to execute the merger. As the champion of the now-rejected agreement, Pritchett resigned.[32]

When Richard Maclaurin assumed the presidency two years later, the search for a site remained unresolved. In April 1909, Charles Stone, a founding partner in the firm of Stone & Webster, invited Maclaurin to dinner at his home on the water side of Beacon Street. They could see the Embankment Company site in Cambridge that had been rejected by the institute before Pritchett resigned (figures 6.26, 6.27). Stone explained that the city would oppose any move that would create more tax-exempt property; it would likely create problems with Harvard as well. In June Harvard awarded Maclaurin an honorary degree, only to follow with a letter from President Lowell a few days later saying that choosing a Cambridge site "would not improbably imperil the

6.26 During the depression of 1893 the Embankment Company went bankrupt. As late as 1910 only a few buildings occupied the Cambridge Esplanade, which extended from the Cambridge (now Longfellow) Bridge almost to Brookline Street. Though most of the buildings were red brick, the International Shoe and Leather Exposition Building of 1908, designed by Edward Graham, was covered with white stucco, a hint of things to come.

6.27 Almost all the lots of the Cambridge Embankment Company remained vacant for the next twenty years. Harvard's President Eliot proposed a merger to MIT, which included an offer of the site later occupied by the Harvard Business School. When that agreement was rejected by the MIT faculty and alumni, the president of MIT resigned, and the new president began negotiations for the Cambridge esplanade property, shown here (upper left) in 1907, looking downstream from the railroad overpass near the Cottage Farm Bridge.

financial stability of both institutions" and might result in a loss of the tax exemption for all educational institutions.[33]

In October of that year a group that included Arthur Shurcliff and the architect Walter Kilham (probably functioning as a site selection committee, although the document is not titled) filed a report with Maclaurin that analyzed various sites in the Boston area. Their review was based on four considerations: accessibility for students, faculty, and the public; the potential to construct a dignified group of buildings "worthy of the institute's importance"; a price that would not use up the funds for buildings and equipment; finally (in an obvious reference to their failed negotiations with Harvard, and perhaps to the land in Brighton purchased by Higginson, Carnegie, and others), a location that would be "independent of the influence of other institutions."[34]

The group reviewed eleven sites, including two adjoining Huntington Avenue, one in West Roxbury, one in Dorchester, and three along the Fenway. Thirteen other sites were "not seriously investigated," including the possibility of an island in the Charles River Basin. They concluded that only three merited further review: the Allston Golf Course, the Riverbank site (the report's designation of the Cambridge Esplanade), and the Fenway parcel (located at the corner of Longwood Avenue and Avenue Louis Pasteur, near the new Harvard Medical School campus as well as a number of other colleges). In their view, the Allston property was "liable to deteriorate in importance." The Fenway was, on the whole, the best site in terms of size, location, and the possibilities for development, which they measured against the new standards of the "City Beautiful": The new institute campus would be "one more group of semi-public buildings in that locality and practically establish an interesting civic center." Their discussion of the Riverbank property was largely a list of problems: the cost of land, the number of owners, the "encroaching manufacturing district," the nearness to Harvard, and Cambridge's objection to more untaxed real estate.[35]

Although a final site decision was not yet made, Maclaurin solicited a contribution toward the new campus from Andrew Carnegie two months later. He was turned down. Carnegie pointed out that he had just given $3,800,000 to the Institute of Technology in Pittsburgh, and he did not "put the Pittsburgh school behind even the Massachusetts Institute of Technology." He added in a postscript: "If I mistake not, I am a part owner of that ground that my friend Lee Higginson and some of us purchased to unite the two institutions, *which should be done*." Maclaurin then approached Coleman duPont of the class of 1884, who offered $500,000 toward the purchase of the Commonwealth Avenue site in Allston.[36]

Perhaps hoping to encourage local support, Maclaurin told a reporter that MIT might have to move where the cost of living was within the school's means. The comment spread, and almost immediately the city of Springfield offered a site. The *Chicago Evening Post* claimed that "We could support a 'Boston Tech' with our loose change, and we wouldn't, like some cities we know of, have to search all the hinterland roundabout to find the money." A spate of letters in support of the institute was directed to Maclaurin, from the mayor and other Cambridge residents.

George Cox, a longtime member of the Cambridge Park Commission, wrote that he had spent nineteen years on "the development of the Cambridge shore, the Dam and the Drawless Bridge. The Basin is the future great water park of Metropolitan Boston, and its proper treatment demands the erection of handsome buildings facing it." The tax question should not even be raised, he said, since the institute would attract taxable property far in excess of the land to be occupied by the school. The conditions at Kendall Square were "quite the reverse from the situation in and about Harvard Square."[37]

The Cambridge City Council passed a resolution in support of a local site, and duPont offered to amend his pledge to contribute to the Embankment property. In March, Maclaurin received a formal resolution from the president and fellows of Harvard College indicating that the president of Harvard should notify the president of MIT that "the Corporation withdraws any objection . . . raised on the ground that the exemption from taxation . . . might endanger the stability of the existing provisions relieving educational institutions from taxation." By the fall of 1911, negotiations were completed with the thirty-five owners of the Cambridge property.[38]

With the site chosen (although not yet announced), Maclaurin embarked on a fund-raising tour that winter to raise money for the new buildings. When he visited Rochester, where a number of MIT graduates were employed at the Eastman Kodak Company, he found that George Eastman was out of town. A meeting of the two men was quickly arranged in New York City, and Eastman pledged $2,500,000. Eastman insisted that the gift remain anonymous, and until 1920 only Maclaurin's wife and secretary (and two of the staff at Kodak) knew the donor; for seven years he was identified as "Mr. Smith."[39]

Only a month after Eastman's pledge, Hiram Mills, one of the institute's distinguished engineering graduates, declined Maclaurin's invitation to contribute ten thousand dollars to the new campus and questioned the structural integrity of the Cambridge site. Although it seems to have created little alarm among the administration, Mills replied to the solicitation by saying that he was unable to advise his friends "to put money into permanent buildings for an institution which by the time it gets to be vigorously performing its use is faced by a continually increasing expense to protect it against the encroachments of the sea, with a distant future when submergence is inevitable."[40]

Mills thought that the "general subsidence of this region" had been sufficient to eliminate the site from consideration, and recent evidence, in his view, only confirmed the hazard. The storage warehouse on Vassar Street had sunk 1.19 feet since its construction, and the metropolitan sewer running through the site was two feet lower after only thirteen years. In his reply to Maclaurin, Mills pointed out that he had recently spoken to one of Maclaurin's advisers. He had plainly said that the proposed campus was within two feet of extreme high tide, and that "before this site has been a seat of learning as long as have been Oxford and Cambridge the extreme high tides will rise to be five feet above the level of the ground here." The advisor's response, according to Mills, was that the school "must not try to look farther ahead than a century or two." The Cambridge property was "unquestionably unfit" for its intended purpose, in Mill's opinion, and his "promptings as an engineer" urged on Mills the burden of asking that, even at this late date, the mistake of choosing the site be corrected.[41]

At some point Maclaurin asked John Freeman (who had directed the study of the proposed Charles River dam in 1901–1902, served as a member of the MIT Corporation, and been president of the alumni association) to evaluate the load-bearing capacity of the site. Freeman not only evaluated the site but produced a plan for the new school, accompanied by a withering indictment of the usual architectural approach to such problems. The typical campus reflected a completely unnecessary deference to the "motive of monumentality" (a phrase that recalls Charles Eliot's criticism of Harvard administrators for allowing donors to determine the size and siting of buildings). If MIT were willing to consider what industrial engineers had learned about modular design and the flow of people and goods in complex processes, the institute could bring about "a vast improvement in the efficiency of college architecture."[42]

Colleges built structures "of widely different architectural types scattered over a campus," wrote Freeman, with "each department, so far as possible, isolated and housed in a separate building so that the professor in charge . . . reigns undisturbed, in a little kingdom of his own, [while] the undergraduate student . . . spends some valuable time and runs much risk of colds in our northern climate, in passing from one lecture to another." The student does benefit from fresh air, "which becomes of greater importance by reason of the wretched ventilation that commonly prevails in college lecture rooms and laboratories. . . ." Freeman indicated, in fact, that he hoped to be named the architect for the new campus.[43]

The concerns of Mills and Freeman are are now only curious footnotes in the story of MIT's renowned riverfront campus. Yet they were following their best professional judgment; Maclaurin was left to resolve their profound professional disagreements.

At some point Maclaurin promised the faculty and alumni that the school would not build factory buildings or skyscrapers, but would create a "great white city" on the river—precisely the approach to architecture that Freeman had railed against. Preliminary studies were completed by Desire Despradelle, a member of the architecture faculty, but following his death in 1912 the institute gave the commission to Wells Bosworth, a graduate of MIT (1889) and of the Ecole des Beaux Arts. In announcing the selection of Bosworth, Maclaurin described his skill in landscape and exposition design, and his ability to bring simplicity and grandeur to the site.[44]

As the design was progressing, Bosworth persuaded Maclaurin and Charles Stone to travel with him to inspect Thomas Jefferson's "academical village" at the University of Virginia. It was, however, the visual focus of the domed library and not the openness of "the Lawn" that Bosworth saw in Charlottesville. In his MIT plan, the space under the dome was to be occupied by the principal auditorium; when that was deleted to save money, he moved the library there to preserve the form.[45]

Bosworth departed from the American college tradition in two fundamental ways. First, he proposed one great structure organized on a grid with connecting corridors, rather than a series

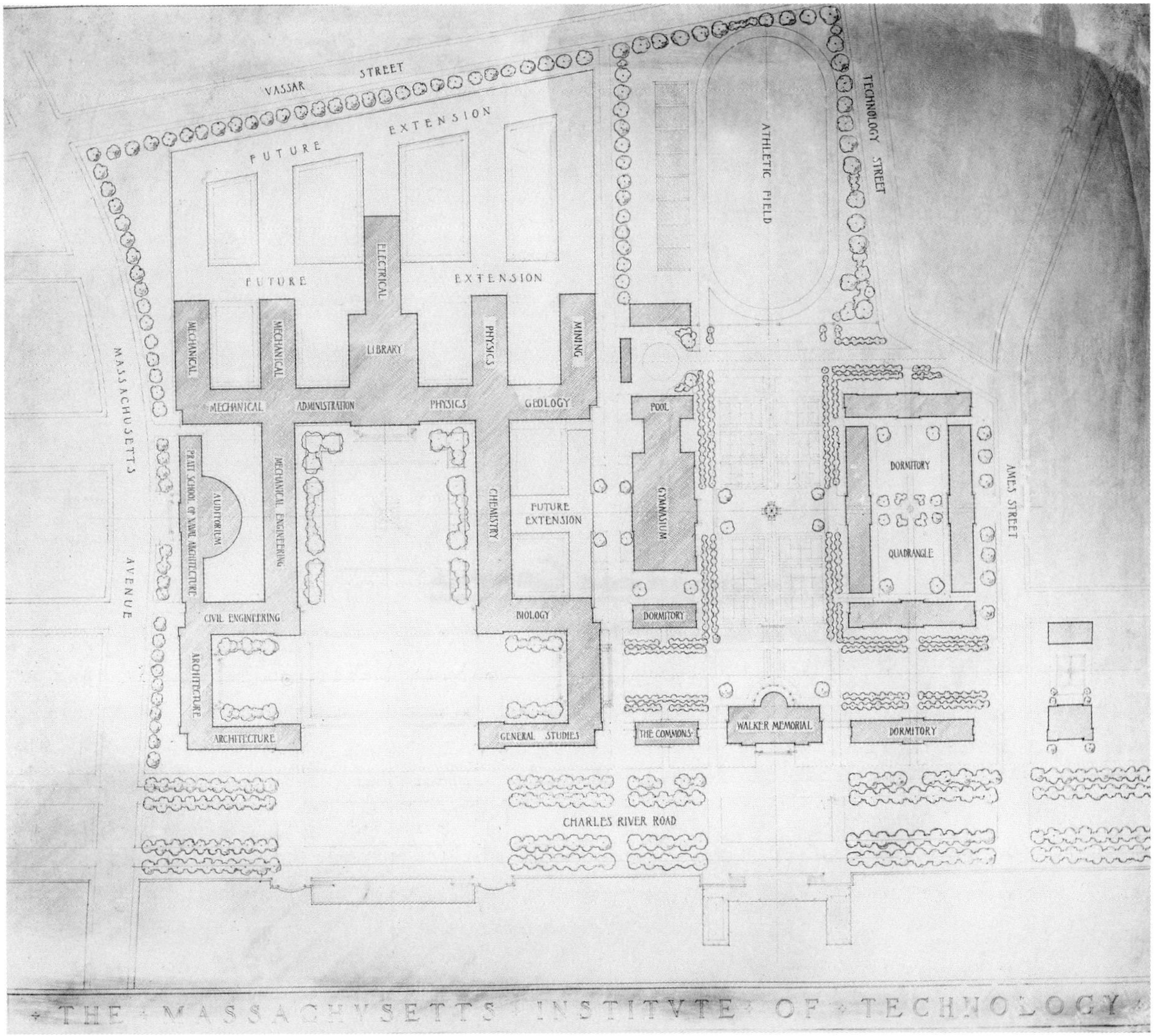
VASSAR STREET
FUTURE EXTENSION
FUTURE EXTENSION
ELECTRICAL
LIBRARY
MECHANICAL
MECHANICAL
PHYSICS
MINING
MECHANICAL
ADMINISTRATION
PHYSICS
GEOLOGY
ATHLETIC FIELD
TECHNOLOGY STREET
POOL
GYMNASIUM
DORMITORY
QUADRANGLE
AMES STREET
MASSACHUSETTS AVENUE
PRATT SCHOOL OF NAVAL ARCHITECTURE
AUDITORIUM
MECHANICAL ENGINEERING
CHEMISTRY
FUTURE EXTENSION
CIVIL ENGINEERING
BIOLOGY
DORMITORY
ARCHITECTURE
ARCHITECTURE
GENERAL STUDIES
THE COMMONS
WALKER MEMORIAL
DORMITORY
CHARLES RIVER ROAD
THE MASSACHVSETTS INSTITVTE OF TECHNOLOGY

6.28 President Maclaurin promised the faculty a “great white city” on the river, and hired Wells Bosworth, an alumnus and graduate of the Ecole des Beaux Arts in Paris, to design the new campus. His plan organized a connected grid of buildings around a central “Great Court” facing the Charles.

of separate buildings (figures 6.28, 6.29). He may, in fact, have been apprised of Freeman's suggestions. The plan left several of the small quadrangles completely enclosed and also created what came to be called the "infinite corridor," extending over three hundred feet from Massachusetts Avenue to the colonnade facing the Great Court and continuing another three hundred feet beyond. The movement of students and faculty happened as much within the buildings as between them. Second, Bosworth's sketches of the severe exterior landscape recalled Mediterranean temples, not a sylvan New World campus. The plan for the Great Court on the river side of the dome included an imposing statue of Athena, but few plantings and almost no lawn. Photographs at the time of the dedication of the campus in 1916 show the expanse of the Great Court with a gravel surface (figures 6.31, 6.32). By the mid-1920s, the gravel had been replaced with grass.[46]

The design for the Great Court and for Walker Memorial also proposed a series of sharply defined terraces that opened onto the river (figures 6.29, 6.30, 6.32). The rows of trees along the embankment road and the uniform line of the seawall were broken, and a pair of stairs framed a long, narrow platform on the water's edge. Even without this more dramatic embrace of the river, Bosworth's architectural Great Court is a fitting complement to Eliot's vision of the Charles as the "court of honor" of the metropolitan district (figure 6.33).

6.29   The classical aura of the Great Court was heightened by the placement of a large statue of Athena in front of the domed main building and by the paved, almost unplanted terraces that stepped down to a boat landing along the water. Automobiles and trees are completely absent from the center of the Esplanade.

6.30 Like the Great Court, Bosworth's design for the Walker Memorial cut through the seawall along Charles River Road (now Memorial Drive) to create a grand staircase down to the river.

6.31 Ralph Adams Cram, who taught in the architecture department at MIT, designed an elaborate barge called the *Bucentaur* to carry the school's charter across the Charles for the dedication of the new campus in 1916.

6.32 Paving and gravel were the primary materials in the Great Court (foreground) and the flanking side courts at the time of their completion, although they were later replaced with lawn.

PROPOSED TREATMENT FOR CAMBRIDGE SHORE FRONT
CHARLES RIVER BASIN
WITH WATER COURT FOR MASS. INSTITUTE OF TECHNOLOGY

6.33 Although Bosworth's plans to step down to the river were not built, even more elaborate schemes to connect to the Charles were later suggested. Several, including this perspective by Arthur Shurcliff, suggested filling the Great Court with water and linking it to the Charles via an inlet under the parkway.

About the same time MIT's classical campus was conceived, and not long after the publication of the island scheme by Ralph Adams Cram for a new St. Paul's Cathedral, a Gothic tower along the river was actually constructed—on solid ground and designed by another Boston architect, R. Clipson Sturgis, for the Perkins School for the Blind. The school was incorporated in 1829 and opened in Boston three years later. After a series of moves, Perkins acquired thirty-odd acres for a new campus in Watertown, which opened in 1912. The focal point of the school is the central stone tower sited on a low hill overlooking one of the most tranquil bends in the basin (figures 6.34, 6.35).[47]

Ten years later, Boston University also adopted the Gothic style for its newly purchased riverfront property along Bay State Road, just downstream of the Beacon Trotting Park, by now the yards of the Boston & Albany Railroad (figures 6.36, 6.37). Founded in 1869, only eight years after the first classes were held at MIT, Boston University began its life in a series of buildings scattered on Beacon Hill. The center of gravity of the university shifted westward to Copley Square in 1907, when the old home of the Harvard Medical School on Boylston Street was acquired. A number of departments moved from other locations to the 1883 building, located behind the magisterial new Boston Public Library.[48]

For decades, the school lived on the edge of insolvency, frequently running deficits from year to year. Lemuel Murlin, who became president in 1911, aspired not only to end the annual losses and to raise faculty salaries, but to make the university one of "the four or five dominating factors in the material, intellectual, and spiritual life of Boston." A significant part of that ambition was Murlin's plan for a new campus. In 1919 he told the trustees that it was time for the university to find "a permanent location with reference to the future development of the city of Boston and the University's position therein."[49]

Less than a year later, the university purchased fifteen acres of land between Commonwealth Avenue and the Charles, extending west from Granby Street to the Cottage Farm Bridge. Three acres

6.34 The Perkins School dominates the narrow river channel above the Arsenal and was even more imposing before the trees obscured the massing of the structure.

6.35 The landmark along the recently completed river parkway in Newton in this view from the early 1920s was the tower of the Perkins School.

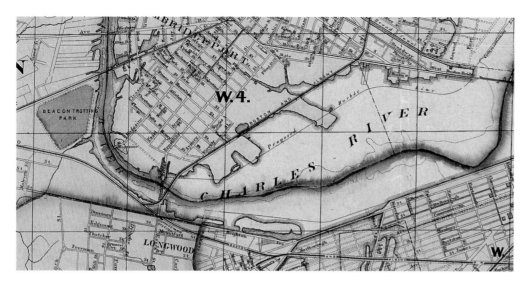

6.36 As late as 1875, Longwood was a peaceful, almost rural suburb near the Charles (lower left). The Boston & Albany Railroad had taken over the line that passed under the Cottage Farm Bridge, but the Beacon Trotting Park (left) still occupied the large riverfront property south of River Street. The irregular mudflats extending upriver along Brighton Avenue in Boston were filled in as part of the development of Bay State Road by Charles Francis Adams and his brother John Quincy Adams II in 1889–1894.

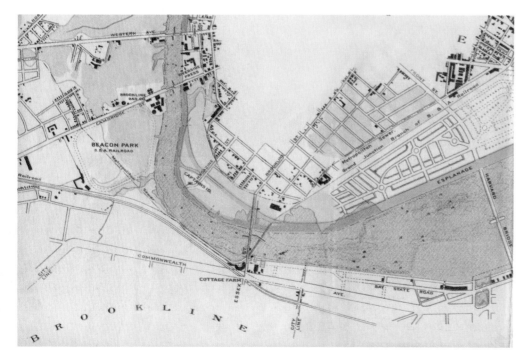

6.37 By 1894, the trotting park had become the Beacon Park yards of the Boston & Albany Railroad, with a roundhouse just upstream of the Cottage Farm Bridge. Boston University purchased fifteen acres immediately downstream of the bridge in 1920 and announced a new plan for the campus two years later.

of vacant land and an acre of tidal flats were acquired from the Riverbank Improvement Company, developers of rowhouses in the area between Deerfield Street and the Cottage Farm Bridge; the other twelve acres, held by twenty-six different owners, included four apartment houses and twelve private residents. Title to the company land included deed restrictions against commercial development, which restricted the height of buildings and reduced the purchase price.[50]

In 1921, Murlin determined that the new campus would require a substantial increase in the endowment. The following year he unveiled a campus plan, which would be dominated by a 400-foot-high tower modeled on St. Botolph's Church in Boston, England (figure 6.38). The fund-raising effort, however, proved exhausting, and the campaign did not raise enough money to begin the new campus; Murlin resigned in 1924.[51]

The depth of the original site between Commonwealth Avenue and the river was shallow, given the university's ambitious plans, although a hundred-foot-wide extension was filled to form a riverside terrace. About 1928 the university successfully petitioned the Boston Zoning Board to raise the height limit from 80 to 155 feet; in October of that year, Daniel Marsh, the new president, released a campus plan prepared by Cram & Ferguson. The future campus was reduced when the MDC made land takings in the 1920s to extend Soldiers Field Road, the planned riverside parkway. The Metropolitan Park Commission had clearly set out its intentions in 1893 to acquire the entire shoreline of the Charles Basin and had made similar takings from Harvard beginning in 1895; Boston University may have been surprised nonetheless by the takings in the 1920s. It is certain that the reduction in available land heightened an already difficult problem for the university's architects. When the MDC offered $25,000 for the loss of land and tidal flats, the university's treasurer countered with a figure of $100,000. That amount was rejected by the MDC, and the university sued. A superior court decision awarded the university $390,000, and the amount was affirmed on appeal.[52]

Daniel Marsh, Murlin's successor, faced the problem of paying the debt from the land acquisition during the Great Depression,

6.38 In a 1923 fund-raising publication, a bird's-eye view of the future Boston University campus underscored the school's role "in service to the city."

and several times the trustees recommended selling the riverfront site. As it happened, the decision to build along the Charles was hastened by MIT. For some years Boston University had rented the Rogers Building on Boylston Street, which MIT still owned. Then in 1938, apparently without warning, the building was sold and the university was given six months' notice to vacate. The Hayden Memorial Building, the first new structure on the Charles River campus, was rushed to completion the following year (figure 6.39).[53]

The university published a revised master plan in 1940, along with drawings and a model of the entire site (figures 6.40–6.41). A joint effort of Cram and Ferguson with Coolidge Shepley Bulfinch and Abbott, the design realized Murlin's original commitment to Collegiate Gothic. The revised 1940 site plan made plain the narrowness of the site; the quadrangles extending east and west of the chapel pushed the buildings to the edge of Commonwealth Avenue and Bay State Road. In a none too subtle marking of the physical context of the site, the published plan also suggested the academic standing to which the university aspired: Arrows on the river side of the campus pointed upriver toward Harvard and downstream toward MIT.[54]

6.40 The centerpiece of the revised 1940 plan by Ralph Adams Cram was a Gothic tower intended to recall St. Botolph's church in Boston, England. A parkway ran along the river's edge.

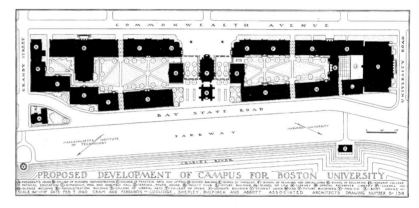

6.41 In the 1940 site plan, arrows point up- and downstream toward the campuses of Harvard and MIT.

6.39 Shocked by an eviction notice from MIT in 1938, Boston University had only a year to vacate the old Rogers Building on Boylston Street and to complete the Hayden Building (right center), the first structure on the school's riverfront property. After the First World War, Commonwealth Avenue attracted a long line of automobile showrooms and related businesses, including the New England headquarters for Shell Oil (left center; the Shell sign was relocated to the Cambridge side of the river in 1944). Down the street was a Howard Johnson's coffee shop.

In April 1928 a new commission was approved by the legislature to consider developing the Charles River Basin. Its objectives were to develop parks, playgrounds, beaches, and promenades along the river; to complete the parkway system connecting Watertown Square with Boston and Cambridge; and to make the basin itself safer and more attractive for boating and water sports. At about the same time Helen Storrow submitted plans for a "huge boat house" along the river to promote rowing in greater Boston schools. Once the commission held several meetings and agreed on the approach to developing the basin, Mrs. Storrow determined to donate one million dollars to the project (figure 6.42).[55]

Almost immediately the commission became embroiled in a debate over a proposed parkway along the river. It was inconceivable, said the commission, that the Charles River should be bordered by highways at all other locations but not have a roadway in the one place where it would do the most to relieve traffic congestion and add to the pleasure and safety of motorists. One newspaper suggested that more cars along the river might not be a bad thing, and pointed to other parks: Franklin Park was "unused" until a parkway was put through it; more people enjoyed Jamaica Pond from cars, but few walked along it; the Arboretum had no cars, but also few people.[56]

The basin commission's large-format report was short but extensively illustrated with photographs, elevations, plans, and perspectives, including large color foldout plans. The landscape architect for the commission was Arthur Shurcliff, who had opened his own office in 1905 and had done numerous projects for the Boston and metropolitan park commissions for more than twenty years (figure 6.43). The first published plan for the embankment itself was almost severe in its mostly open landscape (figure 6.44). Shurcliff's design consisted of a single sidewalk on either side of the parkway, broken only by a boat landing at the end of Dartmouth Street and a large semicircular memorial plaza upstream from the Longfellow Bridge.

6.42 Helen Storrow, shown above canoeing in Maine with her husband James (in one of the few photographs of her ever published), offered the Commonwealth one million dollars to create a memorial to her husband along the river.

An elevation in the report showed the proposed road depressed below the height of the original seawall, making the auto traffic invisible from Back Street but not from the new park. As it was interpreted in newspaper accounts, the commission's report plainly said that a pedestrian on the Esplanade would not even see the automobiles along the roadway; this was to be "an ingenious combination of park and boulevard . . . devised so as to be mutually exclusive." With the parkway depressed, vehicles would not be visible from the "main portion of the Esplanade," which the commission defined as the narrow area between Back Street and the parkway, not the wider portion of the Esplanade between the parkway and the river.[57]

6.43 Soon after an apprenticeship in the Olmsted office, Arthur Shurcliff joined with Frederick Law Olmsted, Jr., to create the first American four-year degree program in landscape architecture. He directed the site development for Colonial Williamsburg from 1929 to 1940 and continued as an advisor there until 1950. This portrait was done 1919 by his friend Charles Hopkinson.

6.44 Prepared at the direction of the Special Commission on the Charles River Basin, Arthur Shurcliff's 1928 plan for the Boston Embankment focused on a grand landing near Brimmer Street. The plan also included a major roadway connecting Soldiers Field Road (which at the time ended at the Cottage Farm Bridge), Embankment Road, and Arlington Street. The 1910 embankment would be widened to compensate for the proposed increase in the width of Embankment Road and Charles Street.

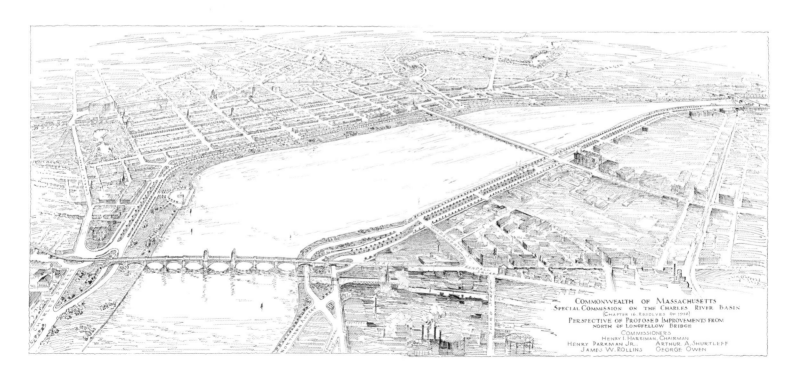

A plan by Perry, Shaw and Hepburn to create a much larger lagoon (extending from Arlington Street to Bay State Road) and to locate the parkway on the water side of the lagoon was included in the report, but the board opposed it because of the additional expense and the proposed siting of the road (figure 6.45).

By now automobile traffic had become an issue not only along the river, but also along the congested radial roadways: The report showed a perspective for new overpasses through the park at Charlesgate that were not constructed at the time but foreshadowed what would be built there in the 1960s (figures 6.46, 6.47).

A group called the Charles River Basin Protective Association was organized to do battle against the highway. They were convinced that the road would be a disastrous safety hazard next to the new park. It was true that a parkway on both sides of the Charles from Boston to Watertown had been suggested as early as the first Boston Park Commission reports and had been supported by Charles Eliot and others in the 1890s. But by the 1920s the nature of automobile traffic had clearly changed. Sylvester Baxter had written in the *Transcript* on the thirtieth anniversary of the metropolitan park system in 1923 that "the parkways and boulevards . . . intended to be strictly subordinate . . . to make the reservations pleasantly and easily accessible . . . have become the primary factor in the scheme of the park system." In a 1925 report on parks and parkways for the city, Shurcliff noted that in "this

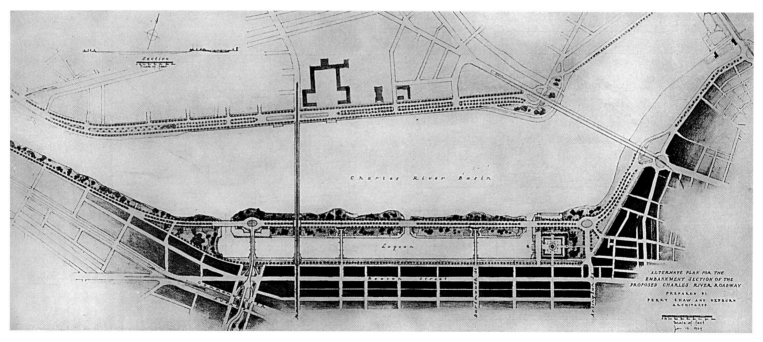

6.45 The 1928 report also included an alternative alignment for the roadway drawn by Perry Shaw & Hepburn, which located the road on the water side of a large lagoon.

6.46 The proposed roadway attracted enormous opposition, including the disapproval of Helen Storrow, and was dropped from the final plans.

6.47 In addition to the proposed riverfront parkway, the commission believed that the constant increases in auto traffic required a redesign of the roads through the Charlesgate section of Olmsted's Emerald Necklace, shown in this Shurcliff plan prepared for the Boston Park Department and included in the 1928 report. The Charlesgate realignment proposed an elevated roadway over Commonwealth Avenue, which intersected with the proposed limited-access parkway at the edge of the river.

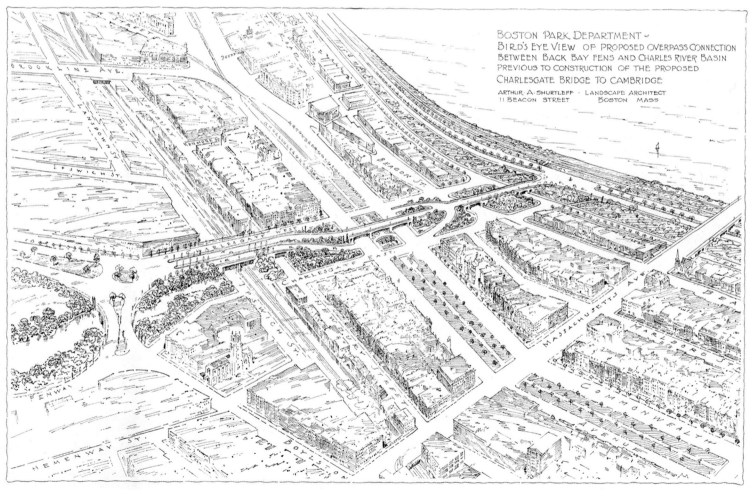

epoch of the revolution of vehicular transportation" there was a powerful temptation to overdevelop the parkways "as a matter of immediate relief and instant economy"; the only antidote was to recognize the parkways as adornments essential to the welfare of the city.[58]

Helen Storrow was also opposed to the road, but she was reluctant to say so in public. When the debate dragged on, she felt compelled to have her attorney read a letter at a hearing indicating her agreement with the Protective Association.[59]

The issue was lively and divisive, the most protracted and public fight over road construction in the city since the advent of auto traffic. According to the *Boston Herald*, the plan for the basin "changes not only from week to week but from day to day." In their coverage of the controversy, the *New York Times* observed that "in no city is unification of public sentiment more difficult to obtain. In none are more numerous or more various plans offered every time a public improvement is proposed. . . . Will the thing be done? Who can tell? This is Boston." In March the road was dropped from the park plans, and the revised legislation was finally approved in June.[60]

After the plan for a four-lane parkway was dropped, the design was considerably revised (figure 6.48). The section of the embankment between the Longfellow Bridge and Berkeley Street was organized in an informal symmetry marked by a restrained use of symmetrical, classically detailed stonework. Behind two arched breakwaters was a boat haven, with a wide granite landing along the shore. On either side of the landing were two large grass ovals, a "Music Oval" edged with linden trees for the Boston Pops concerts (which had begun in 1929) and a nearly matching oval on the other side (figures 6.50–6.52).

The Esplanade from Berkeley Street to the Harvard Bridge was also informal but symmetrical. The semicircular memorial, located along Embankment Road (now Mugar Way) in the 1928 scheme, was replaced by two large granite overlooks, sited to create visible landmarks at the termination of Dartmouth and Gloucester Streets. For the Gloucester Street overlook several schemes were considered (figure 6.49); the executed design includes a circular granite memorial to James Storrow. In between the two formal granite platforms was a long, oval lagoon intended for small pleasure boats, toy boat sailing, and ice skating (figures 6.53–6.56). The sloping banks of rounded stones laid over gravel were chosen not to "escape from an architectural treatment" but primarily to prevent the formation of the steep-sided waves that had bothered boaters on the basin for twenty years.[61]

Like Eliot's work on the Cambridge side of the river, Shurcliff's design was grounded in simplicity and restraint. And he followed his own advice. In 1922, in a chapter he wrote for a book on city planning, he suggested that "monotony of appearance and barrenness of interest are much more likely to be found on shores having a constant water level and little shipping, like the Charles River and the Alster Basin. . . . Insipid, stereotyped, and tiresome results are bound to be created unless the designer vitalizes his plans by keeping close to great matter-of-fact requirements and by giving patient attention to details."[62]

Opened to the public in 1935, the new park was formally dedicated as the Storrow Memorial Embankment the following year. Invoking the language of an earlier generation's urban activists, the chairman of the Metropolitan District Commission said that the embankment "sends hope, health, and goodwill through the streets, factories and tenements of the city." Although completed a generation later, the design and the programmed activities of the embankment were a realization of Olmsted, Eliot, and Baxter's hopes for "landscape design as conservative reform"— design that would heal some of the deep divisions in American society through the provision of a generously planted and carefully maintained public environment.[63]

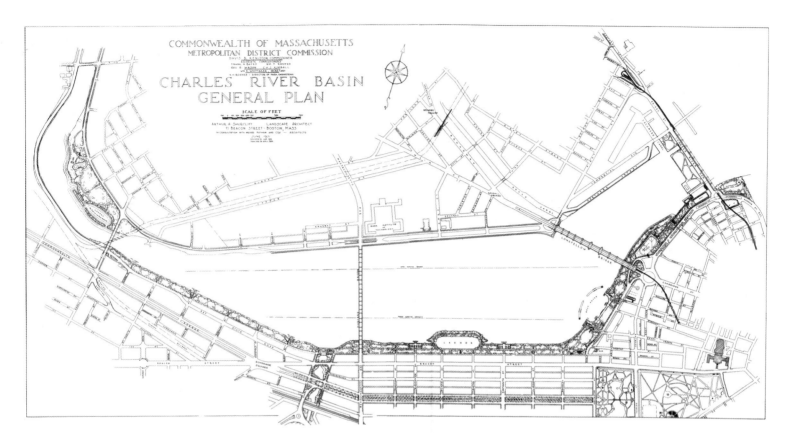

6.48 In Shurcliff's final design, the waterfront promenade all but disappeared, replaced by playing fields and a sloping, grassy "beach." Dedicated as the Storrow Memorial Embankment in 1936, the Esplanade (as it soon became universally known) more than doubled the width of the parkland between the dam and the Harvard Bridge.

6.49 Shurcliff considered several designs for the overlooks at Dartmouth and
Gloucester Streets, including variations with obelisks and fountains.

6.50 Concerts were held on the Boston Embankment beginning as soon as it was completed in 1910; they were also given at several sites along the river in Watertown and further upstream. A whole new era began in 1929 when Arthur Fiedler conducted the first Esplanade concerts of the Boston Pops orchestra in a temporary shell that was taken down at the end of the summer.

6.51 The popularity of the Pops concerts led to the construction of this second temporary shell in 1934. It was replaced six years later by the current shell, designed by Richard Shaw as a memorial to Edwin Hatch and funded from a bequest of his wife Maria.

6.52 Upstream of the Longfellow Bridge (lower right) a curved breakwater created a "boat haven"; between Exeter and Fairfield Streets a shallow lagoon was built.

6.53 When the Storrow Memorial Embankment was dedicated in 1936, the alley traffic along Back Street was separated from the park by the dense line of trees that had been planted in 1911 as part of the construction of the dam. Two walkways ran the full length of the embankment, one at the edge of the 1910 Boston Embankment and the other along the new shoreline.

6.54　A single large, shallow lagoon was constructed between Exeter and Fairfield Streets, designed for small boats in the summer and ice skating in the winter. The "Recreation Building and Boathouse," completed in 1939 (right center), served as a warming house for skaters.

6.55 Overlooks were sited opposite Dartmouth and Gloucester Streets, to provide a visual terminus at the end of each street. In 1936 Helen Storrow joined in the dedication of the new embankment, held at the Gloucester Street Overlook, where a large circular granite marker was placed. The stone was incised with an outline of the basin, the names of the adjoining cities, and a small inscription at the center of the stone with the name of her husband James. In 1949, five years after Helen Storrow's death, a bronze wreath honoring both the Storrows was placed over the earlier inscription, a fitting recognition of their substantial contributions, almost thirty years apart, to the Charles River Basin.

CITY OF BROOKLYN.

PLAN OF A PORTION OF **PARK WAY** AS PROPOSED TO BE LAID OUT
FROM THE EASTERN PART OF THE CITY
TO
THE PLAZA.

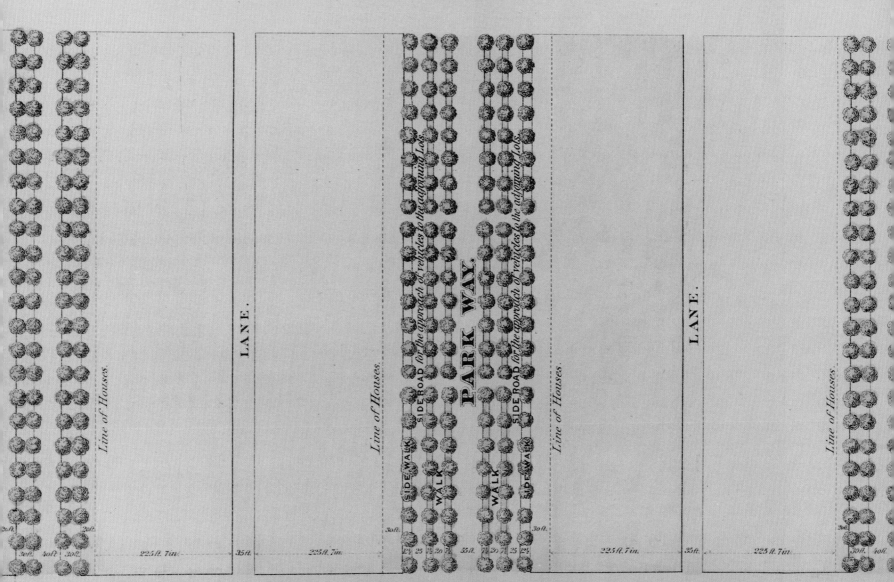

PROPOSED PLAN.

PRESENT PLAN.

Blocks are 255 feet 7 inches
East of Perry Avenue.

Blocks are 262 feet
West of Perry Avenue.

DOUGLASS ST.   DEGRAW ST.   SACKET ST.   UNION ST.

7

Highways and Park Ways

The parkway was not itself a road, it contained a roadway. The strip of land was not just a highway with uniform grassy borders; it was of significantly varying width, depending on immediate topographic and cultural conditions.

Norman T. Newton, *Design on the Land*, 1971

We will have as many motor vehicles as these facilities will accommodate.

Bentley W. Warren, a member of the Charles River Basin Association, predicting in 1929 the number of automobiles on Boston roads by 1950

In 1919, ten years before Boston debated a highway along the Charles, Lieutenant Colonel Dwight D. Eisenhower volunteered to ride in a convoy of 79 U.S. Army vehicles from Washington to San Francisco. The expedition had been organized by General John Pershing to test the condition of the country's 256,000 miles of roads. The question was urgent; in the first two decades of the new century, the number of vehicles had increased from from 8,000 to over nine million. The convoy's two-month trip was evidence enough that the "Good Roads" movement begun in the 1890s, supported by business people, farmers, and groups like the League of American Wheelmen, had not remotely kept pace with the increase in traffic. Pershing later sketched a nationwide highway system that would support military transportation, but his ideas were forgotten by the late 1930s, when Congress requested a study of six national superhighways.[1]

During World War Two, Eisenhower had first-hand experience with the German *Autobahnen*. He later wrote that "the old convoy had started me thinking about good, two-lane highways, but Germany had made me see the wisdom of broader ribbons across the land." Although Congress had actually authorized a 40,000-mile network in 1944, the appropriation was limited and few highways were built. It was not until 1956, when the mechanism of highway tolls was rejected in favor of user taxes, that Congress approved and President Eisenhower signed what he described as the largest public works program "ever undertaken by the United States or any other country."[2]

Frontispiece *City of Brooklyn, Plan of a Portion of Park Way . . .* , 1868

Eisenhower, who was not inclined to involve the federal government in urban issues, received a rude awakening three years later, when he learned for the first time that the Interstate system included urban freeways. Two accounts corroborate his conversation in 1959 with urban planners who described the freeway network planned for the District of Columbia. In July the president ordered a formal study of urban highways, to be produced by 19 full-time staff and three consultants. Nine months later the "Interim Report" delivered a series of recommendations, including the elimination of inner belt highways and the substitution of minimum-length spurs for freeways that went all the way through cities. Seventeen hundred miles were to be eliminated from the system, and there should be comprehensive planning for all urban routes. When the report was presented to Eisenhower in April 1960, he indicated that "the matter of running Interstate routes through the congested parts of the cities was entirely against his original concept and wishes," but that the program was so far along "his hands were virtually tied."[3]

The president of the United States was only one of many city dwellers to be shocked by the extensive plans for urban freeways that sprang up after 1945. Yet in spite of evidence that community opposition appeared in many American cities as soon as urban–freeway construction began, the few histories of Boston transportation present a limited—and sometimes misleading—perspective.[4] The definitive political history of the Central Artery/Tunnel project, for example, asserts that the highway coalition "was unchallenged from the end of World War II until the mid-1960s."[5] In fact, almost every major highway project in Boston, beginning with the proposed embankment highway in 1929, has provoked vigorous opposition.

The following brief outline of Boston's metropolitan highway planning in the past hundred years suggests the ways in which professional perspectives and the region's civic culture were diverging.

Park Ways and Professional Design

The design of roads within and between parks was of great concern to the first generation of American landscape architects. A major innovation in the 1857 design by Frederick Law Olmsted and Calvert Vaux for New York's Central Park was the provision of transverse carriage drives that crossed the park from east to west below the level of the pedestrian ways. In designing Prospect Park in Brooklyn, Olmsted and Vaux proposed in 1868 a new street type they called the "park way" (frontispiece). It would separate carriages from carts and heavy traffic and connect with Central Park and the ocean, extending the scenic values of the parks through residential neighborhoods.[6]

Pleasure drives for suburban Boston had already been described in Gourlay's "Plan for Boston," and more detailed maps and descriptions of such roads were suggested after the Civil War by Copeland, Cleveland, Bowditch, and others (see figures 3.22, 3.24–3.25). In the late 1880s parkways were built as part of Olmsted's plan for the Back Bay Fens, and before Olmsted's retirement in 1895 his completed parkway designs linked the Fens with Jamaica Pond, the Arnold Arboretum, and Franklin Park.[7]

Parkways were included in the Metropolitan Park Commission's report of 1893 as an essential element of the founders' regional vision for the park system, and the river courses were described as ideally situated to connect Boston with its suburbs, but no detailed alignments were mapped in the report. The Boulevard Act of 1894 included an appropriation for the Metropolitan Park Commission to build parkways for a different reason: There was no other regional authority in greater Boston authorized to do such work. Eliot was adamant that detailed planning for the proposed roads was as essential as it was for the proper development of the reservations. He argued that the proposed parkways should benefit the greatest number of people, and therefore the highest priority was to connect the city with the Blue Hills and the Middlesex Fells. The parkways should also include "separate passageways" for street cars as well as lanes for carriages and bicycles.[8]

By 1900, lengthy sections of the Fellsway, the Blue Hills parkway, and several other projects were substantially completed. The Fellsway connected Broadway Park in Somerville with the two southern entrances to the Fells, and the Blue Hills parkway extended to the Neponset River and thence to Franklin Park. Over two miles of lakefront along the Mystic Lakes was integrated with a new parkway, and a short link had been constructed by the MPC between the Cambridge city park at Fresh Pond and Gerry's Landing near the Charles. Two years later a four-mile parkway was completed between Revere Beach and Main Street in Everett.[9]

The increased attention to the planning of city streets and parkways was paralleled by the professionalization of highway design and construction, which occurred in both state and local governments in ways that parallel the development of public parks and reservations. For most of the nineteenth century, the responsibility for roads was seen as a local function. By the 1890s, it was clear that counties and townships were not keeping up with the increasing clamor for more and better rural roads. Under pressure from farmers, bicycle enthusiasts, and politicians, states and the federal government began tentative efforts to investigate highway planning and road construction in suburban and rural areas.[10]

The establishment of the Massachusetts Highway Commission followed the pattern of other state commissions created at the end of the nineteenth century. A study commission was approved first, in 1892 (the same year as the temporary metropolitan park commission). Its membership joined citizen representation with the authority of experts: a member of one of the vocal and well-organized bicycle associations, the city engineer of Chelsea, and the dean of Harvard's Lawrence Scientific School.[9] Their primary focus was on the state of roadways outside the Commonwealth's cities and towns. They conducted a survey of existing road conditions for the 600 miles of highway in every county but Nantucket, did traffic counts on some of the roads into Boston, and estimated the savings of improved construction methods. Their report concluded that roads outside of cities and towns were in deplorable condition, and that only counties or the state could provide sufficient funds. The legislation to establish a permanent highway commission was enacted the following year, creating the first state highway department in the nation.[11]

By the turn of the century, Massachusetts was the only state with minimum engineering standards for state-aided local projects, as well as the only state to expend a significant amount on roads, providing $6.75 million to improve 480 miles of highways between 1894 and 1903. The commission supported demonstration projects and operated outside the boundaries of cities and towns, whose jurisdiction over road construction was well established.[12]

Metropolitan Improvements

A decade later, the Boston Society of Architects assembled a coalition that included the chamber of commerce and a half dozen other business and civic groups to promote a plan for major urban improvements. The 1907 report of their Committee on Municipal Improvements began by analyzing a troubling symptom: Why were there "vast activities in New York and throughout the country," while building operations were almost at a standstill in Boston?[13]

The committee did consider briefly the improvement of the Port of Boston, and even resurrected the century-old idea of inland waterways extending to the Connecticut and Hudson river valleys. The 1907 report found the greatest issues, however, in the heart of the city, where they hoped to "consolidate the population by filling the gaps in the city plan; avoid congestion by enlarging the business district; and keep within the city limits the prosperous and educated class that now goes to the suburbs."[14]

An unnamed committee member offered two reasons for the area's decline. First, large areas of unoccupied space in the heart of Boston, both land and water, cut off communications between sections and neighborhoods of the city, increasing traffic congestion and preventing expansion of the business district. Second, overly restrictive building laws affected height and materials, limiting construction and driving people to the suburbs. Five large vacant spaces were identified. The Boston & Albany Railroad yard separated the Huntington Avenue section from the residential district of the Back Bay between Beacon and Boylston Streets. In the same way, the Boston and Providence yards were blighting the Columbus Avenue neighborhood. South Bay should simply be filled and developed. The last two "vacant spaces" hindering development were more surprising: "the park system of the Fenway, which obstructs the

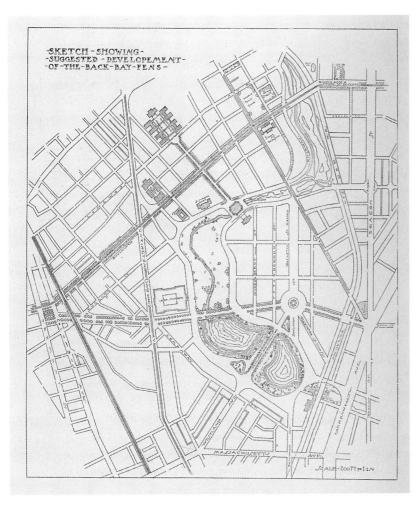

7.1 As the number of automobiles on city streets ballooned, it became obvious to many that the network of local streets would have to change. One of the earliest local proposals came in a 1907 report from the Boston Society of Architects (BSA). While a more axial alignment of streets around the Back Bay Fens might have moved traffic faster, the plan shows little understanding of Olmsted's recently completed design.

city's growth to the southwest"; and the Charles River, which "isolates the Riverbank lands in Cambridge [the future site of MIT], owing to lack of means of communication."[15]

According to the committee, most of these problems could be addressed by changing the street plans, which would not only create "monumental sites" but would cut streets through deserted districts, raise tax valuations, and "add to the riches of the city." If South Bay were filled, a substantial portion of the railroad yards could be relocated there. For the recently completed parks and parkways along the Muddy River and the Back Bay Fens, broad new boulevards would break open the enclosed spaces of Olmsted's pastoral landscapes (figure 7.1). The "adequate" new street leading to the new campus for Harvard Medical School would be "perfected" with "a suitable ending where the new street joins the park." The monumentality of important new buildings such as the Museum of Fine Arts would be revealed, and future structures might then follow their "worthy" example. The "City Beautiful" would reign triumphantly over Olmsted's fusty, outmoded pastoral ideals. Altering the street pattern for the "vacant space" of the Charles River Basin would require building new bridges, whose cost could be reduced by various schemes for creating magnificent building sites on islands in the middle of the river.[16]

The proposal for "Inner and Outer Boulevards" was an early application of the analogy of "the spokes of a wheel" to the growing problem of city traffic (figure 7.2). It was relatively easy, according to the authors, to get from the center of the city to the suburbs. By contrast, the routes from Cambridge to Roxbury, or from Brookline to the Revere Beach Parkway, were "inconvenient and circuitous." The solution was an Inner Boulevard, which would cut through Cambridge on the Grand Junction railroad alignment, then turn southeast across the Fens (where the "Inner Belt" would be proposed fifty years later).[17]

A number of issues identified by the committee were clearly metropolitan in scope. Encouraged by the architects' report, the General Court appointed the Metropolitan Improvement Commission the same year. The new commission's charge was to review "any public works in the metropolitan district" that would

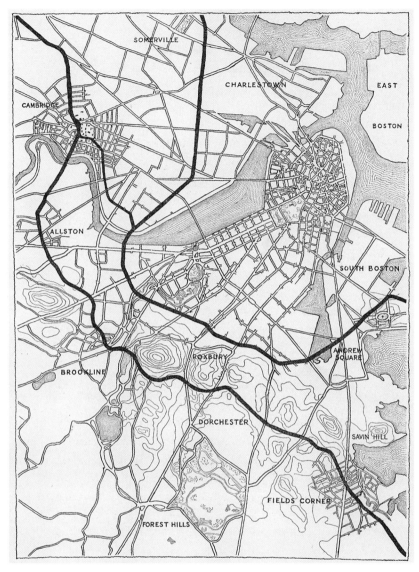

7.2 The 1907 BSA report also promoted the construction of "Inner and Outer Boulevards." The inner boulevard traced an arc extending west from South Boston, cut across the Fens, and crossed the Charles at the Cottage Farm Bridge, following much the same route as the proposed "Inner Belt" of the 1960s.

improve convenience, develop local business, or beautify the district. The commission extended the architects' work on several fronts, with the broader aim of promoting their vision of metropolitan government. The choice of authors for the commission's studies revealed, however, that professional specialization had progressed only so far. Sylvester Baxter wrote on the commercial uses of the rivers and harbors, and the landscape architect Arthur Shurcliff was considered sufficiently equipped to serve as the commission's expert on roads and highway traffic.[18]

The final report of the Metropolitan Improvement Commission in 1909 noted that the broad scope delegated to the commission was "almost as comprehensive as the whole question of the public welfare and progress of the Metropolitan District." The most pressing issue for the commission, however, was clearly transportation or, as they described the problem, a "systematic method of internal communication" that would include highways, the control of traffic and transportation, and the location of docks and terminals. Witnesses at the commission's hearings confirmed that transportation was the most urgent public works question in the district, and that the future prosperity of the state would be contingent on the growth of the city as a commercial port. The longest sections in the final report addressed railroads and terminals, docks, and waterways, and all three were written by civil engineers. Although the emphasis on transportation ignored other important urban public works issues, the commission's aspirations to look comprehensively at all modes of transportation reflected the growing sense that cities could be planned and that professionals would do the planning.[19]

Shurcliff's essay on metropolitan highways, based on eighteen months of investigation, was both naive and prophetic. He correctly diagnosed the weaknesses in the existing street network but grossly underestimated the burdens that would quite soon overwhelm the pattern he described. His deductions assumed that the typical American gridiron plan was "not applicable to the steep, isolated hills, radiating valleys and irregular shoreline" of greater Boston. The "bewilderment of strangers" at the unusual street system of Boston should be of little concern, since with few excep-

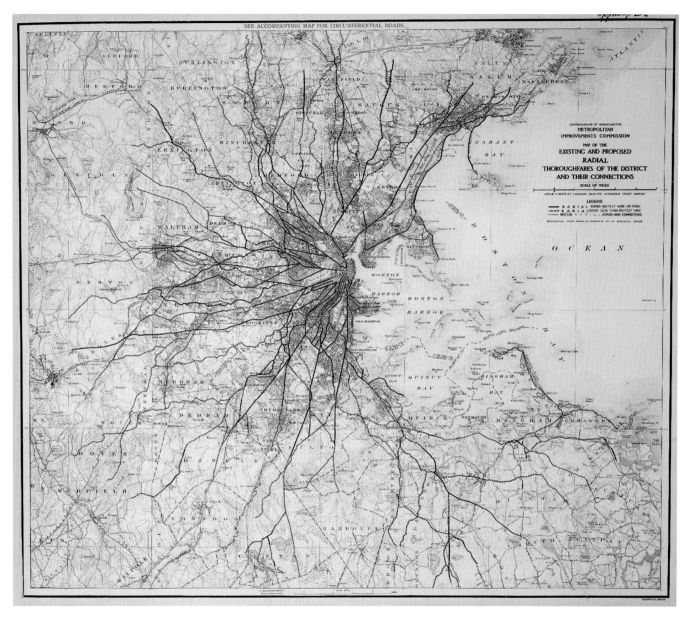

7.3 In the early decades of the twentieth century, landscape architects contributed significantly to the planning of new traffic solutions, especially in the development of parkways. Arthur Shurcliff showed in 1909 that the network of radial streets extending out from the center of the city was far more complete than the "circumferential thoroughfares" connecting the cities and towns surrounding Boston.

Chapter 7

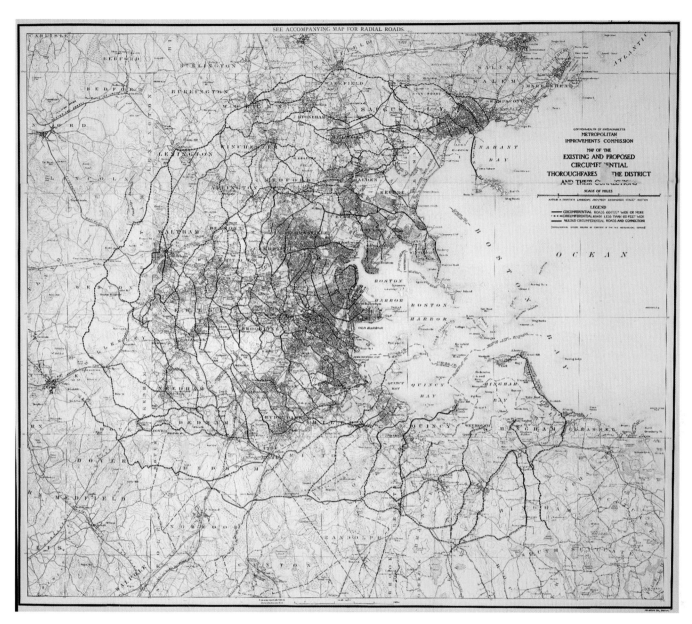

7.4 Shurcliff not only mapped the discontinuities in the routes around Boston, he also proposed alignments for new circumferential roads. It has been suggested that Shurcliff's plans anticipated the need for limited-access beltways around Boston. On the contrary, these drawings illustrate a dense network—more roads, but none as wide as the highways that were subsequently constructed.

tions it is logical for those who know it. Only in the most densely settled sections would it be difficult to adjust highways to modern needs. The radial streets were sufficiently wide and well distributed, but were not being expanded to meet increased demands (figure 7.3). The circumferential roads, on the other hand, were generally "narrow, crooked and broken in their alignment" and unnecessarily increased the load on the radial roadways (figure 7.4).[20]

Shurcliff believed that if the missing connections in the radial and circumferential networks were built, there would be no need to establish "a new general system." He also apparently assumed that parkways would continue to be constructed where the regional road network intersected with the metropolitan reservations; there was therefore no contradiction between his support

for public open space and his recommendation to build new roads through the reservations, for example, south of Spot Pond in the Fells and north of Houghton's Pond on the south side of Great Blue Hill. He identified the need for what was later called the "Northern Artery" from Harvard Bridge in Cambridge to the Wellington Bridge on the Mystic River; the plan also called for a major route from Allston across the Charles past Fresh Pond to Davis and Powderhouse Squares in Somerville.[21]

Like the authors of subsequent studies completed during the next two decades, Shurcliff concluded that additional bridges across the Charles would be required, on either side of the Harvard Bridge and upstream of the Cottage Farm Bridge at Magazine Street (figure 7.5).[22] That approach would have resulted in a finer

7.5 For the circumferential network, Shurcliff proposed four new bridges along the Charles, creating a roadway network that dispersed the traffic across many routes, instead of concentrating it on a few much larger roads.

7.6 To fill out the radial network, the gap in the Charles River Road (now Memorial Drive) is completed, and a new link is proposed between Causeway and Cambridge Streets, rather than expanding Charles Street and narrowing the public space at Olmsted's Charlesbank.

grain and lower maximum speeds for the highway network; the actual average speeds might not have been any lower than the speeds on the highway system that was built after the Second World War. He also proposed a connection from Causeway Street and the Bulfinch Triangle to Cambridge Street south of Charles Street, to avoid increasing the traffic and reducing the size of Charlesbank (figure 7.6).

Since new bridges would be expensive, "earth causeways" could be built in the river to reduce the costs, as Shurcliff and Ralph Adams Cram had illustrated in the 1907 report of the Boston Society of Architects (see figures 6.1, 6.2). The causeways might be islands, or peninsulas perpendicular to the basin, much like the roads crossing the Alster in Hamburg. In either approach, the tree-lined earthworks would save a third to half of the cost of

bridges, make the basin far more popular for boating and skating, and render it "more human in scale." They should not be considered as projects for making land, however, since there was already ample provision for recreation and so much vacant land nearby (most of it in Cambridge) that the islands as building sites or parks would not be needed for some time.[23]

How would all these roadway improvements be realized? Shurcliff cited the successful merger of the metropolitan water and sewer commissions, and he recommended a second merger with the park and highway commissions. A regional agency should execute these improvements without abridging local authority. Yet the report did not describe in any detail how the continuing local opposition to metropolitan government might be overcome.[24]

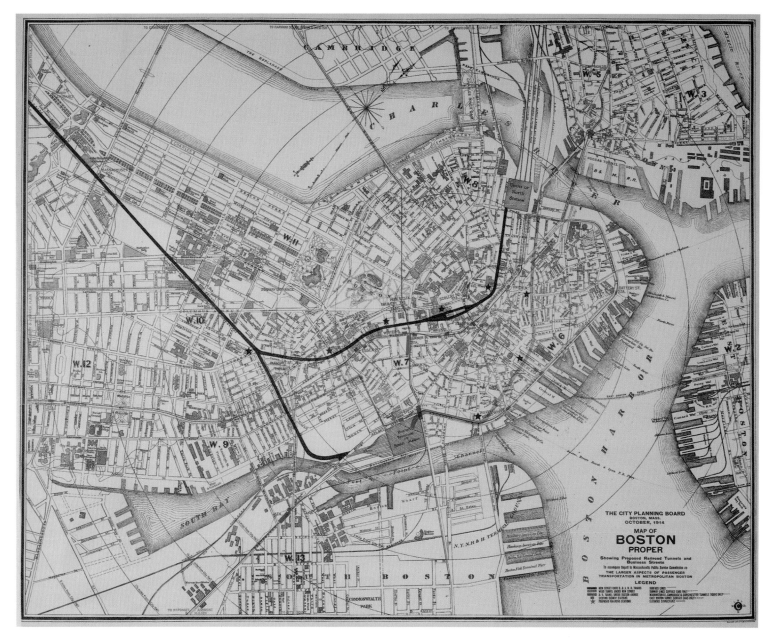

7.7 Seventy years after Robert Gourlay's plan first suggested linking Boston's several railroad stations on the north and south of the city (figure 2.23), the Boston City Planning Board proposed in 1914 to connect North and South Stations with both a "business boulevard" and a railroad tunnel (shown in green). Recognized as a missing link in the regional transportation network for more than a hundred and fifty years, the rail connection was not even considered when the Central Artery was built in the 1950s but was included in the early planning for the depressed Central Artery.

Baxter's contribution to the 1909 report on metropolitan improvements was a general study of "The Water Front of Boston Bay," which described the Charles, Mystic, and Fore Rivers and Lynn Harbor. Baxter was certain the Charles functioned as an essential part of the harbor, and echoed Eliot's observations in 1892 on the obstacles to navigation created by the railroad bridges at North Station. Boating traffic was restricted by the railroad bridges "that fairly roofed the river" and by more than thirty-one acres of platforms used as a switching yard. Shipping on the river had nonetheless doubled between 1891 and 1905, but only the lower Charles saw much activity. Less than a fifth of the commercial traffic went above the Cambridge Bridge; the Watertown Arsenal was now supplied entirely by rail, and the wharf there was "deserted and overgrown."[25]

In spite of the commission's work, improvements were slow in coming. Although it had little to do with the city's economy, the images of islands in the Charles would exercise a fascination into the present among Boston's designers. In the extended chain of Boston urban visions, the most influential images of the 1909 report were the "Inner and Outer Boulevards" and the "Circumferential Thoroughfares." Another report whose influence would persist was the study by the new Boston City Planning Board to link North and South Stations with both a "business boulevard" and a rail tunnel (figure 7.7).

The 1930 Thoroughfare Plan

In the two decades following the publication of the 1909 "Improvements" report, almost nothing came of the ambitious roadway plans. In 1929 the Commonwealth accepted Helen Storrow's additions to the Esplanade, after agreeing to cancel the embankment highway. But at the same moment, the Boston City Planning Board was paying for a traffic study by a New York City consultant that endorsed the construction of a parkway along the lower Charles, following the alignment that the legislators had just rejected, along with nine other "major" projects and fifty-six other road improvements (figure 7.8).

Robert Whitten, the study's author, emphasized transportation's primary role in the city. Echoing Gourlay almost a century before, his 1930 plan asserted that prosperity depended on the "utmost freedom of circulation for goods and persons." In creating that freedom, the roadway network should be designed for as much traffic as will use city streets. The report acknowledged the argument that "it is useless to increase street capacities in central areas as any additional capacity provided will be immediately taxed to the saturation point." It was claimed that this argument, while valid for certain business streets, was not valid for major traffic arteries. This approach, however, failed to define how future capacity would be determined, and how this logic might quickly become circular.[26]

Whitten argued that "the private automobile has long since ceased to be primarily a 'pleasure car.' The number of trips made on city streets just for the pleasure of driving is negligible. Automobiles are used to get somewhere." All these assumptions were linked to Whitten's view that rapid transit would continue to provide for most of the commuting traffic to and from the city; when transit was cheaper and more efficient than the car, people would choose it, saving their car for those trips when it was the more efficient mode. He completely underestimated the preference for auto commuting, even when it was clearly more expensive and less efficient.[27]

Ten major projects were described in the thoroughfare plan, including a proposed elevated "Central Artery" along the route of Atlantic Avenue where there was already an elevated streetcar line (figures 7.9, 7.10). (An elevated highway through downtown had been proposed by William Stanley Parker, chairman of the Boston City Planning Board, in 1923.)[28] Of the ten recommended projects, the first to be constructed was the East Boston (now Sumner) Tunnel, opened in 1934; the second was a road along the Boston side of the river.

The report asserted that the shores of the basin offered the only satisfactory route for the uninterrupted movement of large volumes of traffic to the western suburbs. While acknowledging that the Charles River Basin improvement plan approved by the

7.8 In 1929, the same year that the Commonwealth accepted Helen Storrow's gift for additions to the Esplanade after agreeing not to construct a highway alongside it, the Boston City Planning Board hired Robert Whitten, a New York traffic consultant, who recommended the "parkway" along the Charles (number six on the plan), along with nine other major traffic projects.

7.9 Whitten's plan included an elevated "Central Artery" that ended at Causeway Street near the just-opened Boston Garden. The existing bridges over the Charles, linked to a new arterial road through Somerville, were thought to be adequate for future auto traffic.

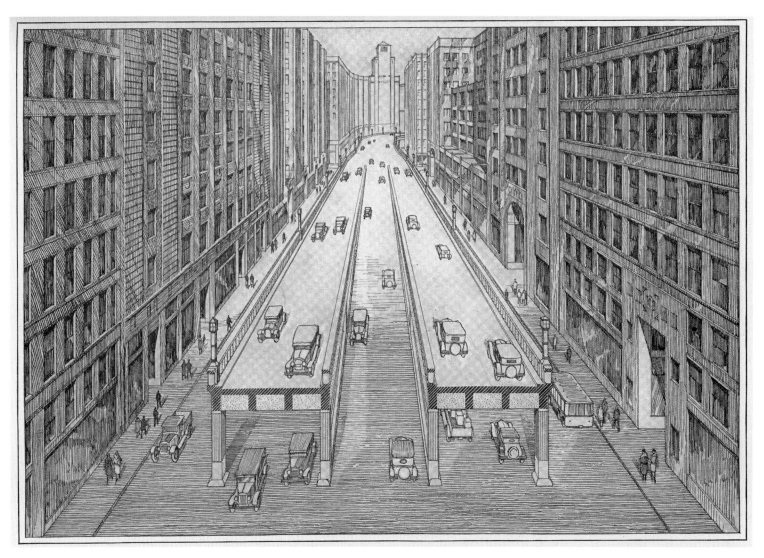

7.10   By the 1930s there were loud complaints about the noise, dirt, and
shadows generated by Boston's elevated streetcar lines, but the city's highway
planners were convinced that the elevated roadway through the center of
Boston (shown in this drawing from Whitten's report) would be a great boon
to the city.

legislature in 1929 provided that no portion of the new park should be used for roadway construction, Whitten believed that congestion along Beacon Street and Commonwealth Avenue would eventually require the building of a basin parkway. This was so, even though the report proposed both a "Roxbury Crosstown" expressway and a "B & A Highway" over the Boston and Albany tracks from the Cottage Farm Bridge to Arlington Square in South Boston (once a change in the trains' "motive power" permitted the construction of a viaduct over the tracks).[29]

In addition to the Basin Parkway, Whitten proposed two other new parkways, one along the Neponset River and the other from the Neponset to the proposed Blue Hills Radial. The report provided only typical sections for the roads, not detailed designs, but even the proposed "expressways" were closer to the model of Commonwealth Avenue than to the limited-access highways later mandated by federal standards after World War II. The expressways included short underpasses to separate traffic and broad medians of trees (figure 7.11). A number of new or extended parkways were also described.

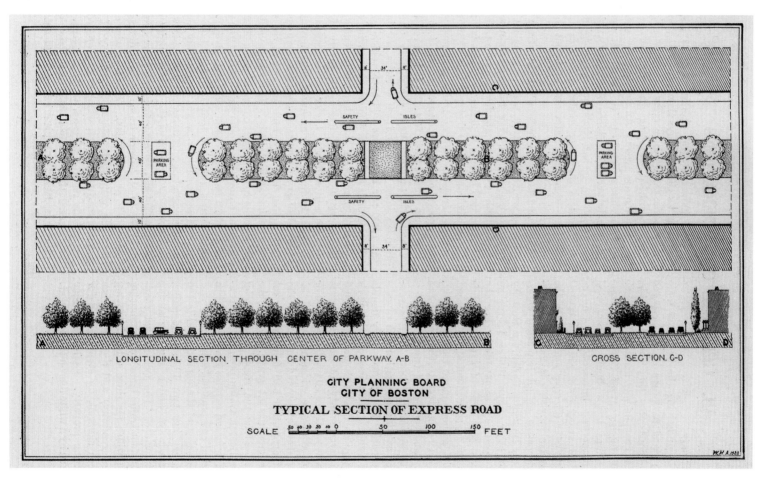

LONGITUDINAL SECTION THROUGH CENTER OF PARKWAY. A-B

CROSS SECTION. C-D

CITY PLANNING BOARD
CITY OF BOSTON

TYPICAL SECTION OF EXPRESS ROAD

SCALE 50 40 30 20 10 0   50   100   150 FEET

7.11 While the proposed Central Artery was elevated, most of the other "express roads" in Whitten's report would be more like boulevards, with trees generously planted in the medians.

A thoroughfare plan should be just one part of a comprehensive city and regional plan, Whitten argued. Traffic ought to be analyzed in relation to "zoning, parks, public buildings, rapid transit" and all the other factors of comprehensive planning. Such an approach, however, was beyond the scope of the 1930 report. Whitten did conduct the first origin and destination studies in Boston, and he applied the logic of cost savings to justify the new roads. For the proposed embankment highway, which was expected to carry ten million cars per year by 1940, the annual savings were calculated at $920,000, based on a rate of two minutes per mile for each driver for a little over two miles.[30]

The Whitten report would define the general alignment of all the major highway projects built during the next thirty years. Although the Great Depression and the Second World War would delay the implementation of these projects for two decades, Whitten's images of the elevated Central Artery vividly represented what many agreed was Boston's most critical highway project.

The 1948 Master Highway Plan and Storrow Drive

A much more comprehensive and ambitious engineering study, the *Master Highway Plan for the Boston Metropolitan Area* (sometimes called the "Maguire plan"), was completed in 1948. It recommended the Esplanade road as a supplemental connection to a proposed belt route that would cross the river just above the Cottage Farm (now Boston University) Bridge. The beltway was to be the hub of a system of radial expressways: southeast, southwest, west, northwest, north, northeast (figure 7.12).

The 1948 plan responded to the logic dictated by the federal Bureau of Public Roads report on *Toll Roads and Free Roads* (1939) and by the federal legislation of 1944 with its description of a national Interstate system. In seeking solutions to the traffic congestion of the 1930s, the *Toll Road* report was committed to uniform solutions applied across the country. While the bureau recognized that the new expressway network would also require the development of parking and transit facilities to function well,

it was authorized to fund only highway facilities. The federal standards mandated a single approach to highway design in both rural and urban areas: the high-speed expressway.[31] The great parkway designs of the 1920s and 1930s (for example, the parkways in Connecticut and New York, now designated historic and engineering landmarks) were ignored.

Finally, to guarantee the implementation of federal standards, it was proposed to raise the share of federal funding significantly above the fifty-fifty split then in place. In 1943 William Cox, a highway engineer and head of the Connecticut highway department, began campaigning against raising the federal share. He wrote to Robert Moses that if the state share were reduced to 25 percent, the states would be 'licked' from the start." The professional relationships between state and federal engineers, he feared, would be shattered; the local expertise in determining final road alignments would be ignored. Thomas MacDonald, director of the Bureau of Public Roads from 1919 to 1953, later was reported to have said that the ninety-ten split in federal funding was "the greatest mistake in highway development."[32]

The new federal mandate, however, proved irresistible. The *Master Highway Plan* rejected the comprehensive but smaller-scaled arterial improvements proposed by Shurcliff and Whitten. The high-speed, limited access radial highways and the connecting Inner Belt proposed in 1948 would be far larger than the "expressways" of the 1930 report.[33]

While consideration of most of the master plan took another two decades, the Esplanade road became an immediate issue. The governor's message to the legislature in 1946 had emphasized that the metropolitan highway system required two projects immediately: a second tunnel under the harbor and the embankment road. The parkway had not even been mentioned in the Special Postwar Highway Commission's report published that year; it said that the major transportation issues in Boston were the harbor tunnel, off-street parking, and the Central Artery. A study prepared by the Metropolitan District Commission (MDC) concluded in a separate study that it would be a mistake to run a highway along the Esplanade; the study

7.12   The creation of the interstate highway system is commonly dated to
1956, the year Congress revised the 1944 "Federal-Aid Highway Act" and
authorized substantial funding to construct the interstates. But many of the
major policy decisions, including the approach to urban highway design, had
already been determined in federal highway reports of 1939 and 1944.
Boston's 1948 Master Highway Plan, with its radial freeways and inner beltway, responded to those requirements and rejected the finer grain of Shurcliff
and Whitten's proposed roadway networks. Missing from the plan is the turnpike extension into Boston, which would have obviated the need for the
highway along the Esplanade.

showed a plan that ended the riverside parkway just east of the Harvard Bridge. The legislature nonetheless authorized the Metropolitan District Commission to prepare plans for extending the embankment road.[34]

The urgency behind these studies reflected the fact that the state was substantially behind in collecting federal matching funds. Highway construction had dropped from an average of a hundred million dollars during the years 1894–1935 to between thirty and forty million in 1947 and 1948. The proponents of the embankment parkway were led by state senator Philip Bowker, a former MDC associate commissioner, and supported by real estate leaders and the Greater Boston Development Committee, a group organized in 1944.[35]

Four years later the committee published a high school textbook on the future development of Boston, called *Surging Cities*. It began with a consideration of ancient urban development and then analyzed in some detail the cities of New York, Boston, Philadelphia, Chicago, and Los Angeles. The authors endorsed the 1930 *Thoroughfare Plan* by Robert Whitten, the "eminent city planning consultant," and reproduced the map of proposed expressways from the frontispiece of the 1948 *Master Highway Plan*.[36] (The textbook included "before" and "after" photographs to suggest the benefits that would follow the demolition of elevated streetcar tracks; the proposed elevated Central Artery, on the other hand, was sketched as an up-to-date element of urban architecture (figures 7.13–7.16).

In spite of the Development Committee's campaign, a broad-based coalition opposed the Esplanade road; according to the *Globe*, they were neighborhood residents, those who thought recreation would lose, and music lovers. They wrote letters to newspapers and the legislature and organized baby carriage marches at the State House. Community leaders from the West End, who probably had as much at stake as any of the adjoining neighborhoods, objected on the same grounds as they had in 1929.[37]

When a bill to construct the embankment highway was drafted in 1948, a group of Boston residents organized the Storrow Memorial Embankment Protective Association. The Protective

7.13 In 1944 the Greater Boston Development Committee was organized to promote the postwar economy of Boston. Four years later the committee published a high school textbook called *Surging Cities*, which focused on the physical and social development of the metropolitan region. Their interests included taking down the now-antiquated elevated streetcar tracks in the city, including the Orange Line on Washington Street.

7.14 The elevated Orange Line was air-brushed out of this 1948 photograph, which was captioned, "Washington Street . . . Soon." The Orange Line was finally demolished in 1987.

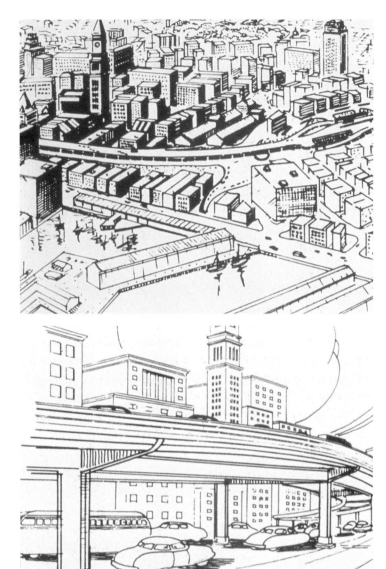

7.15 While promoting the demolition of elevated streetcar tracks, *Surging Cities* also glamorized the Central Artery as a local realization of the "Futurama" vision from the 1939 World's Fair—futuristic, often elevated highways, connecting America's cities.

7.16 These highway visions failed to explain how high-speed elevated roads would be any less ugly and noisy than the streetcar tracks they were to replace.

7.17 The elevated Central Artery was included in the report of the 1946 Special Postwar Highway Commission, but the report did not even mention Whitten's 1930 proposal for a highway along the river. After the most contentious debate in the history of road construction in Massachusetts, Storrow Drive was initially rejected by the legislature and then approved by only a single vote in 1949. This 1951 photo was taken from a building facing Embankment Road, looking upstream from the Harvard Bridge.

Association included among its members some of the same Boston families that had been active in planning for the basin in 1902 and 1929, as well as the secretary of the Trustees of Reservations, the president of Boston University, and Arthur Fiedler, the popular conductor of the Boston Pops. James Storrow III, the son of James and Helen Storrow, was originally on the executive committee, but when the legislature proposed naming the roadway after his father he withdrew from the association.[38]

In justifying the Esplanade freeway, the report asserted in its summary that there was a very strong traffic demand paralleling the Charles River. In fact, the *Highway Plan* appeared to show the heaviest traffic demand from the west of Boston to be south of Newbury Street, as the protective association claimed. The association also cited the master plan's own conclusion that the river freeway would provide only a measure of temporary relief from congestion until the entire beltway was completed. For the opponents of Storrow Drive, the issue was clearly the park versus the freeway; a moderate improvement for drivers would come at enormous cost to the nearby neighborhoods. There were no engineering or geological subtleties, as there had been in 1902 with the Charles River Dam.[39]

An alternative alignment proposed by Senator Richard Lee would connect Boylston Street just east of Massachusetts Avenue with Soldiers Field Road upstream of the Cottage Farm Bridge, avoiding the Esplanade entirely. Two variations were described in the *Boston Herald*. One extended Boylston Street straight across the Fens to intersect with Park Drive; the other linked Boylston Street with an elevated highway built over the Boston and Albany tracks (the route of the turnpike extension in 1969).[40]

The battle was intense, and its last days were covered on the front pages of Boston's newspapers. Senator LoPresti of the West End pleaded on behalf of the neighborhood's underprivileged children. Another state senator claimed that the Storrows' "gift to the people was being turned into a high-speed highway where children will be killed."[41]

On April 12, the Storrow Drive bill was defeated by eight Democrats. But the defeat was short-lived. Two weeks later, the

7.18 At Boston University, the original construction of Storrow Drive included a connection to Bay State Road and new fill in the river (left).

doors of the house chamber were locked. Then the House provided for the required three readings of the bill by adjourning twice and then reconvening. The roadway was passed by one vote (figures 7.17–7.18). Efforts to require a referendum and to make the road a separate bond issue failed.[42]

The opponents of the road did succeed in passing amendments to widen the Esplanade to replace some of the park land to be taken for the freeway, to build two swimming pools, and to depress a section of the roadway (figure 7.19). Arthur Shurcliff and his son Sidney were the landscape architects for the new plan, which extended the single large lagoon by constructing very narrow islands up- and downstream to create a series of smaller lagoons (figure 7.20). The Shurcliffs revised the 1929 plan for overpasses on top of the Charlesgate (which was finally completed in 1966, devastating the park beneath it); they also designed a "Recreation Center" on new fill extending from the remnant of the Charlesbank (figure 7.21). Although Arthur Shurcliff had at first joined in the protest against the highway, his son later said that Arthur "became convinced that the road really was necessary."[43]

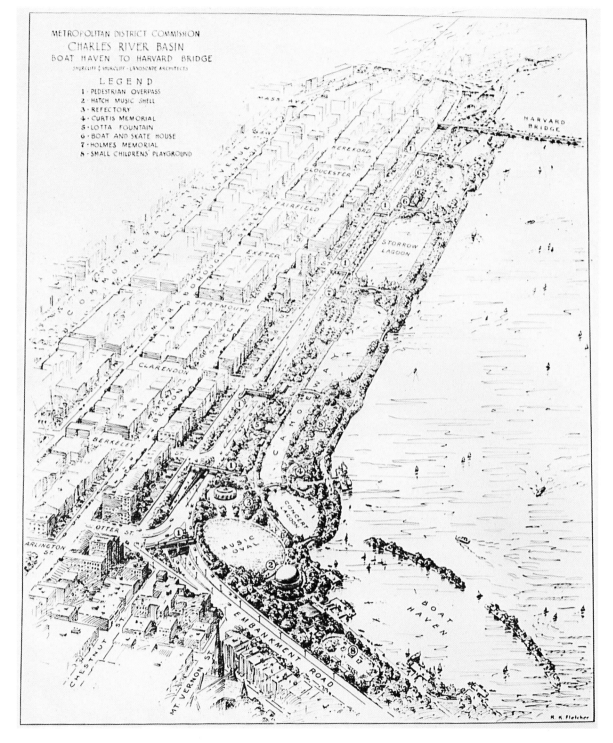

METROPOLITAN DISTRICT COMMISSION
CHARLES RIVER BASIN
BOAT HAVEN TO HARVARD BRIDGE
SHURCLIFF & SHURCLIFF · LANDSCAPE ARCHITECTS

LEGEND
1 · PEDESTRIAN OVERPASS
2 · HATCH MUSIC SHELL
3 · REFECTORY
4 · CURTIS MEMORIAL
5 · LOTTA FOUNTAIN
6 · BOAT AND SKATE HOUSE
7 · HOLMES MEMORIAL
8 · SMALL CHILDRENS' PLAYGROUND

7.19 As a compromise for demolishing a hundred-foot swath of the Storrow Memorial Embankment only fifteen years after it was dedicated, the legislature authorized additional fill in the Charles for new parkland. Arthur Shurcliff and his son Sidney designed the reconfigured Esplanade.

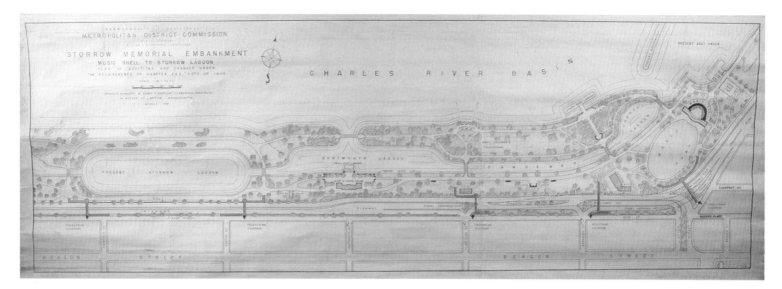

7.20 In their redesign of the Esplanade, the landscape architects proposed two new islands, one from the Hatch Shell to the existing island that formed the Storrow Lagoon and one extending from the upstream end of the lagoon to a point just beyond the Harvard Bridge. Only the downstream filling was completed, as an extension of the existing island.

7.21 Charlesbank was also widened to compensate for the widening of Charles Street, and a pool was constructed to replace the heavily used beach created in the 1930s.

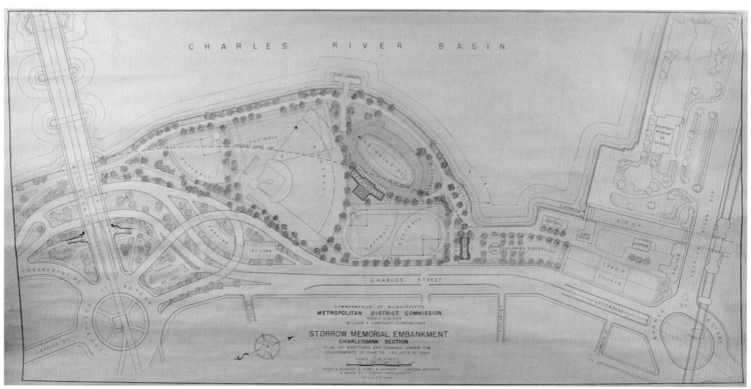

7.22 In 1939, three years after the Esplanade was enlarged, the "Boathouse and Recreation Building" (center) was built on the lagoon. In the winter it was used as a warming house by skaters. The building stood in the way of Storrow Drive and was torn down in 1951.

7.23 The men's field house at Charlesbank (upper left) was demolished in 1951 as part of the second widening of Charles Street along the river edge of the West End.

The new highway demolished both Olmsted's Charlesbank on the edge of the West End and the recreation center between Exeter and Fairfield Streets that had been built as part of the Storrow Embankment construction, completed just thirteen years earlier in 1936 (figures 7.22, 7.23). The loss of parkland at Charlesbank foreshadowed the bulldozing of the entire neighborhood of the West End in the late 1950s, which proceeded with near-unanimous support from the city's business community and from architects and city planners.[44]

Building the First Central Artery

Like the embankment highway, the construction of the original Central Artery also generated vigorous community opposition. Surprisingly, in the case of the artery the protest actually resulted in a major revision to the original plan. At several points along the artery route, lawsuits delayed the demolition of buildings. The butchers in Haymarket Square demanded a new facility before they abandoned their old quarters, but residents and business owners were unable to stop the taking of the first fifty-four parcels of land for the new highway in the North Station area.

Once construction began on the elevated highway along the edge of the North End, the Boston City Council voted to oppose similar demolition in Chinatown and the Leather District. The acting mayor said the destruction of Chinatown would be not only "a grave mistake" but "a cardinal sin." A tunnel design was built instead, even though it resulted in the demolition of almost half the land area of Chinatown.[45]

At the Charles River, Whitten's original plan had proposed only an elevated rotary leading to the northern routes out of the city. Instead, a double-decked steel truss bridge of mediocre design was built over the river (figures 7.24–7.26). It connected with an elevated highway that crossed over City Square in Charlestown and linked with the Mystic River (Tobin) Bridge, which, like the High Bridge over the Charles, was another missed opportunity.

Other changes near the mouth of the Charles reflected the changing view of the city center. "The Front," the park first proposed on the Cambridge side of the river by Charles Eliot in 1894, had been intended as the neighborhood park for East Cambridge, although heavy auto traffic along Commercial Avenue separated the park from the nearby residents (figure 7.27). Community gardens were developed there during the First World War. In 1950 the city determined that its interests were better served by commercial development and sold the entier riverfront between the dam and Longfellow Bridge to private developers. The Cambridge annual report called it the most important piece of industrial development that year. In 1948 the MDC leased the grounds of the park on the

7.24 The new Central Artery crossed the Charles on the double-decked "High Bridge" and connected via an elevated roadway over City Square in Charlestown with the Tobin Bridge, which opened to traffic in 1950. Though its double-decked design minimized the shadow cast on the river, the High Bridge reflected traffic noise from the underside of the upper deck, and its steel truss design continued the Boston tradition of mediocre bridges.

Charles River Dam to the Museum of Science. The museum closed in the open pavilion on the dam and occupied it for more than thirty years; a series of ever-larger buildings was constructed over the next thirty years. A parking garage erected in 1972 filled the entire park space between the O'Brien Highway and the river and severed pedestrian access between Boston and Cambridge on the water side of the park (figure 7.28). As the neglect or abandonment of open spaces up and down the Charles made plain, the commitment to urban parks was clearly on the wane.

7.25 The north- and southbound lanes of the Central Artery met at the High Bridge and then swung to the east over City Square and the Charlestown Bridge. The Warren Bridge (center) was demolished in 1974 for the construction of the new Charles River Dam.

7.26 Traffic from Storrow Drive connected with the Central Artery at Leverett Circle (hidden behind the Registry of Motor Vehicles, upper right, demolished in 2001 for the new artery). Nashua Street passes between the registry and the tracks leading to North Station. Just beyond the registry is the Green Line viaduct across the Charles.

7.27 This aerial photograph was taken in 1925 looking north from Boston toward Cambridge. The Green Line viaduct runs parallel to the dam (left center) and then curves to pass in front of North Station. West of the Green Line and south of the river is the West End (lower left). East of the viaduct a seawall would be built by the Boston & Maine railroad in 1931 to enclose a nearly square parcel of land intended as a switching yard. On the Boston side, depots for the Boston & Maine, Eastern, and Fitchburg Railroads stand in a row on Causeway Street. The Lechmere Canal extends across the upper left of the photograph.

7.28 By 1958 almost every parcel in figure 7.27 had changed. Half of the Lechmere Canal was paved for parking. The open space along "The Front" was replaced by low commercial buildings (GE, Parke-Davis). The Museum of Natural History became the Museum of Science when it moved from the Back Bay in 1949, and in ten years its buildings covered almost all the parkland on the old dam. Downstream of the dam, the unused railyards in Cambridge were filled with one-story warehouses. Interstate 93 was built to connect with the Tobin Bridge and Route 1. The West End would soon disappear, to be replaced by the towers of Charles River Park; Massachusetts General Hospital was a campus of high-rise buildings.

Two projects along the river in Boston were proposed almost as soon as the pavement on Storrow Drive had been poured—new elevated ramps over the Charlesgate section of the Fens to link Route 1 to Storrow Drive, and the extension of the Massachusetts Turnpike to downtown Boston.

Building the turnpike extension into Boston over the railroad right-of-way had been proposed during the acrimonious debates about Storrow Drive. As an authority, the turnpike was independent of the legislature's direct oversight, and it chose to ignore that suggestion. Instead, turnpike director William Callahan announced in 1962 that the authority planned to build that part of the turnpike by filling in eight acres of the Charles just above the Boston University Bridge (figure 7.29). Although the MDC in the 1960s was vigorously pursuing its own road projects elsewhere in the metropolitan parks, this was going too far. MDC commissioner (and former lieutenant governor) Robert F. Murphy proposed instead that the turnpike build a viaduct over the river (an idea only slightly less drastic than the turnpike's), or move their project inland.[47]

When negotiations between the agencies failed, the turnpike authority took the river acreage by eminent domain. The MDC challenged the taking, and the Supreme Judicial Court determined that the turnpike lacked the authority to seize the land. In September 1963, Callahan issued "a terse announcement" that the turnpike would build a bridge three thousand feet long over the New York Central (originally the Boston & Albany) Railroad tracks, the same route that had been proposed as an alternative to the construction of Storrow Drive. (As late as 1977 Storrow Drive with four to six lanes carried 15,000 more cars per day than the turnpike's eight lanes).[48]

Meanwhile, the MDC was busy with plans for more viaducts of its own, just downstream at Charlesgate. The 1929 report that recommended the widening of the Esplanade also described the traffic congestion where the proposed embankment roadway crossed the Charlesgate. Arthur Shurcliff's 1928 design for improving this series of intersections was based on a proposed "Charlesgate Bridge" to Cambridge, with overpasses above

7.29 In 1962 the Massachusetts Turnpike Authority broke ground on the turnpike extension from Weston to downtown Boston. Rather than purchase the air rights above the railroad tracks along the river just upstream of the Cottage Farm (now Boston University) Bridge, the Turnpike proposed filling eight acres of the river itself (dashed line). A year later, the MDC finally succeeded in overturning the proposal, and the highway was built over the tracks.

Commonwealth Avenue and the adjacent streets. Nothing came of the bridge to Cambridge, but the vision of ramps over Commonwealth Avenue persisted. By the late 1950s, the design of limited access roads had changed considerably from Shurcliff's approach, and the plan proposed half a dozen ramps with broader curves that covered most of the riverbank and a large fraction of Olmsted's original design for Charlesgate. Some residents of the nearby neighborhoods were outraged when the "Bowker Overpass" was announced by the MDC, but their objections were easily turned aside, and the project was completed in 1966. In a *Boston Globe* essay on the Back Bay, Bainbridge Bunting concluded that the construction of the Bowker Overpass "desecrated one of the loveliest city parks in America" (figures 7.30, 7.31).[49]

7.30 The construction and subsequent widening of Storrow Drive had already severed the banks of the river from the Charlesgate, Olmsted's link with the Back Bay Fens. After successfully resisting the turnpike's proposal to build in the Charles, the MDC built the Bowker Overpass in 1966, four lanes of elevated highway to connect Route 1 with Storrow Drive, creating a barrier between the Back Bay and Kenmore Square.

7.31 The stone bridge footbuilt as part of the Boston Embankment in 1910 was marooned inside a triangle of elevated ramps. Walkers and joggers along the Esplanade were cut off from the Emerald Necklace.

Hell's Half Acre

Across the river in Cambridge, highway projects in the 1950s and 1960s were far less grandiose, but they generated opposition as vigorous as the Storrow Drive controversies of 1929 and 1949. And when the MDC finally started building the section of riverfront parkway between Gerry's Landing and the Watertown Arsenal, fifty years after the first detailed plans had been completed, activists in Cambridge proposed what was then a radical departure for urban open space: the restoration of the marshes—the same wetlands Charles Eliot had acquired for parks and parkways, saying they "must sooner or later be made useful."[50]

In 1907, plans were completed for a road connecting Mt. Auburn Street in Cambridge with the river entrance to the arsenal at North Beacon Street in Watertown, and the first section from North Beacon to Arsenal Street (now part of Greenough Boulevard) was completed after the river was dammed in 1908. A gravel path a mile and a quarter long was built through the marshes in the area where the road was planned. The rest of the road was postponed, and a portion of the land just downstream of Arsenal Street was transferred by the Metropolitan Park Commission to the U.S. Army as an emergency measure, an "emergency" that lasted until the 1960s.[51] The cleanup of the site that began soon thereafter is still unfinished.

In 1918 the city of Cambridge was permitted to provide lifeguards and portable bathhouses at Gerry's Landing, and a permanent bathhouse was proposed almost annually. A project funded by the federal Works Progress Administration in 1936–1937 included grading, filling, and the construction of walks along the beach (figure 7.32).[52]

With the completion of the Eliot Bridge in 1951, the MDC revived the planning for the road from the new bridge to Arsenal Street, and dumped a gravel base along the road alignment even before the final drawings were finished (figure 7.33).

By far the most famous reaction to the gravel dumping was a 1955 *Harper's* essay by Bernard DeVoto. Although "neither a nature lover nor an outdoorsman," DeVoto was inspired by the

7.32 Gerry's Landing in 1925 was a popular swimming spot just upstream of Mount Auburn Hospital. The Metropolitan Park Commission had determined to build a parkway between the landing and Watertown as early as 1900 and was not interested in developing the beach. In 1918 the city of Cambridge was allowed to provide its own lifeguards and portable bathhouses, which it did until the Second World War.

nature studies pursued by several teenage boys along the Charles in an area they called "Hell's Half Acre." The marsh was hardly pristine wetlands, and by now the river itself was a scandal: "It is foul and noisome, polluted by offal and industrial wastes, scummy with oil, unlikely to be mistaken for water. Still, it *is* a river."[53]

As he had done in lobbying for the national parks, DeVoto advanced an economic argument for preserving this unloved marshland. If leaving the area open "should cost ten or fifty times as much as taking the highway across Hell's Half Acre, it would nevertheless be an economy—a tax and cash economy—so great that a commission endowed with proper business sense could never consider any other course."[54]

DeVoto's essay inspired Annette Cottrell of Cambridge to organize a campaign in 1957 for a thirty-acre nature reservation to be named after DeVoto. By then Richard Simmers and DeVoto's son Mark had identified over 100 species of plants and 40 species of birds in the marsh.[55] Sidney Shurcliff, then the MDC's landscape architect, contributed a plan. Several well-known Cambridge residents joined the cause, including Arthur Schlesinger, José Luis Sert, and Louis Lyons, but Cottrell's neighbors were not unanimously supportive; Bradford Washburn, the director of the Museum of Science, and Ted Storer, the president of a national commercial real estate firm headquartered in Boston, wrote in opposition to her proposed reserve.[56]

In the end, despite three years of hearings and letters and editorials, the road was finally completed in 1966. As one Cambridge city councilor grandiloquently observed, "It is a question of which is more important, the education this wildlife sanctuary might provide for a limited number of students or the economic salvation of Massachusetts and Boston."[57] From then until now, the traffic counts on Greenough Boulevard have been among the lowest of all the sections of roadway along the river.

7.33 In the balancing of traffic pressures and the maintenance of reservations, the MDC's record in the 1950s and 1960s was mixed. Bernard DeVoto, best known for his studies of the western United States, wrote an essay on "Hell's Half Acre" in 1955 that argued against building a road through the marshes upstream of the Eliot Bridge. The road was finally completed in 1966, but the level of auto traffic for this section of the parkway has never reached the level predicted by its proponents.

While the campaign for Hell's Half Acre represented a radical departure in its view of the river environment, another conflict between residents of Cambridge and the MDC ratcheted up the application of the tools of community organizing and public relations. In 1962 the legislature authorized the MDC to build three underpasses along Memorial Drive at River Street, Western Avenue, and Boylston Street (now John F. Kennedy Street), to match the roadway design across the river on Soldiers Field Road. The plan threatened the London plane trees (widely known as sycamores) that Charles Eliot had planted sixty years before, and the MDC's chief engineer could not say "if one tree or all the trees will be taken down" (figure 7.34).[58]

The threat to the trees attracted the attention of the neighbors, including Edward Bernays, widely known as the father of public relations in America and recently retired to Cambridge, and longtime Cambridge resident John Moot. A statehouse hearing in February 1964 drew four hundred people and the attention of

Time magazine. "Present" and "Projected" views of Memorial Drive were shown (figure 7.35), and the testimony in opposition included Paul Dudley White, the renowned cardiologist who had successfully lobbied in 1960 for overturning the ban on bicycles along the Esplanade pathways. The Cambridge Planning Board concluded that "$100,000 of electronically controlled traffic signals would do as well as $6,000,000 worth of bypasses." The legislature nonetheless voted to proceed with the construction.[59]

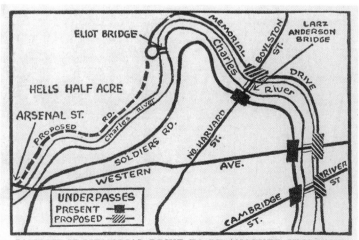

7.34 In 1962 the MDC announced a plan to build underpasses at three intersections on Memorial Drive, to match the grade-separated intersections already constructed directly across the river along Soldiers Field Road.

7.35 The "Citizens Emergency Committee to Save Memorial Drive" mobilized 400 people to attend the State House hearing, which was coverd by *Time* magazine in February 1964. The article included the committee's drawings of "Present" and "Projected" views of Memorial Drive.

The following June, "National Recreation Day" was organized, which Bernays called "a frolic and a protest." While the riverbank in front of the Harvard houses was filled with people, opponents held balloons in a long line to mark the trees and open space that would be paved over (figure 7.36). When the threat continued into the fall, the *New York Times* reported that a "tree patrol" would guard the trees "in the predawn hours," with instructions "to blow a whistle beneath the window of a Harvard housemaster, whose wife has agreed to sound the alarm by telephone."[60]

A new MDC commissioner was appointed, who postponed the construction until a study was completed. The plan finally died a year later. The trees were spared, and the willingness of Cambridge residents to take on the state was reinforced.

Riverbend Park

A few years later, the Cambridge residents who fought to save the sycamores joined to promote a new riverfront "park," dreamed up by Isabella Halsted. John Moot, who later became a board member for the park, believes she was inspired by similar closings along Rock Creek Parkway in Washington, D.C. In 1974 she sent a letter to four hundred residents to see if people would support the closing of Memorial Drive on Sundays from spring to fall. About the same time Halsted attended a charity auction and was the high bidder for a lunch with Senator Edward Kennedy. She described her idea to him, and soon thereafter MDC Commissioner John Sears received a call from the senator. The commissioner agreed to close Memorial Drive—not only between Western Avenue and the Eliot Bridge, but also in front of MIT. On a Sunday in May the following year the drive was closed for the first time.[61]

In 1976 Memorial Drive was closed on Sundays from Memorial Day to Labor Day, and Halsted and the Trust for Riverbend Park raised the money to cover the costs. Nine years later the state legislature finally approved funding and the permanent closing of the drive from April to November. In a letter announcing the state funding, Halsted wrote again to the park's supporters to say that "this is not an appeal for money. Who needs

it? The MDC will pay all operating expenses of the Park, from now on." The letter was signed "gratefully and joyfully, Isabella Halsted."[62] In 1997, a stone bench, the work of the Cambridge sculptor Will Reimann, was installed near Memorial Drive to commemorate her indefatigable efforts to create a day of rest from auto traffic for the riverfront.

The Image of the Road

While some Cambridge residents argued over Hell's Half Acre, MIT professor Kevin Lynch began a series of studies on the "visual quality of the American city." In *The Image of the City* (published in 1960), Lynch considered what he called the "legibility" of Boston, Jersey City, and Los Angeles, and the contributions that visual clarity made to the satisfaction of city dwellers. He sought to determine how residents made sense of the places they lived by asking them for "descriptions, locations, and sketches, and for the performance of imaginary trips."[63]

The visual structure of the historic center of Boston was clear to most residents, Lynch concluded, and the city's visual legibility is strongest along the edge of the Charles (figures 7.37, 7.38). The Common, the gold dome of the State House, and the view across the Charles River Basin from Cambridge symbolized the city. Yet to many the city was "one-sided," and as they moved away from the basin, their sense of the city lost "precision and content." That clarity also dissolved at the lower end of the basin; most people in Lynch's interviews were unable to link the river with Boston Harbor.[64]

Storrow Drive (like the Central Artery) was perceived ambiguously. For pedestrians it was a barrier and made for an unclear connection between the river, Beacon Hill, and the Back Bay. On the other hand, if people imagined themselves in a car on Storrow Drive, the road was perceived as a high-speed path, which contributed to the perception that along the edge of the basin, at least, the city could be visually understood.[65]

The legible structure that contributed so greatly to Bostonians' sense of their city was missing in the observations of

7.36 The Citizens Emergency Committee organized "National Recreation Day" along Memorial Drive in Cambridge in June 1964, with family activities along the river. During the day members of the committee lined up with balloons and had this photo taken to mark the extent of the proposed road construction and to suggest the number of sycamores that would be cut down. Nine months later the legislature authorized a study that effectively postponed the road plan indefinitely.

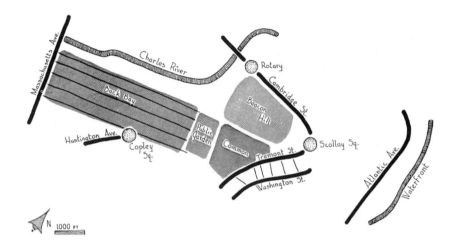

7.37 In his pioneering study *The Image of the City*, MIT professor Kevin Lynch interviewed thirty Boston residents, then sketched what he called "the Boston that everyone knows." The places mentioned most often were Boston Common, Beacon Hill, the Charles River, and Commonwealth Avenue. As this diagram suggests, most of the people were unable to connect the Charles with Boston Harbor.

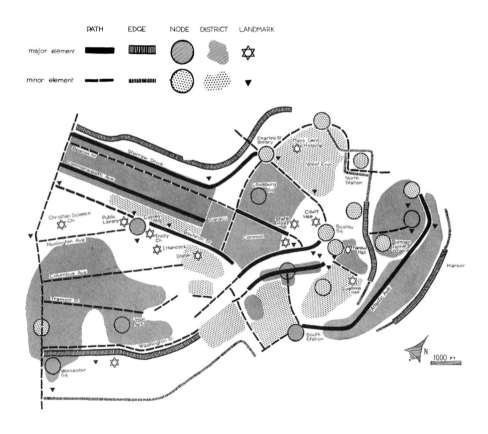

7.38 Lynch analyzed the elements employed by residents to organize and understand the city, which he called paths, edges, nodes, districts, and landmarks. The favorite views of the city were the long views across water. Not surprisingly, one of the most frequently mentioned views was the outline of Beacon Hill as seen from across the Charles in Cambridge.

people in Jersey City and Los Angeles. The new freeways in American cities, according to many urban critics, exacerbated that problem by erecting massive barriers between city neighborhoods. Lynch and his colleagues Donald Appleyard and John Myer were persuaded that well-designed highways could contribute to the life of urban dwellers. By planning for *The View from the Road*, they were convinced that the urban freeways "might be one of our best means of re-establishing coherence and order" on a metropolitan scale. The highway is, or at least might be, a work of art:

> The view from the road can be a dramatic play of space and motion, of light and texture, all on a new scale. These long sequences could make our vast metropolitan areas comprehensible: the driver would see how the city is organized, what it symbolizes, how people use it, how it relates to him. To our way of thinking, the highway is the great neglected opportunity in city design.

Those who were distressed by modern highways focused on the repression of ugliness, rather than on making something positive of the highway experience. The authors acknowledged in passing the parkway tradition, dating back to Olmsted and other nineteenth-century landscape architects, but claimed that the original parkways had been intended primarily for pleasure driving, not "general traffic." In the affluent society of postwar America, they asserted, we could once again choose to make driving more pleasurable.[66]

The design of Boston's Inner Belt would be a good test of this hypothesis, since the highway would cross the basin twice, at Boston University—where drivers and pedestrians could look from the bridge all the way to Beacon Hill—and at the mouth of the river near North Station, the point where the Charles disappeared from sight. The Inner Belt incorporated the existing Central Artery from Charlestown to Roxbury. A new interchange would cut across Roxbury to the Fenway, not far from the Museum of Fine Arts, and cross the Charles just above Boston University. Various routes were considered through Cambridge— from Cambridgeport through Central Square, north of MIT and

then along the river—and then the loop connected again to the Central Artery near City Square in Charlestown (figure 7.39).

Based on their analysis, the authors revised the Department of Public Works (DPW) plan for the beltway, cutting the number of intersections from five to three, and making the road a gently rounded triangle rather than an irregular circle (figure 7.40). One objective was to draw on the surroundings of the three highway segments so they would each have a distinctive character: the Riverway, from East Cambridge to the Boston University Bridge; the Crossing, cutting diagonally through the Back Bay and the South End; and the Centerway, roughly along the alignment of the existing Central Artery. The first and third of these segments would have a strong visual identity because of their relationship to the river and the harbor (figures 7.41, 7.42). Two of the three intersections (in Charlestown and Brighton) were located in rail yards, and the third would be on the Charles, minimizing the disruption of existing street and block patterns.[67]

The visual opportunities in the three-sided plan were appealing (figure 7.43). Yet the difficulties, only some of which were acknowledged in the study, should have been equally clear. Many conflicts existed between the view from the road and the view *of* the road, and they bore directly on issues of legibility and urban structure. If expansive views of the river and the harbor were opened to drivers, they would be lost to the neighborhoods on the opposite side of the road. The triangular scheme forced a crossing at Fort Point Channel, which had been avoided in the 1948 *Master Highway Plan*. The choice of elevated sections (rather than tunnels) across the Fenway seems inconsistent with Lynch's keen observations in *The Image of the City* about the discontinuities between Beacon Hill and the Esplanade created by Storrow Drive.

More fundamentally, the long history of neighborhood resistance to elevated structures—built first for streetcars and later for roadways—might have suggested the possibility of flaws in the basic assumptions of urban freeway design. Nowhere in their argument did the authors raise the issues of scale or urban highway speed limits, or question the fundamental logic of a small number of very large highways through complex old cities like Boston.

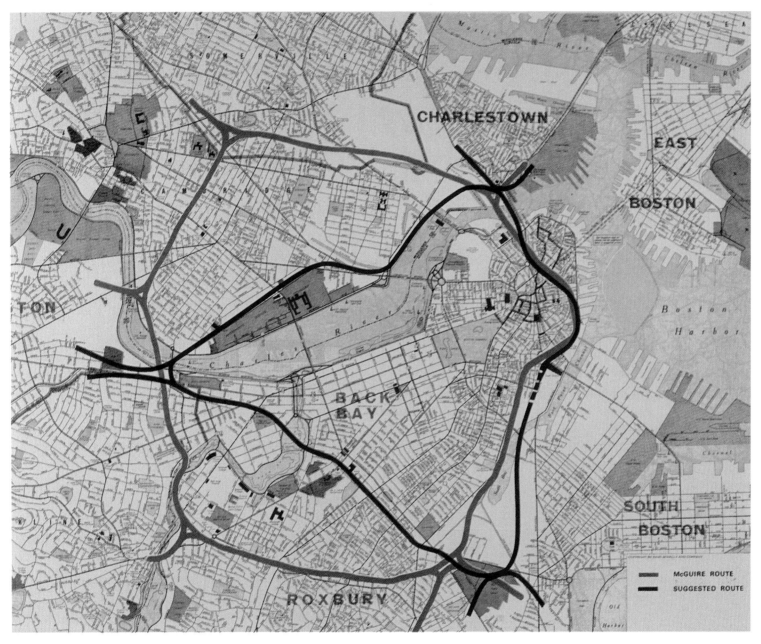

7.39 *The View from the Road* (1964) asserted that the planning of highways was "the great neglected opportunity in city design." Instead of the highway department's five-sided plan for Boston's Inner Belt, a tighter, three-sided plan named each road segment: the "Riverway" ran from Cottage Farm Bridge to Charlestown; the "Centerway" went through downtown and across Fort Point Channel; the "Crossing" cut diagonally across the South End and the Back Bay Fens to Cottage Farm.

7.40 In a photomontage, the three-sided Inner Belt layout was drawn over an aerial photograph of the city. One objective of the revised plan was to give each of the three segments a distinctive character.

7.41 The "Centerway" and "Riverway" sections intersected just beyond the existing Central Artery bridge over the Charles. While the Riverway left almost untouched the half-vacant warehouse parcels adjoining the railroad yards in Cambridge, the intersection with the Centerway multiplied the damage already wreaked on City Square in Charlestown by the previous elevated highway construction of Route 1.

7.42 The "Crossing" segment of the revised Inner Belt divided the South End, cut across Olmsted's Emerald Necklace at the widest point, and erected a barrier the full length of the Boston University campus, already cut off from the river by Storrow Drive.

7.43 The focus on the "view from the road" created driving sequences like this one along the Riverway, as the dome of the State House came into view. Although these drawings look primitive today, they represented the state of the art at the time. The study inexplicably ignored the view of the road as it would be seen from the open areas and dense neighborhoods it would slice through.

Stopping the Inner Belt

Soon after *The View from the Road* was published, the opponents of the mostly elevated Inner Belt succeeded in shifting the state's attention from roadway alignments and design alternatives to the project's fundamental value to the region and its effects on the neighborhoods it would pass through. After Richard Nixon's victory in the 1968 presidential election, Governor John Volpe resigned to accept the president's nomination as secretary of transportation. Lieutenant Governor Frank Sargent was sworn in as acting governor in January 1969 and was almost immediately greeted on the steps of the State House by demonstrators from all over the region. They were protesting the expansion of the airport, the construction of the Southwest Expressway through Fowl Meadow near the Blue Hills, the construction of Interstate 95 through the Lynn Woods, and the proposed demolition of scores of homes to build the Inner Belt.[68]

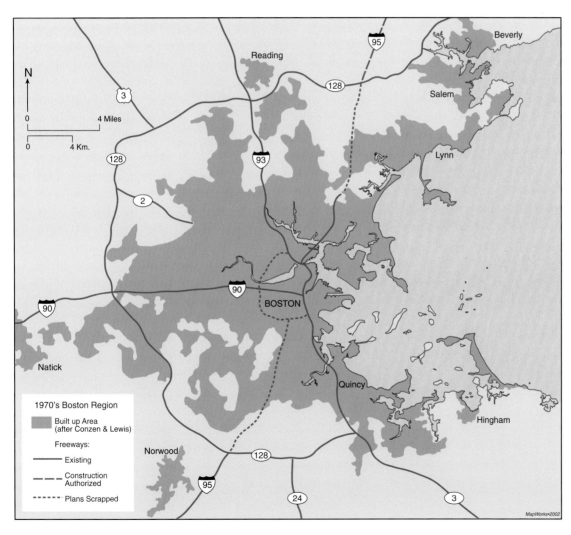

7.44 In 1970 highway opponents persuaded Governor Frank Sargent to cancel both the extension of Interstate 95 through Boston and the Inner Belt highway. The Inner Belt would have cut across the Back Bay Fens and through the middle of Cambridge, with massive interchanges at both ends of the lower basin.

In August Governor Sargent appointed a task force to review the highway controversies, with Alan Altshuler (an MIT political science professor) as chairman and John Wofford (who held appointments at Harvard Law School and the Kennedy School of Government) as executive director. Just before the end of the year the task force drafted a report recommending a restudy of all transportation projects in the metropolitan area. The governor's staff had also consulted with Boston mayor Kevin White, who publicly requested "an immediate halt to any land taking, demolition, or construction now taking place or contemplated for new highways," including the entire Southwest Expressway, the Inner Belt from Somerville through Cambridge and the South End, the third harbor tunnel, I-93, and the Winthrop connector.[69]

Two months later Governor Sargent went on television to say that "nearly everyone was sure highways were the only answer to transportation problems for years to come. But we were wrong." He announced that he had decided to reverse the transportation policy of the state by declaring a moratorium on highway construction inside Route 128 (Boston's "outer beltway").[70]

The governor did exempt two projects from the moratorium, the Leverett Circle Bridge and Interstate 93 through Somerville (figure 7.44). Both of these projects included substantial elevated highway construction, and neither of them required planning studies of any issues besides traffic. In both cases, one of the lessons of the original Central Artery was ignored: that elevated highways through existing communities provoke fierce and tenacious opposition as soon as they are announced.

The Leverett Circle Bridge

Almost unknown except among highway planners and government officials, the Leverett Circle Bridge (sometimes called the Leverett Circle Connector) was the subject of intense, off-and-on combat between the Massachusetts Port Authority (Massport), the MDC, and the cities of Boston and Cambridge. In 1960 Massport offered the MDC $10 million as the authority's share of a bridge linking Storrow Drive with the Mystic River Bridge (figure 7.45).

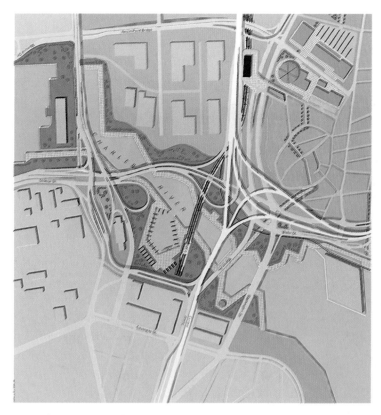

7.45 The Leverett Circle Bridge was promoted at the same time as the Inner Belt as a necessary link between Storrow Drive and Route 1 from the North Shore. In this 1962 plan the connector filled both banks of the Charles below the old dam with highway ramps.

7.46 Newspaper diagrams, like this one in December 1969, made the configuration of the Leverett Circle Bridge look deceptively simple.

Four years later the legislature authorized the MDC to build the bridge, but did not appropriate funds for its construction. In 1966, money was finally authorized to complete a study of the bridge; by this time, planning for the Inner Belt was accelerating and disastrous traffic congestion was already predicted for the merge of Route 1 with the proposed Interstate 93 at the edge of the Charles. Sketch plans published by MassPort called for the demolition of the Green Line viaduct in front of the Museum of Science and the construction of loop ramps near Leverett Circle (figure 7.46). The plan was opposed by city officials, as well as by residents of Back Bay and Beacon Hill. They feared the bridge would increase traffic on Storrow Drive and result in another widening of the road (most of the drive along the river had been increased from four to six lanes only four years after it was opened).[71]

The study dragged on, and the project was caught in the demand of community activists for a halt to highway construction inside Route 128. In his December 1969 letter to the governor requesting a moratorium, Mayor White dropped his opposition to the proposed Leverett Circle Bridge. After the broadcast announcing the moratorium the following February, Sargent indicated that he, too, would not oppose the connector project.[72]

The governor did not, however, intervene to prevent John Sears, the newly appointed MDC commissioner, from undertaking a careful review of the whole idea. A Beacon Hill resident himself, Sears shared the neighborhood concern that the bridge would eventually lead to the widening of Storrow Drive and require filling part of the lagoons.[73]

Section 4(f)

Three years earlier new, uncharacteristically straightforward regulations had been added to federal transportation law that substantially increased the protection for parks, recreation areas, and historic sites. Section 4(f) of the Department of Transportation (DOT) Act of 1966 boldly proclaimed that it is "the national policy that special effort should be made to preserve the natural beauty of the countryside and public park and recreation lands, wildlife and waterfowl refuges, and historic sites." The law prohibited the secretary of transportation from approving any highway or transit projects that require

the use of any publicly owned land from a public park, recreation area, or wildlife and waterfowl refuge of national, State, or local significance as determined by the Federal, State, or local officials having jurisdiction thereof, or any land from an historic site of national, State, or local significance as so determined by such officials unless (1) there is no feasible and prudent alternative to the use of such land, and (2) such program includes all possible planning to minimize harm . . . from such use.

Unlike the far broader and usually much more complex analytical requirements stipulated by the National Environmental Policy Act passed in 1969, Section 4(f), by government standards, was a model of simplicity. First, a determination of significance is to be made by the agency having jurisdiction over the land; second, a written review by the transportation agency is required to show that there is no "feasible and prudent alternative" to the use of the land; third, the transportation agency is to provide "all possible planning to minimize harm" to the land.

The first test of the law to reach the U.S. Supreme Court was *Citizens to Preserve Overton Park v. Volpe* in 1971. Overton Park is a three-hundred-acre park near the center of Memphis, Tennessee; the plans for Interstate 40 through Memphis included a six-lane road that would have separated the zoo from the rest of the park. The U.S. Supreme Court held that parks were not to be taken for transportation projects unless there were "truly unusual factors present in a particular case" or the "costs or community disruption" of alternative highway designs "reached extraordinary magnitudes."[74]

The application of Section 4(f) was also a major issue in the Inner Belt and radial highway studies commissioned by Sargent, and it was cited in the decisions against the alignment of I-95 through the Lynn Woods and Fowl Meadow. The experience of state and local agencies with the new law, however, was still limit-

ed; its applicability to the widening of Storrow Drive could be circumvented by using only state highway funds.[75]

In late 1969 a Back Bay group filed a bill to kill the Leverett Circle bridge. A few months later Sears met with officers of the neighborhood associations of Beacon Hill, the Back Bay, and the Fenway who presented him a petition signed by two thousand people from seventy-four cities and towns; the petition called the bridge an "irrevocable error" that would result in the ultimate destruction of the entire Esplanade. In August, however, Alan Altshuler, the state secretary of transportation, agreed that the bridge was an essential project and that two controls should be established: that neither the Central Artery nor Storrow Drive be widened. A year later the plan was dropped with the tacit approval of Altshuler's office. Edward King, the director of the Msassachusetts Port Authority, was not surprised; King later said he knew when Sears was appointed that the bridge would not be built. Even after his election as governor in 1978, King was not able to resurrect either the "big-build" six-lane version of the Third Harbor Tunnel or the Leverett Connector.[76]

The confrontation over the Leverett Connector would affect highway planning long into the future. Beacon Hill residents, who feared that changes at Leverett Circle would lead to the ruination of the Esplanade, thwarted the consideration of all the proposed tunnel alternatives for the Charles River Crossing in the early 1990s. In the end, a redesigned Leverett Connector would be completed in 1999 as part of the Central Artery/Tunnel project, a change of design so drastic that Leverett Circle itself would disappear in a maze of up- and down-ramps to the depressed Central Artery.

Extending Interstate 93

The second project exempted from the 1970 highway moratorium was the extension of Interstate 93 through Somerville. As with the Leverett Bridge, Mayor White and Governor Sargent agreed not to oppose the construction of I-93 through Somerville to Route 1 at City Square in Charlestown (figures 7.47, 7.48). This construction project was the missing limited-access link between the original Central Artery and the Interstate construction that had divided the MDC's Middlesex Fells Reservation in the 1960s. White's letter to the governor had exempted from the requested moratorium any projects already under contract, and at the time Sargent announced the moratorium the last of four DPW contracts for this section of I-93 was out for bid.[77]

Alan Altshuler said later that there did not seem to be any controversy about I-93 or the bridge when the moratorium was announced. The governor's office was asked if there were any highway projects they could endorse; they said they checked with the city of Boston and with community activists and found no opposition. Others involved with highway planning at that time have suggested that the state did not look hard enough. Lester Ralph, the successful reform candidate for mayor of Somerville in 1970, made the highway project a major issue in his campaign. Everyone, including Altshuler, agreed that soon after the moratorium was announced, "both issues [I-93 and the Leverett Bridge] blew up." Residents of Somerville stood in front of bulldozers and filed a lawsuit to halt construction and change I-93 to a depressed road (figures 7.49, 7.50).[78]

The governor's task force in 1970 made an explicit commitment to look at housing, employment, open space, and pollution—and not just at the highway system. Nothing like that was done for the completion of I-93. The traffic studies alone, however, might have stopped the Interstate had there not been pressure to build at least one highway somewhere. By the end of 1972, according to Altshuler, nobody in the state transportation department wanted to complete I-93 to the Central Artery for fear it would create "traffic pandemonium" at the merge of I-93 and Route 1 on the high bridge over the Charles (figure 7.51).[79]

The decision came down to the money. If the project were suspended, the state would face $10 million in breach-of-contract payments to firms that had already been awarded the construction contracts. On the other hand, completing the $40-million highway would cost the state only $4 million, because the federal government was paying the other 90 percent. The task force had curtly laid out the temptation of federal money before the decision was made to build I-93 through Somerville: "To be blunt, we perceive

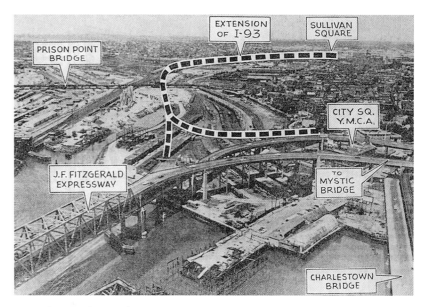

7.47 The completion of Interstate 93 into Boston joined Route 1 (the connection to the Tobin Bridge) just north of the Charles.

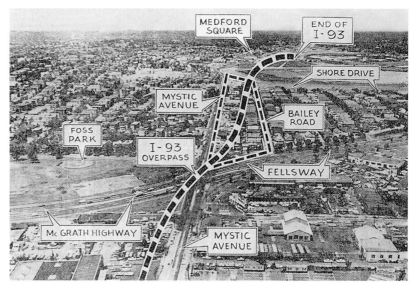

7.48 Somerville residents argued that there was no need to continue the elevated highway simply because it was elevated at the river.

a great mindless system charging ahead. The interstate highways within Route 128 will be built as planned, it appears, not because they are the best public investment—or even the best highway investment—for the money. They will be built solely because they involve ten cent dollars."[80]

There is no better example in Boston of the consequences for transportation planning (predicted as early as the 1940s) once the state share of highway funding was reduced to a small fraction of project costs. The design of the I-93/Route 1 interchange did not meet federal standards and created merges so dangerous that the opening of the completed highway was postponed for months. In addition, given the intense study of these dilemmas by the 1970 governor's task force, it should have been apparent to highway planners how much more difficult this project would make any future resolution of the link between I-93, Route 1, Storrow Drive, and the Central Artery. If any substantive land-use analysis had been completed, it might have revealed the potential of the four hundred acres of nearly empty rail yards in Somerville, an area far larger and better connected to the regional transportation network than the Fan Pier/Pier Four development that attracted so much political attention in the 1980s. To the protestors in Somerville, those concerns paled against the immediate social and economic harm to their city.

7.49 By April 1966 the residents of Bailey Road and Shore Drive had been evicted, just prior to the demolition for Interstate 93.

7.50 Although the residents of Beacon Hill and Back Bay halted the construction of the Leverett Connector, Somerville sought unsuccessfully to delay the highway construction and reconsider its alignment. The appeal of ten-cent federal highway dollars was irresistible. This May 1966 photograph was taken at the corner of Bailey and Temple Roads.

7.51 The completion of Interstate 93 through Somerville (upper left) to the Charles River intersected with Route 1 at the High Bridge. The short weaving distances for traffic were sufficiently hazardous that the highway opening was delayed for several months after its completion. The cofferdam between the Charlestown Bridge and the High Bridge was built for the construction of the new Charles River Dam.

Beyond the two designated park sites more of the
New Basin's complexities and possibilities unfold.
The area is full of both current transportation structures
and sculpturally interesting ruins of older ones. These
old bridge piers may not have to be demolished.
they could become small islands or pedestals for
sculptural events.

8

The Lost Half Mile

Most subjects were unable to interconnect the Charles River and Boston Harbor in any concrete way. Partly this must be due to the screening of the water at the tip of the peninsula by railroad yards and buildings, partly to the chaotic aspect of the water, with its myriad bridges and docks, at the meeting of the Charles River, the Mystic River, and the sea.

Kevin Lynch, *The Image of the City*, 1960

We are escaping a different city; we are in search of a different Mother Nature.

Sam Bass Warner, Jr., 1972

The half mile of the river between the 1910 dam and the mouth of the harbor, a much broader expanse of open water as late as 1830, was almost buried over the next hundred years by road and railway construction. By the 1950s the area was a collage of public and private parcels, cut up by railroads, highways, viaducts, bridges, and a multitude of massive underground pipes and high-voltage electrical lines. The local jurisdiction of the area was divided among Boston, Cambridge, and Somerville; state and federal agencies regulated highways; surface, elevated, and underground rail lines; fish and wildlife, flood control, tidelands, and navigable waterways.[1]

In *The Image of the City*, Kevin Lynch identified the widely shared sense of visual clarity created by the Charles River Basin. At the same time, he found that almost no one could connect the river with the harbor. Lynch speculated that this might be due to the screening of the mouth of the river by bridges, buildings, and rail yards, as well as the lack of continuous paths where the river met the harbor. So many people passed over or around this part of the city without seeing it that in 1986 the writer and editor Max Hall christened the area "the lost half mile" of the Charles.[2]

In 1959 the Boston Society of Architects organized a "Committee on Civic Design," determined to promote a vision of the city's future. The committee streamlined Charles Eliot's image of Boston as a city defined by "the rock hills, the stream banks, and the bay and the sea shores." Boston's greatest asset, according to the

Frontispiece The abandoned railroad trestle at North Station, looking toward the Green Line viaduct and the Museum of Science, 1989.

committee, was water; its second great asset was its hills. The city's structure is "a *line* of water"—the Charles River Basin—and "a *ring* of surrounding hills." Out of these discussions came a 1960 sketch by Kevin Lynch for what came to be called the "High Spine"—a two-block-wide corridor of tall buildings that would extend from the Back Bay Fens to the harbor (figure 8.1).[3]

Although great attention was given to realizing the vision of the "High Spine," little notice was paid to Lynch's proposal for gateways into the city. His sketch showed a southern gateway along the Southeast Expressway, a western gateway along the Charles just upstream of Boston University, and a northern gateway at the junction of the Charles and the harbor. The two gateways along the river echoed Eliot's proposals for new bridges with expansive views at just those locations (see figures 5.11, 5.14).

Neither a gateway nor any other development in the "lost half mile" attracted any attention to the area, which languished in the shadows of the more alluring projects to the west and south. Beginning with the administration of Mayor John Collins, enormous public energy and professional attention were fixed on the urban renewal projects for Government Center and the West End.[4] The Central Artery between Haymarket and the river, completed in the late 1950s, erected an enormous barrier between the commercial establishments in the Bulfinch Triangle and the residents of the North End. Passenger traffic into North Station was dwindling.

Plans for the "lost half mile" would finally be revived in the late 1970s—but not because private capital discovered the potential value of this area, so close to the center of the city, or because of planning or urban renewal efforts instigated by Boston, Cambridge, or the Commonwealth. Hurricanes struck the city in 1954 and 1955, and Cambridge and the Back Bay suffered large losses from flooding. Seven years later the General Court approved the construction of a new Charles River dam on the site of the Warren Bridge; the level waters of the Charles River Basin would be extended a half-mile closer to the harbor. Then while one set of city, state, and federal agencies worked to reclaim this area, christened the New Charles River Basin by the MDC in 1980, anoth-

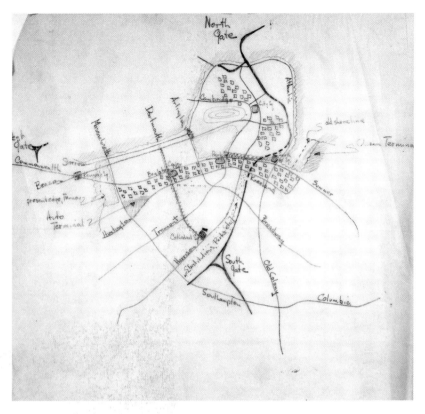

8.1 In 1960 Kevin Lynch sketched a plan christened the "High Spine." It concentrated new high-rise commercial construction south of Boylston Street from the Back Bay Fens to the financial district and Fort Point Channel on the edge of the harbor. Usually overlooked on the drawing are the three proposed gateways into the city, the "South Gate" along the Southeast Expressway, the "West Gate" on the Charles near the Boston University Bridge, and the "North Gate" at the junction of the Charles and the harbor—along the "lost half mile."

er set of agencies created increasingly complex and overlapping regulations that would apply to this peculiar, urban riverfront.

The End of the Line

Charles Eliot had predicted in 1894 that the railroads would sooner or later lose the state permits that allowed them to "temporarily" cover the mouth of the river with timber bridges and switching platforms.[5] That did not come to pass. In fact, the expansion of the railroads at the mouth of the Charles continued into the first several decades of the twentieth century. In 1928 the Boston & Maine Railroad (which by then had acquired the interests of most of the rail lines into North Station) was authorized by the state to build a seawall and to fill permanently much of what remained of the meeting point of the Miller's and the Charles southeast of the Prison Point (now Gilmore) Bridge.[6]

The filling was only part of a much larger plan to consolidate the railroad's interests in Boston. The design for a whole complex of buildings along Causeway Street was presented to the city in glamorous drawings that played up the buildings' spare art deco motifs. The station incorporated a new Boston Garden above the station level and was flanked by an office building on the east and the Hotel Manger on the west. New bascule bridges over the Charles replaced several existing structures, including the original jackknife drawbridge built in the 1830s. In 1929 the buildings of the old McLean Asylum on Cobble Hill (which had been sold to the railroad in 1895) were demolished, the hill was leveled, and when the work was done the railroad gave a dinner for 2,000 people on the site to celebrate.[7] Soon after the dinner, a freight warehouse was constructed on the remains of the once-famous eminence.

The Boston & Maine misjudged its own future. Auto and truck traffic exploded after World War II, and the railroad's passenger service at North Station began a long, slow decline. The elevated structures of Interstate 93, completed in 1972, took acres of the once-vast rail yards, reinforcing the barriers that divided Somerville and separated Cambridge from Charlestown.

City and Regional Plans

It was not just the lower Charles River that seemed to disappear in the minds of Boston residents; after World War II, the neighborhoods on both sides of the river entered what was described as an irreversible decline. The clearance of the West End for public housing was suggested in the late 1930s, and ten years later the Boston Planning Board identified the West End, as well as the North End and the South End of Boston, as sites for slum clearance.[8]

In 1957, the city organized the Boston Redevelopment Authority to take control of the West End urban renewal project. In the grand renewal schemes that were executed in Boston in the 1960s, the proposal for new public open space at the mouth of the Charles was a minor element. It was, however, one more example of the challenges facing the city of Boston in dealing with the plans of numerous state and federal agencies. As Mayor Collins asked in 1960, "Who, if not the City of Boston, is to coordinate the activities of the State Department of Public Works, the Turnpike Authority, the Port Authority, the MDC, and the railroads as they make their presently uncoordinated plans about what to do for Boston?"[9]

Five years later the Redevelopment Authority published its *1965/1975 General Plan for the City of Boston and the Regional Core*. The plan considered regional as well as local transportation and land-use planning issues, and it attempted to assess the potential for both private and public development. The "City of Ideas," according to the report, faced a host of troubling issues: "economic stagnation; antiquated public services; an inadequate transportation system; loss of population; deteriorating housing; and extensive commercial and industrial blight, to name a few." By mid-century, in contrast to growth and prosperity in other parts of the northeast, Boston had the appearance of a city that had "already seen its best years."[10]

Although the analysis of open space and recreation was only a fraction of the report's consideration of public facilities, the plan made two essential points about public spaces. First, a variety of recreational opportunities was essential to Boston's reputation.

Second, the nonrecreational use of Boston's harbor and river shores was a blight; if these spaces were developed for recreation, they would significantly enhance the city's economic soundness. The Neponset River, the Harbor Islands, and Fort Point Channel were seen as major large-scale opportunities. Smaller potential waterfront sites were described briefly, including harbor frontage in East Boston, the North End, the North Station area, and South Boston. The extension of the Charles River Basin to the proposed new dam was included in this list, the first time this project was described in a public planning document. Only the south side of the river was mapped as future open space, however; the complex geometry of the proposed Leverett Connector took most of the Charlestown side of the river (figure 8.2).[11]

The first detailed planning for open space along the New Charles River Basin (New Basin) was a consequence of hurricanes in 1954 and 1955 that caused severe flooding on both sides of the lower Charles. The 1955 storm dumped twelve inches of rain on Boston in two days, and the water in the basin rose more than four feet above normal. Damage was estimated at more than five million dollars. The MDC commissioned several engineering studies of the river, and all the reports concluded that a new dam should be constructed downstream of the 1910 earthen structure, with a pumping station of sufficient capacity to push the flood waters of the river into the harbor even in the face of high storm tides. In 1962 the legislature approved a new dam at the mouth of the Charles, but it did not appropriate funds for its construction. Controversy over the cost of the project led eventually to a comprehensive study of the whole watershed by the Army Corps of Engineers.[12]

To keep up with the corps, Lydia Goodhue of the Wellesley League of Women Voters organized all the league chapters in towns along the river and created the "Charles River Valley Group" in 1963. The following year a lengthy series on the Charles was published in the *Boston Globe*. The Boston Society of Landscape Architects organized a day trip for local officials (reminiscent of the 1892 tours organized by Charles Eliot for the Metropolitan Park Commission), with a morning boat tour of the

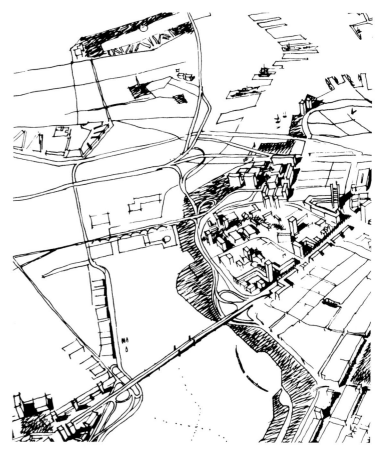

8.2 Studies in the 1960s usually included as an objective the development of public open space to connect the city's neighborhoods. Along the Charles, however, the proposed new highways—the Leverett Circle Bridge and the Inner Belt—would increase the barriers between the North End, the West End, Charlestown, and East Cambridge.

basin and an afternoon bus ride through the river towns from Watertown to Needham.[13]

The result was the organization of the Charles River Watershed Association in 1965, with a charter to take on all the issues that touched on the river for its entire eighty miles. The League of Women Voters supported the new association by pulishing a hundred-page document titled *Charles River Valley: A Guide for Citizens Concerned about Its Future*.[14]

Nathan Pusey, the president of Harvard, organized the very active committee that oversaw the planning being done by the corps, and when the generals proposed a whole series of concrete drainage ditches in the upper valley towns, Rita Barron, the Watershed Association's second director, took up the challenge. In the end, the original plan was transformed into a program of "Natural Valley Storage," at the time the only "nonstructural" flood control project in the country. The corps eventually purchased 3,252 acres and acquired conservation easements on several thousand additional acres, which prevent development on the land. Although many of the Watershed Association's members lived in Boston's western suburbs, they actively supported both the transfer of four acres of federally owned property along the "lost half mile" across from the Museum of Science and the construction of the new dam; a federal appropriation for the dam was finally passed in 1968.[15]

As Olmsted's plan for the Back Bay Fens had seamlessly woven the re-creation of a salt marsh landscape into a program of flood control and sanitary improvement, the proposed new dam, together with the dramatic decline in railroad activities along the river, seemed to open the way for the first time in a century to link the open space of the Charles with Boston Harbor. The 1962 legislation for the new dam granted control of the "lost half mile" of the river and the adjoining lands to the MDC, and extended the same powers outlined in the 1903 and 1909 statutes that had authorized construction of the first dam to create a "water park."[16]

In the mid-1960s the Boston Redevelopment Authority commissioned a study of the Charles Basin and the Muddy River by landscape architect Roy Mann. Responding to the studies of the Charles by the Corps of Engineers, Mann argued that the river should not be analyzed alone but as part of a larger open space system that suffered from truncated links to Boston Harbor and the Back Bay Fens, which had been all but severed from the basin by the construction of the Bowker Overpass (Route 1) over Charlesgate. Tying the basin to the harbor would not only connect the Boston and Cambridge Esplanades with Charlestown and the North End, but would also provide the matrix for real estate development on both sides of the river near North Station.[17]

The Charles and the "lost half mile" also figured importantly in the *Open Space and Recreation Program for Metropolitan Boston* published by the Metropolitan Area Planning Council in 1969, part of the federally funded Eastern Massachusetts Regional Planning Project. Sponsored by the state Departments of Public Works and Commerce and Development as well as 152 of the region's cities and towns, one of the *Program*'s primary goals was to address the relationship of open space systems to transportation facilities and development patterns. The study made several assumptions. First, the United States was becoming a nation of city dwellers; urban areas were expanding at the rate of one million acres a year (no distinction was drawn between urban and suburban populations). Second, rising incomes and increased leisure time were driving a rapid rise in the demand for recreation. In addition to active and passive recreation, the analysis considered the conservation of natural resources and the organization of urban space.[18]

The third of the study's four volumes addressed the three primary rivers of metropolitan Boston and the opportunities they presented for creating continuous open space. The Mystic, Charles, and Neponset Rivers form "the backbone of the inland open space system," dividing the urban area into four roughly equal sectors and providing linear open space within easy walking distance or driving time of every community.[19]

In emphasizing the unique character of the region's rivers, the study echoed the Metropolitan Park Commission's first report of 1893. Like Baxter and Eliot, the authors of the *Open Space and Recreation Program* asserted that the quality of metropolitan life depended as much on the provision of recreation and the enhancement of natural areas as it did on "homes, jobs, or highways." Yet seventy-five years after the first acquisitions along the region's rivers, and in spite of the international renown of the Charles Basin, only 65 of the 224 miles of river banks in greater Boston were in public ownership. The new report repeated the 1893 park commission's recommendation that the shores of all the region's rivers should be publicly owned or controlled.[20]

The *Open Space and Recreation Program* presented the development of the "lost half mile" of the Charles in a clearly delineated regional context.[21] Acknowledging the state legislature's approval of the new Charles River dam seven years earlier, as well as the planned Inner Belt highway construction, the study urged that park land should be acquired immediately upstream of the proposed dam, prior to the start of highway construction (figures 8.3, 8.4). The dam was to be built on the site of the Warren Bridge, which had provided both vehicular and pedestrian connections from City Square and the Navy Yard to North Station. To replace that pedestrian link, the report recommended the construction of a walkway across the locks, the lock gates, and the pumping station at the new dam.[22] Like Boston's 1965 *General Plan*, the *Open Space Program* left blank the Cambridge side of the "lost half mile."

8.3 In 1969 the first comprehensive metropolitan open space plan since 1893 was published. Though the plan proposed a connection between the Boston Esplanade and the harbor, it showed no new open space on the Charlestown side of the river; most of that area was taken up by highway ramps.

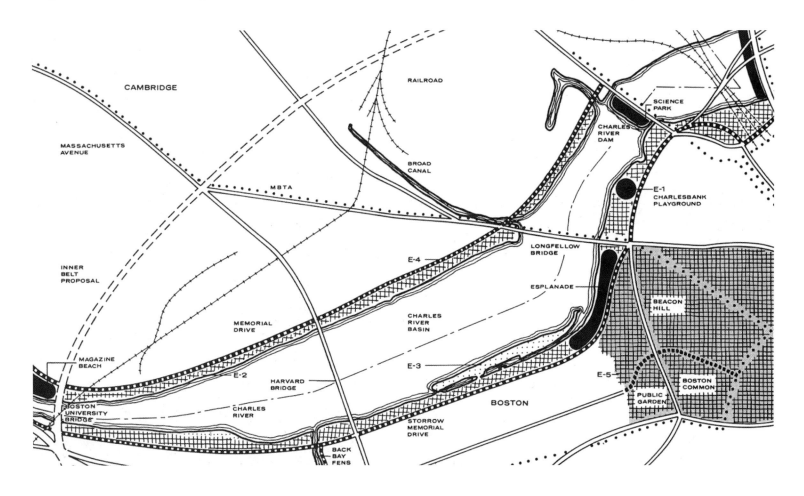

Chapter 8

EXISTING LOCK

RECOMMENDED PROJECT

BOSTON HARBOR

8.4 Many neighborhoods along the river in Boston and Cambridge were flooded during the hurricanes of 1954 and 1955. Following a series of studies by the Army Corps of Engineers and others, the legislature approved a new dam and pumping station downstream of the 1910 dam at Leverett Street. Initially the proposal included an elevated replacement for the Warren Avenue bridge.

Damming the New Basin

Begun in 1974, the dam, locks, and pumping station were completed four years later. Six pumps were installed, each driven by a 2,700-horsepower diesel motor, with a total capacity of more than three million gallons a minute. The new dam had been completed but not opened at the time of the blizzard of February 7, 1978, when the storm tide rose five and a half feet above mean high water, equaling the record high tide of April 1851. The locks and sluices were closed, and after the storm the pumps ran for several days straight.[23]

On either side of the pumping station and the locks, the dam was an earthen structure faced with stone riprap along the Charles and the harbor (figures 8.5-8.7). Fenced pedestrian walkways were built across the new dam and on the lock gates. On the north side of the pumping station a fish passage was built to accommodate the spring spawning runs of alewife and blueback herring, shad, and smelt. Lighted paths on the Boston side extended along the shore as far as the railroad bridges upstream (in anticipation of a future pedestrian crossing over the tracks). Walkways also connected the dam with the commercial buildings that faced Causeway Street. The three-acre park on the north side of the dam, a tree-lined grass oval, was named Revere Landing Park. Although of unexceptional design, these parks and pedestrian ways would later be of crucial legal importance in the debates over the scale and form of the Charles River Crossing.

Unlike the meandering shores and planted meadows of the Fens, which were integral to Olmsted's 1880s design for the Muddy River, the proposed open space upstream of the new dam was not a functional necessity in the new flood control program at the mouth of the Charles. But no property was acquired along the "lost half mile" until the late 1980s; by then the plans for depressing the Central Artery were well advanced.

The North Station Development Plan

From the redevelopment authority's perspective, the riverfront parks were significant as part of a much larger scheme for the Bulfinch Triangle that included a substantially renovated and expanded Boston Garden and North Station. The first step in that scheme was securing the site for a new federal office building. The federal General Services Administration at first preferred a location facing Boston Common, but the redevelopment authority retained the architectural firm of Moshe Safdie Associates to document the benefits of a Causeway Street location and the development that was likely to follow the federal investment in the area. The Safdie study, completed in 1980, included the first elaboration of the urban design opportunities in the "lost half mile" since Eliot's 1894 sketch.[24]

The advantages of the North Station area included well-developed transit and auto access and proximity to Government Center, Faneuil Hall, and the Charles River. The red brick buildings, mostly four to eight stories, established a distinctive character for the Bulfinch Triangle. But there were also obvious reasons for the area's dilapidated state. The elevated structures of the Green Line and the Central Artery, and the rail lines and railroad bridges across the Charles, divided the area, already small, into fragments: the viaduct between Leverett Circle and the artery cut off most of the riverbank; North Station was squeezed between the viaduct and the Green Line. Almost seventy percent of the property was owned by the city or the state, including all of the riverfront except for the Spaulding Rehabilitation Hospital.[25]

Perhaps the most striking aspect of the plan was its optimism about the work to be completed in the first three years. These included "the most important and immediate public initiative," the removal of the Green Line elevated tracks on Causeway Street; a new federal office building; and the renovation of Boston Garden. Those projects would be followed by the permanent relocation of the Green Line. Consistent with the late 1970s preliminary planning for the artery, the plan recommended that in the long term the northbound Storrow connector should be relocated in a tunnel under the Charles, and the southbound Storrow connector rebuilt on grade or in a tunnel. The rail lines on the river side of North Station should be relocated downstream, or rebuilt underground as part of the artery construction. Simplifying the tangle of

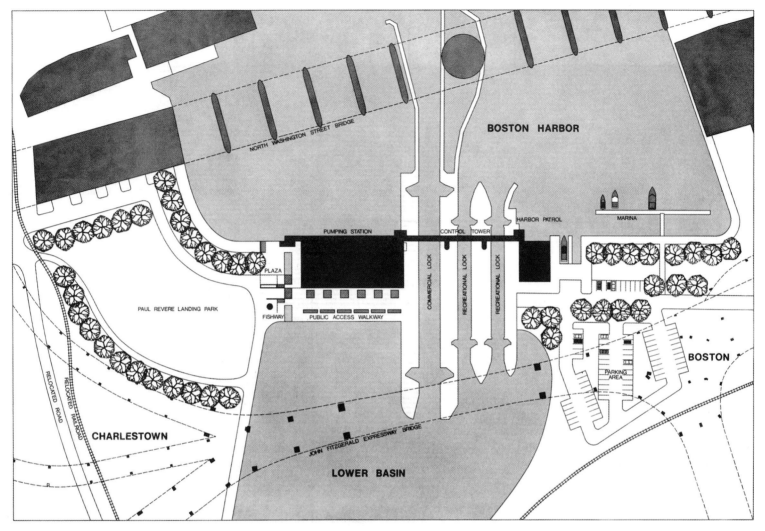

8.5 In the final plan, a new Warren Bridge was deleted. The new dam was an earthen structure with a pumping station and locks in the middle. Although at first planned as a parking lot, the north side of the dam's surface became a large new park, just across Rutherford Avenue from City Square in Charlestown. Walkways were constructed across the lock gates, creating a pedestrian connection between Charlestown and North Station.

8.6 A large cofferdam was created for the construction of the pumping station and locks.

8.7 The red brick of the pumping station echoed the brick warehouses along Causeway and Water Streets. In February 1978, before the completed pumping station had been formally dedicated, a freak winter storm in Boston with hurricane-force winds produced a high tide fifteen feet above mean low water, equaling the all-time record set in 1851. The locks and sluices were closed, and the pumps, running for several days after the storm, pushed the flood waters into the harbor, overpowering the incoming tide.

elevated and underground transportation structures would be crucial if the vision for the area were to be realized.[26]

These publicly funded actions would be followed by a major renovation of Boston Garden and 1,500,000 square feet of private construction, all of it surrounded by "Rockefeller Center–type" open space. Over five hundred thousand square feet of building renovation was expected in the Bulfinch Triangle south of Causeway Street. Along the river eleven hundred units of housing and a four-hundred-room hotel would be developed with connections to Canal Street, the Freedom Trail, and upriver to the Esplanade.[27]

The architects took a bold approach to reconfiguring land uses along the river. Two schemes made only modest alterations in the shoreline, in configurations they labeled "Back Bay Fabric" and "Towers in the Park." Gourlay's 1844 fantasy of an island in the river was revived, in two quite different variations. A plan for "Piers and Canals" would create a "one-of-a-kind environment" like Amsterdam and Venice. A "Mixed Use Island" proposed a single, more articulated island, large enough for new development and open space, with public spaces on both sides of a reshaped river channel (figures 8.8–8.10).[28]

City and state officials succeeded in the primary objective of the *Development Plan*, which was persuading the federal government to build a new office building on Causeway Street. Everything else outlined in the *Plan*, including the "immediate" public-sector initiatives, was delayed—the demolition of the elevated Green Line, the creation of a "super-station" linking the Orange and Green Line with the commuter rail platform, the North Station–South Station rail link. The owners of the Boston Garden later determined to construct a new building, but that, too, became inextricably entwined with the planning for the Central Artery.

The First New Basin Master Plan

In 1980, the MDC responded to the highway planning for the Central Artery and directed the agency's chief landscape architect to draw a "master plan" for the "Proposed New Charles River

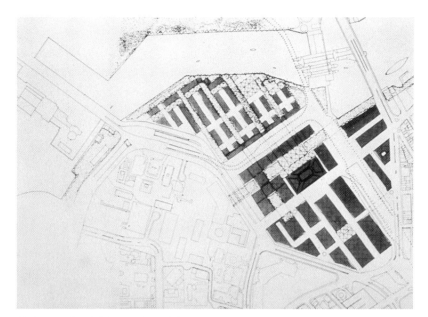

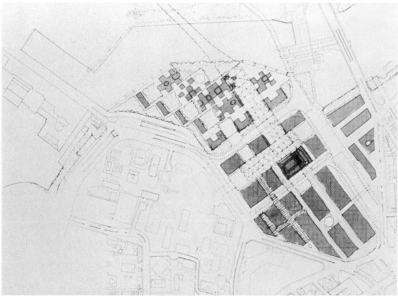

8.8 Hoping to persuade the federal government that the Bulfinch Triangle was a better site for a new federal office building than across from Boston Common, the Boston Redevelopment Authority commissioned a study of the North Station area. In several of the schemes drafted by Moshe Safdie Associates, the commuter rail tracks were relocated or rebuilt in tunnels.

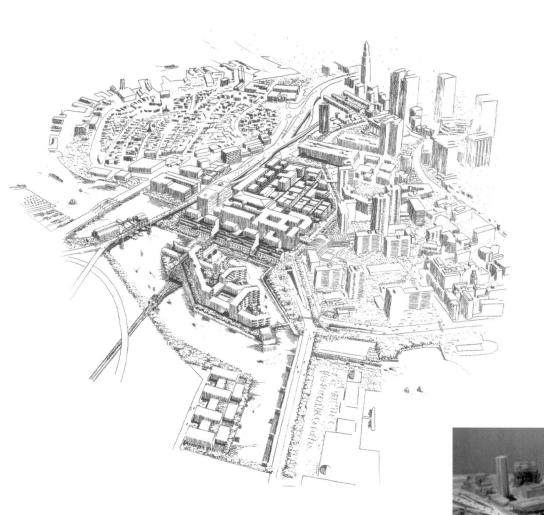

8.9 The North Station study included a proposed island, harkening back to the island proposals of 1905–1920. In this scheme a second river channel would be created directly behind North Station.

8.10 The model of the North Station area shows part of the elevated highway replaced by a tunnel under City Square (lower left), with two sets of ramps coming out of the tunnel and connecting with the artery.

Basin," which consisted of a single drawing (figure 8.11). To establish a formal record of its future intentions, the MDC commissioners voted to endorse the master plan.[29]

The proposed New Basin extended the design approach of the Storrow Embankment. New fill would create an island along Nashua Street, with a lagoon on the landward side, and would enlarge the open space on the water side of Spaulding Hospital (figure 8.12). Continuous pathways would link the New Basin with the esplanades upstream and with the surrounding city. A footbridge was proposed across the lock on the old dam to the pavilion behind the Museum of Science. The drop in elevation from the drawbridge to Leverett Circle created the possibility of a walkway beneath the O'Brien Highway to the new park space along Nashua Street. The narrow channel that was the remnant of the Miller's River would be landscaped on both sides, and a footbridge would be constructed where the Miller's River met the Charles. Walkways would be extended over the railroad tracks, along the harbor side of the old Austin Company (later Stop and Shop) building, and would continue under the Charlestown Bridge to the North End (figure 8.13).

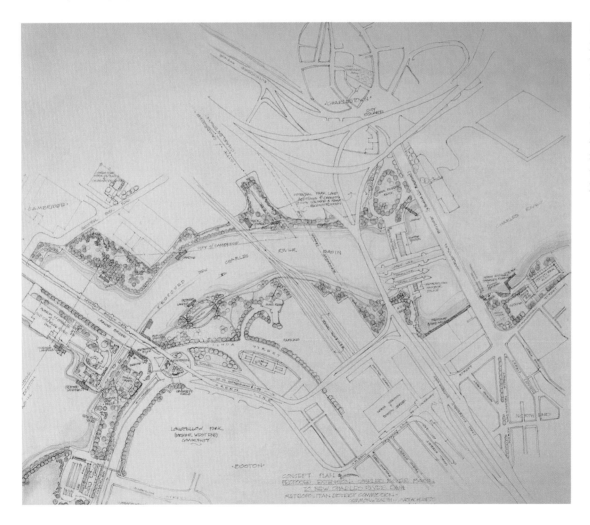

8.11 When it became clear that the proposed Central Artery project would require a new crossing of the river, the MDC developed a plan in 1980 for what it called the "New Charles River Basin." The plan identified potential new public space around the highway construction, and included links and bridges to connect the Boston and Cambridge Esplanades with the harbor.

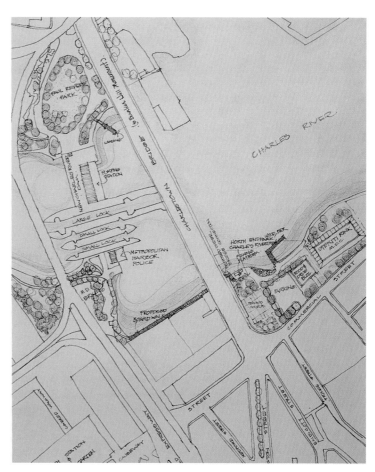

8.12 The New Basin plan included pedestrian bridges over the railroad tracks, large landscaped areas along the inlet at North Point in Cambridge and around the remnant of the Miller's River, and a new island and lagoon near Nashua Street.

8.13 At the new dam, the master plan included a boardwalk under the Charlestown Bridge, creating a continuous pathway from the North End upstream to the Boston Esplanade.

The MDC's plan for the New Basin was pinted in the 1982 environmental impact statement for the north area of the Central Artery project. Although the MDC had always had the power of eminent domain, money for land acquisition was limited, and several years passed without progress on the plan.[30]

Commonwealth Tidelands

A major revision of state law was the impetus for the first open space acquisitions in the New Basin. The state waterways legislation, Chapter 91 of the Massachusetts General Laws, established regulations for construction and development along waterways, including tidelands, rivers, and streams. Following the passage of the original version of Chapter 91 in 1866, the railroads were required to obtain licenses for temporary or permanent fill along the lower Charles, which were routinely granted; there was apparently no interest in providing public access in what was generally viewed as an industrial area.

The origin of Chapter 91 goes back to 1641, when the government of colonial Massachusetts granted ownership rights down to the low tide mark in order to promote wharf building. These grants were subject to a guarantee of public access for fishing, fowling, and navigation, an acknowledgement of the doctrine of public trust in Roman and English law, which recognized broad rights in natural resources as well as the state's obligation as trustee of the public interest.[31]

The law was amended in 1983 to protect "water-dependent uses" of Commonwealth tidelands (fishing, shipping by water, etc.) and to promote other public purposes; in particular, to enhance public access to the water. Chapter 91 licenses would be required for all projects on, over, or under "flowed tidelands," that is, seaward of the present mean high water shoreline. The regulation also applied to "filled tidelands," the area between the present mean high water line and the historic high water line; that jurisdiction was bounded, however, by a line 250 feet from mean high water or the first public way, whichever was further landward (figure 8.14). Along the Charles River in Boston, for example, even

though all structures in the Back Bay were built on filled tidelands, the law would apply only to the area between the river and Storrow Drive, the public way nearest the water.[32]

A new development of a "non-water-dependent use"—for example residential or commercial construction—on filled land would be required to create an appropriate public benefit like waterfront parks or public walkways. Over time, the revised regulations added significantly to the public access in the New Basin, but their application was dependent on the piecemeal pattern of new public and private development. The Chapter 91 licensing procedures constituted one more regulatory overlay in the fragmented, parcel-by-parcel reclamation of the New Basin.[33]

Between 1984 and 1988 the Chapter 91 waterways licenses for three projects along the "lost half mile" mandated the construction of several waterfront pathways and required the transfer of two large parcels of waterfront land for future park development. The first project was to replace the railroad trestles at North Station that burned in 1984, shutting down all the commuter lines into North Station. At least one person realized the opportunity this offered. Roy Mann, author of the 1967 Charles Basin study, had later published *Rivers in the City*, a study of the river fronts in a score of cities around the world.[34] Soon after the trestle fire, his letter to the editor of the *Globe* cited both the 1967 report and Charles Eliot's proposal of 1894. The fire, Mann wrote, was another indication of the hundred-year-old conflict between the surface rail crossing and the frequent proposals for riverfront open space. Instead of rebuilding the trestle, the rail crossing should be buried in a tunnel, which would not only allow for open space at North Station but would encourage taxable private development where the train platforms were located. Mann also pointed out that the highway ramps proposed in Charlestown should be pulled back from the river's edge so that the proposed Esplanade extension "could see the light of day." Mann's proposal was never seriously entertained by any state or local agencies. Instead, a new concrete trestle was built on the site of the old one. The Chapter 91 license for the new trestle required the construction of walkways on the upstream and downstream edges of the new structure; even though

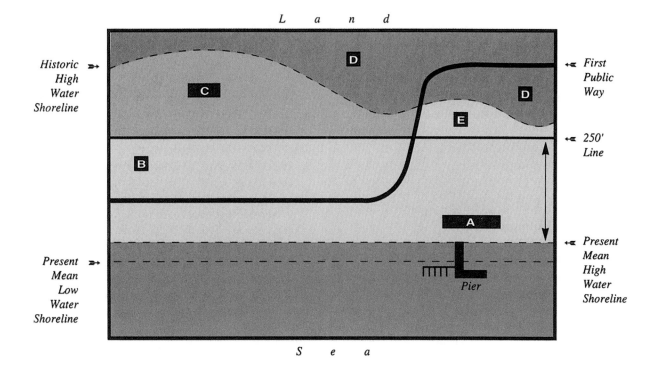

Land

Historic High Water Shoreline ➤

First Public Way ◄

250' Line ◄

Present Mean Low Water Shoreline ➤

Present Mean High Water Shoreline ◄

Pier

Sea

Flowed tidelands – *Chapter 91 license required*

Filled tidelands with buildings A, B & E – *Chapter 91 license required*

Landlocked (*i.e. landward of the first public way and more than 250 feet landward of MHW*) **filled tidelands with building C** – *does not require a Chapter 91 license since the site is not located within a Designated Port Area*

Upland with buildings D – *not subject to Chapter 91*

8.14 Chapter 91 of the state code regulated tidelands and historically addressed fishing, fowling, and navigation between the lines of high and low tide. In a major updating of the statute in 1983, new development on historic tidelands required the provision of public access and public benefits. Chapter 91 decisions were of great significance in acquiring and developing public space along the New Basin.

the walks dead-ended in the middle of the river at the railroad drawbridges, they were seen as an essential next step in linking the fragmented parcels of public land along the river.[35]

Two years later, in 1986, a court-ordered settlement mandated the construction of a new Suffolk County jail. Although in the middle of the city, the "lost half mile" was visually removed from residential neighborhoods and therefore a politically acceptable site for the prison. Again, a Chapter 91 license was required; it mandated the transfer to the MDC of a hundred-foot-wide strip of land on the river side of the jail site, extending from Leverett Circle to Spaulding Hospital. Under the license, park construction was to be completed within two years after the last lease on the property (for a state-run helicopter landing site) expired. It was argued during the jail's planning that the building's function was incompatible with the vision for the New Basin; after its completion, the jail was also criticized for being unnecessarily luxurious.[36]

The most complex waterways license in this area was for the new Central Artery, which had been divided into three study areas: north, central, and south. By the mid-1970s, the Central Artery North Area (CANA) project was split off as an independent project. The state DPW argued that the northern section could be designed to accommodate a depressed Central Artery, and even if the depression of the center section was never approved, the north area project would remove the dangerous weave at the merge of Route 1, Interstate 93, and the Storrow Drive connector.[37] The plans for the north area called for the demolition of the elevated highway over City Square in Charlestown, to be replaced by a tunnel and loop ramps connecting the Mystic River Bridge and Interstate 93. The loop ramps would extend in a rising semicircular arc from the proposed City Square tunnel over the last remnant of the Miller's River and encircle the large plant of the Boston Sand & Gravel Company. The loops would take up most of the portion of the then-vacant rail yards south of the Gilmore Bridge and might also require the demolition of a nondescript assemblage of warehouses in Cambridge.

The construction of the City Square tunnel and loop ramps would dig up the edge of the recently completed Revere

Landing Park between the highway and the dam, and the highway department proposed using the balance of the park as a staging area. The federal Section 4(f) review of the north area project approved the temporary use of the park during construction and required the redesign of the park after the highway was completed. Because the loop ramps were built on filled tidelands, the state Chapter 91 license went beyond the federal 4(f) requirements and mandated that the DPW transfer to the MDC a large portion of the land under the demolished elevated highway and around the new loop ramps as an extension to Revere Landing Park.[38]

The Lechmere Triangle and North Point

While the state DPW was beginning the early planning for the north area project, the Cambridge Community Development Department completed a planning study for redevelopment of the Lechmere Canal area, immediately to the west. Industrial production in the area after World War II had declined dramatically, and many old buildings, including historic landmarks like Bulfinch's Middlesex County Courthouse, were vacant (figures 8.15, 8.16). In 1950 the city sold the park land along the river for the construction of commercial buildings and a hotel. Because the area was zoned for industrial development, with no height limit and no housing allowed, the adjoining residential neighborhood, extending west from Second and Third Streets, feared the possibility of more large-scale commercial development.[39]

Following a two-year planning study of the Lechmere area, the city published its *East Cambridge Riverfront Plan* in 1978. A planned unit development was established, substantially limiting the scale of new construction in the area. A federal Urban Development Action Grant funded the reconstruction of roads, a new parking garage, and a park around the reconfigured Lechmere Canal, completed in 1987. The new park reestablished pedestrian access from the riverfront to the canal, and new commercial and residential structures followed the construction of public improvements (figures 8.17, 8.18).[40]

8.15 In the early 1940s, the Lechmere Canal was largely intact. Community gardens covered much of the area near the water, but were cut off by a busy roadway along the river's edge. The park on the old Charles River dam was separated from the nearby neighborhoods in Boston and Cambridge by heavy traffic.

8.16 By 1975, half of the canal had been filled in. A new hotel occupied a waterfront site next to one- and two-story manufacturing structures. The Museum of Science, which leased the park on the old dam in 1948, occupies almost the entire site from Boston to Cambridge.

8.18 Designed by Carol Johnson Associates and completed in 1987, the Lechmere Canal Park created pedestrian access from the river around the newly configured canal. On the west side of the circular terminus of the canal is the Cambridgeside Galleria mall. Soon after the park opened, tour boats operating out of the canal began plying the river again.

8.17 In the area designated the Lechmere Triangle, the city of Cambridge used federal grants to fund an urban design plan by Dennis Carlone Associates and to create a park along the edge of the Lechmere Canal. Commercial and residential development followed the commitment to public investment in open spaces along the canal.

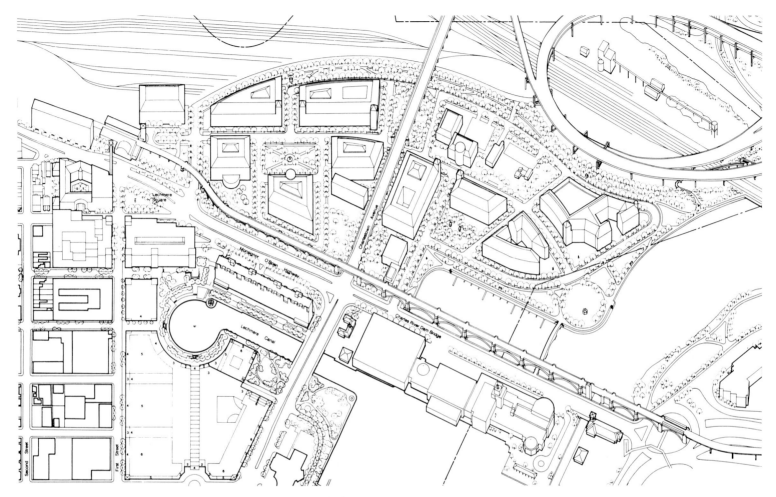

8.19 Following the successful development of the Lechmere Triangle, the city of Cambridge determined to take on the area east of Msgr. O'Brien Highway, the last large development area in Cambridge, which they christened "North Point." Dennis Carlone's urban design plan proposed a boulevard extending in a single arc from East Street to the edge of the Charles just below the Green Line viaduct. At the bend in the seawall (right center), constructed in 1928 by the Boston and Maine Railroad, the North Point plan proposed a circular green space as the focal point of the new neighborhood.

The city followed its successful Lechmere Canal development with a similar process for the area east of the O'Brien Highway on the old rail yards of the Boston & Maine, which the city named North Point (figures 8.19, 8.20).[41] The MBTA's commuter lines from North Station continued to use the railroad's old roundhouse, but much of the old switching yards had been abandoned; only a few warehouses operated in the area. Although about the same size as the Lechmere Triangle, this area was cut off from Cambridge and Charlestown by the Green Line viaduct, the Gilmore Bridge, and the railroad tracks.

The first Chapter 91 license for a private development in the New Basin resulted in a substantial contribution of land and park improvements. In 1988 the city granted a building permit for "Museum Towers," a ten-story hotel and two twenty-four-story apartment towers at North Point. The state Chapter 91 license for Museum Towers required the transfer of an acre of riverfront land to the proposed park as well as the reconstruction of the rubble seawall on the river edge of the project.[42] Although the project was postponed in the collapse of the real estate market in the late 1980s, the city remained confident that its urban design plan demonstrated the potential of the area, which included the largest remaining undeveloped parcels in the city. The plans for North Point would be a primary factor in the conflict that arose ten years later, when the state highway department unveiled its final, much expanded plans for roadway connections to the Central Artery.

Landscape Architecture and Modernism

In the spring of 1987, with funds from a recently passed bond issue, the MDC began planning to complete the missing links in the river corridors of the Metropolitan Park System, including the "lost half mile" of the Charles. By this time, academic and professional debates about the nature of public spaces, as well as several examples of newly constructed public landscapes in eastern Massachusetts, seemed to invite, if not complete revision, then at least thoughtful reconsideration of the 1980 "Master Plan."

Signs of change and discontent in the profession of landscape architecture had multiplied during the previous two decades. As far back as 1965 at a White House Conference on Natural Beauty, Julia Broderick O'Brien (later involved in the 1969 Metropolitan Area Planning Council *Open Space* study and then the director of planning for the MDC) suggested that, as builders of public parks, "We have not shown the ability to design anything much larger than a tot lot which reflects the differences between our way of life and that of Olmsted." The historian Albert Fein completed a study of the profession of landscape architecture in 1972; the following year he proposed a merger of landscape architecture and planning.[43]

In a 1985 essay in *Landscape Architecture*, the only American journal directed to practicing professionals, Steven Krog (himself a landscape architect) described the field as "a discipline in intellectual disarray," plagued by a "deficiency of theoretical discourse." At a 1988 conference on landscape architecture at the Museum of Modern Art he elaborated on his earlier argument, and he concluded that the field was "thoroughly confounded by self-doubt." About the same time John Dixon Hunt, a landscape historian and later chair of the Department of Landscape Architecture at the University of Pennsylvania, asserted that "one of the most striking aspects of modern landscape architecture is its ignorance of history."[44] After almost a hundred years of conscious efforts to establish the profession, how had the discipline of landscape architecture arrived at such a state?

One argument was that the aesthetics of twentieth-century art were, by and large, "fundamentally hostile to nature," precipitating an outright divorce between architecture and the natural world, and "a vital, modern landscape tradition never emerged." Modernism, and its impact on public spaces, however, did not begin in this century. In many fields, historians traced its roots to the late eighteenth century. It was then, according to Hunt, that many of the arts abandoned the notion of "their service to some general, collective public will" and chose instead to pursue individual, largely private expression. At the same time, the Romantic glorification of personal experience meant that every person "could enjoy—nay, could only have—his or her own . . . response to everything around them, including gardens, parks, and the wilderness." The meanings attached to nature and the natural world proliferated, and the production and interpretation of the fine arts became increasingly fragmented.[45]

By the last decades of the twentieth century, landscape architects and urban critics were heatedly contesting the value of the hundred-year-old public spaces designed by Olmsted and his followers. Had people ever responded to these picturesque landscapes as Olmsted had hoped? Did anyone today? Or were these spaces now anachronisms, a hundred years removed from today's kinetic sports and high-speed recreation, irrelevant to Americans who are now "escaping a different city . . . in search of a different Mother Nature"? Had public parks, like other post–Civil War reforms, failed as "structures of social and political intercourse . . . defined for the popular mass by a cultured elite hovering above"?[46]

In this tumult of opinions, how could a public agency define a program for parks and public spaces? Several choices presented themselves, in highly regarded examples of public spaces recently constructed in eastern Massachusetts, especially the state Department of Environmental Management programs for urban heritage state parks and Olmsted historic landscapes.

Public History and Public Landscapes

In the late 1960s a few long-time residents of Lowell, Massachusetts, began discussing the idea of a "Lowell Urban Cultural Park." They hoped to create "a new kind of park" with the aim of making Lowell "a showcase of America's industrial history." Walter Hickel, then secretary of the federal Department of the Interior (which included the National Park Service) endorsed the idea in 1970, but no action was taken by the city or the Park Service. The initial suggestion was followed by a 1973 report assembled by several groups in Lowell, and then the state Department of Natural Resources completed a study in 1974.[47]

Two goals were established: to preserve the cultural heritage of the city; and to increase the public appreciation and enjoyment of Lowell's cultural resources. In particular, there was a specific concern to protect and improve the water-related open space, including the system of locks and canals, so that the citizens of Lowell could "integrate recreation into the daily pattern of their lives." It was hoped that a major commitment by the state would be followed by city, federal, and private investments, so that "the utopian dream of its founders for a humanized cityscape" could be realized.[48]

The new administration of Governor Michael Dukakis, elected in 1974, aggressively developed the program of heritage parks. As Dukakis phrased it, "we don't throw away cities." One of the state's planners elaborated on the importance of bringing a "visible, physical improvement into the heart of a city that hadn't had a nickel of private money invested in it for fifty years." After Lowell, the idea was extended first to Fall River, where the waterfront was a tangle of highways and fuel storage tanks without a single foot of public access; a dozen other Massachusetts cities subsequently received state funding to develop parks designed around local historic resources and themes.[49]

From this historical perspective, the "lost half mile" of the Charles offered the region's ultimate collection of transportation artifacts. This short stretch of river was the site of the Charles River Bridge, the first bridge from the town of Boston to the mainland in 1786; the terminus of the Middlesex Canal, completed in 1803; and the first movable railroad bridge in America. The 1910 Charles River Dam, designated a national Civil Engineering Landmark in 1981, retained its unusual sliding lock gates, at rest in the upper and lower lock gatehouses and secured forever in the open position since the opening of the new dam downstream. Two of the single-leaf rolling-lift bascule bridges (each with a 629-ton overhead concrete counterweight) constructed by the Boston & Maine Railroad in 1931 still halted the traffic of boats for every crossing of commuter trains over the river.[50] On the underside of the Charlestown Bridge, the large steel wheels and gears remained in plain view, although the bridge no longer operated as a rotating span.

At the same time, the still active transportation structures— the commuter rail lines, especially the highway bridge and the double-decked structures extending into Somerville and

Charlestown—visually dominated the area and made it hard for many people to imagine any sort of public space downstream of the old dam. And the existing double-decked highway would be dwarfed by the design for this part of the new Central Artery. In meetings with community groups in Charlestown as late as 1987, artery project engineers were showing drawings of a six-lane bridge over the Charles, even though the decision to widen the project to ten lanes had been made in 1983.[51] The straightforward goal of creating continuous pedestrian links on both sides of the river through this expanding maze of highway bridges and ramps would demand considerable negotiation. Added to that was the challenge of creating safe, visible public spaces in this highway construction zone before much of the adjacent land was developed. Could those issues be resolved in a park aesthetic?

The planners in charge of implementing the new heritage parks programs in Lowell, Holyoke, and Fall River in 1983 were struck as they began work in those cities by the "perilous" condition of the existing public parks. With the exception of a 1978 federal program for "Urban Park and Recreation Recovery," which lasted only two years, there were no state or federal funding programs to support the replanning or restoration of municipal parks. In 1981 a group of historians, designers, park administrators, and community leaders had founded the Massachusetts Association of Olmsted Parks to promote the appreciation and preservation of Olmsted parks. One of their first ventures was a survey of ten parks designed by the Olmsted office in the Commonwealth. In the course of that work, the association found that the firm had consulted on at least 280 parks in more than 150 cities and towns in Massachusetts, many of them by then in terrible condition.[52]

By joining the interest in Olmsted's work with the tools of historic preservation, advocates of "adaptive restoration" of these city parks secured funding for the program in six months. The development of a commitment in the community for stewardship of the parks was as important to the program as the funding for design and construction, and the Olmsted firm's original design intentions provided a significant vehicle for the discussion of historic and contemporary design principles and community values.

In the first five years, the Olmsted landscape program completed construction projects at Buttonwood Park in New Bedford and Elm Park in Worcester, as well as inventories, surveys, and historic landscape reports for a number of other parks.[53]

The Biophilia Hypothesis

At a more fundamental level, several strands of academic research in environmental psychology and biological diversity came together in what was called the Biophilia Hypothesis. Designers and environmental psychologists began investigating landscape preferences in the 1960s. After a series of more general studies, the psychologist Roger Ulrich published a widely read study in 1984 in the journal *Science* titled "View through a Window May Influence Recovery from Surgery" that compared benefits to patients in a hospital where the view on one side of the building was a parking lot and on the other was a park.[54]

That same year the basis of these investigations was profoundly broadened when the biologist E. O. Wilson suggested that the "deep history" of evolution was at work in the human response to certain landscapes. The origins of the human species on the plains of Africa had predisposed not only the body, but also the mind, to life on the savanna, "such that beauty in some fashion can be said to lie in the genes of the beholder." The elements of this partiality were "open tree-studded land on prominences overlooking water." In cities or landscapes where these elements were absent, people went to great lengths to create the "savanna gestalt." This preference was an aspect of a profound human sense that Wilson called *biophilia*. It is, he said, "the innate tendency to focus on life and lifelike processes." Wilson later identified the diversity of plant and animal life as an essential hereditary need of human beings, and a crucial link to the older ethic of conservation.[55]

In many fields, including landscape architecture, the principle of biodiversity was increasingly recognized. The dramatic eradication of well-known but more remote environments like rain forests and tropical reefs was widely and repeatedly publicized, and as these debates continued, the biological diversity of natural areas closer at hand was acknowledged. State and federal legislation sought to protect rivers, wetlands, lakes, and ponds. The city of Boston mapped its "urban wilds," and many park departments and natural resource agencies sought to protect and increase the diversity of plants and animals in undeveloped areas as well as in the interstitial spaces of the urban environment.[56]

Imagining the New Basin

Only a fraction of this expanded view of landscape architecture appeared in the proposals submitted in 1988 to develop the New Basin Master Plan. Although most of the competing design firms edged cautiously toward an assimilation of the history and the massive artifacts of the site, two proposals, both from Cambridge architectural firms, went further. One sought a nexus between landscape architecture and public art, the other joined landscape diversity with the interpretation of the natural and cultural history of the river.

The proposal by Moore-Heder Architects, in a collaboration with a team of landscape architects and artists, asserted outright that it was impossible to repeat in the New Basin the "wide open water and bucolic park space" mode of the old esplanades. The weight of the "overpowering" transportation structures would have to be mastered in the spirit of judo, in their view, to be made integral elements of the design. Such a spirit was beyond the skills of traditional landscape architecture and called for a collaboration with environmental artists. A striking set of photographs illustrated their reading of the existing landscape of the New Basin: the railroad bridges as "giant sculptures of the industrial revolution"; the two unconnected highway ramps originally planned as part of the never-built Inner Belt, "surreal and evocative . . . already a kind of historical exhibit of highway planning." One example of their approach was the suggestion—unique to their proposal—to build a walkway along the downstream edge of the dam, directly underneath the elevated tracks of the Green Line viaduct. Much of what would be significant in the new public spaces, they argued, "is already there, waiting to be seen in a new way" (frontispiece, figure 8.20).[57]

The selected consultant was Carr, Lynch Associates, another Cambridge firm. They, too, asserted that "a bold vision" would be required to "transform obstacles into opportunities." Their analysis began with Kevin Lynch's conclusion in *The Image of the City*, that most people were unable to connect the river with the harbor; their proposal focused on the opportunity to create an identity for the New Basin. This would be done with activities to create uses and attractions, and would be reinforced with interpretive elements and with rich and diverse plant materials. A carefully designed public process would engender a sense of collaboration in the final design choices.[58]

Like a number of other public open space projects in Massachusetts, the New Basin Master Plan was caught in the wake of the regional economic recession and the contraction of the state budget at the end of 1988. Before the consultants could begin work, the funding for the project was withdrawn.

Two years later, after protracted public and private negotiations with the Central Artery project over the impact of the proposed highway bridges over the Charles River, the master plan was revived as one of many "mitigation measures" to be funded as part of the highway construction. Concerned because money for landscape construction is often hard to come by at the end of road projects, the MDC proposed that the state environmental permits for the artery require the New Basin parks upstream and downstream of the artery's Charles River bridges be built before the bridge work started. Anxious to get on with the project, the highway department agreed—although the commitment was never enforced.

8.20 The proposal for developing the New Basin from a team led by Moore-Heder Architects, argued that the "ruins" of existing transportation structures did not have to be demolished, but could become sculptural elements in the new public spaces. The great opportunity along the river's "lost half mile" was to "see what is already there in a new way."

Finally, we returned to this wonderfully monumental view
under the green line, now never seen, that will be made
available to joggers, bikers and walkers - special
spaces and some activities may be created under the
spans. it could become a link between a walkway along
the old locks and a crossing to North Point.
A LOT OF WHAT WILL BECOME THE NEW BASIN PARK IS
ALREADY THERE, WAITING TO BE SEEN IN A NEW WAY !

Boston Sunday Globe

AUGUST 8, 1954

ROTO *Pictorial* MAGAZINE

Boston's $110,000,000 Highway in the Skies

By K. S. BARTLETT

92,000 Tons of Steel, 459,000 Tons of Concrete, and the Widest Vehicular Tunnel in the World to Smash City's Traffic Bottleneck

How soon can we use it?

That's the question most folks ask about the Boston Central Artery.

Then come questions about size, where it starts and ends, how many motor vehicles will use it, why it's unique among Massachusetts highways and unusual anyway.

During recent months the most spectacular part,

construction of the towering steel skeleton of the elevated half of the highway has been watched by scores of thousands in downtown Boston. Many wonder how much steel is needed. Some ask about engineering problems, relatively few about costs.

Here are the answers, or partial answers, to these and some other questions about the great expressway which the Massachusetts Public Works Department is building.

Continued on Page 7

9

The Big Dig

Unlike every other major twentieth-century highway plan in Boston, the primary objective of the early 1970s proposal to depress the Central Artery was not focused on traffic. The elevated artery would be replaced by a tunnel of the same size in the same location. Relatively modest improvements in the location of on- and off-ramps were subsequently developed with the aim of meeting the requirements for federal funding. The passion of its initial proponents derived from the promise it offered to make Boston's historic downtown whole again, to correct what were seen as the disastrous effects of the original elevated highway on the physical character of the city. The idea could not have been more straightforward. As it was later promoted in an eight-page, full-color insert in the Sunday editions of Boston's two daily newspapers in 1989, the proposal was reduced to a simple epigram: "Now you see it, now you don't" (figures 9.1, 9.2).[1]

From the first, however, this uncomplicated concept was seen as a logistical nightmare and a financial impossibility. As the project planning went from preliminary design to final engineering, the constrictions of the city's geography were exceeded by a byzantine

Frontispiece *Boston Sunday Globe,* August 8, 1954

Now you see it.

9.1 The basic concept for reconstructing the artery was summarized in a simple epigram, and circulated in a glossy, full-color brochure in the *Globe* and the *Herald* in 1989.

convergence of local politics with professional culture. The urban design vision for the city center created heightened expectations that ultimately collided with the complete absence of civic vision for the northern portion of the project, the Charles River Crossing. In 1994, the sesquicentennial of Robert Gourlay's proposal for the "scientific planning" of Boston, the design for the depressed Central Artery was still unfinished after more than twenty years of work and hundreds of millions of dollars in consultants' fees.

By that time it was no longer clear that open civic discourse was possible for a project of this magnitude. The federal, state, and local requirements for transportation planning had become so highly specialized that it was nearly impossible even to understand them, to say nothing of weighing incommensurable categories of analysis. Over each professional discipline at work on the design—whether more quantitative, like the chemistry of air quality, or more abstract, like the architecture of the highway structure—hovered the faith in expertise, the sense that only the specialists really understood. When the experts arrived at conflicting solutions, the traffic planners and the highway engineers, with their trip tables and computer-generated alignment drawings, were almost always granted the ultimate authority by state and federal administrators. And since the transportation bureaucracy controlled the budgets for all the other disciplines, there was, in the end, no appealing their decisions.

The protracted battle over the Charles River Crossing became the last remaining obstacle to the construction of the Central Artery. The artery had already been through more than two decades of public discussion, political infighting in Boston and Washington, and an almost incomprehensible bureaucratic history at the state and federal level that culminated in the override of a presidential veto.[2] They were followed by local contests that matched Cambridge against Boston, environmental groups against the downtown business community, and mass transit proponents against the experts from one of the world's largest private engineering and construction enterprises. The river crossing must be seen in its complex relationship to the rest of the project to understand how the plans for public open space along the Charles

Now you don't.

9.2 The initial promotion of the artery emphasized the opportunity for open space in the corridor that would be vacated when the elevated highway was torn down.

became the focal point in the public debate over the largest urban highway project ever planned in the United States.

Discussions of major public works projects have also been hindered by what seems to be an ever-shorter collective memory. The debate over the Central Artery in the 1990s—including the Charles River Crossing—was marked by few open discussions of the relationships between highway planning and other kinds of urban development or even the regional transportation legacy from the previous generation.

Redirecting Transportation in Greater Boston

Following the moratorium announced in 1970, Governor Sargent succeeded in stopping a $6 million "joint development" study of the Inner Belt and using half of the money for a restudy of all the highway and transit projects. The restudy, as it was known at the time, began in July 1971 and was formally called the Boston Transportation Planning Review (BTPR). The restudy organized a public process and later completed the first environmental impact statements under the new National Environmental Policy Act, passed in December 1969.[3]

Draft reports were published on the Southwest corridor, the I-95 North/Blue Line corridor, and the Third Harbor Crossing in 1972, and the governor's office solicited written comments and held public hearings across the metropolitan region. Most private groups and virtually every city or town through which the proposed expressways would pass opposed the highways, including Boston, Cambridge, Somerville, Revere, Saugus, Lynn, Milton, and Needham. After the hearings, Sargent structured an informal process for groups to come to the State House and present their case to him personally. The groups included two coalitions that had been created as part of the restudy process, the Environmental Coalition and the Municipal Coalition, as well as organizations in favor of the expressways.[4]

Later that year Sargent went on state-wide television to announce that he was canceling the Southwest Expressway and I-95 North. Instead, an arterial boulevard would be built in the

"Southwest Corridor," where land and buildings had already been taken for the Inner Belt and the Southwest Expressway. The Orange Line would be relocated to share the existing Amtrak railroad corridor and would be covered so that the Southwest Corridor Park could be built. (Now managed by the Metropolitan District Commission, the popular park provides a pedestrian and bicycle link from the South End to the Emerald Necklace near Harvard's Arnold Arboretum.) The region's existing commuter rail network, which transit plans beginning in the 1940s had slated for discontinuance, would be upgraded. Sargent also endorsed one major highway project that had been analyzed in the restudy: a two-lane tunnel directly from the turnpike to Logan Airport (on airport property, with no land takings in East Boston neighborhoods), to be used only by buses, taxies, and trucks. (A decision on extending the Red Line beyond Harvard Square was deferred until the completion of a draft report; the following year an alignment through Cambridge and Somerville was approved by the communities and the state.)[5]

In deciding to cancel the planning for Interstate 95, Sargent put over $1 billion in federal highway aid at risk, at a time when the state's economy was suffering through a recession. In his announcement he made a commitment to lobbying for a change in federal law so that money collected by the Highway Trust Fund could be also used for transit. With the support of major cities across the country, Congress enacted a transfer provision in the Federal Highway Act of 1974, allowing metropolitan areas to create a public process and examine transit alternatives to approved Interstate highways. That provision enabled Massachusetts to transfer its highway funds to two major transit projects, the relocation of the Orange Line to the railroad corridor and the extension of the Red Line to Alewife.[6]

In his 1972 announcement, Sargent also indicated that the idea of depressing the Central Artery was worth a serious look to determine its feasibility. Suggestd as early as 1925, the revival of the idea had not come from the staff of the restudy, but from a local highway contractor.[7]

Depressing the Central Artery

The community pressure to depress the final portion of the artery in the 1950s signaled the intense public dislike of the elevated highway even before it opened. Although they accepted the highway's function, the neighborhoods assailed the damage caused by its design.

By the early 1970s, as some people saw it, the fierce antipathy to the elevated Central Artery was casting a dark shadow over the rest of the 1948 highway plan. Bill Reynolds, who broached the idea of dismantling the artery during the controversy over the Inner Belt and the Southwest Expressway, was a construction contractor with an engineering degree from MIT. He had been described by the *Boston Globe* as "one of the state's most respected engineer-road builders." He had concluded that while people in other parts of the country loved highways, in Boston people hated them. The reason was the Central Artery. It was like a giant billboard that said "roads are bad" (figure 9.3). If the artery were put underground, then people would love it, and the state could resume building the other expressways in the 1948 *Master Highway Plan*—the Inner Belt and the northeast, north, northwest, west, and southwest radial highways.[8] (This anxiety over the image of the elevated artery is especially striking since Reynolds's proposal surfaced soon after the state had rejected the pleas of Somerville residents to depress I-93 through their city.)

The appeal of the idea was reflected in the multiplicity of images later developed to sustain the basic scheme. It would "heal the scar" of the original intrusive highway, it would "knit the city back together," it would allow the economic lifeblood of the region to flow freely on the new expressways. The political benefits were also obvious. Antihighway people could support a road construction project that would not take any homes, as the extension of the Massachusetts Turnpike into Boston had done. It would not take more property in the North End. It might be possible to include the rail link between North and South Stations. And it would address unemployment among highway construction workers, which would soon reach 14 percent.[9]

9.3 Protests over the design of the northern section of the first Central Artery led to a change in mid-construction; the south end of what was to be an elevated highway was built instead as a "cut-and-cover" tunnel. On the right is the North End; just beyond North Station (upper left) is the "lost half mile" of the Charles.

One of the first people Reynolds approached was Fred Salvucci. As head of East Boston's Little City Hall, Salvucci had served as spokesman for the opposition to Logan Airport expansion; by this time he had joined the mayor's staff. Salvucci thought the idea of depressing the artery was insane. The state, he told Reynolds, would have to post a sign at the Charles River saying, "City Closed for Alterations, Come Back in Ten Years."[10]

Salvucci nonetheless agreed to go with Reynolds to see John Wofford, the director of the restudy. At Salvucci's suggestion, the engineering staff of the restudy completed the first analysis of a depressed Central Artery. Although Salvucci changed his mind, others remained skeptical for their own reasons. State transportation secretary Alan Altshuler regarded the artery proposal as a diversionary tactic, since Salvucci had never supported a highway project, and this one had two obvious, probably fatal, flaws. The first was the enormous logistical difficulty of maintaining existing traffic while the depressed road was built. New developments just underway in the financial district and along the waterfront would be jeopardized by severe congestion during construction. The second problem was paying for the project. Without federal funding it would be impossible. Congressman Barney Frank, then a state representative, spoke for many skeptics when he asked in 1974 if it wouldn't be cheaper to raise the city than to depress the artery.[11]

Initially, the project had nothing to do with the Charles River. In the earliest schemes the depressed highway came out of the ground near Haymarket, just north of the exit from the Sumner Tunnel, and connected with the double-decked high bridge that crossed into Charlestown. Like some other interstate projects of the 1960s, the new road would be only partially covered and would not require mechanical ventilation. Envisioned first as eight lanes, it was reduced after Governor Sargent decided in 1972 that no new roads larger than six lanes would be built inside Route 128. A 1974 study by the Boston Redevelopment Authority evaluated six alternatives for replacing the elevated roadway. The least expensive option was estimated at $360 million and did not increase the capacity of the road. It did not alter the Dewey Square tunnel near South Station, and it did not include funding for the North Station–South Station rail link, estimated to cost $130 million. The existing intersection of Route 1 and I-93 just north of the Charles would be unchanged. Although the study said the artery was technically feasible, the cover letter from the redevelopment authority director stated bluntly that neither the state nor the federal government could afford the project. It should be considered only after higher priorities like the third harbor tunnel and the transit extensions were completed.[12]

After Michael Dukakis defeated Governor Sargent in the 1974 election, he appointed Salvucci secretary of transportation. Dukakis was opposed to the special-purpose harbor tunnel to the airport, the other road project (along with the depressed artery) for which Governor Sargent had allowed studies to continue after the 1971 expressway moratorium. He told people that "we had a Third Harbor Tunnel. It was called the Blue Line." Dukakis did approve additional planning work on the proposed artery, though Salvucci later recalled that the governor "didn't even like the artery. It was the railroad [the North Station–South Station rail link] that convinced him to be for it."[13]

Soon after the new state administration took office, the Federal Highway Administration (FHWA) rejected the request from Governor Sargent to include the artery in the state's interstate highway cost estimate, an essential step in the federal funding process. Salvucci chose to lobby FHWA to reverse its decision without pressing for increased funding, even though he was in favor of the most expensive alternative for the artery—which exceeded the approved budget. A year later, the project was revived under a compromise that recognized the need for significant improvements in the Charlestown (Interstate 93–Route 1) merge and at the other end of the artery near South Station. Planning would be divided into three areas; federal funding would not be available for the center section. FHWA in this case agreed with the state's claim that the north, central, and southern artery projects could "fit together in a unified series" but could also be constructed "essentially independently of one another."[14] The decision to proceed with the north area was supported by the residents of Charlestown, since it would mean the demolition of the elevated

highway over City Square and the construction of a tunnel to the Tobin Bridge. As it turned out, however, once construction began on the tunnel, its design severely limited the options in the subsequent planning for the bridges over the river (an example that helps to explain why segmentation of a large project for the purposes of minimizing environmental review has been an issue in a number of lawsuits as a violation of federal regulations[15]).

The "open study" mode of citizen participation established by the Boston Transportation Planning Review (BTPR) during the Sargent administration, however, was abandoned, and between election years planning for the Central Artery attracted little public discussion, although reports occasionally surfaced in the press. At the beginning of 1977 the project released a cost estimate that totaled almost a billion dollars: the north section would cost $70 million; the center section (depressing the elevated roadway) would be $600 million; and the southern section would cost $150 million. Responding to the new cost estimate, John Larkin Thompson, speaking for downtown business interests, countered that there was no evidence supporting the north–south rail link (without saying what sort of evidence would settle the question), and that if the third tunnel were built there would probably be no need to bury the center or southern sections of the artery.[16]

Dropping the Artery, Promoting the Tunnel

In 1978 Edward King ran against Dukakis in the Democratic primary. King had been ousted as executive director of the Massachusetts Port Authority after Governor Sargent appointed new directors to the authority's board. King represented the conservative wing of the Democratic Party and vigorously opposed the transportation policies of both Sargent and Dukakis. King had actively promoted the Leverett Circle Connector as director of the Port Authority; he had also favored a six-lane general purpose tunnel under the harbor to the airport, but was adamantly opposed to the depressed artery plans. Once elected governor, King made clear how deeply committed he was to his view of the regional highway network. He successfully blocked a move by the lame-duck Dukakis administration to transfer the approved third harbor tunnel funding to mass transit projects; he officially withdrew from federal consideration the state's previous planning studies for the central and southern sections of the artery; and he delayed the studies of the northern section for two years to reconsider the bridge at Leverett Circle.[17]

The third year of the King administration was a bad year for state transportation officials. In the spring of 1981 the Department of Public Works published a report that compared the "no-build" option, two different harbor tunnel alternatives, and a combined artery/tunnel scheme. As they explained in a letter to the Federal Highway Administration soon thereafter, the state had determined to drop the artery because of its "astronomical" cost of $855 million and its impact on 107 businesses and 47 downtown buildings. In May the state transportation secretary was arrested for accepting a bribe, and his replacement found the department in complete disarray. Two months later, federal officials notified the state that they would not fund the environmental impact statement (EIS) for the tunnel. They did not believe the state could finish the EIS by the 1983 national deadline for interstate highway projects, or that the state was capable of managing the tunnel's design and construction. State executives dropped everything to lobby FHWA, which reversed its decision in September and agreed to let the impact study proceed.[18]

The revival of the harbor tunnel study provoked a fierce reaction in East Boston, just as a rematch for governor was shaping up between King and Dukakis. The Coalition against the Third Tunnel was organized, and soon many of the state's elected officials were supporting the coalition. Some people suggested that a lot of the dispute had more to do with King's bad relations with other politicians than it did with the tunnel. In February four members of the state's Congressional delegation—Ted Kennedy, Paul Tsongas, Tip O'Neill, and Ed Markey—signed a letter to the federal secretary of transportation, claiming, among other things, that it was "shortsighted to build another tunnel without first addressing the problems of the Central Artery and its connections with [Interstates] 93 and 95." O'Neill told the

Globe that the only way the tunnel would be built was over his dead body.[19]

James Carlin, the state transportation secretary, responded by not only defending the tunnel but also criticizing the highway policies of both the previous governors. Sargent and Dukakis, he said, refused to acknowledge that "Americans are married to the automobile." The "young activists" (including Dukakis and Salvucci) had fought for the moratorium and then "continued the no-build policy" during Dukakis's term as governor. Carlin said they were wrong:

> What were the results of this highway moratorium? Massachusetts stopped the completion of I-95 from Route 128 into Boston—a bad decision. Massachusetts stopped construction of the Inner Belt from the proposed I-93 to the proposed I-95 in Roxbury—a bad decision. Massachusetts stopped the Leverett Circle Connector from Charlestown to Storrow Drive—a bad decision. Massachusetts decided on a reconstruction of the Southeast Expressway without expanding its capacity—a bad decision. Gov. Dukakis couldn't sell the Federal Highway Administration on depressing the Central Artery, and he was one of President Carter's favorite governors.
>
> What has Massachusetts started and finished in terms of major road improvements inside Route 128 since 1960? The answer is almost nothing. It's a disgrace.

He wondered whether the turnpike extension would have been constructed in the face of "resistance of the no-build environmentalists, utopia-seeking pseudointellectuals, and community groups." Neighborhoods don't want prisons, waste treatment facilities, power plants, or big highways and bridges, he said, but it is impossible to solve "big transportation problems without making people mad." Public officials in Massachusetts should "push those projects that must be built for the long-term good, even if it means jeopardizing their political careers." The proposed Third Harbor Tunnel might, Carlin suggested, be one such test of political courage.[20]

The Dukakis primary campaign focused on corruption and incompetence, not transportation policy, and offered no forceful response before the election to Carlin's challenge on this issue. Salvucci asked Dukakis to trust his professional judgment that there were other options for the tunnel besides the design that East Boston opposed, but those alternatives could not be fully analyzed until after the election. There was no need to antagonize either the neighborhood or the construction industry with superficial explanations. In a campaign speech to construction contractors, Dukakis indicated that he intended to look again at the design of the third tunnel, but by and large he avoided the subject.[21]

There was apparently just one exception to this strategy of avoiding the tunnel controversy. In East Boston just before the primary, Dukakis left his prepared text in his car, and then, throwing caution to the winds, denounced the tunnel: "I don't know why in 1982 we are talking about spending a half billion for another tunnel. There's no reason, no excuse, and no need for it." Except for the local East Boston papers, the statement was not widely reported.[22]

Reviving and Widening the Artery

Dukakis won the primary election easily. Almost immediately, well before the governor took office, Salvucci began recruiting allies to revive the planning for a depressed Central Artery. The urban design benefits were downplayed, in favor of three other arguments: First, the project was essential to the region's transportation network; second, the project's minimal impacts would be mitigated; finally, there was no alternative. Repairing the existing artery would be a traffic nightmare; upgrading it, with or without the Leverett Connector, was indefensible transportation policy.

A few critics were quick to attack Salvucci's public commitments to mitigate the project's "minimal impacts"; Congressman Brian Donnelly called it "blood money for siting decisions."[23] Donnelly's view of mitigation, however, failed to differentiate between those measures required by state and federal regulations to mitigate documented findings of "adverse effects" and measures offered to affected property owners or neighborhoods to deflect political opposition to the project.

Early in 1983, the new state transportation administration approved two crucial revisions in the plans for the depressed artery. The roadway was widened by one or two lanes in each direction, and the North Station–South Station rail link was dropped. Federal transportation officials had never accepted the state's arguments that redesign of the existing six lanes (closing some ramps and adding breakdown lanes) by itself would increase traffic flow. Widening the road addressed that objection, but it also meant a deeper, mechanically ventilated tunnel, with no room for the rail link at the same level as the road. The locomotives used throughout the state's commuter rail network were still diesel-powered, and ventilation in the revised tunnel design would have been extraordinarily expensive.[24]

There was almost no public discussion of these changes or their consequences. No one seemed to notice that for ten years DPW traffic studies had justified six lanes as the right size for the project, given the capacity constraints on I-93 north and south of downtown Boston; now, the engineering analysis rationalized the need for two to four additional lanes, which would substantially increase the cost of the project. The larger roadway was mentioned in passing in the *Boston Globe* in March 1983, and was discussed briefly in a transportation discussion at the Boston College Citizen Seminar in June, when Salvucci argued that the new harbor tunnel wouldn't work without a widened and depressed artery. There was apparently no public reaction to the wider roadway; the Sargent administration's commitment to limit the width of new highways inside Route 128 to six lanes was now eleven years old, and apparently forgotten. Governor Dukakis did, however, react angrily when a front-page story in July announced that Salvucci was working to get approval for the tunnel.[25]

A draft environmental impact report on the tunnel was published in December 1982; a supplemental report including the depressed artery was released the following July, and both were reviewed in public hearings in August.[26] There was no mention of the now-deleted rail link, and both depressed roadway alternatives were drawn at the new width of eight to ten lanes. Residents of East Boston had fought the tunnel for years; now it was the North End neighborhood angered by the revived artery plans.[27]

The most serious criticism of the draft report came in the "Certificate of the Secretary of Environmental Affairs" required by state regulations. According to the certificate, the traffic improvement appeared "surprisingly slight for a $2 billion capital project having top transportation priority for the next decade." The net result of the project would be "simply a shifting of congestion from one location to other locations." The certificate also singled out the project's potential "major impacts" on the Charles River Basin and said that the environmental affairs staff had been unable to find "any meaningful discussion of the issue" in the environmental impact report. There were already two master plans for developing this part of the Charles River Basin, and according to the certificate the Central Artery project appeared to be ignoring both of them. One was the North Station *Development Plan* prepared for the Boston Redevelopment Authority by the office of Moshe Safdie in 1979, which made the river the focal point of the development (figures 8.8–8.10). The other was the MDC's 1980 "master plan" (figure 8.13). According to the certificate, the proposed ramps at Leverett Circle "might be a permanent barrier to that plan."[28]

The 1983 certificate was the first legally mandated review to comment on the conflict between the artery project and the plan to reclaim the river's lost half-mile. Yet the only press coverage was a single article in the *Boston Herald* four months later. The *Herald* raised four issues that were almost universally ignored (until they finally exploded in 1990). First, Fred Salvucci had pushed this "wildly costly project" in the face of massive deficits. Second, promoting the project was made much easier by "a largely uncritical" press. Third, the "most devastating critique of this massive building plan" in the environmental affairs certificate was its impact on the Charles River. Finally, the article quoted the observation of the secretary of environmental affairs, that the $2 billion investment only slightly relocated the traffic congestion.[29]

These last two flaws cited by the *Herald* in their analysis of the environmental impact report—the inadequate consideration of regional transportation consequences and the failure to address the impacts on the Charles—were among the most serious of many problems with the document. State planners recalled later that the report "basically was a mess." The approach was "almost a tacit admission that we know we are not perfect but if we are not unified we won't get a chance to do it at all."[30]

All these objections, the highway planners thought, could be resolved in the project's final design, when there would be another public review. In late September 1983 Governor Dukakis officially endorsed the combined Central Artery/Tunnel project.[31]

More Federal Objections

The combined Central Artery/Tunnel project faced federal criticism on two levels. To the FHWA, the administrative agency responsible for technical review, there appeared to be major engineering flaws in the highway design, as well as significant unresolved environmental impacts. From a political perspective, the substantially increased cost of the artery and tunnel together became a national issue both for the Congress and the White House.[32]

The federal response to the Environmental Impact Statement was released one week after Reagan was reelected in 1984. The tunnel was approved, subject to Congressional authorization, but the depressed artery was flatly rejected. It was found ineligible not just for 90 percent interstate construction funds, but for any federal highway money. A number of major design flaws in the project were pointed out. It added capacity for only 13,000 cars a day—less than a single lane—at a cost of $1.3 billion. It took five parcels protected by Section 4(f), including a parcel owned by the MDC and included in its "New Charles River Basin Master Plan," published by the state highway department just two years previously in its impact statement for the north area project in Charlestown.[33] There were serious operational and safety issues, including sight distances, grades, and poorly designed ramps. The project displaced 97 businesses and restricted access to numerous other businesses during construction, and it required the disposal of a projected two million cubic yards of excavate.[34]

Overarching all the design issues was the question of cost. The Reagan administration was committed to completing the interstate system and had already supported a 1981 transportation bill that eliminated a number of projects and reduced the cost of finishing the national system from $53 billion to just under $40 billion. The combined Central Artery/Tunnel project was large enough by itself to skew the whole budget, and so Ray Barnhart, the FHWA administrator, began a well-publicized campaign in the Western states against "Tip's Tunnel."[35]

State officials countered with a lobbying effort targeted at federal highway officials as well as the Congress. Roger Allan Moore, a Boston lawyer who had worked on Reagan's presidential campaigns since 1968, developed a strategy that included an invitation to Barnhart to come to Boston in 1985 and see the MDC property along the Charles River. A Massachusetts assistant secretary of transportation later recalled the visit:

> Boston Garden is on your left and there is an old building on your right and there is a walkway that comes down to the dam. The walkway was the 4(f) site that they claimed we were impinging. Now if you have ever been in that walkway you know it is all full of pigeon droppings because it is all dank and dark. Needless to say, here is a conservative Republican from Texas [Barnhart, the Federal Highway Administrator] claiming this was an environmental question. It was an embarrassing position [for Barnhart] to be in.[36]

In fact, the status of the "dank and dark" walkway (figure 9.4) was an environmental question, which also made it a legal issue: Under federal law, when is a park a park? In the construction of the new Charles River dam in 1978, Paul Revere Landing Park had been built on the Charlestown side of the earthen dam (see figure 8.5) A walkway had been built across the pumping station and the lock gates, connecting with a sidewalk on the Boston side along the harbor and continuing to Causeway Street (paralleling the High Bridge). At the time of Barnhart and Moore's visit, several hundred people walked each day along these paths from Charlestown to Boston and back, in spite of the pigeon droppings

9.4 A walkway from Causeway Street to the new dam traversed a narrow opening between the old brick warehouses and the High Bridge over the Charles; a walkway along the river passed under the bridge and dead-ended at the railroad bridges upstream. The legal status of these walkways became a critical issue in the design of the new Central Artery bridges over the Charles.

nearby (the steel beams on the underside of the High Bridge made for ideal pigeon roosts).

In 1978 a walk had also been built along the edge of the Boston side of the Charles, from the south lock to the commuter rail tracks, where the path stopped at a chain-link fence. Beyond the fence was a sidewalk built as part of the new railroad trestle (reconstructed after the fire of 1984). These walkways were planned to link the river and the harbor, once connections were built over and adjacent to the tracks. Were these paths "parks"? Was the parking lot under the High Bridge parkland? Was the river itself, under the federal statute, to be considered a significant recreational resource? In a memo written a few months after his walk along the Charles, Barnhart reversed FHWA's November 1984 decision against the depressed artery portion of the project, effectively postponing the resolution of several previous objections, including these questions about parks.

State officials could not, however, put off the issue of federal funding. The deliberations between the state and federal highway agencies over artery funding had been closed for years; some of the artery funding studies that were financed with public money were withheld for months after their completion, limiting public discussion of the project's costs. After the environmental impact statement on the artery was filed in 1983, the enormous increase in the estimated cost made the financing of the project a much more public issue. Massachusetts legislators hoped to avoid the fate of New York City's Westway, the $1.5 billion project on Manhattan's West Side, which was scuttled on the House floor. They crafted a strategy to make sure that a similar vote on the artery appropriation did not occur. A compromise with FHWA was reached late in 1985. The federal surface transportation bill would allow a four-lane harbor tunnel (estimated at $1.25 billion), and the north and south sections ($650 million) would be eligible for interstate completion funds. The centerpiece of the project, however—depressing the artery from High to Causeway streets, estimated at $600 million—would not be eligible.[37]

The compromises in the transportation bill were strongly opposed by the White House, and the likelihood of a presidential veto raised the stakes for both Congress and the White House. Reagan vetoed the transportation bill in March 1986, as expected, saying that he hadn't "seen this much lard since [he] handed out blue ribbons at the Iowa State Fair."[38] He singled out two projects by name, a subway project for Los Angeles and Boston's Central Artery. The brutal battle to override Reagan's veto ultimately came down to a single vote; North Carolina Senator Terry Sanford changed sides, and the bill passed. The project had survived yet another close call. At long last, state officials believed, the political issues they had battled for over a decade were resolved.[39]

For fifteen years, the artery project had faced a series of fundamental questions: Should an "urban beautification" project be eligible for interstate funding if it did not increase the capacity of the highway system? Should the funding for the proposed artery be used instead for public transit improvements? Did the regional transportation network require both a new east–west tunnel and a major increase in the system's north–south highway capacity? Could the state afford its share of the Central Artery/Tunnel project without sacrificing highway construction in the rest of the state? Would the bonding for road-building squeeze out the public funds for other priorities—health, education, public safety, open space? At the end of 1987, with the passage of federal funding, senior artery staff thought these controversies had all been addressed.

Even before these general issues were finally resolved, however, the proposed alignment of the harbor tunnel had aroused heated opposition in both South Boston and East Boston. In South Boston, the connection to the airport required a choice between a bridge and an intricately engineered tunnel; either would affect the property and perhaps the operations of Gillette, the largest manufacturing employer in the city of Boston. Gillette officials determined that a tunnel would be less disruptive and lobbied successfully against a bridge. East Boston neighborhood groups had battled the airport for years and had acquired substantial political skills; their objections were overcome by locating the tunnel entrance on airport property rather than in a residential neighborhood. (figure 9.5)[40]

Two substantial tasks remained before the final design could begin: the plan for design of the Charles River crossing, and the preparation of the Supplemental Environmental Impact Statement for that plan. The first would demand first-class highway engineering skill; the second called for the marshaling of experts in a number of related but distinct disciplines. In 1985 the state had gone outside the Department of Public Works and hired Bechtel/Parsons Brinckerhoff, a joint venture of Bechtel Civil and Parsons Brinckerhoff, two of the largest engineering firms in the world. Their qualifications seemed well matched to the work at hand, which was seen as primarily technical, not political. The institutional debate had been intense, but except for a few outspoken critics, state officials believed they had succeeded in uniting a coalition to support the project.

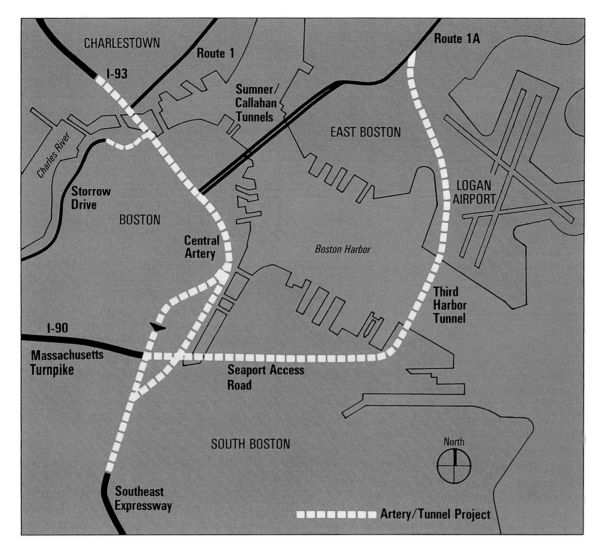

CHARLESTOWN

Route 1

Route 1A

I-93

Sumner/
Callahan
Tunnels

Charles River

EAST BOSTON

Storrow
Drive

BOSTON

LOGAN
AIRPORT

Central
Artery

Boston Harbor

I-90

Third
Harbor
Tunnel

Massachusetts
Turnpike

Seaport Access
Road

SOUTH BOSTON

North

Southeast
Expressway

■■■■■■■■ Artery/Tunnel Project

9.5 The concept plan for the Charles River crossing was published in the glossy 1989 brochure with the headlines "Now You See It, Now You Don't."

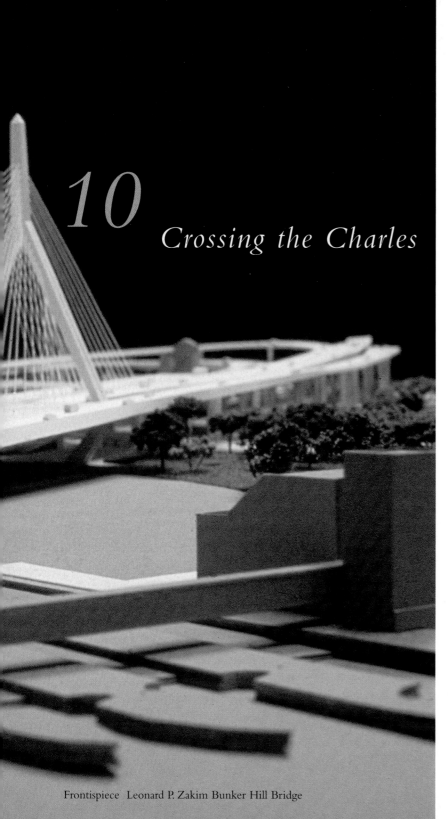

10

Crossing the Charles

Frontispiece Leonard P. Zakim Bunker Hill Bridge

Citizen lawsuits are a terrible way to make public policy.

A plaintiff in the Charles River Crossing Coalition lawsuit, 1995

By the end of 1987, it seemed that the Central Artery project's battles for Congressional funding and federal highway staff approval were over. Preliminary plans appeared to resolve the complexities of engineering technology and construction phasing for the third harbor tunnel and the southern and central portions of the depressed artery. Only then, however, did the enormous difficulties of widening and replacing the highways that intersected near the Charles become apparent.

The state's highway planners and their consultants had been working for almost twenty years on the intricacies of connecting Interstate 93 with Route 1 and the first Central Artery, but the 1983 agreement between state and federal highway agencies to widen the depressed artery had increased the potential complexities enormously. Recent advances in computer-aided design, on the other hand, offered not only extraordinary opportunities to generate alternative highway configurations, but also to make the options comprehensible to the public.

Never before had there been a public works project in Boston with the technical resources of the Bechtel/Parsons Brinckerhoff joint venture.[1] Yet the two firms' skills in three-dimensional electronic imagery were not applied to Scheme Z, the Charles River Crossing alternative selected in 1988 after three years of analysis—even though this was arguably the most difficult area of the project to visualize because of the massive scale of the proposed bridge. No public presentations of Scheme Z's design were made for months after the alternative was selected—no video (though video was prepared for the harbor tunnel design), no computer-drawn elevations or perspectives, not even the centuries-old techniques of three-dimensional models or hand-drawn bird's-eye views.

To cross the Fort Point Channel, engineers initially considered a bridge structure before conceding the issues raised by Gillette and switching to a tunnel design. At the Charles River, Scheme Z was the project's choice—with eighteen lanes of traffic on two bridges—and a local engineer asked why the highway wasn't crossing the river in a tunnel (figure 10.1).

It was a sensible question. Once the construction was completed, three of the four major routes that meet near the Charles would be underground as they approached the river—the tunnel under City Square in Charlestown had just been completed to connect with Route 1 and the Tobin Bridge; a new east-bound Storrow Drive tunnel would be built at Leverett Circle to match the existing west-bound tunnel; and the new underground artery through downtown would still be in a tunnel at Causeway Street. But in Scheme Z, all three of these highways would come out of the ground at the edge of the river and connect with two bridges and a massive set of loop ramps. Why?

The obvious reason for Scheme Z was its lower cost. The proponents of the various tunnel schemes agreed that tunnels were substantially more expensive than bridges—but, they argued, wasn't more than half of the artery/tunnel project about getting rid of an ugly elevated road?[2]

After Congress finally approved funding for the artery project in 1987, the joint venture budgeted 18,800 hours to complete

the final environmental impact statement. By August 1989, 131,520 hours had been billed for work on the impact statement and project staff estimated that another 31,000 hours would be required. Significant conflicts were still unresolved in East and South Boston, and new issues arose downtown. Federal and state permits were required to dump thirteen million cubic yards of dirt on a greatly enlarged Spectacle Island to create two 13-story hills. The Conservation Law Foundation negotiated directly with senior managers and the project's general counsel on a mitigation program to improve public transit.[3]

All of these issues taken together, however, would not generate the controversy over the proposed highway crossing of the Charles River. In 1988 Rebecca Barnes, the artery's director of urban design, had the project's architectural staff build models of the proposed bridges and ramps, and a photograph of the model appeared in the *Boston Globe* in September 1989. A noisy and very public opposition arose, with threats of lawsuits and city council votes against Scheme Z in Boston and Cambridge.[4]

When Scheme Z was approved fifteen months later, John DeVillars, the state secretary of environmental affairs, required the appointment of a "Bridge Design Review Committee" to evaluate alternative designs.[5] Between early 1991 and mid-1992, the forty-two people appointed to the committee invested thousands of hours to master the intricacies of the highway project, and their design debates were widely reported in the press and on local television. For those few months in the twenty years of planning the Central Artery, the project broke through the boundaries of commercial and governmental interests into the wider realm of civic discourse.

WAIT A MINUTE ?!?! IS THIS FORT POINT CHANNEL OR THE CHARLES RIVER?

10.1 David Bryson, *The Boston Informer*, 1994

Redesigning the River Crossing

Not since the study done by John Freeman's team of engineers and scientists for the Committee on Charles River Dam in 1903 would such an enormous range of professional expertise, and so many hours, be devoted to a study of the river. The 1893 reports of Eliot and Baxter, the Freeman report of 1903, and the several dozen volumes of reports produced by the artery project—and the public discussions that followed—help to reveal how deeply the culture of professionalism had taken root. And the work of the Bridge Design Review Committee reveals that it was still possible for citizens to master the work of many different disciplines and to arrive at a broad perspective based on a shared understanding of the public interest.

In the 1985 environmental impact statement, the proposed river crossing design, then called Scheme 5A, was found to be "not consistent with MDC proposals for extension of Charles River Reservation pedestrian walkways along the River's edge"; it also created adverse impacts under state and federal regulations on the river itself and on the proposed park land on the river's margins. Though the 1985 impact statement was approved, Scheme 5A was identified as one of four "major unresolved issues," to be revised and submitted for further review.[6]

Engineers for the joint venture immediately began what would turn out to be a lengthy search for alternatives, but they now faced a new constraint: the Central Artery North Area (CANA) project in Charlestown. The North Area project would remove the elevated ramps that connected with the Tobin Bridge and replace them with a tunnel under City Square. The tunnel would come out of the ground just west of City Square and split into two large elevated loop ramps encircling the Boston Sand & Gravel plant in Cambridge and the last remnant of the Miller's River, which marked the boundary between Cambridge and Charlestown. State highway officials asserted that the North Area project could be built even if the central and southern portions of the artery project were not funded, and it would eliminate the dangerous merge on the existing high-level bridge. In the judgment of Herbert Einstein, a professor of engineering at MIT who later consulted on the river crossing, the North Area project literally cast "boundary conditions in concrete" for the subsequent planning of the crossing.[7]

Within a few hundred yards, Interstate 93 intersected with Route 1 to the east and then with the ramps from Storrow Drive to the west. Instead of the four pairs of connections in a standard

cloverleaf intersection, six sets of ramps were required. The proximity of Charlestown, the proposed North Point development in Cambridge, the river, the new dam, and the tracks entering North Station left very little space on the ground. And there was only one place to put the ramps—in the same place the ramps from the City Square tunnel were coming out of the ground, on the Charlestown-Cambridge line.

Working within these constraints, engineers for the project developed thirty alternatives between 1985 and 1987, designated "A" through "DD." There were three different approaches to the Storrow Drive connections with Route 1 and I-93: in tunnels, on bridges, or with hybrid designs that combined tunnels and bridges. The "A" family of designs made the connections from Storrow Drive to the southbound artery in tunnels just north of North Station, and northbound connections on viaducts above the tunnels. The "M" family included the options that made all the connections in tunnels under the Charles. The "E" family made all of the connections on viaducts. One design from each of the three families was selected for further study: options "S," "T," and "Z" (figures 10.2, 10.3).[8]

Since the hybrid design of Scheme S combined many of the disadvantages of both the tunnel and the viaduct schemes, the analysis focused on the drastic differences between Schemes T and Z (figures 10.4, 10.5). Several arguments weighed against Scheme T. Because of the tunnel connections, it would be more expensive to construct. Some artery staff argued that it would be substantially more difficult to obtain the necessary state and federal permits for the tunnel schemes. There would be over a million cubic yards of muck (much of it contaminated soils) excavated from the bottom of the Charles.

To proponents of the tunnel alternative, however, this line of reasoning seemed at odds with the justification offered for the rest of the project. Permits for similar work would be necessary for the harbor tunnel. More important, from the initial conception of the project, it had been the long-term urban design benefits of depressing the center section of the artery that had justified the cost of excavating thirteen million cubic yards of dirt, relocating all

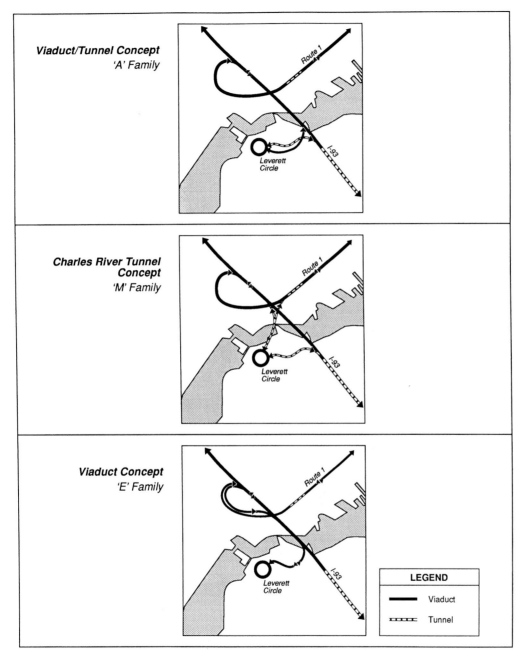

Viaduct/Tunnel Concept
'A' Family

Leverett
Circle

Route 1

I-93

Charles River Tunnel Concept
'M' Family

Leverett
Circle

Route 1

I-93

Viaduct Concept
'E' Family

Leverett
Circle

Route 1

I-93

LEGEND	
————	Viaduct
▭▭▭▭	Tunnel

10.2   As it was first conceived, the depressed Central Artery would come to the surface south of Causeway Street and connect with the existing double-decked High Bridge over the Charles. When the Federal Highway Administration indicated it would not fund the original proposal for a six-lane tunnel downtown, the proposed tunnel width was increased by up to four lanes. One consequence was that the High Bridge would need to be replaced. Three "families" of alternatives for the connection to Storrow Drive were considered: hybrid designs of tunnels and viaducts (the "A" family); tunnels (the "M" family); or viaducts (the "E" family).

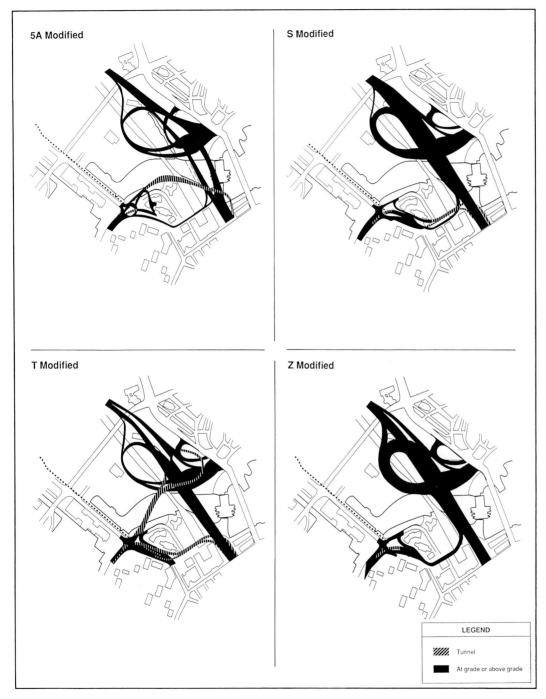

5A Modified

S Modified

T Modified

Z Modified

LEGEND

///// Tunnel

■ At grade or above grade

10.3 Scheme 5A, the 1985 proposal for the river crossing, included two bridges over the Charles for Interstate 93, one on either side of the existing bridge. A tunnel from the Artery under the Charles would have surfaced in the middle of the proposed park along Nashua Street to make the connection to Storrow Drive. All the 1990 schemes located the mainline bridge upstream of the old bridge.

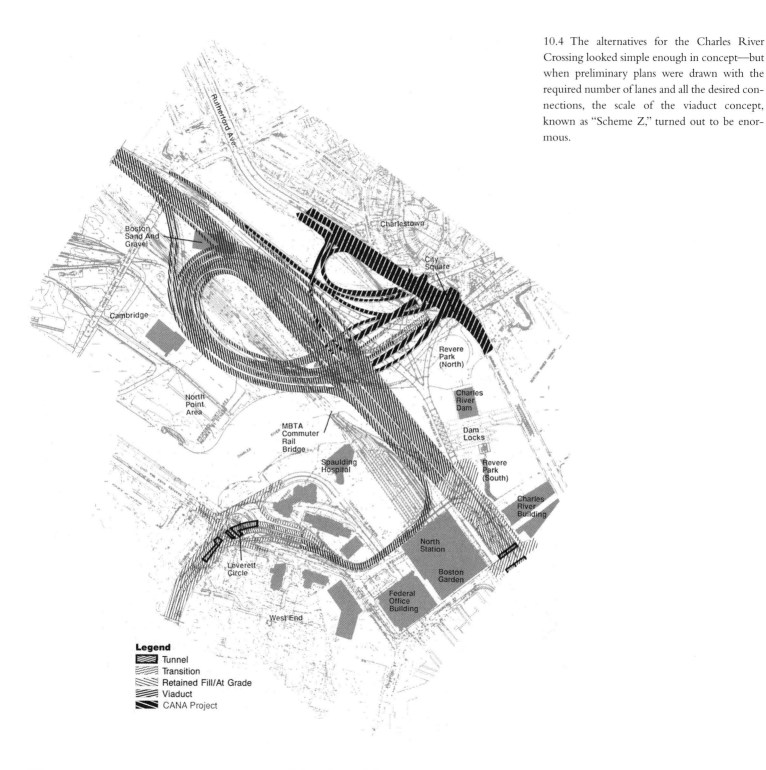

10.4 The alternatives for the Charles River Crossing looked simple enough in concept—but when preliminary plans were drawn with the required number of lanes and all the desired connections, the scale of the viaduct concept, known as "Scheme Z," turned out to be enormous.

Legend
Tunnel
Transition
Retained Fill/At Grade
Viaduct
CANA Project

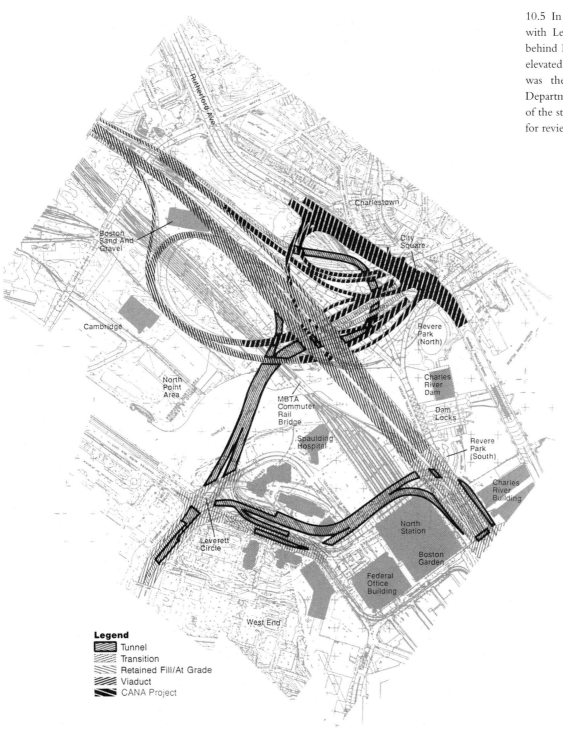

10.5 In Scheme T, tunnels connected the Artery with Leverett Circle, eliminating the viaducts behind North Station and greatly reducing the elevated loop ramps in Cambridge. Scheme T was the preferred alternative of the state Department of Environmental Protection, one of the state agencies with primary responsibility for reviewing the bridge designs.

Legend
- Tunnel
- Transition
- Retained Fill/At Grade
- Viaduct
- CANA Project

the utilities that crossed under the artery, and constantly re-routing traffic during the long years of construction. The state Department of Environmental Protection consistently indicated (first in meetings, and later in written comments on the draft and final impact statements) a strong preference for Scheme T because of the long-term waterway and open space benefits of the tunnel.[9] Another significant potential opportunity was a substantial increase in land available for real estate development, since the highway ramps would be in tunnels. Yet there was no easy way to balance the higher highway construction costs against the funds that would accrue from increased state and local taxes from new building construction in the area, even though ninety percent of the construction costs was expected to be reimbursed by the federal highway trust fund.

Scheme Z made all of the connections on viaducts and required six connecting ramps, two more than Scheme S and four more than Scheme T. The two North Area ramps were about fifty feet high; the stack of six ramps in Scheme Z would be over a hundred feet. The extra ramps were connected to four bridges across the Charles, more than in any other scheme—two five-lane bridges for the mainline traffic, a two-lane bridge downstream for the north-bound on-ramp from Traverse Street in the North End, and a four-lane, double-decked bridge connecting the ramps to Leverett Circle. This configuration required a double crossing of the river for traffic between Storrow Drive and I-93 southbound. (From Storrow Drive, for example, cars would travel north across the river, circle around a loop ramp, and then recross the river to I-93.) This was touted by the project as an advantage, since the lengthened ramps, though more costly, increased the "storage capacity" of the highway—the space available between on- and off-ramps for cars to idle in traffic jams. The additional ramps would take up more land in Cambridge's proposed new development at North Point, further constricting an already difficult site.

With its wider elevated bridges, Scheme Z also had significantly greater impacts, as defined by Section 4(f) of the federal transportation statutes, on the river and the planned public park land along its banks. A number of the project's senior managers were familiar with the federal requirements to minimize impacts on parkland, since they had been involved in the environmental review of the Southwest Expressway (one of the projects canceled by the governor following the 1971 highway moratorium).[10] Staff objections to Scheme Z came from the manager of urban design, the manager of planning and environment, and one of the assistant secretaries of transportation. Martha Bailey, the manager for planning, told Salvucci that Scheme Z was "environmentally unsound and unsound from a community point of view and you name it." She predicted mass protests.[11] Steve Kaiser, a long-time observer of the project who had once worked as a traffic analyst for the state environmental review (MEPA) office, claimed that there were no senior managers except Salvucci who liked the viaduct plan.[12]

In the early summer of 1988 Salvucci overrode the objections of his staff, and on August 14, Scheme Z was announced as the preferred alternative.[13]

Selling Scheme Z

The urban design of the Central Artery air rights, was—for the first decade, at least—the justification for the project. Images of a transformed downtown were crucial in promoting the depressed roadway. For a year after Scheme Z was chosen as the recommended alternative for the Charles River Crossing, however, no perspectives or models of the design were presented to the public.

An early example of this image-less strategy was a plan for two Charles River bridges that was discussed in the neighboring communities in December 1987. Building the new crossing as two three-lane bridges, one on each side of the existing bridge, was one way to maintain traffic until the new crossing was completed. Charlestown community groups reacted angrily to this alternative, since this meant the northbound bridge would be two hundred feet closer to the nearby neighborhood than the existing double decks of I-93. Yet the public presentation of this option, and the newspaper account of it, used no perspective drawings or scale models, only large-scale site plans. A public presentation of Scheme Z was not made in Cambridge until the middle of 1989, and it included no models or renderings, only site plans. Many Charlestown residents, the project's immediate neighbors, were not shown the design for Scheme Z until late 1989.[14]

Rebecca Barnes, who became the project's manager of urban design in 1988, was convinced that models of "beautiful, gateway bridge designs" were essential to the public acceptance of the river crossing. A model of the crossing was completed in August 1989, and photographs of it appeared in the daily papers in mid-September, under a front-page headline, "Artery bridges raise doubts" (figure 10.6).[15] Elizabeth Epstein, director of the Cambridge Conservation Commission, said that the scheme did not seem to fit Boston—it "appears to be a road system like I would imagine in Los Angeles." MDC Commissioner Ilyas Bhatti said he had asked Salvucci in several meetings to find ways to lessen the visual impact of the bridges on the beauty of the river, so that the vision of Charles Eliot for the lost half mile of the river could be realized. Cambridge officials were also concerned about the proximity of the ramps to the planned developments at North Point.[16]

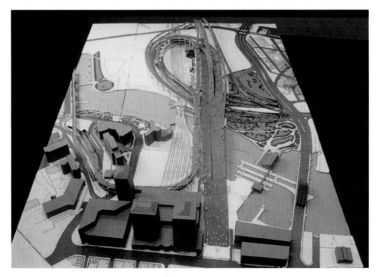

10.6 The breakthrough in the discussion of the Charles River Crossing came when Rebecca Barnes, the Artery's director of urban design, commissioned a model of Scheme Z. A photo of the model appeared in the *Boston Globe* in September 1989, and the public reaction was immediate, widely voiced outrage.

The problem of restricted information was not just an issue for the wider community. Even the professional staffs at other agencies had considerable difficulty getting data and graphic material on Scheme Z from the highway department. Once they did, their reaction, almost without exception, was negative. When he first saw the design, Stephen Coyle, the outspoken director of the Boston Redevelopment Authority, thought it was "horrendous." He was certain it would have to be redesigned, but in a discussion with the Boston Civic Design Commission (a city panel that included a number of the city's best-known designers; its chair was John deMonchaux, the dean of the MIT School of Architecture and Planning) he nonetheless lobbied the commission members to reverse their original vote opposing Scheme Z. After a presentation by Salvucci a few days later, the commission endorsed the proposed crossing.[17]

As the most powerful and articulate voice for urban design issues in the city of Boston's administration, why didn't Coyle challenge Scheme Z and its impact on Charlestown and the Bulfinch Triangle? In an interview with the *Globe* when he left Boston two years later, Coyle said that city officials chose to make their cause the air rights over the future depressed artery, and not Scheme Z; for him, the artery air rights issue was the most important question he faced during his seven years at the Redevelopment Authority. "Providing a pathway for parks and open space and civic uses" on top of the new artery would add more to the quality of life in the city than constructing four or five million square feet of moderately scaled buildings in that space, since "the image of the city is defined by those four or five square miles that are the downtown."[18]

City staff and elected officials in Cambridge, on the other hand, were more concerned with minimizing the adverse consequences in Cambridge of the artery project. The Cambridge Community Development Department began preliminary planning for their side of the "lost half mile" in the 1970s. The city's architects and planners were convinced they could repeat the success of the Lechmere Triangle at North Point, but from their point of view, Scheme Z threatened that prospect. The nested loop ramps

5A Modified

T Modified

10.7 Once the first model of Scheme Z was made public, models of the other schemes were also built for the required state and federal environmental review.

of Scheme Z were more than twice as high as the original North Area design, and they covered the banks of the river at the crucial edge where North Point was to connect with Charlestown and the new developments at North Station (figure 10.7).

The MDC's plans for the area would also be drastically altered if the elevated bridges and ramps of Scheme Z were built. It was difficult, however, for MDC officials to challenge another state agency, and the DPW was one of the most powerful departments in state government even under ordinary circumstances. In this case, the DPW's power was magnified by the billions of federal dollars that would flow from the project into the local economy.

Nine months after Scheme Z was selected, the artery's permitting consultant had not completed an analysis of the impacts of the proposed bridge on the existing and proposed parks or consulted with the MDC, as required under Section 4(f) of federal highway regulations. Concerned that the MDC's clearly stated objectives for the river would be seriously compromised, Commissioner Bhatti wrote to the highway department in May 1989, citing the 1909 legislation that transferred "exclusive care and control" of the Charles River Basin and the parks and parkways along its edges "as part of the metropolitan park system." The letter also quoted the 1962 statute authorizing the new dam, which extended the jurisdiction of the park system to the "waters and lands lying between the present Charles River dam and the [new] dam to be constructed."[19] The commissioner's letter concluded that the statutory language was clear: "The Charles River Basin itself is a park, and . . . this park extends to the new dam."[20]

Highway department officials suggested in subsequent interviews that the MDC was trying to "advance other agendas" and was seeking concessions from the project through "adversarial processes."[21] The MDC, on the other hand, felt that artery proponents were trying to short-circuit the requirements of the Federal Highway Administration, mandated in federal regulations passed in 1966. The implementation of the federal Section 4(f) regulations requires a review of protected resources; a prescribed analysis to determine the preferred alternative; and an analysis of the impacts of the highway design after the preferred alternative had been selected.[22]

Protected resources are defined as recreational, archeological, and historic sites as well as existing and planned park land. The transportation agency must analyze whether there are any "prudent and feasible alternatives" to the taking of park land, and if the effect on significant park land is adverse, "all possible planning" is required to minimize the adverse effects of the project.[23]

Mitigation usually includes the replacement of land and facilities or monetary compensation to enhance the remaining park land. Section 4(f) applies to portions of rivers contained within the boundaries of existing or planned parks, and to bridges over park and recreational resources "if the bridge harms the purposes for which these lands were established." And "the entire property" must be considered, "not just the portion of the property being used for the [transportation] project."[24] Since the MDC had jurisdiction of almost all the land along the New Basin—Nashua Street, North Point, and Paul Revere Park—as well as of the river itself, the Charles appeared to be clearly protected under Section 4(f).

The federal statute requires the selection of the alternative with the least impact on parkland, even if that alternative is substantially more costly. Project officials, on the other hand, had made a public commitment to Scheme Z as the preferred alternative. They feared the loss of federal funding if a more expensive river crossing were required.

The All-Tunnel Plan

In 1989 a radical alternative to Scheme Z was developed by Steve Kaiser. He had been invited in November 1988 to a briefing at which a model of Scheme Z was shown. Although he felt there was no chance whatever to consider other options, Kaiser thought someone should put on record an alternative to the river crossing "in the interests of history," to demonstrate that not everyone had acquiesced to the awful design proposed by the project. The obvious option, in his mind, was to continue the approach that had spawned the whole project—to bury not only the existing downtown segment of the highway, but also the High Bridge over the Charles. (figure 10.8)[25]

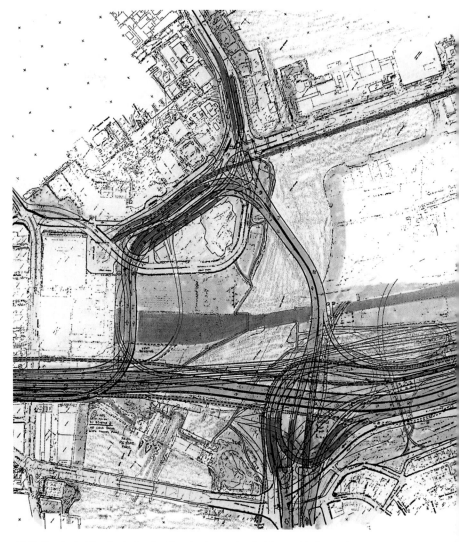

10.8 Frustrated by the lack of vision in the project's thirty-odd alternatives, Steve Kaiser, a traffic analyst with a Ph.D. in mechanical engineering from MIT, developed early in 1990 what he called the "all-tunnel" plan, in which not only the ramps but also the "mainline crossing" were in tunnels. By replacing the existing bridge with underground structures, the all-tunnel plan would open several dozen acres for commercial or residential development.

When Kaiser's December 1989 letter to the secretary of transportation proposing a tunnel crossing went unanswered, Kaiser determined to come up with a design himself. The following April he mailed to Salvucci Version 3.02 of what he called the "all-tunnel plan."[26] After showing the plan for the first time in the summer of 1990 to the East Cambridge Planning Team (an advocacy group for the Cambridge neighborhood closest to the highway project), Kaiser made additional revisions.[27]

In spite of the likely cost, the all-tunnel scheme seemed to many people to be a legitimate alternative to Scheme Z—perhaps even legally mandated under Section 4(f) of the federal regulations because it drastically reduced the impacts of the highway on the planned parks. And the cost of the tunnel would be greatly reduced if the 1983 decision to increase the number of lanes were reconsidered.

Public and Private Opposition

Early in 1990 scattered public criticism of Scheme Z appeared in meetings and in the press. In January a federal EPA official called the proposed collection of bridges and ramps "the single ugliest structure in New England," a phrase that would be frequently repeated in the press and in public discussions.[28] In April 1990, the *Globe* asked Environmental Affairs Secretary DeVillars about rumors of an impending conflict between his office and the highway department. DeVillars responded that the artery project was "essential not only for the future of the metro-Boston economy, but an important piece of a strategy to improve air quality." But he also indicated that there were a number of environmental issues to resolve.[29]

The escalating objections to Scheme Z in 1990 were the subject of increasingly frequent news stories as the year went on. A visible schism developed between the *Globe* editorial board, who supported the project, and the paper's reporters and columnists. The press coverage of the artery debate became increasingly graphic; even when pictures or maps were not included, visual descriptions were often used to convey the magnitude of Scheme Z. While the stories seldom described the proposed riverfront open space in any detail, the image of extending the Esplanade figured often in depictions of what was wrong with the proposed river crossing. This image-making helped to enlarge the range of issues beyond the realm of the traffic engineers and, for a time, opened the discussion to a broader public.

On the last Sunday in June, two of the *Globe*'s columnists filled the entire front page of the "Arts" section with their views of Scheme Z. In a piece on how he "learned to stop worrying and love Scheme Z," M.R. Montgomery compared the bridge with the Eiffel Tower. He observed that "to make a grand bridge, you must have great approaches—bare, open, undeveloped shores—but Scheme Z must link the quirky cow paths of Boston and Charlestown with the awesome modernist crush of I-93." We should not worry, he assured readers, that Scheme Z would block the views—the bridge itself would be the view. "Like Grand Coulee or Hoover Dam, like the Long Beach–San Diego Freeway stack in Los Angeles or the Quaker Oats silos in Cedar Rapids, Iowa, it will be concrete, undecorated, unabashed, unglamorous."[30]

Robert Campbell, the paper's Pulitzer prize-winning architecture critic, included a close-up photo of the model to illustrate the construction of what he called "a Great Wall across the Charles" (figure 10.9). He quoted at greater length the January comment of EPA that this would be "the ugliest structure in New England" because "it will be a low, dark roof over the Charles." Next to this Great Wall of Concrete would be the "Stadium of Ramps." In another image that would be repeated often in public meetings, he suggested that the artery was following "some perverse law of physics: 'if you push it down in one location, an equal and opposite mass will pop up somewhere else.'"[31]

The present condition of the area was irrelevant, Campbell wrote; thirty years ago the downtown waterfront was also an industrial wasteland. The community should simply say that "the Great Wall of Concrete and the Stadium of Ramps of Scheme Z" are counter to the premise on which the new artery was advanced, that is, to improve the quality of life on the city's water edges. One

Caution: HIGH BRIDGE AHEAD

Artery plan includes an awful scheme for a Great Wall across the Charles

10.9 A schism developed at the *Boston Globe* between the editorial board, which supported Scheme Z, and the paper's columnists. Robert Campbell, the *Globe*'s architecture critic, wrote that the Artery was obeying "some perverse law of physics: 'if you push it down in one location, an equal and opposite mass will pop up somewhere else.'"

sure sign that the project needed improvement was the "rush to judgment," the increasingly repeated threat that any further opposition would kill the project. The myriad experts working on the project did not vouchsafe the public good, Campbell implied; in fact, they could easily obscure it. The community should not allow itself to be drawn into discussions of traffic planning or the countless other technical questions that surrounded this project, since professionals "have a way of rendering amateurs impotent by seducing them into debate about technicalities."[32]

The increasing public criticism of Scheme Z came in the final months of the Dukakis administration and heightened the anxiety of CA/T managers over the approvals yet to be acquired from state and federal agencies. In August the state's mediation service was asked to convene a discussion with the DPW, the MDC, and the cities of Boston and Cambridge.

Meanwhile, the Conservation Law Foundation, a Boston nonprofit advocacy organization, wrote to the MDC commissioner in July, asserting that state officials had pressured the MDC to sign a Section 4(f) statement denying the significance of the river and the public lands along its banks. The letter emphasized that under Massachusetts law, "the Charles River itself, as well as the land along its banks, is a park."[33]

A week after the foundation's letter, the assistant general counsel of the National Trust for Historic Preservation wrote to the Federal Highway Administration and to Secretary DeVillars. If state officials had requested the MDC to make a formal declaration that the Charles River was not subject to Section 4(f), the letter pointed out, such action would "subvert the purpose and intent" of the transportation statute. The trust "has a long history of leadership in the enforcement of Section 4(f)" as well as "a strong institutional interest in protecting the integrity of this important mandate."[34] Two months later, the trust's vice president for law and public policy formally filed comments on the draft environmental impact statement on the artery project. Scheme Z would cast a permanent shadow "of several acres over recreational lands and waters," and would "create a concrete 'ceiling' over several hundred feet of existing pedestrian walkways." The number and types of bridge alternatives studied for the Charles River Crossing seemed "severely limited, especially given the five billion dollar project budget." The trust's second letter also noted that the impact statement did not discuss a full tunnel option, even though that alternative would clearly preserve the parkland in the New Basin, and that artery project officials had not replied to two public document requests for studies that analyzed alternatives to Scheme Z.[35]

The prospect of a lawsuit from the National Trust over Section 4(f) made the MDC determination of the status of the river and the adjacent MDC-owned land a crucial issue. Both CLF and the National Trust agreed to join the state's mediation process.

In August Secretary DeVillars announced in an interview that he intended to "extract every last ounce of environmental and recreational benefit that the law and common sense allow" in his review of the project, including $20 million for improvements along the Charles and $25 million for a park on Spectacle Island, where the project proposed to dump most of the ten million cubic yards that would be excavated to build the new artery and tunnel. He also hoped to force the project to design a suspension or cable-stay bridge on the river by requiring a reduction in the number of bridge piers in the Charles.[36] The *Globe* characterized the statement as a "weekend raid on Salvucci's turf," and indicated that many of these requirements were being raised for the first time. Salvucci would not comment on the requirements, but the next day another member of the governor's cabinet denied that there was any dissension between the offices of transportation and environmental affairs.[37]

The concern of the Conservation Law Foundation over the river crossing was not the foundation's primary issue with the artery project; for several months the foundation had been negotiating a multi-billion-dollar program of public transit mitigation, to compensate for the project's impact on traffic and air quality.[38] In the fall, with the state's mediation process going nowhere, staff from the foundation and the National Trust began meeting privately with artery lawyers. A letter from the foundation to the artery project in early November indicated that the foundation would withdraw its objections to Scheme Z provided the project agreed "to a set of mitigation measures that approximates what would flow from the 4(f) accounting which we consider to be ultimately the legally correct one."[39] In other words, the foundation would not require a review of an all-tunnel scheme or a determination that Schemes S and T were "prudent and feasible alternatives" to Scheme Z, provided the adverse effects of Scheme Z were fully mitigated.

While the closed negotiations among the highway department, the Conservation Law Foundation, and the National Trust were taking place, Bob Weinberg, a long-time colleague and friend of Salvucci, was asked to mediate the highway department's dispute with the MDC. A marathon session on November 9, 1990, with senior staff and legal counsel from the two agencies resulted in an agreement by the artery project to fund most of the mitigation measures the MDC had proposed, including all the public

open space along the river, and a letter from the MDC to the Federal Highway Administration.

The November 9 letter from the MDC became the basis for the required Section 4(f) evaluation, written by artery project staff and cosigned by FHWA; it was also crucial in the subsequent lawsuits filed against the project. The letter did not withdraw the assertion in the MDC commissioner's May 1989 letter, that the river and the planned parks on MDC-owned riverfront land were protected park land as defined in the federal statute. But the letter did not repeat that assertion or make the "determination of significance" required under federal regulations.[40]

The letter stated that the MDC had designated "the portion of the Basin extension river surface area upstream of the railroad bridge, for park and recreational purposes." However, such a partial designation is not in the public record.[41] The New Basin had been the subject of designation by the MDC once, in the vote on the 1980 master plan, which defined the New Basin as the entire length of the river between the old and new dams (see figure 8.11). That 1980 New Basin master plan had also been published in the 1982 impact statement on the Central Artery North Area and reviewed in the 1983 certificate issued on the artery project by the state secretary of environmental affairs.[42]

The Section 4(f) evaluation for Scheme Z, included as part of the environmental impact statement, found that the river was a protected resource upstream of the proposed highway crossing, but not where the bridge would be built (figure 10.10). The evaluation recognized a small taking of 4(f) land on the Boston side of the river, but left out most of the public open space just west of Paul Revere Park, previously designated under the separate Central Artery North Area (CANA) highway project, which the MDC had asserted in its May 1989 letter was part of the park plan.

In other words, the entire river basin was a protected resource—except in the area where the new bridge would be built.

The agreement later signed between the highway department and the MDC stated that the proposed mitigation measures were subject to the availability of federal and state funding. Since the final Section 4(f) evaluation concluded that the river and most

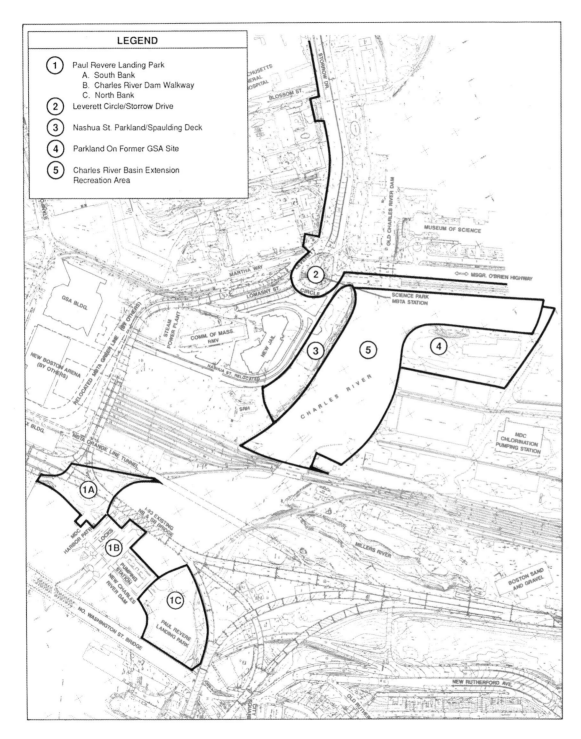

LEGEND

1. Paul Revere Landing Park
   A. South Bank
   B. Charles River Dam Walkway
   C. North Bank
2. Leverett Circle/Storrow Drive
3. Nashua St. Parkland/Spaulding Deck
4. Parkland On Former GSA Site
5. Charles River Basin Extension Recreation Area

10.10 The environmental impact statement for the artery project asserted that the water surface of the Charles River was a significant resource for open space and recreation—except where the highway was to go.

of the planned parkland under the highway bridges were not protected resources under the federal statute, FHWA was legally obligated to pay for only a small fraction of the proposed park developments. And the commitment in the state environmental impact report to fund the parks could be overturned by a future administration. Some open space advocates feared that the financial burden of the artery project might lead the legislature to determine that the cost of all the promised public spaces exceeded state funds available for the project.

Another issue raised by critics of the artery was that there appeared to be an explicit strategy of minimizing the required public discussions and substituting in their place more and more private bargaining. The public mediation that included the MDC was displaced by closed negotiations that included only the artery, the Conservation Law Foundation, and the National Trust. Senior staff of the trust had seen firsthand the pressure brought to bear on the MDC, and their first two letters to FHWA had been unequivocal in endorsing the MDC's 1989 position that the river was a protected resource under the federal statute. In their final comments, however, the trust concurred with the December Section 4(f) finding;[43] they had apparently agreed with the compromise proposed by the foundation.

As troubling as the limited public discussion of design alternatives were the efforts to keep the judgments of the project's own experts from the public view. Restricting the production and circulation of visual images of the river crossing was one example. Another example occurred in the summer of 1989, when project administrators were asserting that the schemes for tunnels under the Charles were unbuildable. An in-house study concluded that the project had not done sufficient test borings to evaluate the permitting and construction difficulties of tunnel designs for the river crossing. The study disappeared, and project administrators did not respond to requests from the city of Cambridge and from the Conservation Law Foundation for copies of the study under the state's freedom of information statutes. MIT professor Herbert Einstein later confirmed that borings from the river bottom indicated a "normal level of pollution . . . not a severely toxic mess"; it

was, he said, incorrect to say that environmental concerns ruled out the tunnel options.[44]

For many people, the most troublesome issue was the project's estimated cost, which was rising substantially faster than the rate of inflation. Commitments had been made to federal officials that the cost, inflation excepted, would not increase. The level of federal funding for various pieces of the project was uncertain, and the possible use by the artery project of non-Interstate federal money, intended for road projects across the state, jeopardized the support of state legislators outside metropolitan Boston. Here, too, project officials avoided public discussion. The New York firm of Lazard, Freres was hired to analyze funding alternatives, and completed a draft before the beginning of the public comment period. But project officials insisted the report was incomplete and therefore could not be released until after the comment period ended.[45]

What had happened to citizen participation in the twenty years since the "open study" of the Inner Belt? Fred Salvucci, the artery project's mastermind and champion, had years of experience with Boston's Little City Halls program, had vocally supported the East Boston neighborhood's opposition to airport expansion, had never forgiven the Turnpike Authority for the condemnation and relocation process that took his mother's home in Brighton. One long-time observer of the project suggested that Salvucci, a person "born of process—the balancing of issues, ideas and interests that defines government," at some point in the twenty years of discussion decided that "to get things done, big things, one must do more than participate. One must control the process."[46]

On the other hand, it could be argued that at crucial points in the project's history, for example, the decision to widen the artery, that the project was severely constrained in both design and cost issues by Congress and the Federal Highway Administration.

Managing the politics of the artery had been made both easier and more difficult because of the nature of its financing. Unlike the two battles over Storrow Drive or the protracted conflict over the Inner Belt, the project never came to the legislature for a one-time, yes-or-no vote. Instead, legislators had only to include enough money in state bond bill legislation to match the federal dollars;

because of the artery's massive scale, the funding would stretch over four different four-year federal transportation appropriations.

For a time in 1990, however, it looked like the artery might become an election issue. Before the primary elections in September, Steve Kaiser suggested to the artery staff that if the state would undertake a technical analysis of Version 4.0 of his all-tunnel plan, he would not raise the issue during the gubernatorial campaign.[47] In a few weeks Kaiser's proposal had been transferred to the artery's computerized database. It appeared to fit within the project's seemingly innumerable physical constraints and was found to be technically feasible. The joint venture staff, however, concluded that there would be serious permitting problems even though the state DEP, one of the state agencies that would have to grant permits for the project, consistently indicated its preference for schemes that included tunnels. DEP argued in comment letters on the artery project's impact reports that the environmental issues for Charles River tunnels were an order of magnitude less than those for depressing the artery or building the Third Harbor Tunnel. The artery, for example, had to dispose of ten million cubic yards of dirt for the harbor tunnel, while the Charles River tunnels were estimated to require the disposal of only a tenth of that amount.[48]

The artery review of Kaiser's all-tunnel design also determined that the plan would cost an additional $400 million. This was a far more serious objection, since even after the 1987 veto override, Congress continued to scrutinize the project closely. In mid-September, only a few weeks after the all-tunnel scheme was analyzed by artery engineers, the chairman of the Senate Finance Committee proposed revisions in the highway program, including a drastic reduction in the Central Artery project.[49]

In October Kaiser presented the all-tunnel plan to a public meeting in Cambridge; several weeks later he delivered Version 5.0 to the MDC, the Boston Redevelopment Authority, and the Federal Highway Administration.[50] Whatever the disputed boundaries of the existing and planned park land might be, Kaiser's design was clearly the most "green" of all the alternatives. It would eliminate not only the proposed "Stadium of Ramps" and the

"Great Wall" over the river; it would also take down the double-decked barrier of I-93 between Cambridge and Charlestown.

The all-tunnel plan was vigorously promoted by the Committee for Regional Transportation, a group funded primarily by the owner of a parking and shuttle business near the airport who was suing the artery project over the proposed taking of his property by eminent domain. Kaiser was among the founders of the group, whose members included Charlestown and Cambridge residents as well as active members of the local Sierra Club and the National Railroad Passengers Association. The group hired an engineering firm, legal counsel, and a public relations consultant, and was a major factor in altering the terms of the public debate in the fall of 1990.[51] In a lengthy *Globe* essay, Dun Gifford, another member of the Committee for Regional Transportation, challenged the state's argument that this part of the Charles River was an unredeemable wasteland. It was ironic, he wrote, that artery planners who disparaged the "lost half mile" were claiming at the same time they could turn Spectacle Island, once a garbage dump, into a "glorious park" with the excavate from the Third Harbor Tunnel.[52]

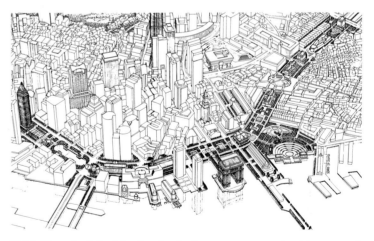

10.11 Once the federal funding for the Artery was approved, a debate ensued over the future use of the corridor once the elevated highway was demolished. The city of Boston hired the Spanish architect Ricardo Bofill to develop a plan for the corridor surface that devoted three-quarters of the surface to open space.

In the face of increasing opposition to Scheme Z, the artery project's managers tried to redirect public attention to other aspects of the project, in particular to the project's public arts program and to the open space above the depressed artery. Four different plans were developed; taken together, they raised some of the same fundamental issues about urban open space that wold be debated during the subsequent planning for the New Charles River Basin: How important is open space? How much open space is enough? When all the construction is finished, should the city look as if the artery had never existed? What are the roles for public and private development?

In 1988 the BRA had selected two consultants to advise them on the future artery open space, Alex Krieger of Boston and Ricardo Bofill, a Spanish architect described by the *Globe* as an avant-garde neo-classical designer. Although Stephen Coyle suggested at the time that the choice of Bofill would "elevate the profile" of the open space design, his work for the BRA made no discernible contribution to the public debate (figure 10.11).[53]

Two years later the *Globe* published full-page drawings and a lengthy discussion of proposals from both the BRA and Alex Krieger, as well as a separate proposal from the Boston Society of Architects (figures 10.12–10.14). The BRA advocated using most of the twenty-seven acres for parks, including an urban arboretum and a winter garden. The architects proposed buildings for most of the parcels. Krieger suggested a literal middle ground: buildings on alternating parcels, to frame what he called "a fantasy of seven Copley Squares." All three plans agreed that surface roads should run the length of the corridor, and that the major connections from the city to the water that were broken by the old artery, like State Street, should be visually highlighted as boulevards. The plans also shared a recognition of the activities and historic character of surrounding districts—for example, more active uses near Quincy Market, and low-density residential development near the North End.[54]

"Knitting back the city" meant, to architects, erecting buildings on this historically built-upon swath of land. Coyle challenged

10.12 The Boston Redevelopment Authority produced a plan that showed twenty of the twenty-seven acres developed as public space.

10.13 The plan by the Boston Society of Architects proposed building structures on three-quarters of the corridor, arguing that, "like anything, you can have too much park."

10.14 Alex Krieger laid out what he called "a fantasy of Seven Copley Squares" on every other parcel of open land.

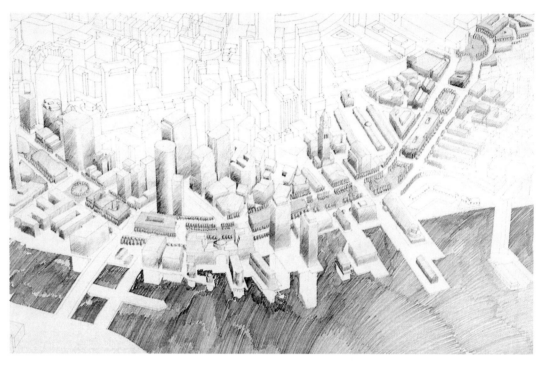

that interpretation of the metaphor: "Which city are you knitting back to which city? Are we talking about knitting back Governor Winthrop's Boston, or the city of Frederick Law Olmsted, or James Michael Curley's Boston, or the post–Civil War city, or the new Boston? When you really get the read of Boston, you see that it's really six or seven cities woven together. So what are we supposed to knit to what?" The five million square feet opened up by the demolition of the old artery could be developed, but more construction downtown would divert investment from other parts of Boston. The city administration was more interested in moving growth out to the neighborhoods. Coyle was convinced that if ten citizens were brought into City Hall, and all the "lawyers, architects, developers, and planners"—all the professionals—were just thrown out of the process, "the citizens who remained would all go for a park."[55]

The Boston Society of Architects took the opposite view and argued for buildings along the entire length of the corridor. As Larry Bluestone, the cochair of the BSA task force, put it, "like anything, you can have too much park. Look at City Hall Plaza— it's too much plaza. . . . So size itself is not what makes a good public space." Besides, he contended, the city was trying to develop Harborpark along the waterfront; open space above the new artery would create a second string of parks parallel to the first, and only a half block away, in the center of the city.[56] That argument did not acknowledge that Harborpark, for most of its planned length, was only a narrow public walkway along the water's edge.

Like Coyle, Alex Krieger saw Boston as a patchwork city, but his conclusions were very different from the BRA's. Since Boston had to grow by filling along the shoreline, the land under the artery offered the opportunity to create a new, identifiable district with a variety of buildings, taller near the downtown and lower near the North End. On alternate parcels between the buildings, landscaped squares would relate to the nearby neighborhoods and would reconstruct the links across the artery, staying true "to the most basic intent of Boston originally . . . its connection to the sea."[57]

In this scheme, large squares would face Rowe's Wharf, Central Wharf, and Long Wharf. Reducing the amount of new parkland, and constructing new adjacent buildings might offer the means for long-term park maintenance, an issue that troubled many open space advocates. Even if the artery paid for the construction of parks in East Boston, City Square in Charlestown, the Charles River, as well as Spectacle Island, who would maintain them? Post Office Square, almost everyone's favorite example of public space created through a successful private design and construction process, also charged the abutters who built the park for its upkeep.

Krieger's plan literally divided the difference between the BRA plan (75 percent open space) and the BSA proposal (75 percent built space). He feared, though, that his proposed design guidelines would be subjected to "the reaction against anything that is bold or visionary." There was "a risk that the highway planning will overwhelm the town planning, the townscape planning," he suggested, as if that had not already happened.[58]

The boldest strategy to overcome the opposition to Scheme Z was the change to a long-span bridge design that would reduce the number of piers in the river and provide the city with a landmark structure at the northern gateway to the downtown. Though more expensive than the seventeen-pier design, the new crossing, supported by two large towers, was expected to defuse the opposition of environmental groups and the U.S. Coast Guard. A cable-stayed bridge design was announced in October, and engineers rushed to develop the design in time to receive the required approvals before the Dukakis administration left office.[59]

Politicians Join the Opposition

By December 1990, opposition to Scheme Z was surfacing on many fronts, and for several weeks stories appeared in the Boston papers almost daily, accompanied by images that tried to communicate the scale and impact of the proposed bridges (figure 10.15). The transportation imperatives that led to Scheme Z were not at issue. The accounts consistently challenged the plan as a failure on urban design grounds, or because the public process was seen as manipulative, distorted, or simply bogus.

A lengthy, front-page *Boston Globe* article on December 2 reported claims that the state's environmental review process had been compromised for the artery. The state's environmental review of the artery's draft impact statement at the end of the summer had been altered by other state officials after Secretary DeVillars left for Europe. Favorable comments about Kaiser's all-tunnel plan had been deleted, and requirements for public transit improvements had been weakened.[66] A state environmental official, speaking anonymously, said there had been "a complete prostitution of the process." As community activists had been saying since the spring, "project officials for months refused to make non-blueprint illustrations of Scheme Z available." Only in the last months of 1990 were community leaders finally able to understand the size and scale of the project.[60]

Two days later, the state representative for the North End and part of Charlestown filed a bill that would halt the construction of Scheme Z and require a citizens' panel to review a redesign of the bridge. The *Globe* also described the all-tunnel option for the first time.[61] Later that same week, Kaiser presented his tunnel plan to the BRA, the MDC, and to the regional FHWA administrators. He acknowledged that the all-tunnel scheme would cost up to $1 billion more than Scheme Z, but it would avoid "re-creating the Central Artery on top of the Charles River," and would also accommodate the North Station–South Station rail link. One federal official said it would be up to the state to determine if the plan should be adopted. The director of environmental review for the EPA said the all-tunnel plan was "a serious proposal that deserves serious consideration." He was also interested in a variation of the plan that located two-thirds of the crossing in tunnels.[62]

The outgoing Dukakis administration had until January 2, 1991, to complete the state review process and approve Scheme Z. In the weeks before that deadline, the *Globe* twice published lengthy reviews of Scheme Z, including extensive photographs, maps, and charts. Three broad arguments were made in favor of the design. First, tunnels generally cost more than bridges; each alter-

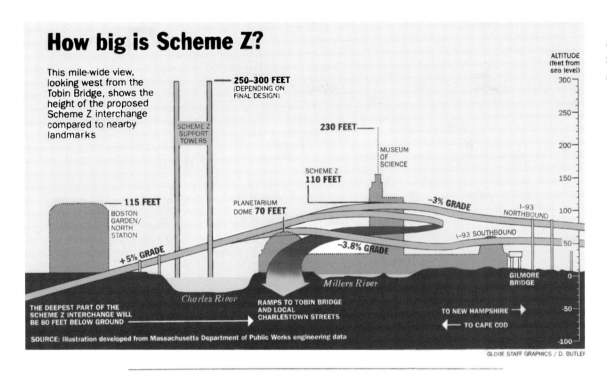

How big is Scheme Z?

This mile-wide view, looking west from the Tobin Bridge, shows the height of the proposed Scheme Z interchange compared to nearby landmarks

250–300 FEET (DEPENDING ON FINAL DESIGN)

SCHEME Z SUPPORT TOWERS

230 FEET

MUSEUM OF SCIENCE

SCHEME Z **110 FEET**

115 FEET
BOSTON GARDEN/ NORTH STATION

PLANETARIUM DOME **70 FEET**

−3% GRADE

I-93 NORTHBOUND

I-93 SOUTHBOUND

+5% GRADE

−3.8% GRADE

GILMORE BRIDGE

Charles River

Millers River

THE DEEPEST PART OF THE SCHEME Z INTERCHANGE WILL BE 80 FEET BELOW GROUND

RAMPS TO TOBIN BRIDGE AND LOCAL CHARLESTOWN STREETS

TO NEW HAMPSHIRE ➤

◄ TO CAPE COD

SOURCE: Illustration developed from Massachusetts Department of Public Works engineering data

ALTITUDE (feet from sea level)
300
250
200
150
100
50
0
−50
−100

GLOBE STAFF GRAPHICS / D. BUTLER

10.15 Scheme Z required that cars cross the river twice to go from Storrow Drive to the southbound artery.

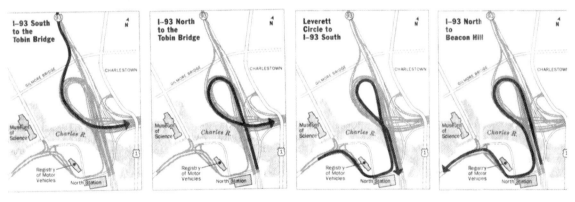

I-93 South to the Tobin Bridge

I-93 North to the Tobin Bridge

Leverett Circle to I-93 South

I-93 North to Beacon Hill

Four scenarios for navigating Scheme Z by automobile.

Is this wild and crazy ride in your future?

native with more tunnel and less viaduct would cost more, up to $1.7 billion more for the all-tunnel plan. Second, some unspecified complications would affect the Orange Line and North Station commuter trains. Finally, Scheme Z, according to Salvucci, was the only plan that did not contain tunnels or ramps that would conflict with the new Boston Garden. (Subsequent analysis in 1992 found solutions to the last two problems; by then, the cost of two years' additional design work plus the delay in construction was approaching the cost of the all-tunnel plan.) A spokesperson for the project argued in the *Globe* that the internal review of more than two dozen different schemes should make people feel better about supporting Scheme Z as the final choice. Many people took issue: Dan King, a Charlestown resident and a member of the Committee for Regional Transportation, concluded that when "they say they've done 31 versions and this monstrosity is the one that works best, that's not a reason to accept it. That's a reason to ask for our money back."[63]

On its editorial pages, the *Globe* continued to defend Scheme Z, repeating arguments and images that Robert Campbell had eviscerated in a lengthy article six months earlier. One editorial said that the area along the riverbanks was "a grimy combination of railyards, the I-93 overpass and a cement factory. Most of it can never become parkland."[71] Another editorial three weeks later claimed that the issue of the Charles River crossing "is more aesthetic than environmental. That section of the Charles, littered with warehouses and rail yards, can never be as beautiful as the Esplanade nearby. Even an ugly bridge would do little environmental harm."[64] The paper's editorial writers did not mention that by this time, the artery project had already promised to fund the construction of these same forty-plus acres of planned open space that could "never become parkland" (figure 10.16).

In the middle of December a *Globe* writer sought out the views of design professionals. Several architects and planners echoed earlier comments that the project had failed to make information about Scheme Z available when it was selected eighteen months earlier. One noted that the architectural model had been completed only six months ago, and even for professionals who work with them every day, "models can be very deceptive." They also suggested new images and visual comparisons to explain the bridge design. Tony DeMambro, a Boston architect, elaborated on Campbell's "perverse law of physics": the project was like squeezing a sausage; the artery goes underground, but the bad stuff appears somewhere else. Another designer suggested that the state was building "a parking garage over the Charles." The Scheme Z interchange would be taller than the State House and as big as Boston Common, and, according to one opposition group, would be the largest highway intersection in the world.[65]

The Boston Civic Design Commission had first voted against Scheme Z in August, and then reversed the vote a few days later. Now John DeMonchaux, the chair of the commission, said that the challenge was "to bring more information out into the open." Alex Krieger, a member of the Design Commission, was more blunt. The state, he said, was "trapped in a mess of its own making, out of a reluctance to air its plans in a timely manner."[66]

The *Globe* cited only one professional who supported Scheme Z. Gary Hack, a city planner and professor at MIT as well as a consultant to the Artery Business Committee (a downtown group organized to advance the project), was "virtually a lone voice of support for Scheme Z." The opposition to the bridge design, according to Hack, was the result of an attitude that "man-made things ought to be secondary to natural things"— we don't like parking lots because we don't like to look at them, he said, but we all want to drive.[67]

The Boston City Council voted unanimously to oppose Scheme Z on December 20. The Cambridge and Somerville city councils followed a few days later. More bills were filed in the state legislature to kill the project.[76] Finally the project's staunchest backers reversed themselves. The Artery Business Committee announced its opposition and then hired Perini International, a large local engineering and construction firm, to evaluate the all-tunnel alternative.[68]

On January 2, the last day in office of the outgoing Dukakis administration, Secretary DeVillars approved the environmental impact report for the entire Central Artery/Tunnel project, includ-

10.16 The MDC's plan for the New Charles River Basin was based on the simple concept of creating uninterrupted paths from the Cambridge and Boston esplanades to Charlestown and the North End. The dilemmas would be in the details—footbridges over wetlands and railroad tracks and under fourteen lanes of highway, and public spaces for yet-to-be-developed sites.

ing Scheme Z. Two major requirements were imposed on the Charles River Crossing. First, the project would be obligated to fund the design and construction of new public open space on the forty-plus acres of land owned or controlled by the MDC, with no dollar limit specified for the total cost. Second, a design review committee would be established to identify "improvements in the Scheme Z crossing so as to make it as aesthetically pleasing and environmentally harmless as possible—in short, to develop a beautiful, architecturally significant, and environmentally friendly bridge structure." The committee was to begin its work no later than February 1, and DeVillars cautioned that the work of the committee should not jeopardize the Artery project by "endless review and delay."

The Bridge Design Review Committee

William Weld, the newly elected governor, appointed Robert Taylor as Secretary of Transportation and Construction. Faced with the deadline of organizing the design review committee by the beginning of February, Taylor quickly came to two decisions. He appointed as chair of the committee Stanley Miller, a Republican with close ties to the new governor and a former chair of the Newton Planning Board; and he hired as facilitator to the committee Jack Wofford, the director of the Boston Transportation Planning Review from 1971 to 1973 who later served as Deputy General Counsel in the federal Department of Transportation under President Jimmy Carter.[69]

Secretary Taylor then faced the task of appointing the committee. Its membership would be large, since it was required to include citizens from East Cambridge, Charlestown, and the North End; representatives from fourteen organizations and agencies: the Boston Society of Architects, the Charles River Watershed Association, the Conservation Law Foundation, the Boston Preservation Alliance, the MDC, the Massachusetts Historical Society, Move Massachusetts 2000, 1000 Friends of Massachusetts, the Building Trades Council, the Artery Business Committee, and the Committee for Regional Transportation; staff from three Boston city agencies: the Redevelopment Authority, the

Transportation Department, and the Parks Department; and three members appointed by the Secretary of Environmental Affairs.[70]

That list wasn't long enough, as Taylor saw it, and he determined to add staff from the city of Cambridge, the Metropolitan Area Planning Council, the office of the mayor of Boston, the Boston Environment Department; representatives from the Boston Greenspace Alliance, the National Trust for Historic Preservation, the American Planning Association, the Sierra Club, Massachusetts General Hospital, the Greater Boston Chamber of Commerce, and five independent architects and engineers. (No one was invited from Somerville, perhaps because the city was a few hundred yards north of what was the project's northern boundary at the Gilmore Bridge—a boundary that, like so many other aspects of the project, would later expand.)[71]

Several of those groups had threatened lawsuits, and someone suggested that the opposition shouldn't be allowed on the committee. Taylor replied that "if we don't have the people who are suing us at the table, how can we expect to get an agreement?"[72]

The committee might easily have come and gone, yet another example of institutional failure—large, unwieldy, politically expedient but ultimately unproductive. Instead, the members of the committee, and the many people who listened in on their discussions, demonstrated that as inexpert citizens it was possible to understand a project of extraordinary complexity and to connect its detailed issues with the larger concerns of the public realm. Like the groups that were organized during the debates over the Inner Belt—the protestors as well as the state's restudy—the bridge committee took on experts from profoundly different professional cultures: the quantitative worlds of traffic planning and highway engineering, the visionary inclinations of city planning and urban design, and the skills of negotiation and political compromise.

Three subcommittees were created, to focus on bridge design, open space, and traffic and transportation. With little publicity, Secretary Taylor approved a budget of $500,000 so that the committee could hire independent experts in three areas: bridge design, tunnel design, and transportation planning. He also committed a substantial amount of the project budget to developing and analyzing new alternatives for the river crossing.[73]

From the beginning, participation in the bridge committee meetings regularly exceeded the forty-two appointed members. The meetings compelled the attendance of a large retinue from the joint venture staff, representing the disciplines of traffic planning, highway engineering, architecture, landscape architecture, and urban design; often, design-related issues required expertise from the legal, regulatory, environmental permitting, cost estimating, and budgeting groups. More remarkable was the large number of interested citizens who came, even though they were seldom invited to participate: residents of affected neighborhoods, professionals not collecting consultants' fees on the project, and observers of the city-making process. Attendance at the meetings was often double the size of the committee.

Committee members broached several major conflicts immediately. The committee was split over the issue of recommending changes that would increase the cost or delay the project. Specific design alternatives divided the committee in different ways. Cambridge and Boston residents were often on opposite sides; changes that improved the design on one side of the river often made it worse on the other side. The project boundaries were established as fixed and not subject to discussion (athough they were later altered).

The committee gave itself ninety days to complete its review, even though that date was several weeks after the legal deadline facing the groups who had threatened to sue to stop Scheme Z.[74]

In April, following two months of intensive work, two very different prospects were presented to the committee. One was as sweeping as Gourlay's original 1844 plan for the Back Bay; in fact, it took the re-creation of the Back Bay as the model for the "lost half mile." A single image tellingly embodied this vision, elaborated by two local architects, Peter Roudebush (who had worked on the 1970 Boston Transportation Planning Review) and Brad Bellows. The two architects superimposed on a black-and-white photograph of the vast acreage of the old Boston & Maine yards a green and blue image of the Esplanade and the neighborhood of the Back Bay (figure 10.17). This representation graphically demonstrated that the area surrounding the highway project was as large as all of the Back Bay and all of the Esplanade.

Two economists working with Roudebush and Bellows outlined a plan for tax increment financing, where the increase in property values would be taxed to help fund the more expensive highway alternatives. They pointed to the Back Bay, where the state paid for the filling, donated nine acres of land to churches and schools, and still made $3.4 million between 1856 and the last land auction in 1886. The four hundred acres north of the Charles might generate four to six billion dollars in new development over time. Because of the perceived financial obstacles to the all-tunnel plan, Kaiser, Bellows, and Roudebush later drew up an alternative with two-thirds of the river crossing in tunnels and a bridge of only four lanes, which they compared to the Longfellow Bridge. The reactions of committee members ranged from enthusiastic interest to complete skepticism.[76]

More startling was the response of the bridge committee to the proposals of the Swiss bridge designer Christian Menn. While in Boston to give a lecture at the Harvard Graduate School of Design, Menn was invited by David Wallace, a local architect and a consultant for the artery to inspect the site of the Charles River Crossing and asked if he would be interested in designing a new bridge. Soon thereafter he was hired by the bridge committee.[74]

Menn's first presentation to the committee took only a few minutes, and was as spare and elegant as the bridge schemes he presented. His design intentions were straightforward. First, there should not be a conflict between the bridge and its environment. The design should make Bostonians proud, not litigious. Finally, there should be order, unity, and attention to detail. The immediate reaction of the committee, even before anyone responded to Menn's proposal, was an almost audible sense of unexpected delight.[78]

The preceding weeks of contentious debate had seemed to focus on which scheme was disliked the least by the fewest people. Now, quite suddenly, there was a sense that a range of graceful and harmonious choices was possible. The adversarial spirit that

10.17 Peter Roudebush and Brad Bellows, two local architects, demonstrated photographically that the space in the New Basin and the vacant rail yards nearby (left center) was as large as all of Back Bay and all of the Esplanade (lower right).

had exploded in opposition to Scheme Z at the end of 1990 dissipated in the anticipation of this new opportunity. The proposed bridge alternatives seemed to cast a new light not only on the crossing itself, but on every related issue: ramps, pedestrian access, adjacent land development, new public spaces.[79]

Menn subsequently developed three different bridge designs, to accommodate the bridge widths required by the tunnel and nontunnel variants of the river crossing, one with eight lanes and two towers, one with ten lanes and six towers, and a third with two decks (four lanes over eight lanes) and two towers. The towers in all the designs were at least a hundred feet lower than the preliminary bridge scheme by the joint venture. Menn also addressed the loop ramps, the connection between Route 1 and I-93. In Scheme Z, the ramps came out of the ground as soon as they passed under City Square in Charlestown, directly under the mainline bridge. Menn proposed that the ramps remain in tunnels until they passed under the bridge, because they obscured the north tower of the bridge behind a screen of piers and roadway structures and created a concrete backdrop for pedestrians walking along the river.[80]

The drama of Menn's designs seemed to eclipse the investigations into tunnel construction by the other internationally renowned expert hired by the committee, Professor Herbert Einstein of MIT. Based on the scheme first proposed by Steve Kaiser, Einstein analyzed alternative methods of tunnel construction, and outlined the likely cost savings. His ideas were not developed to the same level of engineering detail as Menn's bridges and the tunnel schemes never seemed financially feasible to many members of the committee. In May the traffic and transportation subcommittee reported that although three subcommittee members wanted to continue the study of the all-tunnel plan, the other eleven members felt the alternative was "unaffordable" (in the revised estimates the plan was still about $500 million more than the next most expensive alternative). After a general discussion of alternatives, the bridge committee agreed to end further study of the all-tunnel plan, and the chairman acknowledged the contribution that Steve Kaiser's visionary scheme had made to the project.[81]

As the discussion of Menn's bridge designs continued, variations and sub-variations were developed based on the bridge committee's first twelve or thirteen numbered schemes. A number of the open space advocates on the committee favored the double-deck bridge designs. Since they were narrower in width and took less parkland, committee members argued, they appeared to be required by the Section 4(f) regulations. That approach, however, was seen as narrow and legalistic by some of the architects on the committee, who saw the single-deck designs as more "visually elegant." The improved visual profile of the bridge, they argued, more than compensated for the increased width of the concrete "roof" above the pedestrian paths and the river, and their view prevailed.

The committee worked a month beyond its original deadline to consider a new option that proved infeasible. By mid-June the committee had narrowed its preferences to three options. All of the options eliminated the double crossing of the river. Scheme Z's three bridges were replaced by a single bridge, and the height and width of the bridge designs was about one third less than the Scheme Z bridge. All of the bridges incorporated design improvements based on the work of Christian Menn. The six ramps at North Point had been reduced to two or three; CIP 5 (a variation of Scheme T) had two tunnels under the river and CIP 8 had a single tunnel. CIP 3 (like Scheme Z) was an all viaduct scheme. Based on the improvements in all the schemes, the committee voted unanimously to recommend the abandonment of Scheme Z. Stan Durlacher, the Assistant Secretary of Transportation from 1991 to 1993 credited these substantial improvements to the open, multi-disciplinary process that the committee had sustained throughout its intense efforts to resolve the crossing design.[82] It appeared that CIP 5 (a variation of Scheme T) would be approved, in spite of the opposition of the Beacon Hill delegation. Many members of the committee, however, were visibly startled when the formal vote was taken. The staff from the city of Boston, who had supported this variation in numerous formal and informal discussions, all voted against the scheme. Richard Dimino, the Boston transportation commissioner, had lobbied at the last minute in favor of CIP 8; this effort was supported by Stanley Miller, chair of the bridge committee. In counting the votes, Miller refused to accept the absentee votes of several committee members, and Scheme 8, opposed by the city of Cambridge and two environmental groups, was declared the winner by a vote of seventeen to fifteen. The mayor of Cambridge immediately announced that the city would proceed with its lawsuit.[83]

Another year of public and private discussions followed. In March 1992 the bridge committee unanimously agreed on "CIP 8.1D, Modification 5," an awkward name that reflected the numerous sub-variations it incorporated. "Mod 5" (as the committee came to call this option) included a three-lane tunnel under the river connecting Leverett Circle with City Square, replacing some of the loop ramps. One transportation consultant suggested that the scheme failed the test of simplicity; any design that visually complex should not be built. The numerous and subtle differences among the schemes, over which committee members and the project staff had labored for so many months, were difficult to summarize in project publications and in press reports. Committee members joked that even they now had trouble telling the variations apart.

On the same day as the committee vote, the Conservation Law Foundation announced that the foundation had agreed to a federal court order that would enforce major public transit improvements as a part of the artery project; consequently its lawsuit would be dropped. The two biggest threats to the project, the lawsuits over transit mitigation and the design of Scheme Z, appeared to be resolved. The state secretary of transportation optimistically declared that the ghost of New York City's Westway was finally laid to rest.[84]

The press coverage of the vote for "Mod 5" noted that there remained opposition to the design from some Beacon Hill residents. In fact, the resistance to Mod 5 was much more serious than the news report suggested. The city of Boston had hired its own traffic consultant (with money provided by the CA/T Project), and two months after Mod 5 was approved the Boston Traffic Commissioner announced that the city had developed a new variation of the bridge design.[85] The decision was not final after all.

A New Bridge Design

At the end of September 1992, the artery's permitting consultants filed a "Notice of Project Change" for the scheme with the state Environmental Affairs office. The notice was required under state regulations because the previously approved project would now be substantially revised. In a major reversal of years of previous arguments, the notice described at length the many benefits of tunneling under the Charles instead of building viaducts to connect Leverett Circle with City Square.[86]

A few weeks later, Richard Taylor, the state secretary of transportation, resigned. He was replaced by James Kerasiotes, the state highway commissioner. Kerasiotes had objected in March to aspects of the settlement with the city of Cambridge under which the city agreed to drop its lawsuit if some variation of Scheme 8.1D were built. The new secretary rejected this scheme early in 1993 without consulting the Bridge Design Review Committee; in fact, Kerasiotes never called a meeting of the committee, asserting that the committee's task was the development of a series of design standards, not the approval of a final design.[87]

Concerned by this abandonment of both the process and the committee's consensus choice, an informal association organized in 1992 called the "Artery Focus Group" (whose membership included some downtown businesses, representatives of the New Boston Garden Corporation, Massachusetts General Hospital, and the Beacon Hill Civic Association) convened its own search for a bridge solution. The most promising alternative included a tunnel downstream (rather than upstream) of the commuter rail bascule bridges across the Charles, in the same alignment as the proposed Leverett Circle bridge in Scheme Z and its later variations. This tunnel alignment had been rejected earlier in the bridge committee's design review, because of its location between the Orange Line tunnel and the rail bridges; now, it appeared the scheme's advantages justified moving the bascule bridges, which were over sixty years old and scheduled to be replaced soon after the completion of the Artery Project. Supporters of the proposal included Fred Salvucci, who had never before endorsed a tunnel design.[86]

The new scheme addressed many of the concerns raised by the city of Cambridge and the Charles River Crossing Coalition, an affiliation of nonprofit organizations that included Cambridge Citizens for Livable Neighborhoods, Citizens for a Livable Charlestown, and the Charles River Watershed Association. Members of the coalition had sued to stop Scheme Z, and their action had been joined in federal court with the city of Cambridge lawsuit against the project. The two cases were still pending when the "Artery Focus Group" design was developed. Representatives of Cambridge and the coalition were approached by state highway officials about their support of the new alternative and their willingness to drop the lawsuits, but were given only a few days to decide. They were wary of the new scheme, since they had looked at dozens of tunnel schemes during the past two years that seemed promising in concept, but that later proved impossible, either because of engineering constraints or political opposition. Neither lawsuit was withdrawn.[89]

The state took the new option off the table, and the December 1993 environmental impact report endorsed the all-viaduct scheme as the preferred alternative. It had fewer and lower loop ramps in Cambridge, but still had two bridges over the Charles. The cable-stayed bridge was ten lanes wide, and would later be described by the artery project as the widest bridge of its type in the world (two of the ten lanes were cantilevered outside the cables on the downstream side). The Leverett Circle bridge just upstream was four lanes wide, and it was connected to a set of tunnels and elevated ramps that would fill a substantial portion of the land between the new Boston Garden and Leverett Circle.[90]

Once the construction was completed, three of the four highways that meet at the Charles River would be underground as they approached the river—Storrow Drive at Leverett Circle, the new underground artery at Causeway Street, and the Route 1 tunnel just completed under City Square in Charlestown. But all three of these highways would come out of the ground at the edge of the river to meet the new bridges. Some Cambridge critics immediately labeled this design "The Son of Z." In 1994, the new alternative was approved by state and federal agencies, and the coalition and Cambridge proceeded with their lawsuit (figure 10.18).[91]

10.18 The Charles River Crossing Coalition, which included Cambridge Citizens for Livable Neighborhoods, Citizens for a Livable Charlestown, and the Charles River Watershed Association, was organized to oppose the variations of Scheme Z developed by the artery project. In 1994 the coalition produced this postcard to suggest the scale of the of the bridges over the Charles and to raise money for a lawsuit to stop what critics called "The Son of Z."

The New Basin: The Other Regional System

The work of the bridge committee focused extraordinary attention on the proposed extension of the Charles River esplanades, the most public discussion of the "lost half mile" since the regional open space study of 1969. During the frequent bridge design meetings that addressed the proposed pathway connections along the river, Julia O'Brien, the MDC's Director of Planning, repeatedly advanced the idea that in the "lost half mile" two substantial regional systems crossed: the metropolitan park system and the regional transportation network. It was critical, she said, that there be a genuine crossing of the two systems, not the overpowering of the park connections by the transportation structures. Over time, the opportunity to link the river and the harbor with over forty acres of new parks and greenways became, for several committee members, the primary justification for permitting such huge highway structures in the center of Boston. No one on the committee challenged the necessity of the highway project; the issue was whether the thirty-year-old plan to link the Charles with Boston Harbor was still possible, given the scale of the road construction.

Some people felt that neither the most sophisticated planning, nor any level of creative design along the river by architects or public artists, could overcome the barriers to public access initially created by the railroads and now to be greatly expanded by the proposed Charles River Crossing. According to this view, the east-west pedestrian links under the new highway bridge would be dark and dangerous, especially on the Boston side, even if they could be engineered.

In approving Scheme Z on his last day in office in January 1991, outgoing secretary of environmental affairs John DeVillars required not only the creation of the Bridge Design Review Committee but also a citizens advisory committee for the New Basin. Seven of the New Basin Advisory Committee members would be appointed by DeVillars's successor as secretary of environmental affairs, and the mayors of Boston and Cambridge would each appoint seven members. This formal approach to public discussion reflected the increasingly bureaucratic character of city

design, as well as the continuing (sometimes ambivalent) state commitment to the community participation that had been aggressively promoted by activist groups in Boston since the planning of the Inner Belt in the 1960s. The state appointments included the directors of two nonprofit environmental groups, the Boston Greenspace Alliance and the Charles River Watershed Association; two lawyers with backgrounds in environmental issues; and two state environmental officials. The mayor of Boston appointed the director of the city's environmental department, a senior park department staff member, and five Boston residents. Cambridge was also represented by two city staff members, as well as five Cambridge residents, including two architects, an active member of state and local bicycle groups, and a resident of the nearby condominiums on Lechmere Canal. Seven members of the advisory committee were also members of the artery project's Bridge Design Review Committee.[92]

One month after the committee's vote in favor of the river crossing known as "8.1D" in March 1992, the highway department finally transferred the money to the MDC to begin the New Charles River Basin Master Plan.[93] Neither the planners from the MDC nor the agency's design consultants referred to the 1970s work of the Boston Transportation Planning Review, but the advisory committee meetings followed the same approach to community participation.[94] The committee functioned in an advisory role, not as a forum for decision-making; unlike the bridge committee, no votes were taken. Where a clear consensus was reached, the MDC generally followed the committee's recommendations. The MDC actively solicited participation from neighborhood organizations and other interest groups, and the meetings were open to anyone, not just the twenty-one appointed members.

It was clear to most members of the advisory committee, especially those who had been through a year of the bridge committee meetings, that the new highway bridges across the Charles would dwarf the engineering works that had dominated the river and shoreline spaces between the railroad bridges and the new dam. Nonetheless the committee members, especially those from city agencies in Boston and Cambridge, clearly hoped that the realization of the New Basin Master Plan would establish an appropriate setting for new commercial and residential development in the upper half of the "lost half mile." In meetings of both the Bridge Design Review Committee and the New Basin Advisory Committee, several designers spoke frequently about creating a public landscape that would respond appropriately to the scale of the existing transportation artifacts and the new highway. Yet they all found this verbal abstraction extraordinarily difficult to translate into landscape images, and no one could point to real places where this idea had been realized at this scale. The committee maintained its optimism that somehow the park spaces, pathways, and pedestrian bridges would tie the edges of the "lost half mile" together, in spite of the design character and the enormous scale of the proposed artery bridges.[95]

At the committee's first meeting, Julia O'Brien, the MDC director of planning and a former student of Kevin Lynch, cited some of Lynch's observations about Boston and the Charles River in his *Image of the City*. She described Lynch's pioneering methods of inviting city residents to make diagrams that marked out their perceptions of the places they lived. She then asked committee members to draw the New Basin as it now existed. A presentation of the history of the New Basin included photographic evidence of the reclamation of the basin above the old dam and suggested that the historic esplanades were completely fabricated environments, just as the spaces in the New Basin would be.[96]

The advisory committee first considered general objectives, then park programming, and finally landscape design. There was strong support for the conditions established in the 1990 environmental review documents, which required the construction of pedestrian and bicycle connections both up- and downstream, to establish links between the river and the harbor, from the Esplanade in Boston to the North End, and from Cambridge to Charlestown and the Navy Yard. The committee also concurred with the required connections across the river, at or near the commuter rail bridges. The existing walkways across the old and the new dam, though not on the list of required mitigation measures, presented opportunities for substantial improvement. There

was general agreement that the New Basin should include spaces for active as well as passive recreation, and that both the enjoyment and safety of the New Basin would be enhanced by park programming and interpretive activities—a Charles River visitors center, for example. The greatest concern of the committee was all too familiar to almost every park agency in America: could these public spaces, once built, be maintained? And given the issue of future maintenance, how should these spaces be designed now?[97]

Following the first months of planning by Carr, Lynch, Hack and Sandell of Cambridge, the MDC's consultants, two alternatives were developed. The "New Esplanade," the first schematic design, was based on the formal vocabulary of Arthur Shurcliff's Esplanade design of the 1930s (figure 10.19). The large geometry of this approach was arguably closer in scale to the existing and proposed engineering works in the New Basin, and represented "the familiar and comfortable nineteenth-century pattern pushing its way through these large structures to reach the sea." The second alternative, "Charlesbank Meadows," was compared with Olmsted's design for the Fens. It would "create landscapes that evoke pastoral, natural areas" in an urban setting without recreating them." This scheme would appear as if "nature had reclaimed this ragged edge of the city and then been developed into a park" (figure 10.20).[98]

The advisory committee was divided over these alternatives. The large geometry of the "New Esplanade" seemed appropriate, but the cost of the formal elements—the granite detailing—was a major concern. There was more enthusiasm for the "Meadows," in particular for the introduction of more diverse plantings than in the "Esplanade" approach. The contrary view was that the naturalistic approach was plainly overwhelmed by the scale of the new highway construction. The design solution was a synthesis of the two schemes, which sought to maintain "the reverence for nature, in its curving forms and details, while welcoming the large elements of the urban landscape as parts of the whole. The design is based on the reconciliation of opposites—space and mass, centrality and extension, nature and culture—that characterized the Baroque architectural synthesis."[99]

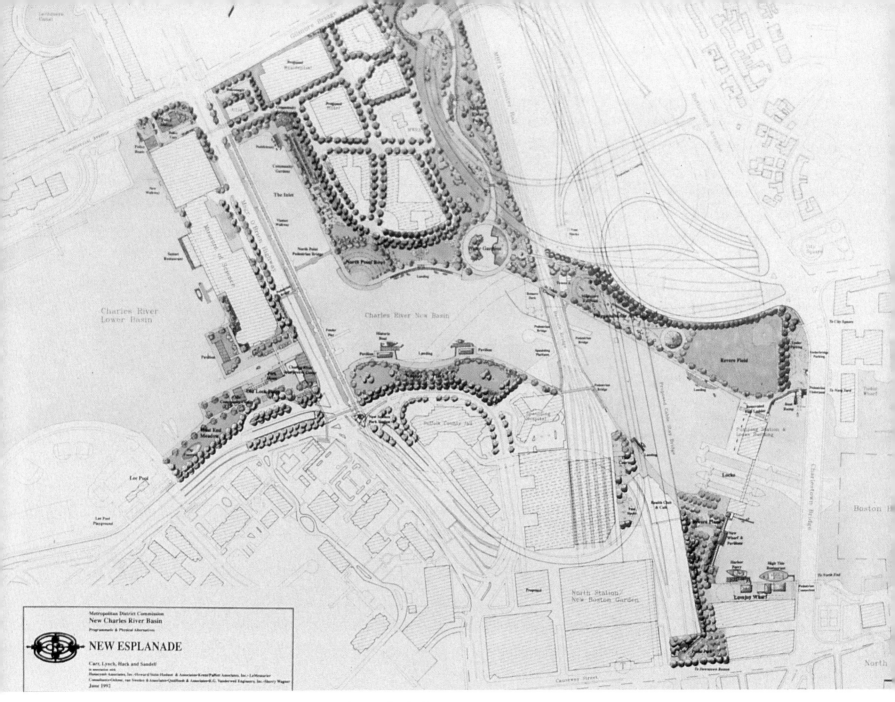

10.19   Carr, Lynch, Hack, and Sandell, the master planners for the New Basin, developed two alternatives. One, called the "New Esplanade," was geometric in plan and formally detailed.

Chapter   10

10.20 "Charlesbank Meadows," the second alternative for the New Basin, was more naturalistic and more diversely planted, consciously echoing Olmsted's Back Bay Fens.

10.21 North Point Park, the largest of the new public spaces in the New Basin, included a shallow water feature for small boats, which connected with the main channel of the river.

This synthetic approach shared a number of elements with the MDC "Master Plan" of 1980 (figure 8.11). The MDC scheme had proposed an island and lagoon on the Boston side of the river, but the 1980s construction of the new jail on Nashua Street since that first plan had narrowed the available land. In the Carr Lynch plan, strongly geometric islands (including a large circular island) and a winding lagoon were laid out at North Point. Substantial areas of new fill in the river were proposed on both sides of the river, extending a history of land-making that began in the seventeenth century (figures 10.21-10.24). The regulation of waterfront construction had changed substantially since 1980, however, and during the public review of the master plan it was suggested that neither the state Department of Environmental Protection nor the Army Corps of Engineers would allow the realization of the plan's vigorous geometry.

The greatest departure of the 1995 master plan from Charles Eliot's nineteenth-century vision of the river was its commitment to public art and public history. The MDC's Reservations Division, created in 1984, had developed extensive interpretive programs that presented the natural and cultural history of individual sites and reservations.[100] But the Metropolitan Park System was seldom presented to the public as a linked network of parks, established to reveal and "reserve" the natural character of the region.

The Master Plan proposed the renovation of Guy Lowell's 1910 structures on the first Charles River Dam, with one or more of the buildings devoted to interpreting the history of the park system and the region. The theme would be "connections": the river and its margins as a system of visible connections between the natural and the built environment, as a place linking the past, the present and the future, and as a place where connections would be established among the people who came to the river. This set of connections among people, though, was not cast in the nineteenth-century sense of the middling crowds learning from association with their betters; this would be a mingling of equals in the city's increasingly diverse citizenry.[101]

There would also be spaces for public art, including a pair of beacons framing the view from the New Basin to the old locks and to the Longfellow Bridge beyond. In all the public discussions of the master plan, the approach to public art elicited the strongest dissent. A group called the Reclamation Artists had been organized in the late 1980s; its members included the architect Lajos Heder, whose photographs of the New Basin sought to capture its essence in the Moore-Heder proposal for the master plan in 1988 (chapter 8 frontispiece, figure 8.21). Their aim was to focus attention on areas of neglected urban land by creating temporary outdoor installations of public art, open to any artists interested in participating. By the spring of 1994 the Reclamation Artists had produced four installations along the Charles, and were included in an exhibit on "Public Interventions" at Boston's Institute for Contemporary Art. They took exception to the clean, carefully landscaped sites suggested for large-scale art works in the New Basin. Mags Harries wanted instead an area that could be dug up, rearranged, reconstructed—transformed by "the big loud things" on the site. As an alternative to the long elevated pedestrian bridges over the railroad tracks, Harries and Heder proposed a floating walkway under the railroad bridges. Laura Baring-Gould told the *Globe* that "Olmsted should end at the viaduct."[102]

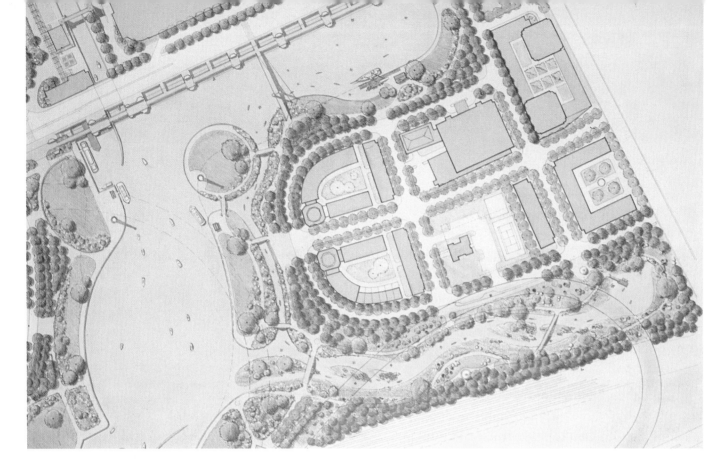

10.22 Two islands at North Point Park were created by the shallow water channel, which also extended under the highway ramps.

10.23 At Nashua Street Park, where the reconstruction of the existing rip-rap slope was required, a new seawall was proposed to match the curve of the seawall on the Cambridge side, establishing a very visible symmetry for the primary water surface of the lost half mile.

10.24 Two towers with beacons, one on the round island at North Point (lower right) and one along Nashua Street, would announce the creation of the New Basin.

In the advisory committee meetings, many of the committee members disagreed with the artists. The values associated with pastoral open spaces in the city were, for them, still valid, a perspective that became apparent in the meetings held to discuss the design of the first park to be built in the New Basin.[103]

The Parks and the Bridges: Under Construction at Last

In 1994, the design of Paul Revere Park began, the first public space to be built as mitigation for the environmental impacts of the highway bridges across the Charles. The park was a reconstruction of the open space that had been completed on the northern, earthen portion of the dam in 1978. Less than ten years later, the park became a construction staging zone for the new highway tunnel that passed under City Square and came out of the ground just north of the park.[104]

The community's preferred approach to the design of the park was expressed in several public meetings. To establish the scale of the park, the design consultants showed that the area was large enough to accommodate a baseball diamond with longer foul lines than Fenway Park. Charlestown residents were unanimous in rejecting ball fields. They said they wanted "a real park," and they described what Olmsted called a "country park"—a planted, pastoral oasis.[105] Their preference was shared by the park planners and by the MDC. When the park was formally dedicated in 1999, there was space in the park for sound art and mosaics, interpretive sculpture, and public programming (figures 1.1, 1.2, 10.25, 10.26)—but the matrix of those spaces was a shaded, oval greensward (figure 10.27).

In 1997, two years before the park was opened, a federal judge ruled in favor of the artery in the lawsuit filed by Cambridge Citizens for Livable Neighborhoods, the Charles River Watershed Association, Citizens for a Livable Charlestown, and the city of Cambridge. The decision rejected the assertion by the plaintiffs that the tunnel alternatives had been inadequately reviewed under the National Environmental Policy Act. In determining that only part of the river was a recreation resource under Section 4(f) of the Department of Transportation Act, the ruling reviewed the legislation in 1903, 1909, and 1962, as well as the November 1990 MDC letter to the Federal Highway Administration, dismissing as irrelevant earlier correspondence and prior actions by the Commission.[106]

In short, the construction of the two bridges over the Charles could begin at last.

The state environmental review for the Charles River bridges had required that construction should commence on all of the parks not in the construction right-of-way before the work on the bridges began. In the end, the parks took much longer; work began on Nashua Street Park in the fall of 2001, and the construction of North Point Park was scheduled to start about nine months later. By then the Leverett Circle bridge had already opened, and all but the last section of the cable-stayed bridge was complete. The legislature determined to recognize both the nearby neighborhood and a recently deceased community leader in naming the new structure the Leonard P. Zakim Bunker Hill Bridge.

10.25 At the edge of the large grass oval, Susan Gamble rendered in ceramic tile a 1775 map of the British march to Lexington and Concord, with text from Paul Revere's own description of his famous ride.

10.26 "The Charlestown Bells" were created by Paul Matisse (right, holding a silver umbrella). Mounted on the water side of the railing upstream of the pumping station at the new dam are twenty-eight rainbow-colored pipes of spun aluminum. Rubber-coated hammers are connected to stainless steel levers installed on the walkway side of the railing so that pedestrians can play the bells as they cross the dam.

10.27 During the construction of the City Square tunnel in Charlestown, Paul Revere Park was a construction staging area. When the residents of Charlestown were asked what should be done when the park was restored, they agreed they wanted "a real park." After some discussion, it became clear that they meant a passive park with a large open greensward.

10.28 The Leonard P. Zakim Bunker Hill Bridge under construction.

11

Urban Visions and the Future of the River

It is an easy matter to lay out a New Town—*to display wonders with the compass and square, but our business is to correct the obliquities of time and recover from dirt and distortion.*

Robert Gourlay, Edinburgh, 1829

Nothing less than "The Future of America" was the title H. G. Wells chose for a series of articles in *Harper's Weekly* recounting his visit to the United States in 1906. After his first stop in New York City, he took the Fall River steamer to Boston. Wells wanted to understand how Boston, once the leading city of the colonies, had been eclipsed by raucous, flamboyant New York. On his arrival in Boston, he found himself "in a singularly short space of time . . . climbing into a tremulous impatient motor-car with three enthu-siastic exponents of the work of the Metropolitan Park Commission," including Sylvester Baxter. The three men present-ed Wells with "a neatly tinted map, large and framed and glazed," and set off "to explore a fresh and more deliberate phase in this great American symphony, this symphony of growth" (figure 11.1)[1]

Extending fifteen or twenty miles from the State House, the region had been "planned out and prepared for growth." The woodland reservations and the banks of the streams and rivers and meres had been made into parks, and tree-lined avenues a hundred and fifty yards wide had been built. The "fair and ample and shady new Boston, the Boston of 1950," Wells wrote, "grows visibly before one's eyes." Wells compared "the disciplined confidence" of these proposals with "the blind enlargement of London," and con-fessed to moments when it all seemed too good to be true. "All cities do not grow," he told Baxter. "Cities have shrunken." Yet he could not deny the unfolding vision he saw:

> If possible, it is more impressive even than the crowded large-ness of New York to trace the serene preparation Boston has made through this [Metropolitan Park] Commission to be widely and easily vast. New York's humanity has a curious air of being carried along upon a wave of irresistible prosperity, but Boston confesses design. I suppose no city in all the world (unless it be Washington) has ever produced so com-plete and ample a forecast of its own future as this Commission's plan of Boston.[2]

11.1 In a series of articles in 1906 about "The Future of America," H. G. Wells described the "serene preparation" of Boston's Metropolitan Park Commission for a future city that would be "widely and easily vast." His tour of the regional parks included a drive along the Middlesex Fells parkway.

With Baxter as his guide, Wells could easily see the grander vision—that parks and reservations were only the first step in the realization of greater Boston's future.

Public Space and a "Journalism of Ideas"

The conversations of H. G. Wells and Sylvester Baxter are just one of many Boston examples of what Lewis Mumford called a "journalism of ideas," a public discourse that begins with particular subjects like architecture and urban design and then expands its view to illuminate broader social concerns. The historian Thomas Bender has argued that in the writings of Frederick Law Olmsted, "architectural and general cultural and political issues converge"; and, in a larger sense, "his purposes and career as a designer cannot be understood apart from his purposes and career as a writer."[3] Yet in our recent enthusiasm to restore the public spaces of Olmsted and his successors, we have paid much less heed to their writings than to their drawings.

In fairness, that is not entirely our fault. Most of Olmsted's discussions of landscapes and public space were delivered in professional reports; they were not easy reading and were not circulated to a broad public.[4] Olmsted never attempted a systematic summary of his design principles for public spaces, but he actively promoted the writing by others whose skills he thought exceeded his own. Eliot's descriptions of landscapes in his correspondence prompted Olmsted to reply that he had not seen "such justly critical notes . . . on landscape architecture" from anyone in a generation. Eliot should "write for the public, a little at a time if you please, but methodically, systematically." It was part of his "professional duty to do so."[5]

Eliot willingly accepted this calling, and he wrote three dozen essays and several lengthy and widely circulated reports in his brief career, none more important than the 1893 report to the Boston Metropolitan Park Commission. Sylvester Baxter took a different path to the same calling. Starting from his interests in parks and municipal administration, he saw the campaign for metropolitan reservations as the first step toward larger questions that he believed could be addressed only by a regional approach to government. It was therefore not surprising that Baxter and Eliot chose to work together to promote the metropolitan park system. They were sufficiently persuasive that in seven years the Metropolitan Park Commission was able to acquire almost nine thousand acres of natural reservations, including the banks of the Charles River extending from the lower basin as far as Newton and Wellesley. Their campaign to engage business and political leaders in a series of twelve "inspection tours" of proposed parks in greater Boston in 1892 was, in fact, an extended traveling discourse on the subject of cities and public spaces.

At several points in Boston's city building, however, its citizens have not waited for professionals to show the way, as the history of the Charles River makes plain. Seeing connections between design and some of the larger issues confronting the community, they have enticed or provoked designers into joining them in extended public discussion. The post–Civil War campaign for parks in Boston was organized by the city's elite, who persuaded Olmsted first to speak in Boston and then to accept the commission for the Back Bay Fens. In much the same way, the 1894 campaign to construct a Charles River dam did not succeed immediately; in fact, James Storrow vigorously took exception to Eliot's support of a compromise proposal to build a dam at Cottage Farm. And Storrow's success in organizing and finally gaining legislative approval for the Charles River Dam in 1903 is more than a reflection of the social status of that generation's city fathers. It was also a consequence of a generation of extensive public discussion in Boston about metropolitan open space. Edward Filene took these public conversations a step farther in 1909 when he assembled the committee for "Boston–1915," which produced a remarkable exhibition and the journal *New Boston*, both of which aimed at engaging all of Boston's residents in the ongoing design of the city.

Over a hundred and fifty years, we should not be surprised to find great changes in the language of these public discussions. Robert Gourlay was absolutely certain in 1844 that if land in America were "rightly laid out, and honestly disposed of," beginning with his "New Town" in the Back Bay, pauperism would end.

At the well-attended 1876 public meeting in Faneuil Hall to discuss public parks, the Reverend J. P. Bodfish, taking Olmsted's ideas a step farther, urged "the men who possess capital to look out and provide for the wants and necessities of the poor, on whom they depend to a great extent; for capital cannot be independent of labor."[6] Olmsted's decades of experience in New York, however, tempered his hopes for changes in society. In his famous 1870 speech in Boston, he urged the creation of "a ground to which people may easily go after their day's work is done, and where they may stroll for an hour seeing, hearing and feeling nothing of the bustle and jar of the streets. . . . We want, especially the greatest possible contrast with the restraining and confining conditions which compel us to walk circumspectly, watchfully, jealously, which compel us to look closely upon others without sympathy."[7]

A generation later President Eliot made a less direct link between rich and poor in arguing for the Charles River Dam. He concluded his testimony at the 1901 public hearings with the assertion that "great modern communities do not exist ultimately for commerce, but commerce exists for them. Nor do municipalities exist for profit in money, but for the people who live in them, and the supreme object of any city should be the happiness of the community."[8] His words were recited in 1929 and again in 1949 when a highway was proposed through the Esplanade, his community vision still seen as fitting for the cause at hand.

The public concern for the poor so often expressed in the earlier rhetoric of park design—even the vestiges of that discourse in our own references to diversity—has been criticized for its implicit fear of urban disorder. The creation of parks, it has been argued, was just one more mechanism to sustain the security and economic superiority of the rich. A more recent critique of parkmakers and other arbiters of morality and refinement, drawing on Freud, claims that nineteenth-century civility was only a facade, a barrier to expressions of the "real" self.[9]

In fact, like all public works, parkmaking has always drawn on a variety of motives—"to make money, to display the city's cultivation, to lift up the poor, to refine the rich, to advance commercial interests, to retard commercial development, to improve public health, to curry political favor, to provide jobs."[10] The fact that the wealthy also benefited from parks and urban reservations does not lessen the importance of such improvements to all of the city's residents. The idealistic rhetoric of the leaders of the Boston park movement, including the proponents of the Charles River Basin—Olmsted, Baxter, Eliot, James and Helen Storrow—was matched by their lifelong participation in public life. And the spaces they helped create have proven strikingly adaptable to the changing life of the city.

At the beginning of the twenty-first century, our sense of the nature of urban communities has shifted. The MDC's 1995 master plan for the New Charles River Basin is peopled by pedestrians, bicyclists, and skaters, by visitors making historical and thematic connections, by "communities coming together."[11] The diversity of the community is expressed in a more vague vocabulary of activities and interests, not of social or economic status.

The *Charles River Basin Master Plan: The Second Century*, published in 2002, addresses the existing conditions of the historic basin, not the justification for new public spaces. It addresses the undeveloped areas of the basin like Hell's Half Acre, but its focus is the task of maintaining existing landscapes and managing activities for the thousands of walkers, joggers, skaters, and cyclists; the rowers and sailors at fifteen boathouses and four yacht clubs; the people who rent boats and take boat tours. Like the New Basin master plan, the *Second Century* report reflects the participation of scores of volunteers, who contributed an estimated 4,000 hours in workshops, subcommittee sessions, and large, open discussions. The resulting plan describes the historic basin as five coexisting systems: a living landscape; a collection of significant prehistoric and historic resources; a "ribbon of narrow parklands"; a network of paths and parkways, for both commuters and park users; and an aquatic recreation area. The balance of the plan is an elaboration of these five systems: the requirements for maintaining historic structures, the opportunities for improving the natural landscape, the challenges of public safety and enormous popularity.[12] It is this interconnected set of relationships that is both the challenge and the glory of the basin.

A Community of Interests

Neither the old language of public space nor a new one will make any difference, though, unless we still identify with local communities. Profound social and economic changes have disabled the discourse of city building in our own time. The multiplication of professional specializations, the powerful, inescapable influence of federal and state governments, and the transformation of local business and social elites by the global scale of public and private enterprises—all serve to disconnect people from places.

Nineteenth-century landscape architects pushed back against the centrifugal movement of the professions by promoting their discipline as the "mother art" of modifying the earth for human habitation, carefully nurturing the subsidiary arts of building and gardening. Early in this century, landscape architects like Frederick Law Olmsted, Jr., took the lead in establishing the new profession of city planning and then struggled to connect with every discipline that promised to make the metropolis comprehensible—economics, public health, sociology, political science. Architects, however, were convinced that their much older profession already encompassed a comprehensive view of human communities. Building on the visions of Daniel Burnham and other architects of the "City Beautiful," they christened this broader perspective "urban design."[13]

On the one hand, the nature of their work makes city designers more aware than other professionals of the physical environment of their local communities. Yet their interests also push designers and their clients toward the largest possible geographic realm for their professional practice. The effects of travel on cultural and professional life, noted as early as the advent of the railroads, changed the nature of community life in small towns across America. The Unitarian minister Henry Bellows described the consequences in 1872:

> Thousands of American towns, with an independent life of their own, isolated, trusting to themselves, in need of knowing and honoring native ability and skill in local affairs—

each with its first-rate man of business, its able lawyer, its skilled physician, its honored representative, its truly selectmen—have been pierced to the heart by the railroad which they helped to build. . . . It has annihilated their old importance . . . removed the necessity for any first-rate professional men in the village, destroyed local business and taken out of town the enterprising young men, besides exciting the ambition of those once content with a local importance, to seek larger spheres of life.[14]

While the scope of professional work narrowed, its geographic scale increased. The relative ease of travel also widened the reach of professionals in government, making possible more extensive state and federal influence of local and regional design.

Baxter and Eliot were convinced that a vision of regional public stewardship would triumph over these centrifugal forces. But by the middle of the twentieth century, it was clear that few in greater Boston shared that vision. The "Boston Contest" of 1944 is perhaps the most dispiriting landmark in the history of regional concerns. Led by the Boston Society of Architects, the contest sought "master programs" to guide the future of greater Boston. Many familiar names were there—Charles Francis Adams (son of the first chair of the Metropolitan Park Commission in 1893); the president of Boston University; deans from Harvard, MIT, and Boston University; the president of the Chamber of Commerce. But even the imprimatur of renowned author and urbanist Lewis Mumford and the rest of the distinguished jurors on the committee could not persuade Boston's politicians that the first prize should be implemented.

The winning team of six Harvard professors, including Carl Friedrich and Talcott Parsons, began with the observation that while the MDC had adopted some of the methods of metropolitan government, its authority overlapped with several counties and all the cities and towns in the metropolitan district without providing for the direct participation of citizens. The professors proposed that the MDC should be "*democratized, expanded, and constituted as a federation of all the local government authorities* in the area." Without this essential step, the other reforms essential to the realization of metropolitan government would not occur (figures 11.2, 11.3).[15]

In the realm of Boston politics, no one paid much attention. The region's cities and towns jealously guarded their centuries-old prerogatives, in spite of—or perhaps because of—the increasing authority asserted by a growing number of state and federal organizations.

The Future of the River

The increased authority of government is even more apparent in the series of decisions that were made, beginning in the late 1930s, about highways and transportation. Two policies in particular stand out: the designation of a national highway system with a fixed number of miles and the provision for ninety-percent federal funding of highways. Both of these policies were first discussed in the late 1930s; the highway network was authorized in 1944 and the provision of billions of "ten-cent" federal dollars was approved in 1956. Highway engineers predicted at the time that relationships previously built on professional competence would be transformed by the pressures to conform to the opinions of federal officials. Responding in part to the state-by-state ceiling on interstate highway miles, Boston's *Master Highway Plan* of 1948 abandoned the fine-grained network of arterials that Shurcliff and Whitten had advocated; the federal government would fund only the network of fewer, larger expressways required by the interstate program.

The cancellation of the Inner Belt in 1971 would have been politically impossible if the state had been required to return the federal highway money. Instead, state officials successfully lobbied to transfer the federal highway subsidy to transit improvements. The opportunity for the state to make its own professional choices—to reconstruct the depressed artery with only six lanes and include in the project the North Station–South Station rail link—was apparently not available in 1983, when the Federal Highway Administration insisted that the Central Artery project be widened

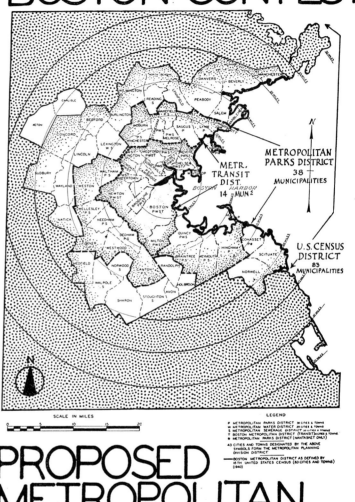

11.2 The winning entry in the "Boston Contest" of 1944 was a proposal for "expanding and democratizing" the metropolitan parks district as a federation of local governments.

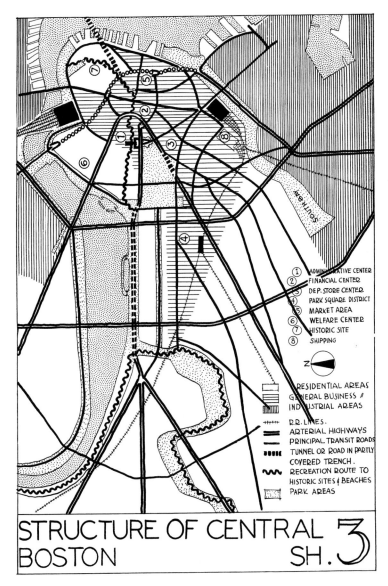

The following legend appears within the figure:

① ADMINISTRATIVE CENTER
② FINANCIAL CENTER
③ DEP. STORE CENTER
④ PARK SQUARE DISTRICT
⑤ MARKET AREA
⑥ WELFARE CENTER
⑦ HISTORIC SITE
⑧ SHIPPING

RESIDENTIAL AREAS
GENERAL BUSINESS ↗
INDUSTRIAL AREAS
R.R. LINES.
ARTERIAL HIGHWAYS
PRINCIPAL TRANSIT ROADS
TUNNEL OR ROAD IN PARTLY
COVERED TRENCH.
RECREATION ROUTE TO
HISTORIC SITES ↓ BEACHES
PARK AREAS

STRUCTURE OF CENTRAL BOSTON SH. 3

11.3 In the new central Boston, the riverfront would be extended to the harbor and a roadway constructed in a tunnel under the Esplanade.

if the state wanted federal funding. The substantial increase in the scale of the project vastly multiplied the cost and design conflicts that followed.

As the largest public works project in the nation's history, the artery project faced a series of seemingly intractable issues. The most visible disagreement was the debate over how to cross the Charles. To review "Scheme Z," the proposed set of bridges and ramps over the river, the Bridge Design Review Committee was appointed in 1991. In a few months, committed amateurs became literate in the languages of traffic planning, highway engineering, urban design, and a host of related disciplines. They weighed incommensurable variables from all of these specialties, and came to see the effects of traffic and construction alternatives on all the surrounding neighborhoods. For a little over a year, the design of the highway was the starting point for wide-ranging discussions of how Boston would change because of this unfathomably huge project.

Yet all these questions were distorted by the ultimate issue, which was to protect the federal money appropriated for the Central Artery. When the Bridge Committee was unilaterally dissolved and its recommendations ignored eighteen months later, there was a deafening silence from the design community. Since almost every design and engineering firm in the region was under contract to the artery project, or hoped to be, that was perhaps to be expected. The committee, and a wider public who had participated in the hundreds of hours of review, were worn down and outlasted by state and federal administrators, whose responsibility was, at some point, to stop weighing alternatives and build the highway.

The Central Artery project was the realization of a simple scheme—the demolition of an ugly, elevated highway that cut though the heart of Boston and the creation of a series of public spaces. The critics of Scheme Z had no disagreement with that purpose. They argued that the "lost half mile" of the Charles was a reminder of a larger vision, that the several hundred acres of abandoned rail yards just north of the river and the surrounding neighborhoods belonged to a metropolitan vision of a city linked together by public spaces.

Did the delays that followed the meetings of the Bridge Design Review Committee add $1.3 billion to the cost of the artery, as some state officials have claimed? Or could much of that additional cost have been avoided if the committee's recommended design been promptly built in 1992? How much would have been saved if Scheme Z had been recognized as a political disaster in the making, as then-senior staff members in the state highway department suggested in 1988?[16] Given the enormous complexities throughout the life of the artery project of estimating costs, these questions are unlikely to be answered. Yet they are exactly the sorts of issues that follow inevitably from a commitment to the community that public discourse will be honest and open.

"Fireworks and Hypocrisy"

Like the Central Artery project, the Charles River Basin is also the realization of a simple idea, though not finished now and perhaps always to remain unfinished. The founders of the metropolitan parks were practical enough to see that the water edges of rivers and shores could provide open space without taking large tracts off the tax rolls. Charles Eliot told the Cambridge park commissioners that in 1894 Fresh Pond and the Charles River offered the city "eight hundred acres of permanently open spaces provided by nature without cost." Capturing their edges for the public opened "these now unused and inaccessible spaces with their ample air, light, and outlook."[17]

Yet behind these matter-of-fact statements was a transcendentalist vision of the mystical power at the edges and margins of the natural world. The human craving for landscapes is most deeply realized where the earth connects with water and sky. Emerson, whose writings these park advocates knew well, declared that "in every landscape the point of astonishment is the meeting of the sky and the earth." The New England teacher Horace Mann put it more plainly: "Water is to the landscape what the eye is to the face."[18]

A hundred years ago Eliot was convinced that reservations of scenery had become the cathedrals of the modern world. Are they now? The historian Sam Bass Warner, Jr., has argued that at the end of the twentieth century, "we are escaping a different city; we are in search of a different Mother Nature." It is not just the highways everywhere, cutting off spaces like the Charles from surrounding neighborhoods. Across the country, "greenways" are created on former railroad beds, along canals, and in other once-unimaginable "public open spaces"; Olmsted is acclaimed as the "father of greenways." Greenways, however, are no longer simply peaceful byways for "restoring the tired souls of townspeople."[19] Many of us now jog, sunbathe, cycle, and skate in places where, until recently, such activities were forbidden. Scenic reserves for many people have become landscapes of speed and motion.

In the campaign for the creation of the basin, Eliot argued that "as a drainage channel, an open space, a parkway, a chain of playgrounds and a boating course," the river would "perform its highest possible service to the metropolitan community."[20] He did not live to see the banks of the river filled with automobiles, though Baxter did; could either of them have imagined the quiet pathways filled with cyclists and skaters?

The writer Adam Gopnik has recently suggested that Olmsted, at least, would likely have found room for all of these activities. In his travels through the southern United States in 1852–1853 as a reporter for the newly founded London *Times*, Olmsted compared the "vertical" society of of the South with the "horizontal" society of the northern states:

> In a Northern community a man who is not greatly occupied with private business is sure to become interested in social enterprises. . . . School, road, cemetery, asylum, and church corporations; bridge, ferry, and water companies; literary, scientific, art, mechanical, agricultural, and benevolent societies; all these things are managed chiefly by the unpaid services of gentlemen during hours which they can spare from their private interests. [Our young men] are members and managers of reading rooms, public libraries, gymnasiums, game clubs, boat clubs, ball clubs, and all sorts of clubs, Bible classes, debating societies, military companies; they are planting road-side trees, or damming streams for skating ponds, or rigging diving-boards, or getting up fireworks displays, or private theatricals; they are always doing something.

11.4 The Boston Esplanade, July 4, 1995.

In his later years Olmsted struggled to write a manuscript—never finished—in which he hoped to describe the "foundation of civilized society." According to Gopnik, Olmsted understood that "fireworks and hypocrisy were the foundations of liberal government: on the one hand, a commonplace civilization of people playing their own games; on the other, an organized pretense that one group's games were just as good as the next group's" (figure 11.4).[14]

From this perspective, the skaters who crowd the Esplanades are as welcome as the walkers and the bikers. And we are obligated to make room for the powerboaters as well as the rowers and sailors, while at the same time we protect the spaces that shelter birds and birdwatchers—to make places for as many people and interests as we can.

A City on a Hill

"The City on a Hill" is the oldest and among the most enduring of all the images of Boston. The image belongs first, of course, to the city of the seventeenth century. Two hundred years later, visionaries and park promoters described the scenic vistas from the ring of hills surrounding the city, but they also acknowledged Beacon Hill as the literal and symbolic center of Boston.

Today, Beacon Hill is invisible from Boston Harbor. Yet because of the height restrictions in the historic districts of Beacon Hill and the Back Bay, and the creation of the "High Spine" to channel development south of those districts, the city is graced, along the Charles, with enduring views of the hill. For those who live or work in Cambridge and Boston it is a frequent view, not like the occasional visit to the top of the tallest building. But is this a view only for the privileged? Does the river offer anything to those for whom Harvard and MIT and Boston University represent wealth and status? What do these spaces mean to those who cannot afford the schools or the hospitals—or even the apartments nearby? And what of all the residents of the greater Boston region who seldom see the river?

These questions matter, because the hill, the colleges and church steeples, the hospitals and the towers of commerce, and the river are emblems of the city's character. They represent, as Henry James said about his old neighborhood on the hill, "the history of something as opposed to the history of nothing." Set apart by the expanse of the Charles, the golden dome of the State House and the red brick of Beacon Hill appear more prominently in our mind's eye than all the tall boxes that surround them (figure 11.5). Whether seen often or remembered from a distance, the hill and the river constitute an ensemble that remains Boston's great public space.

11.5 Randall Imai, view of Beacon Hill from Cambridge.

12

Views from the River

For generations, the river and its valley were enough. The low rapids at the fall line of the Charles—the boundary between fresh water and the tidal estuary—made for an abundance of alewife, herring, and shad, and drew native Americans to the shores of the Charles.

The shoreline began moving in the seventeenth century, when the low rapids at the falls in Watertown were built over to make the first dam in the Bay Colony. The margins of the river became sites for houses and commerce. Two hundred years later, when the pleasures of the river seemed at risk, Bostonians decided that the stewardship of the Charles would be public. The landscapes along the river, built up piecemeal by individual choices, would now be changed dramatically.

By the 1950s, the riverfront had been completely made over for most of its length. Almost every green thing, almost every spade of dirt along the Charles was brought there. And our view of its history has changed as the river has been transformed.

Today, the faded letters on the plaque in honor of Sir Richard Saltonstall's 1630 landing near the corner of Mount Auburn Street and Coolidge Hill Road get hardly a glance from passers-by. There was a time when we told our stories by such markers; now we look for other ways.

The following visual narratives sketch the history of the riverfront not as a single chronology but as many chronologies of a series of places, each one adding to the views from the river.

Frontispiece   Cambridge, the Charles River, and the Brighton marshes, 1901.

12.1 Charles River Bridge, looking toward Charlestown, 1786.

12.2 Charles River Bridge (lower left), Charlestown Bridge, looking toward Boston, 1899.

12.3 Charlestown Bridge looking toward City Square, 1909.

The Charlestown Bridge

In Boston's town meetings, a bridge to replace the Charlestown ferry was considered as early as 1720, and a charter was finally granted in 1785. Harvard College claimed that the new bridge would render their ferry privilege worthless; the issue was resolved when the college agreed to accept an annual payment of £200.

With a span of fifteen hundred feet, the new structure was said at the time to be the only bridge of any size in America (figure 12.1). There were then no bridges over the Merrimack, the Connecticut, the Hudson, the Delaware, the Susquehanna, or the Potomac. The proprietors celebrated the opening of the Charles River Bridge on Bunker Hill Day, June 17, 1786.

The wooden bridge was replaced in 1899 with a steel swing bridge built just upstream. In the photograph looking from City Square in Charlestown toward Boston, miscellaneous sign-covered wooden structures line the length of the old bridge (figure 12.2). The new bridge is nearly complete and its rotating center span, mounted on a round steel gearbox, rests in the open position. Steel columns for the elevated railway are in place. In the background (upper right) are the crenellated towers of the Fitchburg Railroad Station, one of three depots fronting on Causeway Street.

The 1909 view toward Charlestown shows the convergence of the Charles River and the Warren Bridges near City Square (figure 12.3).

In the foreground upstream of the bridge in 2001 (figure 12.4) are the fender piers and locks of the new Charles River Dam. At the Charlestown end of the bridge is the new City Square Park. The 1959 elevated highway that connected the Tobin Bridge with Interstate 93 has been replaced by a tunnel under City Square.

12.4 Pumping station and Charlestown Bridge, 2001.

12.5 Warren Bridge and railroad trestles across the Charles, 1911.

12.6 Charlestown Bridge, Warren Bridge, and the rail yards, 1925.

Warren Bridge, the New Dam, and the New Charles River Basin

The first Warren Bridge was opened just three hundred feet upstream of the Charles River Bridge in 1828, following the first use of the veto power by a Massachusetts governor and a lawsuit that was finally resolved as the first case on monopolies to be decided by the U.S. Supreme Court.

The Boston & Lowell Railroad built the first railroad bridge over this part of the river in 1835. Soon thereafter other bridges and trestles were built by the Boston & Maine, Fitchburg, and Eastern Railroads.

Looking toward Charlestown in 1911 (figure 12.5), the Warren Bridge extends from left to right across the bottom of the photograph. Just upstream are the railroad bridges over the Charles, which appear to fan out and multiply as they get closer to the railroad stations along Causeway Street. In the distance can be seen the just-completed viaduct for the Boston Elevated Railway (upper left, now the Green Line to Lechmere Station).

In 1925 railroad depots lined Causeway Street (figure 12.26). Three years later the Boston & Maine built a new North Station (with a new Boston Garden above the waiting room) and four new bascule bridges across the river. Only two remain, both hidden behind the "High Bridge," the double-decked structure completed in 1955 to connect the first Central Artery with the elevated highways over City Square in Charlestown and the Tobin Bridge (figure 12.7).

The Warren Bridge, once the primary route into Boston from the North Shore, was replaced by the new Charles River Dam and Pumping Station and the Col. Richard Gridley Locks (lower right), named for the first head of the Army Engineers, who had directed the fortifications erected for the Battle of Bunker Hill. The pumping station was completed but had not yet been dedicated when the "Blizzard of '78" struck on February 7. The six 2700-horsepower diesel pumps (with a capacity of three million gallons per minute) were fired up and pushed the floodwaters of the river into the harbor against a high tide of fifteen feet above mean low water, which equaled the record set in 1851.

12.7 Charles River Dam, the High Bridge, and the Leonard P. Zakim Bunker
Hill Bridge, 2001.

12.8 The West End, 1886.

12.9 The West End and Charlesbank, about 1895.

12.10 Charlesbank men's gymnasium and the Charles River Dam, 1910.

In 1880 the Boston Park Commissioners approved a plan for a new park to be built along the waterfront of the city's West End (figure 12.8) between Craigie's Bridge and the West Boston Bridge (renamed the Longfellow Bridge in 1927). A new seawall was constructed, leaving the Massachusetts General Hospital and other enterprises separated from the river by the park, named Charlesbank.

Near the West Boston Bridge, a play area for women and girls was built with play equipment and "sand courts." Downstream a large outdoor gymnasium for men and boys extended from the bend in the seawall (figure 12.9, lower right) to Leverett Street. At the upstream end of the gymnasium was a large "lavatory building." To the left of the lavatory the cupola of the Charles Street Jail is visible; to the right, on the horizon, is the West Boston Bridge.

Between 1905 and 1910 the Charles River Dam was constructed adjacent to Charlesbank. The 1910 photograph of the park and the dam (figure 12.10) was taken from the bridge tender's tower of the lower lock gate house. The old park house is visible just beyond the upper lock gate house, at the end of the lock. At the left edge of the photo a portion of the sliding lock gate is visible. On the horizon is the Cambridge (now Longfellow) Bridge, completed in 1907.

The Charlesbank fieldhouse was demolished by the second widening of Charles Street in 1951, at the same time Storrow Drive was constructed between the Longfellow Bridge and Boston University (see figure 7.23). The demolished tenements of the West End, torn down in the late 1950s, were replaced by Charles River Park ("If you lived here, you'd be home now"), reflecting the visions of early twentieth century architects for towers in a park (figure 12.11). On the horizon is the realization of Kevin Lynch's idea of the "high spine" along Boylston Street, which protects the Back Bay historic district by allowing high rises to the south.

12.11 Charles River Park, Charles Street, and Charlesbank, 2001.

12.12 Craigie's Bridge, Lechmere Point, and Cobble Hill, 1810.

12.13 Charles River Dam, lower lock gate house, and streetcar viaduct, about 1911.

Craigie's Bridge, the Charles River Dam, and the Green Line Viaduct

Cobble Hill in Charlestown (now Somerville) was sufficiently remote from Boston in 1791 that Joseph Barrell directed Charles Bulfinch to design a country estate there. In an 1810 drawing (figure 12.12), the elaborately landscaped villa rises in the distance beyond the recently completed Craigie's Bridge (lower right). Upstream of the bridge a few scattered houses have been built at Lechmere Point; in the distance beyond the bridge is Powder House Hill.

The photograph taken a hundred years later (figure 12.13) shows the first Charles River Dam, laid out as a park connecting Boston and Cambridge. The lower lock gate house with its bridge tender's tower (left foreground) faces the viaduct of the West End Street Railway. In between is the new roadway built on the dam, which follows the alignment of the bridge in the 1810 drawing. Guy Lowell, best known in Boston as the architect of the Museum of Fine Arts, designed the park and the five structures on the dam: the upper and lower lock gate houses, the open pavilion, the boathouse, and the stables.

Today traffic backs up on the dam most of the day, and from April to November the queues include recycled World War II DUKW (duck) boats (figure 12.14). The duck boats carry sightseers through downtown streets and then into the Charles just downstream of the viaduct for a ride upstream to the Longfellow Bridge.

12.14 O'Brien Highway and the Green Line viaduct, 2001.

12.15 Charles River lock and open shelter, 1910.

12.16 Charles River Dam, looking toward Cambridge, about 1947.

12.17 Charles River Dam and the Museum of Science, 1951.

The Charles River Dam and the Museum of Science

Completed in 1910 (figure 12.15), the dam was still a quiet, open park in 1947 (figure 12.16) when Bradford Washburn, the director of the Museum of Natural History, began looking for a new home. With a lease from the Metropolitan District Commission (MDC), the renamed Museum of Science covered Lowell's exquisite little pavilion with siding and moved in (figure 12.17).

By 1976 the Museum had built a series of structures, including the planetarium—and were still using the pavilion as office space (figure 12.18). Twenty-five years before, the city of Cambridge had sold "The Front"—the site of a proposed park that was never developed—and the first generation of commercial structures filled the property, including General Electric, Parke-Davis, and the Charter House (now the Sonesta) Hotel.

The Washburn Pavilion, carefully restored by the Museum, now offers one of the river's most urbane views (figure 12.19). The Longfellow Bridge still marks the horizon, but an entire new generation of taller buildings lines the Cambridge riverfront, including the stepped balconies of "The Esplanade" condominiums designed by Moshe Safdie & Associates and completed in 1989.

12.18 Charles River Dam and the Museum of Science, 1976.

12.19 Charles River lock and open shelter, 2001.

12.20 Lechmere Canal and East Cambridge, 1920.

12.21 Lechmere Canal, 1949.

The Lechmere Canal

The Lechmere Canal was created by filling behind new seawalls, not by digging a channel through dry ground. In 1874 seawalls were built on the mudflats of East Cambridge, which were flooded at high tide. Fill was dumped behind the seawalls to make new land (with access to the harbor) for the burgeoning nineteenth-century industries of East Cambridge—glass, furniture, pipe organs, and slaughterhouses.

Although on the edge of the Charles River water park, the canal continued to support extensive industry, as the 1920 view makes clear (figure 12.20). The cupola of the Middlesex County Courthouse designed by Charles Bulfinch is visible on the horizon (left center).

The canal itself was truncated when the city of Cambridge determined to renew the area. Working from an urban design plan by Dennis Carlone, the city commissioned Carol R. Johnson Associates to design a park around the edge of the canal. The provision of well-designed public space was instrumental in securing financing for the CambridgeSide Galleria mall (figure 12.22), designed by Arrowstreet Architects and opened in 1988.

12.22 Lechmere Canal and CambridgeSide Galleria, 1999.

12.23 Broad Canal, 1919.

The Broad Canal

Dug in 1805, the Broad Canal was part of an enterprise intended to develop the marshes near the Cambridge end of the West Boston Bridge. The promoters convinced Congress to declare Cambridge a port of entry, thus giving Cambridgeport its name, and created a network of canals and docks along both sides of Main Street, with a branch leading to the Miller's River. The Broad Canal originally extended almost three-quarters of a mile inland, but was reduced to its present length between 1966 and 1968 as part of the Kendall Square urban renewal project (figures 12.23, 12.24).

Hoping to promote commerce in the area, the city never implemented Olmsted, Olmsted & Eliot's plan for a park and bathing beach between the Broad and Lechmere Canals. During the First World War the legislature allowed land that was originally taken for park purposes to be used for industrial development instead. No manufacturer was interested in building on land leased from the city, however, and in 1946 the frontage on Cambridge Parkway was put up for sale (figure 12.24).

By the end of the twentieth century (figure 12.25), a number of historic buildings near the canal had been renovated, and new high-rise office buildings were built along the canal.

12.24 Broad Canal, 1958.

12.25 Broad Canal, 2000.

12.26 West Boston Bridge.

12.27 West Boston Bridge, 1864.

The Longfellow Bridge

The West Boston Bridge was completed in 1793, only seven years after the opening of the Charles River Bridge downstream (figure 12.26). At 3,483 feet, it was more than twice as long as the earlier bridge. Canals and dikes were soon built around the bridge on the Cambridge side and the Concord Turnpike (now Broadway) and the Middlesex Turnpike (now Hampshire Street) were opened, with the hope that the village of Cambridgeport might become a major shipping destination. The commercial fortunes of the village, however, were rapidly eclipsed by East Cambridge.

In 1864 the view from the bridge was dominated by the Charles Street Jail (left center), just west of the Massachusetts General Hospital (designed by Charles Bulfinch) and Harvard Medical School (figure 12.27). Upstream of the bridge the dome of the State House marks the crown of Beacon Hill.

By the end of the century, river traffic had long since passed its peak, and Cambridge and Boston aspired to building a beautiful, draw-less bridge. A major campaign was begun, and the federal government finally relented.

Edmund Wheelwright was the architect for the new Cambridge Bridge (renamed the Longfellow Bridge in 1927), which many consider Boston's finest bridge. The clearance required by the War Department suggested an arched profile for the structure that Wheelwright turned to great advantage. Though the site did not offer dramatic heights from which to spring the bridge, the width of the basin ensured that the bridge would be visible from much of the riverfront in both Boston and Cambridge (figure 12.28).

12.28 Longfellow Bridge, 2002.

12.29 The Back Bay from the State House, 1858.

12.30 The Back Bay from the State House, 1898.

The Back Bay

Four years before the 1858 photograph was taken from the dome of the State House, the state and the two corporations operating mills and dams in the Back Bay reached an agreement to abandon the mills along the Great Dam and the Cross Dam and to fill the mud flats (figure 12.29).

Initially, three trains of thirty-five cars each ran twenty-four hours a day hauling gravel fill from Needham. By the 1880s the Back Bay had become a neighborhood of elegant row houses, centered on the Commonwealth Avenue mall and ending at the Back Bay Fens, Frederick Law Olmsted's recently completed park that connected with the Charles River (figure 12.30).

Early in the twentieth century, the Back Bay eased into a genteel decline as many families moved to the suburbs and the rowhouses were subdivided into apartments. After a few contested cases, the height restrictions in the Back Bay were upheld, and a revival of the neighborhood's fortunes began in the 1980s. Today its architectural distinction is one of the city's great assets (figure 12.31).

12.31 The Back Bay from the State House, 1999.

12.32 The water side of Brimmer Street looking downstream, 1904.

12.33 The water side of Brimmer Street and Embankment Road, about 1911.

The Boston Esplanade along Embankment Road

The back side of Brimmer Street was an unprepossing assortment of stables in 1904 (figure 12.32). Among its few landmarks were the Union Boat Club (right) and the steeple of the Church of the Advent. The filling of what was then called the Boston Embankment was authorized in 1903 when the first Charles River Dam was approved by the legislature.

The widest part of the embankment—three hundred feet—was between the West Boston (now Longfellow) Bridge and Berkeley Street. Here a tree-lined street called Embankment Road (now David Mugar Way) was laid out (figure 12.33). Elegant granite steps led from the Longfellow Bridge to the embankment, and a new boathouse for the Union Boat Club was built on the riverfront.

The embankment (now universally known as the Esplanade) was transformed in the 1930s (figure 12.34). Helen Storrow contributed one million dollars in honor of her husband, who had led the successful campaign for the dam in 1901-1903. A breakwater was added in front of the Union Boathouse, and in 1941 the Community Sailing Boat House was completed (left center).

12.34 The Esplanade from Longfellow Bridge, 2002.

12.35 The Embankment looking west toward Harvard Bridge, 1911.

12.36 The Storrow Memorial Embankment, 1936.

Back Street, like most of the riverfront in Boston, was lined with "the unmentionable parts of private houses" until the Boston Embankment was completed in 1910 (figure 12.35). From Berkeley Street to Charlesgate West, a new seawall was built a hundred feet north of the existing seawall. The embankment was not heavily planted, according to the Metropolitan Park Commission, in part because the property owners on the water side of Beacon Street did not want their view interfered with.

In the early 1930s, the width of the embankment was doubled according to a design by the landscape architect Arthur Shurcliff. Along the edge of the widened embankment Back Street remained as a narrow alley (figure 12.36). The old walk along the water then marked the middle of the park. Upstream the Storrow Lagoon, set off by the Dartmouth and Gloucester Street Overlooks on either side, had been created by filling a dike around it.

The most drastic change visible today (figure 12.37) is the displacement of the 1910 portion of the esplanade by Storrow Drive, approved in 1949 as a four-lane limited access roadway.

Since the opening of the Storrow Embankment (the Esplanade) in 1936, bicycles had been banned from its walkways. In 1960 the famous Boston cardiologist Paul Dudley White (who had a few years before gone for a bike ride with Mayor Richard Daley along Chicago's lakefront) approached the MDC about lifting the ban on bikes. He thought Americans needed more exercise, and the river offered miles of pathways and superb views. A one-year trial was approved, and the following year the ban was permanently rescinded.

12.37 The Esplanade, 1999.

12.38 The Boston Embankment near Dartmouth Street, 1907.

12.39 The Embankment from the Harvard Bridge, 1910.

The Boston Esplanade Looking East toward Beacon Hill

The seawall north of Back Street, the alley behind the houses on the water side of Beacon Street, was constructed in several stages between the mid-1840s and the early 1880s. At low tide the mud-flats extended out from the seawall several hundred feet to the shallow main channel of the river. Filling for the Boston Embankment began in 1907 at the same time the new seawall was completed, a change from the usual nineteenth-century technique. The usual method was to drive wooden piles, then build a wooden platform on top of the piles, and finally construct on the platform a heavy seawall of large, rough-cut granite blocks. In 1907, the filling was underway before the piles were driven for the seawall (figure 12.38). Another departure from past practice was the use of concrete for the seawall, with granite used only for the capstones.

The new plantings in 1910 are sparse, reflecting the concern of many residents on the water side of Beacon Street that their views not be obstructed (figure 12.39). Though the construction of the dam was seen by some as a plot led by, among others, Harvard rowing interests, the construction of a second vertical seawall did nothing to reduce the steep-sided waves that reflected off the seawalls on both sides of the river in moderate winds. When the Storrow Memorial Embankment was designed in the early 1930s, the river's edge was gently sloped along the Boston side.

When Storrow Drive was proposed in 1948, it was to be a six-lane, limited-access roadway; part of the compromise in 1949 was a reduction in the road's width to four lanes. The interchanges at the Harvard Bridge and near Arlington Street were apparently designed to accomodate the original plan, however, and only three years after Storrow Drive was completed, the road was widened to six lanes east of Massachusetts Avenue.

12.40 Storrow Drive from the Harvard Bridge, 2002.

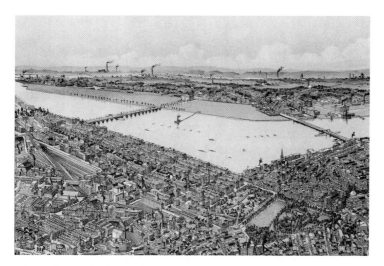

12.41 The Cambridge Esplanade, 1899.

12.42 The Cambridge Esplanade and the Harvard Bridge, about 1910.

The Harvard Bridge, the Cambridge Esplanade, and MIT

Charles Davenport's 1870s vision for the Charles River included elegant residences along the Back Bay as well as facing what he called the Cambridge Esplanade. Davenport and his associates formed the Charles River Embankment Company to implement his plan. Although his development foundered in the panic of 1893, a thousand feet of seawall was built, and the two-hundred-foot Esplanade was deeded to the city, almost twenty years before the Boston Embankment was built on the other side of the Charles. An 1899 bird's-eye view (figure 12.41) marks the Cambridge Esplanade with a row of trees on either side of the Harvard Bridge; the Grand Junction Railroad runs along the back side of the undeveloped property.

The house lots remained waterlogged and unsold until 1912. The MIT faculty had rejected a proposed merger with Harvard in 1903, even though the proposal included a site for a new campus on the Brighton marshes (now the home of the Harvard Business School). MIT acquired the part of the Embankment Company's property east of Massachusetts Avenue between the railroad and the river and moved to Cambridge in 1916 (figure 12.42). Over time the Institute acquired the remaining land and buildings west of Massachusetts Avenue and in 1937 converted the Riverbank Court Hotel (built in 1900) into a dormitory. The draw was removed from the Harvard Bridge in 1924.

In the 1960s MIT built Eastgate and Westgate, high-rise apartment towers that defined the long, narrow wedge of the now-densely built campus (figure 12.43). This 1999 photograph will soon be outdated, as the Institute began half a dozen major building projects at the end of the twentieth century.

12.43 MIT and the Harvard Bridge, 1999.

12.44 Charlesgate from the Braemore Apartments, about 1920.

12.45 Charlesgate and the Back Bay Fens, 1954.

Charlesgate at Storrow Drive and Route 1

The Back Bay Fens was the first park designed by Frederick Law Olmsted after he was hired by the Boston Park Commissioners in 1878, and Olmsted repeatedly explained that his plan was first a sanitary improvement to address the flooding of Stony Brook and then a park only by the ingenuity of its design. The Fens, wrote Olmsted, would be filled with the "tints, lights, and shadows and movement of salt-marsh vegetation."

He envisioned Charlesgate as the meeting point of the Back Bay Fens with the Charles River (figure 12.44). It includes one of the most significant park structures ever designed—the bridge over the Muddy River at Boylston Street, the work of Olmsted's Brookline neighbor and erstwhile collaborator, the architect H. H. Richardson (figure 12.45, center).

In 1951 the construction of Storrow Drive cut off the Charles from the Fens. A second great indignity was visited on Olmsted's park and its connection to the river when the Bowker Overpass was completed down the middle of the Charlesgate in 1966 (figure 12.46). The view from the rooftops is deceptive (see figure 7.30). Although only four lanes wide, the elevated roadway has turned what was once the open, green front yard for hundreds of apartment dwellers into a deeply shadowed, neglected assemblage of failing plants and deteriorating concrete structures.

12.46 Charlesgate from the Braemore Apartments, 2001.

12.47 The Fens Gate House and Harvard Bridge, 1909.

12.48 The Fens Gate House, June 1951.

12.49 The Fens Gate House, about 1954.

Charlesgate and the Fens Gate House

As part of the Charles River Dam construction in 1905–1910, the Boston Marginal Conduit, a large sewer, was built at the same time along the entire length of the embankment. A gate house was built at the junction of the marginal conduit and the Stony Brook conduit coming from the Fens (figure 12.47).

Since the Charles was now a freshwater lake, the marshes created by Frederick Law Olmsted in the Fens were no longer flooded with salt water twice a day. In their 1910 report to the city parks department, Arthur Shurcliff and the firm of Olmsted Brothers pointed out that some of the marshes near the river were turning into mud and fresh-water swamp. They also made detailed recommendations for a revision in the original design completed two decades before.

The city's solution, however, was to fill part of the Fens with dirt from the construction of the Boylston Street subway, to plant grass and erect fences for ball fields. The landscape architects thought this was a "savage waste" of a park that had been created at enormous cost. They suggested this made no more sense than meeting the city's obligation to Boston's children by filling the reading rooms of the new Public Library with swings and gymnastic apparatus.[1]

In his original design, Olmsted had also envisioned a connection for boats from the Back Bay Fens to the Charles. Boating on the Fens never became popular, and the connection was never built. As part of their 1910 report, the landscape architects suggested that with the water level in the Charles and in the Fens now the same, it would be easier and even more important to establish the link between the two parks (figure 12.48). For fifteen years nothing was done, so in 1925 Arthur Shurcliff and the Olmsted Brothers firm wrote another report for the city; like the first, it, too, was ignored.

The widening of Storrow Drive in 1954–1955 (figure 12.49) created an elevated barrier at the mouth of the river, cutting off the Esplanade from the Fens.

12.50 The Fens Gate House and the Route 1 overpass, 2001.

12.51 Boston Athletic Association Boathouse, International Boat Day, 1913.

12.52 The construction of Storrow Drive, 1951.

On International Boat Day in 1913, several new buildings had been just completed on Charles River Road (now Memorial Drive) upstream of the Harvard Bridge, including the Boston Athletic Association Boathouse (figure 12.51, left center), the Ford Motor Company assembly building (figure 12.52, left) and the Gray and Davis Company (figure 12.52, right). The Boston Athletic Association had proposed a boathouse on the embankment next to the Union Boat Club, but their plans changed after some residents of Brimmer Street threatened a lawsuit. It looked at the time as if the industrial area between the River Street and Essex Street (now Boston University) Bridges would extend downstream and overtake Charles Davenport's planned residential development.

MIT moved across the river from the Back bay in 1916, and eight years later leased the boathouse. In 1965 MIT completed a new boathouse downstream, and Boston University bought the old building. Today the institute has gone well beyond the bounds of Davenport's development. Riverbank Court is now MIT's Ashdown House, an undergraduate dorm. The warehouses along the river have been torn down or converted to commercial space, and a new Hyatt Hotel was built in 1972, designed by Graham Gund Architects (figure 12.53). MIT built the Pierce Boathouse downstream in 1965, and Boston University took over the old boathouse; it was replaced in 1999 by a larger structure designed by Architectural Resources Cambridge (ARC).

12.53 Boston University Boathouse and the Hyatt Regency, 2002.

12.54 Magazine Beach, 1906.

12.55 Magazine Beach, 1935.

Captain's Island, a five-acre hillock surrounded by salt marsh (just upstream of the present Boston University bridge), was conveyed about 1637 by the town of Cambridge to Daniel Patrick, one of the two military commanders in the colony. It was passed to the family of Francis Dana, and then was sold to the Commonwealth in 1817. A powder magazine was erected there, and before long both the beach on the island's river edge and the street leading to it were named for the magazine.[2]

The Cambridge Park Commission, organized in 1893, determined that Captain's Island, then covered with pitch pine, would become the largest park in the city's park system. Seven years later the Olmsted office incorporated the granite blocks of the powder magazine in a new bath house. The commissioners reported in 1899 that "Captain's Island bathing beach is unequalled by any artificial beach in this vicinity. The water of the river is clean, and its temperature much higher than the water at Revere Beach."[3]

In 1906, the beach looked out on the Brookline Gas Works, assorted other industries, and the yards of the Boston & Albany Railroad (figure 12.54). The rail yards were named "Beacon Park," after the "pleasure grounds" established earlier on the site. Thirty years later, the view across the river had changed very little (figure 12.55).

As soon as the temporary dam on the Charles was completed in 1908, some people voiced suspicions about the fresh water, but the beach remained popular (figure 12.55). The concern for water quality finally led the MDC to build a swimming pool nearby in 1951, and the beach was planted in grass (figure 12.56).

12.56 Magazine Beach, 2002.

12.57 Western Avenue Bridge, 1909.

12.58 Western Avenue Bridge, about 1924.

The Western Avenue Bridge

The first Western Avenue Bridge was built by the proprietors of the West Boston Bridge to connect Main Street with what was called in 1830 the Watertown Road (now Western Avenue). Tolls were charged on both bridges until they were transferred to the cities of Cambridge and Boston in 1858. In the 1909 photograph, the Cambridge shore is dominated by the Electric Light Company building, completed in 1901. On the horizon just beyond is the tower of Harvard's Memorial Hall. At the far left are the twin smokestacks of the West End Street Railway power plant (figure 12.57).

Desmond and Lord, the architects for the new Western Avenue Bridge, were chosen in a design competition that also included the Arsenal Street and the River Street Bridges. The Western Avenue Bridge was opened in 1924 (figure 12.58).[4]

Today the horizon is punctuated by Harvard buildings. The white towers of Lowell House and Dunster House now compete with the diamond-shaped screens on the roof of the Leverett House towers and with the concrete towers of Mather House and Peabody Terrace. On the left are the red brick Soldiers Field Park apartments designed by Benjamin Thompson in 1975 to meet the requirement for density without building towers. Against some community opposition, Harvard broke ground in 1999 to build its first high-rise on the Boston side of the river (see figure 12.56, right).

12.59 Western Avenue Bridge, 2001.

12.60 The Charles upstream of Western Avenue, 1897.

12.61 Harvard boathouses, about 1895.

Charles Follen McKim, who later designed the Harvard Business School and the Weeks Bridge, suggested in the 1890s that the "inch-plank architecture" of the Riverside neighborhood in Cambridge—the area between Mt. Auburn Street and the river—should be acquired and demolished. Along the river was the college coal wharf (leased to Richardson and Bacon, figure 12.60, lower left), three sheds for Harvard rowing (figure 12.61), and the collection of buildings of the Riverside Press (just downstream of the Western Avenue Bridge), which included a boathouse owned by workers at the press.

The salt marsh across the river in Brighton between North Harvard Street and the River Street Bridge (center) was still empty but would be acquired a few years later and offered to MIT as their future home, provided they agreed to a merger with Harvard. MIT turned down the offer, and the site remained vacant until the Harvard Business School was constructed in 1923–1926.

The city of Cambridge had chosen not to be part of the metropolitan park district, but the city's new park department hired Charles Eliot as their landscape architect. He immediately persuaded the city that its greatest open space was the river itself, and access to it could be had for almost nothing by purchasing the banks of the river. Meanwhile, as late as 1898, Harvard College was selling land between the river and Harvard Yard.

The city park department acquired almost the entire Cambridge riverfront in 1894 and moved or demolished the intruding boathouses and commercial structures.

In 1963 Peabody Terrace was completed, a work by José Luis Sert, dean of the Harvard Graduate Schol of Design. It is a visual link to Sert's Boston University Law School tower and to the utopian visions sketched by the French architect Le Corbusier of skyscrapers planted in expanses of green.

12.62 Peabody Terrace, Harvard University, 2001.

12.63 The first Weld Boathouse, about 1896.

12.64 The second Weld Boathouse, about 1911.

The Weld Boathouse and the Harvard Houses

The first Weld Boathouse was built in 1890 near the Boylston Street (now Anderson) Bridge (figure 12.63). Immediately behind it was the power plant of the West End Street Railway. Just downstream was the college coal wharf, leased to Richardson and Bacon (right).

After completing a small section of Charles River Road (now Memorial Drive) between Boylston and Ash Streets as a demonstration project in 1897, the city demolished half of the college coal wharf to extend the parkway downstream. By 1902, most of Richardson & Bacon's building had been demolished for the extension of Charles River Road; the first Weld Boathouse was replaced by a grandiose fireproof structure in 1907 (figure 12.64). Behind the new boathouse a second smoke stack had been constructed.

The glory of the river is the assemblage of red brick buildings erected by Harvard. A group of alumni organized by Edward Forbes assembled the land, and three freshman dormitories were completed in 1913. With a gift from a Yale graduate, residential colleges on the model of Oxford and Cambridge were constructed in 1930, incorporating the earlier dorms. Eliot House was constructed on the site of the old railway power plant (figure 12.65).

Today, the open courtyards and prominent towers of the Harvard houses, in graceful sequence along Eliot's tree-lined parkway, are the epitome of Georgian revival architecture in America.

12.65 Eliot House and the Weld Boathouse, 2001.

12.66 Mt. Auburn Street, 1878.

12.67 Memorial Drive, about 1949.

12.68 Memorial Drive, about 1951.

Memorial Drive Upstream of the Anderson Bridge

In 1878 the mudflats along the river above the Boylston Street (now Anderson) Bridge extended to the edge of Mount Auburn Street (figure 12.66).

As a demonstration project, the Cambridge park commissioners began construction of the Charles River Road (now Memorial Drive) just upstream of the bridge, "where park-like effects might be most quickly and easily obtained." After some difficulty filling and stabilizing the marshy banks of the river, the area was graded and the first London plane tree (sycamore) was planted on April 22, 1897. The roadway ended at Bath (now Hawthorne) Street, where travelers continued on Mt. Auburn Street.

The Cambridge Hospital acquired nine acres near Mount Auburn Street in 1883, and opened its first building three years later. For patients with contagious diseases a two-story "pest house" was erected in 1891 near the river and its fresh air and as far as possible from the main buildings (figure 12.67, center). After decades of being confused with the Cambridge City Hospital, the Cambridge Hospital in 1946 changed its name to Mount Auburn Hospital. On the horizon at the left is the tower of Mt. Auburn Cemetery, designed by Jacob Bigelow and completed in 1852.

Continuous parkways on both sides of the river were first proposed in the 1890s. Various plans were advanced to shift the bed of the river, taking some of the parkland from the Brighton side and increasing the narrow strip of land that separated Mt. Auburn Street from the river. In the end the Brighton bank was not disturbed, but some fill was added on the Cambridge side when Memorial Drive was finally extended beyond the hospitals about 1950 (figures 12.68, 12.69).

12.69 Memorial Drive, 2002.

12.70 Gerry's Landing, about 1910.

12.71 Gerry's Landing, 1935.

Gerry's Landing and Hell's Half Acre

A small creek once drained into the Charles from a point near the marker on Mt. Auburn Street east of Coolidge Hill Road. The marker commemorates the landing in July 1630 of a group of English settlers led by Richard Saltonstall. By about 1635 the inhabitants of Watertown had moved two miles west. Sir Richard's Landing took the name of Elbridge Gerry after he moved into the estate nearby.

The Metropolitan Park Commission planned to build a parkway along this stretch of the river as early as 1900; a bridge was proposed in 1911 (figure 12.70). Grading was completed with emergency relief funds for a road from the landing to Arsenal Street in 1915, and a walkway twenty feet wide was built through the marsh along the future road alignment.

Swimming at the landing had become so popular that in 1918 the city of Cambridge asked the Metropolitan Park Commission for permission to hire lifeguards and build a men's bathhouse. Two years later the city park department borrowed a voting booth to serve as the women's bathhouse, a practice that continued for more than ten years. The city complained in 1933 that the beach and its "most undesirable" dressing facilities presented "a barren spectacle"; the state should incorporate in their roadway plans "a modern bathing beach." The following year the New Deal's Emergency Relief Administration covered the cost of building two small, portable bathhouses (figure 12.71).[5]

After the Second World War, the poor water quality of the Charles led to the replacement of riverfront beaches with large, public swimming pools, often in the same locations as the old beaches. Gerry's Landing was disrupted by the construction of the Eliot Bridge in 1951, a memorial to Charles W. Eliot and to his son, Charles Eliot. When Bernard DeVoto wrote about this stretch of the river four years later in a widely read *Harper's* essay titled "Hell's Half Acre, Mass.," he defended the area between the new bridge and Arsenal Street upstream as the last undeveloped stretch of the Charles, worth far more as a natural area than as a parkway filled with cars (figure 12.72).

12.72 Hell's Half Acre and Greenough Boulevard, 2001.

12.73 The Arsenal wharf, 1875.

12.74 North Beacon Street Bridge and the Arsenal wharf, about 1910.

12.75 North Beacon Street Bridge perspective, 1915.

After the War of 1812, the U.S. War Department determined that the arsenal at the Charlestown Navy Yard was too close to the harbor and possible attack by Great Britain. A new site was selected downstream of Watertown Square, and the earliest buildings were constructed in 1819 from the designs of Alexander Parris, who later designed Quincy Market in Boston. Thirteen buildings were constructed around two quadrangles. The War Department required that every bridge on the river between the harbor and the arsenal be built with a draw, a stipulation that led to major debates over the replacement of the West Boston (now Longfellow) and Boylston Street (now Anderson) Bridges.

A gas house, gasometer, and foundry were built by the Arsenal on the edge of the river just downstream of the North Beacon Street Bridge between 1865 and 1867 (figure 12.73). The projecting seawall probably dates from that time.

In 1906 the Arsenal granted the park commission the right to construct Charles River Road through the Arsenal, provided the commission demolish the three buildings on the site of the road, which was opened three years later (figure 12.74). The current North Beacon Street Bridge, designed by the architects Haven and Hoyt for the Metropolitan Park Commission, dates from 1917 (figure 12.75).[6]

12.76 North Beacon Street Bridge and the Arsenal wharf, 2002.

12.77 Galen Street Bridge, before 1906.

12.78 Galen Street Bridge and Watertown Square, about 1910.

12.79 Galen Street Bridge and Lewandos, about 1910.

Roger Clapp and the "Dorchester Men"—a party of about ten—landed on a knoll just downstream from Watertown Square in June 1630 and "were informed that there were hard by us 300 Indians." They exchanged biscuit cakes for bass, but were soon ordered to "come away" to Mattapan.[7]

After establishing a small settlement near what is now Mt. Auburn Hospital in Cambridge, the Watertown proprietors led by Sir Richard Saltonstall moved westward to Meetinghouse Common (a triangular area bounded today by Mt. Auburn and Belmont Streets and Hillside Road). At about the same time a mill and dam were constructed along the Charles near the falls (upstream of the present Galen Street Bridge). Because the threat of famine was great the town fathers wrote in 1635 that "there be too many inhabitants in the town and the town thereby [is] in danger of being ruinated."[8]

The Watertown settlement did survive the first decade, and town records mention a footbridge near the mill in 1641. Seven years later a bridge sufficiently strong to bear "a loaden horse carrying a sack of corn" was built across the Charles nearby. The mill and the bridge attracted other commercial ventures, and over time the center of Watertown shifted from Meetinghouse Hill to the north bank of the river, between the dam and the bridge. In about 1718 a wider bridge was built; it remained until 1906 (figure 12.77).[9]

The Metropolitan Park Commission acquired land along almost the entire length of the Charles in Watertown beginning in the 1890s, and with the anticipated creation of the freshwater Charles River Basin, the banks of the river near the square were landscaped and a new, stone arched bridge was completed over the river in 1907 (figure 12.78).

The largest building in the square in 1910 was "Lewando's Cleansers, Dyers, Launderers," marked in large letters on the top of the building (figure 12.79). The residues from cleaning and dyeing were dumped in the river, mingling downstream with the offal from the Brighton Abbatoir. Lewando's was recently renovated as the Riverbend Office Park (figure 12.80).

12.80 Galen Street Bridge and Riverbend offices, 2001.

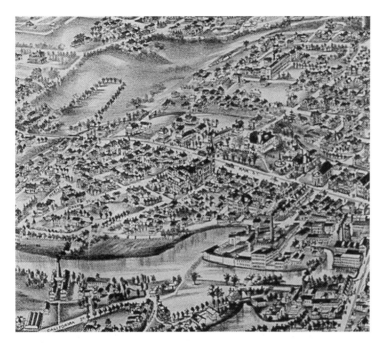

12.81 Bird's-eye view of the Watertown Dam, 1868.

12.82 Watertown Dam, 1910.

Watertown Dam

A fish weir was authorized by the General Court in 1632 at the falls two miles north of Roger Clapp's 1630 landing site, the upper reach of the Charles River tidal basin. Although a dam is not mentioned in the legislative records, Thomas Mayhew wrote to Governor Winthrop in June 1634 to borrow a team of oxen "to carry the timber for building the mill at Watertown." A dam and mill race were constructed about the same time (upstream of the present Galen Street Bridge). By 1663 a fulling mill had been erected along the river, and about ten years later a second grist mill was built nearby on Beaver Brook.[10]

More enterprises were drawn to the river, and by the middle of the nineteenth century the mill race defined a large island of mills and assorted other structures (figure 12.81).

Following the establishment of the Metropolitan Park Commission in 1893, Charles Eliot surveyed the riverfront land from Boston and Cambridge to Watertown, Waltham, and Newton. Over three hundred acres along the Charles were acquired between Watertown Square and Hemlock Gorge in Newton—and then forgotten. In 1908 the construction of the Charles River Dam (the site now occupied by the Museum of Science) stabilized the water level in the basin all the way to the Watertown Dam (figure 12.82).

A revival of interest in the upper Charles began in the late 1980s. The MDC negotiated with over one hundred owners and abutters in Watertown, Waltham, and Newton to reclaim the margins of the river, and paths, walkways, and overlooks were constructed on both sides of the Charles, including a new overlook on the north side of the dam (figure 12.83). With the new parks and pedestrian bridges along the New Basin at the mouth of the river, it will soon be possible to walk along the Charles from Boston Harbor to Route 128 in Newton.

12.83 Watertown Dam, 2002.

About the Charles River Conservancy

On December 21, 2001, the winter solstice, the Charles River Conservancy lit four bridges that connect Cambridge with Allston and Brighton to demonstrate the visual power of this potential improvement and to hasten the restoration of these architecturally significant bridges. John Powell, a sculptor and light artist designed and orchestrated the illumination.

The Charles River Conservancy, founded in 2000, is dedicated to the stewardship and renewal of the 500 acres of public parklands along the Charles River from Boston Harbor to the Watertown Dam.

Working with volunteers, community organizations, and government, corporate, and institutional partners, the Conservancy engages in the planning, maintenance, and restoration of parks, pathways, and bridges along the almost 10-mile-long river basin in Boston, Cambridge, Newton, and Watertown, Massachusetts. Its mission includes advocacy and extends to a broad program of education and service learning as well as to introducing new recreational opportunities such as a skatepark and swimming areas. The Charles River Conservancy endeavors to increase the access, beauty, enjoyment, and safety of this "democratic common ground" for all.

The Conservancy depends on the time and energy of thousands of volunteers and the generous financial support of individuals, corporations, and foundations. Among the first groups to help with the Conservancy Volunteers program were BostonCares, Single Volunteers Boston, and local colleges.

Grants for the Charles River Conservancy to strengthen the organization, its activities, and its projects have come, in part, from The Boston Foundation, the George H. and Jane A. Mifflin Memorial Fund, the Harold Whitworth Pierce Charitable Trust, the Tomforde Foundation, the Fuller Foundation, the Boston Foundation for Architecture, the William P. Wharton Trust, the NLT Foundation, the Cambridge Community Foundation, the Tony Hawk Foundation, the Unity Foundation, the Architectural Heritage Foundation, and the Massachusetts Cultural Council.

To learn more about the Charles River Conservancy, to volunteer, or to donate, go to www.charlesriverconservancy.org

Notes

Introduction

1. Anthony Sutcliffe, *Toward the Planned City: Germany, Britain, the United States, and France, 1780–1914* (Oxford: Basil Blackwell, 1981), 197; Walter Creese, "The Boston Fens," *The Crowning of the American Landscape: Eight Great Spaces and Their Buildings* (Princeton: Princeton University Press, 1985), 183.

2. Kevin Lynch, *The Image of the City* (Cambridge, Mass.: MIT Press, 1959), 19–21.

3. Lee Marc G. Wolman et al., "Boston's Charles River Basin," *American Society of Civil Engineers, Journal of the Boston Society of Civil Engineers Section* 67 (Summer 1981): 199.

4. The history of the Charles Basin is briefly considered in Walter Muir Whitehill, *Boston: A Topographical History* (Cambridge, Mass.: Belknap Press of Harvard University Press, 1959; rev. ed. 1968); Bainbridge Bunting, *Houses of Boston's Back Bay* (Cambridge, Mass.: Belknap Press of Harvard University Press, 1967); Cynthia Zaitzevsky, *Frederick Law Olmsted and the Boston Park System* (Cambridge, Mass: Belknap Press of Harvard University Press, 1982; Creese, "The Boston Fens." The exhibit catalog by Alex Krieger and Lisa J. Green, *Past Futures: Two Centuries of Imagining Boston* (Cambridge, Mass.: Harvard University Graduate School of Design, 1985) includes short chapters on the basin and the metropolitan parks. Alan Emmet, *Cambridge, Massachusetts: The Changing of a Landscape* (Cambridge, Mass.: Harvard University Department of Landscape Architecture, 1978) traces the changes to the Cambridge side of the river. The creation of the metropolitan park system is an important part of David Schuyler's *The New Urban Landscape*, but the integral place of Boston's river reservations and parkways in ordering a topographical pattern for the region is not discussed. Daniel Schodek's study of American engineering landmarks includes the Charles Basin, but the story resolves all the contentious issues in less than ten years and focuses on a single MIT engineer; "The Charles River Basin," *Landmarks in American Civil Engineering* (Cambridge, Mass.: MIT Press, 1985), 297–301. Lewis Mumford is among the few urban critics to recognize the significance of Eliot's proposed reclamation of the Charles as central to this new metropolitan framework, in *The Culture of Cities* (New York: Harcourt, Brace, Jovanovich, 1938), 220. The most coherent account of the basin's development is found in Max Hall's essay, *The Charles: The People's River* (Boston: Godine, 1987), 34–60.

5. Geoffrey Blodgett recognized this difference in reclaimed rather than reserved nature, and has suggested that Revere Beach "sprang from the imagination of Charles Eliot" and was the "finest single product of the [metropolitan park] commission"; *The Gentle Reformers: Massachusetts Democrats in the Cleveland Era* (Cambridge, Mass.: Harvard University Press, 1966), 126. It will be argued here that while Eliot's design for Revere Beach was realized in his lifetime, his work to create a widely shared image of public open space on the Charles had a far more profound affect on the urban life of the region.

6. Max Hall, "The People's River: How Mankind Has Changed the Charles," *Harvard Magazine* 86 (July–August 1984), 36.

7. Paul Boyer, *Urban Masses and Moral Order in America, 1820–1920* (Cambridge, Mass.: Harvard University Press, 1978); Robert Wiebe, *The Search for Order, 1877–1920* (New York: Hill & Wang, 1967); Richard Bushman, *The Refinement of America: Persons, Houses, Cities* (New York: Alfred A. Knopf, 1992).

8. Bushman *Refinement*, 145–148; William R. Taylor, "New York and the Origin of the Skyline: The Commercial City as Visual Text," *In Pursuit of Gotham: Culture and Commerce in New York* (New York: Oxford University Press, 1992), 23–34; Spiro Kostof, *The City Shaped: Urban Patterns and Meanings through History* (Boston: Little, Brown, 1991), 279–336; Michael Holleran, "Boston's 'Sacred Skyline': From Prohibiting to Sculpting Skyscrapers, 1891–1928," *Journal of Urban History* 22 (July 1996): 552–585.

9. Sam Bass Warner, Jr., *The Urban Wilderness* (New York: Harper and Row, 1972), 46; Roy Rosenzweig and Elizabeth Blackmar, *The Park and The People: A History of Central Park* (Ithaca: Cornell University Press, 1992), 15–18.

10. Henry James, *Charles W. Eliot, President of Harvard University, 1869–1909* (Boston: Houghton Mifflin, Riverside Press, 1930), 1:56–57.

11. Thomas Bender, "The Erosion of Public Culture: Cities, Discourses, and Professional Disciplines," in *The Authority of Experts: Studies in History and Theory*, ed. Thomas L. Haskell (Bloomington: Indiana University Press, 1984), 4, 6.

12. One Bostonian's view of Boston Common and its underground garage (above which no trees can be planted) is found in Robert Lowell's "For the Union Dead," *For the Union Dead and Other Poems* (New York: Farrar, Straus & Giroux, 1964), 70–72.

> . . . One morning last March,
> I pressed against the new barbed and galvanized
> fence on the Boston Common. Behind their cage,
> yellow dinosaur steamshovels were grunting
> as they cropped up tons of mush and grass
> to gouge their underworld garage.
>
> Parking spaces luxuriated like civic
> sandpiles in the heart of Boston.
> . . . .
>
> . . . Everywhere,
> giant finned cars nose forward like fish;
> a savage servility
> slides by on grease.

Chapter One

1. Dr. Eliott Talks on Life Work," *Boston Sunday Herald,* April 2, 1911.

2. Michael P. Conzen and George K. Lewis, *Boston: A Geographical Portrait* (Cambridge, Mass.: Ballinger, 1976), 5–9.

3. Susan E. Maycock, *East Cambridge: Survey of Architectural History in Cambridge*, rev. ed. (Cambridge, Mass.: MIT Press, 1988), 2.

4. Charles Eliot, "First Report of the Charles River Improvement Commission" (March 1892), in [Charles Eliot], *Charles Eliot, Landscape Architect* (Boston: Houghton Mifflin & Co., 1902), 559–560. Although the river had been much altered in its particulars when Eliot wrote, the extensive marshes of Soldiers Field still remained to suggest the character of the estuary.

5. Dena F. Dincauze, *Charles River Archeological Survey* (Cambridge, Mass.: 1968), 19.

6. Ives Goddard, Smithsonian Institution, interview by author, September 24, 1992.

7. Dincauze, *A Preliminary Report on the Charles River Archeological Survey,* 26–28.

8. Alex Krieger and David Cobb with Amy Turner, ed., *Mapping Boston* (Cambridge, Mass.: MIT Press, 1999), 82.

9. Whitehill, *Boston,* 9, 21, 23, figures 15, 16.

10. Peter Tufts, *Plan of Charlestown Peninsula in the State of Massachusetts* (Boston, 1818).

11. The 1630 settlement, originally called "Newtowne," was renamed "Cambridge" in 1638, two years after Harvard College was founded.

Bainbridge Bunting and Robert H. Nylander, *Old Cambridge: Survey of Architectural History in Cambridge* (Cambridge, Mass.: MIT Press, 1973), 15.

12. Maycock, *East Cambridge*, 2; Whitehill, *Boston*, 11.

13. Thelma Fleishman, *Charles River Dams* (Auburndale, Mass.: Charles River Watershed Association, 1978), 1–2, 24. The dam is not mentioned in the records of the General Court, perhaps because the right to construct a fish weir had already been given on the same site two years earlier.

14. Bunting and Nylander, *Old Cambridge*, 15.

15. Whitehill, *Boston*, 11–12.

16. Ibid., 21.

17. Thomas Pemberton, "A Topographical and Historical Description of Boston, 1794," *Collections of the Mass. Historical Society*, 1794, vol. 3 (Reprint: Munroe & Cornhill, 1810), 245; Maycock, *East Cambridge*, 16–17; Whitehill, *Boston*, 48–52; Christopher Roberts, *The Middlesex Canal, 1793–1860* (Cambridge, Mass.: Harvard University Press, 1938), 5. Hancock was the best-known of the proprietors, but Russell is credited as the leader of the project in Stanley I. Kutler, *Privilege and Creative Destruction: The Charles River Bridge Case* (Philadelphia: Lippincott, 1971), 9.

18. Caleb H. Snow, *A History of Boston* (Boston, 1828), in Whitehill, *Boston*, 49; Kutler, *Privilege and Creative Destruction*, 9, 15; *American Recorder* 1 (June 20, 1786): 56.

19. Roberts, *Middlesex Canal*, 21–22; Mary Stetson Clarke, *The Old Middlesex Canal* (Melrose, Mass.: Hilltop Press, 1974), 3.

20. *Report to the Proprietors of the Middlesex Canal, at their Meeting January 25, 1809*, 3.

21. It is not clear how long the sunken tow-line functioned; in 1826, a petition to build a new bridge to Charlestown described how shipments of lumber on the canal were transferred to wagons in Charlestown to be transported over the old Charles River Bridge to Boston. See Kutler, 23.

22. Edward Chase Kirkland, *Men, Cities, and Transportation: A Study in New England History* (Cambridge, Mass.: Harvard University Press, 1948), 64; Clarke, 122, 129-130.

23. Roberts, *Middlesex Canal*, 25.

24. *Columbian Centinel*, January 21, 1792.

25. Kutler, *Privilege and Creative Destruction*, 13–14

26. Cambridge Historical Commission, *Cambridgeport. Survey of Architectural History in Cambridge, Report Three* (Cambridge, Mass.: MIT Press, 1971), 17–18.

27. Ibid.

28. Judy D. Dobbs, *A History of the Watertown Arsenal, Watertown, Massachusetts, 1816–1967* (Watertown, Mass.: Army Materials and Mechanics Research Center, 1977), 1–3.

29. Maycock, *East Cambridge*, 17–19.

30. Ibid., 19–20; Kutler, *Privilege and Creative Destruction*, 15.

31. Maycock, *East Cambridge*, 21–22.

32. Ibid., 28–29, 130, 176.

33. Whitehill, *Boston*, 60–62. For a recent argument that this railroad was the first in America, see Frederick Gamst, "The Context and Significance of America's First Railroad on Boston's Beacon Hill," *Technology & Culture* 33, no. 1 (1992) 66–100. Depositions from the lawsuits are the principal source of information on both the land development and the rail road that was developed; Nancy Stein Seasholes, "Landmaking and the Process of Urbanization: The Boston Landmaking Projects, 1630s–1888" (Ph.D. dissertation, Boston University, 1994), 126.

34. Whitehill, *Boston*, 79.

35. Ibid., 88.

36. Seasholes, "Landmaking and the Process of Urbanization," 220–221. The Back Bay project is also described in Whitehill, Winsor, and Shurtleff.

37. Uriah Cotting, *The Boston and Roxbury Mill Corporation*, [Boston?: s.n., 1818], 21.

38. Ibid., 22–23.

39. Seasholes, "Landmaking and the Process of Urbanization," 222; Whitehill, *Boston*, 90.

40. John Olmsted wrote in 1905 that "in 1875 it became apparent that this population had at least one great problem before it which could not be solved effectively by the independent action of the separate municipalities. The problem was the problem of sewage disposal." "The Metropolitan Park System," 56. As the 1878 Massachusetts Board of Health report makes clear, 1875 was the year the board began investigating the problem.

41. *Boston Daily Advertiser*, June 10, 1814, in Whitehill, *Boston*, 90.

42. Cotting, 1–20.

43. Josiah Quincy, *Municipal History of the Town and City of Boston during Two Centuries* (Boston: C.C. Little & J. Brown, 1852), 26–27.

44. Kutler, *Privilege and Creative Destruction*, 18–20.

45. Ibid., 31–33.

46. Ibid., 35–36, 45.

47. Ibid., 54–58.

48. Ibid., 75.

49. Ibid., 106–108, 74–75.

50. Ibid., 76–77; Joseph Story to Charles Sumner, 25 January 1837, in *The Life and Letters of Joseph Story, Associate Justice of the Supreme Court of the United States, and Dane Professor of Law at Harvard University,* ed. William W. Story (Boston: Little, Brown, 1881), 266.

51. February 14, 1837, in Story, *Life and Letters of Joseph Story,* 268.

52. Kutler, *Privilege and Creative Destruction,* 87–93.

53. Ibid., 112–116.

54. Maycock, *East Cambridge,* 31–32.

Chapter Two

1. Robert Fleming Gourlay, *Plans for the Improvement of Edinburgh—No. 1,* [1829], British Library; Ralph Waldo Emerson, "The Poet," 1844; Robert Fleming Gourlay, *Plans,* 1844, 37, 14, 19.

2. Oscar Handlin and Mary Flug Handlin, *Commonwealth: A Study of the Role of Government in the American Economy: Massachusetts, 1774–1861* (Cambridge, Mass.: Harvard University Press, 1947; rev. 1969).

3. Bushman, *Refinement,* xiv.

4. Ibid., xvii, xix.

5. Thomas Jefferson, *Notes on the State of Virginia,* Query XIX, quoted in Leo Marx, *The Machine in the Garden: Technology and the Pastoral Ideal in America* (New York: Oxford University Press, 1964), 125.

6. Bushman, *Refinement,* 139.

7. Whitehill, *Boston,* 22–46.

8. On the influence of Bulfinch in Boston, see Whitehill, "The Boston of Bulfinch," in *Boston,* 47–72; Harold and James Kirker, *Bulfinch's Boston* (New York: Oxford University Press, 1964); Harold Kirker, *The Architecture of Charles Bulfinch* (Cambridge, Mass.: Harvard University Press, 1969).

9. Edward G. Porter, "Demolition of the McLean Asylum at Somerville," *Proceedings of the Massachusetts Historical Society,* Second Series, 10 (1895–1896): 549–550.

10. Ibid., 549; Cynthia Zaitzevsky, "Education and Landscape Architecture," in *Architectural Education and Boston: Centennial Publication of the Boston Architectural Center, 1889, 1989,* ed. Margaret Henderson Floyd (Boston: Boston Architectural Center, 1989), 20; Nina Fletcher Little, *Early Years of the McLean Hospital* (Boston: Countway Library of Medicine, 1972), 149. One nearby example of the gentleman architect was Christopher Gore, who designed the grounds of his estate along the Charles in Waltham.

11. Tamara Plakins Thornton, *Cultivating Gentlemen: The Meaning of Country Life among the Boston Elite, 1785–1860* (New Haven: Yale University Press, 1989), 22–24, 27–32, 106–107; Bunting and Nylander, *Old Cambridge,* 80.

12. Harold Kirker, *Architecture,* 211–215, 307–317. On moral management and therapeutic landscapes, see Andrew Scull, "The Discovery of the Asylum Revisited: Lunacy Reform in the new American Republic," *Madhouses, Mad-Doctors, and Madmen: The Social History of Psychiatry in the Victorian Era,* ed. Andrew Scull (London: Athlone, 1981), 148–159; and Kenneth Hawkins, "The Therapeutic Landscape: Nature, Architecture, and Mind in Nineteenth-Century America" (Ph.D. dissertation, University of Rochester, 1991). Charles Bulfinch was sent off to inspect hospitals and asylums in New York, Philadelphia, and Baltimore, and then retained by the hospital to design two new wings for the Barrell estate as well as the hospital's first structure in Boston.

13. Josiah Quincy, *A Municipal Hisotry of the Town and City of Boston during Two Centuries* (Boston: C.C. Little and D. Brown, 182), 378.

14. Quoted in Whitehill, *Boston,* 15.

15. Ibid., 59–60, 65–66.

16. Seasholes, "Landmaking and the Process of Urbanization," 239–242.

17. Quoted in Seasholes, 242.

18. Ibid., 243.

19. Quoted in Blanche Linden-Ward, *Silent City on a Hill: Landscapes of Memory and Boston's Mt. Auburn Cemetery* (Columbus: Ohio State University Press, 1989), 161, 164–165. On the background of Quincy's actions to promote public health, see John B. Blake, *Public Health in the Town of Boston, 1630–1822* (Cambridge: Harvard University Press, 1959), 220–242.

20. Lucius Paige, *History of Cambridge* (Cambridge: Riverside Press, 1877), 236.

21. Henry C. Binford, *The First Suburbs: Residential Communities on the Boston Periphery, 1815–1860* (Chicago: University of Chicago Press, 1985), 24, 110; Paige, *History of Cambridge,* 238.

22. Binford, *Suburbs,* 110; Paige, *History of Cambridge,* 238.

23. Bigelow later taught a course and wrote a text on "technology," a word he coined to describe "the application of science to the useful arts."

24. The group convened by Bigelow included Gen. Henry Dearborn, John Lowell, Judge Joseph Story, Edward Everett, and Nathan Hale (whose father had been a classmate at Yale of James Hillhouse, the organized of New Haven's rural New Burying Ground). Linden-Ward, *Silent City on a Hill,* 167–173.

25. Ibid., 177–178.

26. Samuel Eliot Morison, *Harrison Gray Otis, 1765–1848: The Urbane Federalist* (Boston: Houghton Mifflin, 1969), 201; the description by Captain George Talcott, the Arsenal's superintendent, is quoted in Dobbs, *History of the Watertown Arsenal*, 1–3. See also Edward Francis Zimmer, "The Architectural Career of Alexander Parris (1780–1852)" (Ph.D. dissertation, Boston University, 1984), 1:301–312.

27. Dearborn's cemetery committee originally included Bigelow, Brimmer, John Lowell, Abbott Lawrence, and Thomas Handasyd Perkins; now with the addition of Joseph Story, Edward Everett, Daniel Webster, and others, it was increased to twenty men. Linden-Ward, *Silent City* 175–182; Acts of 1831, chap. 69.

28. Story, *Life and Letters of Joseph Story*, 2:65–67.

29. Linden-Ward, *Silent City on a Hill*, 208, 210.

30. Ibid., 210–212, 258–294.

31. Nathan Hale, *Remarks on the practicability and Expediency of Rail Roads from Boston to the Hudson River and from Boston to Providence* (Boston: W. L. Lewis, 1827), iv.

32. Quincy, *Municipal History*, 285–286.

33. Ibid., 100, 103; Charles Francis Adams, Jr., "The Canal and Railroad Enterprise of Boston," in *Memorial History of Boston*, ed. Justin Winsor (Boston: Ticknor & Co., 1881), 4:122.

34. In addition to Perkins and Nathan Hale, the group included Josiah Quincy, Jr., Royal Makepeace, and Emory Washburn of Worcester and Theodore Sedgwick of Stockbridge. Five of the men were members of the legislature; Perkins was the only conspirator of wealth. Kirkland, *Men, Cities, and Transportation*, 102–104.

35. *Boston Daily Advertiser*, March 14, 1829.

36. Charles Francis Adams, Jr., "Canal and Railroad Enterprise," 4:122.

37. Ibid., 4:124; Stephen Salsbury, *The State, the Investor, and the Railroad: The Boston & Albany, 1825–1867* (Cambridge, Mass.: Harvard University Press, 1967), 112–132.

38. *Report of the Board of Directors of Internal Improvements* (Boston: Daily Advertiser, 1829)

39. *Report of the Directors of the Boston & Worcester Rail Road Corporation* (Boston: Steam Power Press, 1832), 24; Salsbury, *The State, the Investor, and the Railroad,* 100–102.

40. Ibid., 101–102.

41. *Boston Evening Transcript*, April 4, 1834; Christopher Columbus Baldwin, *Diary of Christopher Columbus Baldwin, Librarian of the American Antiquarian Society, 1829–1835* (New York: Johnson Reprint Corp., 1971), 316.

42. Lewis Mumford, *The City in History: Its Origins, Its Transformations, Its Prospects* (New York: Harcourt, Brace & World, 1961), 458–465.

43. N. I. Bowditch, *A History of the Massachusetts General Hospital to August 5, 1851*, 2d ed. with a continuation to 1872 (Boston: The Trustees, 1872), 150–151, 673.

44. Whitehill, *Boston,* 102–109.

45. Ibid., 101; *The Inaugural Addresses of the Mayors of Boston* (Boston: Rockwell & Churchill, 1894), 1:136; City of Boston, *Report of the Special Committee of the Board of Aldermen on the Memorial of D. Sears, and the Petition of J. C. Warren and Others, July 2, 1849* (City Document no. 36, Boston, 1849), 3.

46. Krieger and Green, *Past Futures,* 28.

47. William Smith, *Robert Gourlay*, Bulletin of the Department of Historian and Political and Economic Science in Queen's University (Kingston, Ont.: Jackson Press, 1926), 1–20; Lois Darroch Milani, *Robert Gourlay, Gadfly: The Biography of Robert (Fleming) Gourlay, 17789–1863, Forerunner of the Rebellion in Upper Canada, 1837* ([Thornhill, Ont.]: Ampersand, 1971), xi; Gourlay, *Plans*, 1. Milani's biography, the lengthiest account of Gourlay's life, does not mention Gourlay's city designs.

48. Gourlay, *Plans*, 1, 10, 14, 18.

49. Ibid., 1, 14.

50. Ibid., 9–10; Robert Gourlay, *A Plan of a Pagoda and Flower Garden in the Common, Submitted to the Citizens of Boston* (n.p., 1843).

51. Gourlay, *Plans*, 17–20.

52. Ibid., 1, 23.

53. Ibid., 24.

54. Ibid., 16.

55. Ibid., 38.

56. Ibid., 17.

57. Ibid., 18–19.

58. Ibid., 35.

59. Ibid., 35, 37.

60. Gourlay, *General Plan.*

61. Charles Caldwell, "Thoughts on the Moral and Other Indirect Influences of Rail-Roads," *North American Review* 2 (April 1832): 292, 293.

62. Ibid., 293.

63. Marx, *Machine in the Garden.*

64. Quoted in Leo Marx, "The Railroad-in-the-Landscape: An Iconological Reading of a Theme in American Art," in *The Railroad in American Art: Representations of Technological Change*, ed. Susan Danly and Leo Marx (Cambridge, Mass.: MIT Press, 1988), 5, 195.

65. Ibid., 69, 70.

66. Susan Danly, "Introduction," in Danly and Marx, *Railroad in American Art*. See also Joseph Garland, *Boston's North Shore* (Boston: Little, Brown, 1978), 84–89.

67. Sam Bass Warner, Jr., noted this flaw in the pastoral vision in "The Search for the Meaning of Landscapes," *Journal of Urban History* 15, no. 3 (May 1989): 326.

Chapter Three

1. George Snelling, *Remarks* [Memorial and Letters], (Boston, 1860), 3; Henry James, *The Bostonians*, 1886; Zaitzevsky, *Frederick Law Olmsted*, 96; Bunting, *Back Bay*, 389; Whitehill, *Boston*, 149.

2. Fletcher Steele, "Robert Fleming Gourlay, City Planner," *Landscape Architecture* 6:1 (October 1915): 1–14; Krieger and Green, *Past Futures*, 28.

3. Seasholes, "Landmaking and the Process of Urbanization," 355; Whitehill, *Boston*, 149–150.

4. Whitehill, *Boston*, 149–150. In this version of Sears's plan, the Boston and Providence Railroad line runs straight into the shallow waters of the proposed lake, without connecting to the company's depot south of the Botanic Garden; that defect is corrected in other versions of his proposal. See Krieger and Green, *Past Futures*, 28.

5. Seasholes, "Landmaking and the Process of Urbanization."

6. Ibid., 272, 354.

7. Resolves of 1850, chapter 111.

8. Resolves of 1852, chapter 79; Seasholes, "Landmaking and the Process of Urbanization," 355, 356. In 1855 the board was renamed the Commissioners on the Back Bay.

9. Seasholes, "Landmaking and the Process of Urbanization," 357.

10. Ibid., 358–361.

11. Whitehill, *Boston*, 152-153.

12. Seasholes, "Landmaking and the Process of Urbanization," 362.

13. Ibid., 362–364; Whitehill, *Boston*, 151.

14. Seasholes, "Landmaking and the Process of Urbanization," 365–366.

15. Commonwealth of Massachusetts, *Acts of the General Court*, 1859, chapter 210; Zaitzevsky, *Frederick Law Olmsted*, 33–34.

16. Quoted in Seasholes, "Landmaking and the Process of Urbanization," 366–367.

17. Schuyler, *The New Urban Landscape*, 101; *The Papers of Frederick Law Olmsted*, vol. 3, *Creating Central Park, 1857–1861*, ed. Charles E. Beveridge and David Schuyler (Baltimore: Johns Hopkins University Press, 1983), 354–357. For a summary of the development of Fairmount Park in Philadelphia, Druid Hill in Baltimore, and Brooklyn's Prospect Park, see Schuyler, *The New Urban Landscape*, 102–127.

18. Snelling, *Remarks*, 3. Nancy Seasholes generously shared this reference to Hamburg's water park, which is the earliest known illustration published in Boston of the Alster Basin.

19. Ibid., ii.

20. Ibid., 11, 13, 14; City of Boston, *Report of the Hearing Before a Committee of the House of Representatives of Massachusetts on the Occupation and Improvement of the Commonwealth Flats on Charles River* (November and December, 1869, City Document no. 128, 1869), 251.

21. Snelling, *Remarks*, 22, 23, 26. Sumner later donated his copy of Snelling's memorial to Widener Library at Harvard. The simile of "the face without eyes" is the inverse of Horace Mann's observation that "water is to the landscape what the eye is to the face" (quoted in Creese, 192).

22. Ibid., 20, 29, 31.

23. Ibid., 56.

24. Commonwealth of Massachusetts, Committee on Charles River Dam, *Evidences and Arguments before the Committee on Charles River Dam* (Boston: Wright & Potter, 1903), 491.

25. Snelling, *Remarks*, 43–44, 49–50.

26. Ibid., 17. A century later this generalization about Hamburg persists; see Hermann Hipp, *Freie und Hansestadt Hamburg: Beschichte, Kultur und Stadtbaukunst an Elbe und Alster* (Köln: DuMont, 1989), 11.

27. Hipp, *Freie und Hansestadt Hamburg*, 12–14, 28–32.

28. Nancy Seasholes, "Gaining Ground: Boston's Topographical Development in Maps," *Mapping Boston*, 124–127.

29. Harvard Corporation Records, 4:597, quoted in *Sibley's Harvard Graduates*.

30. Samuel Eliot Morison, *Three Centuries of Harvard, 1636–1936* (Cambridge, Mass.: Harvard University Press, 1936), 206; Bainbridge Bunting, *Harvard: An Architectural history*, completed and edited by Margaret Henderson Floyd (Cambridge, Mass.: Belknap Press of Harvard University Press, 1985), 57; Susan E. Maycock and Charles M. Sullivan, *Old Cambridge* (Cambridge, Mass.: MIT Press, forthcoming 2003).

31. City of Boston, Report on Free Bathing Facilities (City Document no. 102, 1866), 1–17.

32. Morison, *Three Centuries of Harvard,* 315; Maycock and Sullivan, *Old Cambridge*; *Ballou's Pictorial Companion,* June 20, 1857.

33. City of Boston, *Report and Accompanying Statements Relating to a Public Park for the City of Boston* (City Document no. 123, 1869), 44–45.

34. Ibid., 3, 9–10, 269.

35. Ibid., 73–74, 75–77.

36. Richard Sennett has traced this imagery from William Harvey's seventeenth-century discovery of circulation in the human body. See his *Flesh and Stone: The Body and the City in Western Civilization* (New York: Norton, 1994), 255–270.

37. City of Boston, City Document no. 128 (1869), 78, 80, 94.

38. Ibid., 101.

39. Ibid., 123–158, 209–244.

40. Ibid., 264–267.

41. Zaitzevsky, *Frederick Law Olmsted,* 32–47.

42. [Horace William Shaler Cleveland], *The Public Grounds of Chicago: How to Give Them Character and Expression* (Chicago: Charles D. Lakey, 1869), 8. Before moving to Chicago, Cleveland worked with Olmsted and Vaux on Prospect Park in Brooklyn. See William H. Tishler, "H.W.S. Cleveland," in Tishler, ed., *American Landscape Architecture: Designers and Places* (Washington, D.C.: National Trust for Historic Preservation, 1989), 24–30; and Karl Haglund, "Rural Taste, Rectangular Ideas, and the Skirmishes of H. W. S. Cleveland," *Landscape Architecture* 66 (January 1976): 67–70, 78.

43. [Cleveland], *Public Grounds of Chicago,* 9.

44. Ibid., 10, 12; *Boston Evening Transcript,* November 10, 1869.

45. City of Boston, City Document no. 123 (1869), 36–37.

46. Robert Morris Copeland, "The Park Question," *Boston Daily Advertiser,* December 2, 1869. On Copeland, see Zaitzevsky, *Frederick Law Olmsted,* 227, n. 21.

47. Ibid.

48. Ibid.

49. Ibid.

50. "Letter from Uriel H. Crocker," in City of Boston, City Document no. 123 (1869), 91–92.

51. Ibid., 90, 93; *Boston Daily Advertiser,* December 18, 1869.

52. Commonwealth of Massachusetts, *Acts of the General Court,* 1870, chapter 283.

53. On the founding of the American Social Science Association (1865) and other national professional groups, see Burton J. Bledstein, *The Culture of Professionalism: The Middle Class and the Development of Higher Education in America* (New York: Norton, 1976), 80–92.

54. Olmsted, *Public Parks,* 68.

55. Zaitzevsky, *Frederick Law Olmsted,* 37; Charles River Dam, *Evidences* (1903), 492.

56. Robert Morris Copeland, *The Most Beautiful City in America: Essay and Plan for the Improvement of the City of Boston* (Boston: Lee and Shepard, 1872), 14.

57. Zaitzevsky, *Frederick Law Olmsted,* 38; Copeland, *The Most Beautiful City in America,* 14, 44.

58. Zaitzevsky, *Frederick Law Olmsted,* 39; *Boston Daily Advertiser,* June 13, 1874.

59. [George A. Shaw], *Speech of Hon. George A. Shaw in the Common Council of the City of Boston, March 25, 1875, On the Subject of Public Parks* (Boston: n.p., 1875), 19.

60. Zaitzevsky, *Olmsted,* 39–41.

61. City of Boston, *Report on the Establishment of a Public Park* (December 3, 1874, City Document no. 105, 1874), 3, 7–11.

62. Ibid., 11–13.

63. Zaitzevsky, *Frederick Law Olmsted,* 41–42.

64. *Cambridgeport,* 22; Maycock, *East Cambridge,* 73–74.

65. Maycock, *East Cambridge,* 73.

66. *Cambridgeport,* 27; Maycock, *East Cambridge,* 74.

67. *Cambridgeport,* 31–32; "A Leaf from Massachusetts of Today, Issued for the World's Columbian Exposition" (Boston: Columbia Publishing Co., 1893).

68. Ibid., 32–33.

69. MIT acquired Riverbank Court (now Ashdown House) and the armory (now DuPont Gymnasium).

70. Zaitzevsky, *Frederick Law Olmsted,* 43–44.

71. City of Boston, *Second Report of the Board of Commissioners of the Department of Parks for the City of Boston* (April 24, 1876, City Document no. 42, 1876), 1.

72. Ibid., 4–5.

73. Ibid., 16, 18.

74. *Parks for the People: Proceedings of a Public Meeting held at Faneuil Hall, June 7, 1876* (Boston, 1876), 13, 41–42; Zaitzevsky, *Frederick Law Olmsted,* 46.

75. Zaitzevsky, *Frederick Law Olmsted*, 46–47.

76. Ibid., 55–57

77. Frederick Law Olmsted to Francis W. Lawrence, January 28, 1890, quoted in Creese, "The Boston Fens," 175.

78. Zaitzevsky, *Frederick Law Olmsted*, 81–82.

79. Ibid., 83–84.

80. *Fifth Annual Report of the Board of Commissioners of the Department of Parks for the Year 1879* (City Document no. 15, 1880), 18; *Twelfth Annual Report of the Board of Commissioners of the Department of Parks for the Year 1886* (City Document no. 24, 1887), 10–13.

81. *Fifteenth Annual Report of the Board of Commissioners of the Department of Parks for the Year 1889* (City Document no. 15, 1890), 39; *Kim Townsend, Manhood at Harvard: William James and Others* (New York: Norton, 1999), 99–102.

82. *Sixteenth Annual Report of the Board of Commissioners of the Department of Parks for the Year 1890,* 44; *Seventeenth Annual Report of the Board of Commissioners of the Department of Parks for the Year 1891* (City Document no. 26, 1892), 75–77; Suzanne M. Spencer-Wood, "Domestic Reform and the Design of Cities, Parks and Playgrounds," unpublished paper presented at Radcliffe College, February 20, 1992, 6.

83. Commonwealth of Massachusetts, Metropolitan Park Commission, Minutes, November 2, 1892; *Twenty-fourth Annual Report of the Board of Commissioners of the Department of Parks for the Year Ending January 31, 1899,* 13.

84. Morison, *Three Centuries of Harvard,* 411–412, n. 1.

85. Eleanor McPeck, Keith Morgan, and Cynthia Zaitzevsky, eds., *Olmsted in Massachusetts: The Public Legacy* (Brookline: Massachusetts Association for Olmsted Parks, 1983), 13–14.

86. [Eliot], *Charles Eliot,* 211, 212.

87. Ibid., 211, 213.

88. Maycock, *East Cambridge,* 71–73.

89. Ibid., 202–204.

90. Ibid., 205.

91. Ibid., 49, 206.

92. City of Boston, *Sixth Annual Report of the Board of Health* (May 1, 1878, City Document no. 68, 1878), 3.

93. William P. Marchione, *The Bull in the Garden: A History of Allston-Brighton* (Boston: Trustees of the Public Library of the City of Boston, 1986), 22, 29–31, 73–77; the 1898 maps produced by the Sanborn Map Company name some of the riverfront structures that are unidentified on the 1894 *Joint Board* map.

94. Commonwealth of Massachusetts, Joint Board Upon the Improvement of Charles River, *Report of the Joint Board consisting of the Metropolitan Park Commission and the State Board of Health Upon the Improvement of Charles River from the Waltham Line to the Charles River Bridge* (House Doc. no. 775, April 1894), ix. Cited below as Joint Board, *Charles River* (1894).

95. *Boston Daily Advertiser,* June 13, 1874.

Chapter Four

1. Sylvester Baxter, "Report of the Secretary," 1, 9; Charles Eliot, "Report of the Landscape Architect," 90; in Massachusetts, Metropolitan Park Commission, *Report of the Board of Metropolitan Park Commissioners* (House Doc. no. 150; January 1893), cited below as *MPC Report* (1893); Jack Shepherd, *The Adams Chronicles: Four Generations of Greatness* (Boston: Little, Brown, 1975), 424. Thomas S. Hines, *Burnham of Chicago: Architect and Planner* (New York: Oxford University Press, 1974), 101, 115, quotes Daniel Burnham, the chief architect of the Chicago Fair, on the color of the buildings and Charles Eliot Norton, Harvard professor of Fine Arts, on their arrangement.

2. [Henry Adams], *The Education of Henry Adams* (Boston: Houghton Mifflin, 1974), 340.

3. For a discussion of Olmsted and J. J. R. Croes's 1876–1877 plans for the Bronx, see Schuyler, *The New Urban Landscape*, 174–179. *MPC Report* (1893), 91. Creese, "The Boston Fens," 167, describes the metropolitan park system as "Eliot's Emerald Necklace," an oversimplification of the plan.

4. On the role of Frederick Law Olmsted in the campaigns for Yosemite and Niagara Falls, see Laura Wood Roper, *FLO: A Biography of Frederick Law Olmsted* (Baltimore: Johns Hopkins University Press, 1973), 271–290.

5. Sylvester Baxter, transcripts, University of Leipzig; Humboldt University, Berlin. Baxter's study in Germany predates by a decade the study tours of English and American experts that Christiane Crasemann Collins dates to the 1890s. Collins, "A Visionary Disciple: Werner Hegemann and the Quest for the Pragmatic Ideal," *Center: A Journal for Architecture in America* 5 (1989), 75.

6. Zaitzevsky, *Frederick Law Olmsted*, 123.

7. Sylvester Baxter, "An Aboriginal Pilgrimage," *Century* 24 (1881–1882): 526–536; Cyrus Field Willard, "The Nationalist Club of Boston (A Chapter of History)," *Nationalist* 1, no. 1 (May 1889): 16–20; see also Baxter's articles, "What Is Nationalism?" *Nationalist* 1 (May 1889): 8–12;

"Why the Name, Nationalism?" *Nationalist* 1 (July 1889): 82–83; [Sylvester Baxter] "Sylvester Baxter," in James Phinney Baxter, *The Baxter Family: A Collection of Genealogies* (n.p., 1921), 94–102. See also Curtis M. Hinsley, "Boston Meets the Southwest," in *The Southwest in the American Imagination: The Writings of Sylvester Baxter, 1881–1889,* ed. Curtis M. Hinsley and David R. Wilcox (Tucson: University of Arizona Press, 1996), 5-18.

8. [Eliot], *Charles Eliot,* 5–31; Charles Eliot, unpublished autobiography.

9. [Eliot], *Charles Eliot,* 32–34; Zaitzevsky, "Education."

10. Keith N. Morgan, "Introduction to the 1999 Edition: Charles Eliot, the Man behind the Monograph," in [Charles W. Eliot] *Charles Eliot, Landscape Architect* (Amherst: University of Massachusetts Press, 1999), reprint of the 1901 edition.

11. Shepherd, *Adams Chronicles,* 379; [Eliot] *Charles Eliot,* 286–291; Edward Chase Kirkland, *Charles Francis Adams, Jr., 1835–1915, The Patrician at Bay* (Cambridge, Mass.: Harvard University Press, 1965), 187.

12. Charles Eliot, "The Waverly Oaks," *Garden and Forest* (March 5, 1890): 117–118.

13. Charles Eliot to Gov. William Russell, December 19, 1890, quoted in [Eliot], *Charles Eliot,* 356.

14. Sylvester Baxter, *Greater Boston: A Study for a Federalized Metropolis Comprising the City of Boston and Surrounding Cities and Towns* (Boston: A.J. Philpott & Co.), 1891. Baxter, "Greater Boston." Baxter believed that his use of the term "Greater Boston" predated its use in New York City, a reflection of Baxter's fascination with place names as well as the long-standing rivalry between the two cities.

15. Lawrence W. Kennedy, *Planning the City upon a Hill: Boston Since 1630* (Boston: Northeastern University Press, 1992), 67–70; *Boston Daily Advertiser,* March 7, 1872, quoted in Martha H. Bowers and Jane Carolan, *The Water Supply System of Metropolitan Boston: 1845–1926* (Boston: Metropolitan District Commission, 1984), 9, 11.

16. Baxter, *Greater Boston,* 3, 8.

17. Baxter's recollection that Eliot proposed a joint effort to realize the park system is found in his "Wonderful Progress During the Past Seven Years of Work on the Great Metropolitan Park System," *Boston Sunday Herald* (May 20, 1900), 41; and in Baxter, "Greater Boston's Metropolitan Park System," *Boston Evening Transcript,* Part Five (September 29, 1923), 1.

18. Charles Eliot to Mary Eliot, February 1892.

19. Eliot first proposed that the association be called "The Trustees of Massachusetts Scenery." The name chosen, "The Trustees of Public Reservations," was the source of some confusion, since the organization was privately organized and funded; in 1954 it became "The Trustees of Reservations." Gordon Abbott, Jr., *Saving Special Places: A Centennial History of the Trustees of Reservations: Pioneer of the Land Trust Movement* (Ipswich, Mass.: Ipswich Press, 1993), 12.

20. Charles Eliot to Gov. William Russell, December 19, 1890, quoted in [Eliot], *Charles Eliot,* 356.

21. Minutes of the Temporary Metropolitan Park Commission, August 30–November 2, 1892; cited below as MPC Minutes.

22. MPC Minutes, September 14, 26, 30; October 3, 10, 1892.

23. MPC Minutes, September 14, 26; October 10, 14, 1892.

24. IMPC Minutes, September 14; October 10, 1892.

25. For a discussion of the Charles River Improvement Commission, see below.

26. MPC Minutes, November 2, 1892.

27. MPC Minutes, November 12, 1892.

28. MPC Minutes, November 15, 26; December 3, 6, 8, 1892; January 5, 9, 12, 16, 1893.

29. *MPC Report* (1893), 82.

30. [Eliot], *Charles Eliot,* 383.

31. The drawings were done by W. Bodwell; the color map was prepared by Charles Eliot.

32. *MPC Report* (1893), 2–3.

33. Ibid., 4–6.

34. Ibid., 8–11.

35. Ibid., 12–13.

36. Ibid., 14–18.

37. Ibid., 16, 19–20.

38. Ibid., 25.

39. Ibid., 51.

40. Ibid., 62–81.

41. Gourlay, *Plans,* 37; *MPC Report* (1893), 91.

42. *MPC Report* (1893), 82.

43. Ibid., 82–110.

44. Ibid., 83–84.

45. Ibid., 85–86.

46. Ibid., 87–88, 89.

47. Ibid., 90–91.

48. Ibid., 91–92.

49. Ibid., 97–98.

50. Ibid., 98–104.

51. Ibid., 108–109.

52. Baxter considered Eliot's "comprehensive reservation of the banks of the three rivers" unique in a system of park development; see Baxter, "Wonderful Progress," 40; Lewis Mumford wrote in *The Culture of Cities* (Harcourt Brace Jovanovich, 1938), 220, that Eliot added to Olmsted's conception of the park system "the further necessity of using the riverside and sea-coast areas" to create a complete environment where the country and the city were "continuously inter-related and inter-penetrating."

53. Ibid., 106, 109.

54. Ibid., viii–ix.

55. Ibid., x–xiii.

56. Ibid., xiii–xvi.

57. The characterization of Boston politics in this period as "both high-handed and liberal" is from Martin Meyerson and Edward C. Banfield, *Boston: The Job Ahead* (Cambridge, Mass.: Harvard University Press, 1966), 106; Kirkland, *Charles Francis Adams, Jr.*, 188; Baxter, "Wonderful Progress," 41.

58. *MPC Report* (1895), 1.

59. *MPC Report* (1896), 44–45; (1897), 26.

60. For a concise summary of the commission's administration during its first three years, see Charles Eliot, "The Boston Metropolitan Reservations," *New England Magazine* 15 (September 1896), 117-121.

61. Charles Eliot, *Vegetation and Scenery in the Metropolitan Reservations of Boston: A Forestry Report Written by Charles Eliot and Presented to the Metropolitan Park Commission, February 15, 1897* (Boston: Lamson, Wolffe, 1898), 8.

62. Eliot, *Vegetation and Scenery*, 9; *MPC Report* (1895), 31.

63. Olmsted, Olmsted & Eliot to the Metropolitan Park Commission, June 22, 1896, quoted in *Charles Eliot*, p. 655; Eliot, *Vegetation and Scenery*, 9, 22.

64. Charles Eliot, "The Necessity of Planning," *Garden and Forest* (August 26, 1896), 342; Eliot, *Vegetation and Scenery*, 9, 22.

65. *MPC Report* (1895), 32; Eliot, *Vegetation and Scenery*, 22–23.

66. *MPC Report* (1897), 51.

67. Maycock and Sullivan, *Old Cambridge;* Minutes of the temporary Metropolitan Park Commission, November 1, 1892.

68. City of Cambridge, *Report of the Committee on Public Parks* (Cambridge, 1892), 10.

69. Ibid., 7–8, 10, 11.

70. Cambridge Park Department Report, 1894, 100; also cited in Charles Eliot, 423.

71. Maycock and Sullivan, *Old Cambridge.*

72. Henry Yerxa, "European Out-door Life," *Cambridge Chronicle,* September 13, 1894.

73. Ibid.

74. Cambridge Park Department, 1896, 6; Maycock and Sullivan, *Old Cambridge.*

75. Maycock and Sullivan, *Old Cambridge;* Cambridge Park Department, 1915, 12.

76. James Russell Lowell, *The Complete Poetical Works of James Russell Lowell* (Boston: Houghton Mifflin, 1911), 70.

77. William Brewster, *The Birds of the Cambridge Region of Massachusetts,* Memoirs of the Nuttal Ornithological Club, no. 4 (Cambridge, Mass.: The Club, 1906), 33.

78. [Charles Eliot], "Landscape Architects' Report," *MPC Report* (1897), 43.

79. Olmsted to Partners [John Olmsted and Charles Eliot], October 28 and November 1, 1893, Olmsted Papers, Library of Congress. As Keith Morgan has pointed out, all but the first of these parks were initiated and directed by Eliot; see Morgan, "Introduction," xviii–xix.

80. Charles Francis Adams, diary, October 3, 1894; June 10, 11, 13, 1895.

81. *Charles Francis Adams, 1835–1915, An Autobiography* (Boston: Houghton Mifflin, 1916), 185.

82. *MPC Report* (1898), 7.

83. *MPC Report* (1900), 74. Very little additional land was acquired during the next twenty years.

84. *MPC Report* (1905), 30–31; Andrew Wright Crawford, "The Development of Park Systems in American Cities," *Annals of the American Academy* (1905), 223.

85. Collins, "A Visionary Discipline," 79–80.

Chapter Five

1. Charles Eliot, "Boston Metropolitan Reservations," 117–118; George Santayana, *Persons and Places: Fragments of Autobiography*, William G. Holzberger and Herman J. Saatkamp, Jr., eds. (Cambridge, Mass.: MIT Press, 1986), 138–139.

2. John P. Marquand, *The Late George Apley* (Boston: Little, Brown, 1936), 122, 147.

3. Ibid., 149.

4. Ibid., 151.

5. Ibid., 150.

6. *First Report of the Charles River Improvement Commission*, 1892; in [Eliot], *Charles Eliot*, 557–558.

7. Ibid., 559.

8. Ibid., 559–561.

9. Ibid., 563–569.

10. *MPC Report* (Janaury 1895), 38–39.

11. [Eliot], *Charles Eliot*, 564, 565.

12. Ibid., 570–571.

13. Joint Board, *Charles River* (1894), vii.

14. Ibid., 34.

15. Ibid., xv, xvii. This argument for having the parks "constantly under view" has been extended to city neighborhoods in general. See, for example, Jane Jacobs, *The Death and Life of Great American Cities* (New York: Vintage, 1963), 35–41.

16. Board of Harbor and Land Commissioners of Massachusetts, *Charles River Dam: Evidences and Arguments before the Board of Harbor and Land Commissioners and Report Thereon* (Boston, 1894).

17. Ibid., 5.

18. Ibid., 48, 50.

19. Ibid., 57–58, 58.

20. Ibid., 405, 407.

21. Ibid., xix–xx.

22. Santayana, *Persons and Places*, 138–139.

23. Joint Board, *Charles River* (1894), 36.

24. Acquisition maps, Metropolitan District Commission Archives.

25. *Arborway Update* (October 1998), 9; Joint Board, *Charles River* (1894), 41.

26. Joint Board, *Charles River*, 42.

27. *Charles River Dam, Evidences* (1903), 494; [Eliot], *Charles Eliot*, 592.

28. [Eliot], *Charles Eliot*, 592.

29. *Report of the Cambridge Bridge Commission* (Boston: City of Boston, 1909), 22–23.

30. *Cambridge Bridge Commission*, 23; *Dictionary of American Biography* (1936), 61; "William Jackson," *Journal of the Association of Engineering Societies* 46 (February 1911): 148–149.

31. *Cambridge Bridge Commission*, 23–26.

32. Ibid, 30–31.

33. Ibid, 41.

34. Ibid, 30–31.

35. Ibid, 32–33.

36. Ibid, 35.

37. *Boston Herald*, January 17, 1899.

38. Constance K. Burns, "The Irony of Progressive Reform, 1898–1910," in Ronald P. Formisano and Constance K. Burns, *Boston, 1700–1980: The Evolution of Urban Politics* (Westport, Conn.: Greenwood Press, 1984), 142.

39. *Boston Transcript*, March 27, 1901.

40. Charles River Dam, *Evidences* (1903), 155–156.

41. Henry Greenleaf Pearson, *Son of New England: James Jackson Storrow, 1864–1926* (Boston: Todd, 1932), 35–36.

42. *Boston Herald*, January 17, 1899; Henry L Higginson et al., *The Improvement of the Charles River Basin* (Boston, 1901); Lee, Higginson & Co. et al., *The Proposed Commission to Investigate the Feasibility of Turning Charles River Basin into a Water Park* (Boston, 1901). Charles River Dam, *Evidences* (1903), 153.

43. John R. Freeman, "Some Problems of the Charles River Dam," paper presented to the Boston Society of Civil Engineers, June 24, 1903, published in *American Society of Civil Engineers, Journal of the Boston Society of Civil Engineers Section* 67 (Summer 1981): 217.

44. Deborah A. Cozort, "John Ripley Freeman and the Honest Doubters of Boston: How the Charles River Dam was Won," *American Society of Civil Engineers, Journal of the Boston Society of Civil Engineers Section* 67 (Summer 1981): 209–211; Charles River Dam, *Evidences* (1903), 453. Fitzgerald would later defeat Storrow in the fiercely contested mayoral election of 1910; the margin was 47,177 to 45,775, with a record turnout of 90% of the city's eligible voters (see Burns, "The Irony of Progressive Reform," 153–159).

45. Charles River Dam, *Evidences* (1903), 423–431.

46. Ibid., 343–344.

47. Quoted in Hall, "The People's River," 44.

48. Charles River Dam, *Evidences* (1903), 159–160, 178.

49. Norman T. Newton, *Design on the Land* (Cambridge, Mass.: Belknap Press of Harvard University Press, 1971), 320–336. On President Eliot's involvement in the profession of landscape architecture, see Creese, 200–204.

50. Charles River Dam, *Evidences* (1903), 135–136. These paragraphs from Eliot's testimony would be cited in 1929 and again in 1949 when highways through the Boston embankment were proposed. See below.

51. A recent history on American hydraulics concluded that Freeman was the most influential engineer in his field. Wolman et al., "Boston's Charles River Basin," 200. For parallel careers that place the professionalization of engineering in context, see Sam Bass Warner, Jr., "Charles A. Stone and Edwin S. Webster," *The Province of Reason* (Cambridge, Mass.: Harvard University Press, 1984), 52–66.

52. Freeman, "Charles River Dam," 218, 220.

53. Ibid., 220; Freeman to William Otis Crosby, May 11, 1903, in Cozort, "John Ripley Freeman and the Honest Doubters of Boston," 221.

54. Cozort, "John Ripley Freeman and the Honest Doubters of Boston," 203.

55. Commonwealth of Massachusetts, Committee on Charles River Dam, *Report of the Committee on Charles River Dam appointed under resolves of 1901, chapter 105, to consider the advisability and feasibility of building a dam across the Charles River at or near Craigie bridge* (Boston, 1903), 38.

56. Ibid., 39.

57. Cozort, "John Ripley Freeman and the Honest Doubters of Boston," 208, 212. Freeman then had to argue for months with Pritchett over his fees.

58. *Report . . . on Charles River Dam . . .*, 108.

59. Ibid., 109.

60. After graduating from Harvard College, Lowell completed the course in architecture at the Institute of Technology and then spent four years in Europe. He studied at the Ecole des Beaux Arts in Paris, and worked there for the famous landscape architect Edouard Andre. On his return to Boston in 1900, he opened his own office, and was appointed a lecturer in landscape architecture at MIT, a position he held through 1913. See the *National Cyclopaedia of American Biography* (New York: White & Co., 1931), 21:48. Lowell's best-known Boston building is the Museum of Fine Arts, completed in 1907.

61. Commonwealth of Massachusetts, *Second Annual Report of the Charles River Basin Commission* (Public Doc. no. 71, October 1, 1904), 16.

62. Ibid., 17–18.

63. Schodek, *Landmarks in American Civil Engineering*, 299.

64. Ibid.

65. *Basin Commission* (October 1, 1904), 17; (December 1, 1908), 24–25.

66. John F. Fitzgerald, Richard C. Cabot, John D. Adams, and George U. Crocker, "Popularizing the Basin," *New Boston* 2 (October 1911): 198; *MPC Report* (December 1910), 8–9.

67. Fitzgerald, Cabot, Adams, and Crocker, "Popularizing the Basin," 198.

68. Earl F. Gates, "The Charles River Lower Basin: Wanton Waste of Recreation Resources," *New Boston* 2 (August 1911): 162. Daniel Schodek, *Landmarks in American Civil Engineering* (Cambridge, Mass.: MIT Press, 1987), 299, concludes that the basin "was an immediate success." Gates's article was one of numerous contemporary opinions to the contrary.

69. Leonard Ware, *Helen Osborne Storrow, 1864–1944, A Memoir* (Northampton, Mass.: n.p., 1970), 19; Robert P. Bellows, "Developing the Basin: An Island for Recreation and Boating Purposes," *New Boston*, 2 (October 1911): 199; Commonwealth of Massachusetts, Joint Board on Metropolitan Improvements (Boston, 1911), 27.

Chapter Six

1. Hiram Mills to Richard Maclaurin, April 18, 1912; *Cambridge Tribune,* fiftieth anniversary edition, 1928, 8; *New York Times,* January 29, 1929, 6E.

2. Eliot had suggested courses in landscape architecture at Harvard after Shurcliff's mechanical engineering studies at MIT. Although he left the Olmsted office about 1907, Shurcliff was a consultant for forty years to both the Metropolitan Park Commission (the Metropolitan District Commission after 1919) and the Boston Park Department. In 1930 he changed his last name from Shurtleff. Arthur A. Shurcliff, "Autobiography," 46.

3. Boston Society of Architects, Committee on Municipal Improvements, *Report Made to the Boston Society of Architects by its Committee on Municipal Improvements* (Boston: Alfred Mudge, 1907); Shurcliff, "The Development of the Charles River Basin," *New Boston* 2 (November 1911): 246–248.

4. Boston Society of Architects, *Report* (1907), 13.

5. Joint Board, Final Report . . . on Metropolitan Improvements (1911), 27–28, 95–103.

6. "The Exposition in 1915," *New Boston* 1 (May 1910): 36.

7. Boston–1915, *Boston–1915, Official Catalogue of the Exhibits Shown at Its First Exposition of Boston, November 1–17, 1909* (Boston, 1909).

8. Gates, "The Charles River Lower Basin"; Arthur Coleman Comey, "The Alster Basin in Hamburg," *New Boston* 2 (October 1911): 204–208; Fitzgerald et al., "Popularizing the Basin."

9. Gates, "The Charles River Lower Basin," 165–166.

10. *MDC Annual Report* (1926), 5.

11. City of Boston, *Report of the Mayor's Committee on Proposed Memorial . . .* (Boston, 1921); *Cambridge Tribune,* fiftieth anniversary edition, 1928, 8.

12. Zaitzevsky, *Frederick Law Olmsted*, 57.

13. Bunting, *Harvard*, 124.

14. Beth Andrea Mandelbaum and Marjorie Kitchen FitzSimons, "Edward Forbes: City Planner," in *Edward Waldo Forbes, Yankee Visionary* (Cambridge, Massachusetts, 1971), 58.

15. Charles Moore, *Life and Times of Charles Follen McKim* (Boston: Houghton Mifflin, 1929), 98.

16. Morison, *Three Centuries of Harvard*, 412; Henry Lee Higginson, *Addresses by Henry Lee Higginson on the occasion of presenting the Soldiers' Field and the Harvard Union to Harvard University* (Boston: Merrymount Press, 1902), 6.

17. Bunting, *Harvard*, 116–117, 120–121.

18. Bunting, *Harvard*, 119; Townsend, *Manhood at Harvard*, 111, 190.

19. Bunting, *Harvard*, 117–119.

20. Bunting and Nylander, *Old Cambridge*, 186; Morison, *Three Centuries of Harvard*, 445; Mandelbaum and FitzSimons, "Edward Forbes," 60. The Class of 1880 Gate, now blocked off from behind by Lamont Library, was built as the focus of the DeWolfe Street axis.

21. Paul Venable Turner, *Campus: An American Planning Tradition* (Cambridge, Mass.: MIT Press, 1985), 169–177; on "The University as City Beautiful," see 169–177; *Harper's Weekly* 53 (December 18, 1909), 18.

22. *Harper's Weekly* 53 (December 18, 1909), 18; Bunting, *Harvard*, 179.

23. Mandelbaum and FitzSimons, 59, 66.

24. Ibid., 67.

25. Bunting and Nylander, *Old Cambridge*, 186–187; Mandelbaum and FitzSimons, "Edward Forbes," 64–86.

26. Morison, *Three Centuries of Harvard*, 471-472.

27. Marquand, *The Late George Apley*, 330; Morison, *Three Centuries of Harvard*, 472.

28. Douglass Shand-Tucci, "Charlesbank Harvard: Radical Innovation, Architectural Masterwork," *Harvard Magazine* 83 (November–December 1980): 28.

29. Douglass Shand-Tucci, *Harvard University: An Architectural Tour* (New York: Princeton Architectural Press, 2001), 309.

30. Samuel C. Prescott, *When MIT Was "Boston Tech," 1861–1916* (Cambridge, Mass.: Technology Press, 1954), 69, 193.

31. Ibid., 192–201.

32. Ibid., 201.

33. Ibid., 249–250; Francis Ernest Wylie, *MIT in Perspective: A Pictorial History of the Massachusetts Institute of Technology* (Boston: Little, Brown, 1975), 44.

34. Arthur Rice, Arthur A. Shurtleff, Henry J. Carlson, and Walter Kilham, report to Richard Maclaurin, October 27, 1910.

35. Ibid.

36. Andrew Carnegie to Richard C. Maclaurin, December 7, 1910: Prescott, *When MIT Was "Boston Tech,"* 250–251.

37. Prescott, *When MIT Was "Boston Tech,"* 251; George Howland Cox to Richard Maclaurin, February 4, 1911.

38. The President and Fellows of Harvard College to Richard C. Maclaurin, March 13, 1911. The final conveyance of the property took place in March 1912; Prescott, *When MIT Was "Boston Tech,"* 264.

39. Prescott, *When MIT Was "Boston Tech,"* 289.

40. Hiram Mills to Richard Maclaurin, April 18, 1912.

41. Ibid.

42. Fred Hapgood, *Up the Infinite Corridor: MIT and the Technical Imagination* (Reading, Mass.: Addison-Wesley, 1993), 53, 55.

43. Ibid., 52, 55.

44. *Cambridgeport*, 128; Prescott, *When MIT Was "Boston Tech,"* 276.

45. Wylie, *MIT in Perspective*, 45.

46. Turner, *Campus*, 196; *Cambridgeport*, 128.

47. *Boston Sunday Globe*, February 9, 1913, 4.

48. Nancy Lurie Salzman, *Buildings and Builders: An Architectural History of Boston University* (Boston: The Trustees of Boston University, 1985), 35. The Medical School moved to a newly constructed campus in the classical style on Longwood Avenue.

49. Kathleen Kilgore, *Transformations: A History of Boston University* (Boston: Boston University, 1991), 127–128.

50. Boston Transcript, March 10, 1920; cited in Warren O. Ault, *Boston University: The College of Liberal Arts, 1873–1973* (Boston: Boston University, 1973), 146; Kilgore, *Transformations*, 128–129. The chairman of the association was Charles Francis Adams, Jr., who had chaired the Metropolitan Park Commission from 1892 to 1895.

51. Kilgore, *Transformations*, 129, 142-144.

52. Salzman, *Buildings and Builders*, 10, Kilgore, *Transformations*, 148. On the Cambridge side of the river, the riverfront parkway had already been developed when Harvard and MIT laid out their new buildings. The construction of Storrow Drive in 1951 as a limited-access highway rather than a parkway, however, greatly multiplied the volume and speed of traffic on the edge of the Boston University campus.

53. Kilgore, *Transformations*, 184.

54. *Boston University* (Boston: The University, ca. 1940).

55. "Mrs. Storrow Gives Million to Make Charles River Basin Splendid Water Playground," *Boston Herald,* August 24, 1928; Ware, *Helen Osborne Storrow,* 19.

56. Commonwealth of Massachusetts, Special Commission on the charles River Basin, *Report on Proposed Improvements of the Charles River Basin* (Boston, 1929), 10; *Boston Herald*, March 21, 1929, 1, 4.

57. Ibid., 6, 7.

58. *Boston Evening Transcript*, September 29, 1923, quoted in Newton, *Design on the Land*, 333; Shurcliff, *Future Parks, Playgrounds and Parkways* (Boston: Boston Park Department, 1925), 46; Shurcliff, "Park Development and Recreation at Boston," *Parks and Recreation* 32 (October 1949), 20.

59. Ware, *Helen Osborne Storrow*, 19; *Boston Globe*, March 20, 1929, 16.

60. *New York Times*, January 29, 1929, 6E; *Boston Herald*, March 21, 1929, 1, 4; Acts of 1929, ch. 371.

61. Shurcliff, "Autobiography," 46.

62. Arthur Shurcliff, "Nov-Navigable Waters," in John Nolen, ed., *City Planning* (New York: Appleton, 1916), 221–222.

63. *Boston Herald*, September 11, 1936; Geoffrey Blodgett, "Landscape Design as Conservative Reform," in *Art of the Olmsted Landscape*, ed. Bruce Kelly, Gail Travis Guillet, and Mary Ellen W. Hern (New York: New York City Landmarks Preservation Commission and Arts Publisher, 1981), 111–122.

Chapter Seven

1. Norman T. Newton, *Design on the Land: The Development of Landscape Architecture* (Cambridge, Mass.: Belknap Press of Harvard University Press, 1971), 597; *Boston Transcript*, March 27, 1929; James Tobin, *Great Projects* (New York: Free Press, 2001), 232–233; Gary T. Schwartz, "Urban Freeways and the Interstate System," *Southern California Law Review* 49, no. 406 (1976): 422.

2. Tobin, *Great Projects*, 235; Schwartz, "Urban Freeways and the interstate System," 426–438.

3. Ibid., 444–447.

4. Alan Lupo, *Rites of Way: The Politics of Transportation in Boston and the U.S. City* (Boston: Little, Brown, 1971); Allan K. Sloan, *Citizen Participation in Transportation Planning: The Boston Experience* (Cambridge, Mass.: Ballinger, 1974); Ralph A. Gakenheimer, *Transportation Planning as Response to Controversy: The Boston Case* (Cambridge, Mass.: MIT Press, 1976).

5. David Luberoff, Alan Altshuler, and Christie Baxter, *Mega-Project: A Political History of the Central Artery/Third Harbor Tunnel Project* (Cambridge, Mass.: Kennedy School of Government, Harvard University, June 1994; revised ed. April 1996), I-2.

6. Charles Beveridge, *Frederick Law Olmsted: Designing the American Landscape* (New York: Rizzoli, 1995), 46–48; Zaitzevsky, *Frederick Law Olmsted*, 31.

7. Zaitzevsky, *Frederick Law Olmsted*, 37–38, 39, 92–94.

8. MPC Report (January 1895), 42.

9. MPC Report (January 1899), 13, 67; MPC Report (January 1898), 81, 83; MPC Report (January 1901), 69; MPC Report (January 1903), 51.

10. Bruce E. Seely, *Building the American Highway System: Engineers as Policy Makers* (Philadelphia: Temple University Press, 1987), 11–16.

11. Comonwealth of Massachusetts, *Acts of the General Court,* 1892, chapter 338; Seely, *American Highway System*, 13; Arthur W. Dean, "Massachusetts Highways," *Proceedings of the Boston Society of Civil Engineers* 16 (December 1929): 496–499. Prof. Nathaniel S. Shaler was an authority on geological and topographical surveys, and on the geology of road construction, and he established the first university courses in highway engineering.

12. Seely, *American Highway System*, 16, 22.

13. Boston Society of Architects, Committee on Municipal Improvements, *Report Made to the Boston Society of Architects by its Committee on Municipal Improvements* (Boston: A. Mudge, 1907), 7.

14. Ibid., 8.

15. Ibid.

16. Ibid., 3.

17. Ibid., 8.

18. Commonwealth of Massachusetts, Metropolitan Improvement Commission, *Public Improvements for the Metropolitan District. Report of the Commission on Metropolitan Improvements appointed under Resolves of 1907, chapter 108, to consider the subject* (Boston: Wright & Potter, 1909), 40.

19. Ibid., 3, 5–6.

20. Ibid., 188, 211.

21. Ibid., 195.

22. Ibid., 218.

23. Ibid., 218–219.

24. Ibid., 46–48, 212.

25. Ibid., 296–297. In the *Public Improvements* report Baxter claimed that the Charles Basin was by then "popularly known as 'Charlesmere,'" although there is no evidence that anyone else ever used the word.

26. Boston City Planning Board, *Report on a Thoroughfare Plan for Boston* (Boston, 1930), Robert Whitten, consultant, 22–23.

27. Ibid., 23.

28. City of Boston, Tenth Annual Report of the City Planning Board, 1923, Appendixes 4–6.

29. Boston City Planning Board, *Thoroughfare Plan*, 6–8, 101–102, 113.

30. Ibid., 102.

31. Jonathan Lewis Gifford, "An Analysis of the Federal Role in the Planning, Design and Deployment of Rural Roads, Toll Roads and Urban Freeways," Ph.D. dissertation, University of California, Berkeley, 1983, 134–140, 152–185; Warner, *Urban Wilderness*, 38–41.

32. Mark H. Rose, *Interstate: Express Highway Politics, 1939–1989* (Knoxville: University of Tennessee Press, 1990), 24; Seely, *American Highway System*, 17.

33. Maguire, Charles A. and Associates, *Master Highway Plan for the Boston Metropolitan Area* (Boston, 1948).

34. Commonwealth of Massachusetts, Special Post-war Highway Commission, *Report of the Special Post-War Highway Commission* (Boston, 1946); Commonwealth of Massachusetts, Metropolitan District Commission, *Study of the Traffic Situation in Boston by the engineers of the Metropolitan District Commission* (Boston, 1946).

35. *Boston Globe*, April 15, 1949, 17.

36. Theodore T. McCroskey, Charles A. Blessing, and J. Ross McKeever, *Surging Cities, A Secondary School Textbook in Two Parts* (Boston: Greater Boston Development Committee, 1948), 51, 195–198.

37. *Boston Globe*, April 15, 1949, 1, 17.

38. Letter to the House of Representatives from the Storrow Memorial Embankment Protective Association, April 18, 1949; Donald C. Starr, interview by author, May 23, 1984.

39. Maguire, *Master Highway Plan,* 20; Storrow Memorial Embankment Protective Association to the House of Representatives, April 18, 1949; Starr interview.

40. Undated newspaper article, "Charles River Basin" file, Frances Loeb Library, Harvard University Graduate School of Design.

41. *Boston Globe*, April 13, 1949, 1, 7.

42. *Boston Globe,* April 13, 1949, 1; April 29, 1949, 1.

43. Karen Madsen, ed., *An Interview with Sidney N. Shurcliff on Arthur A. Shurcliff, Conducted by Melanie L. Simo, Introduced by Charles W. Eliot II, 1980* (Watertown, Mass.: Hubbard Educational Trust, 1992), 6.

44. On the West End, see Herbert J. Gans, *Urban Villagers: Group and Class in the Life of Italian-Americans*, updated and expanded edition (New York: Free Press, 1982); Sean M. Fisher and Carolyn Hughes, eds., *The Last Tenement: Confronting Community and Urban Renewal in Boston's West End*, with a foreword by Herbert J. Gans (Boston: Bostonian Society, 1992).

45. Thomas H. O'Connor, *Building a New Boston: Politics and Urban Renewal, 1950 to 1970* (Boston: Northeastern University Press, 1993), 80–85.

46. City of Cambridge, *Mid-Century Cambridge, Annual Report, 1950*, 45.

47. *Boston Globe*, December 29, 1962, 1, 2.

48. *Boston Globe*, September 6, 1963, 1, 4; City of Boston, [ital] *Boston Transportation Fact Book and Neighborhood Profiles* (May 2002), 7. In 1977 the average weekday traffic volume on Storrow Drive was 91,000 cars, compared with 77,000 cars on the turnpike; ten years later traffic on Storrow Drive had increased to 103,000 cars per day, and the turnpike traffic had jumped to 109,000 cars per day. By 1999 traffic on Storrow Drive had leveled off at 106,000 cars per day, while turnpike traffic had increased to 121,000 cars per day.

49. *Boston Globe*, April 18, 1965, 24A. *Boston Globe*, July 18, 1967. Bunting's series of essays was drawn from his *Houses of Boston's Back Bay* (1965). As noted above, state senator and former MDC associate commissioner Philip Bowker was among the active proponents of the construction of Storrow Drive in 1949.

50. *MPC Report* (1897), 43.

51. *MPC Report* (1903), 52; (1908), 59; (1910), 42; (1915), 57–58; *Christian Science Monitor*, November 11, 1957.

52. Senate Document no. 100, 1937; *MDC Report* (1937), ff. 20.

53. Bernard DeVoto, "The Easy Chair: Hell's Half Acre, Mass.," *Harper's* 211:1264 (September 1955), 11, 13. DeVoto does not indicate in the essay that one of the boys was his son Mark.

54. Ibid., 13.

55. *Harvard Crimson,* October 24, December 10, 1957; Mark DeVoto, interview by author, July 11, 2002. Bernard DeVoto died in November 1955, two months after his *Harper's* essay was published.

56. "Hell's Half Acre" file, MDC Secretary's Office.

57. *Cambridge Chronicle-Sun*, n.d.; in MDC Archives.

58. *Boston Globe*, Nov. 17, 1963, 72.

59. *Time,* February 12, 1964, 21.

60. *New York Times*, November 15, 1964.

61. John Moot, interview by author, Cambridge, Mass., September 5, 2001; John Sears, interview by author, Boston, August 5, 2002.

62. Isabella Halsted, undated letter from "People for Riverbend Park."

63. Lynch, *Image of the City*, 2, 15.

64. Ibid., 17, 20.

65. Ibid., 23.

66. Kevin Lynch, Donald Appleyard, and John R. Myer, *The View from the Road* (Cambridge, Mass.: MIT Press, 1964), 2, 3.

67. Ibid., 45.

68. Luberoff, *Mega-Project* (1996), I-6–I-9.

69. Ibid., I-9–I-10; John G. Wofford, letter to author, August 10, 2002.

70. Lupo, *Rites of Way*, 94, 106, 107.

71. *Boston Globe*, May 18, 1960; *Boston Evening Globe*, August 31, 1964, 1, 9; *Boston Herald*, August 16, 1964; *Boston Globe*, April 25, 1967, 52; Luberoff, *Mega-Project* (1994), 211–213.

72. Lupo, *Rites of Way*, 107, 271.

73. Sears interview.

74. *Citizens to Preserve Overton Park. Inc., v. Volpe,* 401 U.S. 402, 412–413.

75. *Boston Globe*, March 10, 1970; Title 49, United States Code, Section 1653(f), quoted in [Federal Highway Administration], "Section 4(f) Policy Paper," September 24, 1987, 1; Sloan, *Citizen Participation in Transportation Planning,* 107–112.

76. *Boston Globe*, March 10, 1970; *Boston Globe*, May 17, 1970, 64.; *Boston Globe*, August 6, 1970; *Boston Globe*, August 22, 1971; Luberoff, *Mega-Project* (1994), 5–6.

77. Lupo, *Rites of Way*, 271.

78. Ibid., 106–110.

79. *Boston Globe*, November 26, 1987, 28.

80. Ibid.; Lupo, *Rites of Way*, 96–97.

Chapter Eight

1. Lynch, *Image of the City*, 62; Sam Bass Warner, Jr., "Open Spaces," review of *FLO: A Biography of Frederic Law Olmsted,* by Laura Wood Roper, *New Republic,* March 23, 1974, 30.

2. Lynch, *Image of the City,* 20; Max Hall, "The Lost Half Mile on the Charles," *Boston Globe*, May 25, 1986, 65.

3. Boston Society of Architects, Committee on Civic Design "The Architects' Plan for Boston," (1961?); Robert S. Sturgis, "The Architects' Plan for Boston," *American Institute of Architects Journal* 37:1 (January 1962), 34-39; Robert S. Sturgis, "Urban Planning: Changing Concepts," in *Architectural Education and Boston: Centennial Publication of the Boston Architectural Center, 1889–1989,* ed. Margaret Henderson Floyd (Boston: The Center, 1989), 111–118.

4. O'Connor, *Building a New Boston,* 122–140.

5. [Eliot], *Charles Eliot,* 592.

6. Peter Stott, *A Guide to the Industrial Archeology of Boston Proper* (Cambridge, Mass.: MIT Press, 1984), 52–53; L. Peter Cornwall, "North Station—A Pictorial Essay," *B&M Bulletin* 10, no. 2 (Winter 1980–1981): 5–16.

7. *Somerville Journal,* August 30, 1929; September 25, 1931; May 19, 1994. Although Barrell's country estate and its hilltop site were leveled, "Cobble Hill" persists as the name of a railroad switching station on the remains of the hill.

8. O'Connor, *Building a New Boston,* 125–126.

9. Ibid., 191.

10. Boston Redevelopment Authority, *1965/1975 General Plan for the City of Boston and the Regional Core* (Boston, 1965?), 74–75.

11. Ibid.

12. Hall, *The Charles,* 66–67. An incomplete list of previous studies is given in Department of the Army, New England Division, Corps of Engineers, *Water Resources Development, Interim Report on Charles Rover for Flood Control and Navigation, Lower Charles River, Massachusetts* (Waltham, Mass., May 1968), 3–4. Additional studies completed by various consultants between 1956 and 1973 are filed at the MDC Archives.

13. James Ayres, *The Charles River: Its Problems and Possible Solutions* (Boston: Boston Globe, 1964); League of Women Voters, *Charles River Valley: A Guide for Citizens Concerned About Its Future* (n.p., 1968). At least two more editions were published during the next three years.

14. Ibid.

15. Hall, *The Charles,* 67, 74–75. In a remarkable departure from the typical civil engineering solutions to flood control, the Corps of Engineers study also recommended "Natural Valley Storage" along the upper Charles in Medfield and Millis. The purchase of 3,200 acres of existing wetlands (as well as easements on several thousand additional acres) obviated the need to construct artificial flood storage areas.

16. Commonwealth of Massachusetts, *Acts of the General Court,* 1962, chapter 550. The jurisdction established by these statutes would be critical in the lawsuits filed in 1990 over the Charles River Crossing element of the proposed Central Artery.

17. Boston Redevelopment Authority, *Boston's Scenic Corridor: The Parkland of the Muddy River and the Charles River Basin* (Boston, 1969), Roy

Mann, Landscape Architect. Incomplete copy, Government Documents, Boston Public Library.

18. Commonwealth of Massachusetts, Metropolitan Area Planning Council, Metropolitan District Commission, and Department of Natural Resources, *Open Space and Recreation Program for Metropolitan Boston*, vol. 1 (Boston: April 1969), 5.

19. Commonwealth of Massachusetts, *Open Space and Recreation Program for Metropolitan Boston*, vol. 3, *The Mystic, Charles and Neponset Rivers* (Boston: April 1969), 5.

20. Ibid.

21. By contrast, the MDC regional master plan of 1956, although it recommended the acquisition of large tracts in the suburbs, did not describe the possibility of linking the Charles with Charlestown, the North End, and the Harbor. Commonwealth of Massachusetts, Metropolitan District Commission, *Study and Recommended Program of Development of Park and Reservation and Recreational Facilities of the Metropolitan Parks District*, Edwards, Kelcey and Beck, consultants (Boston, 1956).

22. *Open Space and recreation Program,* 3:5, 36.

23. Hall, *The Charles*, 69–70. The permanent opening of the locks at the old dam to stabilize the water level in the New Basin was delayed until the ten-story-deep Prison Point Pumping Station was completed in February 1981.

24. Kennedy, *Planning the City,* 207. Moshe Safdie and Associates, *A Development Plan for the North Station District* ([Boston], [1980]).

25. Ibid.

26. Ibid.

27. Ibid.

28. Ibid.

29. Minutes of the Metropolitan District Commission, June 12, 1980.

30. Louis Berger and Associates, *North Area Central Artery: Final Report* (Boston, July 1982), 338.

31. William L. Lahey, "Waterfront Development and the Public Trust Doctrine," *Massachusetts Law Review* 55 (1985): 55–57.

32. Ibid., 61–66. This limited jurisdiction granted after-the-fact approval to all post-1863 construction landward of the roads and parkways along the Charles. Licenses granted for specific purposes like the railroad bridges, trestles, and switching yards extending from North Station, applied only to the original use; new structures on such filled land would be subject to the new regulations.

33. Commonwealth of Massachusetts, Department of Environmental Protection and Massachusetts Coastal Zone Management, *Chapter 91: An Introduction to the Massachusetts Public Waterfront Act and Its Regulations* (n.p., n.d.), 4–15; see also Lahey, "Waterfront Development and the Public Trust Doctrine," 55.

34. Roy Mann, *Rivers in the City* (New York: Praeger, 1973).

35. Roy Mann, letter to the editor, *Boston Globe*, April 23, 1984; Commonwealth of Massachusetts, Department of Environmental Protection, Chapter 91 Waterways License no. 1952, April 18, 1989.

36. Hall, "The Lost Half Mile," 86.

37. Boston Redevelopment Authority, *Central Artery Corridor: Central Area Planning Study* (Boston: October 1977), 7. In fact, when the Charles River Crossing was finally designed in the early 1990s, the earlier design for the north area ramps had to be substantially redesigned, and an already constructed ramp connection to City Square had to be demolished in 1997.

38. Commonwealth of Massachusetts, Department of Environmental Protection, Chapter 91 Waterways License no. 3302, May 18, 1993.

39. Maycock, *East Cambridge,* 43–45, 53–54.

40. Ibid., 53–54; City of Cambridge, Community Development Department, *East Cambridge Riverfront Plan* (Cambridge, Mass., May 1978).

41. City of Cambridge, Community Development Department, *North Point Revitalization Plan: Summary of Goals and Objectives* (October 5, 1987).

42. Commonwealth of Massachusetts, Department of Environmental Protection, Chapter 91 Waterways License no. 3156, December 30, 1992.

43. Julia J. Broderick, cited in *Beauty for America: Proceedings of the White House Conference on Natural Beauty* (Washington, D.C.: U.S. Government Printing Office, 1965), 531; Albert Fein, *A Study of the Profession of Landscape Architecture: Technical Report* (McLean, Va.: American Society of Landscape Architects Foundation, 1972); Albert Fein, "A Merger of the Professions of Planning and Landscape Architecture," *New York Planning Review* 15 (Summer 1973): A 30–32.

44. Steven R. Krog, "The Language of Modern," *Landscape Architecture* 75:2 (1985), 56; Krog, "Whither the Garden?" in *Denatured Visions: Landscape and Culture in the Twentieth Century*, ed. Stuart Wrede and William Howard (New York: Museum of Modern Art, 1991), 94; John Dixon Hunt, "The Dialogue of Modern Landscape Architecture with its Past," in *Modern Landscape Architecture: A Critical Review*, ed. Marc Treib (Cambridge, Mass.: MIT Press, 1993), 134.

45. Wrede and Adams, *Denatured Visions,* 4; Hunt, 136.

46. Warner, "Open Space," 30; Geoffrey Blodgett, "Landscape Design as Conservative Reform," 122. For contrasting views of the Olmsted legacy, see Albert Fein, "The Olmsted Renaissance: A Search for National Purpose," in *Art of the Olmsted Landscape,* ed. Bruce Kelly, Gail Travis Guillet, and Nary Ellen W. Hern; Tony Hiss, *The Experience of Place* (New York: Knopf, 1990), 42–48.

47. Massachusetts Department of Natural Resources, Office of Planning, *A Proposal for an Urban State Park in Lowell, Massachusetts,* August 1974, 2. The origin of the Massachusetts heritage state parks program is discussed in Hiss, *The Experience of Place,* 208–210; while the later efforts of state planners are described, there is no mention of the early discussions among Lowell residents. For an extended review of public history in urban settings, see Dolores Hayden, *The Power of Place: Urban Landscapes as Public History* (Cambridge, Mass.: MIT Press, 1995), 4–78.

48. *Proposal for . . . Lowell* (1974), 5.

49. Hiss, *The Experience of Place,* 209–210.

50. Stott, *A Guide to the Industrial Archeology of Boston Proper,* 54–55.

51. Luberoff, *Mega-Project* (1996), II-7–II-8.

52. Christopher M. Greene, "Reviving the Olmsted Vision," in *First Interim Report, Olmsted Historic Landscape preservation Program* (Boston, April 1990), 6–7; McPeck et al., *Olmsted in Massachusetts,* i. The National Association for Olmsted Parks was founded a year earlier, in 1980.

53. Ibid., 9–28.

54. Ervin H. Zube, *Landscape Assessment: Values, Perceptions, and Resources* (Stroudsburg, Penn.: Dowden, Hutchinson, and Ross, 1975); Roger Ulrich, "View through a Window May Influence Recovery from Surgery," *Science* 224:420–421.

55. Edward O. Wilson, *Biophilia* (Cambridge, Mass.: Harvard University Press, 1984), 109–110, 1. Edward O. Wilson, "Biophilia and the Conservation Ethic," in *The Biophilia Hypothesis*, ed. Stephen R. Kellert and Edward O. Wilson (Washington, D.C.: Island Press, 1993), 31–41. See also the extensive bibliography in the same volume in Roger Ulrich, "Biophila, Biophobia, and Natural Landscapes," 127–137.

56. Boston Redevelopment Authority, *Boston Urban Wilds: A Natural Area Conservation Program* (Boston, 1976).

57. Moore-Heder Architects et al., "The New Charles River Basin: Proposal," 1988.

58. Carr, Lynch Associates, Inc., "Proposal for the New Charles River Basin," 1988, 1–15. To develop a rich and diverse landscape, Carr, Lynch proposed to collaborate with Wolfgang Oehme and James van Sweden. On the twenty-year collaboration of Oehme van Sweden, see "Wolfgang Oehme and James van Sweden: New World Landscapes," *Process Architecture* 130 (1996).

Chapter Nine

1. Mumford, *The City in History* (1961), plate 47; Luberoff, *Mega-Project* (1996), I-14.

2. The most comprehensive single source on the Central Artery project is David Luberoff, Alan Altshuler, and Christie Baxter, *Mega-Project: A Political History of the Central Artery / Third Harbor Tunnel Project* (Cambridge, Mass.: Kennedy School of Government, Harvard University, June 1994; revised ed. April 1996). A more personal point of view is found in Steve Kaiser, "A Grass-Roots Perspective on the Battle of Scheme Z," (September 1993, photocopy); see also http://libraries.mit.edu/rotch/artery/kaiser.htm

3. Luberoff, *Mega-Project* (1996), I-6–I-11; Wofford, August 10, 2002.

4. Wofford, August 10, 2002.

5. Luberoff, *Mega-Project* (1996), I-11, I-16I-17; Wofford, August 10, 2002.

6. Luberoff, *Mega-Project* (1996), I-10; Wofford, August 10, 2002.

7. Luberoff, *Mega-Project* (1996), I-12–I-13.

8. *Boston Globe,* June 13, 1983, 17. Luberoff, *Mega-Project* (1996), I-13.

9. Ibid., I-13–I-14.

10. William Kramer, "Transportation Policy in Massachusetts (C)," Kennedy School of Government, 1975, 5.; Luberoff, *Mega-Project* (1994), 22.

11. Luberoff, *Mega-Project* (1996), I-13–I-14; Wofford, August 10, 2002.

12. Ibid., I-19–I-21; Boston Transportation Planning Review, Central Artery Summary Report, 1972; Boston Redevelopment Authority, Central Artery Depression Preliminary Feasibility Study (Boston, 1974), cited in Luberoff, *Mega-Project* (1996), I-25.

13. Luberoff, *Mega-Project* (1994), 19; Interview, 1991; quoted in Luberoff, *Mega-Project* (1994), 29.

14. Luberoff, *Mega-Project* (1996), I-23–I-27; Boston Redevelopment Authority, Central Artery Corridor: Central Area Planning Study (Boston, Mass.: October 1977), 7. In 1993, temporary ramps were constructed and one newly built ramp was abandoned, because the revised design of the river crossing was no longer compatible with the original north area plans; the hope that the projects could be designed independ-

ently proved impossible to carry out. The state auditor issued a report criticizing the ramp demolition as an example of unnecessary waste.

15. Federal Highway Administration memorandum, "The Development of Logical Project Termini," November 5, 1993.

16. *Boston Herald,* January 2, 1977.

17. Luberoff, *Mega-Project* (1996), I-31–I-33; Wofford, August 10, 2002.

18. Ibid., I-33–I-34.

19. *Boston Globe,* June 1, 1982; February 21, 1982.

20. *Boston Globe,* August 11, 1982, 15.

21. Luberoff, *Mega-Project* (1996), II-3–II-4.

22. Ibid., I-35.

23. Ibid., II-12.

24. Ibid., II-7–II-9.

25. *Boston Globe,* March 9, June 13, July 7, 1983, 1; Luberoff, *Mega-Project* (1996), II-1. In the language of the state's environmental review requirements, the artery/tunnel was not found to be a "major and complcated" project, since it was only replacing an existing road. Hence no citizens' advisory committee was required.

26. The federal review requires an Environmental Impact Statement (EIS); the state review process requires an Environmental Impact Report (EIR). Often, although not always, a single document is submitted as an Environmental Impact Statement/Report (EIS/R).

27. *Boston Herald,* August 24, 1983.

28. Commonwealth of Massachusetts, Executive Office of Environmental Affairs, "Certificate of the Secretary of Environmental Affairs on the Supplemental Draft Environmental Impact Report, Project Name: Third Harbor Tunnel and Depressed Central Artery," August 29, 1983.

29. *Boston Herald,* December 22, 1983.

30. Luberoff, *Mega-Project* (1996), II-22–II-23.

31. Ibid, II-2–II-23,

32. Ibid., III-1–III-38.

33. Berger, *North Area Central Artery.* 338, 347.

34. *Boston Globe,* November 18, 1984.

35. Luberoff, *Mega-Project* (1994), 87.

36. Luberoff, *Mega-Project* (1996), III-19; [Federal Highway Administration], "Section 4(f) Policy Paper," September 24, 1987. According to Luberoff, "the state argued that the 4(f) obstacles cited by FHWA letter were trivial because the sites officially classified as parkland were not actual parks"; Luberoff does not, however, point out that designated parks are also protected under Section 4(f).

37. Ibid., III-24–III-26. The state could use Interstate reconstruction funds for the artery, although that would cut into highway maintenance projects in other parts of the state.

38. Ibid., III-33; *Washington Post,* March 28, 1987.

39. Luberoff, *Mega-Project* (1996), III-30–III-38.

40. Gillette, East Boston objections.

Chapter Ten

1. Thomas P. Hughes, *Rescuing Prometheus* (New York: Pantheon, 1998), 212–214.

2. Kaiser, "Battle of Scheme Z," 16.

3. Luberoff, *Mega-Project* (1994), 155; Luberoff, *Mega-Project* (1996), IV-16–IV-18.

4. *Boston Globe,* September 14, 1989.

5. Commonwealth of Massachusetts, Executive Office of Environmental Affairs, "Certificate of the Secretary of Environmental Affairs on the Final Supplemental Environmental Impact Report, project name; Central Artery/THT," January 2, 1991.

6. Federal Highway Administration and Massachusetts Department of Public Works, *Final Environmental Impact Statement and Final Section 4(f) Evaluation, Third Harbor Tunnel, Interstate 90/Central Artery, Interstate 93* (August 1985), 11–12.

7. Herbert Einstein, comments, "Scheme Z On-line Archive," http://libraries.mit.edu/rotch/artery/forum4.html; Berger, *North Area Central Artery,* 35–51.

8. Commonwealth of Massachusetts, Department of Public Works, *Final Supplemental Environmental Impact Report* (November 1990), IIB 1–6.

9. Ibid., IV 5.2–30.

10. Sloan, *Citizen Participation in Transportation Planning,* 107–112, reviews in detail the Section 4(f) issues for the proposed Interstate 95 routes through the Lynn Woods, the Saugus Marshes, and Fowl Meadow.

11. Luberoff, *Mega-Project* (1996), IV-24.

12. Kaiser, "Battle of Scheme Z," 22.

13. Luberoff, *Mega-Project* (1996), IV-24.

14. *Boston Globe,* December 11, 1987, 34.

15. Rebecca G. Barnes, "Comments," http://libraries.mit.edu/rotch/artery/forum4.html; models were later built of Schemes 5A and T, and photographs of the models were included in the 1990 environmental impact reports.

16. Luberoff, *Mega-Project* (1994), 217; *Boston Globe,* September 14, 1989, 1, 14.

17. Luberoff, *Mega-Project* (1996), IV-34; *Boston Globe,* December 13, 1990, 81.

18. Stephen Coyle, interview, October 1991; quoted in Luberoff, *Mega-Project* (1996), IV-25; *Boston Globe,* January 19, 1992, 68.

19. Commonwealth of Massachusetts, Acts of the General Court, 1909, Chapter 524; 1962, Chapter 550.

20. M. Ilyas Bhatti, MDC Commissioner, to William V. Twomey, CA/T Project Director, May 1, 1989.

21. Luberoff, *Mega-Project* (1994), 218.

22. [Federal Highway Administration], "Section 4(f) Policy Paper," September 24, 1987. The legislation has been revised several times, but the required review is still known as Section 4(f) after the section in the original statute.

23. Ibid., 3–6.

24. Ibid., 6, 16, 20.

25. Kaiser, "Battle of Scheme Z," 16–17.

26. Stephen H. Kaiser to Frederick Salvucci, December 12, 1989; April 2, 1990.

27. *Cambridge Tab,* October 9, 1990, 3.

28. *Boston Globe,* January 31, 1990, 17, 18.

29. *Boston Globe,* April 8, 1990, 25, 37.

30. *Boston Globe,* June 24, 1990, B29, B33.

31. Ibid., B29, B32.

32. Ibid.

33. Stephen H. Burrington to M. Ilyas Bhatti, July 13, 1990 (emphasis in the original).

34. Elizabeth S. Merritt to John DeVillars and Alexander Almeida, July 20, 1990; in *Final Supplemental Environmental Impact Report,* November 1990, IV 5.5–355.

35. David A. Doheny to John DeVillars and Alexander Almeida, September 21, 1990, in *Final Supplemental Environmental Impact Report,* November 1990, IV 5.5–351–2. Given the record of the National Trust in litigating transportation cases, it is puzzling that Luberoff does not mention the direct involvement of the trust's legal staff in the 1990 discussions of Scheme Z.

36. *Boston Globe,* August 26, 1990, 1, 78, 79.

37. *Boston Globe,* August 27, 1990, 13, 15.

38. For a discussion of CLF's transit issues, see Luberoff, *Mega-Project*

(1996), chapter 4, 16–18, 37–38, 45–46; chapter 5, 25–36.

39. Stephen H. Burrington to Douglas McGarrah, November 1, 1990.

40. M. Ilyas Bhatti to Anthony Fusco, November 9, 1990, in Commonwealth of Massachusetts, Department of Public Works, *Central Artery (I-93)/Tunnel (I-90) Project, Final Supplemental Environmental Impact Statement* (January 1991), Appendix 3.

41. Ibid.

42. Berger, *North Area Central Artery,* 338.

43. David A. Doheny to John DeVillars and Alexander Almeida, December 23, 1990, 1.

44. Stephen H. Burrington to Frederick Salvucci, December 11, 1989, 2; Herbert Einstein.

45. Costas, "The Power Broker," *Boston Business Journal* (June/July 1990), 22.

46. Ibid., 72.

47. Kaiser, "Battle of Scheme Z," 16–17.

48. *Final Supplemental Environmental Impact Report* (November 1990), IV 5.2-25–5.2-33.

49. *Boston Globe,* September 12, 1990.

50. *Boston Globe,* December 7, 1990, 29, 33.

51. Luberoff, *Mega-Project* (1996), IV-32–IV-33.

52. K. Dun Gifford, "The Artery Project: Unnecessary Surgery?" *Boston Globe,* October 21, 1990, A21, A24.

53. *Boston Globe,* August 16, 1988, 17, 18.

54. D. C. Denison, "The 27-Acre Opportunity," *Boston Globe Magazine,* October 14, 1990, 18–21, 31–43.

55. Ibid., 36, 37.

56. Ibid., 39.

57. Ibid., 42.

58. Ibid., 43.

59. Luberoff, *Mega-Project* (1996), IV-42–IV-43; Kaiser, "Battle of Scheme Z," 39.

60. *Boston Globe,* December 2, 1990, 37, 44, 45. A statement not in the original draft was added, which excused the project's failure to file a "Notice of Project Change," even though Scheme Z was "a massive change" from the interchange in the 1985 report. Had the artery complied with the requirement, said the *Globe,* Scheme Z would have been subjected "to the public debate it is now undergoing months or years sooner. "

61. *Boston Globe,* December 5, 1990, 1, 28.

62. *Boston Globe,* December 7, 1990, 29, 33.

63. *Boston Globe,* December 9, 1990, A18.

64. *Boston Globe,* December 15, 1990, 26; January 7, 1991, 14.

65. *Boston Globe,* December 13, 1990, 81.

66. Ibid.

67. Ibid.

68. *Boston Globe,* December 20, 1990; Luberoff, *Mega-Project* (1996), IV-43.

69. Luberoff, *Mega-Project* (1996), V-1–V-2.

70. "Certificate of the Secretary of Environmental Affairs on the Final Supplemental Environmental Impact Report, Project Name: Central Artery/THT," January 2, 1991, in Commonwealth of Massachusetts, Department of Public Works, Central Artery (I-93)/Tunnel (I-90) Project, Final Supplemental Environmental Impact Statement (Boston, January 1991), Appendix 1, 7.

71. Wofford, letters. For more than a decade, artery staff insisted that FHWA would not allow any construction beyond the Gilmore Bridge. Before the end of the bridge committee meetings a year later, design changes in the river crossing required the breaking of that boundary. Members of the committee raised the possibility of moving the concrete plant a few hundred yards north, into the old, half-empty rail yards of the Boston & Maine, so that the loop ramps would be further away from the riverbank. That move was said to be too costly and outside the project limits. Several years later, when the final design of the Leverett Circle bridge was completed, the connecting ramp was extended all the way to Sullivan Square.

72. John G. Wofford, interview with author, Boston, August 12, 2002.

73. *Boston Globe,* April 4, 1991, 21.

74. *Boston Globe,* February 2, 1991, 25, 28.

75. *Boston Globe,* April 14, 1991, A27, A28.

76. Ibid.

77. *Boston Globe,* August 6, 2001, B1.

78. *Boston Globe,* April 29, 1991, 30, 33.

79. Ibid.

80. Bridge Design Review Committee, "Christian Menn, Preliminary Concepts," April-May 1991.

81. Bridge Design Review Committee minutes, May 17, 1991.

82. Ibid., June 21, 1991.

83. Luberoff, *Mega-Project* (1996), V-15–V-16; *Boston Globe,* June 22, 1991, 26.

84. *Boston Globe,* March 14, 1992, 31.

85. *Boston Globe,* March 13, March 18, 1992; *Boston Globe,* May 22, 1992, 22.

86. Commonwealth of Massachusetts, Massachusetts Highway Department, "Notice of Project Change: Area North of Causeway Street" (Boston, September 1992).

87. Luberoff, *Mega-Project* (1996), V-20–V-24. In the final weeks before it was submitted for review in 1990, Scheme Z had been reduced from eighteen to sixteen lanes by dropping the two-lane northbound on-ramp cantilevered from the bridge towers on the downstream side. The decision to drop the on-ramp was widely criticized at the time (see above), and the design approved in 1994 restored the two cantilevered lanes.

88. Ibid.

89. Ibid.

90. Ibid., V-23.

91. Ibid.; Federal Highway Administration and Massachusetts Department of Public Works, *Charles River Crossing, Central Artery/Tunnel Project, Boston, Massachusetts, Final Environmental Impact Statement/Report* (December 1993).

92. New Charles River Basin Citizens Advisory Committee minutes, February 1992.

93. The funding had been promised "immediately" during the intensive negotiations over Section 4(f) with the park agency more than fifteen months before. Some observers of the artery believed that the delay was deliberate, since it put off the publication of the park plan (which in turn might have required a revised 4(f) determination) until after a river crossing design had been approved.

94. On the citizen participation process of the Boston Transportation Planning Review, see Sloan, *Citizen Participation in Transportation Planning,* 35–36, 41–42.

95. Commonwealth of Massachusetts, Metropolitan District Commission, *New Charles River Basin Master Plan,* Appendix, A–6, A–7.

96. Ibid. There was no discussion at the time of the enormous structure then being planned by the MBTA to replace the old Boston & Maine roundhouse just beyond North Point.

97. Ibid.

98. Commonwealth of Massachusetts, Metropolitan District Commission, *New Charles River Basin Master Plan,* 23; New Charles River Basin Master Plan Appendix, A–16.

99. *New Charles River Basin Master Plan,* 24.

100. Otile McManus, "Wrestling with an Octopus," *Boston Globe Magazine,* March 2, 1986, 56.

101. *New Charles River Bason Master Plan* 24, 35–46.

102. "Reclamation Artists at North Point, April 30–May 28, 1994"; *Boston Globe,* May 11, 1994; *New Basin Master Plan,* Appendix, A-41 (July 23, 1992); John Chandler, "The Wasteland Reclaimed," *Art New England* (February/March 1993), 18–19.

103. *New Basin Master Plan,* Appendix A, 40–41.

104. Ibid., 105–108.

105. Author's notes.

106. U.S. District Court, District of Massachusetts, *Daniel E. Geer, Jr., et al. v. Federal Highway Administration et al.,* "Memorandum and Order," August 4, 1997.

Chapter Eleven

1. Robert Fleming Gourlay, *Plans for the improvement of Edinburgh.—No. I.* Edinburgh, [1829], British Library; H. G. Wells, "The Future in America: A Search after Realities," *Harper's Weekly* 50 (1906): 1018.

2. Wells, "Future in America" (1906), 1018.

3. Thomas Bender, "Architecture and the Journalism of Ideas," *Design Book Review* 15 (1988): 47.

4. Laura Wood Roper, *FLO: A Biography of Frederick Law Olmsted* (Baltimore: Johns Hopkins University Press, 1973), 403.

5. *Charles Eliot,* 207.

6. Olmsted, "Public Parks," quoted in Greene, 9.

7. *Parks for the People,* 1876, 2.

8. Charles River Dam, *Evidences* (1903), 135-136.

9. Richard Bushman, "The Genteel Republic," *Wilson Quarterly* 22 (Autumn 1996): 22.

10. Rosenzweig and Blackmar, *The Park and the People,* 18.

11. Commonwealth of Massachusetts, Metropolitan District Commission, *New Charles River Basin Master Plan,* 9–11; *New Charles River Basin Master Plan Appendix,* A12–A19.

12. Commonwealth of Massachusetts, Metropolitan District Commission, *Master Plan for the Charles River Basin: The Second Century* (Boston, 2002), 7–12.

13. Schuyler, *New Urban Landscape,* 180–195.

14. Quoted in Thomas Bender, "The Cultures of Intellectual Life: The City and the Professions," in *Intellect and Public Life: Essays on the Social History of Academic Intellectuals in the United States* (Baltimore: Johns Hopkins University Press, 1993), 9.

15. *The Boston Contest of 1944: Prize Winning Programs* (Boston: Boston University Press, 1945), 7–8.

16. Adam Gopnik, "Olmsted's Trip," *New Yorker* (March 31, 1997), 98, 100.

Chapter Twelve

1. "Report of Olmsted Brothers," *Boston Parks Department Annual Report,* 1911, 48–59.

2. Emmet, *Cambridge,* 5; *Cambridgeport,* 15.

3. City of Cambridge, Park Department, *Annual Report* (1899), 8.

4. MDC Annual Report (1923), 3.

5. City of Cambridge, *Report of the Park Commissioners* (1933), 16.

6. MPC Annual Report (1915), 34; 1917, 8.

7. Quoted in Roger Thompson, *Divided We Stand: Watertown, Massachusetts, 1630–1680* (Amherst: University of Massachusetts Press, 2001), 144.

8. Ibid., 51.

9. Ibid., 93.

10. Quoted in G. Frederick Robinson and Ruth Robinson Wheeler, *Great Little Watertown: A Tercentenary History* (Watertown: Watertown Historical Society, 1930), 38.

Glossary and Gazetteer

4(f) See **Section 4(f)**.

Anderson Memorial Bridge Donated in honor of Nicholas Longworth Anderson by his son Larz, this structure is most frequently called by the son's name. The bridge required the approval of the War Department to be built without a draw. It was built on the site of the Great Bridge (1662), which was replaced by another wooden structure in 1862.

Arsenal Street Bridge One of three bridges included in a competition held by the MDC in 1923, the bridge was designed by Robert D. Andrews and completed in 1925. It replaced an earlier bridge built by the proprieters of the West Boston Bridge in 1824.

Artery Project See **Central Artery/Tunnel Project**.

Back Bay Originally a body of water extending from the foot of the Common to **Sewell's Point** in Brookline (now Kenmore Square). The bay was dammed along the line of present-day Beacon Street in 1821 to provide power for tide mills. The largest filling project—the eastern portion of the bay—began in 1855 and was largely complete by 1880. The Back Bay became a neighborhood of elegant rowhouses.

Back Bay Fens A flood control project designed by Frederick Law Olmsted to give the appearance of a salt marsh landscape, largely completed by 1890.

Barrell Mansion Designed by Charles Bulfinch for Joseph Barrell on Cobble Hill (also called Pleasant Hill), the estate was acquired by the trustees of the Massachusetts General Hospital in 1816 and expanded for use as the McLean Asylum. The property was bought in 1895 by the Boston & Maine Railroad, which demolished the buildings and leveled the site, and the hospital moved to Belmont Hill.

Barrell's Creek See **Miller's River**.

Basin See **Boston Basin, Charles River, Charles River Basin**.

Boston Basin The low-lying area inside the ring of hills that extend in an arc around the city. The most visible boundaries of the Boston Basin are the Middlesex Fells on the north, Prospect Hill in Waltham and Belmont Hill on the west, and the Blue Hills south of the city.

Boston Embankment See **Boston Esplanade**.

Boston Esplanade The formal boundaries of the Esplanade in Boston are Charles Circle and the Boston University Bridge. The first fill in this area was completed in 1910 and was called the Boston Embankment. To honor her husband James, who had led the campaign to complete the first **Charles River Dam** in 1901–1903, Helen Storrow donated one million dollars to the state in 1929. The Boston Embankment was widened, the Storrow Lagoon was created, and the expanded park was dedicated as the James J. Storrow Memorial Embankment in 1936. By then it was widely known simply as the Esplanade. Additional fill was added to the park and the lagoon was extended in 1949–1951 as part of the construction of James J. Storrow Memorial Drive (Storrow Drive), a highway that Helen Storrow had opposed in 1929.

Boston University Bridge Erected in 1928 as a replacement for the 1850 Essex Street Bridge (sometimes called the Brookline Street Bridge), the Cottage Farm Bridge was renamed for Boston University in 1949.

Bridge Design Review Committee (BDRC) Mandated by the state when the **Charles River Crossing** of the Central Artery project was approved in 1990, the committee considered alternatives to Scheme Z and met from February 1991 to November 1992. The committee hired Dr. Christian Menn of Switzerland as a consultant, and Menn later designed the cable-stayed bridge built across the Charles River.

Broad Canal As part of the development of Cambridgeport, Broad Canal was built in 1806 and extended almost to today's Central Square. It was reduced to its present length between 1966 and 1968 as part of the Kendall Square urban renewal project.

Brookline Street Bridge See **Boston University Bridge**.

Bulfinch Triangle See **North Cove, Mill Pond**.

Bunker Hill Bridge See **Leonard P. Zakim Bunker Hill Bridge**.

CA/T See **Central Artery/Tunnel Project**.

Cambridge Bridge See **Longfellow Bridge**.

Cambridge Esplanade The name given by Charles Davenport in the 1870s to his development on the Cambridge side of the river between the **Longfellow Bridge** and the **Boston University Bridge**. Begun in 1883, the development went bankrupt ten years later. Most of the site was acquired by MIT, whose new campus opened in 1916.

CANA See **Central Artery North Area Project**.

Canal Bridge See **Craigie's Bridge**.

Central Artery North Area (CANA) Project Planned as part of the **Central Artery** project, the CANA project replaced the elevated highway between the first Central Artery (Interstate 93) and the Tobin Bridge (Route 1) with a tunnel under City Square in Charlestown. Construction on the CANA project began before the design was completed for the **Charles River Crossing**.

Central Artery/Tunnel (CA/T) project The largest highway project to date in the United States, the artery includes a tunnel connecting the Massachusetts Turnpike (Interstate 90) to Boston's Logan Airport and a tunnel to replace the elevated Central Artery built in the 1950s through downtown Boston. The project also includes two bridges over the Charles River, including the cable-stayed **Leonard P. Zakim Bunker Hill Bridge**.

Chapter 91 A section of the Massachusetts General Laws, Chapter 91 requires a state permit to fill tidelands. It also requires the provision of public access and other public benefits for new developments built on filled tidelands.

Charlesbank A park designed by Frederick Law Olmsted for the West End neighborhood of Boston, it included the first outdoor gymnasiums for men and women in the United States. A waterfront promenade extended from **Craigie's Bridge** (now the **Charles River Dam**) to the Longfellow Bridge.

Charles River The longest river within the borders of Massachusetts, the Charles begins in Hopkinton and winds for eighty miles to Boston Harbor. A slow-moving river, it flows at an average of about 370 cubic feet per second (one-twentieth the flow of the Merrimack River in Lowell). The Boston Marathon also starts in Hopkinton but takes only twenty-six miles to arrive in Boston.

Charles River Basin Originally the name of the tidal estuary that extends for almost nine miles from Boston Harbor to the natural fall line, now the site of the **Watertown Dam** (upstream of the **Galen Street Bridge**). Today the name refers to the freshwater lake of the same extent created by the first **Charles River Dam** in 1908. The river between the dam and the Boston University Bridge is sometimes referred to as the Lower Basin; from the **Boston University Bridge** to the **Watertown**

Dam is called the Upper Basin. In 1978 a new dam was completed a half mile downstream of the old dam, and the lock gates of the old dam were taken out of service. The area between the old and new dams, informally christened "the lost half mile," is known as the New Charles River Basin or the New Basin.

Charles River Bay An early name for the body of water between Charlestown and East Cambridge. See also **Miller's River.**

Charles River Bridge Completed in 1786, the Charles River Bridge connected Boston with Charlestown. It was replaced by the present **Charlestown Bridge** in 1899.

Charles River Crossing The name for the new bridges over the Charles built as part of the **Central Artery** project, so called because the choice between bridges and tunnels (or some combination of both) to cross the Charles had not been made when the project began.

Charles River Dam After decades of debate, a dam on the site of Craigie's Bridge was approved in 1903 and constructed in 1905–1910. A temporary wooden dam was built to close off the basin in 1908. Hurricanes in 1938, 1954, and 1955 caused extensive flooding in Boston and Cambridge, and a new dam and pumping station were completed in 1978 just upstream of the **Charlestown Bridge.**

Charles River Park A private development built along the river on the site of the West End neighborhood, which had been leveled by the city with federal urban renewal funds in the late 1950s.

Charles River Road See **Greenough Boulevard, Memorial Drive.**

Charles Street Once a riverfront street, it runs from Boston Common to Leverett Circle. The part of the street between Charles Circle and Leverett Circle has been widened three times, in the early 1930s, in 1949–1951, and in 1999–2004. It is not officially part of Storrow Drive.

Charlestown Bridge Also called the North Washington Street Bridge, it was completed in 1899. Its center span opened on a circular pivot (still in place) for masted vessels.

Cobble Hill See **McLean Asylum.**

Cottage Farm Bridge See **Boston University Bridge.**

Craigie's Bridge Also known as Canal Bridge, its leading promoter was Andrew Craigie. It originally connected Barton's Point (now Leverett Circle) in Boston with Lechmere Point in Cambridge. The name is now applied to the draw bridge built as part of the first **Charles River Dam** in 1905–1910.

Eliot Bridge Completed in 1951, the bridge is a monument to Charles W. Eliot, president of Harvard from 1869 to 1909, and to his son Charles, the landscape architect for the Metropolitan and Cambridge Park Commissions.

Embankment, Embankment Road See **Boston Esplanade.**

Esplanade See **Boston Esplanade, Cambridge Esplanade.**

Environmental Impact Statement (EIS), Environmental Impact Report (EIR) Projects that exceed thresholds established under the National Environmental Policy Act (NEPA) are required to file an EIS. The Massachusetts Environmental Policy Act (MEPA) may require projects to file an EIR. A single document, an EIS/R, may be filed to meet both state and federal requirements.

EOEA The Massachusetts Executive Office of Environmental Affairs. The EOEA secretary is a cabinet-level position reporting directly to the governor.

EOTC The Massachusetts Executive Office of Transportation and Construction. The EOTC secretary is a cabinet-level position reporting directly to the governor.

Essex Street Bridge See **Boston University Bridge.**

Galen Street Bridge Built about 1907, the present stone arch bridge at Watertown Square replaced earlier structures from about 1647, 1667, and 1719.

General Court The Massachusetts legislature, officially the "Great and General Court."

Gerry's Landing Long known as "Sir Richard's Landing" after Richard Saltonstall, one of the founders of Watertown, the landing took the name of Elbridge Gerry after he inherited the nearby house now known as Elmwood.

Gibbon's Creek See **Miller's River.**

Greenough Boulevard The last section of riverfront parkway built along the basin, Greenough Boulevard (between the Eliot Bridge and Arsenal Street) was completed in 1966. Its construction through Hell's Half Acre was protested by Cambridge neighbors.

Harvard Bridge Named for John Harvard, the bridge opened in 1891. It was rebuilt in 1924 and 1990.

Hell's Half Acre The area near **Gerry's Landing** was given this nickname first by students at a nearby school and then in a 1955 article by the historian Bernard DeVoto.

Larz Anderson Bridge See **Anderson Memorial Bridge.**

Lechmere Canal Built in 1874, the canal resulted from landmaking (not from digging through solid ground) for industries in East Cambridge.

Leonard P. Zakim Bunker Hill Bridge The most visible addition of the Central Artery project to the Boston skyline, the cable-stayed bridge resulted from the efforts of the Bridge Design Review Committee in 1991–1992. It was designed by the Swiss engineer Dr. Christian Menn and named for Boston civil rights leader Leonard Zakim (1953–1999).

Leverett Circle Bridge Also called the Leverett Circle Connector, this early 1960s project proposed a highway link between the Tobin Bridge and Leverett Circle. This connection is now made by the smaller of the two bridges over the Charles built by the **Central Artery** project.

Longfellow Bridge Designed by Edmund Wheelwright, the Cambridge Bridge opened in 1907. It replaced the West Boston Bridge, built in 1793. The U.S. Congress overruled the War Department and allowed the new bridge to be built without a draw. It was renamed in 1927 for the poet Henry Wadsworth Longfellow.

Lower Basin See **Charles River Basin.**

McLean Asylum In 1816 the founders of Massachusetts General Hospital bought the estate of Joseph Barrell on the top of Cobble Hill in Charlestown (now Somerville) and opened the McLean Asylum. In 1835 the first of several railroads was built near the asylum, which finally sold the property to the Boston & Maine Railroad in 1895 and moved to Belmont. The railroad demolished the asylum buildings and leveled the hill.

MDC See **Metropolitan District Commission.**

Memorial Drive Charles River Road was planned by Charles Eliot and the Cambridge Park Department as a parkway along the full length of the city's riverfront boundary. The first segment of the road was built between Boylston (now John F. Kennedy) and Bath (now Hawthorne) Streets and the first London plane trees were planted there in 1897. In 1921 the parkway was transferred to the MDC, and two years later it was renamed Memorial Drive.

Metropolitan District Commission (MDC) In 1892 the legislature created the Metropolitan Park Commission (MPC) as a temporary board to consider the opportunities for "reservations of scenery" in greater Boston. The commission produced a landmark report in January 1893 and was made a permanent commission in June of that year. Funding for the new reservations was apportioned among the cities and towns of the park district. In 1919 the Metropolitan Park Commission was merged with the Metropolitan Water and Sewer Commission to create the Metropolitan District Commission. After the passage of "Proposition 2½" in 1980, a limitation on property tax increases, the assessment of cities and towns was replaced by funding through the annual state budget.

Metropolitan Park Commission See **Metroplitan District Commission.**

Middlesex Canal Opened in 1803, the canal connected Boston with the Merrimack River. Just as the canal became profitable in the 1830s, the Boston & Lowell Railroad was built on almost the same route. The canal finally shut down in 1852.

Mill Dam Approved by the legislature in 1814 to generate power for tide mills, the dam between Charles Street in Boston and Sewell's Point in Brookline was completed in 1821. Western Avenue (now Beacon Street) was built on its surface.

Miller's Creek, Miller's River A broad, shallow stream in East Cambridge, the Miller's River, known earlier as Gibbon's Creek, was filled in during the nineteenth century for industrial development.

Mill Pond A dam across the natural causeway (now Causeway Street) was built in 1643 to create the Mill Pond.

MPC See **Metropolitan District Commission.**

Mushauwomuk See **Shawmut Peninsula.**

New Charles River Basin, New Basin See **Charles River Basin.**

North Cove Located between the North End and the West End of Boston, the cove was divided by a natural causeway accessible at low tide. A mill dam was built across the cove on the line of the causeway in 1643.

North Beacon Street Bridge Built just upstream of the Watertown Arsenal wharf, the bridge was designed by Haven and Hoyt and completed in 1917.

North End Almost four hundred years after the settlement of Boston, the North End remains a residential neighborhood facing the waterfront of Boston Harbor.

North Washington Street Bridge See **Charlestown Bridge.**

River Street Bridge The design of the current bridge by Robert Bellows was chosen in a competition held by the MDC in 1923, and the bridge opened three years later. The first bridge on this site was built in 1810.

Section 4(f) The federal transportation act of 1966 requires in Section 4(f) that publicly owned parks, recreation areas, wildlife refuges, or historic sites may not be taken for federally funded transportation projects unless there is "no prudent and feasible alternative." If such land is taken, "all possible planning" is required to "minimize harm."

Sewell's Point, Sewall's Point Located near today's Kenmore Square, Sewell's Point was the western end of the "Great Dam," built when the Back Bay was separated from the Charles.

Shawmut Peninsula The name is probably a transliteration of the Algonkian word *mushauwomuk,* "where there is a big river," and referred to the entire river valley. English settlers shortened the word and applied it to the peninsula on which Boston was established in 1630.

Sir Richard's Landing See **Gerry's Landing.**

Storrow Memorial Drive, Storrow Memorial Embankment See **Boston Esplanade.**

Town Cove At the foot of King (later State) Street, Town Cove extended from Lewis Wharf on the north to Rowe's Wharf on the south sand inland as far as Congress Street.

Upper Basin See **Charles River Basin.**

Warren Bridge Built in 1828 just upstream of the **Charles River Bridge,** the Warren Bridge was the subject of the first monopoly case heard by the United States Supreme Court, which ruled in favor of the new bridge's proprietors in 1837.

Watertown Dam Built about 1634, the dam was constructed at the fall line of the Charles River, and marked the boundary between the tidal estuary (the **Charles River Basin**) and the fresh-water river.

Weeks Bridge The John W. Weeks Bridge is the only footbridge that spans the Charles. It was designed by McKim, Mead & White, the New York architectural firm responsible for the first buildings of the Harvard Business School on the Boston side of the footbridge.

West Boston Bridge See **Longfellow Bridge.**

West End The Boston neighborhood located between Beacon Hill and the North End, this area was the largest slum clearance project in Boston. Long after most of the tenements were demolished in the 1950s, highrise apartments known as Charles River Park were built.

Western Avenue Bridge Designed by Desmond and Lord and completed in 1924, the bridge was one of three whose architects were chosen in a competition held by the MDC. The first crossing on the site was a toll bridge built by the West Boston Bridge proprietors in 1824.

Zakim Bridge. See **Leonard P. Zakim Bunker Hill Bridge.**

A Chronology of the Charles River Basin

1630   The town of Boston is established on the Shawmut Peninsula.

Watertown is settled, and the meetinghouse is located at what is now Mt. Auburn and Traill Streets.

Newtowne (changed to Cambridge in 1638) is officially designated the capital of the Massachusetts Bay Colony and settled the following year.

1634   Boston Common is set aside on the edge of the Back Bay of the Charles River.

A mill dam is built in Watertown at the fall line of the river.

c. 1641   A footbridge is built near the Watertown dam.

1643   A mill dam is built across the mouth of North Cove (now Causeway Street).

1662   The Great Bridge is completed between Cambridge and Brighton.

1786   The Charles River Bridge is opened on the site of the ferry between Boston and Charlestown, from North Washington Street to City Square.

1793   West Boston Bridge connects Cambridge Street in Boston with Main Street in Cambridge.

1800   A bath house on the river is built for Harvard College students in Cambridge.

1809   Canal (Craigie's) Bridge is opened from Leverett Street (now Lomasney Way) in Boston to Lechmere Point in Cambridge.

1810   River Street Bridge is built in 1810. It is rebuilt in 1884 and 1920 and replaced in 1925.

1814   A proposal is published for a dam across the Charles (along a line just above the Harvard Bridge) and a mill dam (along present-day Beacon Street, from Charles Street in Boston to Sewell's Point in Brookline).

1819   The U.S. War Department relocates the Charlestown Arsenal to Watertown and for the next eighty years requires that every bridge on the Charles River Basin be built with a draw.

1821   The Mill Dam (on some maps the "Great Dam") is completed (along the line of present-day Beacon Street) between Boston and Brookline. Mills are built along the Cross Dam.

1824   A toll bridge at Western Avenue connecting Brighton and Cambridgeport is built by the proprietors of the West Boston Bridge. It is rebuilt in 1879 and 1910, and replaced in 1924.

1828   The Warren Bridge is completed. A lawsuit over the bridge, filed by the owners of the Charles River Bridge just down stream, is finally resolved by the U.S. Supreme Court in 1837.

1835   The Boston & Worcester and Boston & Providence Railroads construct causeways across the Back Bay.

The Boston & Lowell Railroad builds a trestle across the Miller's River in East Cambridge and a bridge across the Charles to Boston.

Braman's Baths, one of the earliest public baths and swimming schools, opens at the foot of Chestnut Street.

1844   Robert Gourlay proposes a freshwater Charles River Basin with a new town built by the state on fill in the Back Bay.

c. 1844   The first boat house is built and rented to four student clubs at Harvard that owned boats.

1850   The Essex Street (Brookline Street) Bridge is opened. In 1928 it is replaced by the Cottage Farm Bridge (renamed for Boston University in 1949).

1851   The Union Boat Club is organized and builds a boathouse on the water side of Brimmer Street. A second boathouse is completed nearby in 1870. When that structure is cut off from the river by the completion of the Boston Embankment in 1910, the club completes the present boathouse on the edge of the Embankment the following year.

1854   The Tripartite Indenture between the state, the Boston & Roxbury Mill Corporation, and the Boston Water Power Company settles land claims in the Back Bay.

1859   In a petition to the legislature to preserve the open water between Marlborough and Newbury Streets, George Snelling compares Hamburg's Alster Basin with the Charles River Basin and includes a view of the Alster.

1866   The city of Boston constructs six floating bathhouses, including two on the Charles.

1869   Workers at Riverside Press in Cambridge organize the Riverside Boat Club and build their first boathouse at the foot of Albro Street.

1869–   Public debates on the creation of Boston parks include
1870   discussions of a "water park" along the Charles.

1875   The Boston Parks Department is established. Frederick Law Olmsted designs the Back Bay Fens, linked to the river at the Charlesgate; the Fens are largely completed by 1890.

1881   The Charles River Embankment Company is founded by Charles Davenport; the seawall on the Cambridge side is begun in 1883, halted in the depression of 1893, and finally completed by the city.

1890   Harvard dedicates Soldiers Field. In 1902 Harvard Stadium opens as the country's largest football stadium and largest reinforced concrete structure.

1892   Charlesbank, designed by Frederick Law Olmsted as an outdoor playground and waterfront promenade for Boston's West End, is completed.

1893   The permanent Metropolitan Park Commission is established, and the first regional park plan in America is published.

1894   The Cambridge Park Commission is authorized and acquires the first public park land on the river. The first London plane trees are planted along Charles River Road (now Memorial Drive) in 1897.

Report of the Joint Board on the Improvement of the Charles River recommends damming the river above Craigie Bridge and filling for a new row of house lots along the Boston side.

1903   The first Charles River Dam at Craigie's Bridge is approved after a major study of engineering and environmental issues.

1907   The Cambridge Bridge opens, the first bridge on the river to be built without a draw since the U.S. War Department relocated the Charlestown Arsenal to Watertown in 1819. The bridge is renamed in 1927 to honor the poet Henry Wadsworth Longfellow.

1905–
1910   The Charles River Dam is constructed on the site of Craigie's Bridge, and a park is laid out on the earthen dam that connects "The Front" in Cambridge with Charlesbank in Boston. A new seawall is constructed and new land is filled on the Boston side between Cambridge Street and Charlesgate West to create the Boston Embankment.

1913   The Anderson Memorial Bridge, a monument to Nicholas Longworth Anderson given by his son Larz, is opened (the bridge is usually called after the son's name).

1913   Harvard freshman dormitories are completed along Charles River Road (now Memorial Drive).

1916   MIT dedicates a new riverfront campus by transporting the university's charter on a barge across the river from its original building in the Back Bay.

1927   The John W. Weeks Bridge, the only footbridge spanning the basin, is opened.

1928   The city of Boston closes its last floating bathhouse on the river.

1936   Storrow Memorial Embankment (now universally known as the Esplanade) is dedicated after proposals to include a highway along the river are rejected by the legislature.

1939   Boston University completes its first building on the riverfront campus just below the Cottage Farm (now Boston University) Bridge.

1949   The Museum of Science moves from the Back Bay to the park on the first Charles River Dam.

1949   Storrow Drive legislation is defeated, then passed by one vote, authorizing a four-lane highway through the Esplanade (the highway was completed in 1951 and expanded to six lanes in 1954–1955).

1962   A new Charles River dam and pumping station are approved, with authorization to extend the level basin from the old dam to the Warren Bridge and to acquire riverfront land.

1966   The Bowker (Route 1) Overpass is completed over the outlet of the Back Bay Fens at Charlesgate.

1969   The Metropolitan Open Space Plan endorses extending the Esplanade from the Museum of Science to Charlestown and the North End.

1978   The new Charles River Dam and pumping station are completed, and the level basin is extended to Boston Harbor. Although not yet dedicated, the pumping station is put in service during the "Blizzard of '78" when the high tide equals the record of fifteen feet. Paul Revere Park is completed on the surface of the earthen dam north and south of the pumping station.

1980   The MDC publishes a plan for the "New Charles River Basin" to connect the Boston and Cambridge Esplanades with Boston harbor.

1990   The Central Artery/Tunnel project is approved, including the "Scheme Z" crossing of the Charles River; funding for park construction along the New Basin is required to mitigate the highway impacts along the river.

1992   A cable-stayed bridge design for crossing the Charles River is approved after months of work by the Bridge Design Review Committee.

1999   Paul Revere Park (north of the new Charles River dam) is reconstructed as the first park in the New Charles River Basin funded by the Central Artery project.

2002   The Leonard P. Zakim Bunker Hill Bridge is opened to thousands of pedestrians on Mother's Day, in anticipation of an imminent opening to vehicular traffic.

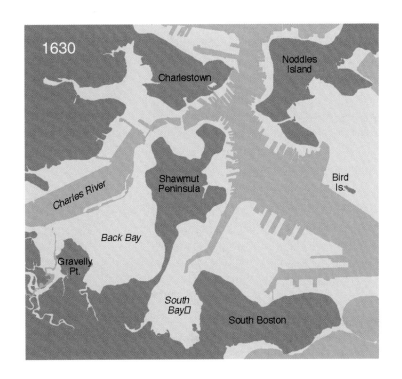

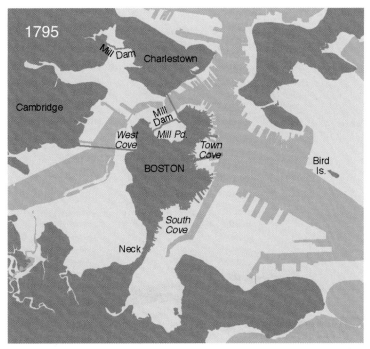

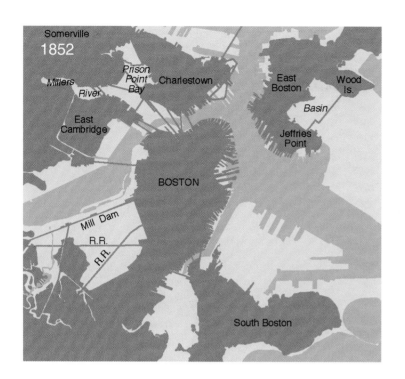

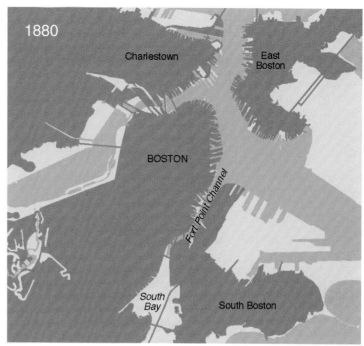

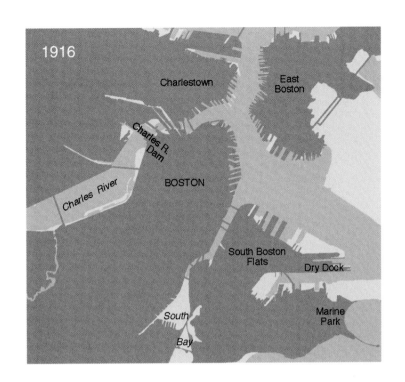

1916

Charlestown

East
Boston

Charles R.
Dam

Charles River

BOSTON

South Boston
Flats

Dry Dock

South
Bay

Marine
Park

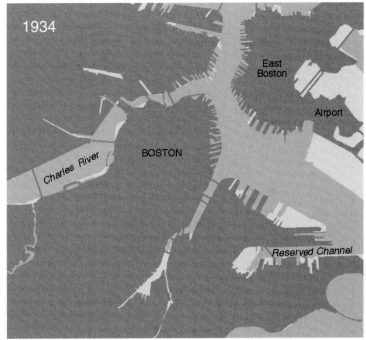

1934

East
Boston

Airport

Charles River

BOSTON

Reserved Channel

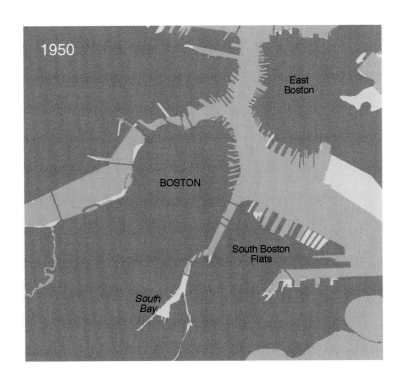

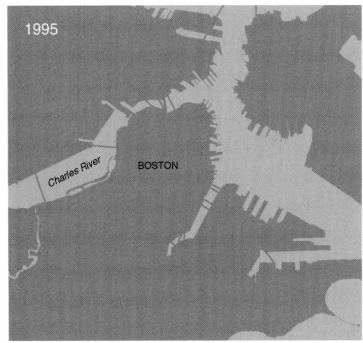

Illustration Credits

7.51 Interstate 93 and Route 1 at the Charles River, 1974. Photograph by Jack Maley. Courtesy of the MDC Archives, Boston

Chapter Eight

Frontis. Abandoned railroad trestle in Cambridge near North Station, 1989. Lajos Heder and Mags Harries

8.1 *High Spine,* by Kevin Lynch, 1960. Courtesy of Robert S. Sturgis

8.2 Open space along the Charles, Boston Redevelopment Authority, *1965/1975 General Plan for the City of Boston and the Regional Core* (Boston, [1965?])

8.3 The Charles River Basin. Commonwealth of Massachusetts, Metropolitan Area Planning Council, Metropolitan District Commission, Department of Natural Resouces, *Open Space and Recreation Program for Metropolitan Boston, vol. 3, The Mystic, Charles and Neponset Rivers.*

8.4 "Charles River Locks and Dam," undated. Courtesy of the MDC Archives, Boston

8.5 New Charles River Dam, site plan. C. E. Maguire, *Charles River Dam Design Review Report* (December 1973). Courtesy of the MDC Archives, Boston

8.6 New Charles River Dam during construction, c. 1976. Courtesy of the MDC Archives, Boston

8.7 New Charles River Dam, elevation. C. E. Maguire, *Charles River Dam Design Review Report* (December 1973). Courtesy of the MDC Archives, Boston

8.8 *Site plan alternatives. A Development Plan for North Station,* 1980. © Moshe Safdie and Associates

8.9 *Perspective drawing. A Development Plan for North Station,* 1980. © Moshe Safdie and Associates

8.10 *Photograph of model. A Development Plan for North Station,* 1980 © D. Litz

8.11 *Concept Plan, Proposed Extension, Charles River Basin to New Charles River Dam,* Metropolitan District Commission, James Falck, Landscape Architect, 1980. Courtesy of the MDC Archives, Boston

8.12 *Concept Plan, Proposed Extension, Charles River Basin to New Charles River Dam,* Metropolitan District Commission, James Falck, Landscape Architect, 1980, detail. Courtesy of the MDC Archives, Boston

8.13 *Concept Plan, Proposed Extension, Charles River Basin to New Charles River Dam,* Metropolitan District Commission, James Falck, Landscape Architect, 1980, detail. Courtesy of the MDC Archives, Boston

8.14 Flowed and filled tidelands, Commonwealth of Massachusetts, Department of Environmental Protection and Massachusetts Coastal Zone Management, *Chapter 91: An Introduction to the Massachusetts Public Waterfront Act and Its Regulation (n.p., n.d.)*

8.15 The first Charles River Dam in 1948. Photograph by Bradford Washburn. Courtesy of the Museum of Science, Boston

8.16 The first Charles River Dam, 1975. Photograph by Bradford Washburn. Courtesy of the Museum of Science, Boston

8.17 Lechmere Canal Park, model, Carlone & Associates. Photograph by Alan Ward

8.18 Lechmere Canal, undated. Photograph by Jerry Howard. Courtesy of Carol R. Johnson Associates

8.19 "North Point, Housing & Office Scenario," drawing by Carlone & Associates. City of Cambridge, Community Development Department, *North Point Revitalization Plan: Summary of Goals and Objectives* (October 5, 1987)

8.20 View from under the Green Line viaduct, 1988. Lajos Heder and Mags Harries

Chapter Nine

Frontis. *Aerial Camera's Eye View of the Central Artery . . .,* from *the Boston Sunday Globe, Roto Pictorial Magazine,* August 8, 1954. Courtesy of Laurence Lowry

9.1 "Now you see it." Central Artery/Tunnel Project Supplement, *Boston Globe,* July 1989. Author's collection

9.2 "Now you don't." Central Artery/Tunnel Project Supplement, *Boston Globe,* July 1989. Author's collection

9.3 Construction of the Central Artery, c. 1954. Courtesy of the State Transportation Library

9.4 The Charles River Dam, the Central Artery, and the High Bridge. Photograph by the author

9.5 Schematic plan for the Central Artery/Tunnel project. Author's collection

12.1   *The Charles River Bridge,* by John Scoles for the *Massachusetts Magazine* 1, no. 9 (September 1789): frontispiece. Courtesy of William Marchione

12.2   Charles River Bridge and Charlestown Bridge. Courtesy of the Bostonian Society/Old State House: Elevated Railway Collection

12.3   Charlestown Bridge looking toward City Square. Courtesy of the Bostonian Society/Old State House: Elevated Railway Collection

12.4   Pumping station and Charlestown Bridge, 2001. Photograph by Peter Vanderwarker

12.5   Warren Bridge and North Station railroad trestles, 1911. Courtesy of the Society for the Preservation of New England Antiquities

12.6   The North End and North Station District, 1925. Photograph by Fairchild Aerial Surveys. Courtesy of the Boston Public Library, Print Department

12.7   Charles River Dam, the High Bridge, and the Leonard P. Zakim Bunker Hill Bridge, 2001. Photograph by Peter Vanderwarker

12.8   West End Seawall. City of Boston Archives, Department of Parks, Annual Report, 1886

12.9   The West End and Charlesbank, c. 1895. Courtesy of William Marchione

12.10   Charlesbank men's gymnasium and the Charles River Dam, 1910. Photograph by Luther H. Shattuck. Courtesy of the Massachusetts State Archives, Boston

12.11   Charles River Park, Charles Street, and Charlesbank, 2001. Photograph by Peter Vanderwarker

12.12   View of the Joseph Barrell Mansion, 1810. Courtesy of the Society for the Preservation of New England Antiquities

12.13   "Aqueduct," Boston, Mass. Postcard by A. Israelson & Co. Courtesy of the Society for the Preservation of New England Antiquities

12.14   Monsignor O'Brien Highway and the Green Line viaduct, 2001. Photograph by Peter Vanderwarker

12.15   Charles River lock and open shelter, 1910. Photograph by Luther H. Shattuck. Courtesy of the Massachusetts State Archives, Boston

12.16   Charles River Dam, looking toward Cambridge, c. 1947. Photograph by Bradford Washburn. Courtesy of the Museum of Science, Boston

12.17   Charles River Dam and the Museum of Science, 1951. Courtesy of the MDC Archives, Boston

12.18   Charles River Dam and the Museum of Science, 1976. Courtesy of the MDC Archives, Boston

12.19   Charles River lock and open shelter, 2001. Photograph by Peter Vanderwarker

12.20   Lechmere Canal and East Cambridge, 1920. Courtesy of the Massachusetts State Archives, Boston, 1920

12.21   Lechmere Canal, 1949. Photograph by Bradford Washburn. Courtesy of the Museum of Science, Boston

12.22   Lechmere Canal and CambridgeSide Galleria, 1999. Photograph by Peter Vanderwarker

12.23   Broad Canal, 1919. Courtesy of the Massachusetts State Archives, Boston

12.24   Broad Canal, 1949. Photograph by Bradford Washburn. Courtesy of the Museum of Science, Boston

12.25   Broad Canal, 2000. Photograph by Peter Vanderwarker

12.26   West Boston Bridge, undated. Brighton-Allston Historical Society Archive

12.27   West Boston Bridge, 1864. Courtesy of the Bostonian Society/Old State House

12.28   Longfellow Bridge, 2002. Photograph by Peter Vanderwarker

12.29   Back Bay from the State House, 1858. Photograph by Southworth and Hawes. Courtesy of the Trustees of the Boston Public Library, Print Department

12.30   Back Bay from the State House, 1898. Courtesy of the Boston Public Library, Print Department

12.31   Back Bay from the State House, 1999. Photograph by Peter Vanderwarker

12.32   The water side of Brimmer Street. Photograph by James A. Wells. Courtesy of the Society for the Preservation of New England Antiquities

12.33   Embankment Road, c. 1911. Courtesy of the Bostonian Society/Old State House

12.34   The Esplanade from Longfellow Bridge, 2002. Photograph by the author

12.35   The Embankment looking west toward Harvard Bridge, 1919. Courtesy of the Massachusetts State Archives, Boston

12.36   The Storrow Memorial Embankment, 1936. Courtesy of the MDC Archives, Boston

12.79   Galen Street Bridge and Lewandos, 1910. Courtesy of the Massachusetts State Archives, Boston

12.80   Galen Street Bridge and Riverbend Office Park, 2001. Photograph by Peter Vanderwarker

12.81   Bird's-eye view of Watertown. Courtesy of the Watertown Free Public Library

12.82   Watertown Dam, 1910. Courtesy of the Massachusetts State Archives, Boston

12.83   Watertown Dam, 2002. Photograph by the author

A Chronology of the Charles River Basin

diagrams © The Muriel G. and Norman B. Leventhal Family Foundation; cartography by MapWorks, Herb Heidt and Eliza McClennen, Norwell, Massachusetts

About the Charles River Conservancy

Frontis.   Lighting of the River Street, Western Avenue, Weeks, and Anderson Bridges, December 21, 2001, by John Powell. Photograph by Bob O'Connor

Endleaves: © 2001 Charles River Conservancy; orthophoto source: Massachusetts Executive Office of Environmental Affairs, MassGIS, 1995 data

Index